CUNNINGHAM

John Winton

SAPERE
BOOKS

CUNNINGHAM

Published by Sapere Books.

20 Windermere Drive, Leeds, England, LS17 7UZ,
United Kingdom

saperebooks.com

ISBN: 978-1-80055-399-6.

'In the Eastern Mediterranean we found in Admiral Andrew Cunningham an officer of the highest qualities and dauntless courage.'
Winston S. Churchill, *The Second World War*

TABLE OF CONTENTS

FOREWORD

THERE WAS a gale-force wind, clouds raced across the sky, and the sea was rough as I stood with members of my family and the Board of Admiralty on the flight-deck of HMS *Hampshire* thirty-five years ago. The ship was hove to in the Channel, south of the Nab Tower, and we had come to bury at sea one of Britain's most distinguished Admirals, Andrew Browne Cunningham — 'ABC' to the Navy, Andrew to his friends, Uncle Ned to his relations. As the Chaplain of the Fleet concluded the service, a bright shaft of sunlight illuminated the ship and the coffin was committed to the deep.

As a young lieutenant, I stood there thinking about the great-uncle who had inspired me to join the Royal Navy and wondering about those qualities of leadership that he had so successfully brought to bear during a remarkable career in which he had seen active service in the Boer War and two World Wars.

I thought too about the many happy weekends I had spent with the Cunninghams at the Palace House in Bishop's Waltham during the last few years of my uncle's life. He had no doubt mellowed by then, but he still had an air of purpose and little escaped his penetrating gaze. Moreover his racy humour and a mischievous streak were not far below the surface. He was a devil at Racing Demon; he could not bear to be beaten on the croquet lawn; and he drove his car like an attacking destroyer — woe betide the oncoming traffic if he decided to overtake. Furthermore, he derived enormous boyish pleasure out of simple pranks; one got incredibly adept at fielding, with one's sideplate, butterballs flicked with great accuracy on the tip of the Admiral's knife from the far end of the table. All in all, he was the greatest fun and the best of company.

Those weekends gave me the unique opportunity to study and understand the character of a man who, from young cadet to First Sea Lord, devoted his action-packed life to his country and was single-minded in his determination to ensure that the Royal Navy played a key role in its future.

ABC was the epitome of destroyer captains at a time when fine seamanship, iron discipline, dashing ship-handling, aggressive tactical manoeuvring and a fighting spirit inspired great confidence in the Fleet. He was a man of uncanny foresight, exceptional stamina, supreme courage and sometimes ruthless action; he was vigorous, decisive and resolute in the face of adversity. No one could have been better placed to command the Mediterranean Fleet and bring all his experience and ability to bear in those dark days in the early 1940s. He could well be described as an Admiral of Destiny.

John Winton draws heavily on ABC's personal letters and wartime diaries to build up a picture of his personality and thus expose the merits and indeed the flaws in his character. There can be no doubt that, in command, he was in his element, and the United Kingdom was lucky to have such a man at such a time. Equally there can be little doubt that, despite an uneasy relationship with the Prime Minister, ABC's offensive spirit and willingness to take risks appealed to Churchill. However, when he became First Sea Lord, he was clearly less than comfortable in the cut-and-thrust of Whitehall: administration was anathema to him and he was not an intellectual. Nevertheless, he had a shrewd, perceptive, pragmatic intellect and his formidable reputation as a bluff, straightforward, highly accomplished fighting Admiral carried him through and ensured that he wielded great influence in the higher direction of the war. That said, he was outspoken in his views and was an exceptionally hard taskmaster who abhorred inefficiency and demanded the toughest standards, but, behind this, lay shining honesty, wise counsel, deep humanity and genuine modesty; and thus he was held in the highest esteem.

So HMS *Hampshire* returned to harbour that day and all those present knew that they had paid homage to one of our greatest fighting sailors who had given a lifetime of sterling service to his country in the Royal Navy that he so loved.

Admiral Sir Jock Slater, GCB, LVO, ADC
First Sea Lord and Chief of the Naval Staff
Ministry of Defence London, 1998

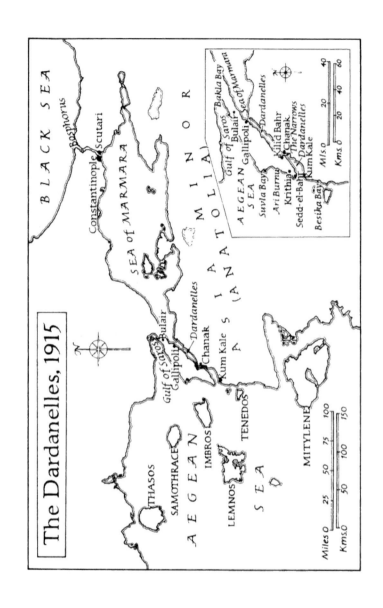

The Dardanelles, 1915

BLACK SEA

Bosphorus

Constantinople · Scutari

SEA of MARMARA

A S I A M I N O R

(A N A T O L I A)

Bulair
Dardanelles
Gulf of Saros
Gallipoli
Chanak
Kum Kale

AEGEAN SEA

THASOS

SAMOTHRACE

IMBROS

LEMNOS

TENEDOS

MITYLENE

Miles 0   25   50   75   100
Kms 0   50   100   150

Inset:

Bakla Bay
Gulf of Saros
Bulair
Dardanelles
AEGEAN SEA
Gallipoli · Sea of Marmara
Suvla Bay
Ari Burnu
Kilid Bahr
Chanak
Krithia
The Narrows
Sedd-el-Bahr
Dardanelles
Besika Bay
Kum Kale

Mls 0   20   40
Kms 0   20   40   60

12

Greece and Crete, 1941

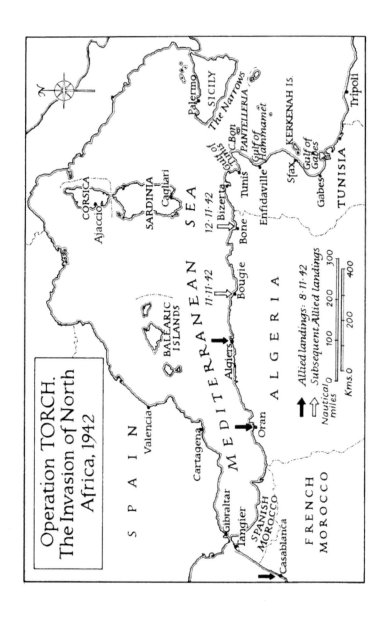

Operation TORCH.
The Invasion of North
Africa, 1942

Operations HUSKY and AVALANCHE, 1943

Milan
Venice
Trieste
YUGOSLAVIA
Genoa
I T A L Y
A D R I A T I C
Split
S E A
Dubrovnik
ELBA
CORSICA
Ajaccio
Rome
Bari
Brindisi
Anzio
Mt. Vesuvius
Naples
Salerno
Taranto
AVALANCHE
5th (U.S.) Army
T Y R R H E N I A N
S E A
Pizzo
Messina
Bagnara
Cagliari
Palermo
C. Spartivento
Mt. Etna
Str. of Messina
SARDINIA
The Narrows
S I C I L Y
Catania
Bizerta
C. Bon
Licata
Syracuse
Gela
Bone
Tunis
7th (U.S.)
8th (Br.) Army
PANTELLERIA
Army
HUSKY
GOZO
Valetta
MALTA
Sousse
T U N I S I A
LAMPEDUSA
MEDITERRANEAN SEA

Miles 0   50   100   150   200
Kms. 0   75   150   225   300

Allied Landings

1: EARLY DAYS IN THE NAVY

TO HIS NAVAL contemporaries, he was Andrew. To the sailors on the lower deck, he was 'Cutts'. To the Royal Navy as a whole, he was always 'ABC'.

He liked punctuality, bawdy stories, dogs, gardens and gardening, party games after dinner and the company of the young. Especially, he loved fishing; he always thought more of a man, whether British politician or French admiral, if he were a fellow fisherman. He disliked conversation before breakfast, personal publicity, and Admiral 'Ernie' King's anglophobia. He loathed General Montgomery.

Ashore, he was a poor and reluctant administrator. Afloat, he was one of the most brilliant handlers of ships and men the Royal Navy has ever produced. He was a shrewd judge of men, slow to award his trust, but once convinced he trusted absolutely. He was a very good friend to many and a benefactor to some. He followed the subsequent careers of those who had served under him and, if they had served him well, put in effective and influential good words for them. But he had a brutal streak and was a pitiless critic of lesser men, such as Tom Phillips, whom he thought promoted above their deserts. He knew how to use his staff, but sometimes drove them to distraction. He was a bully, who liked people to stand up to him. Somebody once compared him to a bear: warm and cuddly, but with sharp claws.

He could be childish, petulant and wilfully exasperating. But he was also supremely brave and physically robust, with a towering self-confidence which gave confidence to others. One First Lord of the Admiralty, A.V. Alexander, told the House of Commons that he had 'that touch of magic' which inspired those under him with something of his own spirit, and described him as 'the greatest sea captain since Nelson'. Winston Churchill once gave him a signed portrait, inscribed to 'Andrew Cunningham The Great Admiral of the Mediterranean.'

In action, Cunningham had a natural talent for battle and an instinctive knowledge of the way a tactical situation was developing. The Spaniards always believed that Sir Francis Drake possessed a magic mirror in which he could see where all their ships were. In a sense, Cunningham inherited Drake's mirror.

Above all, Cunningham was devoted to the Royal Navy. To the end of his life he was convinced that there was no Service or profession to compare with it.

Such a man should have come from a naval family, admirals all. In fact, his family were clerical and medical. His grandfather, John Cunningham, was parish minister at Crieff, a fashionable health resort in Perthshire, for forty-one years, and in 1886 was Moderator of the General Assembly of the Church of Scotland.

His father was Daniel John Cunningham, who went to Edinburgh as a medical student in 1870 and became one of the most distinguished anatomists of his day — Professor of Anatomy at the Royal College of Surgeons of Ireland in 1882 and, a year later (and for the next twenty years), Professor of Anatomy at Trinity College, Dublin, where he was the most popular lecturer in the university.

In 1878, Daniel Cunningham married Elizabeth Cumming, the eldest daughter of Andrew Browne, minister of the parish of Beith in Ayrshire. Their third child was born at 42 Grosvenor Square, Rathmines, Co. Dublin, on 7 January 1883, and was christened Andrew Browne Cunningham. They already had a daughter and a son, and were to have another daughter and another son, thus achieving what Cunningham described years later as 'a full house sons up'.

He signed his letters home as 'Ned'. The younger members of his family called him 'Uncle Ned'. He acquired the nickname at an early age, supposedly from a popular song of the era, with the refrain: 'There was an old n****r and his name was Ned, And he had no hair on the top of his head.'

Ned had a happy childhood in Dublin, with an English governess and a succession of German governesses to teach what his father regarded (because of its use in science) as the most important foreign language. At nine years old, Ned was bilingual in English and German.

Their father was a somewhat remote and awe-inspiring figure (the Irish cook's worst threat was 'I'll tell the Doctor on yez') but he took them on fishing trips and to Dublin zoo and across to St Andrews for what Ned always remembered as wonderful summer holidays. Their mother, whom they all adored, was in Ned's words 'a wonderful manager with a very sweet temperament' and she often acted as intermediary and advocate for her children against their father's wrath.

Ned went to school in Dublin and then to Edinburgh Academy, as a dayboy, staying in term time with his aunts, his mother's sisters, Connie Jean and Helen ('Doodles') Browne at 28 Palmerston Place. Although he had many friends and relatives in Edinburgh and continued to enjoy visits there for the rest of his life, he always distanced himself mentally from that city, regarding the 'Edinburgh influence' as inward-looking, complacent and provincial.

He had always been interested in boats and the sea, but he was still surprised to get a telegram from his father: 'Would you like to go into the Navy?' Egged on by his aunts, he replied:

18

'Yes. I should like to be an Admiral.' Edinburgh Academy was just starting a 'Navy Class', but Ned was sent to Mr Foster's school, at Stubbington House, Fareham, a 'crammer' for the Navy.

Ned inherited his family's brains, but not their energy. He never had to work hard and was always lazy. Mathematics was easy, but he 'could not abide Latin, French and English and was quite useless at them'. He was mediocre at sports, uninterested in cricket, but he did play hockey and soccer.

At the end of the 1896 autumn term, the Navy Class went up to London to take the Civil Service Examination. Ned passed top of the Stubbington House boys, and fourteenth out of the total of sixty-five accepted.

HMS *Britannia*, which Mr Cunningham, as he now was, joined as a Naval Cadet on 15 January 1897, shortly after his fourteenth birthday, was the old wooden-walled training ship, laid down in 1860 as the 131-gun *Prince of Wales*. She was moored in the river Dart above the town of Dartmouth in 1869, replacing an older and smaller *Britannia*. Another old wooden wall, the two-decker accommodation ship *Hindustan*, lay close upstream of her and the two ships were connected, stem to stern, by a walkway.

Britannia's masts and rigging had been removed, except the foremast, which was still rigged for cadets to climb on, with a safety net below it. The upper deck was largely built over with classrooms, model rooms and cabins for ship's officers. The guns had been removed and the gun-decks were used as dormitories, messrooms, bathrooms and promenades.

Cadets spent four terms in the *Britannia*. As the number of terms in a year had just been increased from two to three, Cunningham's term would undergo in sixteen months the same curriculum of studies and naval training which had taken their predecessors two years. A cadet gunner, who was a warrant officer, and four chief petty officers, were responsible for discipline. Each term had a lieutenant as divisional officer, responsible for his cadets' performance at work and play (a system that survives to this day).

The two senior terms lived in the *Britannia*; the first termers, or 'news', and the second termers, in *Hindustan*. Every cadet slept in a hammock and kept his clothes and belongings in his sea-chest. All four terms ate, by terms, on four long tables in the large cadets' messroom which was the assembly space for morning prayers, inspections and evening preparation, and was also where the cadets spent their spare time, reading, writing letters or larking about.

Britannia had a rigorous, spartan regime of hard exercise and hard discipline. The day began, winter and summer, with a bugle call at 6.30 a.m. and a plunge into a cold salt-water bath, and it proceeded strictly upon its laid-down course. The passing hours were marked by bugle call and ship's bell: muster, morning studies and drills, disperse, breakfast, muster, prayers, studies, dismiss, dinner, cadets land for sports and sailing, recall, shift clothing and boots, studies, tea, prayers, cadets turn in, rounds, pipe down.

The syllabus included mathematics and navigation, seamanship, some French, some grudging instruction in 'Steam' and a little naval history taught by Hamilton Williams — 'Badger Bill'. His book *Britain's Naval Power* was on the list of compulsory books to be bought by every cadet, along with those on algebra, trigonometry, Euclid, spherical trigonometry, navigation and nautical astronomy, Inman's *Nautical Tables*, an atlas, Nares' and Alston's *Seamanship*, a bible, prayer book and *Hymns Ancient & Modern*. For his third term every cadet had to provide himself with a sextant.

Cunningham did not find the classroom work hard, and had time in the evenings to become a proficient chess player. After classes, there were cricket and football, tennis, walks in the Devon countryside, cross-country runs, and the *Britannia* Beagles. Cunningham was much more interested in the river than the playing fields. *Britannia* inspired in him a lifelong pleasure and skill in sailing. There were twenty gigs and skiffs (painted blue and known, as they still are at Dartmouth today, as 'blue boats') in which Cunningham spent every hour he could. There were also six larger cutters, the tender *Wave* in Dartmouth harbour for exercises and sailing drills, and the sloop *Racer* for longer cruises to sea for a week.

Cunningham was a little surprised, much later in life, to find himself recalled by others in his term as a particularly aggressive amateur pugilist, who loved a scrap. He did not think of himself as particularly quarrelsome as a boy. Nevertheless, 'Meat Face' they called him, and 'Fight You on Sunday' was his well-remembered invitation to some bloody and Homeric fights up on the playing fields, where scores were settled.

Britannia punishments varied from a public caning, from six to twelve strokes, depending upon the offence, inflicted by a muscular petty officer in front of all the cadets assembled on the quarterdeck, to a range of minor punishment routines, numbered in order of severity from No. 1 to No. 7. These involved turning out earlier and going to bed later, extra drill with poles or heavy rifles, stoppage of pocket money and standing on deck facing the bulkhead for an hour.

In his first year Cunningham led a comparatively blameless life, with only two very minor offences. But in his final term, in the spring of 1898, like many boys (possibly with the onset of puberty), he seems to have begun to pit himself against the

Britannia disciplinary system. From December 1897 to March 1898, Cunningham was punished nine times, for offences such as talking in study after being cautioned, skylarking or being improperly dressed at muster, improperly marching to study, misbehaviour in the messroom, and, late in March, when he was within only a few days of leaving *Britannia*, disobeying Cadet Captain's orders.

Perhaps because of this sudden spate of misdemeanours, he did not become a cadet captain. In April 1898, he passed out tenth in his term list. Late Victorian naval education has been criticised for its narrowness, but Cunningham's passing certificate shows what he himself called the 'formidable list' of subjects taught to boys of fifteen:

> Religious Knowledge; Algebra; Geometry; Plane Trigonometry, Practical and Theoretical, and its application to useful problems in Navigation, Surveying, etc.; Spherical Trigonometry, and its application to simple Astronomical problems; Navigation, Practical and Theoretical, so far as to determine a Ship's position both by Dead Reckoning and Observation according to the ordinary daily practice at Sea; Protracting Geometrical and Nautical Problems; the construction of Charts and their use in the practice of Navigation; the use of the Sextant, Azimuth Compass, Barometer, Thermometer, etc., and the principles of their construction; Elementary Physical Science; French and Drawing, Naval History; Geography and Astronomy; Drawing, Freehand and Mechanical.

This same certificate testified that Mr Cunningham had shown a good proficiency in the use of the Sextant and Artificial Horizon, and had paid 'much' attention to the various branches of study. He gained first-class certificates in mathematics and seamanship, second-class certificates in

French and extra subjects. He could swim, and his conduct had been 'Very Good'.

The result was that Mr Cunningham gained seven months' sea-time, or advanced seniority, so that he would serve only one month at sea as a Naval Cadet, before being rated up to Midshipman, without any more examinations, on 15 June 1898.

The cadets were asked where they would like to go. At that time, the Navy had ships all over the world. One of Cunningham's best friends, Henry Archer Colt, chose the Cape of Good Hope and West Africa Station, which sounded far away and romantic enough for Cunningham too, with a chance of active service with a Naval Brigade ashore. He went on leave to Dublin, thought no more about it, and was surprised by the official brown envelope with the Admiralty franking, the first of many in his life. He and Colt were both appointed to the cruiser *Fox*, on the Cape Station. They sailed from Southampton, bound for Cape Town, in the RMS *Norman* on 21 May 1898.

After a voyage of seventeen days, RMS *Norman* steamed under the dramatic shape of Table Mountain. But the two cadets were disappointed to find that *Fox* was up the east coast of Africa, and not expected back for some weeks. Meantime, they joined the flagship *Doris*, at Simonstown.

Doris, a 5,600-ton second-class cruiser, had a tiny and grossly overcrowded gunroom, intended for only fifteen midshipmen but now, with the two newcomers, occupied by twenty-nine. The food was indifferent and very expensive and the midshipmen had to have their meals in three shifts. Cunningham's pay as a cadet was one shilling a day, plus fifty pounds a year, which his parents had to pay to the Admiralty.

There were two Captain Protheros in the Navy List of that time: Prothero the Good and Prothero the Bad. *Doris'* Captain was Reginald C. Prothero, the Bad. The sailors liked him and had the greatest respect for him, because he was absolutely fair and consistent. But, with his piercing, hawk-like eyes, great hooked nose, booming tempest-shaking voice and bristling black beard, Prothero the Bad was quite the most terrifying man Cunningham had ever encountered. If a midshipman annoyed him, or got in his way on the bridge, he would simply pick the boy up, one fist grasping his collar and the other the seat of his trousers, and drop him over the bridge screen onto the deck below. Cunningham and Colt were therefore greatly relieved when *Fox* arrived on 2 July.

Fox was a typical Victorian armoured cruiser, of 4,360 tons, built at Portsmouth and completed in 1895, coal-fired, with a top speed of about 18 knots, and a complement of 318 officers and men. With her usual headquarters at Zanzibar, *Fox* patrolled the whole eastern coast, from Simonstown up to the Horn of Africa. She had no wireless and, except for the cables picked up at ports she visited, was completely cut off from the flagship at the Cape and the Admiralty in London. Her Captain, Frank Hannan Henderson, one of three brothers who all achieved flag rank, thus had virtually a free hand to go wherever and do whatever he wished.

For Cunningham, it was a free and joyous existence and he had a year of almost complete enjoyment. There were only eight in the gunroom, and they were all the best of friends. In harbour, Cunningham was Midshipman of a sailing cutter on alternate weeks and was able to indulge his delight in sailing. The British residents had constructed a links at Zanzibar and Cunningham began to play golf — another lifelong love.

But after a year, *Fox*'s three-year commission came to an end and the ship went home. In May 1899, Cunningham and Colt had to rejoin *Doris*. It was back to the bad old days of overcrowding, poor and expensive food, few recreations and nothing to occupy the midshipmen's minds except an hour or two's indifferent instruction, which they did their utmost to avoid.

Even sailing the cutter became hard work. False Bay, outside Simonstown, was notoriously stormy, especially in a south-easterly gale when the Bay became a lee shore. But Prothero the Bad refused to use the steam pinnace provided and insisted that midshipmen sail their boats whatever the weather. Many a midshipman and his crew were washed up on the beach and had to wait there until the weather moderated.

Cunningham survived these and other mishaps. In February 1900, while coaling ship, he was very nearly killed when he fell between *Doris* and the collier. Luckily, despite rope burns on his hands, he was able to pull himself out of the water a few seconds before the two hulls ground together.

Cunningham's luck changed when the Boer War broke out on 12 October 1899. A Naval Brigade of about 400 men, half of them Marines, from *Doris*, *Monarch* and *Powerful*, with four 12-pounder guns, landed at Simonstown on 19 November. Commanded by Captain Prothero, the Naval Brigade went up country by train to join Lord Methuen's force and on 25 November suffered severe casualties at Graspan, on the railway south of Kimberley. Major Plumbe, RMLI, of *Doris*, and one of *Doris*' midshipmen, C.A.E. Huddart, were among those killed.

Prothero the Bad, armed only with his walking-stick, led his men from the front and, being almost as broad as he was tall, made an excellent target. The Boers had the temerity to shoot him. He was badly wounded and returned to hospital in Simonstown.

Cunningham was bitterly disappointed not to be chosen for the Naval Brigade. He was particularly annoyed when a midshipman junior to him was chosen. 'I am fearfully sick at present at not getting up to the front,' he wrote to his mother. 'It is enough to make a saint swear to see these people about a year junior to you and only about two months on the Station going up and you sitting down here doing absolutely nothing.'

Cunningham seized his chance when Major Peile, Plumbe's replacement, arrived on board. Hearing that Major Peile was just about to leave for the front, he asked if he could go as his aide-de-camp. The Major agreed, if Cunningham could get permission.

There was no time to go through the usual channels. So, in what he always regarded as the single bravest act of his whole life, Cunningham woke Prothero the Bad from an after-lunch nap, and stammered out his request. But Prothero the Bad merely growled and wrote out the necessary approval. When the train left that evening, 28 February 1900, Cunningham was on it.

After the train journey and a week's trek by ox-waggon, he joined the Naval Brigade on 7 March for several months of hard campaigning, of forced marches and living off the countryside. Major Peile's marine servant caught a stray horse on the veldt for Cunningham to ride. It was blind in one eye and Cunningham had to start it off at ninety degrees to the direction he actually wanted to go. He was not much of a horseman but, as he told his mother, 'I can't ride but I can stick on.'

The Naval Brigade entered Bloemfontein on 15 March, and were inspected by Lord Roberts, who was a friend of the

Cunningham family. They were now commanded by Captain John Edward Bearcroft, of the cruiser *Philomel*, who evidently had a low opinion of Cunningham and may well have been piqued when Lord Roberts asked to meet Cunningham who, somewhat to his embarrassment, was summoned to shake hands with the great man. 'Skipper forgot to introduce me to Bobs,' Cunningham wrote to his mother, 'and did not give 3 cheers. The Skipper made an ass of himself per usual.'

For the next seven weeks the Naval Brigade stayed in camp on a hill some three miles north of Bloemfontein, where living conditions were shockingly insanitary and eighty-nine officers and men of the Brigade were taken ill with typhoid, enteric fever and dysentery. Cunningham, on the other hand, thrived on the life. His letters were buoyant. He had a balaclava helmet and his binoculars ('the best in the Brigade') sent out from home. In return he sent back some 2½d. South African stamps, likely to be rare because 'only 2,800 were printed'.

His only problem (but a large one) was Captain Bearcroft. When the Naval Brigade at last moved off to advance on Pretoria, Bearcroft pointedly left Cunningham behind, with two 12-pounder guns for the defence of Bloemfontein. 'I have had very bad luck all thro' that old pig Bearcroft who has left me behind here,' he wrote furiously to his mother on 13 May. 'There was really no necessity for anyone being left with these two guns at all.'

He might have stayed in Bloemfontein indefinitely, had not Lord Roberts ridden into the Naval Brigade's camp one evening and asked for him. Finding that Cunningham had been left behind, he ordered Bearcroft to send for him. This, too, was not likely to endear Cunningham to Bearcroft who, almost certainly, thought that this midshipman had used family influence to get round his orders.

However, Cunningham joyfully set off and after a journey of a week rejoined the Naval Brigade in time for the final advance on Pretoria, which surrendered on 4 June. Lord Roberts' force entered the city the next day. By now the Naval Brigade was a tatterdemalion band, unwashed and unshaven, with khaki uniforms almost in rags. Casualties in action and disease had reduced their numbers to about 100 sailors, seventy marines, ten naval officers and four marine officers. But they squared their shoulders and marched into the main square of Pretoria to 'A Life on the Ocean Wave' played by the fifes and drums of the Guards.

On 10 June the Naval Brigade took part in Lord Roberts' crucial battle against Botha at Diamond Hill, some twenty miles east of Pretoria. On 14 June, young Ned wrote to his mother, with a touching mixture of seasoned campaigner and schoolboy, describing how they had been 'chasing Brother Boer out towards Middleburg, trying to round them up and surround them', how they had 'marched about eight miles and did absolutely nothing, though fairly heavy firing was going on all round us', and how

we then moved on about three miles when a Boer gun had the impudence to chuck four shells at us. They missed us altogether, and two fell among the R.F.A. whom they could not see, but nobody was hurt. We then came into action and fired between thirty and forty rounds meeting with no response, so stayed there for about an hour and a half and then got an order to join the Guards' Brigade. The sun was setting as we came up with them. There was a row going on between our infantry and the Boers. Rifle shots and volleys and artillery were all banging away together, and a few stray bullets came whistling round us, but not at all close. In the night John Boer fled and left nothing behind, so it was a complete victory.

28

The sailors were now campaigning in some of the most dramatic and beautiful scenery in the world. Peak after mountain peak, range after range, shrouded in clouds and mist, rose before them as they advanced to the east. The road, often cut into the steep mountain sides, wound through rocky ravines and narrow passes. At the top of every slope, the valley floor opened below, with the snake-like column of the Army and its supply train, guns, mule teams, oxen, waggons, infantry and squadrons of outriding cavalry winding away into the blue distance.

However, they had no time to enjoy the views. They marched at a great pace, and covered ninety miles in nine days. In many places, the road was not much more than a rough stone and shale-strewn track. The guns sometimes had to be physically manhandled up the steeper slopes. Going downhill was even harder than going up. The sailors had to man drag-ropes to prevent guns and carriages taking charge and careering out of control.

On 5 September, Cunningham left for Pretoria. Professor Cunningham had just arrived in South Africa, as a member of a Royal Commission to investigate the medical arrangements for the troops, and Lord Roberts ordered young Cunningham back from the front to see his father.

The rigours of campaigning had so altered Cunningham that his father failed to recognise him. He spent a pleasant week in great comfort in the hospital train provided for the Commissioners, before leaving to rejoin the Naval Brigade. He spent ten days in the mess of the Guards escorting Lord Kitchener and completed the last twenty-five miles of his journey, through the good offices of Lieutenant Walter Cowan, Kitchener's naval ADC, sitting in a corner of the guard's van of His Lordship's special train, with Lord Kitchener himself, whom Cunningham thought 'a most forbidding-looking man', seated in the middle in an armchair.

The campaign was over for the Naval Brigade. At the end of September 1900, they were ordered back to their ships. Cunningham was glad to go. Although he had had a break at the end, after seven months he was tired of the war, with its 'day after day of hard marching and very little real fighting', he wrote. 'I was only seventeen.'

Given the option of going home or staying on the Station, Cunningham chose to go home. Before leaving in October, he collected his back pay, which included five shillings a day field service allowance. To his great surprise, he was given a bag of 100 gold sovereigns. He was lucky to lose only twenty-five pounds playing poker on the way home.

Cunningham never regretted his experience in the Boer War. It was very good training for a young man to have to fend for himself and his sailors, to be forced to improvise and to live off his wits in unfamiliar circumstances in a strange country. As he said, it taught him responsibility and self-reliance. It brought him into close contact with the Army, which he found useful in the years to come. Above all, it made him aware of 'the cheerfulness and endurance, and the many other sterling qualities, of that versatile and adaptable person the British sailor'.

Nevertheless, he doubted whether the Boer War did him much good from a purely Service point of view. Nor did it.

Cunningham's next appointment was to HMS *Hannibal*, one of eight pre-Dreadnought battleships of the Channel Squadron. He joined her, at Portsmouth on 7 January, his eighteenth birthday, in time for a solemn naval occasion.

On 1 February, *Hannibal* was among the British and foreign warships in the Solent as the Royal Yacht *Alberta*, bearing the coffin of Queen Victoria who had died at Osborne on 22 January, steamed slowly through their lines.

Cunningham was greatly impressed by the spectacle — 'a dark, lowering afternoon with occasional shafts of wintry sunlight, and all the ships "manned" by long rows of silent seamen with guards and bands on their quarter-decks'.

He thoroughly enjoyed his time in *Hannibal*. It was a happy gunroom, which included Henry Colt. The gunroom mess was large, and positively palatial compared with *Doris'* 'poky, overcrowded little dungeon'.

After seven months, Cunningham was appointed in July 1901 to the brig HMS *Martin*, tender to the boys' training ship HMS *St Vincent*, at Portsmouth. The Captain was a character, Lieutenant Samuel Montagu Agnew, who creased his trousers 'athwartships' instead of the usual fore-and-aft, and who 'handled his brig as though she were a high-powered, twin-screw steamship'.

Martin had only two midshipmen, so Cunningham changed from being just one of a crowd of 'warts', to a ship's officer with responsibilities. After some experience, he was allowed to handle the ship. He took charge of drills. He even had a cabin. Agnew had a quick temper and a sarcastic tongue. It was a rare drill that did not end with Cunningham having his leave stopped for the rest of the commission. But all was forgiven and forgotten the next day. Once again, Cunningham enjoyed himself and was always glad that he had served in the old sailing Navy.

Like all his term, Cunningham was now preoccupied with examinations and certificates which were important in determining sub-lieutenants' seniority.

Midshipmen had to serve three-and-a-half years, and reach the age of nineteen, before they could be promoted sub-lieutenant. On 7 January 1902, his nineteenth birthday, Cunningham took his seamanship examination on board the old battleship *Repulse* at Chatham and passed with a first-class certificate. He could take off his midshipman's white patches, and put up the single bright gold stripe.

After leave, he went for navigation and pilotage courses at the Royal Naval College, Greenwich, where, with the attractions of London so close, he did just enough work to get a second-class pass in navigation. But pilotage was something Cunningham knew he was good at, and he confidently expected a first class. So he was bitterly disappointed to get only a second.

He had another disappointment, again as a result of his time in South Africa. There had been many awards and promotions for the Naval Brigade. All the midshipmen were noted for early promotion — all, that is, except Cunningham, although he had served ashore longer than any of them and had actually been mentioned in dispatches in the *London Gazette*.

Cunningham was naturally very disappointed by the omission, but he could not have been really surprised. After all, in his opinion, Bearcroft 'was the last man on earth who should have been appointed after Prothero was wounded', and 'was a perfect ass and perhaps I showed I thought it'. So he had to be content with Queen Victoria's South Africa Medal (1899-1902), with its red, blue and orange ribbon, and four clasps: 'Belfast', 'Diamond Hill', 'Orange Free State' and 'Cape Colony'.

Professor Cunningham was convinced that his son's treatment had all been a mistake and ill-advisedly rushed to his offspring's defence. He wrote to the Admiralty, stating that his son had landed on 28 February 1900 and had served ashore until 12 October, 'being present at all the operations between

Poplar Grove and Komati Poort'. But, as anybody in the Navy could have warned the Professor, it was no use. The chilling reply was: 'Captain Bearcroft had not recommended Midshipman Cunningham'.

After Greenwich, Cunningham's term went down to Portsmouth, to the Royal Naval College, inside the dockyard, where they were accommodated while they did courses in gunnery at HMS *Excellent*, Whale Island, and in torpedoes at HMS *Vernon*.

It was sometimes said of Cunningham that it was a pity he never specialised and 'had his mind stretched'. He remained a non-specialist, a 'salt-horse', and was always sceptical about 'experts' and 'specialists', especially gunnery specialists.

This attitude may well have stemmed from his experience at Whale Island, where everything was done to make sub-lieutenants' lives miserable. They were constantly chivvied and chased about the Island. Being shouted at on parade or for some minor offence merely made Cunningham feel mutinous and glad to get away from 'the detestable place'. He left on 13 March 1903 with a second-class certificate and (as a result of a peccadillo) an unsatisfactory report on his general conduct.

At *Vernon*, the instruction was good, conditions more human, and Cunningham gained a first-class certificate. With his two 'ones', in seamanship and torpedoes, and his three 'twos', in navigation, pilotage and gunnery, he did not earn any advanced promotion, but he became a fully fledged sublieutenant, with seniority of 14 March 1903. Some months later, he received his commission, a handsome sheet of stiff parchment, written in elegant copper-plate, signed by Admirals Sir John Fisher and John Durnford, and endorsed by His Majesty King Edward VII.

Cunningham's first ship as a fully commissioned officer was the new battleship HMS *Implacable*, in the Mediterranean. Her Captain was Prothero the Bad, who was getting old and more crotchety and eccentric than ever. The ship had an uneasy atmosphere, with Prothero the Bad attempting to impose his own draconian regime and rigid discipline.

Cunningham was mate of the messdecks, with no responsibility and very little to do. He did not keep watches at sea and not often in harbour. After six months, he was longing for a proper job and when he heard of a vacancy for a sub-lieutenant in the destroyer HMS *Locust* he applied and was successful. He left *Implacable* on 17 September 1903 with, he thought, both the Captain and the Commander glad to see the last of him.

Many a time Cunningham blessed the impulse which had caused him to apply for that vacancy. *Locust*'s Captain, Lieutenant A.B.S. Dutton, was notoriously hard to please and quick to reprimand if matters went awry, but he demanded a great deal of his sub-lieutenant. Thus, Cunningham suddenly found himself personally responsible for the discipline, efficiency, welfare and cleanliness of a 355-ton destroyer and her ship's company of sixty.

Locust was a 'B' Class destroyer, 30 knots, coal-burning, with four funnels. Living conditions were hard but Cunningham thrived on the life and the responsibility, and when Dutton left after three months he gave Cunningham a report to gladden his heart.

Cunningham was promoted Lieutenant on 31 March 1904, and took passage home to Portsmouth in his old ship *Hannibal*. He always recalled with affection and pride his sub-lieutenant's time in Mediterranean destroyers and, as he shrewdly noted, there were some up-and-coming destroyer captains in that flotilla, all likely to remember a young sub-lieutenant who had done well in *Locust*.

His next ship was HMS *Northampton*, a barque-rigged cruiser, completed in 1878. Since 1894 she had cruised around the seaports of the British Isles recruiting young men, nicknamed '*Northampton* riggers', for the Navy. These cruises had been very successful and, when Cunningham joined her at Campbeltown on the Mull of Kintyre in June 1904, *Northampton* was accompanied by two smaller cruisers, *Cleopatra* and *Calliope*.

Northampton was supposed to proceed under sail as well as steam, but Cunningham never saw her do so. Perhaps this was just as well, because the 'riggers' laid aloft and scrambled along the yards 'rather like a lot of plough-boys', and whenever they did try and make sail on passage, the ship at once flew up into the wind.

Cunningham was one of two lieutenants borne for watch-keeping duties and at first had nothing to do with the boys' instruction. However (and not before time, in Cunningham's opinion), the Admiralty reorganised the training of new entries. Lieutenants were appointed to take charge of the boys' welfare and instruction, with one officer specially detailed to organise the training of all 300 boys on board. To Cunningham's satisfaction, *Northampton*'s Captain, A.J. Horsley, gave this job to him.

Cunningham's days in *Northampton*, and in the 'more modern' (completed in 1892) cruiser *Hawke*, to which they transferred in November 1904 when *Northampton* paid off for the last time, were some of the happiest in his career. He believed that every lieutenant should do at least a year in the training service. 'To teach, one had to learn how.'

Hawke was one of a newly formed Training Squadron, the others being the cruisers *St George* and *Edgar*, with boys from the training ships, and *Isis* and *Highflyer*, with naval cadets. Cunningham had one of *Hawke*'s four divisions, of some seventy boys, but also took charge of instruction. He kept watches at sea but not in harbour.

Early in 1905, the Squadron went across to the West Indies. The Navigating Officer went down with measles halfway across the Atlantic and Cunningham took over his duties.

The Squadron had its snobberies. '*Northampton* riggers', entered direct from shore without going through any of the training establishments, were rather looked down on as being uncouth and half-trained. Six months older than the average and supposed to be underweight and physically weaker, they had an extra half-pound of beef a day. Cunningham was therefore delighted when *Hawke*'s cutters' crews thrashed the rest.

When *Hawke* paid off in May 1906, Cunningham was not chosen to recommission her, as he had hoped. Instead, after leave at home in Edinburgh, he went to the cruiser HMS *Scylla* for the Naval Manoeuvres of 1906.

The manoeuvres of June 1906, an extended trade defence exercise in the eastern Atlantic, had the most ominous implications for the Royal Navy in the two world wars to come. War was supposed to have broken out between a stronger (Red) naval power, commanded by Admiral Sir Arthur Knyvet Wilson, with the Channel Fleet at Milford Haven, and supported by the Mediterranean Fleet under Admiral Sir Charles Beresford at Gibraltar, and a weaker but still formidable (Blue) naval power, under Vice-Admiral Sir William May, at Berehaven in southern Ireland. Several shipping companies co-operated by agreeing that their merchant ships would pretend that they were sunk or captured during the exercise.

The exercise scenario virtually restricted Blue to an attack on merchant shipping on passage to and from the British Isles, the South Atlantic and the Mediterranean. May disposed his ships in search lines off the Portuguese coast stretching some 200 miles out into the Atlantic. This 'ill-fated disposition', as one naval pundit called it, exposed May to attack by Wilson from the north and Beresford from the south, and May's ships indeed suffered several casualties.

But there was one very disquieting aspect, which was ignored or glossed over. While Red was attacking Blue's battle fleet, Blue's smaller ships carried out a short but successful *guerre de course*. In the eight days of the exercise, 400 ships (merchant ships or warships acting as merchant ships) passed through the area. Of those, ninety-two were liable to attack and fifty-two were adjudged sunk or captured.

The two slow, unarmoured, third-class Blue cruisers *Scylla* and her sister ship, *Sappho*, sank or captured ten ships. A few Blue destroyers accounted for twelve more ships. Thus twenty-two ships (nearly half the total) were sunk or captured by what the pundits called 'these insignificant vessels'.

The exercise showed conclusively how vulnerable ships sailing individually were to attacks by ocean raiders, and therefore how vitally necessary it was to introduce convoy in time of war. In fact, exactly the opposite conclusion was drawn. Blue's attack on shipping was judged 'strategically unsound'. Official opinion was that 'on the outbreak of war, ship-owners would prefer to be left with a free hand as to the action of their vessels'. All the experts insisted that the destruction of the enemy's battle fleet must continue to be the

Navy's primary objective in war. Exercise evidence was manipulated to support that theory.

From *Scylla* Cunningham went to the 9,800-ton 22-knot armoured cruiser HMS *Suffolk* in the Mediterranean Fleet. When her Captain, Rosslyn Wemyss, joined her in September 1905, he was warned that *Suffolk* was 'the worst ship in the Navy', with discontented officers, unwilling sailors, and the ship herself constantly in the dockyard with engine defects.

Rosslyn Wemyss, known universally as 'Rosy', appeared more courtier than naval officer. With his aristocratic birth and bearing, his monocle, his villa in Cannes, his wealth and his abundance of friends and social connections, he presented an unusually *boulevardier* image for a naval officer. But behind that seemingly dilettante façade, there was a very shrewd, knowledgeable and capable professional, who was to rise to be First Sea Lord.

When Cunningham joined *Suffolk*, he found her a very happy ship and her unusual Captain, he said, 'under an air of complete insouciance, concealed shrewdness with a very alert mind and a mass of professional knowledge'.

Always quick to learn from his superiors, Cunningham noted how Rosy handled his officers, always most courteously, although he could be severe if the occasion warranted it. When Cunningham was doing duty as navigating officer, he made an error in working out the ship's noon position. Rosy noticed it, leaned over Cunningham's shoulder, put his finger on the chart and politely pointed out where Cunningham had gone wrong. 'It was true,' said Cunningham, 'I had. Together we corrected the mistake.'

The fleet went on at least two and sometimes three cruises a year, to the Greek islands, to the Italian ports, the Aegean and the south of France, carrying out exercises on passage. There were quarterly gunnery and torpedo practices. Combined manoeuvres with the Atlantic Fleet were usually held once a year.

The Commander-in-Chief, Admiral Sir Charles Beresford, 'Charlie B' as he was known, was a very capable, much liked and respected flag officer, with many ideas on training and tactics. He ran a very 'flagshippy' flagship, insisting on the strictest ceremonial. He demanded absolute silence at all times. All orders had to be given by signs. Nobody was allowed to cheer, even when their ship's boats won the regatta, but they had to clap politely. Cunningham himself fell foul of this rule, by making too much racket in *Suffolk*'s picket boat when the ship's cutters, trained by him, won the squadron obstacle race. Rosy Wemyss was unmoved by a snorting signal from the flagship. The victory was properly celebrated in the cuddy.

Suffolk won the squadron sports and the regatta — the sure sign of a good ship. Her crack cutter regularly beat all comers and her sailors made a steady income from betting, until Nemesis arrived in the shape of the Channel Fleet cruiser *Argyll* with her specially built racing cutter. After an epic race over three miles, *Argyll*'s boat won by half a length, and £658 — a colossal sum for those days — changed hands from the Mediterranean to the Channel Fleet.

Cunningham kept watches, at sea and in harbour, was in charge of sailing and organised the training of the ordinary seamen and boys. It was a busy and a fulfilling life, but he had set his heart on a destroyer command. With only four years' seniority, he was barely eligible, but when *Suffolk* paid off at Devonport in April 1908, he asked Rosy Wemyss, whom he knew had some influence at the Admiralty, if he would put in a good word for him. Rosy promised he would do his best.

On leave in Edinburgh, Cunningham waited impatiently for the post every day. He knew it was more likely he would get another battleship or a cruiser and serve another commission, two more years at least.

But Rosy did not let Cunningham down. The 'long official envelope from the Admiralty arrived one morning early in May. I tore it open. I was appointed to HMS *Hecla*, at Portsmouth, for H.M. Torpedo Boat No. 14, in command... I was delighted at the prospect.'

2: DESTROYER COMMAND

CUNNINGHAM JOINED *TB 14* on 13 May 1908 in the Tidal Basin at Portsmouth and sailed at once with her sister ship *TB 13* to Campbeltown to join their depot ship *Hecla* and the other twenty to twenty-five TBs of the 4th (Portsmouth) Flotilla. They were brand new torpedo boats, numbered 1 to 36, built as 'Coastal Destroyers', armed with two 12-pounder guns and three 18-inch torpedo tubes. Turbine driven and oil-fired, they could do 26 knots. They were very small at 270 tons (Cunningham had no cabin, just one of the four bunks in the wardroom) but they were good seaboats.

The flotilla spent the summer at Campbeltown, with gunnery or torpedo exercises every forenoon and afternoon, then returned to harbour in time for a round of golf at Machrahenish. They had reduced complements and seldom spent a night at sea. In September, the flotilla went south, to lie up for the winter in Fareham Creek, going to sea occasionally for exercises.

Professor Cunningham was now Dean of the Faculty of Medicine at Edinburgh University, but he was in poor health and in the summer of 1909, when *TB 14* was at Oban preparing to take part in the combined fleet exercises, Cunningham received a telegram that his father was dying. He went home on compassionate leave and was able to see his father before he died on 23 June 1909.

His next command was the 30-knot coal-burning destroyer *Vulture*, but he thought her 'distinctly inferior', and complained to his Captain (D), Reginald Tyrwhitt, of his 'Irishman's rise', at which Tyrwhitt was somewhat annoyed. However,

Cunningham's luck held and he exchanged into the beautiful little destroyer *Roebuck* — fast, handy and economical on fuel and with a captain's cabin which was a palace compared to the cramped hole in *Vulture* and the bunk in *TB 14*. But *Roebuck* paid off with boiler trouble in December 1910.

Cunningham had now commanded destroyers for two-and-a-half years and was due to go to a big ship. But once again he went to his Captain (D), the melodiously named Mortimer L'Estrange Silver, and asked him to put in a good word.

To his delighted amazement, Cunningham was appointed in command of the destroyer *Scorpion*. One of the new *Beagle* Class, she had only been completed three months. She was 900 tons, with one 4-inch gun on the fo'c'sle, three 12-pounder guns and two 21-inch torpedo tubes, and could do 27 knots.

Scorpion had turbines but was coal-fired. Coal and turbines, as Cunningham said, made a bad mixture. Oil was a much cleaner and more efficient fuel, but every drop of it had to be imported from abroad, nor did Great Britain yet have the oil storage, the tankers or fuelling facilities required. Therefore, after some changes of Admiralty minds over their design, the *Beagles* were coal-burning — the last Royal Navy destroyers to be so.

Cunningham joined *Scorpion* at Harwich on the afternoon of Saturday 11 January 1911. On Sunday morning, when he had just started rounds of his new ship, he received a signal to repair at once on board the light cruiser *Boadicea* which wore the broad pennant of the Commodore (D), who had already been round his flotillas in his barge that morning and had noticed mud on *Scorpion*'s port anchor.

This was Cunningham's first encounter with Rear-Admiral Sir Robert Arbuthnot. Arbuthnot was a 'big ship' man, and he brought highly unwelcome and much resented 'big ship' methods and attitudes to his destroyer flotillas. He was a harsh disciplinarian and a hard driver, who insisted upon the exact letter of the last and least considered law. He frequently ordered destroyers to spend weekends at sea, after a hard week's exercises, as punishment for minor misdemeanours, and often placed officers under arrest, as a means of stopping their leave. At sea, he would signal his displeasure by telling a captain to consider himself under arrest and turn over his command to his First Lieutenant — thus, incidentally, giving many a junior officer invaluable experience.

That first Sunday morning, Cunningham explained that he had only joined *Scorpion* the day before. Arbuthnot mellowed at once, and this, as Cunningham said, was the first and last time he was in trouble with Arbuthnot.

On 24 June 1911, *Scorpion* was at the Spithead Naval Review, to commemorate the Coronation of HM King George V. The British warships alone stretched for more than twenty-six miles, with forty-two battleships, four battlecruisers, thirty armoured cruisers, thirty-seven protected cruisers, eight scouts, fifteen torpedo gunboats, sixty-eight destroyers, eight submarines, and seven depot ships.

After the Review, the flotilla returned to Harwich. Under Arbuthnot, there were no rounds of golf; in fact, the flotilla was nicknamed the 'Outer Gabbard Yacht Club', from the Outer Gabbard Lightship, far out in the North Sea, which was their usual rendezvous. Three weeks out of four, Arbuthnot took his destroyers to sea at noon on Mondays and kept them at sea until Thursday night for hectic programmes of gunnery and torpedo exercises. Even if it was too rough or too foggy for exercises, Arbuthnot's ships went to sea just the same.

On Fridays, and during the fourth week, there were harbour drills. In spare moments, there was coaling ship and then hands to cleaning stations. Always Arbuthnot was ready, binoculars to his eyes, to detect defects and omissions. 'Our every little fault or failing was noted, and corrected,' Cunningham wrote.

Cunningham himself drove *Scorpion* and her ship's company very hard. In his zealous desire to succeed, his behaviour and his language sometimes exceeded the bounds of what was felt to be acceptable. In 1912 a Court of Inquiry investigated the punishment of a leading signalman of *Scorpion*. The verdict, entered on Cunningham's service record, was that he 'was informed that Their Lordships are highly displeased with his conduct (losing his temper and making use of improper and exasperating language to a subordinate) and warned him to be more careful of his language in future'.

On a dark night in November 1911, the flotilla was approaching the Straits of Dover, on passage back to Harwich after exercises at Portland, when *Scorpion* collided with the *Fynn*, a three-masted wooden sailing ship, which capsized and sank.

The Board of Inquiry established that the collision was wholly *Scorpion*'s fault. *Fynn* had been beating down Channel when *Scorpion*'s officer of the watch mistook her red port navigation light for one of the flotilla's in the column to starboard. The Admiralty paid *Fynn*'s owners compensation. *Scorpion* spent four months under repair in Chatham dockyard.

Cunningham was lucky again. Although a captain was always held responsible for everything that happened in his ship, he was evidently not blamed for the accident and his career was unaffected.

Arbuthnot left in July 1912. The flotilla, with sixteen *Beagle* Class destroyers, became the 3rd Flotilla. The new Commodore (D), Cecil Lambert, was almost as hard a taskmaster as Arbuthnot. Training continued in the North Sea in all weathers.

In the autumn of 1913, the 3rd Flotilla went out to the Mediterranean, arriving in Malta in November. The famous Malta social season was in full swing, with parties, balls, picnics and sports. But Cunningham seems to have become a confirmed bachelor at an early age, almost wedded to the Navy, and virtually uninterested in women. While others went 'poodle-faking', he spent his spare time playing golf or sailing.

In February 1914, a new Captain (D), C.P.R. Coode, arrived and there was an immediate hardening of the flotilla atmosphere. Coode made coaling ship, for example, fiercely competitive, knowing that war was coming and that shorter coaling times meant that his flotilla would be ready for sea more quickly. Coaling rates soared from a leisurely thirty or forty tons an hour, which had been regarded as reasonable, up to ninety or a hundred. *Scorpion* held the flotilla record, of 120 tons an hour.

That summer of 1914, the Mediterranean Fleet went on its customary cruises, to Corfu, the Aegean islands, and the eastern Mediterranean. But on 28 July the fleet was ordered to sail in haste for Malta to coal and store for war. On 2 August, on a peaceful Sunday afternoon, when most of the sailors were ashore, the 3rd Flotilla was ordered to raise steam with all dispatch. They sailed next day at noon, with warheads on torpedoes and live ammunition, to patrol off Malta. The order to commence hostilities reached them in the early hours of 5 August 1914.

Half of the 3rd Flotilla went home, but Cunningham stayed, against his will. Nelson may have sought and gained a bed of laurels in the Mediterranean, but for Cunningham and his contemporaries honour and glory were to be found in the

North Sea, where everybody expected the first act to be a cataclysmic clash between the British and the German battle fleets, which everybody believed would result in a decisive win for the British. By contrast, the Mediterranean was expected to be a backwater.

At the outbreak of war, the German Navy had the battlecruiser *Goeben* and the light cruiser *Breslau* in the Mediterranean. They were sighted off the coast of North Africa by both the French and the British on 4 August, but hostilities had not begun and no action could be taken.

It was assumed that the German ships intended to head west for the Atlantic. In fact, they steered east and when, on the evening of 6 August, they emerged from the southern end of the Straits of Messina and turned northeast towards the Adriatic, only the light cruiser HMS *Gloucester* was still in touch.

That evening, the 3rd Flotilla was ordered to join the 1st Cruiser Squadron, led by Rear-Admiral Sir Ernest Troubridge, flying his flag in *Defence*. Early on 7 August they were steaming at 19 knots (the cruisers' full speed) to intercept. Troubridge signalled that they would probably be in action at 6 a.m. This, Cunningham said, 'thrilled us to the marrow'.

The C-in-C, Admiral Sir Berkeley Milne, had been ordered by the Admiralty on 30 July: 'Do not, at this stage, be brought to action against superior forces, except in combination with the French, as part of a general battle.' Milne passed this on to Troubridge who, in the early hours of 7 August, decided that he could not intercept *Goeben* until two hours after dawn. A battlecruiser in daylight was 'superior forces'. Therefore at 4 a.m. Troubridge reduced speed and called off the chase.

Meanwhile Milne, with three battlecruisers, was still west of Malta, proceeding at leisurely speed. The whole enterprise petered out in disappointment and later acrimony. *Goeben* and

Breslau reached Constantinople on 10 August. Their arrival was a major propaganda and diplomatic success for Germany and played a large part in bringing Turkey into the war on the side of the Central Powers. Troubridge was later court-martialled for abandoning the chase, but was acquitted.

The Admiralty ordered Troubridge to take *Defence* and all his destroyers, with their parent cruiser *Blenheim*, to the Dardanelles, where a blockade was to be set up, in case the German ships attempted to escape.

The Dardanelles blockade was the dreariest period of Cunningham's naval career. The destroyers patrolled the entrance, working two days on, two days off, stopping and (when the weather permitted) boarding all steamers entering or leaving the Straits. Fresh food soon ran out at sea: 'we are living on chickens and stale eggs,' Cunningham wrote to his mother.

There was no proper base or harbour, so the island of Tenedos, off the coast of Asia Minor, was used as shelter; when the wind blew from the north, they anchored on the south side, and vice versa. Notice for steam was seldom more than two hours. There was shore leave occasionally, but nothing to do ashore.

What Cunningham called the 'more literary-minded' flotilla officers started *The Tenedos Times*, typed and issued monthly from Captain (D)'s office in *Blenheim*. It had three editors, one of them Gerald Dickens, Captain of *Harpy* and a grandson of the novelist Charles. It ran to seven issues and contained much doggerel verse, parodies of Lewis Carroll, cartoons, watercolours and occasional articles.

Great Britain's ultimatum to Turkey over *Goeben* and other acts expired on 31 October. On the next day, *Scorpion* and her 'chummy' ship *Wolverine* were dispatched to Vourlah Bay, in the Gulf of Smyrna, to investigate a report that a Turkish ship was being fitted out as a minelayer there.

When they entered the Gulf at daylight, they saw a large yacht of about 500 tons alongside Vourlah jetty, but, though she proved to be armed with at least two guns, they were not sure she was a minelayer. Nor were they sure they were definitely at war with Turkey (war was not officially declared until 5 November).

The destroyers withdrew for instructions and were told to make the yacht surrender or destroy her. A Turkish lieutenant came out in a four-oared boat but left *Wolverine* in a hurry, and, when he was halfway inshore, waved his hand as though to give a sign. The yacht immediately burst into flames forward and aft. Both destroyers then contributed several rounds of 4-inch. *Scorpion*'s first shell (her first ever fired in anger) blew away the yacht's funnel.

There were some heavy explosions, which also sank a smaller vessel alongside. Cunningham felt they could have gone in and brought the yacht out as a prize. But *Scorpion* and *Wolverine* had taken part in the first hostilities against Turkey.

Vice-Admiral Carden, who had relieved Troubridge, was instructed to bombard the outer forts of the Dardanelles defences, and *Scorpion* and *Wolverine* rejoined the flag for the first bombardment on 3 November. The British bombarded the forts at Sedd-el-Bahr and Cape Helles, on the European side, while the French dealt with Kum Kale and Orkanieh on the Asiatic side.

It was difficult to establish just what the bombardments achieved, but they certainly alerted the Turks and the Germans and the defences were strengthened. Because Carden's ships departed and did not return, it was reported in Constantinople that they had been driven off.

Apart from a ten-day spell in Malta, where *Scorpion* was refitted for the action to come, *Scorpion* continued her dreary and monotonous patrolling. But, in the New Year of 1915, there were rumours of a forthcoming naval assault on the Dardanelles.

The plan for the Dardanelles, as it finally emerged, was for warships to force the Straits, successively reducing the coastal forts by bombardment, eventually penetrating to the Sea of Marmara and, ultimately, occupying Constantinople so as to force Turkey out of the war, relieve pressure on the Russians on the Eastern Front, and provide a decisive counterbalance to the main Allied campaign on the Western Front. No troops were to be landed. It was to be a purely naval undertaking.

The scheme, whose most enthusiastic and powerful protagonist was Winston Churchill, the First Lord of the Admiralty, ignored the wisdom of previous centuries: ships were no match for forts. As Nelson said, with first-hand experience, 'any sailor who attacked a fort was a fool'.

Even if the Narrows were forced, every ship passing up or down would still have to run the gauntlet of hostile shores; sooner or later, troops would surely have to be landed to secure at least one side of the Straits. If the fleet did reach Constantinople, there was no guarantee that the Turkish Government would necessarily capitulate.

There was also a danger from mines. The Dardanelles was perfect for minefields. Experience of mines during the Russo-Japanese war had shown how effective they were, and their designs had since been improved.

Cunningham had his own misgivings about the plan. As he said, 'It sounded just too easy; but few of us in the destroyers had all that touching faith in naval gunnery.'

The first bombardment was on 19 February 1915, the anniversary of Admiral Sir John Duckworth's passage of the Dardanelles in 1807. This was an omen: Duckworth's ships were virtually unscathed on the way up, but were subjected to enormous volumes of shot from every fort on the way down, so that some were very badly knocked about.

It was a brilliant morning, of bright winter sunshine, with the sea almost flat calm, and the lightest of breezes — jolly bombarding weather. To Cunningham and the other watchers, the shooting by the battlecruiser HMS *Inflexible* (wearing the flag of Vice-Admiral Carden), the battleships *Triumph*, *Cornwallis* and *Albion*, and the French battleships *Suffren* and *Bouvet*, certainly looked impressive. Hits could be clearly seen on the earthworks ashore.

The forts made no reply. The defences appeared to be overwhelmed by the weight of fire, and there were no signs of life anywhere. At 4.40 p.m. Vice-Admiral Carden signalled ships to cease fire and to go closer inshore to examine the forts' damage.

Suddenly, to everybody's intense surprise, the forts opened fire, as though they had not been touched. The bombardment began again, but with the light fading, the overriding need to conserve precious ammunition, and the risk of a night torpedo attack on his big ships, Carden signalled the cease fire at 5.50, although one fort, ominously, was still firing as his ships withdrew. Carden intended to resume on the morrow. It was reckoned that only another hour's bombardment would be needed to finish off the forts.

The weather broke next day and the bombardment could not be resumed until 25 February, when the ships were ordered to 'destroy each individual gun by a direct hit'. Working in pairs, the ships steamed into the jaws of the Narrows and fired until the range was down to 3,000 yards.

The forts soon showed that they had by no means been destroyed and returned fire, but eventually the persistence of the bombardment had some effect. By 3 p.m. the shore batteries were practically silenced. The minesweeping trawlers closed the coast, and began sweeping at 4 p.m. Escorted by destroyers, including *Scorpion*, the sweepers carried on under cover of darkness. By daylight they had cleared a wide channel for four miles up the Straits. No mines were found.

When three battleships entered the Straits the next morning, they were constantly harassed by fire from howitzers and field guns which they could not pin down. The shore batteries had been enormously strengthened since the first bombardment of November 1914. Clearly, the forcing of the Dardanelles was not going to be as simple as it may once have appeared.

The naval bombardments had only destroyed about a third of the heavy guns. More direct action was needed. On 26 February, marines from *Vengeance*, and a demolition party of sailors under the ship's Torpedo Officer (and Cunningham's *Britannia* term-mate) Lieutenant-Commander E.G. ('Kipper') Robinson, landed to destroy fort guns and a bridge across a river. For this exploit, and for his work with the minesweeping trawlers, 'Kipper' Robinson was awarded the Victoria Cross (the second of Cunningham's term: Midshipman Basil Guy had won the VC at Tientsin during the Boxer Rising in 1900).

More parties were landed and their reports made it clear the bombardments were doing little real damage to the forts. Neither were the minesweepers, upon whom everything ultimately depended, making the expected progress. Slow and encumbered by their sweeps, the trawlers could not make proper headway against the strong Dardanelles currents and were very vulnerable to shore-battery fire. A dangerous impasse was reached. The minefield batteries prevented the minefields from being swept. But until the minefields were swept, the big ships could not get close enough to knock out the minefield batteries.

The destroyers were busy escorting the bombarding big ships by day, and themselves firing at targets of opportunity, and shepherding the minesweepers by night. At first, Cunningham expected to be hit and when fired at manoeuvred rapidly out of the way. But he and his ship's company soon became 'strangely phlegmatic'. One sailor, Leading Torpedoman Love, was sitting on the upper deck, reading a Wild West thriller, when a Turkish shell pitched alongside with a loud explosion and a column of smoke and spray. Love looked up, said 'Another redskin bit the dust', and carried on reading.

But the Turks' shooting improved. Escorting the minesweepers became, as Cunningham said, 'distinctly nasty'. All sorts of Turkish guns 'let us have it'. Occasionally a shell fell into the water close by with 'a heavy sort of splodge'.

The weather continued stormy and constantly interrupted bombardments and landings. In one letter home Cunningham remarked that the ship was rolling heavily as he wrote. But though it was very cold, his ship's company were warmly clothed. 'Don't send woollies,' he wrote in February. 'The Navy League have sent seventeen boxes since Christmas, and we are trying to find some ships to take the surplus.' Instead, he asked for some Edinburgh shortbread, and a large map of Europe.

It was a rare Sunday morning that did not find Cunningham at his desk in his cabin dealing with his personal mail. 'Things are bucking up splendidly,' he wrote to his mother, on 6 March. 'Everything is much more interesting now.'

Scorpion and the other destroyers were certainly kept busy, escorting bombarding ships, covering landings by marines and demolition parties and shelling shore targets.

In mid-March it was decided, and not before time, that the trawlers were unsuitable for minesweeping. *Scorpion* and the other *Beagles* were converted into fast minesweepers by equipping them with sweeps and kites, streamed from their quarterdecks. They worked in pairs with the gear suspended between them, sweeping at 14-15 knots, or faster if the risk of parting the gear was accepted.

On 16 March Vice-Admiral Carden's health broke down, and he was relieved by de Robeck. Rosy Wemyss, then Admiral-in-Charge at Mudros, was the senior, but de Robeck was Carden's second-in-command and much more in touch with affairs, so Rosy with typical generosity agreed to serve under him.

On 18 March 1915 another great operation was launched, to silence the batteries once and for all, and then sweep through the Narrows to clear the way through into the Sea of Marmara at last.

Carden had always used his big ships in 'penny packets', sending them singly, or at the most in threes. By contrast de Robeck, a much bolder officer, intended to use all eighteen capital ships available to him.

Cunningham expected *Scorpion* and the other *Beagle* Class destroyers, all by now fully efficient as fast minesweepers, to take part. Instead, half lay at anchor off Tenedos for the whole day. Cunningham spent the afternoon playing bridge, listening to the distant thunder of the guns, intercepting wireless reports, and champing with exasperated impatience.

The intercepted reports were nearly all of bad news. *Inflexible* was mined and badly damaged and returned that evening with her fo'c'sle nearly awash and her ship's company mustered aft on the quarterdeck. She was, as Cunningham soon learned, the visible evidence of a disastrous day.

Several bombarding ships were hit by shore fire. The French battleship *Bouvet* blew up and sank so quickly only a handful of men were rescued. *Irresistible* struck a mine and had to be abandoned after her ship's company had been taken off.

The minesweeping trawlers tried to sweep further up but came under such intense fire that they all turned back. De Robeck decided that the battleships could not be left inside the Straits after dark and there was no chance of clearing the minefields that night. When he saw that *Irresistible* had been abandoned, he hoisted the General Recall. But the day's disasters were not over. *Ocean* then struck a mine as she was withdrawing under heavy fire and she too was abandoned.

As the stricken battleships had not actually been seen to sink, *Scorpion* and the other destroyers went up that night to look for them. But they had both sunk in deep water. So ended yet another and, as it happened, the last attempt to force the Narrows by naval action.

Lord Kitchener, the Secretary of State for War, had hitherto taken the view that no troops were required or could be spared from the Western Front, while Winston Churchill had continued to argue that the Navy could achieve everything on its own. But now it was clear, as it had been for some time to those on the spot, that the present tactics were not, and never would be, enough to subdue the Dardanelles.

Kitchener reported to the War Council that the situation on the Western and Eastern Fronts had so changed that the 29th Division could be released. In the event, the 29th Division (18,000 men), and five battalions (Nelson, Drake, Hood, Anson and Howe) of the Royal Naval Division and the Portsmouth and Deal battalions of the Royal Marines (11,000 men), 34,100 men of the Australia and New Zealand ('Anzac') Corps, and a French division of 18,000 men — a total of 81,100 men — were all available. Almost without anybody noticing it, and certainly without anybody planning it, the assault on the Dardanelles had become a very large combined operation.

When the first troops arrived at Mudros Bay, it was found that their transports had been loaded according to the bureaucratic direction of a Mr Graeme Thomson, the Admiralty's civilian Director of Transports, who had no experience or notion of war. Troops were embarked in one transport, their stores and equipment in another. Gunners were separated from their guns, which were separated from their ammunition. Port facilities at Mudros Bay were quite inadequate, so General Ian Hamilton, the newly appointed Army Commander, had to send or divert ships to Alexandria, 700 miles away.

Thus, the main landings were further delayed, and the Turks given more time to prepare their defences. While minesweeping or patrolling off the coast by night, Cunningham could actually hear from *Scorpion*'s bridge the sounds of spades and the thudding of mallets, as Turkish working parties dug trenches and earthworks, and erected posts for barbed wire.

On 31 March, de Robeck and some of his staff embarked in *Scorpion* to see for themselves what the Turks were doing to their defences. As lunch time drew near, Cunningham became 'rather fussed' and sent down to ask what fare *Scorpion* could give their guests. After several days on patrol, destroyers were often down to 'Bare Navy' — bully beef and ship's biscuit. *Scorpion*'s victuals consisted of bully beef and rice pudding made with condensed milk so Cunningham was immensely relieved when de Robeck said that they had brought their own food with them.

While de Robeck was in *Scorpion*, he had a word with the galley staff who told him they were 'almost as bare as Mother Hubbard's cupboard'. The following morning, just before *Scorpion* sailed from Mudros, de Robeck's barge came alongside with chickens, loaves, butter and all manner of good things. It was an example of leadership and consideration which was not lost on Cunningham. Can one wonder, he wrote, 'how greatly John de Robeck was liked and admired for this and many other little acts, of kind thoughtfulness?'

Scorpion was joined by one of *Irresistible*'s survivors, Midshipman Robert Adamson. He is 'the laziest young rascal I've ever seen', Cunningham told his aunt, Helen Browne (always addressed by her family nickname, 'Doodles'). Adamson 'joined with only what he stood up in (wretched youth) and two mufflers and two towels and a tin of cigarettes (the latter he thinks I have not seen. He is only sixteen)'.

Another junior officer who served in *Scorpion* was Sub-Lieutenant Francis Flynn, from the battleship *Canopus*. He had noted the destroyers coaling at Tenedos:

> Two destroyers, moving fast, appeared, returning from a Dardanelles patrol. One made for the collier and came alongside, handled with great precision. While the berthing wires were still being rove, men and equipment came pell-mell on to the collier's deck and down into her hold. Derricks were swung out, bags filled, and, with scarcely any sound other than from the winches, the hoists were swung over and dumped on the *Scorpion*'s upper-deck. Everyone contributed to the intensive competition. The finish was as sharp and efficient as the beginning.

Flynn particularly noted *Scorpion*'s Captain, a 'red-faced

Lieutenant Commander' with 'markedly penetrating blue eyes', and volunteered to serve in his ship because he wanted to learn from this tough, professional naval officer. Cunningham lost no time in finding out what his new Sub-Lieutenant was made of; within twenty-four hours, Flynn was officer of the watch on the bridge, on his own, in complete charge of the ship, for the first time in his life.

> At the mouth of the Dardanelles, two mine-sweeping trawlers came down towards us. I did not like the idea of altering course to avoid their sweep as it would certainly arouse my captain, so I was relieved when the skipper of one of the trawlers leant over his bridge and beckoned me on. Meanwhile ABC had come on deck aft, and, believing that I was going to foul the ship, rang down the after engine-room telegraphs to half astern. I promptly put my bridge telegraphs to half ahead again and waited for an explosion. On ABC's arrival I explained my actions. He gave me a searching and unsmiling look and said nothing at all.

Flynn found that Cunningham did have a keen sense of humour and a simple, almost childlike, sense of fun. He was easy to amuse, although exchanging jokes with him was like putting one's hand in the cage to pat the tiger. Cunningham very seldom raised his voice: 'Perhaps the *Scorpion* was so highly trained it was unnecessary.'

Scorpion was now fully involved in the preparations for the great amphibious operation planned for the end of April. Early on the 17th the submarine E. 15 ran aground under the guns of a fort in the Straits. Her Captain and some of her crew were killed and the rest were made prisoner. *Scorpion* took part in attempts, eventually successful, to destroy the submarine's hull *in situ*.

When the destroyers returned to Mudros, they found the bay crammed with shipping. Rosy Wemyss and his staff had transformed Mudros from a sleepy little fishing haven into the busiest port in the Mediterranean, with warships of all kinds, store ships and auxiliaries, and some fifty troop transports carrying the 29th Division and the Anzac Corps. The nearby hillsides were covered with large tended camps for British, Australian, New Zealand, Indian and French troops.

The Allied landings at Gallipoli were intended to secure the heights overlooking the Straits on the European side, to safeguard the warships when, in due course, as everybody expected, they resumed the forcing of the Narrows.

Scorpion and the other seven *Beagles* had the task of sweeping inside the Straits to allow the battleships on the right flank of the Army to come close inshore and subdue the defenders during that critical period while the landing force was getting ashore.

Bad weather delayed the landing until 25 April, giving the Turks even more time to prepare their defences. But the day itself was ideal. From *Scorpion*'s bridge, Cunningham witnessed a thrilling, unforgettable sight: a sea, flat calm and burnished like a mirror; destroyers packed with troops and towing boats with more troops; troop transports further out, waiting to unload; closer in, late but rapidly nearing 'V' Beach, the converted collier *River Clyde* carrying over 2,000 troops and towing with her the boats which would form a landing pontoon. Closer inshore, Cunningham could see huge clouds of smoke and dust from exploding shells as the battleships and cruisers pounded the Turkish positions which seemed surprisingly quiescent.

Stunned fish in their thousands rose to the surface, but the Turks were relatively unharmed. When the bombardment lifted, there was a short but fatal delay while *River Clyde* ran in, grounded and began to get out her boats. The Turks manned their defences again and opened fire.

The soldiers, packed like sardines in their boats and weighed down with equipment, were shot in ordered ranks, just where they sat. When *River Clyde*'s specially designed gangways crashed down, more soldiers poured out and tried to get ashore, but were machine-gunned as they emerged. As the leading ranks fell, more men appeared unknowingly behind them, as though queuing up for slaughter. *River Clyde* did her best to protect her charges. Her Captain and his ship's company won five Victoria Crosses between dawn and dusk. But for a time the sea off Cape Helles did run dark, not with wine, but literally with blood.

After making three or four sweeps, the destroyers lay off the beaches waiting for orders. By a decision of almost incredible stupidity (whose, Cunningham could never afterwards discover) the destroyers had been given the strictest orders not to open fire in support of the soldiers ashore.

Scorpion lay for some time off 'V' Beach, only five hundred yards from a trench full of Turkish troops. Cunningham could actually see 'our infantry lying flat on their faces on the beach under withering fire, and every now and then one or two men dashing out to cut the wire in front of them, only to be quickly shot down. It was a tragedy and a mortifying situation for a well-gunned destroyer.'

At first, the Turkish defenders were too busy to notice the destroyers. But on the second and subsequent days, life became uncomfortable. The destroyers were very vulnerable whilst sweeping, when they had to steam in pairs, on steady courses, at about 12 knots against currents of 2-3 knots, unable to manoeuvre because of the sweep gear streamed between their sterns.

On 27 April, the third day of sweeping, *Scorpion* and her 'chummy ship' *Wolverine* were some distance further up the Straits than on previous days, and had just passed the sweep wires and were opening out, only some seventy yards apart, when a shore battery opened a very accurate fire.

Two shells passed over *Scorpion*, two pitched between the ships, and the fifth hit *Wolverine* square on the bridge, killing her Captain, a midshipman RNR, and the Coxswain. Later, *Scorpion* was hit on the fo'c'sle by a shell which passed between the legs of the gunlayer of the 4-inch, and penetrated to the seamen's messdeck below.

The damage-control stoker petty officer arrived somewhat breathlessly on the bridge to report that the messdeck was on fire. Cunningham 'coldly replied, "Then put it out"'. As *Scorpion* was still connected to *Wolverine*, there was not much else he could have said. In fact, there was some damage to kit lockers and gear on the messdeck (which enabled *Scorpion*'s sailors to get new kits free) but no fire. There were a few shrapnel holes in the ship's side, patched up by *Blenheim*.

But, as the days went by, several destroyers were hit and needed more than patching up. Soon it was clear that minesweeping by day was too expensive in destroyers to be a practicable proposition. Also, the right flank had established only a toe-hold, and did not have the reserves of men and ammunition to break out of their initial beach-head positions.

On the night of 12/13th, *Scorpion* and *Wolverine*, now commanded by Lieutenant-Commander Adrian Keyes, Cunningham's term-mate, who had been beach-master at 'Y' Beach on 25 April, were on patrol when they intercepted gleeful German signals reporting three torpedo hits on an

English *Linienschiffe*. In fact, the battleship HMS *Goliath* had been torpedoed and sunk by a Turkish torpedo boat manned by Germans. Judging by the increasing strength of the radio signals, the enemy was returning up the Straits.

The two destroyers were racing up towards the Narrows to cut off the intruder when Cunningham received a signal by shaded lamp from Keyes — 'Submarine in sight to starboard. Am about to ram.' As the searchlight beams swept around, there indeed was a U-boat, lying apparently unsuspectingly on the surface. Keyes, a submariner himself, hastened into the attack. But then Cunningham 'saw a boil of water under the *Wolverine*'s tail as she went full speed astern'. The 'U-boat' was E. 15, high and dry. Keyes had recognised her just in time. 'Then the heavens opened up with guns of every calibre and we came out of it in a hurry.' They never did see the enemy torpedo boat.

On 25 May, the battleship *Triumph* was torpedoed off 'Y' Beach, on the open, western side of the peninsula. *Scorpion* was patrolling about six miles away and at once went full speed to reach the spot. Boats were lowered to rescue a couple of survivors, but most were picked up by the destroyer *Chelmer*, commanded by another of Cunningham's term-mates, Lieutenant-Commander Hugh England.

Two days later the battleship *Majestic* was torpedoed at anchor, with antitorpedo nets rigged, off Cape Helles. Cunningham acknowledged it was a very fine performance by the U-boat commander. *Scorpion* searched vainly for the U-boat.

There was no means of detecting submarines, other than by eyesight, or of destroying them, except by ramming or gunfire. One scheme tried was for whalers to be sent away armed with the ship's blacksmith, his 40 lb sledgehammer, and some canvas bags. When a periscope was sighted, a canvas bag was to be slipped over it, thus blinding the U-boat commander. If all else failed, the blacksmith was to smash the periscope glass with his hammer. Cunningham was scornful: 'like little Audrey, we laughed and laughed!'

After the losses of *Triumph* and *Majestic*, the battleships were withdrawn from fire-support duties. For the next six months, some of the hardest of Cunningham's life, *Scorpion* and *Wolverine* were used as mobile batteries, providing fire support for the left flank of the Cape Helles front. They worked forty-eight hours on, forty-eight off, one destroyer on station, the other at anchor at two hours' notice for steam.

Their fire was mostly indirect, using spotting corrections sometimes provided by an aeroplane overhead but usually by a spotting officer, a hardy Royal Marine called Lieutenant Gordon Seath, who lived ashore with his signalmen.

The destroyers fired by day and by night at targets as requested by the Army, anchoring offshore to shine searchlights on enemy positions. Their existence was a mixture of tedium and danger, an unrelenting round of drills, divisions, coaling, steaming up to the line, firing, withdrawing, landing casualties, patching up damage and returning again.

On 28 June, *Scorpion* supported an advance on Cape Helles' left flank. Her 4-inch gun, which had fired between three and four thousand rounds and was 'rapidly becoming a smooth-bore', bombarded deliberately for almost two hours before the advance was due to begin, and as rapidly as it could be reloaded in the ten minutes before zero hour. As the troops were about to go over the top, the gun became so hot it would not run out properly and remake the firing circuit after the recoil. It was no time for any gun to stop firing, so the gun's crew short-circuited the contact with a 4-inch piece of wire. It was unorthodox, and certainly against regulations, but it worked. 'How Whale Island would have solved the problem,' Cunningham wrote, 'I do not know.'

That evening, Cunningham received a signal that the troops ashore were relying on *Scorpion*'s fire until the morning. So at sunset he anchored within 600 yards of the front line, and shone both searchlights in front of the trenches, to detect any movement by the Turks. He then had his supper, and turned in in his clothes on the settee in the charthouse.

At midnight, Cunningham was woken by several heavy books falling on him from the rack above his head, and his First Lieutenant, Sub-Lieutenant John G. Nicolas, calling down the voice-pipe: 'Captain, sir, things are getting pretty hot up here.'

The Turks were trying to shoot out *Scorpion*'s searchlights before making their counter-attack and Cunningham had never known 'the air more thick with rifle and machine-gun bullets'. The searchlights were extinguished, the petty officer manning the after light was shot in the stomach, and *Scorpion* had to move into deeper water, dragging her anchor with her.

But no sooner had the *Scorpions* weighed their anchor and repaired their lights than they received an urgent signal from the front line that the Turks were preparing for a massed attack. *Scorpion* went back and opened fire again. Cunningham later heard that between 300 and 400 dead Turks were counted in front of the trenches at dawn. As Cunningham said, 'The Army was very glad to have us.'

Two days later, Cunningham heard that he had been selected for promotion to Commander in the latest half-yearly list. He had served three years and three months as a lieutenant-commander, and was therefore comparatively junior for promotion. 'I fell out of bed with surprise,' he wrote to

Doodles. 'It means', he told his mother, 'that I have popped up about 250 places [in the Navy List] on this deal, and I am naturally delighted, though it is hard on the fellows over whose head I have jumped.'

The promotion was a very welcome new topic for his weekly letters home, in which he was constantly complaining of never having much to say. Censorship and security prevented him commenting in detail on his doings. He could only say that 'The destroyers out here are known as the "Suicide Club". Pleasant what?' and that three Taube aircraft had flown over and 'to our astonishment, one of them opened fire on us. We parted friends, neither of us having done the other any harm.'

Cunningham was much concerned for his sailors' health and welfare, and for their families. He sent his mother the addresses of any sailors' families living near Edinburgh. He noticed that his mother had to spend twopence for the stamp on every letter and, twopence being a large sum from a sailor's pay of a few shillings a day, thought of the men's wives having to do the same. He arranged football matches and runs ashore, and whenever possible had hands to bathe over the ship's side.

He was therefore very pleased and relieved when *Scorpion* went to Malta for almost a whole month's rest and maintenance in October 1915. He himself played ping-pong and did jigsaws in his spare time, and 'took a room at the Club for a week and tried to forget there was any such thing as sea'.

When *Scorpion*, with splinter-proof matting fitted around her bridge, arrived to take up her old post on the left flank in mid-November 1915, there were rumours of retreat and evacuation. The operations at Suvla in August, intended to break the stalemate, had failed. The campaign had long since degenerated into a bloody and futile slogging match, with thousands of casualties on both sides.

On 17 December *Scorpion* was back on the left flank at Helles. Cunningham amused himself by chasing a rat around the charthouse in between shoots to support a diversionary attack being staged to cover the evacuations at Suvla and Anzac. 'The rat you enquire so tenderly about', he later told his mother, 'was kicked over the side one night so that was the end of him.'

The Suvla and Anzac evacuations were carried out successfully in calm weather on the nights of 18/19 and 19/20 December. *Scorpion* spent Christmas Eve 1915 on the left flank, firing and being fired on, and on Christmas Day took a party of war correspondents back to Mudros. On Boxing Day, Captain (D) C.P.R. Coode came on board and presented Distinguished Conduct Medals to members of *Scorpion*'s ship's company. On 1 January, Coode himself was awarded the DSO. 'Our Captain D got a DSO the other day,' Cunningham wrote home, 'a poor reward for all he has done but he seems quite pleased and doubtless will get something else later.'

The evacuation of Helles began on 29 December and ended in the early hours of 9 January 1916. After a furious Turkish attack on 7 January, which was largely quelled by gunfire support from warships offshore, the final evacuation took place as planned. 'By 5.30 a.m. the last man was off the peninsula,' Cunningham wrote. 'Whereas a loss of thirty to forty per cent had been expected, the evacuation had been carried out with the loss of one sailor killed. So ended the Dardanelles campaign, a failure but a very gallant one.'

At the end of February 1916, *Scorpion* and *Wolverine* were sent to the Dodecanese, to patrol the 150 miles of the transport route between Rhodes and Nikaria. After a month, Cunningham was given a roving commission, to take *Scorpion* and *Wolverine*, with three trawlers, eleven drifters and a collier, all under his own orders, and establish a base at Port Laki, on the island of Leros. They were to patrol between Samos in the north and Rhodes in the south, investigate bays and inlets on the Turkish mainland, capture or sink any craft they found which might be useful to the Turks, and to shell any villages which fired on them.

It was an exciting kind of coastal warfare, full of incident and interest, which was in many ways similar to the small-ship actions of the Napoleonic wars. Demolition parties in picket boats, with Maxim machine-guns mounted, were sent into tiny coves by night, to search for and destroy Turkish caiques. Many of the villages were only too ready to fire on the ships. The heavy bullets the Turks used went straight through the destroyers' bridge protection. Special steel plating, provided by *Blenheim*, had to be fitted (these, incidentally, sent the ships' compasses haywire so that all navigation had to be done by eye).

Cunningham was greatly assisted by the local intelligence service provided by Lieutenant-Commander John Myres, RNVR, scholar, anthropologist, ethnologist and in civilian life Wykeham Professor of Ancient History at Oxford. He spoke Greek fluently and had travelled widely all over the Middle East. Myres also helped with naval victualling, in a way which had Homeric echoes of the Trojan wars, by organising roving bands of well-armed Anatolian peasants to round up the Turks' cattle and drive them to the coast, where they were slaughtered for Cunningham's ships.

Cunningham had heard in February the news of the award of a Military Cross to his soldier brother Alan. In March, he had a telegram from London, 'from Farrant, one of my many First Lieutenants', he told his mother. 'Heartiest congratulations', but he did not know what for. It was, as he found out, for his

DSO, published in the *London Gazette* of 14 March 1916, for his services in the Dardanelles. It was also, as Cunningham himself realised very well, an award to everybody in *Scorpion*. He was pleased to see, in the same list, a DSO for his term-mate James Somerville, Fleet Wireless Officer.

Cunningham's 'many First Lieutenants' were reputed to join and then leave *Scorpion* at a famous rate. Neither the Navy List, admittedly often out-of-date in wartime, nor *Scorpion*'s deck log, which recorded officers' joinings and departures, bear out the legends, but one sketch in fleet theatricals at Mudros began with a loud splash, and 'Good God, what was that?... Only another First Lieutenant being flung out of the *Scorpion*?

Sub-Lieutenant Richard Symonds-Tayler, who won a DSC as midshipman of one of *Agamemnon*'s picket boats, joined *Scorpion* in October 1916, for a stormy but eventually rewarding relationship with Cunningham:

> ABC expected nothing but the best, and yet he was most patient in training me, an inexperienced youngster. 'Oh *miserable* Sub, what *are* you doing!' was a common cry. I was frequently addressed as 'Boy', or 'You young devil!', and these forms of address were used when we met in later years. After a few months, the then First Lieutenant left, and I became ABC's 13th First Lieutenant.
>
> From then onwards, instead of 'miserable Sub', the cry was 'First Lieutenant, what *do* you think you're doing!' when things were not as he wished them to be. He helped, advised and guided me in the running of the ship, which was extremely clean and efficient.
>
> Life was strenuous, discipline was very strict, and one had to be on one's toes all the time. He had an eye like a hawk and the 'balloon' went up frequently. Having delivered a 'rocket', usually on the quarterdeck, I well remember him saying: 'Right, come and have a drink'. Down we would go to the

wardroom, and the incident was never mentioned again. I never heard him admonish anyone in the wardroom, where all was jolly and cheerful.

Occasionally, after a particularly bad 'rocket', I was sent to my cabin under arrest! There I remained, sometimes for several hours, till I was sent for and released. In spite of all this, I knew that ABC was a friend who trusted me and who, if need be, would stick by me through thick and thin.

I loved serving under him. I had a wonderful year in the *Scorpion*, and I was ever grateful for the advice, experience and training I received.

Cunningham, who was careful with his money to an almost legendary extent, nevertheless proposed Symonds-Tayler for the Union Club in Malta, found him a seconder, and paid his entrance fee and first year's subscription.

Symonds-Tayler provided an unexpected bonus in return. He was regularly sent two huge fruit cakes, each weighing at least 8 lbs, from home every week. Cunningham much enjoyed the cakes, but preferred them without orange peel. He told the Sub to write and ask his mother to leave that ingredient out of the recipe.

Of the numerous dismissals from his ship, Cunningham himself said, perhaps with tongue a little in cheek, that although he might have no great opinion of a particular officer's ability, another captain might be more tolerant or understanding and the fairest way was to arrange a change as soon as possible.

He was as severe with the ship's company. Minor offences in the Navy were punished by extra drill and work, or stoppage of leave or pay. More serious offences, carrying penalties of confinement to cells, or detention ashore, disrating or loss of good conduct badges, were punished 'by warrant', an official document containing details of the offence and the punishment awarded, read out publicly before the assembled ship's company and the offender himself.

Warrants are unusual in destroyers, with their 'small ship' spirit, and are even rarer in destroyers engaged on strenuous active service. But in just over six months of 1915, while operating in the Dardanelles, *Scorpion* had an average of about one warrant a month, when men were discharged to cells in some larger ship.

In July 1916, Cunningham took *Scorpion* back to Devonport for refit (two stokers were discharged to Royal Navy Barracks for cell punishment the day before *Scorpion* paid off). Cunningham himself returned to the Mediterranean after a fortnight's leave to assume temporary command of the destroyer *Rattlesnake* ('I do not care for *Rattlesnake*,' he wrote to his mother; 'there are bugs in the charthouse') and to take part in the seizure of Salamis and the Piraeus in September 1916.

Cunningham rejoined *Scorpion* for her new commission at Mudros on 2 October 1916. By that stage of the war there was heavy dilution of regular naval ratings with men who had joined for 'hostilities only'. Cunningham did not like what he called 'conscripts'. 'They are not the same,' he told his mother; 'a very poor crowd of men after the late ones but they will doubtless be all right in time.'

Cunningham exerted himself to ensure that his new ship's company became 'all right'. The 'black list men' under punishment began to fall in for extra work and drill in the dog-watches, when (by no coincidence at all) the rest of the hands were piped to bathe. Soon there were no black list men. But the warrants continued at the rate of one or two a month for as long as Cunningham was in command. Five were read on one day in May 1917.

Early on 30 November, *Scorpion* was rammed from right ahead by *Wolverine*, who should have been her next astern. *Wolverine*'s officer of the watch had mistaken a light ashore for *Scorpion*'s stern light and both officers of the watch had then ordered their helms put the wrong way.

Scorpion was badly damaged, with a great hole driven in her side, extending from the fo'c'sle deck down to her keel. She was patched up and went back to Malta for permanent repairs, arriving neatly in time for Christmas 1916.

In the New Year, *Scorpion* was employed largely in escorting convoys, which had, at long last, been introduced in the Mediterranean. They were very effective, cutting losses down to nil, at least where Cunningham was involved. He never lost a single ship from any convoy he escorted.

By the summer of 1917, even Cunningham himself realised he had been in *Scorpion* and in the Mediterranean long enough. He was offered the job of Commander (D) of all destroyers based on Malta, a very responsible and worthwhile appointment. The Cunningham of 1915 or even of 1916 would have jumped at it. But it seemed to him that the exciting times in the Mediterranean were now over. Home was the place to be.

By September 1917 Cunningham was writing, rather sadly, 'I am now the sole survivor of the old flotilla.' Everywhere were ships and men who knew not Joseph. Captain Coode had gone to the Admiralty, as Director of Operations (Foreign), in May. In August Symonds-Tayler, 'one of the best I've ever had', went home for subs' courses and the new sub-lieutenant 'does not impress me very favourably'. In October, Cunningham wrote to Coode to ask if he could get him a ship under Commodore Tyrwhitt at Harwich, or under Keyes at Dover. Coode replied that he would do his best.

In December, Cunningham was selling his armchairs and disposing of other furniture and bulky gear before going home. *Scorpion* sailed for England in January 1918 with mail and passengers who included the Governor's ADC and a small Scottish terrier, the property of a Miss Nona Christine Byatt. Cunningham had never met Miss Byatt, nor even knew her name, but he understood she had either gone or was going shortly home. He was to take her dog home and deliver it into quarantine.

Scorpion finally paid off at Devonport on 29 January 1918 (after three final warrants, read on 23 January, discharging three prisoners to *Vivid* [HM Barracks, Devonport] for cell punishment). The ship's company sent the surplus from their canteen fund to Pearson's Holiday Fund, to pay for an outing for children on 29 June, the anniversary of their hectic night on the left flank at Helles.

So Cunningham left *Scorpion*, after seven years and three weeks. Many years later he wrote:

> I am not unduly sentimental. Ships are expendable; but the *Scorpion* *was* a staunch little vessel. I knew all her particular idiosyncrasies, all her dents and patches, almost every bolt and rivet. Even now I think I could find my way blindfold along her upper deck. In the long time I was in her we had many memorable experiences in peace and war, and I had as shipmates some quite wonderful officers and men.

3: CAPTAIN, RN

CUNNINGHAM SPENT A quiet leave staying with his
mother in Edinburgh, waiting for his next appointment. With
his proven ability, wartime experience, early promotion and his
DSO, he could have had any appointment for the asking.
There were developments taking place in the Navy, in plans, in
aviation, and in the conduct of convoy warfare, which it would
have profited a man of his energy and ability to experience. But
his heart was firmly set on destroyers.

The appointment, albeit a temporary one, was disappointing:
Ophelia with the 14th Flotilla in the Grand Fleet. He joined her
at Port Edgar, on the Firth of Forth, on 11 February 1918, and
was not impressed. She was not up to Mediterranean standards
— for the rest of his life, Cunningham associated the
Mediterranean with excellence. In his opinion, the Grand Fleet
destroyers were stale, spending long periods at sea in vile
weather without the same chances of action against the enemy
as the Mediterranean destroyers. As for the Grand Fleet
destroyer depot ships, Cunningham found them
uncooperative, compared with *Blenheim*, and apt to look upon
their destroyers as nuisances.

Cunningham was only six weeks in *Ophelia* but in that time
he introduced some 'Mediterranean' improvements in ship's
routines and working hours. Captain (D) and Commodore (D)
of the Grand Fleet tried to persuade him to stay. But Roger
Keyes, now Vice-Admiral, Dover Patrol, had promised
Cunningham the first vacancy. Cunningham also knew that
some special operation was brewing and was anxious not to
miss it. The signal on 28 March 1918, appointing him to

command the destroyer *Termagant*, did not come a moment too soon.

He joined *Termagant* at Hull, where she was refitting, and found her as deficient as *Ophelia*. He was soon writing to his mother to tell her that he, who abhorred paperwork, had just spent from 9.30 a.m. to 5 p.m. on a 'good spring day' clearing up the backlog left by his predecessor.

Termagant sailed on 17 April, Cunningham still intending to take part in the special operation — the blocking of the Zeebrugge canal on 23 April. But they were too late to take what Cunningham called 'any really interesting part'.

Life in the Dover Patrol was as arduous as in the Dardanelles. *Termagant* was one of a division of four destroyers normally based at Dunkirk, escorting troopship convoys across the Straits by day, and patrolling the eastern end of the area by night. She spent her first eighteen consecutive nights at sea, with her ship's company at action stations almost the whole time. Cunningham thrived on the life, only chafing at what he considered the dullness of it all. The other destroyer captains, who knew his reputation, soon discovered that the half had not been told them. 'The younger COs wondered with some apprehension', said Lieutenant-Commander F. Dalrymple-Hamilton, commanding *Murray*, 'as to whether our shortcomings would be too obvious to one who had seen so much active service for so long. In fact we expected a good "shake-up". This in my case was not long in coming, as the next time the patrol put to sea I was hailed from the *Termagant* and told "IF YOU DON'T KEEP OUT OF MY WAY I'LL SINK YOU"!'

Cunningham could turn a Nelsonian blind eye, at some risk to his career. One day towards the end of May 1918, when he was 'having a thoroughly dull time' escorting the monitor *Terror* on patrol off the net barrage, he noticed heavy firing inshore. Then he saw four German destroyers steaming out from the land, and led the four escort destroyers at full speed towards them, signalling to Captain C.W. Bruton in *Terror* that he had sighted the enemy and was about to engage.

Cunningham pretended he had not seen furious flashing from *Terror*, and an inconclusive action ensued in which the number of enemy destroyers rose to thirteen. The weather was rough and the gunnery was very bad on both sides.

On *Termagant*'s return, there was an acrimonious exchange of signals with Captain Bruton who wanted to know why Cunningham had gone off without his permission and why he had ignored six recall signals. Cunningham replied that the recall signals had been read incorrectly and that he had signalled 'enemy in sight' six times without reply.

Bruton reported Cunningham's conduct to Commodore Larken, at Dunkirk. However, Larken was an old friend whom Cunningham had known in the Aegean, and he made light of the affair. For an officer of less standing and repute than Cunningham, the matter would have had serious repercussions.

Cunningham took action to improve *Termagant*'s gunnery, organising 1-inch rifle-aiming practice to train his guns' crews in laying and firing. But the real problem remained the amount of sea-time the Dover Patrol destroyers had to do; they simply did not get enough chances for gunnery.

An attempt to block Ostend with the *Vindictive* in May had failed. Keyes put it down partly to a failure in ship-handling. He wanted an expert ship-handler to try again. He asked Cunningham, who was delighted by the compliment and accepted at once.

The old battleship *Swiftsure* was to be taken between the breakwaters at Ostend and run into the western bank. A cruiser following would ram her stern and force her across the Channel. Both ships would then be scuttled as they lay.

Cunningham was able to choose the officers, and his first choice was his First Lieutenant in *Termagant*, Wilfred Joe Williams, 'a magnificent man' Cunningham called him, promoted from warrant rank because of his exceptional ability. A volunteer crew was to be provided from Chatham, where *Swiftsure* was being prepared for her task. When Cunningham and Williams arrived in Chatham Barracks, they were amused to hear that the gossip amongst *Termagant*'s ship's company was that they had both been thrown out of the ship for being too hard on the sailors.

After three weeks of frantic work, selecting and training the crew, mounting machine-guns and mortars, placing explosives in the double bottoms, sand-bagging the conning tower, and making arrangements to take off the ship's company afterwards — Cunningham had no intention of finishing the war in a German PoW camp — Cunningham took *Swiftsure* down the Medway to Sheerness.

But the situation had changed, as Keyes explained, when he came on board *Swiftsure* to break the news that their great venture was off, only three days before it was due to take place. The Germans had ceased to use Ostend for U-boats going to and fro from Bruges, and they had also laid a large minefield off Ostend which it was not likely *Swiftsure* could cross.

Both before and after the Armistice, *Termagant* was 'chiefly employed in taking the great ones over to France or bringing them back': Prince Albert, later King George VI, on his way to represent his father at the official entry of the King and Queen of the Belgians into Brussels; the Duke of Connaught, with whom Cunningham had a three-day 'run ashore in Belgium'; Admiral Beatty, to 'whom we were glad to show a sample of

Dover weather in the shape of a south-westerly gale'; and 'Rosy' Wemyss, by then First Sea Lord and the British Naval Representative at the signing of the Armistice in Marshal Foch's special train in the Forest of Compiègne.

In November 1918, Lloyd George took passage from Boulogne to Dover in a south-easterly gale so bad Cunningham advised him not to sail. But Lloyd George was not to be put off and during a 'frightful passage of above five hours' lay on Cunningham's bunk, reading the *Daily Chronicle*. *Termagant* was rolling gunwales under, even inside Dover harbour. Cunningham 'conducted the Prime Minister to the gangway. I said goodbye and told him that when I said "Go" he was to step forward and let go of everything. I waited until the downward roll, gave the word, and he obeyed orders, to be fielded neatly by the gunner and four sailors and put into the cabin. I admired his courage in a difficult situation, for the weather was really dreadful.'

After the Armistice, it was a time for taking stock. It had been a long and a bitter war, in which the Navy had lost 254 warships, including thirteen battleships and sixty-four destroyers, and suffered nearly 40,000 casualties, with another 29,000 casualties in the Royal Naval Division.

Cunningham had nothing to fear from post-war economies. He was awarded a Bar to his DSO on 20 February 1919. He was known and respected by many senior officers. Contemporaries called him 'the superman from the Dardanelles'. The sailors called him 'Cutts', a curiously apt name for one of his dedication and abrasive manner.

He had few friends outside the Service and almost no interests. Apart from his leaves, he lived on board ship. At thirty-six years old, he was a confirmed bachelor, with no hint of any romantic attachment or even close friendship with a particular woman. He enjoyed family life vicariously, through his goddaughters, his sister's children.

During Cunningham's last weeks in *Termagant* there was an outbreak of Spanish influenza. Cunningham, typically, did not succumb but at one point *Termagant* had only twenty-six fit men out of 150. One of them was a young, recently rated Leading Seaman, E.G. Buckingham, nicknamed 'Duke', who became a temporary wardroom steward (all the cooks and stewards had flu), and then Cunningham's Coxswain.

Once again, Cunningham could have had any appointment for the asking. Once again, he applied for another destroyer and on 1 March 1919 was appointed in command of HMS *Seafire*, destined for the China Station. He took 'Duke' with him, after overcoming opposition from the drafting authorities, who insisted that Buckingham, a Portsmouth rating, could not possibly be drafted to *Seafire*, a Devonport ship.

Cunningham had a short way with bureaucracy. He considered the difficulty 'to be nothing more nor less than a piece of obstructionist red tape'. When he was for a few days acting as Captain (D) at Dover, he ordered Buckingham's papers to be transferred to *Seafire*, and heard no more about it. Buckingham was Cunningham's Coxswain for the next eighteen years.

The China flotilla was temporarily abolished, for reasons of economy, and Cunningham never served on that Station (in fact, he never passed through the Suez Canal during his naval career). *Seafire* went to the Baltic, under Rear-Admiral Walter Cowan, flying his flag in the cruiser *Curacoa*, commanded by Cunningham's term-mate, Charles Little, now a captain.

Curacoa, with *Seafire* and *Scotsman* in company, sailed first for Oslo, where *Curacoa* delivered millions of pounds' worth of gold bullion, then to Copenhagen, and finally through a thick fog (which did not deter Cowan from steaming at 22 knots regardless of navigational hazards and minefields) to Libau, the port of the newly independent Republic of Latvia.

Formerly a Russian province, Latvia had been given national status under the treaty of Brest-Litovsk in March 1918. The Republic had been proclaimed on 18 November 1918 and recognised by HM Government, who provided the Latvian Army with arms and munitions. There was a large German Army occupying much of the country, supported by the 'Baltic barons', the landowners who wished Latvia and Estonia to become Baltic provinces in union with Prussia, and there were the Russian Bolshevik armies in Estonia who had already invaded Latvia from the north and who were opposed to everybody — the British, the Latvian Republic, the German Army and the Baltic barons included.

The British sailors played their traditional roles as peacemakers and bringers of food and comfort, especially to the children, 'pitiable, lean, ragged little scarecrows with pale faces and sunken eyes who gathered abreast of the ship holding out their bony arms and crying plaintively, "Mister! Mister! Please bread!" It took our kind-hearted sailors no time at all to improvise a soup kitchen on the jetty.'

The situation ashore changed from day to day. There were rumours that the German Army had toppled the Latvian Government, then that the Bolsheviks were coming, and then that the Latvian Government had regained control. *Seafire*'s and *Scotsman*'s people often wondered what was going to happen next. The jetty alongside the destroyers was often a miniature battleground. First, German machine-guns positioned at the end of it had to be dislodged. This was done by manning *Seafire*'s guns and sending the Germans a polite message 'to say that if they did not remove their machineguns immediately they would be blown away. They went.'

The Germans retaliated by building a large wooden barrier across the wharf. It took them two days. When it was ready, Cunningham went out and asked the officer in charge if they were finished. When he assured Cunningham it was, *Seafire* and *Scotsman* shifted berth further along the wharf, 'where, as before, we were soon being visited by the people with their children'. When German staff officers rode down to the jetty, an enterprising sailor sounded a long blast on *Seafire*'s siren, which emptied every saddle and bolted the horses.

Seafire and *Scotsman* were relieved at the end of April 1919. Cunningham was sorry to leave Cowan's command but glad for his sailors' sake to get home. He paid *Seafire* off at Devonport in November. He had enjoyed his time in her and had an excellent recommendation from Cowan, who wrote that 'Commander Cunningham has on one occasion after another acted with unfailing promptitude and has proved himself an officer of exceptional value and unerring decision.' A second Bar to his DSO, for distinguished service in *Seafire*, was gazetted on 8 March 1920.

Cunningham had what he thought was 'rather a frosty reception and was told nothing' when he went to the Admiralty to enquire about his next appointment. He was not even allowed to see the Naval Assistant to the Second Sea Lord (whose office was responsible for officers' appointments). So, he called upon Captain Coode, who made some pungent remarks about the Second Sea Lord's office, and told Cunningham to have lunch with him, when he would have some good news: that he would shortly have command of another destroyer and meanwhile was to go on leave.

As usual Cunningham went to Edinburgh where on 1 January 1920 an official letter arrived from the Admiralty. Cunningham left it unopened while he went to play golf. He opened it just before dinner, to find he had been promoted to the rank of Captain. 'It was a real surprise, I had only done four-and-a-half years as a commander and was still about a week under the age of thirty-seven. I was the junior promotion of the batch, and in those days, five-and-a-half or six years as a commander was by no means unusual.'

Cunningham's first appointment as a captain, which could only have been the result of some extraordinary whim of the Naval Secretary's office, was as President of Sub-Commission 'C' of the Naval Inter-Allied Commission of Control in Germany, in charge of the demolition of the defences and harbour works of the Frisian island of Heligoland which had been handed over to the Germans in 1890.

Cunningham arrived on Heligoland in September 1920. There was very little to do, except to watch the explosions and, in a winter of constant gales, the giant rollers smashing against the cliffs. Cunningham was glad to go home in October 1921, before another winter came on.

In February 1922, Cunningham joined the Senior Officers' Technical Course at Portsmouth, where students attended lectures on gunnery, torpedoes, signals and anti-submarine warfare at the various specialist schools, so as to broaden their outlooks and bring them up-to-date in the latest doctrines, tactics and technical developments. Having served in destroyers for years, Cunningham realised there was now much in the Navy that was entirely new to him and that the course would have been to his ultimate professional advantage, but he was appointed Captain (D), 6th Destroyer Flotilla in the Reserve Fleet, and left before the end.

The appointment was a good one, at a time when many naval officers, including some of Cunningham's contemporaries, faced a bleak future. This was the era of the 'Geddes Axe', named after the First Lord of the Admiralty, Sir Eric Geddes, the ex-railwayman turned politician who had been largely responsible for Jellicoe's dismissal as First Sea Lord in 1917, and was arguably one of the least tactful men in twentieth-century public life.

The 'Geddes Axe' removed one third of the captains and scores of commanders, lieutenant-commanders, lieutenants and sub-lieutenants from the Active List and put them into enforced retirement on meagre pensions. Many who had expected to remain in the Navy until the usual age for retirement were thrown on the beach at an age when it was difficult, if not impossible, to make a new start in life. There were many cases of extreme penury and hardship, which did not encourage parents to put their sons into a profession which treated them so harshly. As Cunningham said, 'The "Geddes Axe" was one of the greatest injustices, and incidentally the worst advertisement, the Royal Navy ever suffered.'

None of this affected Cunningham personally. He had a busy life in the 6th Flotilla at Port Edgar, which was conveniently near his home in Edinburgh, and later, in December 1922, as Captain (D) of the 1st Flotilla in the Atlantic Fleet.

In the flotilla leader HMS *Wallace*, Cunningham drove his ships as hard as the exercise programme and the fuel allowance permitted. He was as severe and as unpopular as ever with those he thought back-sliders and conceded that he 'may have been rather outspoken in my strictures'.

Cunningham was always dangerous in the mornings. Flynn, his First Lieutenant in *Seafire*, said that shortly before 8 a.m. the faithful Buckingham would appear in the wardroom, with coffee percolator, to prepare Cunningham's breakfast. At 8.12½ a.m., and never a second later, Cunningham would appear and 'if anyone else was still at table, the silence was as oppressive as before a heavy thunder storm'.

'Cunningham had three favourite phrases, frequently repeated, which have remained ingrained in my mind down the years,' said one young officer in *Wallace*, Sub-Lieutenant Godfrey Brewer, who was himself to become a notable destroyer captain, '"Duty is the first business of a sea officer", NDBGZ (No Difficulty Baffles Great Zeal), and "Intelligent anticipation must be your watchword" — not bad principles for any walk of life.'

Cunningham knew that the lower deck called him 'Cutts' and disliked the name, as shown in this account of an incident by Mr A.D. Browning, Yeoman of Signals in *Wallace*:

> One cold, wet and windy day, the Flotilla was engaged in picking up torpedoes after an exercise, the captain being in a bad mood. A signal came from *Vancouver* requesting permission to send a seaman to hospital. The captain signalled approval, adding 'What is the matter with this rating?' Back came the reply: 'He is suffering from CUTTS.' Everyone on the bridge heard me spelling out each word as it was received. In a raging temper the captain shouted to me: 'Make to *Vancouver*. Captain AND, repeat AND, leading signalman repair on board *Wallace* immediately.'
>
> In answer to the captain's 'Well?' the captain of the *Vancouver* said: 'Sir, I told the leading signalman to make reply that the rating was suffering from lacerations.' Turning to the signalman the captain said, 'And why didn't you?' The signalman said: 'Sorry, sir, I couldn't spell "lacerations", so made "cuts" — only one T.'

A grin spread over Cunningham's face as he said to the signalman: 'Jones, you were never at a loss for a prompt — and apt — reply when you were my leading signalman in the *Seafire*, and you don't really expect me to believe that, do you?' Turning to the Flotilla Signal Officer he said: 'Make to the flotilla "During the morning's exercise only one ship displayed the slightest sign of personal initiative. Congratulations — *Vancouver*."'

Such generosity took any sting out of the incident. Nobody of any spirit could be annoyed with Cunningham, or resent his criticisms for long, for he asked no more of anybody else than he manifestly could do himself. One morning at Scapa Flow, said Brewer,

> a typical Scapa gale was blowing; all ships had two two anchors down and steam for slow speed to ensure safety. All ships were yawing wildly when suddenly *Warwick*, anchored astern of us, was struck by a particularly strong gust, and was obviously going to drag ashore. 'Get up on the fo'c'sle, Sub, and start weighing,' said Cunningham. In almost less time than it takes to tell we had weighed, steamed around, anchored close ahead of *Warwick*, got a wire out to her, hove in our cable and off she came. Almost immediately came a signal from the Admiral: 'That is one of the finest bits of seamanship I have ever seen.'

Cunningham protested when he heard that he was to be relieved in May 1924, but, with so few ships and so many officers clamouring to go to sea, his period in the Reserve Fleet was counted as full sea-time. He was consoled to be appointed Captain-in-Charge of HMS *Columbine*, the destroyer base at Port Edgar, in October 1924.

It was an odd appointment for a bachelor. Cunningham had the use of 'a small corrugated iron house with two reception and four bedrooms overlooking the [destroyer] pens' where he lived in great comfort.

In March 1926, when Vice-Admiral Sir Walter Cowan was appointed C-in-C, North America and West Indies Station, he asked Cunningham to be his Flag Captain and Chief Staff Officer in the cruiser *Calcutta*. Cunningham jumped at it, being 'delighted at the idea of serving with a man for whom I had so great an admiration'.

Not everybody would have jumped at the chance of being Cowan's flag captain. Cowan was a brave and very dedicated officer who demanded the highest standards. He had a DSO and more medals as a lieutenant than many admirals had on retirement.

But, rightly or wrongly, justly or unjustly, Cowan's name was associated with mutiny. There was unrest in the battleship *Zealandia* when he commanded her in 1914, principally caused by the insensitive behaviour of the executive officer, but even Cowan's friends would have agreed that he himself could have been more perceptive. There were mutinies in 1919 in the 1st Destroyer Flotilla after returning from the Baltic and in the cruiser *Vindictive* at Copenhagen. Cowan could not be held responsible, but some said he could have done more to represent the men's grievances to an Admiralty which failed to recognise that service in the Baltic in 1919-20 was as hard and dangerous as any in the war just ended.

There was a mutiny in Cowan's own flagship, the cruiser *Delhi*, brought on by the grievances of those serving in the Baltic, but aggravated by the inconsiderate behaviour of Cowan's Flag Captain, Geoffrey Mackworth. Cowan then asked Mackworth to accompany him as Flag Captain in the battlecruiser *Hood*, where in 1921 there was another mutiny, again precipitated by Mackworth.

84

Cowan was hasty and quick-tempered, liable to lash out reprimands without pausing for thought. But Cunningham had the confidence in his own ability and the temperament necessary to be able to mediate between his superior and his juniors.

At 4,200 tons, and with a complement of 400 plus an admiral and his staff, *Calcutta* was small and overcrowded as a flagship. Cunningham took with him from Port Edgar his Commander, Henry Maltby, and thirty specially selected boy seamen with their own divisional lieutenant.

There were four 'C' Class cruisers and two sloops on the Station, to show the flag, keep in touch with the Royal Canadian Navy and answer calls for assistance from any of the governments of the West Indian islands in the event of civil disturbances. The Station included both coasts of North America and the whole of the Caribbean, an area so vast that no Commander-in-Chief could visit it all during the two years of his appointment.

Cowan arrived in June 1926 and *Calcutta* set off on a cruise to Canada, where at Montreal they berthed in a basin with a 6-knot current running past the entrance. Cunningham managed the tricky entry successfully but *Capetown*'s Captain, a navigating officer, rammed his ship's stem hard against the dockside wall. Cowan made a remark after Cunningham's own heart: 'There you are, when you get a gunnery officer as captain his ship never hits the target, a torpedo officer loses all his torpedoes, and a navigator always hits the wall!'

Captain J.A.G. Troup, later an admiral but then in command of *Cairo*, another 'C' Class cruiser in the Squadron, commented that Cunningham had 'an intense will to win (and he won), combined with a determination invariably to "play the game"'. But although *Calcutta* did well at drills and sport, she soon settled into the familiar pattern of a very pleasant existence, with lengthy cruises to attractive and hospitable ports, where social duties and sport predominated over everything, and where the main demands on her officers were an inexhaustible supply of polite conversation, great tolerance to alcohol, and stamina on the tennis court and the dance floor.

Late in October 1926, a hurricane was reported heading for the coast of Florida. In the expert opinion of *Capetown*'s Captain and the Squadron Navigating Officer, the hurricane would pass 300 miles north of Bermuda. But local opinion held that the centre of the hurricane would strike Bermuda.

The Station Orders laid down that when a hurricane approached, ships were to anchor in the Great Sound, between Ireland and Hamilton Islands. But Cunningham doubted the wisdom of the Orders and decided to leave *Calcutta* alongside the dockyard wall.

By five o'clock the next morning, a full gale was blowing from the southeast. Heavy seas were breaking over the reefs and filling the lagoon so that the water level in the dockyard rose by five feet and the wharves and jetties were all awash. *Calcutta*'s wooden catamarans floated above the jetty, and no longer acted as fenders.

Just after noon, there was a flat calm. The centre of the storm was passing overhead. Cunningham and Maltby had extra hawsers passed, until the ship had no fewer than forty wires connecting her to the shore.

At 1.30 it came on to blow again from the north-west very much harder than before. The anemometer registered 138 m.p.h. before it blew away. The hawsers were snapping like string, the stern wires carried away and *Calcutta* was in grave danger of running aground on a breakwater to leeward. By going full ahead on both engines, Cunningham managed to crash the bow against the entrance to the dock. Maltby, dressed only in bathing trunks and an old uniform reefer jacket, leapt ashore with some fifty sailors, to secure the ship.

The sloop *Valerian*, which had been at sea during the hurricane, did not reply to signals. Cunningham and the Squadron Navigating Officer worked out where she was likely to be. *Capetown* picked up a Carley float with twenty-nine survivors. The rest of *Valerian*'s officers and men had gone down with her when she capsized at about 1.30 p.m. on 21 October. Nothing of *Valerian* was ever found.

Entertainment ceased to be a pleasure and became hard work. 'I am feeling the consequences of too much high living,' Cunningham wrote home. 'What with this and the sticky hot weather I am busy manufacturing excuses for not going to dances.'

There was, however, a long-term result from one visit, to Trinidad during the spring cruise of 1927. Cunningham stayed with the Governor, Sir Horace Byatt, whose sister Miss Nona Byatt acted as his hostess. Miss Byatt, Cunningham discovered, was the lady whose Scottie dog he had taken home from Malta in *Scorpion* in 1918. He very much enjoyed his stay at Government House, the surf-riding, the bathing, and the informal atmosphere.

In particular, Cunningham enjoyed the company of Miss Byatt. Their acquaintance prospered. But it was one of the most discreet courtships in naval history In his otherwise informative memoirs, Cunningham vouchsafed no details whatsoever. And, although the spectacle of the Captain of *Calcutta* 'poodle-faking', to use the naval term, could hardly have escaped the notice of the entire Station, no contemporary reference seems to have survived.

In November 1927, Cunningham took *Calcutta* home to pay off in Chatham. The Admiralty had decided to replace the 'C' Class cruisers abroad with the slightly larger and new 'D' Class. Cunningham commissioned *Despatch* with virtually the same ship's company in December.

Once back on the Station, *Despatch* returned to the old routine of visits and hospitality but with her range greatly enlarged. The visits were as physically punishing as ever. Cunningham's own account stresses the number of times he went to bed at 3 or 4 a.m. exhausted. At a dinner in Ecuador, the guests had to stand for forty-five minutes while the band played the National Anthems several times over. At Valparaiso, there were race meetings, picnics, luncheons, cricket and football matches, sight-seeing tours, receptions, dinners, dances 'and I cannot remember what else. Every officer and man was fully occupied.' On one day, Cunningham visited the Chilean Army, had champagne, beer and speeches, followed by a dinner and, after an exhausting day, 'finally flopped into bed at 4 a.m. next morning'. They sailed for Antofagasta and another gruelling programme, 'almost completely exhausted after eight days of entertainment and quite glad to get to sea'.

Despatch returned to Bermuda in April 1928, by which time Cunningham knew he was to be relieved in July Cowan was also to be relieved in August. They spent the last days in farewell parties and turning over affairs to the new Commander-in-Chief and his staff. Cunningham had had a memorable commission in *Calcutta* and *Despatch*. He had thoroughly enjoyed himself and was sorry to leave *Despatch* and her magnificent ship's company. 'However, I felt it was high time to get back to the Navy and bring myself up-to-date in the latest developments.'

Cowan had hauled down his flag for the last time. It was left to Cunningham to write Cowan's professional *nunc dimittis*:

> His ideals of duty and honour were of the highest, and never
> sparing himself he expected others to do the same... To say
> that he inspired us is no exaggeration. Hasty he undoubtedly
> was; but if in his haste he unjustly hurt people's feelings or
> wounded their susceptibilities he was at pains to make amends
> at the earliest possible moment. I have spent no happier years
> at sea than when serving with Sir Walter in the *Calcutta* and
> *Despatch*.

Cunningham knew there was no chance of another sea-going command so soon, but he was surprised to be offered a course at the Army Senior Officers School at Sheerness, to start in September 1928. In spite of his own disclaimers, he was a very good student. He doubted whether learning how to establish defensive positions on ridges in deep snow or how to obtain greatcoats on a cold night after a battle were of much practical use to a naval officer, but he appreciated the value of living in a mess for three months with officers of another service.

At the end of 1928, Cunningham again enquired at the Admiralty about his future and, to his 'horror', found himself nominated for the next course at the Imperial Defence College, in Buckingham Gate, London.

The object of the course, attended by senior officers from the Navy, Army and Royal Air Force, was to prepare the students for higher command by giving them some knowledge of each other's problems. The Army and the RAF took the course seriously, specially selecting students from 'highflyers' marked for promotion. The Navy, in Cunningham's opinion, sometimes just sent whoever was available, so that some of the naval students were of inferior calibre to their fellows. But, as

Cunningham said, 'I should not complain as otherwise I do not think I should have been selected.'

He thoroughly enjoyed the course and always said that his year at the IDC was one of the most interesting and valuable he ever spent. His old friend and term-mate James Somerville, also a captain, was on the teaching staff.

Besides lectures, the students went on expeditions to naval establishments, RAF stations, and to the 1914-18 battlefields in France and Flanders. Cunningham made his first flight in an aeroplane, a four-hour flight which he recalled as 'a chilly and rather dull proceeding'. The pilot was a fellow student, Wing-Commander Charles Portal.

While on the course, Cunningham renewed what he called his 'acquaintance' with Miss Byatt, who had returned to England after her brother had been relieved as Governor of Trinidad. The acquaintance ripened and in October 1929 the couple became engaged to be married.

Cunningham's next appointment was in command of the battleship HMS *Rodney* in the Atlantic Fleet. He and Nona decided to get married before the ship left. They were married from Sir Horace's house at Bishop's Stortford on 21 December 1929, with Henry Maltby as best man. Cunningham had 'many complimentary messages on my courage in taking on a wife and the largest battleship in the Navy at the same time'.

Nona Byatt was by then well into middle age and no beauty. She was an inordinately shy woman who often seemed in awe and, some would say, even frightened of her husband. Flag lieutenants had to talk to her for some time before she began to relax and 'thaw out'. But, when they met her next day, she would be back in her shy shell and had to be 'thawed out' all over again.

Andrew and Nona Cunningham shared a love of gardening, fishing, dogs and country life. They were never to have children of their own, but they relished the company and lives of their young relatives.

Cunningham had joined *Rodney* at Devonport on 15 December. With their unusual arrangement of nine 16-inch guns in three turrets placed forward along a fo'c'sle of enormous length, and a massive slab-sided control tower aft, *Rodney* and her sister *Nelson* tended to head up into the wind. Hence they could be difficult to handle in shallow water or in certain wind and sea conditions.

Cunningham had never served in anything approaching *Rodney*'s 35,000 tons and he had early experience of her awkwardness when he led the Atlantic Fleet out of Portland harbour. Handling *Rodney* as though she were a destroyer, Cunningham ordered too many engine revolutions. The propellors churned the shallow water without moving the ship, and in the moderate breeze *Rodney* would not turn towards the narrow entrance. The fleet's departure was delayed and Cunningham was chastened, but not surprised, to receive a stinging signal from the C-in-C, Admiral Sir Ernie Chatfield.

The fleet exercised on passage to Gibraltar, where Nona arrived from England. Their stay at Gibraltar was the only honeymoon the Cunninghams had. Cunningham took *Rodney* to sea for exercises during the week and made expeditions into Spain with Nona at the weekends.

After taking part in the annual Combined Exercises, when the Atlantic and Mediterranean Fleets went to war with each other, *Rodney* went back to Devonport in April to recommission. The Commander, R.L. (Bob) Burnett, most of the lieutenant-commanders and some of the lieutenants stayed, but some 700 newly joined ratings marched down to the ship

91

and life on board was 'well-regulated chaos' until they had settled in.

Burnett was a physical-training specialist and *Rodney*'s boxing team won the battleship tournament. Her Royal Marine tug-of-war team beat the fleet and then beat all comers at Olympia. In Falmouth Bay in July, *Rodney*'s crews swept the board. Cunningham 'rather fancied' himself as a boat-sailor and should have won the galleys' race but was dismasted and, having ignored Burnett's advice to take a spare mast, struggled home on a jury rig; Burnett's face, he said, 'was a picture'.

Rodney had no fewer than nineteen executive lieutenant-commanders and lieutenants, resulting, as Cunningham said, 'in work which should have been done by a midshipman or petty officer being consigned to a lieutenant'.

Cunningham did his utmost to dissuade young officers from going to big ships. Writing in September 1930 to Lieutenant John Grant, who had asked for advice on whether to go as Flag Lieutenant to Admiral Howard Kelly on the China Station, he said that; as a flag lieutenant,

> you are a sort of pekinese trained to fetch and carry. I admit they are necessary and there are several nicely mannered young men in HM Service who are very fitted for these jobs and nothing else. I do not think a 'live man' like I think you are should touch one of these jobs. An ex-social flags is always looked on with suspicion in another ship as a general service officer, always put down as useless to start with.
>
> Big ship time is said to be necessary to us all. I have never found it so. The best officers to be found in big ships have come from submarines or destroyers. I would far rather be first lieutenant of a TBD than about 10th down the list of lieutenant commanders and lieutenants in a battleship... I have always maintained there is more real discipline in destroyers than in big ships, and of course we are always so

much more in touch with our men. The skipper of a destroyer gets soaked to the skin on the bridge just the same as any sailor, but his opposite number walks dry-skinned from his luxurious cabin where he has been sitting aloof from all goings on, to an equally luxurious bridge. [Grant went to the destroyer *Watchman* as first lieutenant.]

Yet, when one of Cunningham's own officers wanted to volunteer for something more exciting and challenging, he could not have been more obstructive. When Sub-Lieutenant Bob Whinney, President of *Rodney*'s gunroom mess, volunteered for flying duties, he 'was summoned to appear at 9 a.m. in frock coat and sword on the quarterdeck before the Captain. This meant trouble. I wondered what I had done.

'"Why did you join the Navy, boy?" asked the Captain.

'"To go to sea, Sir," I said, wondering what next.

'"Well, don't join the Fleet Air Arm. Take your name out. That's all."

'That was the end of that. I was dismissed.'

The 16-inch guns in *Rodney* were new and complicated and still troubled by 'teething problems'. Cunningham did not suffer such things lightly. The brunt of his competitive temper fell upon Lieutenant-Commander Geoffrey Oliver, the Gunnery Officer. But 'behind all his ferocity there was the kindest heart imaginable,' said Oliver, himself a future admiral. 'I think it was these two "opposites", laced with an almost boyish sense of humour, that captivated and bound us to him.

'At what was for me and for ABC our first 16-inch full-calibre battle practice shoot, at the fateful moment when, with target in sight at 20,000 yards, guns trained on and elevated, I reported to the bridge from the Control Tower: "Ready to open fire" — there was a pause. Up the voice-pipe came:

93

"Captain wants to speak to you, Sir." Then: "That you, Guns?"
"Yes, Sir." "Lift up your heart!'"

Lieutenant-Commander Stuart Paton, the Torpedo Officer, discovered that when anything went wrong in his department, and it often did, there would first be an explosion. But if the trouble involved any higher authority outside *Rodney*, Cunningham himself would take the blame and say, 'Mind you don't do it again!' 'I would have walked bare-foot through Hell for such a man.'

Cunningham left *Rodney* on 15 December 1930. He had enjoyed commanding her, and such an appointment was essential for future promotion. But, as he wrote to Grant in April 1931, 'I hated the Atlantic Fleet routine, one always seemed to be clinging like a limpet to one's Home Port and the sailors counted the hours till they got back again. West Countrymen are very extreme in that way — they think there is no place on earth but the West Country.'

Cunningham had no immediate appointment, nor did he want one. His stomach was still troubling him and he went up to Edinburgh in March 1931 for a 'further piece of butchery on my insides'. He was then informed that he was to be appointed Commodore of the Royal Naval Barracks, Chatham, early in July He found Chatham naval barracks rather a soulless machine with everything done by regulation and precedent. To Cunningham's mind, not enough allowances were made for the special circumstances of individuals. In his opinion, what was needed was more of the personal touch.

Never was a personal touch needed more than in 1931. The lower deck had no proper channels through which complaints, grievances or even suggestions could be heard and redressed without fear of victimisation. A great gulf, social and mental, had widened between the wardroom and the lower deck. The junior officers believed they could do nothing effective to help the sailors, so they did nothing. Senior officers tended to look upon men who requested to put in a complaint as little better than mutineers, and treated them henceforward as 'marked men'.

This uneasy situation was aggravated in September 1931 when the Government announced cuts in Service pay which bore particularly hardly on the lower rates. Such cuts could never be announced mildly or inoffensively, but the Board of Admiralty (led by Admiral Sir Frederick Field, who was now First Sea Lord) handled the matter with a scarcely credible incompetence and disregard of human nature which might have been calculated to exacerbate the situation. They failed to impress upon the Government, and very probably did not realise themselves, the real consequences of the pay cuts upon sailors and their families. They made no attempt to brief or warn senior officers in the fleets beforehand. They fumbled the promulgation of the cuts, so that rumour and press reports preceded the official announcement.

The upshot was that some ship's companies in the Atlantic Fleet refused to take their ships to sea from Invergordon for exercises. It was a very polite mutiny and a non-violent one. But it forced the country off the gold standard and sent a galvanic shock throughout the Royal Navy. There were extensive and prolonged investigations and recriminations, with a determination in some quarters to try and expunge all memory of Invergordon by applying the screw of discipline even more tightly Some sailors, with impeccable Service records, were discharged SNLR (Services No Longer Required) and a few were subjected to courses of physical 'training' which were unpleasantly close to punishment.

Cunningham blamed the officers, and especially the officers in bigger ships who had fallen out of touch with their sailors and knew nothing of their family problems. Cunningham did not absolve himself, nor was he mealy-mouthed about what had happened. 'A mutiny it certainly was. It has no other name. We were all to blame.'

There was little trouble at Chatham. *Repulse*, who had recently commissioned with 1,000 Chatham ratings, had been at Invergordon but was not involved in the mutiny. Cunningham nevertheless acknowledged that the men were justified in feeling they had a grievance. He invited everyone who wished so to do to come and see him and state his case. He spent days in interviews and saw some 500 men. Some were victims of their own foolishness and lack of thrift, but many lived on the very edge of poverty. Young married men with children could just manage, by pinching and scraping, but they had little or nothing left over for sickness, family emergencies, or amusements.

Rodney was deeply involved in the mutiny. She was dubbed 'the directing ship' of the 'sailors' soviet', and was one of the first to refuse to go to sea. Some of the loudest 'continuous cheering' — the signal to mutiny — came from her upper decks.

Some said that it would never have happened had Cunningham and Bob Burnett still been on board. Cunningham himself was not so sanguine. 'Invergordon has left me most volcanic, but at the same time sore at heart,' he wrote to Grant, in December 1931, 'I feel that a show of firmness would have brought all the good elements (probably 95%) of the ship's companies on to the side of law and order. But it is easy to criticise and one must avoid it as one would probably have done no better oneself.'

Certainly Cunningham was fortunate to be out of *Rodney*. In the general mood of scapegoat hunting he might well have suffered the same fate as her Captain, Roger Bellairs, who handled the most difficult situation in his ship as well as anybody, and better than most, but was relieved of his command when *Rodney* paid off, and not given another sea command (although he was promoted to Rear-Admiral).

Cunningham himself had a proposal for removing 'the iron curtain' which existed then (and until long after the Second World War) between Chatham, Devonport and Portsmouth, whereby every warship was entirely manned by men from one or other of those ports. 'Why should not the crew, most of whom were specialists or highly-skilled technicians be drawn from all three?' Cunningham and his Secretary, Lieutenant-Commander A.P. Shaw — whom Cunningham had first met when Shaw was Rear-Admiral (D)'s Secretary in the 1st Flotilla in 1923, became Cunningham's Secretary in 1932 and served him for the next fourteen years — drew up a scheme for central drafting. But the idea was far ahead of its time, and they were forced to abandon it because 'nobody seemed to want it'.

Cunningham was promoted Rear-Admiral on 24 September 1932, after being a captain for the then unprecedented time of twelve years and nine months. Time on the Captains' List had been getting progressively longer since the war. But Cunningham was philosophical. It had all been good experience and he was still under fifty.

That autumn of 1932, Admiral Sir William and Lady Fisher came to Chatham and dined with the Commander-in-Chief. Cunningham and Nona were also invited and after dinner Cunningham found himself firmly placed beside Fisher. He did not warm to Fisher and disagreed with him over several points during a long conversation. Some days later Cunningham discovered that Fisher, who was just about to relieve Chatfield in the Mediterranean, had been looking for a Chief of Staff. He had been 'vetted' for the job, which went to somebody else.

But all was for the best in the end. Cunningham left Chatham in February 1933, to go on half-pay on leave in Scotland, and then to a Technical Course at Portsmouth. On 1 January 1934 he was appointed Rear-Admiral (Destroyers) on the Mediterranean Station — 'the one appointment I would have chosen above all others'.

4: REAR-ADMIRAL (DESTROYERS) IN THE MEDITERRANEAN

CUNNINGHAM ARRIVED IN Malta with Nona on New Year's Eve 1933 and next morning took over from the outgoing RA(D) in about twenty minutes. ('I have never believed in protracted turns-over'). He and Nona also took over their predecessors' house, the Casa Pieta, in Guardamangia. It was on a hillside overlooking Pieta Creek and from his balcony Cunningham could look down Marsamxett Harbour as far as Sliema Creek and watch the destroyers coming and going, 'though at too great a distance for detailed criticism'. Also, on 1 January 1934, he became a Companion of the Order of the Bath.

Cunningham flew his flag in the light cruiser *Coventry*, with H.E. Horan as his Flag Captain. He commanded three flotillas, the 1st, 3rd and 4th, each with a flotilla leader and eight destroyers. There was also a destroyer depot ship, *Sandhurst*.

The Mediterranean Fleet was then at the height of its power and pomp. There was the 1st Battle Squadron, of five battleships; two cruiser squadrons, the 1st and 3rd, each with four cruisers; the aircraft carrier *Glorious*, with her two attendant destroyers; and the 1st Submarine Flotilla, of four submarines, with their own depot ship.

The Commander-in-Chief, flying his flag in the battleship *Queen Elizabeth*, was Admiral Sir William Fisher, known as 'the great Agrippa' (from the *Strumwelpeter* rhyme, 'Now tall Agrippa lived close by — So tall, he almost touched the sky'). He was indeed a tall, handsome and very imposing man, the very figure of an admiral. He was widely regarded as the admiral likeliest to go to the very top. Because he died prematurely; and never commanded a fleet in war, he is now almost totally forgotten.

At first, Cunningham found Fisher very difficult to get on with, but, when he came to know him better, he had the greatest admiration for him and 'realised that for some months after one had joined his flag his attitude of aloofness and the odd things he said were intended to try out and test the newcomer'.

Jutland still threw a long shadow over the Navy of the 1930s. Destroyers trained for a mass torpedo attack by three or four or even more flotillas on an opposing battle fleet during a major daylight fleet action. Cunningham doubted whether such attacks would ever happen again. However, they were the very best sort of training for destroyer captains. When large numbers of destroyers were manoeuvring at full speed and at close quarters, while flotillas deployed, attacked and regrouped, their captains were tested to the limits in their ship-handling, quickness of reaction, judgement of speed, time and distance, and their ability to weigh up and accept risks. 'Laggards', said Cunningham, ominously, 'soon showed up.'

Laggards tended not to be appointed to Mediterranean destroyer flotillas. Geoffrey Oliver arrived in Malta with no previous destroyer time whatever, strongly suspecting that Cunningham had put his name forward for destroyers to 'wean me from Gunnery and put me through the hoop: for my Captain (D)'s first words on greeting me were: "We didn't ask for you, you know!"' It was Oliver's first command and 'Work was incessant, often thrilling, sometimes terrifying, but never dull. At sea and in harbour there was only one standard for A.B. Cunningham and he saw that he got it. He missed nothing that deserved a "bottle" and the rare receipt of "Manoeuvre well executed" was something to be marked with a white stone.'

Captains bringing their destroyers into Sliema Creek, approaching their berths stern first, soon learned that they were under constant observation from those famously bloodshot eyes gazing down the harbour from Casa Pieta. 'Nothing was thought of a C.O. who didn't bring his ship in with the pendant numbers — which were painted on the stern — entirely covered by the stern wave,' said Oliver. 'I believe his unrelenting drive and "brinkmanship" to have done much to make the quality of so many Second World War captains.'

When Commander Louis Mountbatten, then commanding *Daring*, went to sea for the day with Cunningham in *Coventry*, he

> watched this absolute wizard handle 36 ships entirely by himself. In spite of rather red and watery eyes he always saw everything first, long before the officer of the watch, the lookout or the Yeoman of Signals. No move escaped his eagle eye. It was the greatest one-man performance I have seen on the bridge of a ship, and I never forgot it.

Cunningham's eyesight was legendary and prompted some apocryphal stories. According to Mr E.J. Freestone, a leading signalman in *Coventry*, one of Cunningham's captains was surprised to receive the signal: 'The left ear of the bowman of your motor-boat needs attention.' The sailor was hustled down to the sickbay, but nothing could be found amiss with his ear. He was examined next by the Flotilla Medical Officer, and then sent ashore to the Fleet ear nose and throat specialist in Bighi hospital. If anything, the man's hearing was above average. Finally, the ship had to ask for an explanation. 'There was a fag behind it.'

Cunningham was very fond of the signal branch who, he said, 'were born liars, always had an answer, and stuck together like thieves'. He could read morse and semaphore as well as any signalman and better than most. He joked with them on watch, pitting his skill against theirs, pulling their legs about their speed in reading semaphore, criticising their handwriting: 'If you took that to a chemist,' he once said, looking at a signal Freestone had just taken down, 'I'm sure he would give you something for it.'

In March, the Mediterranean (Red) Fleet took part in the annual Combined Exercises with the Home (Blue) Fleet, held in the Atlantic off Gibraltar. The exercises, in which Fisher comprehensively outwitted and outmanoeuvred Admiral Sir W.H.D. Boyle, C-in-C of the Home Fleet, took place in appalling weather.

The Red (Mediterranean) ships had to steam into a steep head sea from the moment they rounded Cape St Vincent. A giant wave smashed through *Glorious'* lower hangar doors and crushed six aircraft. The weather was too bad for peacetime flying and *Glorious'* aircraft took no part. The Red destroyers had to reduce to 5 knots and finally were almost hove to. Cunningham was anxious for their welfare. Some were reporting severe straining and cracks across their upper decks. However, he decided that on the whole they were doing better than *Coventry*, who was taking enormous green seas and pitching horribly.

In the darkness Cunningham's destroyers kept in touch with each other by switching on their masthead lanterns for a few seconds. The weather had moderated when the destroyers made their attack but there were still some excitements. *Coventry* was leading a flotilla at 19 knots and following hard after the enemy, with all ships darkened and not showing navigation lights, when Cunningham suddenly saw what appeared to him to be a motor-boat, dead ahead, and coming right at him at high speed.

It was, in fact, the bow wave of the destroyer *Delight*, who was retiring out of the action on an exact opposite course to *Coventry*, and the two ships were closing each other at a combined speed of 38 knots. Cunningham shouted 'Hard a port!' which by the old orders relating to movement of the tiller (changed a year previously) would put starboard wheel on. Realising the error, Captain Horan shouted 'Hard a starboard!' The helmsman, with two contrary orders, very sensibly did nothing. *Delight* passed down Coventry's starboard side at a distance of about three yards and vanished into the night astern.

The destroyers' searchlights and starshell gave Fisher the final bearings he needed as his darkened battle fleet stalked their opponents. When the range was down to less than 7,000 yards, Fisher turned his battle fleet into line ahead of his adversary, thus 'crossing the T'. All Fisher's heavy ships switched on their searchlights and fired starshell to denote the moment of opening fire.

The brilliant glare of the searchlights and the glow of starshell silhouetted the superstructures and fighting tops of Boyle's ships, steaming unsuspectingly onwards, their guns still trained fore and aft. Some of Boyle's ships did return fire, but it was still a total and crushing victory for Fisher.

It was also another vindication of the value of night-fighting, not lost on Cunningham, whose destroyers had done very well, although he, with perhaps too much modesty, wrote that 'I could take little credit as I had been with them for only three months. But to me they had certainly shown excellent seamanship in very bad weather, and a high degree of training, efficiency and proper initiative whenever their chance came. I felt very proud of them.'

Coventry and her flotillas returned to Malta in April 1934. Malta in April was very pleasant. The spring rains were normally over, a cooling breeze blew from the north-west, and the sun had yet to reach the torrid height of August. Malta in early summer was at its best, a tiny island, with walled fields, still green, with carnival processions in the streets, and market stalls selling bread and cakes, and flowers — red, white and purple anemones, arum lilies, violets and roses.

Other roses came out from England every year. Naval wives joined their husbands, and often brought their younger sisters, their cousins or nieces or young female family friends with them. There were parties and dances on board the ships, and plenty of young bachelor naval officers as partners. Many ship-born flirtations blossomed into romance and then, as they were intended to do, into marriage. The Navy, which traditionally took a bleak view of its officers marrying, had its own terminology for this annual female influx. The shoals of hopeful girls were known as 'the fishing fleet', the ladies' lounge in the Union Club in Valletta was 'the snake-pit', the ladies' swimming pool at the Sliema Club, 'the Pool of Disillusionment'.

The social life of Malta in the 1930s still leaves a warm glow in the memories of all who enjoyed it. The very scenery was spectacular and thrilling. Valletta, a city built to withstand a siege, the great yellow stone fortresses of St Angelo and St Elmo, and the three cities of Senglea, Cospicua and Vittorioso, together formed a setting like the backdrop of an opera stage. Dawn in Grand Harbour, with early sun glinting on the water and lighting the battlements, church bells tolling from far and near, the tinkling of goats' bells and the shrill cries of their herdsmen, was like the opening prologue to the last act of *Tosca*.

There was a cocktail party, a dance, a reception or a dinner almost every night, on board a ship, at Admiralty House, the Commander-in-Chief's residence in Valletta, at the Admiral Superintendent's house in Vittorioso, at the resident regimental garrison's mess, at the Union or the Marsa or the Sliema, or in somebody's private house. There were performances by leading companies from Rome and Naples at the Opera House in Strada Real, where some wardrooms took season tickets, and amateur performances by the Malta Amateur Dramatic Society. There was football at Corradino, shooting at Ricasoli, tennis, golf and horse-racing at the Marsa, polo for those who could afford it, picnics with swimming and 'sloggers' — sloe gin — at St Paul's Bay, and boat trips to Comino and Gozo.

Drink was cheap: Marsavin, the local wine, at a few pennies a bottle, or 'Red Infuriator'. For the sailors there was cricket or football at Corradino, followed by 'babies' heads' (a particularly glutinous form of steak and kidney pudding), washed down with Farson's Beer. Afterwards, there was Strada Stretta in Valletta, better known as 'The Gut', whose legendary ladies were in waiting to relieve the sailor of his money and his tensions.

Cunningham and Nona were very generous with their hospitality, especially to the younger flotilla officers. Casa Pieta was generally full of young men, and sometimes even the dog had to share his bedroom. Casa Pieta's drawing room, with its marble floor, was big enough for dances and there was a sub-lieutenant who could play the bag-pipes, always dear to Cunningham's heart, so there were eightsome reels, Petronella and Strip the Willow on the tennis court.

Cunningham's nieces came out with the fishing fleet and were company for Nona during the ships' frequent absences. The fleet cruised around the Mediterranean rather in the manner of a Tudor court on progress, normally going to the Riviera and North Africa in the autumn and winter, to the Greek islands and Yugoslavia in the heat of the summer.

The ships exercised intensively *en route* between ports, with full and subcalibre shoots at surface or air-towed targets; night encounters between capital ships; scouting, reporting and shadowing by cruisers and aircraft; torpedo attacks by destroyers, aircraft, submarines or torpedo boats; air attacks on the fleet, at sea and in harbour; and exercises in convoy, in station-keeping and in sending armed landing parties ashore.

The presence of an aircraft carrier, normally *Glorious* or *Furious* for much of the 1930s, lent flexibility and unpredictability to fleet exercises. Over the years, under Chatfield, Fisher and later under Dudley Pound, the Mediterranean Fleet gained considerable experience of the advantages and the problems of operating a carrier with the fleet.

When Lieutenant Keighly-Peach, one of the first naval officers to qualify as a pilot, joined *Coventry* in February 1935, he was

> wheeled along the quarter-deck to the after end, where a rather red-faced little man was standing gazing across Sliema harbour. It was ABC and he turned to greet me as his new Staff Officer (Operations) but his eyes immediately alighted on the flying badge on my sleeve. 'Do you intend to keep that thing on your sleeve whilst on my staff?' he said.
>
> Somewhat abashed by this opening gambit, I said yes I did, as it was part of the recognised uniform for the FAA. No reply to that. However later on during the subsequent spring

cruise, we were approaching Gibraltar with a view to intercepting the Home Fleet which had the aircraft carriers *Furious* and *Courageous* on their side. Suddenly out of the sky appeared a great many torpedo-carrying aircraft (Blackburn Ripons, I think) which attacked us from all angles. ABC was *furious* — and outwardly expressed the view that they would 'all have been shot down and NO hits on our side'. I always think that his views on aircraft at sea underwent a great change that afternoon…

Often there was no respite for the fleet in harbour. On one occasion, when the fleet returned to Malta after a long cruise, Fisher ordered certain ships to store for war forthwith, with fuel, stores, provisions, water and ammunition, and to signal when they were complete. This was the sort of signal made when there was trouble brewing somewhere and ships might be needed to aid the civil power. The officers and ship's companies of the ships designated, who had been looking forward to seeing their wives and families, worked hard all day instead, wondering where they would be going. At midnight, when they reported ready, they learned that it had all been an exercise. Their imaginative C-in-C had been satisfying himself that his ships could get ready within a certain time if the emergency arose.

The most important harbour activities by far were the annual fleet regattas. At the sailing regatta, held at Split in Yugoslavia in October, Cunningham won the Commander-in-Chief's Cup.

In 1935, Cunningham went home for King George V's Jubilee Review at Spithead in July. There were 157 British warships, with various liners, yachts and fishing vessels. The eleven heavy ships and eighteen cruisers present were imposing enough, but, as Cunningham remarked, 'nothing to compare with the Review in July 1914'. However, there was one new element; 100 aircraft of the Fleet Air Arm roared overhead in a fly-past 'and came dipping down in salute in a long glide', Cunningham said. 'It was a beautiful day and the spectacle was impressive.'

Cunningham returned to Malta at the end of July in the cruiser *Despatch*, with a new flag captain, Guy L. Warren. There were rumours of crisis in Abyssinia. The second summer cruise had been drastically shortened and — the surest sign of the gravity of the situation — the fleet regatta had been postponed.

On 12 August, the Mediterranean Fleet began to prepare and store for war (thus justifying Fisher's seemingly capricious exercises) and sailed from Malta on the 29th. Fisher had wanted to stay but was overruled by the Admiralty. Malta was only sixty miles — about twenty minutes' flying time in a fighter — from Sicily. The *Regia Aeronautica* was still largely an unknown quantity, but there were rumours of Italian suicide squadrons, and the British fleet in Grand Harbour might have been too tempting a target for a pre-emptive strike. Malta had no anti-aircraft defences, and there was a shortage of anti-aircraft ammunition at Malta, at Aden and in Egypt.

Thus Fisher had to sail for Alexandria, which controlled the Suez Canal, but had no docking facilities for anything larger than a 'C' Class cruiser, where the fleet arrived on 2 September.

During the summer of 1935 Italian transports carrying troops and stores to Eritrea were passing through the Suez Canal in a steady stream. The obvious international reaction would have been to close the Canal to Italian ships. The League of Nations protested and the international community hesitated, but Mussolini ignored or derided them all.

Fisher was confident that his fleet could defeat the Italian fleet, blockade Italy, and prevent her sending any more forces to Eritrea or bringing any back. He was determined to attack the Italians on their own doorstep immediately after war was declared. On the night after the declaration, a strong force of cruisers and destroyers was to sweep up the coast of Sicily and into the southern entrance of the Straits of Messina, to bombard harbours and installations and, as Cunningham (who was to command the force) said, 'generally to make ourselves obnoxious'.

To guard against a possible 'mad dog' attack by Italy, there was a general world-wide move of Royal Navy ships towards the eastern Mediterranean where the fleet began a period of intensive exercises and weapons training. The sweep up to Messina was rehearsed, and showed that no Italian ships at sea between the east coast of Sicily and the 'toe' of Italy could escape.

Cunningham now had some forty-five destroyers in five flotillas under his command and he drove them as hard as ever. 'I very soon became aware of RA(D)'s ruthless attitude to the Italian aggression,' said Lieutenant-Commander C.R.L. Parry, Squadron Torpedo Officer, 'and he was constantly making plans against their naval forces and territory. He set a high standard of training for the numerous ships now under his command, special attention being given to day and night firings and exercises at high speed, anti-aircraft firings, look-out organisations, and other matters connected with small ship actions... Numerous intriguing night encounter exercises were hatched up.'

Cunningham knew that risks had to be run and 'no omelette could be made without breaking eggs'. In one exercise, *Echo* and *Encounter* found themselves scraping alongside each other at 28 knots, requiring three months' dockyard repairs. One young destroyer captain, Lieutenant-Commander R. Gotto, 'contrived a pretty devastating collision when retiring at very high speed after firing (torpedoes). When it was all over I went in due course with my Captain (D) to see the great man. I felt, at once, that I was not being "carpeted" but that I was receiving very genuine sympathy.'

The elderly *Despatch* could not keep up with high-speed destroyer exercises. When the new, larger (5,200 tons) and faster (32½ knots) cruiser *Galatea* arrived in October, Cunningham suggested that, to avoid his having to lead his forces from the rear, he should move to her. According to Parry, *Galatea* was 'at once seized by ABC... A splendid example of peacetime piracy!'

When Italy invaded Ethiopia on 5 October, the Mediterranean Fleet, for all its warlike stance, was not sure whether it was at peace or war and responded by holding the postponed fleet regatta in Alexandria harbour on 8 and 9 October. The following day the refitted *Queen Elizabeth* arrived, flying the flag of the C-in-C designate, Admiral Sir Dudley Pound. But the Admiralty decided it would be inopportune to change C-in-Cs in the middle of a crisis, and Fisher remained in command. Pound then made the unprecedented offer to act as Fisher's Chief of Staff, which Fisher accepted, and hoisted his flag in *Queen Elizabeth*.

Although fleet training continued, by March 1936, the crisis was considered to have eased enough for Fisher to give up his command. On the 18th, he took his fleet to sea for the last time, for a day of exercises laid on for distinguished guests, including the High Commissioner and several Egyptian politicians. After a farewell dinner in *Renown* given by the flag officers and captains of the fleet, Fisher returned to *Queen Elizabeth* in a galley pulled by admirals, escorted by a double-banked cutter pulled by captains.

Next morning, *Queen Elizabeth* steamed slowly out of harbour, with Fisher standing on top of 'B' turret to take the salute. The fleet paraded guards and bands, manned the side and cheered Fisher out to sea. Cunningham had 'never heard cheers more hearty nor heartfelt. We were losing a friend, and a great commander.'

Fisher thought well of Cunningham — 'a great trump' he called him in a letter home. For his part, Cunningham conceded that Fisher was a difficult man to know, with rather an aloof manner, little sense of humour or time for fools and laggards, but he had great understanding of human nature, and Cunningham considered him an outstanding leader and a great man.

Cunningham himself was relieved as RA(D) by James Somerville some three weeks after Fisher left. 'There were few commanding officers of destroyers who were not on the platform at Alexandria when we left,' Cunningham wrote. 'I felt most deeply this final severance from the destroyer service, with which, except for a few short intervals, I had been intimately connected since 1908.'

When Cunningham went to the Admiralty he was disappointed to be told that he could expect no further employment until 1938. He tried to be philosophical. 'Such is the way of life in the Navy,' he said, 'where many are called and few chosen.' However, he was to be called much sooner than anybody expected.

The idea of two whole years away from the Navy was appalling. After years of short commons and cuts under OUNE (Owing to the Utmost Need for Economy), the Navy was at last getting some new ships, and more were being laid down. There was a sense of change, of great events impending.

Meanwhile Cunningham would spend his days gardening and walking the dog.

Cunningham was promoted Vice-Admiral on 22 July 1936, which made him too senior for the Tactical, Technical and War Courses which he had attended as a Rear-Admiral, and which would have helped to keep him up-to-date. But he did all he could to stay in touch, visiting and corresponding with serving friends, and calling as often as he could on Fisher, who was now Commander-in-Chief, Portsmouth.

With the prospect of two years on half-pay, Cunningham and Nona took Palace House, at Bishop's Waltham, near Southampton, on a long lease. It was a large, handsome, mellow red-brick house, dating partly from the fifteenth century, with additions in the seventeen, eighteenth and nineteenth centuries. They never regretted the decision and years later they bought it.

On 13 May 1937, Cunningham and Nona went to Westminster Abbey for the Coronation of His Majesty King George VI. Cunningham attended the Naval Review, as one of the VIP guests, including twenty admirals, who were passengers in the SS *Van Dyck*, following astern of the Royal Yacht. There were 141 ships of the Royal Navy and Royal Fleet Auxiliary. Of the seventeen foreign warships present, the new German 'pocket' battleship *Admiral Graf Spee* attracted much attention.

The celebrations were tinged with sadness. Admiral Fisher died on 24 June and Cunningham and Nona went to his funeral, which included a simple but very moving service on *Victory*'s quarterdeck.

One illness deprived Cunningham of a friend, but another restored him to active employment. Vice-Admiral Sir Geoffrey Blake, commanding the Battle Cruiser Squadron and Second-in-Command of the Mediterranean Fleet, and a physical fitness fanatic, had suffered a stroke. Instead of resting, he kept up his usual punishing routine and was eventually struck down by two heart attacks.

Offered the command temporarily until Blake had recovered, Cunningham 'leapt at the opportunity', packed enough gear to last him two or three months and within a week was on his way, leaving the long-suffering Nona to carry on furnishing and fitting out Palace House on her own.

Cunningham arrived in Grand Harbour at 7 a.m. on 15 July 1937. He was met by Blake's Flag-Lieutenant, James Munn, and, despite Munn's protestations, went straight on board the battlecruiser *Hood* — Blake's flagship, and now his. Everybody in *Hood* had hoped and expected that Cunningham would not appear until at least 8.30 (the Captain, Arthur Pridham, was still in his bath and not at all pleased to hear that the Admiral was on board). Cunningham was mischievously pleased to have caught them all on the wrong foot. It was just the sort of beginning he would have wished.

HMS *Hood* was middle-aged, having been launched in 1918, but she was still the largest and most beautiful warship in the world. Time and the Second World War were to show that *Hood*'s power was more appearance than reality. There were layers of rust under the innumerable coats of paint, and she had a serious weakness in her deck armour which made her fatally vulnerable to long-range plunging fire. But, in the 1930s, the 'Mighty 'Ood' was still the pride of the fleet.

Cunningham particularly admired the admiral's quarters. To somebody who had spent so many years in small ships, it was like a palace, with 'large airy cabins on the deck above the quarterdeck with great windows instead of the ordinary portholes'.

The Battle Cruiser Squadron consisted of *Hood* and *Repulse*, but Cunningham was also responsible for administrative purposes for the carrier *Glorious* and the fleet repair ship *Resource*. He was in charge of the training of fleet personnel as well. So he soon discovered that he had a full-time job. He took on Blake's secretary and staff, whom he found to be a most efficient body of officers. The Flag Captain, Arthur Pridham, was one of the most able gunnery officers of his day; as Cunningham waspishly remarked, his 'specialisation in gunnery had not impaired his ability in ship-handling, and it was a pleasure to see him bring the great 42,000 ton *Hood* stern first into her tight berth in Bighi Bay'.

Cunningham thought James Munn might not like to stay on with another admiral and gave him twenty-four hours to make up his mind. Munn decided to stay, saying innocently, 'After all, sir, there must be many worse jobs than being your flag lieutenant,' at which Cunningham laughed and laughed.

Cunningham's first call was on his new chief, Dudley Pound. The two men could hardly have been more different. Pound was a technical specialist, a torpedoman, a 'big ship' man, who had never served in a destroyer and had only ever had two commands, the battleship *Colossus* (which he commanded at Jutland) and the battlecruiser *Repulse* after the war. He was an 'office wallah', a hard-working and dedicated planner and administrator.

Somebody once said of Pound: 'He is the most even-tempered man in the world — he's always angry' He tended to look for scapegoats. If a man ever offended Pound, he never forgave nor forgot. He could be brutally rude to subordinates, issuing reprimands of a severity and a length which the offence often did not deserve. He drove himself very hard, at work and play. After a full day's exercises at sea, he would leave the ship at 5 a.m. the next morning, shoot for a couple of hours, return on board, bathe and breakfast, and then do a day's work, after which he would go to some function, to a party or a dinner, before coming back on board and working until 2 a.m.

At their first meeting, Pound told Cunningham that he [Cunningham] 'should freely express his views, especially if he felt there was anything wrong with the fleet or if he disagreed with any of the Commander-in-Chief's actions. I held exactly the same opinion, and though there were few questions upon which we ever disagreed I did not hesitate to say what I thought.'

When Admiral Blake went home as a cot-case that August, Cunningham saw that his 'temporary' appointment would last at least four or five months, so he cabled Nona to let Palace House and come out and join him. Once again, Nona packed and followed and was on her way by the end of July. Cunningham meanwhile found a flat in a new block close to their old house at Casa Pieta. He did not feel that his own 'technique' was up to the business of engaging the maids and so left this to Nona, who arrived in Malta early in August.

The main fleet exercise of 1937, codenamed SZ, was between the familiar Red and Blue fleets, with Red attempting to pass a convoy along the 320-mile passage from Malta to Argostoli, on the Greek island of Cephalonia. Blue, based at Navarino, tried to inflict damage on Red, and, if Red gained harbour, to inflict more damage before Red's harbour defences could be erected. It was, as the staff at the RNC Greenwich candidly said later, 'an exercise representing (roughly) conditions which might arise in a war with Italy'.

It was a hectic and complicated four-day exercise, of night encounters, antisubmarine incidents, air reconnaissance and shadowing, with minefields to be negotiated, attacks by cruisers, destroyers, motor-torpedo boats, submarines, and carrier-borne and shore-based aircraft.

One persistent problem, that of operating a carrier with the rest of the fleet, reoccurred. A carrier had to steam into the wind, often at very high speeds, to launch and recover her aircraft. The wind direction might not suit the fleet's course and an aircraft carrier operating her aircraft could quickly become detached from the main body.

Commenting on this years later, Cunningham wrote that the solution 'of course, was for the carrier to operate in line with the fleet and under its protection, though at that time this was anathema to all captains of aircraft-carriers. Hard experience and losses under war conditions quickly altered their point of view. Under the heavy umbrella of the fleet's anti-aircraft fire they were also much less liable to damage through bombing or torpedo attack.'

Although Cunningham wrote those comments with the advantage of the added perspective of the Second World War and all its carrier experience, he still seemed unaware of the inherent contradiction in his solution. If a carrier had to go, literally, where the wind listeth to operate her aircraft, she could not possibly remain with the fleet. The true solution, brilliantly executed by the US Navy's Task Forces in the Pacific, was for the fleet to conform to the carrier, and not the other way about.

In September, *Hood* returned to Malta to prepare for a tour of duty off the Spanish coast, where the Civil War had been in progress since July 1936. The Royal Navy's tasks were primarily humanitarian, and the first was the evacuation of British tourists, residents and businessmen. But the Navy also evacuated thousands of Spaniards, of both sides, and nationals of many other countries. British ships often found themselves in the position of mediators and were fired on, or bombed, by both sides.

The Navy resisted attempts by both sides to impose blockades on international shipping. The arrival of *Hood* and *Repulse*, with their 15-inch guns, cooled several inflamed situations.

In August 1937 the Italians lent the Nationalists four so-called 'legionary' submarines which, with Spanish liaison officers on board, operated from Malaga. These submarines began an indiscriminate campaign of sinkings which was a modern form of piracy.

The Admiralty authorised counter-attacks on submarines which attacked British merchantmen. Pound issued rules of engagement to the Mediterranean Fleet which were, however, so cautiously worded and hedged about with reservations as to make any captain pause long for thought before taking action.

In September 1937 an international conference was held at Nyon, a village near Geneva, where it was agreed that Great Britain would be responsible for waters around Gibraltar, Malta, Cyprus, and part of the Aegean. Italy, who with Germany boycotted the conference, was allocated the Tyrrhenian Sea, if she agreed, which she never did. However, the Admiralty knew through intelligence that the Italians had already called off the submarine campaign.

Although the main objects of the Nyon Conference had thus already been achieved, Pound initiated the Nyon patrols along the Spanish coast, with destroyers from the Mediterranean and Home Fleets, and the two RAF flying-boat squadrons from Malta who were stationed at Arzeu, near Oran, on the Algerian coast.

Hood returned to Malta in November 1937, for 'four days of hectic lunching, dining and dancing' to mark the visit of the

French C-in-C, Admiral Abrial. The news was that Admiral Blake was recovering and would be out in Malta by December. Cunningham and Nona planned to go home overland, by car. Casa Pieta had rather spoiled them for entertaining, but they used the splendour of *Hood*'s palatial facilities. Cunningham had a large dinner on St Andrew's Night, with two eightsome reels going at once in the dining cabin.

A picture of 'Uncle Ned', as he was known to his numerous nephews and nieces, is exactly caught by James Munn's sister, later the Marchioness of Aberdeen:

> I found after a very short acquaintance that one's only hope was to give as good as one got in the way of chaff. After one big dinner party in the *Hood* he ticked me off for taking so long — with the other female guests — powdering our noses after dinner: twenty minutes he said we took. I pointed out that his accommodation for such functions was entirely inadequate, and, with ten lady guests, this amounted to two minutes each, which, in my view, was not excessive.
>
> A few nights later I did the unforgivable thing of keeping the barge waiting at the Customs House steps when it was fetching ladies for a formal dinner-party. It seemed full of irate wives of admirals, and as the Flag-Lieutenant's sister I was a very low form of life. At the top of the gangway of the *Hood* 'Uncle Ned' met us, and last to be greeted, I said it was entirely my fault we were late and I was very sorry. His reply came back in a flash: 'Apology not accepted — one minute each tonight!'

In the New Year of 1938, Cunningham's appointment was made permanent, as Admiral Blake had retired. Cunningham and Nona set about house-hunting in Malta in earnest, and arranging for all their goods and chattels to come out from England.

In February Cunningham heard that he would probably be appointed Deputy Chief of the Naval Staff at the Admiralty in the autumn. He was 'rather horrified at the prospect', and did his best to escape it.

Later in February, Admiral Sir Roger Backhouse, C-in-C Home Fleet, arrived in Malta in his flagship *Nelson*. He was First Sea Lord designate and at dinner in Admiralty House Cunningham had the chance of a long private talk with him. 'I explained that I felt quite unsuitable for the appointment of D.C.N.S.; that I had practically no staff training, and was not good at expressing myself on paper. It was all to no purpose. Sir Roger just smiled, and said in his usual charming way that he wanted me to come. So that was that. Instead of taking houses in Malta we began to think of going home again.'

Cunningham was unaware that he was being closely observed at this time by John Godfrey, Captain of *Repulse*:

ABC's instinct was to resist any suggestion made and to demand VSOV (Very Senior Officer Veneration). It is a great pity that none of his COs *made* him specialise. He would have been a better admiral if his mind had been well stretched as a Lieutenant. He was stubborn, contemptuous of big ship service, and regarded destroyer service as an end in itself and not as an interlude in a career that ended at the top. Some talent-spotter should have seen to it that as Commander and as Captain he had a big ship appointment as second-in-command and an Admiralty appointment, either operations, plans or intelligence. It would have broadened his mind, introduced him to the machinery of government, tempered his tendency to be contemptuous of big ships, admin., and 'staff work'. His concept of running capital ships like destroyers was sheer nonsense. By neglecting the sublime (to quote Kempenfelt) aspects of his profession he threw his career out of balance but tried to protect himself by belittling everything but destroyer work and command.

Godfrey spoke with some feeling, because he had personal experience of Cunningham's attitude to administration and reforms. He listed some of the many suggestions and requests he had made, with Cunningham's response, if any, in italics:

> Extension of family welfare organisation at Portsmouth. *No reply.* Insurance of cars hired by subordinate officers. *No reply.* Scheme for ameliorating the lot of Maltese tradesmen owed large sums of money by officers who have left the Station. *Not approved for general adoption.* Advocating better publicity for the work of the Navy. *No reply.* Advocating training of young engineer officers in divisional work to help them look after the men they command. *Present training sufficient.* Appointment of executive officers to Captain Ships. *No reply.* Plea for 6 month trial of re-institution of General Mess Committee. *No such organisation needed.* Installation of very small bathroom weighing machines in sick berths as diagnostic aids in lieu of the butcher's steel-yard which had been used from time immemorial. *Hurrah!!!* [Godfrey's comment] *Approved and adopted.* Proposal to train more catapult crews. *Not approved.*

In March 1938, the Spanish Civil War was slowly swinging in Franco's Nationalists' favour on land, against a steadily darkening international scene. Even in Malta, the anti-aircraft defences had at last been strengthened, and civil defence, air-raid and gas attack exercises had been held during the last year.

The fleets assembled at Gibraltar to prepare for the larger war which now clearly lay ahead. There was no major exercise, but twelve smaller exercise serials: dusk attack, convoy escort, night encounters, and massed destroyer and air attacks on the battle fleet.

Although the Navy still had commitments around the coast of Spain, from Bilbao to Perpignan, over eighty ships took part. In one serial, Cunningham said, 'Once more I learnt the unwisdom of one's aircraft carrier operating apart from the fleet.' *Glorious* and *Courageous* were both 'sunk' by each other's aircraft in one early exchange, which led to Pound remarking, prophetically, that 'Armoured carriers may be the only satisfactory solution to the problem of bomb attacks.'

There was another lesson to be learned, the deadly threat to capital ships posed by airborne torpedo strikes, which was seemingly lost on both Pound and Cunningham. *Courageous* flew off a strike of twenty-four *Swordfish* armed with torpedoes to attack the battle fleet, which was steaming at 19 knots. One Swordfish squadron got four hits on *Warspite*, Pound's flagship (and two more aimed at her ran on and hit *Nelson* instead); a second squadron got three hits on *Revenge*, and a third five hits on *Royal Oak* — fourteen hits in all.

Glorious flew off eleven fighters, ten Swordfish to make flight' torpedo attacks and another eighteen Swordfish actually armed with torpedoes, to attack the Battle Cruiser Squadron. They scored three dive-bombing hits on *Hood* and two on *Repulse*, three flight' and two actual torpedo hits on *Hood*, and a torpedo hit on *Repulse*. This was a lesser number of hits than *Courageous*, but the battlecruisers were steaming at the higher speed of 26 knots.

Both carriers launched a combined strike of forty-six Swordfish and eleven fighters against all seven battleships steaming at 19 knots. They achieved no fewer than seventeen torpedo hits on *Nelson*, the Home Fleet flagship, two hits on *Rodney* and one each on *Malaya* and *Royal Oak*. Of forty-six torpedoes fired, twenty-one hit, for the loss of five Swordfish adjudged shot down.

However, battleship staffs continued to denigrate and discount such results. Indignant aircrew rightly complained that 'It didn't matter how many hits you achieved on the battleships, they always said, "Oh it'll be quite different when all the guns are firing at them, they'll never come as close as that".' Hits by Swordfish which were judged shot down were disallowed, although in wartime a torpedo might well run on and hit even after the aircraft had been shot down.

Hood arrived in a deserted Grand Harbour on 20 August. Pridham, who was also about to be relieved, brought the great ship into Bighi Bay for the last time with a tremendous flourish, going rapidly astern and then ordering full ahead to bring her to a standstill, while the sailors on the fo'c'sle and quarterdeck passed the wires in record time.

Cunningham was relieved by Vice-Admiral Geoffrey Layton. Nona was all packed and ready to leave. They left Malta in a P&O liner on 24 August for Marseilles, whence they travelled overland and from London went straight home to Palace House.

5: COMMANDER-IN-CHIEF, MEDITERRANEAN FLEET

'I FELT A great joy in being at sea again,' Cunningham wrote, 'steaming at high speed in perfect weather to what I have always considered is the finest appointment the Royal Navy has to offer.' It was 2 June 1939, and Cunningham was on board the cruiser *Penelope* which was taking him from Marseilles to Alexandria, where he was to relieve Dudley Pound as Commander-in-Chief of the Mediterranean Fleet.

Cunningham's period in the Admiralty had proved to be just an interlude, of only a few months. On 24 September 1938, during the Munich crisis, he was summoned to the Admiralty for duty, but found that for the first week he was to assist Admiral Sir William James, whom he was to relieve. Admiral James did not need any assistance. In fact, he was very much better at the job than Cunningham would ever be, but watching him at work at least gave Cunningham an excellent insight into what he himself would have to do.

Roger Backhouse had relieved Chatfield as First Sea Lord in November 1938. Professionally, he was a brilliant naval officer, who had rightly risen to the top, but he was temperamentally incapable of delegating work and responsibility and insisted upon seeing and doing everything himself, even down to minute details which could, and should, have been left to his staff. Thus papers and signals descended upon him in a never-ending avalanche. He was at his desk early in the morning and stayed till late in the evening. He had no hobbies and could never be induced to take a real rest or a holiday.

Cunningham had 'friendly arguments' when trying to persuade Backhouse to unload some of the burden and he did achieve one 'great triumph', when Backhouse turned over to him all matters connected with the Spanish Civil War, which, by February 1939, was coming to an end with a Nationalist victory. In this, as in his dealings with everything else at the Admiralty, Cunningham's personality blew through the corridors of Whitehall like a fresh — and not entirely welcome — sea breeze.

For someone so unpractised in bureaucracy and so uninterested in (and even disdainful of) the labyrinthine intrigues of Whitehall, Cunningham could not have gone to the Admiralty at a more difficult and delicate time. The Navy was engaged upon the greatest peacetime expansion in its history. The Naval Estimates of March 1939, at £147,779,000, were the largest ever recorded in peacetime. Over two hundred warships were under construction, from battleships and aircraft carriers down to the small *Hunt* Class destroyers (which Cunningham always claimed had their genesis in a suggestion of his own to Backhouse).

Manpower was to be increased by 14,000 to 133,000. Lord Chatfield's campaign to regain control of the Navy's air arm had at last been almost wholly successful. The Fleet Air Arm's personnel was to be expanded from 3,000 in 1939 to over 10,000 by 1942 (a figure which was actually overtaken by the war) and a huge aircrew training programme was under way.

Cunningham rarely left his desk before 8 p.m. every evening. He took a flat in Westminster, where he stayed during the week, but he very wisely got away from Whitehall every weekend he could and went down to Palace House, where he worked with Nona in the garden from Saturday afternoon, returning to London on Sunday evening or Monday morning.

But every Monday morning, the problems of the rearmament returned. New problems arose every few days — 'the arming of merchant vessels and the conversion of anti-submarine vessels; the industrial capacity of the country to provide new ships, guns, ammunition and war stores of every sort and kind; the defence of ports against air and other attack; air raid shelters at the dockyard ports; and the hurrying on of radar, or "radio location" as it was first called'. (The first primitive Type 79 RDF was fitted to *Rodney* in August 1938 and to *Sheffield* in November.)

In December 1938, the Germans announced that they intended to invoke the terms of a clause in the 1935 Anglo-German Naval Agreement allowing them to build up their submarine strength (normally 60 per cent of the British) to 100 per cent in exceptional circumstances. Cunningham headed a delegation to Berlin to try to dissuade Adolf Hitler, on the grounds of the adverse effect such an action would have upon British public opinion. It was not an argument likely to impress the Fuhrer, nor did it. Cunningham's party returned empty-handed, although Cunningham did have the chance to meet and sum up Admiral Raeder, the German naval C-in-C.

On 14 February 1939 Cunningham went to Buckingham Palace to be knighted by King George VI and invested with the insignia of a KCB. The pressure of work in the Admiralty was now such that he had to hurry back to his office immediately after the investiture to attend a meeting.

Roger Backhouse's health was failing badly. As First and Principal ADC to the King, he attended Court on 15 March, when he looked, in Cunningham's words, terribly ill. It was his last public appearance. He came to the Admiralty for an hour or two one afternoon and had papers sent to his bedside, but he showed no real signs of recovery and much of the burden of his work fell on Cunningham.

Cunningham had the constitution of an ox and struggled on for some time. He drafted in Vice-Admiral Charles Kennedy-Purvis as a Deputy First Sea Lord, to help with routine work, and as a result the height of the pile of papers and dockets in his basket was greatly reduced.

Meanwhile, international affairs went from bad to worse. On 14 March, German troops marched into Czechoslovakia. On Good Friday, 7 April, Cunningham was just sitting down to lunch at Palace House when he was called to the telephone. He was to return to London at once, as a matter of extreme urgency, to see the Foreign Secretary. Italy had invaded Albania.

The Admiralty's first task was to extricate ships of the Mediterranean Fleet which, by some malignant coincidence, were visiting Italian ports. On 13 April, when Parliament had reassembled, Winston Churchill told the House he could 'well believe that if our Fleet had been concentrated and cruising in the southern parts of the Ionian Sea the Albanian adventure would never have been undertaken...' He absolved British Intelligence from any blame. He seemed to think that ministers, and the Admiralty, had been warned in good time but had neglected to take any action, chiefly because it had all happened during a weekend.

Writing his own account of the Second World War, Churchill described the 'careless dispositions' of the Mediterranean Fleet, scattered as it was, with its five great capital ships, one at Gibraltar, another in the eastern Mediterranean and the other three 'lolling about inside or outside widely-separated Italian ports'.

The words 'lolling about' stung Cunningham. In his own dismissal of Churchill's charges, he stated

> categorically that Italy's intention was *not* known at the Admiralty, and that, to the best of my belief, neither the Foreign Office nor the Government was aware of it... In 1939 our intelligence about anything inside Italy was sparse, almost nonexistent. We had no subterranean access to Italian secret documents or decisions, and were as surprised as anybody when Mussolini risked incurring the severe displeasure of the Vatican by invading Albania on Good Friday.

The Mediterranean Fleet assembled south of Malta, entered harbour, refuelled and replenished with stores, and then sailed for Alexandria.

This decision to abandon the fleet's base at Malta was forced upon the Navy by the other two Services. As Cunningham explained,

> The R.A.F. experts considered Malta to be incapable of defence against the scale of air attack that might be expected from the aerodromes in Sicily, a bare sixty miles away. The Army accepted the R.A.F. views, so both were unwilling to consider what they thought was a waste of money and material on defending a fleet base that so obviously could not be utilised if Italy came into the war against us. How wrong they were.

It was by now clear that Roger Backhouse was not going to return to duty for some months (in fact, he died on 15 July that year). The obvious solution would have been to recall Lord Chatfield. His health was sound (he lived to be ninety-four) and he was a man of formidable administrative talents and vast experience. Instead, it was decided to offer Dudley Pound the post of First Sea Lord and Cunningham that of Commander-in-Chief, Mediterranean, with the acting rank of Admiral.

Cunningham was relieved by Rear-Admiral Tom Phillips and spent a hectic week settling his affairs and getting ready to leave for the Mediterranean. By the time he left London on 31 May, he had packed all his gear, paid a flying visit to his relations in Edinburgh, winkled Shaw out of his job in the Admiralty to come as his Secretary, chosen a young lieutenant called Walter Starkie as his Flag Lieutenant, and let both the flat in Westminster and Palace House. It was particularly hard to leave Palace House, in spring, with the garden looking at its best and 'the orchard a riot of bluebells and narcissi which we never knew existed. However, there could be no real regrets in view of where I was going.'

As *Penelope* bore him eastward, to what was nothing less than his appointment with destiny, Cunningham was greatly touched and encouraged by the hundreds of letters of congratulation he had received, all confident that he was the man for the job. He shared that confidence. He had served more than ten of his forty-two years in the Navy in the Mediterranean, in eight different ships. He knew the Mediterranean, its climate and its geography, better than any other officer serving. He knew its harbours and its coasts, from Gibraltar to Gallipoli, from Split to Sfax. He knew its people, from the King of Greece to the dghaisamen of Grand Harbour, and he was personally acquainted with many of the senior officers of other Mediterranean navies, some of whom were now to become his opponents. 'It always seemed to me that ABC was a gift from the Gods to us at that moment in history,' wrote Admiral Sir William James.

Penelope arrived in Alexandria on 5 June. Cunningham at once called on Pound in *Warspite*. Pound's flag was hauled down at sunset and the two dined together that evening, Pound briefing Cunningham on the situation in the Mediterranean, Cunningham bringing Pound up to date with the news from home.

Pound left at 4 a.m. the next morning in a flying boat for England. Cunningham saw him off and went on board *Warspite* officially at 9 a.m., when his flag was hoisted. The rest of the fleet was at sea and *Warspite* sailed at once to join them.

The Mediterranean Fleet then had the 1st Battle Squadron, of *Warspite* (the fleet flagship), *Barham*, *Malaya* and *Ramillies*; the 1st Cruiser Squadron, of three *County* Class cruisers; the 3rd Cruiser Squadron, of four light cruisers; three destroyer flotillas, and the depot ship *Woolwich*; the aircraft carrier *Glorious*; a flotilla of submarines, with the depot ship *Maidstone*; and a flotilla of motor-torpedo boats.

Cunningham, from now on always known to his fleet and the rest of the Navy as 'ABC', took over most of Pound's staff, including his Chief of Staff, Commodore Algernon Willis — 'Com' as ABC called him. The two men took to each other at once, in an immediate attraction of opposites. They complemented each other so well that they made a formidable combination of C-in-C and Chief of Staff, and they became lifelong friends. In the years to come, each was to owe the other a great deal, and they understood each other with almost telepathic accuracy.

ABC thought Willis 'an exceptionally brilliant officer... Full of imagination and new ideas, most painstaking and thorough in all he undertook, a good and firm disciplinarian, I found our views coincided on nearly every subject.' But 'Algie' was not a nickname bestowed, as many are, out of affection. As ABC realised, Willis had almost no sense of humour. He was somewhat rigid in his outlook, a stickler for correct procedures. In a curious way, just as he advised and supported ABC, so Willis himself needed ABC's reassurance and support. In short, a man of Algie Willis' somewhat sombre nature needed to have his leg pulled.

Though he said he knew ABC only slightly, Willis felt honoured to be asked to stay on. Of ABC, Willis wrote that 'he was a wonderful man to serve, though at times rather difficult, which was understandable seeing the great responsibilities he had. Quite different to Pound, ABC well understood how to use a Staff, and I personally found everything much easier. Sometimes I disagreed with him violently which he seemed to appreciate. He had no use for "yes men".'

Other members of the staff were C.E. Hotham as Captain of the Fleet, and Victor Crutchley, VC, in command of *Warspite*, with Commanders Royer Dick, Staff Officer (Plans); Geoffrey Barnard, Fleet Gunnery Officer; W.P. Carne ('William the Silent'), Fleet Torpedo Officer; Tom Brownrigg as Master of the Fleet; Eustace Guinness as Staff Officer (Intelligence); 'Tim' Shaw once more as Secretary; and, when he arrived from RNC Dartmouth where he had been a term officer, Walter Starkie as Flags.

All these were, as ABC said, 'a very happy party in the dining room', and most of them were to serve ABC for four years. The only early departure was the Staff Officer (Operations) who, as his successor said, 'argued, lost his temper and was fired'. The successor, Commander Manley Power, known as 'Lofty' as much for his manner as his height, was a submariner, because the job was traditionally a 'submariner's perk'.

Lofty Power was very probably the ablest officer on ABC's staff. He had not wanted the appointment, but never regretted it. He quickly learned the art of survival. 'ABC was a bully,' he said. 'If he was not stood up to he could become unbearable.

Fortunately very early I had a couple of show downs with him and hence the pattern of a long, fruitful and stormy relationship founded on mutual respect.'

The most pressing prospect was war against Italy. ABC's own belief, forcibly expressed, was that 'our policy against Italy was to cut off her supplies, interfere with her communications, bombard her ports, destroy her submarines, and later on, when our military build-up was complete, to conquer Libya and the Italian colonies in East Africa.' If, as a result, the Italian fleet came out, then 'we should welcome the meeting.'

The loss of one or more battleships in the Mediterranean would have great propaganda value for the enemy and would influence Japan's decision whether to enter the war. Therefore the opinion at home was that battleships should be held back from bombarding the Libyan and Sicilian coasts because they might eventually be needed in the Far East for a war against Japan.

ABC thought this policy mistaken. His ships were in danger from air and submarine attack wherever they went in the Mediterranean. He believed they were actually safer at sea than in such a poorly defended harbour as Alexandria.

While ships continued to use Malta for its good dockyard facilities and experienced work force, Alexandria became the fleet base, although its defences were, in ABC's word, 'feeble': there was no airfield for the Fleet Air Arm, no docking facilities for anything larger than a 'C' Class cruiser, and no proper storage for ammunition and explosives. However, there were deep-water berths alongside the wharfs and a range of warehouses which became naval stores. An ammunition dump was built in the desert to the west of the city, an airstrip was constructed at Dekheila near the coast, and a large floating dock was eventually brought out from Portsmouth.

With its cosmopolitan night-life, and its tourist trips to Cairo, the Pyramids and Pompey's Pillar, Alexandria was very popular with the fleet. There were plenty of playing fields, a golf course, tennis courts, magnificent sea-bathing and an excellent Fleet Club for the sailors in the old converted Greek hospital. ABC had taken over Pound's house in Alexandria which was, he said 'the most lovely little house, with a beautifully kept garden, exotic flowers, and an aviary full of love-birds of every hue'. As the new Chief, he embarked upon a social routine so hectic that he broke a tooth and had to have it out (incidentally, his first extraction for thirty-five years).

Warspite arrived in Malta for a short docking on 8 July 1939. Nona arrived by P&O two days later. Her main task was the refurbishment of Admiralty House, the C-in-C's official residence, which, in the days of the Knights of St John, had been the Auberge d'Avignon. It had a handsome main staircase, leading up to the first-floor landing with two balustraded balconies where, on the walls to either side, were two plaques with the names engraved of all ABC's predecessors since 1792, who included Hood, Hotham, John Jervis, Keith, Nelson and Collingwood.

On 30 July, *Warspite* and four destroyers sailed for a visit, which had almost the importance of a formal diplomatic mission, to Istanbul, to be followed by a visit to Cyprus. Before leaving, ABC arranged for Nona and his niece Hilda Bramwell, his sister's youngest daughter, to take passage in the yacht *Aberdeen*, and meet the fleet at Alexandria.

Aberdeen's passage was not quite the innocent pleasure cruise it seemed. On her way, she visited various small ports in southern Greece, the western end of Crete, and the islands of Kithera and Anti-Kithera, where her officers made quick surveys of anchorages, depths of water, and harbour facilities, if any. Some of these little anchorages might well be used by British tankers in a war with Italy. The information gained *by Aberdeen* was to prove very useful in 1940.

Meanwhile, *Warspite* and her escort were enjoying the last hospitality of peace. The Turks had organised an almost ceaseless round of luncheons, dinners, balls, regattas, and football and cricket matches.

Warspite gave a dance — the last of peacetime. The US Ambassador brought three beautiful daughters, and then tried to get away from the dance early. 'I warned him it was hopeless,' ABC told Doodles. 'Every time he attempted to get his flock together some young officer in attendance on the fairies removed him for another glass of champagne.'

Warspite joined the fleet to exercise an attack upon 'Italian' convoys on passage from the Italian coast to Libya and Tripolitania. Ironically, the Italian fleet had just carried out a similar exercise, with the ships representing the 'British' working from Rhodes. ABC hoped that this meant that the Italians would put to sea when war came.

The fleet returned to Alexandria on 15 August 1939. With a fine sense of priority, the fleet was holding a regatta in Alexandria harbour when the news came. ABC was standing with Willis on top of *Malaya's* 'A' turret, watching the races, when the signal was handed up to him: Great Britain was at war with Germany.

ABC wrote to Doodles, 'I never expected to find myself in the position when war was declared of having nothing to do but to go ashore and have tea with Nona. But so it happened. What a senseless business!'

Another signal from the Admiralty that evening, which the fleet received 'with considerable satisfaction', was 'Winston is back'.

In the Atlantic, a five-year battle began with the torpedoing of the Donaldson liner *Athenia* on the evening of 3 September. But in the Mediterranean, ABC had nothing to do. 'It does seem queer,' he wrote to Doodles on 4 September, 'dining on board with Nona and a few women when there's a war on. We are the unemployed.'

Convoy was instituted in the Mediterranean at once. ABC thought it a waste of effort. He would have preferred to rely on anti-submarine patrols in the Straits of Gibraltar to keep German U-boats out of the Mediterranean and let merchant shipping proceed freely on its lawful occasions. 'If we had a ship or two sunk,' he wrote to Pound, 'it would not take long to institute convoy.'

Pound and ABC both set great store upon their correspondence. Pound, who always began his letters 'My dear Andrew', kept ABC up to date on general naval affairs and operations and wrote, 'I do hope you will not hesitate to remark quite frankly on anything I write, the more we discuss things the better and the easier for me to make any necessary decision when the time comes.'

Within a month, the Mediterranean Fleet had begun to disperse. By December, ABC was left with three small 'C' Class cruisers and five 1918-vintage 'V' & 'W' Class destroyers manned by the Royal Australian Navy. However, he knew the Mediterranean would not remain a backwater. When he said farewell to *Warspite*'s officers and ship's company he told them he would see them back in the spring.

Meanwhile, ABC had to fly his flag ashore. He favoured Alexandria, nearer Cairo, where General Sir Archibald Wavell and Air Chief Marshal Sir William Mitchell (relieved, in May 1940, by Air Chief Marshal Sir Arthur Longmore), the Army and Air Force Commanders-in-Chief, both had their headquarters. However, despite Malta's continuing deficiencies in antiaircraft defences, the Admiralty decided that ABC should base himself there, where accommodation and communications were better than in Alexandria, and ABC would be in closer touch with the French.

The Cunninghams moved back to Malta in November 1940. Their new furniture had arrived; hardly a priority cargo in wartime, as ABC said, but very welcome. Nona's redecoration schemes were finished and were well worth the trouble. 'To me as a mere man,' said ABC, 'it was very lovely.'

Some hundreds of sailors' wives and children, many of them none too well off, had been left at Alexandria and Malta. Nona saw to their welfare, helped by Hilda Bramwell and some officers' wives.

Hilda had also been busy in other ways, as ABC and Nona discovered when she became engaged to Walter Starkie at the end of November. She was 'such a sweet good-tempered child,' ABC wrote to Doodles, 'and a very good head on her shoulders'. However, 'the lad has nothing but his pay, which is unfortunate'. ABC thoroughly approved that Hilda 'had had the sense to break away from the Edinburgh medical circle'.

He was not so sure of his sister Liz, Hilda's mother, whose last words to her daughter were 'not to get engaged to a naval officer'. Parental approval was slow in coming but in December, ABC wrote that 'the two are very happy' and 'beginning to think of matrimony'.

As British naval strength in the Mediterranean dwindled, while the French remained the same, it was possible the French might demand overall control of naval policy in the theatre, a prospect which greatly alarmed both Pound and ABC.

From the outset of the war, the Government's policy in the Mediterranean was obscure. ABC, Wavell and Mitchell (whom 'Com' Willis called 'The Lords of the Middle East') had had their first official meeting on board *Warspite* in Alexandria harbour on 18 August 1939, when it had become clear that none of the Services had any detailed instructions on their action in the event of war.

A conference was held in February 1940, at Cairo, and continued in March, at Aleppo, between the three British C-in-Cs, the French and the Turks, from which there was little tangible result other than the appointment of Admiral Sir Howard Kelly as British liaison officer in Ankara.

On the sidelines of the war as he was, ABC eagerly followed from a distance the doings of those who had served with him in the Mediterranean. He grieved for the destroyer *Gipsy*, 'one of ours from the Mediterranean', sunk by a magnetic mine off Harwich on 21 November, and rejoiced when the submarine *Salmon*'s Captain, Lieutenant-Commander Bickford, 'one of ours', sank U.36. The war came much closer when the destroyer *Duchess* collided with *Barham* and sank in the Western Approaches on 12 December 1939. Among those drowned was her First Lieutenant, George Murray, a cousin of ABC's, who had a young wife and a small child living in Malta. It fell to Nona to go round and break the news.

ABC believed that the Maltese were not taking the black-out, or the war, seriously enough. In January 1940 he wrote, 'this island badly wants a bomb dropped on it. The Governor has been pushed by the Maltese to do away with most of the wartime restrictions, so cars roar about all night, and places of entertainment remain open as they like.' Malta 'is only a little farther than the Shetlands from the nearest German air base. They are in a way bad people, these Maltese, they expect to get all the loaves and fishes from the Imperial connection and escape all the responsibilities.'

At home, it was the coldest winter of the century. Even in Malta there were unheard-of flakes of snow. In February there was a private tragedy, when Charles Hotham, the Captain of the Fleet, committed suicide with his own shot-gun. 'Poor man,' wrote ABC, 'too long abroad, I think.' It transpired that Hotham had been invalided home from Malta, with suicidal tendencies, some twelve years earlier.

In April 1940, the 'Phoney War' ended at last, with the German invasion of Denmark and Norway. For ABC, there was stirring news of 'Wash' Warburton-Lee ('one of my lads out here when I was RAD, such a fine chap — he can ill be spared') who took his destroyers into Narvik and won a posthumous Victoria Cross.

ABC had decided that Walter Starkie was too able a young officer to go on serving in an operational backwater and he prepared to have him relieved. But Starkie preferred to stay in Malta, and marry Hilda. The wedding took place in St Paul's Anglican Cathedral, Valletta, on Wednesday, 24 April 1940. ABC gave the bride away, and with his notorious zeal for punctuality delivered her to the cathedral door rather more promptly than was altogether seemly for a bride on her wedding day, indeed an unwary Group Captain and his wife who arrived simultaneously with the bride and jocularly asked ABC's permission to go on in was very disconcerted to be barked at: 'No, you're late!'

After the wedding, ABC began to get his fleet back again. *Warspite* arrived on 10 May, ABC's prophecy having come true. He and his staff were glad to move back into their old quarters. 'I think the men were glad to see us also,' ABC wrote to

Doodles. 'There is a cachet about being fleet flagship which extends to the most junior rating on board.'

On 23 May, ABC informed the Admiralty that his initial object was to secure control of the sea communications in the eastern Mediterranean and the Aegean, and to cut off Italian supplies to the Dodecanese. This limited object did not envisage cutting the sea communications between Italy and Libya, a decision brought about by lack of light naval forces and aircraft and the fact that a military offensive against Libya was no longer contemplated. He added that this did not mean that the central Mediterranean would be neglected, but he intended to carry out an early sweep in this direction with his heavy ships.

Churchill (now Prime Minister) made up his mind that ABC's policy was defensive. Pound, who often had to mediate between Churchill and the Navy, signalled to ABC on 5 June: 'It has been suggested that the Naval Object as outlined in your message of May 23rd, is purely defensive, but I have never interpreted it as being such, and I know it is your burning desire to make as many opportunities for hitting the enemy hard as your limited forces will permit.'

This should not have needed saying to a man of ABC's record and professional stature. Salt was rubbed in by another Admiralty message to ABC, 'to signal his exact dispositions and intended movements in the immediate future more fully than had previously been necessary'.

ABC replied next day with his detailed intentions and dispositions, and a message to Pound:

> You may be sure that all in the fleet are imbued with a burning desire to get at the Italian fleet, but a policy of seeking and destroying his naval forces requires good and continuous air reconnaissance, and a means of fixing the

enemy when located. I am far from well provided with either requirement, whereas the Italians have both. Indeed my chief fear is that we shall make contact with little or nothing except aircraft and submarines, and I must get the measure of these before attempting sustained operations in the Central Mediterranean. It must not be forgotten that the fleet base (Alexandria) and repair facilities are exposed to enemy air attack, with very limited fighter protection, and there is no alternative.

ABC deeply resented the imputation that he was acting defensively. It was, he said,

in the sort of 'prodding' message received by me on June 5th that Mr Churchill was often so ungracious and hasty. We realised, of course, the terrible mental and physical strain under which he was labouring; but so were we. Such messages to those who were doing their utmost with straitened resources were not an encouragement, merely an annoyance. Moreover, as they implied that something was lacking in the direction and leadership, they did positive harm.

When war did come, the fleet was, as ABC said, once again quite imposing, on paper at least. At Alexandria on 9 June were four battleships; the 7th Cruiser Squadron, of five cruisers; the 3rd Cruiser Squadron, of four cruisers; 'a mixed bag' of twenty-five destroyers; the aircraft carrier *Eagle*, just joined from the China Station; a dozen submarines, also from the China Station; the fleet repair ship *Resource* and the submarine depot ship *Medway*. The French, under Vice-Admiral Godfroy, had the battleship *Lorraine*, three 8-inch gun cruisers, one 6-inch gun cruiser, and three destroyers.

On 4 June, the Admiralty estimated that Italy was likely to enter the war between 10 and 20 June. But, on the afternoon of 10 June, Count Ciano informed the British and French Ambassadors in Rome that Italy would be at war from 11 June.

ABC acted on the earlier estimate. At 4 a.m. on 10 June, hours before the declaration of war, he sent the 2nd Destroyer Flotilla and two flying boats on an anti-submarine sweep, to attack any submarines which attempted to leave their declared areas without escort. The Mediterranean Fleet heard the news that Italy had entered the war at 7 p.m. on 10 June. The fleet went to two hours' notice for steam.

Warspite, *Malaya*, *Eagle*, the 7th Cruiser Squadron and nine destroyers sailed from Alexandria at 1 p.m. on 11 June for a 'coat-trailing' expedition, and were joined at sea by *Calypso* and *Caledon*. They headed for Crete, to steam along the southern coast to a point about eighty miles south of Cape Matapan, where the cruisers and the aircraft searched westwards until dark. The cruisers then moved south to attack any Italian patrols off Benghazi and Tobruk at daylight on 12 June. The French meanwhile would sweep up the Aegean and off the Dodecanese.

ABC had expected his ships to spend most of the daylight hours beating off air attacks. In the event, just one aircraft was sighted by the cruisers *Liverpool* and *Gloucester* when they were engaging Italian minesweepers off Tobruk on the 12th. But the cruiser *Calypso* was torpedoed at about 2 a.m. on 12 June, south of Crete, by the Italian submarine *Bagnolini* and sank with the loss of one officer and thirty-eight ratings.

Worse still, a chance of the very kind ABC longed for was missed. The OIC (Operational Intelligence Centre) in Alexandria received D/F (Direction Finding) bearings revealing Italian ships, including the cruiser *Garibaldi*, north of Derna. But because of W/T congestion, the signal to ABC was sent off too late to be of use. The bearings showed that

Garibaldi had been close enough to engage. Coming so soon after the loss of *Calypso*, the whole incident had been, as ABC sharply signalled, 'most regrettable'. Procedures were improved and D/F signals given a much higher priority.

Italian submarines had laid mines off Alexandria in the fleet's absence. The fleet was 'poverty-stricken as regards minesweepers', and entered harbour, very cautiously, on 14 June. The destroyers counter-attacked and claimed to have sunk two submarines, but no Italian submarines were lost off Alexandria at that time.

The Italian Navy entered the war with some 100 submarines, of which it was reported on 18 June that some fifty were at sea. But by the end of June no fewer than ten had been captured or sunk.

Much of this success was due to good intelligence. 'Intelligence about Italy was sparse,' ABC wrote, after the war; 'we had no subterranean access to Italian secret documents or decisions.' In fact, a high proportion of Italian codes were being read regularly by the Government Code and Cypher School (GC&CS) at Bletchley Park. The Italian Navy's most secret high-grade cypher, and its general naval code book, were both being largely read as early as 1937. So, too, was one of the two codes used by Italian naval attaches in embassies abroad.

There was another source. At the outbreak of war in September 1939, the British and Italian naval staffs in the Mediterranean came to an arrangement, 'to avoid incidents', Willis said, whereby the Italians 'informed us of the movements of their submarines and provided surface escorts'. The only condition, 'was that we shouldn't let the Germans know. This was very reasonable.'

The arrangement worked well until MEIC (Middle East Intelligence Centre) in Cairo referred to it in their widely circulated 'magazine of titbits'. The High Commissioner in Egypt 'blurted it out' to King Farouk, whose entourage was full of Italians, whence it got back to Rome, who made a 'well-justified complaint' through the British Ambassador. 'My remarks to the Head of MEIC', said Willis, 'were unprintable.'

In January 1940, when the first brief and incomplete translations of German 'Enigma' machine decrypts obtained by GC&CS at Bletchley Park began to be circulated in Whitehall, the Admiralty had warned C-in-Cs at home and abroad that they might receive intelligence derived from high-grade signal intelligence (Sigint), sent to them in the Flag Officer's cypher in messages prefixed by the codeword HYDRO.

In June 1940, Italian submarines were still using the general naval code book, which was being read almost currently by the GC&CS. For some weeks after the outbreak of war, the Mediterranean OIC could therefore continue to identify the whereabouts of individual Italian submarines, their patrol areas, their numbers and order of battle. More cryptographic material, documents and code books were captured when *Galileo Galilei* surrendered to the trawler *Moonstone* in the Red Sea on 19 June. A new general code book, which the Italian Navy had planned to introduce in July, was captured from *Uebi Scebeli*.

These cryptographic successes were only temporary. Further intelligence value could have been derived from the capture of *Galileo Galilei*, had not pictures of *Moonstone* towing the submarine into Aden harbour appeared in the British press. In general, the Italian Navy's cypher security was excellent (very much better than the German Navy's). On 5 July, the Italians began to use a new, separate cypher system for their submarines and, on the 17th, new cypher tables for their surface ships.

The setbacks of June 1940 and further losses by the end of the year dealt a blow to the Italian submarine service's morale from which it never recovered. Italian submarines never achieved the strategic success which their numbers should have guaranteed.

Meanwhile, the brunt of the war fell upon Malta, which was being bombed by night and by day. The anti-aircraft gun defences were still insufficient and there were no fighters. At the request of Air Commodore Maynard, AOC in Malta, ABC authorised the use of some Sea Gladiators, originally intended as replacement aircraft for *Glorious* (which had been sunk with great loss of life off Norway on 8 June). Three of them, unpacked from their crates, assembled and flown by the RAF under their nicknames of 'Faith', 'Hope' and 'Charity', were for a time Malta's only air defence.

There was an almost unbelievable sequel: a signal some weeks later from an Admiralty stores department, demanding to know why ABC had allowed Fleet Air Arm spares to be turned over to the RAF. Admiralty bureaucrats, in their positions of personal safety at home, had yet to realise there was a war on. ABC said: 'I wondered where the official responsible had been spending his war.'

He was relieved to hear that the civilian population of Malta (on whom he had once wished a bomb would drop) were bearing up under the onslaught. With a wife and two nieces on the island, he was as concerned as any officer or man in his fleet. It had been suggested that Nona should leave but she decided that it was not right and proper for the C-in-C's wife to be among the first to go. So she stayed and was soon running Admiralty House as 'a sort of hostel for lonely wives'.

ABC kept his ships busy, in war as in peace. 'Destroyers were sweeping for submarines; a cruiser and more destroyers were operating in the Dodecanese; British submarines were on passage through the Aegean to the Dardanelles and Doro Channel, as well as on patrol off Augusta, Taranto, and the Straits of Otranto. French submarines were working off Rhodes, Leros, the Straights of Messina and Tripoli.'

On 20 June an Anglo-French force under Vice-Admiral John Tovey, flying his flag in *Orion*, with *Lorraine*, the cruisers *Neptune* and *Sydney* and four destroyers, sailed to bombard Bardia. Five more destroyers sailed to sweep along the Libyan coast as far as Tobruk. The French cruisers *Suffren* and *Duguay Trouin* and three British destroyers sailed in support.

The bombardment took place on 21 June. But this was the last operation in which French ships took part. ABC had planned an Anglo-French sweep between the south of Italy and Libya for 22 June. But this was cancelled by the Admiralty. The French were about to sign an armistice.

For some time ABC had been concerned by the news from France, where the situation 'seemed hourly to be becoming more desperate', because of the presence of the French squadron in Alexandria. ABC got on very well with Godfroy, the French Commander, who was 'one of the best type of French naval officer'; he spoke excellent English, having married an English wife ('now deceased').

But Godfroy, 'full of fight at the outset... faded out as a belligerent' after Pétain asked for an armistice. ABC observed that the French in Alexandria had faith in Pétain and Weygand and 'resented their new government being called unconstitutional. They had no use for General de Gaulle.' Some of the younger men wanted to fight on. One complete destroyer's crew said they would have been glad to fight under the British flag.

When news came of the French capitulation on 24 June, ABC knew that Godfroy was a very honourable man who would not hamper British operations in any way. But it meant that the United Kingdom now had no allies. Next morning, 25 June, ABC was walking up and down *Warspite*'s quarterdeck, 'feeling rather depressed', when an Admiral's barge came alongside.

It was Jack Tovey, who was actually smiling as he came up the gangway. Tovey had caught a curious mood, of relief, almost of exhilaration, which many at home in England were feeling: if we had no allies, then we would have nobody to let us down either. 'Now I know we shall win the war, sir,' said Tovey. 'We have no more allies.' ABC's depression vanished. He could not feel downcast in the face of such optimism.

6: THE FRENCH FLEET AT ALEXANDRIA, AND THE ACTION OFF CALABRIA, JULY 1940

THE FRENCH MIGHT have surrendered, but the war went on. ABC constantly urged his captains to take aggressive action, to implant in the enemy's mind the fear that ABC's ships were ever ready to attack whenever he might venture to sea.

Thus ABC was delighted to hear on 28 June that Jack Tovey with the 7th Cruiser Squadron had intercepted three Italian destroyers some seventy-five miles west-south-west of Cape Matapan. The cruisers opened fire at extreme range and the action developed into a high-speed chase. The Italian destroyers were faster than the British cruisers and two escaped, but the third, *Espero*, was hit and sunk.

It was good shooting to hit such a small, fast-moving target at extreme range. But ABC's joy was tempered, and his scepticism about the gunnery branch revived, by the 'tremendous expenditure' of shell to sink that single 1,100-ton destroyer. As he said, when 'pumping out twelve gun salvos the ammunition just melted away'. The fleet now had only some 800 6-inch shells in reserve which, shared equally, would leave the cruisers at only half their normal outfit. The nearest 6-inch shells were at Durban, some 6,000 miles away.

Meanwhile, there was the pressing problem of what to do about the French ships at Alexandria. ABC might like and respect Admiral Godfroy, but the British ships could never sail for operations against the enemy and leave behind operational

French warships which might sail at once, for Beirut or Toulon.

The main units of the French fleet were distributed between Mers-el-Kebir (the naval base at Oran), Dakar, Casablanca, Sfax and Alexandria, with the most powerful force, including two battleships and two battlecruisers, at Mers-el-Kebir.

Plans were made to give the French ships at Oran the choices of sailing to British ports to continue the fight; of sailing to British ports with reduced crews who would be repatriated if they wished; sailing to a French port in the West Indies where they would be demilitarised; or scuttling in harbour. Otherwise, the French ships were to be destroyed where they were.

The task of carrying out this policy was given to James Somerville, who had just taken command of Force H, of *Hood*, *Valiant*, *Resolution*, *Ark Royal*, two cruisers and eleven destroyers, newly formed to fill the naval vacuum created in the western basin of the Mediterranean by the French surrender.

At Alexandria, ABC was asked on 28 June for his views on the best way to seize the French ships with the 'minimum risk of bloodshed and hostilities'. To ABC,

> the idea was utterly repugnant. The officers and men in the French squadron were our friends. We had had many cordial social contacts with them, and they had fought alongside us. Vice-Admiral Godfroy, moreover, was a man of honour in whom we could place implicit faith. Suddenly and without warning to attack and board his ships, and in the course of it probably to inflict many casualties on his sailors, appeared to me to be an act of sheer treachery which was as injudicious as it was unnecessary.

ABC was sure matters could be settled by negotiation. The

French could not go to sea without his consent. Lack of supplies, pay for the ships' companies and the urgent wishes of his men to go home to protect their families would shortly bring Godfroy to terms. ABC also suspected that the ordinary French matelot had markedly different views from those of his admirals. Besides, he did not believe the French really wanted to surrender their fleet to the Germans or the Italians.

ABC signalled his arguments against the proposed action to the Admiralty on 30 June. Next day he received a more moderate reply: the French ships at Alexandria were to be secured for our own use if this could be done without bloodshed. Any Frenchmen who wanted would be repatriated, but any who chose to stay would have Royal Navy rates of pay and conditions of service.

If the French ships could not be secured for British use, then they could remain at Alexandria with skeleton crews and in a non-seagoing condition. The British Government would be responsible for the pay of the French sailors and the upkeep of the ships. Otherwise, the ships were to be sunk at sea.

ABC was instructed to put these alternatives to Godfroy at 7 a.m. on 3 July, the hour specified precisely because action to be taken against the French ships at Mers-el-Kebir was timed to begin early that day.

Godfroy must have guessed what was in the wind when he received ABC's invitation for such an unusually early hour, but he and his Chief of Staff arrived punctually. ABC was on deck to receive them, with a Royal Marine guard and band.

The meeting was friendly but formal. They spoke English, with Royer Dick, who spoke fluent French, interpreting any point of difficulty. Godfroy was helpful and cordial, but flatly rejected the proposal that the French ships be put at the disposal of the British Government. He had to consult his own

Government and, in any case, how could his ships fight under any flag except the French? He, his officers and men would be classed as deserters.

This was not a promising beginning. But ABC asked Godfroy to tell his sailors about the proposals and to make it clear that every man was free to make up his own mind. ABC pointed out that these were good terms and he could, if he wished, publish them to the French squadron over Godfroy's head, although he preferred not to do that.

Godfroy seemed to be becoming more amenable, the more so when ABC repeatedly reminded him that surely his object was not just to prevent his ships from falling into enemy hands but also ultimately to preserve them for France.

ABC passed on to the second option: that the French ships be immobilised in Alexandria, with the British Government undertaking to pay and supply the crews left on board, and the ships only to be used by the British if the enemy broke the terms of the armistice. At this, Godfroy 'brightened up considerably' and said he thought he could accept it, but would need a little time to think about it.

When Godfroy was given the third option, of taking his ships to sea and sinking them in deep water, it 'evoked no enthusiasm'. ABC's point that this would defeat Godfroy's main object, of preserving the ships for France, seemed to help him to concentrate upon the second option, although he did demur at the crews' being removed from their ships.

ABC impressed upon Godfroy that he must make up his mind himself and he must do it quickly He also said that by agreeing to one of the options Godfroy would, of course, only be yielding to *force majeure* and could therefore come to an agreement with his honour intact. ABC said he hoped Godfroy would choose the second option.

ABC had played his hand with a diplomatic skill which astonished his staff. They all believed Godfroy would choose the second option. ABC signalled as much to the Admiralty. Godfroy's reply was therefore a bitter disappointment: he could not reconcile with his military duty the proposal that his ships would fight alongside ABC's. That ruled out the first option. He was inclined to recommend the second option to his superiors, who alone could authorise him to disarm his ships in a foreign port under duress from a foreign power. If Godfroy had to make the decision, as ABC had told him he must, then he could not authorise the second option on his own.

ABC's insistence that Godfroy alone must take the decision thus seemed to have backfired. Godfroy now felt bound to choose to take his ships to sea and sink them. He asked for forty-eight hours, to arrange for the safety and transport of his crews.

ABC said he had received Godfroy's decision with profound regret and had no alternative but to accept it. 'I am therefore under the painful necessity', he concluded, 'of asking you to proceed to sea to carry out your purpose at 1200 on Friday, 5th July.'

Meanwhile, ABC was still under orders from London to disarm the French squadron by nightfall. But he was sure that if scuttling could be postponed, and the French ships were demilitarised, they would sooner or later rejoin his fleet or at least return into Allied hands.

ABC wrote Godfroy a private and personal letter, asking if a compromise was not possible. Could Godfroy not make some gesture to the British Government? Would he be prepared to remove the oil from his ships and the warheads from his torpedoes? The question of the crews could be left until later.

To ABC's great joy and relief, Godfroy agreed. The French ships were discharging their oil by 5.30 that afternoon. ABC signalled his success to the Admiralty.

Throughout the day, news from Oran showed that events there were moving towards a great tragedy. Finally, ABC learned that at 5.45 that afternoon, 3 July, Somerville's ships had opened fire. The battleship *Bretagne* had blown up and sunk, and a number of other warships were badly damaged. Over 1,000 French sailors were killed or missing. Somerville's signals gave ABC 'a clear impression of his utter repugnance at having to carry out his drastic orders'. ABC himself felt that the action had been 'almost inept in its unwisdom'.

A signal that evening expressed the Admiralty's dissatisfaction with ABC's negotiations with Godfroy: 'Admiralty note that oil fuel is being discharged by French ships. Reduction of crews, especially key ratings, should however begin at once by landing or transfer to merchant ships, before dark tonight. Do not, repeat NOT, fail.'

This was the sort of signal which made ABC grit his teeth with rage, and stump indignantly up and down his quarterdeck. Apart from being unhelpful, it showed no understanding whatever of the explosive atmosphere in Alexandria. Furthermore, it ordered action 'before dark' but it had been sent off after sunset at Alexandria. 'As it was impossible to implement it,' ABC said, 'we ignored it completely.'

ABC always believed that Churchill, not the Admiralty, was the author of that signal. Churchill was determined to convince the world, and especially the United States, that the surrender of France made no difference to the British will to fight on and, clearly, Great Britain had to take some action to dispose of a powerful French fleet which might be used against her.

ABC knew events at Mers-el-Kebir might affect Godfrey's state of mind, so he was not surprised to receive a formal note from him, handwritten in French, saying that he had been ordered by his Admiralty to sail and so was stopping the discharge of oil fuel pending further events. However, his intentions remained unchanged from those he expressed in writing that morning.

Willis went to reason with Godfroy, but having been ordered to proceed to sea, using force if necessary, Godfroy flatly refused to continue discharging oil, or to disembark any of his men, or to sail voluntarily and sink his ships in deep water (although he had already agreed to do so and his last letter to ABC had said that his intentions 'remain unchanged').

Godfroy made it clear that if he were allowed out of Alexandria harbour he would make a run for it, realising that would mean battle. He was resigned to staying in Alexandria with his crews still on board, if necessary. If he were faced with any demand backed by force he would scuttle his ships inside the harbour.

Thus by the evening of 3 July as ABC said, they were back where they started. He and his staff pondered the alternatives. They could attempt to seize the French ships by boarding, which would almost certainly lead to bloodshed. They could sink the French ships where they were. This too was likely to lead to bloodshed and might well result in French ships being sunk in awkward places.

ABC decided to face Vice-Admiral Godfroy with a demand to intern or surrender his ships. He signalled a brief account of what had happened and his appreciation of the situation to the Admiralty soon after midnight and finally went to bed, tired and worried, in the small hours of 4 July.

He was woken just before 7 a.m., for yet another letter from Godfroy, who during the night had received a full account of what had happened at Mers-el-Kebir. He now totally repudiated each and every undertaking he had given.

When ABC dressed and went on deck he found that the French ships were raising steam and clearing their guns for action. The very crisis ABC had tried so hard to avert had arrived, and with the very worst possible outcome in prospect: a pitched naval battle inside Alexandria harbour.

But even now, as ships' boats were laying out kedge anchors so that his battleships could be kedged around until their broadsides bore on the French ships, even as his destroyers and submarines were being warned to torpedo the French ships at once if they opened fire or attempted to move from their berths, even as the tompions were being removed from his ships' gun barrels, ABC still did not despair of negotiation.

He knew that the French ships would need some six to eight hours to raise steam. That might just be long enough to appeal to the French sailors over their admiral's head and, not to be mealy-mouthed about it, try to make them disloyal to him.

Royer Dick composed a message to all the French officers and men. It stressed their helplessness, emphasised the British desire not to fight them or kill them should they try to escape, and repeated the generous terms the British Government offered, which they could accept with dignity and honour.

The message was flashed several times to all the French ships. They did not acknowledge it, but ABC knew that their signalmen would take it down and its contents would soon get round the ships. A bizarre regatta was organised: boats cruised around close to the French squadron, holding up large blackboards, with the same message written on them.

Every French ship had had a British ship allocated to look after her. The captains of the British ships were told to board their opposite numbers and try to reason with the French captains.

There were many comings and goings in the French ships. Mass meetings were held on the fo'c'sles or quarterdecks. Meanwhile, luckily, the telephone remained connected between *Warspite* and Godfroy's flagship, the cruiser *Duquesne*. Royer Dick kept in contact with ABC's French liaison officer, who was working to persuade his countrymen to accept a peaceful settlement. The two were able to discuss matters informally, as between friends, and to suggest possible courses of action, without involving or committing their respective admirals.

After lunch, the French captains could be seen going on board *Duquesne*. After an hour, Godfroy signalled that he wished to call on ABC.

The upshot was all that ABC had hoped for. Godfroy, yielding to *force majeure*, agreed that oil fuel was to be discharged forthwith and ships were to be placed in a condition where they could not fight. The question of the ships' companies was to be further discussed but it was agreed they would be reduced. 'Never in my life', ABC said, 'have I experienced such a whole-hearted feeling of thankful relief.' He drafted a signal to the Admiralty, which gave him the greatest satisfaction to send, giving the outcome of his negotiations.

ABC had personally brought off a dramatically successful diplomatic coup. Later that day, he received a message of congratulations from the First Lord, the First Sea Lord and Mr Churchill. Hitherto his staff had regarded ABC affectionately but warily. This unsuspected talent for patient and subtle diplomacy came as a complete surprise. 'ABC's moral courage and width of view-over this period', wrote Royer Dick, 'is the moment when one first realised his qualities of greatness. Of course we knew him as a fine dashing leader, but his handling of the French problem was masterly and one wonders how many others would have had the breadth of mind let alone the moral "guts" to disregard his instructions. That was truly Nelsonic.'

ABC did not let success affect his sense of humour. On the night of his agreement with Godfroy, Italian high-level bombers bombed Alexandria. During the raid, tracer bullets from an anti-aircraft battery ashore began to stream very low across *Warspite*'s quarterdeck. ABC was told that it was an Egyptian battery, firing to keep their morale up. 'They aren't doing *my* morale much good!' he said. 'At this rate I shall soon be wearing a tin hat over my backside!'

With France out of the war and Italy still in, the balance of sea power in the Mediterranean had changed so much to Britain's disadvantage that Pound began to consider whether the Mediterranean was still defensible. The Atlantic, which he regarded, quite rightly, as of paramount importance, must be safeguarded even if that involved the abandonment of the western Mediterranean.

On 17 June 1940, ABC had received a message from Pound that if France made a separate peace, every endeavour would be made to obtain control of the French fleet beforehand, or failing that, to have it sunk. If this situation did arise, Pound continued, the protection of our vital Atlantic trade would become a formidable problem unless we could hold the Straits of Gibraltar, which could only be done by moving the British fleet there from the eastern Mediterranean.

Pound said he realised the strong political and military objections to such a step up, but the Atlantic must come first. Pound asked for ABC's views, while himself suggesting that part of the fleet should go to Gibraltar westward through the Mediterranean, instead of round the Cape of Good Hope. If the Army lost control of the Canal, then the Navy should be prepared to block it.

All ABC's instincts rebelled against such suggestions, but he replied the same day with his detailed proposals for withdrawing the Navy. Once again, ABC said, 'I stressed the importance of Malta. If the fleet left the Mediterranean, the morale of the Maltese would collapse, and it would only be a matter of time before the island fell. I concluded by saying: "If the decision is made to let Malta go, and a start is made now, it should be possible to evacuate some quantity of the valuable fleet stores now there and personnel not essential for the defence."'

All this talk about evacuation and retreat made Churchill bristle, and he vehemently resisted any such policy which, as he said, 'though justified by the strength of the Italian Fleet, did not correspond to my impressions of the fighting values, and also seemed to spell the doom of Malta'.

On 18 June, lest his previous signal had 'sounded somewhat acquiescent', ABC signalled again to say that, although it might be feasible to move the faster units of the fleet westward through the Mediterranean and the rest through the Suez Canal, 'the effects of this withdrawal would mean such a landslide in territory and prestige that I earnestly hoped such a decision would never have to be taken.'

No doubt the Chiefs of Staffs were impressed by ABC's confidence and his optimism that he could both stay in the eastern Mediterranean and handle the Italian fleet. At any rate, they did not recommend withdrawal to the War Cabinet. Churchill himself took an even stronger line: in a minute to Pound of 15 July, he wrote that 'It is now three weeks since I vetoed the proposal to evacuate the eastern Mediterranean and bring Admiral Cunningham's fleet to Gibraltar. I hope there will be no return to that project.'

'On 3 July, all Commanders-in-Chief were informed that it was intended to maintain the fleet in the eastern Mediterranean. I do not know how near we came to abandoning the eastern Mediterranean,' ABC wrote, 'but if it had come to pass it would have been a major disaster, nothing less.'

ABC's most pressing problem now was Malta. In peacetime, Malta was largely supplied from Sicily, Italy and Tunisia — all now enemy territory. In spite of Malta's long history of sieges, the civil authorities had made no preparations for laying in emergency supplies in case the island were cut off, and within a few weeks of the outbreak of war there were severe shortages.

As a first step, several hundred of '*les bouches inutiles*' were evacuated, among them the families of officers and men whose ships had left the Mediterranean, including, of course, Nona, Millie and her sister. They were to be transported to Alexandria, in a 'fast' convoy of three ships. A second 'slow' convoy was made up of four ships with naval stores. Both convoys were to be covered by the fleet, which sailed from Alexandria on the evening of 7 July.

Submarine activity seemed to indicate that the Italians had established a patrol line to safeguard some major naval operation. In fact, the Italian Navy was also passing a convoy of five merchant ships, with important cargoes including tanks and petrol bound for Benghazi, which sailed from Naples on 6 July, escorted by two battleships, *Giulio Cesare*, wearing the flag of the Italian C-in-C, Admiral Angelo Campioni, and *Conte di Cavour*, with sixteen cruisers, and thirty-two destroyers.

157

Early on 8 July a signal was received from the submarine *Phoenix* that at 5.18 that morning she had sighted two enemy battleships and four destroyers, steering south, about 200 miles east of Malta and 220 miles north of Benghazi.

ABC's ships were south of Crete, steaming north-west at 20 knots, the most the old and unmodernised *Royal Sovereign* and *Malaya* could do. Not long after daybreak, they were found by Italian aircraft from the Dodecanese and were attacked by high-level bombers. Heavy, persistent and accurate bombing went on for most of that day The bombers were mostly too high for the fleet's guns to reach them and were virtually invisible. The first indication of an attack was often the high-pitched whistling of descending bombs. The constant tension, with the feeling that the next bomb, by the law of averages, must hit, was discouraging and frightening.

Up ahead, Tovey's cruisers were also under almost continuous bombing attacks which achieved only near-misses until the evening, in the last attack of the day, when the cruiser *Gloucester* suffered a direct hit on her compass platform. Her Commanding Officer, Captain R.F. Garside, was killed, with six other officers and eleven ratings, and three officers and six ratings were badly wounded.

Luckily, this was the only casualty from the hundreds of bombs dropped that day. This comparative lack of success encouraged the widely held belief that Italian high-level bombing was ineffective. In fact, 'their reconnaissance was highly efficient,' ABC wrote, 'and seldom failed to find and report our ships at sea. The bombers invariably arrived within an hour or two. They carried out high-level attacks from about 12,000 feet, pressed home in formation in the face of the heavy anti-aircraft fire of the fleet, and for this type of attack their accuracy was very good.'

The enemy was sighted again, by a flying boat from Malta, who at 3.10 p.m. on 8 July reported two battleships, six cruisers and seven destroyers, about 100 miles north-west of Benghazi. The Italian heavy ships were still steering southward, covering the convoy, but very shortly afterwards, at 3.20, they left the convoy to carry on to Benghazi and turned to the northward, where they were sighted again, steering north, an hour later.

By this time the Italians, who at that stage of the war had a very able code-breaking service, knew that ABC's ships were at sea. Italian naval strategy in the central Mediterranean was defensive, the main concern being to keep open the supply routes to North Africa. The purpose of this sortie, the arrival of the convoy in Benghazi, had been accomplished. There was little to be gained and much to be lost by a confrontation with ABC's fleet. The Italian High Command ordered Campioni to avoid battle until noon the following day, by which time the British ships should be well within range of bombers from bases in mainland Italy.

The change of course suggested to ABC that the Italian ships were, indeed, covering an important convoy to or from Benghazi. He decided to postpone the sailings of the convoys from Malta while he headed towards Taranto at best speed, to try and get between the Italian ships and their base. That night ABC's ships steamed north-west along the coast of Greece, heading towards the 'toe' of Italy.

At 4.40 on 9 July, *Eagle* flew off a dawn Swordfish search to the west. This was the first time *Eagle* had sailed with the fleet. Her hard-worked air group, with its twenty-two aircraft, carried out all reconnaissance, shadowing, gunnery spotting, anti-submarine patrols, fighter combat air patrols (CAPs) and torpedo strikes.

By 6 a.m. on the 9th, *Warspite* was steering westward, about sixty miles west of Navarino. Tovey's cruisers were some eight miles ahead, while *Eagle* and the two slow battleships were astern. At 7.32 flying boats found Campioni's main fleet, range 145 miles, bearing 280° (almost directly ahead of ABC's fleet), and reported it very accurately as two battleships, sixteen to eighteen cruisers, and twenty-five to thirty destroyers.

Eagle flew off search aircraft during the forenoon and, from their reports, the enemy was believed to be some ninety miles from *Warspite*, bearing 2950. At 11.45, nine Swordfish were launched to carry out a torpedo attack. But ninety miles was still a considerable range, which left plenty of room for error. The Swordfish failed to find the main Italian fleet, which had altered course to the south, and attacked the rear ship of a cruiser squadron. They claimed one hit, but in fact all the torpedoes missed. Fortunately the wind, although only a breeze, was from the north-west, so *Eagle* was able to continue to steer towards the enemy while flying off and recovering her aircraft.

By 1.40 p.m. aircraft reports had revealed that the enemy had turned north again. At 2.15 ABC decided he was now well placed between the Italian fleet and Taranto, and turned his ships west. He had ordered the damaged *Gloucester* to drop back and escort *Eagle*. Thus Tovey had only four cruisers, with not much more than half their normal outfit of ammunition. *Warspite*'s speed was limited by *Royal Sovereign* who could barely make 20 knots at full stretch. However, ABC felt that any opportunity was welcome and ordered *Warspite* to push on ahead to support Tovey's cruisers.

At 12.35, *Eagle*'s aircraft reported the enemy ships only thirty miles to the west. It was good weather for fighting, a perfect

Mediterranean summer day, with visibility between fifteen and twenty miles.

The first smoke, of cruisers and destroyers, was sighted by *Orion* at 2.27. ABC's ships were by then well spread out, with *Warspite* some ten miles behind Tovey's cruisers, *Malaya* and *Royal Sovereign* ten miles astern of her, and *Eagle*, *Gloucester* and two destroyers ten miles to the east. This risked ABC's ships coming under fire piecemeal and being defeated in detail by a superior force. But ABC had made his own estimate of the Italian Navy's fighting capacity and pressed on.

The enemy capital ships were first sighted by *Neptune* and thus it fell to Captain Rory O'Conor to signal at 3.08: 'Enemy battle fleet in sight.' It was a thrilling moment — the first such report since Commodore Goodenough in the cruiser *Southampton* sighted Scheer's High Seas Fleet at Jutland in 1916, and the first in the Mediterranean since Nelson sighted Brueys at the Nile in 1798.

Enemy cruisers opened fire at 3.15 on Tovey's ships who replied at once, but with sixteen cruisers against four and a proportion of 8-inch cruisers against 6-inch, they were outnumbered, outgunned and outranged. The enemy fire improved with practice, and matters were beginning to go awkwardly for Tovey when *Warspite* came up in support and opened fire at 3.26, at a range of 26,400 yards.

ABC went up from his flag-deck to the compass platform to get a better view and was delighted by the sound and spectacle of the first 15-inch salvo, saying: 'That'll make Their Lordships push their chairs back!'

At 3.30 the enemy ships made smoke and turned away. They came into sight again at 3.50 and three minutes later *Warspite* opened fire on *Giulio Cesare*, at a range of 26,000 yards. The Italian ships had reopened fire at 3.48, at a range of 29,000 yards. The enemy's gunnery seemed to ABC initially good, but 'accuracy soon fell off as his ships came under our fire'.

Under fire from both enemy battleships, *Warspite* was shortly straddled, the closest salvo pitching about two cables (400 yards) on her port bow. But *Warspite* herself was shooting fast and well and at 4 p.m. ABC was watching the towering splashes of *Warspite*'s salvoes through his binoculars when he saw a great orange-coloured flash at the base of *Giulio Cesare*'s forward funnel and a column of black smoke.

It was an undoubted hit, at the prodigious range of thirteen miles, which did considerable damage to *Giulio Cesare*'s upper deck, causing 115 casualties, wrecking some of her secondary armament, and reducing her speed from 27 knots to 18.

With his usual scepticism towards gunnery, ABC later said that this hit 'might perhaps be described as a lucky one'. However, it had an immediate effect upon Campioni, causing him to turn his ships away behind smoke and break off the action.

Warspite ceased fire at 4.04, when, as ABC said, the whole western horizon was 'overlaid with a thick pall of smoke behind which the enemy became completely hidden'. *Malaya* had opened fire twice, firing four salvoes each time, but they were all well short. *Royal Sovereign*, though straining to close the enemy at full speed, was never within range and did not fire.

Some enemy destroyers, estimated at two flotillas, worked across to starboard of their main fleet and delivered what ABC called a 'half-hearted' torpedo attack. No tracks were actually seen but the enemy destroyers turned away to the westward, having presumably fired, and retired making smoke. For a time there was spasmodic firing by ships on both sides, with everybody firing at whatever they could see in range whenever the smoke cleared. *Warspite*'s spotting aircraft overhead reported no hits by anybody.

Enemy destroyers continued to dodge in and out of their smoke screen, while ABC's destroyers fired whenever they could see a target. Evidently the enemy attacked with torpedoes again, for tracks were seen. The battleships also fired at the enemy destroyers, *Warspite* firing a few salvoes of 6-inch, and *Malaya* firing one, until the enemy disappeared into the smoke screen. Once again, *Royal Sovereign* did not fire.

ABC had the benefit of considerable information about the enemy's signals, from captured Italian fleet code books. 'We intercepted most of the Italian Admiral's signals,' ABC told Pound later, 'as we had the decodes on board, from one of the sunk submarines, and most interesting they were.'

Some of Campioni's signals, broadcast in plain language at the height of the action, appealed to ABC's ribald sense of humour. He particularly relished Campioni's choice of phrase in signalling to the Italian Naval Command that he was 'constrained to retire'. When ABC saw an intercept of a signal from one of Campioni's cruisers, asking permission to return to harbour, he said 'Reply: Approved'.

None of ABC's ships had seen or detected any Italian submarines, but there was always the chance they were there and ABC realised that it would be foolhardy to continue to press on further to the west. He told Pound later that 'I walked into the trap with my eyes open,' but discretion was still the better part of valour on the day. The fleet altered to a course of 340° at 4.35 and now steered north, to work to windward of the smoke screen. By 5 p.m. the leading destroyers were well clear of the smoke. But the enemy was out of sight, having retired at high speed.

As ABC's ships approached the coast, they were attacked by swarms of high-level bombers who picked out *Warspite* and *Eagle* as the most conspicuous targets. Tovey's cruisers and many of the destroyers were also bombed. It was, as ABC said, 'most frightening. At times a ship would completely disappear behind the great splashes, to emerge as though from a dark, thick wood of enormous fir trees. I was seriously alarmed for the old ships *Royal Sovereign* and *Eagle*, which were not well protected. A clutch of those eggs hitting either must have sent her to the bottom.' But once again, no ship was hit and no serious damage was done, although there were many near-misses and some minor casualties from splinters.

By 5.35 ABC's fleet was only twenty-five miles from the Calabrian coast. This was near enough. Course was altered to south-west, but when it was clear that the enemy ships had given up the fight and there was no chance of intercepting them before they reached the Straits of Messina, ABC turned his fleet round to steer for a position south of Malta.

Warspite's spotting aircraft had remained directly over the Italian fleet during the bombing attacks and reported that the enemy was in a state of 'dire confusion', being bombed by its own aircraft. *Warspite* was still intercepting Italian plain language signals and ABC was delighted to hear Campioni's furious complaints.

The two convoys had sailed from Malta, escorted by destroyers, and covered by *Royal Sovereign* and *Eagle*. During the forenoon of 11 July the slow convoy and its escort were found and bombed by Italian aircraft but, although over 100 bombs were dropped, there were no casualties or damage to any of the ships.

Warspite and four destroyers had pushed on ahead at 19 knots to return to Alexandria. They too were bombed that afternoon. 'Bombed to hell all day,' Geoffrey Barnard noted in his diary; '23 attacks in 10 hours. It was the first time I was really frightened. 36 bombs within a cable of the ship. I was never more pleased at darkness.'

The bombs did no actual damage to *Warspite* but their cumulative effect over a long period made ABC understandably short-tempered, so that it was wise to tread like Agag around the flag bridge. 'ABC slept in his chair between each attack,' said Commander W.P. Carne, the Fleet Torpedo Officer, who had already had his head bitten off for not wearing his tin helmet, and for failing to fall on his face when he heard the whistle of an approaching bomb.

At least, he sat still with his eyes closed, and if he did not sleep he was a very good actor. When other men were frankly frightened as they heard the whistle of the bombs, ABC's reaction was to become quite furious at his inability to hit back. These attacks only lasted a few seconds but at the time it was just as well to keep clear of him. Just before 4.00 p.m. we were attacked by 12 planes from the port quarter. We saw them a long way off and put up a good barrage, but they came steadily on. I obediently fell on my face as the first 12 bombs fell close. As I was getting up ABC turned to me and said in a furious voice: 'That was a very determined attack.'

This seemed to me to be a very obvious remark, not calling for a reply [Carne was known as 'William the Silent'] and as I once more heard the whistle of bombs I again fell on my face. These straddled us: three to port, nine to starboard. As I again got to my feet a red face was thrust into mine and a voice thick with rage said: 'I said that was a very determined attack!'

Thinking that there was enough war going on outside the ship without starting a new one on the Admiral's bridge, I hastily gave a soft answer, saying 'Yes, it was a determined attack.'

Just then I heard the third lot of bombs arriving and once more took up a recumbent position. These fell close alongside. The resulting noise, smoke, spray, and chaos were such as to make it difficult to believe that I was still alive. As I got up I found two closed fists being shaken in my face. From a face purple with rage, through clenched teeth came the strangled words: 'Why the hell didn't you say so the first time?'

Tovey and the cruisers rejoined at 7 a.m. on 12 July. Tovey himself in *Orion*, with *Neptune*, was detached to strengthen the escort of the fast convoy. But it was not long before the bombers arrived again. *Warspite* survived another seventeen attacks. ABC remembered one 'most virulent attack' in particular, 'when twenty-four heavy bombs fell along the port side of the ship simultaneously, with another dozen on our starboard bow, all within two hundred yards, but slightly out of line'. Looking across, ABC saw *Sydney* 'completely disappear in a line of towering pillars of spray as high as church steeples. When she emerged I signalled: "Are you all right?" to which came the rather dubious reply from that stout-hearted Australian, Captain J.A. Collins, "I hope so".'

Three attacks, in which twenty-five bombs were dropped, were made on *Eagle* and the 1st Battle Squadron. *Eagle* was an old ship and near-misses shook up her hull and damaged her aircraft refuelling system, with later consequences.

Fighters arrived overhead later in the afternoon but no more attacks developed. *Warspite* entered Alexandria at 6 a.m. on 13 July. The fast convoy and escort arrived three hours later.

At sea, ships were still being bombed. But *Eagle*'s three Gladiators, ably led by Keighly-Peach, shot down the shadower and two bombers, and badly damaged a third. Blenheim fighters from shore also arrived during the afternoon. The ships arrived in Alexandria at 8.15 a.m. on 14 July, the slow convoy and its escort at 9 a.m. on the 15th. Miraculously, in spite of the hundreds of bombs dropped and the many near-misses, *Gloucester* was the only ship actually hit.

The Italians made the most of their propaganda opportunities. A special news bulletin broadcast from Rome on 10 July claimed that 'On the 9th July, three groups of enemy units were sighted by our aircraft and submarines in the eastern Mediterranean, proceeding westwards. Violent attacks were carried out by our aircraft, several enemy ships being struck, some set on fire and one sunk.'

The newspapers had a photograph of 'a British battleship on fire'. It was actually *Royal Sovereign*, whose sailors did not know whether to be indignant or amused by this photograph of their ship at full speed and, because she was long past the first flush of youth, belching smoke.

Rome and Berlin radios both stated that

> The victorious naval engagement off the Italian coast is the greatest naval battle of the war and perhaps one of the most decisive sea fights of all time; worthy to rank with the great achievements of the republic of Venice and Genoa in sweeping the barbarians from the Middle Seas. Mare Nostrum is no longer a rhetorical expression, but an established fact. *British dominion of the Mediterranean is at an end.*

The broadcast stated that over 1,000 bombs had been dropped on Malta to date. 'Malta is to be bombed until it is Italian.'

By contrast, ABC was disappointed, because the main Italian battle fleet had not been properly brought to battle. It could be called 'a draw', although that single long-range hit on the Italian flagship had a psychological effect out of all proportion to the physical damage done. The enemy was never again to seek action against British heavy ships.

ABC expressed his disappointment in a 'hasty note' he scribbled to Pound as soon as he got into harbour (in fact, at the time of writing some of his ships were still at sea):

> But there is one serious thing, their battleships and 8-inch cruisers straddled us comfortably at 26,000 yards and more and I don't think any ship but *Warspite* crossed the target... I must have one more ship that can shoot at a good range.
>
> Tovey was also up against six to seven 8-inch cruisers and about four to five 6-inch cruisers and, of course, could make no headway as they obscured themselves in smoke at about 22,000 yards. I know I said I could do without 8-inch cruisers but I would dearly like the *York* and *Exeter*.
>
> Naturally after the shooting was over and we were chasing towards the land, we took the bombs. I suppose not far short of a hundred planes and some very heavy bombs. *Eagle* had a charmed life.
>
> My heart was in my mouth lest *Royal Sovereign* should be hit as, if she had taken one of the nests of bombs that were dropping about, I think she'd have gone to the bottom or, at any rate, as we were only 25 miles from the Calabrian coast, we would have had to sink her. In fact I don't think it is a bit of good taking these unprotected old battleships up to the coast unless we are fully prepared to lose one.
>
> Don't think I am discouraged. I am not a bit, but with our facilities at Alexandria also within bombing range, the damaged ship is a nightmare especially over 900 miles away from her base.
>
> Perhaps the worst is yet to come. We left the vicinity of Malta on Thursday after the slow convoy, and all forces were continuously bombed that day up to about 22 miles from Sicily and nightfall. Next morning it started again off Cyrenaica on *Warspite* and cruisers at 9 a.m. and continued till

4 p.m. by which time the Dodecanese were also in action. The *Royal Sovereign*, *Eagle* and *Malaya* are at this moment being bombed continuously passing between Crete and Libya. Literally we have had to fight our way back to Alexandria against air attack.

You suggested that the *Illustrious* might come here. We want some fighters badly. We also want an anti-aircraft cruiser and a couple of convoy sloops.

There is one thing on the bright side. I do not think we need expect anything very dashing from the Italian fleet.

7: REINFORCEMENTS FOR ABC'S FLEET

NONA AND THE two nieces, Dorothy and Hilda, had seen no sign of the enemy during the fast convoy's passage to Alexandria but they had heard of the action against the Italian fleet and were alarmed to see *Warspite* alongside the jetty, listing quite sharply. In fact, she had been deliberately listed so that her side bulges could be examined for damage from near-misses.

There had been, by Nona's reckoning, seventy-two raids on Malta in the twenty-nine days since Italy had declared war. The two nieces had borne up very well. But ABC told Doodles, 'Nona is a bit nervy but don't tell her I said so.' In fact, it was September before he was able to write that Nona was 'at last rid of neuritis'.

Sir Miles Lampson, the Ambassador to Egypt, offered ABC the Ambassador's Residency in Alexandria. It was some six miles from the harbour, with plenty of rooms so that the Cunninghams could entertain suitably, and offer hospitality and a bed for the night to officers who had been at sea for weeks on end. There was a large and somewhat neglected garden which the Cunninghams set about replanting and restocking.

The nieces were both trained VADs but could get no war work to do. Eventually Dorothy worked as an occupational therapist ('the army had never heard of it', said ABC) in the joint Navy/Army hospital in Alexandria. She had no salary and no official status, but steadily worked herself upwards until she was the Middle East authority on Occupational Therapy.

Hilda was a trained dietician and served on a committee supervising patients' food. She was also able to see a great deal of her husband who was impatient for a change of appointment, nearer the action.

ABC tried to get Starkie a destroyer command, but was told politely but firmly by Captain Claud Barry, the Naval Assistant to the Second Sea Lord, that Starkie was too junior and if he did get a command 'he would be going right over the heads of a number of Destroyer No. 1's who have had the heat and burden of this war in this particularly bad winter, which really would be rather unfair'. Starkie was appointed First Lieutenant of the destroyer *Juno*. The new Flags was Lieutenant Hugh Lee, DSC, from the destroyer *Jervis*.

On 18 July, when the Australian cruiser *Sydney* and five destroyers met two Italian cruisers, *Giovanni delle Bande Nere* and *Bartolomeo Colleoni*, off Cape Spada on the northern coast of Crete, the Italian ships were timidly handled and, after a prolonged gun action which became a chase, *Sydney* brought *Bartolomeo Colleoni* to a stop. She was dispatched by the destroyers' torpedoes. The destroyers were bombed while picking up 545 survivors. ABC issued a general warning against the unnecessary risks of picking up survivors from enemy ships.

ABC might have established a moral ascendancy over the Italian fleet, but Italian anti-submarine forces had unquestionably inflicted a defeat upon him. The submarines in Malta and Alexandria had well-trained and experienced captains and crews, but they were all large 'O', 'P' and 'R' Class boats from the China Station, easy to spot from the air in the clear waters of the Mediterranean — 'too big, too old and their auxiliary machinery too noisy for work out here', ABC said. Three of the four Malta boats were lost in the first fortnight and there were further losses in July and August. ABC decided that the COs were 'rather too gallant' and forbade them to cross the 200-fathom line unless in hot pursuit of an important enemy target.

In July 1940, it was decided to augment Malta's fighter strength. HMS *Argus* sailed from the United Kingdom, with twelve Hurricanes embarked, on 24 July for Operation HURRY. ABC's fleet put to sea to cover an Aegean convoy and a diversionary attack and landing on Castelorizzo. Somerville's Force H also sailed, and *Ark Royal*'s aircraft carried out an attack on Cagliari as a diversion.

The scale of the bombing raids on Malta was such that the Hurricanes were badly needed. However, the civilian population had been bearing up very well. They were amused by Italian radio claims, that 'we have destroyed Malta's railway' (there had been no railway in Malta for twenty years), 'the coal mine' (there never had been a coal mine in Malta) 'and have sunk HMS *St Angelo*' (a fort built of massive masonry, overlooking Grand Harbour).

ABC's ships and the convoy were both heavily bombed. No ship was hit but *Malaya* and *Eagle* had to return to harbour with defects. But the enemy seemed confused by all the comings and goings and remained in harbour. *Argus* flew off the Hurricanes without mishap and all arrived safely. Stores and ground crews arrived later by submarine.

Pre-war, ABC's behaviour suggested he was never totally convinced of the importance of air power at sea. He persisted in the belief that the main object of aircraft was to slow down an enemy ship sufficiently for the fleet to be able to overhaul her and dispatch her with gunfire. But the Mediterranean, even before the arrival of the *Luftwaffe*, began his conversion to a belief in air power at sea which was observed by Somerville.

After ABC's ships had been exposed to heavy air attack before and after the action off Calabria, Somerville noted 'I am amused to find that Andrew B. has quite changed his tune as a result of his recent experiences.'

Somerville himself was under constant, irritating pressure from London, to 'do something' with Force H and especially with *Ark Royal*. He was naturally loath to risk a valuable and vulnerable carrier in confined waters in the central Mediterranean to achieve only a pin-prick effect upon the enemy. He also resented the fact that his caution might be construed in London as 'cold feet'. After he had cancelled the diversionary attack by *Ark Royal* planned to take place while ABC was in action off Calabria, he wrote bitterly, 'People at home will be thinking I hadn't the guts to go on. Seemed to me it required far more not to.'

As ever, ABC drove his ships very hard, and was always reluctant to spare them for refitting. Power had to act as advocate on behalf of the increasingly desperate ships' captains. According to him, ABC had a complete disregard of maintenance problems. So Power 'resorted to all sorts of stratagems to disguise how many ships were boiler-cleaning', because ABC 'either could not or would not believe that these were highly complex ships with highly stressed machinery quite different from the little coal-burning *Scorpion* he had commanded with such success in World War One'.

On 17 August ABC went to sea in *Warspite* with *Malaya*, *Ramillies* and *Kent*, screened by twelve destroyers, for a bombardment of Bardia, and Fort Capuzzo, near Solium, which went off satisfactorily; but ABC doubted its real value. Although he himself had suggested them, ABC thought such operations using heavy ships were unjustifiable so long as the war in the Western Desert was static.

Italian bombers arrived as expected in considerable numbers, but this time RAF Blenheims, with *Eagle*'s Gladiators flying from Sidi Barrani, together shot down twelve bombers — 'a heartening sight for the fleet,' as ABC said, 'which the sailors thoroughly enjoyed'.

Reinforcements for ABC's fleet were to sail from the United Kingdom on 20 August. Operations were also planned to deliver personnel, equipment and stores to Malta by the reinforcement ships on their passage westwards, and by a merchant ship convoy from Alexandria. These operations were codenamed Operation HATS.

It was also intended to reinforce the Army with an armoured brigade, including fifty Matilda tanks. As these precious tanks would be of no use to anybody whilst they were at sea, it was essential to cut their passage time to the minimum.

Characteristically, Churchill favoured the bolder plan of sending them direct through the Mediterranean instead of round the Cape of Good Hope, which would take weeks longer. He could not 'see why the large numbers of ships assigned to the Mediterranean should not play an active part from the outset'. Warships, he minuted to Pound, 'are meant to go under fire'.

ABC was asked for his opinion. His reply on 11 August was non-committal: only time and experience would show. The convoy of four 16-knot 'MT' (Mechanical Transport) ships might get through safely, or all four might be sunk.

Pound argued vehemently that the four 'MT' ships would jeopardise the whole of HATS. No feint or diversionary operation could possibly work: as soon as the ships entered the Mediterranean, the enemy would know at once that their destination was Malta and would have two full days in which to prepare air and surface forces in the Sicily area. The warships would be restricted to the 16 knots of the 'MT' ships and therefore be less able to evade attacks by destroyers or motor-torpedo boats in the Sicilian Narrows.

Churchill deployed all his considerable powers of persuasion to make Pound change his mind. But Pound would not be moved and took reassurance from ABC's signal of 11th — 'Your reply that all of them might be sunk was exactly what I expected.'

Churchill was 'both grieved and vexed'. But he knew Pound very well, and had every confidence in his judgement. Churchill could have appealed to the Cabinet over Pound's head but forbore.

The 'MT' convoy sailed on 22 August and the option to route it through the Mediterranean was left open until it passed Gibraltar, in case Wavell's situation had by then deteriorated so that any risk had to be run to reinforce him. In the event, land, sea and air reconnaissances on 25 August showed no enemy activity. The convoy passed Gibraltar on 26 August and went on round the Cape.

ABC's reinforcements, the carrier *Illustrious*, the battleship *Valiant* and the anti-aircraft cruisers *Coventry* and *Calcutta*, sailed from Gibraltar on 30 August, escorted by eight destroyers, with *Renown*, *Ark Royal*, *Sheffield* and seven destroyers of Force H in support.

Force H was to accompany the HATS ships until they were south of Sardinia and then turn back. The HATS ships would go on and meet ABC's fleet. *Valiant* and the two cruisers would disembark personnel, guns, stores and ammunition in Malta, while the destroyers refuelled.

ABC left Alexandria early in the morning of 30 August, flying his flag in *Warspite*, with *Malaya*, *Eagle*, *Orion*, *Sydney* and nine destroyers, heading for a position west of Crete. The cruisers under Tovey (who had since August become Vice-Admiral, Light Forces [VALF] and second-in-command to ABC), with three destroyers, had already sailed to make a detour through the Kaso Channel and the southern Aegean before meeting ABC south-west of Cape Matapan at noon on 31 August. The convoy for Malta — the merchant ships *Cornwall* and *Volo* and the oiler *Plumleaf* escorted by four destroyers — had left Alexandria on the evening of 29 August.

The convoy was attacked from the air in the afternoon of 31 August, and *Cornwall* was hit aft. However, steering by main engines, she kept up with the convoy which reached Malta on the morning of 2 September.

In the evening of 31 August, aircraft and submarines reported that the Italian fleet was at sea: two battleships, seven cruisers and eight destroyers, only 130 miles to the north-west and steering south-east, i.e. closing. It was the sort of situation ABC longed for, but his main concern was for the convoy, now fifty miles to the south. He closed the convoy and kept some twenty miles to the north-west of it, in the direction of the threat, during the night.

ABC hoped for a fleet action the next day, but the enemy ships had vanished. It was not until the evening that a flying boat from Malta sighted them at the entrance to the Gulf of Taranto when they were obviously returning to harbour.

The HATS ships were sighted at 9 a.m. on 2 September. There were more bombing attacks that day, but now *Illustrious* was there with her twelve Fairey Fulmar fighters. With a top speed of about 250 m.p.h., the two-seater Fulmar was slow by contemporary fighter standards, but it was sturdy and had eight wing-mounted .303 Browning guns. The Fulmars and the fire power of *Calcutta* and *Coventry* transformed the fleet's air defence, and five bombers were shot down.

By midnight the whole fleet with HATS reinforcements was steaming to the eastward. But it was not long before two bombers arrived. *Illustrious'* Fulmars shot them both down, to the loud cheers of the ship's companies who, ABC said, 'had had just about as much as they could stand of being bombed without retaliation'.

The fleet now had two ships, *Valiant* and *Illustrious*, fitted with RDF, which extended the detection range of approaching aircraft out to forty or fifty miles, 'which was a very welcome let-up for the anti-aircraft guns' crews'.

On the return passage to Alexandria, ABC split his fleet into two divisions, one passing north and the other south of Crete, to make attacks on the Dodecanese islands, and also to provide cover for a convoy coming south from the Aegean. At dawn on 4 September every available aircraft from *Illustrious* and *Eagle* was launched to attack the two airfields on Rhodes, where the aircraft were based which gave the fleet so many sleepless nights in Alexandria.

The airfields were certainly 'well basted', as ABC said, but unfortunately, owing to the vagaries of the wind, *Eagle* was fifteen minutes late in launching and Italian fighters were airborne when her Swordfish arrived over the target. Four Swordfish were lost, with their crews. 'They were the cream of the Fleet Air Arm,' ABC said.

There were more air attacks south of Kaso, but they were broken up and driven off. The ships reached Alexandria without damage or casualties on 5 September. Churchill sent a signal on 8 September congratulating ABC on the success of HATS, but regretting that the armoured brigade was still three weeks away from its scene of action and going on to refer to the 'high importance' of striking at the Italians that autumn, and 'the advantages of gaining the initiative'.

ABC was 'harassed and not a little irritated' by this 'prodding' signal which, with its needling phrases such as 'the paper strength of the Italian Navy', and its emphasis on offensive action, suggested that Churchill was again accusing ABC of lying on the defensive.

ABC replied at once, with barely controlled politeness:

> Please thank the Minister of Defence for his telegram. I hope that it has been made clear to him that the pre-requisite of successful operations in the Central Mediterranean is constant and complete air reconnaissance, that area in which respect we still fall far short, and that operations of the Fleet are drastically limited by the number of destroyers available.

This was one of several sharp rejoinders whilst ABC was in the Mediterranean, recalled by Churchill in later years. But ABC did not suffer consequences at the time.

ABC was always being urged to move his headquarters to Cairo. It would make consultations between the Commanders-in-Chief and their staffs much easier and would relieve ABC of the inconvenience of frequent time-consuming journeys to Cairo. But although Wavell and Longmore appealed to the Chiefs of Staff for support, ABC steadfastly refused. He believed, and Pound backed him up, that as long as he had a fleet and the chance of meeting the enemy, his place was in his flagship, sharing the same dangers and difficulties as his officers and men.

As a compromise, ABC appointed Captain H.G. Norman, who had served under him at Port Edgar years before, as an additional Chief of Staff in Cairo. Norman was to 'report back to ABC everything of importance but not to bother him with unnecessary detail, and to co-operate with the Army and the RAF as much as possible but not to land ABC with awkward commitments. In other words, I would always be in the wrong!'

ABC cut his visits to Cairo to the minimum, and never stayed a moment longer than he had to. He flew up in the back seat of a Fairey Fulmar on the day of a C-in-C's meeting and flew back as soon as it was over.

In Alexandria, ABC began with a staff conference after breakfast and spent the forenoon dealing with paperwork, which he abhorred, or visiting ships or shore establishments under his command, which he loved.

ABC usually went ashore in the afternoons, for tennis or golf, and would be back at about six o'clock for more paperwork. On dark nights he dined ashore at the Residency. When there was a moon and Italian air raids began again he dined on board. He always returned to *Warspite* at about half-past ten and slept on board.

ABC's staff kept the same routine because it annoyed him to send for an officer and find that he was ashore. A run ashore was rare for ABC's staff. 'Went ashore with Lofty Power,' wrote Geoffrey Barnard, on 13 July 1940. 'First time since the Italian war. Run round the town, came off 0400.'

ABC's staff, of about fifty, including personal retinue and communications personnel, was minute compared with Combined HQ in Cairo, which eventually rose above a thousand. Consequently they were very hard-worked, though ABC often used to remark (much to his staff's annoyance) that he had never known a staff officer to die of overwork.

Vian once said: 'The C-in-C ought to be put in a refrigerator when we get back to harbour and not let out till we get to sea again!' According to Willis, ABC was totally uninterested in administration, his only response being the occasional exasperating sally at somebody's expense. However, Lieutenant

Dick Wheeler, who arrived in May 1940 to serve on ABC's secretarial staff for the next four years, did not agree that ABC's impatience with administration was because he did not understand it. 'I am sure that this was not the case at all — as an operational commander he could not afford to be bound by administrative details — if he did so he would never get at the enemy at all — he had to take the line that the enemy would be hit *in spite* of any administrative difficulties.'

Barnard was not one of the 'inner circle', of Willis, Royer Dick, Power and Tom Brownrigg, and he often felt excluded, denied the consolation, which would have compensated for many hours of toil, of being privy to ABC's most intimate friendship. 'Getting very cross and bored with this endless bloody job,' he wrote, on 25 October 1940.

It was Power who bore up best, to the climate, to wartime life on the staff, and to ABC. It was

> ABC's boast that in me he had a man who never gets tired. How little he knew... I practically never went ashore. All the other staff officers who were potential reliefs were never fully in the picture and I found it took so much time and thought to turn over to them all with which my mind was stocked, it was not worth while for a few hours ashore.

Power often argued with ABC, to the dismay of Willis, 'who was basically horrified by my argumentative attitude to the C-in-C and was always trying to shut me up'. But Power came to exercise more and more influence over ABC.

> I had acquired a reputation for producing operation orders of unusual brevity and clarity. ABC had acquired the habit of signing my orders without reading them — merely saying 'I suppose this is alright. I can't understand your Staff College jargon anyhow.' I was by far the most junior and

inexperienced Commander on the staff but it had come about that he relied on me completely and implicitly where the conduct of operations was concerned, although we had many vitriolic arguments about them.

ABC preserved a sceptical, hard-to-please attitude towards even the 'inner circle', as though they would become mere purveyors of paperwork if they were not carefully watched and did not have their legs regularly pulled. Used to Pound's methods, the staff produced draft orders for six days of forthcoming fleet exercises. ABC read them and wrote across the title page: 'Too long, too complicated.'

The staff reduced the orders to fifteen pages, which Pound would have regarded as a mere precis. ABC read the redrafted orders and then wrote, 'I agree with the second sentence of paragraph 29, and little else.' The praised paragraph read: 'The Fleet will be manoeuvred by the Commander-in-Chief.' With no written orders, the exercises were conducted by signal from the flagship.

ABC always wrote in red ink. He refused to accept typewritten drafts, saying that if drafts were typed he would never know who had suggested what. Willis had to write his comments in green pencil, Power in brown.

Under Pound, the Staff Officer (Operations) used to appear on the flag bridge with an armful of staff tactical books. When Power came onto *Warspite*'s bridge on the first day at sea in the war against Italy, ABC said: 'Put all those books away. We're at war, we ought to know what to do by now.'

He was sceptical about new 'instrumentalisms', including radar. When *Valiant* joined, ABC was unconvinced about her radar's merits. On 3 September 1940, when the fleet was again attacked without warning by Italian bombers, one of *Valiant*'s midshipmen, Roddy Macdonald, wrote in his Journal, 'Being taken unawares is no fault of the RD/F itself, but more that of unintelligent deduction of the data provided by it. The C-in-C appears to distrust it, because he had actually forbidden the use of it this forenoon.'

Next day, Macdonald wrote: 'The Commander-in-Chief made a general signal to the fleet giving his poor opinion of the anti-aircraft lookout kept by ships. At the same time he ordered all RD/F transmitters to close down probably because there is a danger that the beam can be picked up, D/Fed and our position discovered. The danger of this seems out of proportion to the danger of shadowers and the actual attack by aircraft. However it served the purpose of exercising the lookouts.'

The long-expected but cautious Italian offensive in the Western Desert, which began on 13 September 1940, made it all the more necessary to attack their lines of communication across the Mediterranean. But first there was the abortive, ill-advised and well-advertised (by the Free French in London) attempt to land Free French forces at Dakar, in French West Africa, on 23 September.

The affair inevitably caused unease amongst the French in Alexandria, but once again ABC's personal standing with Godfroy stood the test. Godfroy announced that he would take no offensive action, but if there was any attempt to seize his ships, he would scuttle them in shallow water in Alexandria harbour. Thus ABC was able to sail shortly after midnight on 28/29 September for Operation MB.5, to reinforce Malta.

On 30 September, one of *Illustrious'* aircraft sighted the Italian battle fleet, of five battleships (including the new 35,000-ton, 31-knot, 15-inch-gunned battleships *Littorio* and *Vittorio Veneto*), eleven cruisers and some twenty-five destroyers, only eighty miles north-north-west of the British fleet.

However, ABC decided to press on with his main object of landing troops in Malta. His decision not to seek action was sensible, but the similar decision by the Italian Admiral Campioni was inexplicable. ABC's ships had been sighted and accurately reported by Italian aircraft. Campioni must have known that he outnumbered his enemy, and his own battleships were newer, faster and had a greater gun range.

The whole episode showed that ABC was achieving his object of 'defeating the enemy's mind', well described by Brownrigg:

> The Fleet had just returned, the men were tired and the ships required maintenance. Intelligence was received that a very old and inoffensive Italian torpedo-boat had sailed from Taranto for Tobruk. ABC said to us: 'Send out a division of destroyers and sink her.' We protested that the destroyers should boiler-clean, and that in any case the Italian was doing, and could do, no harm. ABC then said: 'We must never let the enemy think that it is safe to go to sea: we must make him realise he is only safe when in harbour. Contrariwise, our Fleet must feel that it is natural for them to be at sea. Go on, send the destroyers and sink the poor inoffensive bugger!'

Jack Tovey struck his flag after MB.5 and went home on leave, to be appointed Commander-in-Chief, Home Fleet. He wrote to ABC that it was 'the job I have always wanted' but he had been worried and rather alarmed to find himself apparently being vetted as a possible relief for ABC himself. 'I could not hope to fill your shoes.'

Tovey dined with Churchill, who remarked that Cunningham had been 'pussy-footing' with the French fleet in Alexandria. This, Tovey said, got 'me rather on the raw'.

Tovey knew who was responsible for his appointment. He wrote to ABC:

> It was only thanks to your most generous recommendation that I was even considered as a possible starter. It is quite impossible for me to give you any idea of what I owe you, from the first moment I served under you at Port Edgar you have been an inspiration to me and I can only hope I have succeeded in learning something of what I could from you. In the early part of the war when they took away all my command but apparently had no use for me, I found myself losing my self-confidence and it has only been your friendship and trust in me that has helped me to regain it. This appointment, which I have got entirely thanks to you, has put the finishing touch and I feel a new man: if only I can be a credit to you, I shall be more than satisfied.

Tovey's relief was Rear-Admiral H.D. Pridham-Wippell, an ex-destroyer officer and a friend of ABC's from his Dardanelles days. Command of the Battle Squadron went to Captain Bernard Rawlings, Captain of *Valiant*, with the rank of acting Rear-Admiral. Pridham-Wippell's first operation was MB.6, the October convoy for Malta, which had an unusually quiet outward passage. The return began equally quietly, but in a night action in the early hours of 12 October the cruiser *Ajax* sank two Italian destroyers and crippled a third, *Artigliere*, which was dispatched by *York* next day.

ABC signalled in plain language to the Italian Admiralty, giving the position of the floats *York* had left for *Artigliere*'s survivors, who were picked up in due course. But on 16 October, ABC had one of those signals, from the First Lord but motivated from another quarter, which left an unpleasant after-taste: 'The Prime Minister is also very pleased... but asks me to say that in view of feeling of public here suffering under intensive and ruthless attacks, it might well be to exclude from future communiqués reference to gallantry of enemy or to compromising one's fleet's position for benefit of enemy.' As ABC said, 'I may have been wrong; but on this occasion the Italian destroyers *had* fought well. As for compromising the fleet's position, the *Ajax*'s action must already have caused the enemy to be aware of our presence.'

By October 1940, Malta was being supplied more or less regularly, and the island's immediate needs were being met. Along the North African coast, bombardments at Bardia and other places by the shallow-draught gunboats *Ladybird*, *Aphis* and *Gnat*, originally designed for the rivers of China, were so successful that the enemy moved troops and vehicles inshore and there was actually a shortage of targets.

However, the submarine situation remained unsatisfactory. Four 'T' Class, more suitable for the Mediterranean than the 'China' boats, arrived during October. But, in fact, this gave only ten boats on patrol: four were refitting, and, as yet unknown to ABC, *Rainbow* and *Triad* were lost in October. By the end of the month, seven submarines — a third of the total strength — had been lost, while the submarines had sunk only six merchant ships of 21,500 tons and the Italian submarine *Diamante*.

Anthony Eden, the Secretary of State for War, arrived in Alexandria on 15 October. ABC had met him when he came out to the Middle East in February and had not been particularly impressed. However, he had found Eden's dinner conversation so interesting that the two had remained at the table talking for some time, without noticing that everybody else had gone. 'He's a nice man,' ABC said, 'perhaps a little full of Anthony Eden but he has the right ideas about winning the war.'

Eden, for his part, liked ABC, whom he thought 'shrewd as well as fiery, and cheerful good company. I like him more and more.' ABC took Eden to the Fleet Club, where 5,000 sailors gave him a 'terrific reception. He was mobbed going out and his back thumped. Being a politician, he loved it.'

Eden had come to find out, for Churchill, what Wavell was doing and what his intentions were. Wavell knew this, and during the conferences he and his Army Commander, General Maitland Wilson, had with Eden, he guarded from Eden, as he guarded from Churchill, the plans he was formulating for an offensive in the desert later in the year.

On 28 October, the Italian Minister in Athens presented a note which accused the Greeks of violating neutrality by allowing their territorial waters and ports to be used by the British. British tankers had indeed occasionally been stationed in Greek anchorages where British ships had refuelled from them. When the Italians discovered this, they bombed British ships in Greek waters. The Greeks had protested and demanded that the British tankers be withdrawn.

The Italian note had been intended as an ultimatum which, as the Italians expected, the Greeks rejected. A few hours later, Greece was at war with Italy.

Eden and the Commanders-in-Chief agreed that Egypt was strategically vital, while Greece was not. However, some help would have to be sent to Greece. Wavell planned to send a battalion to Crete which he had previously ear-marked for Malta. Longmore sent a squadron of Blenheims to Greece. ABC sailed from Alexandria on 29 October with four battleships, the two aircraft carriers, four cruisers and three destroyer flotillas for a sweep into the Ionian Sea. By 31 October, the fleet was to the west of Crete, covering the arrival of ships and troops at Suda Bay.

The Italian invasion of Greece meant that ABC could now use Suda Bay, on the northern coast of Crete, as an advanced base. The first convoy sailed from Alexandria on 29 October and reached Suda Bay on 1 November. Troops and stores were disembarked that day and the net-layer *Protector* laid one anti-submarine net, but an effective boom defence was not installed for some months and, as time would show, Suda Bay was never a safe anchorage.

Nothing was seen in the Ionian Sea and the Italian fleet was reported to be at Taranto and Brindisi, so *Warspite* and *Illustrious* returned to Alexandria on 2 November and the rest of the fleet arrived the following day.

After HATS, there was COAT — the operations in November 1940 to resupply Malta with troops and guns, and Hurricanes from *Argus*, to send convoys to Greece and Crete and to pass reinforcements for ABC through the Mediterranean.

Like HATS, COAT was a complicated undertaking. *Argus* was delayed in the United Kingdom, but 2,150 troops, with guns and tanks, reached Gibraltar by liner on 6 November. There, after dark, the troops transferred to the ships which were going to join Cunningham: the battleship *Barham* took 700 men, the 8-inch-gun cruiser *Berwick* 750, and the 6-inch-gun cruiser *Glasgow* 400. Three destroyers took fifty each and three more Force H destroyers, who would return to Gibraltar, another 150. These ships, with Force H, sailed from Gibraltar on 7 November. Guns, tanks and vehicles were to follow by merchant ship later that month.

Meanwhile, two convoys had sailed from Alexandria on 4 November: AN.6 with coal, stores and aviation spirit for Greece and Crete; and MW.3, consisting of five store ships for Malta and two ships with anti-aircraft guns, fuel and petrol for

Suda Bay. The cruisers *Ajax* and *Sydney*, with troops and antiaircraft guns sailed from Port Said, also for Suda. They were to join Cunningham after disembarking their troops and stores. The main fleet, made up of the four battleships, *Illustrious*, two cruisers and thirteen destroyers, sailed on 6 November.

MW.3 reached Malta on 9 November, after a comparatively uneventful passage. Such air attacks as developed were dispersed by *Illustrious'* Fulmars. *Ark Royal* launched a Swordfish bombing strike against Cagliari on the morning of 9 November. The enemy retaliated with a determined and heavy bombing attack which the Fulmars were unable to break up. *Barham* and several other ships suffered close near-misses.

While Force H returned to Gibraltar, ABC stood on to the west to rendezvous with *Barham* and the other reinforcements who joined his flag at 10.15 a.m. on 10 November and then proceeded into Malta to disembark their troops.

Barham and the other ships had been late at the rendezvous and ABC signalled to Somerville: 'I nearly caught a chill waiting one and three-quarters of an hour at rendezvous for a COAT. I still have no trousers but propose to take off Mussolini's in due course.'

8: TARANTO, NOVEMBER 1940, AND THE *LUFTWAFFE*'S REVENGE, JANUARY 1941

AT DAWN ON 11 November 1940, the fleet was steaming to the north-east, closing the enemy coast to carry out an air strike on the Italian battle fleet at Taranto.

Air strikes on ships in defended anchorages had been exercised by the Mediterranean Fleet since the early 1930s. A plan to strike the Italian fleet in Taranto had been mooted at the time of the Abyssinian crisis in 1935.

Rear-Admiral Lumley Lyster, in command of the Carrier Squadron, was a gunnery officer but he had commanded *Glorious* in the Mediterranean before the war, and knew more than most gunnery officers about the potential of air power. He had discussed a Taranto strike with Pound, who was then C-in-C in the Mediterranean, and when he returned to the Mediterranean, flying his flag in *Illustrious*, he brought up the subject in his first meeting with ABC, who approved of the idea.

Success depended upon good photographic reconnaissance of Taranto harbour, which was provided by Glenn Martin Marylands of No. 431 Flight RAF flying from Malta. The Swordfish would have to be fitted with long-range sixty-gallon internal auxiliary fuel tanks, so that the carriers would not have to approach dangerously close to the enemy coast to launch aircraft, which were not available until *Illustrious*' Swordfish of 815 and 819 Squadrons joined the fleet in September 1940.

A strike from *Illustrious* and *Eagle* was originally planned for 21 October — Trafalgar Day — but had to be cancelled because of a hangar fire in *Illustrious*. A new date was fixed — 11 November — when the shipping movements for COAT, and the phase of the moon, would be suitable.

But two days before, *Eagle* developed defects in her aircraft fuelling system, which had been shaken up by near-misses, showing how accurate the much despised and derided Italian high-level bombing had actually been. In the event, to the great disappointment of her air group and ship's company, *Eagle* did not take part, but five of her Swordfish, and twelve aircrew, six pilots and six observers, from 813 and 824 Squadrons, transferred to *Illustrious* for the strike. As a result, only twenty-one Swordfish were available on the night, instead of the thirty originally intended.

Photographs of Taranto were taken on the afternoon of 11 November. *Illustrious* flew an aircraft into Malta to collect them. Five battleships were in the outer Mar Grande and a sixth was just entering the harbour. By the time the Swordfish took off, the whole Italian battle fleet would be anchored in the outer harbour.

At the same time as the Taranto raid, Pridham-Wippell, flying his flag in *Orion*, with *Ajax* and *Sydney* and the destroyers *Nubian* and *Mohawk*, was to carry out a sweep of the Straits of Otranto, to disrupt the convoy route which ran regularly between the Italian mainland and Albania. This force took departure just after 1 p.m. on 11 November.

At 6 p.m., *Illustrious*, four cruisers of the 3rd Cruiser Squadron and four destroyers were ordered in the time-honoured naval phrase 'to proceed in execution of previous orders', codenamed Operation JUDGMENT, taking with them the high hopes and good wishes of the whole fleet.

'Good luck then to your lads in their enterprise,' ABC signalled *Illustrious*. 'Their success may well have a most important bearing on the course of the war in the Mediterranean.' ABC himself settled down to spend the night 'on tenterhooks'.

The flying-off position was some 170 miles south-east of Taranto. The first wave of twelve Swordfish — six armed with torpedoes, four with bombs and two with flares — led by Lieutenant-Commander K. Williamson, CO of 815 Squadron, took departure at 8.57 p.m. One of the torpedo-droppers made better speed to the target than the rest and his arrival, some twenty minutes early, alerted the defences. There was already some intense anti-aircraft fire as the bombers and flare-droppers peeled off and headed for the eastern side of the harbour.

By the light of the three-quarter moon, and aided by the glow of the flares, Williamson and the other torpedo-droppers approached through fierce flak at a height of about thirty feet. Williamson's torpedo hit *Conte de Cavour* under her fo'c'sle. *Littorio* was also hit on her starboard bow, and again on her port quarter. The other torpedoes, though all were dropped at low height and at close range, either missed, exploded prematurely, or failed to explode. Meanwhile, the bombers and the flare-droppers, who also had bombs, attacked vessels in the inner harbour.

Williamson's aircraft crashed, he and his observer becoming prisoners-of-war, but the rest returned safely to *Illustrious*, after a flight of 4½ hours.

The second wave of nine Swordfish — five with torpedoes, two with bombs and two with flares and bombs — led by Lieutenant-Commander J. W. Hale, CO of 819 Squadron, began to take off at 9.13 p.m. Eight took departure at 9.34 p.m. One was delayed, took off later and caught up the rest. A torpedo-dropper had to return prematurely because its overload fuel tank fell off.

The second wave found the defences still fully stirred up. But once again the bombers and flare-droppers fulfilled their tasks and the four torpedo-droppers attacked through an intense flak barrage at low height, hitting *Caio Duilio* on her starboard side, and *Littorio* for the third time. *Littorio* was actually hit by a fourth torpedo, which failed to explode. A torpedo aimed at *Vittorio Veneto* ran wide. A Swordfish attacking the cruiser *Gorizia* was shot down and its crew were lost.

The seven survivors of the second wave landed on at about 3 a.m. and *Illustrious* rejoined the fleet at dawn on 12 November. Debriefing had shown the probable success of the raid. ABC signalled by flag: '*Illustrious* manoeuvre well executed' which, as he said himself, 'was an under-statement'.

Pridham-Wippell's force rejoined at 11 a.m. that forenoon. ABC signalled 'I trust you had many opportunities of using your heavy mashie?' Pridham-Wippell, a notable golfer who played for the Navy, 'replied in the affirmative'.

They had indeed 'enjoyed a riotous night', intercepting a convoy of four merchant ships, escorted by a destroyer and a torpedo-boat. Two ships were sunk, two more set on fire and left sinking.

A second strike on Taranto was planned for the following night but a bad-weather report caused it to be cancelled.

The results far exceeded the wildest hopes and decisively tilted the strategic balance of capital ships in the Mediterranean, literally overnight. *Littorio* was put out of action for nearly a year. The hit on the older *Caio Duilio* did such serious damage that she had to be beached hurriedly to stop her foundering. *Conte de Cavour* was so badly flooded forward that she settled on the bottom in shallow water, with her fo'c'sle awash. She was eventually raised, but took no further part in the war. The cruiser *Trento* had suffered one hit which failed to detonate. There was minor damage and fires in hangars and a seaplane base, and slight damage from near-misses to two destroyers in the inner Mar Piccolo.

Captain Boyd told *Illustrious'* ship's company, 'This will cheer the entire free world.' 'Just before the news of Taranto the Cabinet were rather down in the dumps,' Pound wrote to ABC, 'but Taranto had a most amazing effect upon them.' ABC said that 'as an example of "economy of force" it was unsurpassed. In a total flying time of about six and a half hours — carrier to carrier — twenty aircraft had inflicted more damage upon the Italian fleet than was inflicted upon the German High Seas Fleet in the daylight action at the Battle of Jutland.'

The Italian Navy moved the remaining heavy ships still able to steam away from Taranto to west coast ports such as Naples, La Spezia and Genoa, where they were safer from air attack but, of course, were much less of an immediate danger to Allied convoys to and from Malta. As they now had to approach through the Straits of Messina, they were also more easily spotted by RAF reconnaissance aircraft.

Understandably, the enemy made strenuous efforts to locate the fleet during the return passage to Alexandria. On the morning of 12 November, three Cant flying boats were shot down by *Illustrious'* Fulmars. The last engagement actually took place over the fleet and ABC 'saw the large bulk of the Cant dodging in and out of the clouds with three Fulmars diving in after her. There could only be one end, and presently a flaming meteor with a long trail of black smoke fell out of the sky, and splashed into the sea just ahead of the fleet. One could not help feeling pity for the Italian airmen who had undertaken a hopeless task in their unwieldy aircraft.'

When the fleet arrived in Alexandria on 14 November, ABC was showered with congratulatory messages, from the Admiralty, Admiral Godfroy, men who had served with ABC in the past, and from His Majesty the King. Somerville, remembering ABC's remark about Mussolini's trousers, signalled: 'Our best congratulations on so successful a debagging accompanied by such a lovely crack on the navel. Another one like that and our friend will join Uncle George singing alto in the choir' (a reference to the chorus of a bawdy gunroom song). ABC's reply was sympathetically Rabelaisian: 'Thank you for your 0850/13 November. Uncle George now learning to pipe tune of 'Black-Shirt Black-Shirt, have you lost your [Code Group Corrupt].'

Air Chief Marshal Sir Arthur Longmore paid a special visit to Alexandria to congratulate the aircrews, which, besides being much appreciated, was historically appropriate. Lieutenant Arthur Longmore, RN, then serving in the Royal Naval Air Service, dropped the first aerial torpedo, from a Short seaplane in the Solent on 28 July 1914.

It was therefore a great pity that such a sweet victory should have been soured by the graceless manner in which the honours and awards were given and announced. Rumour in the fleet was that Williamson and Hale were to receive the Victoria Cross. Certainly *Illustrious'* sailors expected nothing less, with lesser awards pro rata, for everybody who had taken part.

Consequently, disappointment was a pale word for the feelings of *Illustrious'* and *Eagle's* ship's companies when they heard, and only then as late as 20 December, that Williamson and Hale were awarded DSOs, and their observers DSCs. The pilot and observer of one of *Eagle*'s Swordfish also received DSCs. Nobody else was to receive anything. There were reports that *Illustrious*' angry sailors actually tore down the notices announcing the decorations from the ship's notice boards.

Lyster was made CB, Boyd and Bridge both CBE, in the next New Year's Honours List. Finally, and not a moment before time, on 20 May 1941, six full months later, DSOs were awarded to the pilot and observer of a third Swordfish and DSCs to thirteen other aircrew. Eighteen more were mentioned in dispatches. Not one officer or rating of the maintenance and non-flying personnel in *Illustrious* received any recognition at all. As Captain Boyd wrote, with feeling, in his official dispatch, 'This arm has had a long struggle with adverse opinions.'

The responsibility for this bungling (it was nothing less) of the awards must be laid at ABC's door. The Honours and Awards Committee would have endorsed his every recommendation. He was not only Commander-in-Chief, he was actually the senior officer afloat at the time. Here was a clear-cut, dramatic victory, which had been brought about in a new way, and from which the maximum amount of publicity for the Royal Navy's achievements should have been gained (the BBC nine o'clock news the following evening announced the Taranto raid with the comment: 'The RAF does it again'). No better way could have been found of publicising the Navy, and at the same time giving great satisfaction to the fleet, than by rewarding those who accomplished the Taranto raid with a spectacular range of decorations.

Whatever lofty language ABC might have used to describe Taranto in later years, it seems that, at the time, and for some time afterwards, he quite failed to grasp the magnitude of the victory. Lyster and Boyd were surprised and disappointed by ABC's manner, seemingly unimpressed and almost unenthusiastic, at their first meeting in Alexandria.

Some inkling of his failure of imagination, that he might not have given proper credit where it was due, seems to have lingered. In 1949, ABC was guest of honour at a Taranto Night Dinner, held every year by the Fleet Air Arm on the anniversary to celebrate the victory. 'I confess', he said in his after-dinner speech, 'that it was some time before I realised what a tremendous stroke it was. I think Admiral Lyster and Captain Boyd were rather disappointed by the matter of fact way in which I looked at it. And it is true enough', he went on, trying to make amends to his hosts, 'that at first I regarded it as just one of those things that always happened when the Fleet Air Arm were at work!'

With the enemy's battleship threat so much reduced, ABC's own battleship strength could also be reduced. He suggested that he could do without *Ramillies* and the Admiralty were glad to get her home for escorting Atlantic convoys. The Admiralty also suggested the return of *Valiant* but ABC replied that she and *Warspite* were the only two battleships he had with the fuel endurance and the gun range to take on the Italian battle fleet.

At this time, ABC went to see General Wavell about the question of Alexandria's defences against air attack, which were, in ABC's phrase, 'really bad'. Italian bombers had been a problem since the start of the war but now, evidently goaded by events at Taranto, they were coming over almost every day.

The fleet provided its own anti-aircraft defence, which was enough to deter the enemy, but this meant an added strain on the guns' crews who already spent long hours standing to at sea. ABC referred specifically to anti-aircraft batteries and fighters which were being withheld from Alexandria for the defence of other places in Egypt which had never been attacked. Wavell was sympathetic and there was what ABC called a steady improvement.

There were also plans to reinforce Malta's air defences. After COAT, Somerville signalled to ABC: 'I trust goods to your esteemed order arrived safely. Further consignment will follow shortly in a very [repeat] very plain van' — a reference to 'the old pantechnicon of an *Argus*'.

On 17 November 1940, *Argus* flew off two flights of six Hurricanes for Malta, each flight led by a Skua. Ground crews and stores arrived safely in *Newcastle*, but because of faulty navigation and aircraft not being flown at their most economical cruising speed, eight Hurricanes and one Skua ran out of fuel and were lost.

After HATS and COAT, there was COLLAR, another complicated series of linked operations, to reinforce ABC and Malta, and pass convoys east and west. Pridham-Wippell sailed from Alexandria on 23 November, flying his flag in *Orion*, with the 7th Cruiser Squadron, *Malaya*, *Ramillies*, *Eagle*, and nine destroyers. Convoy MW.4 of four ships, escorted by *Calcutta*, *Coventry* and four destroyers, sailed for Malta.

ABC sailed on 25 November, with *Warspite*, *Valiant*, *Illustrious* and nine destroyers. ABC had now established such a command over the eastern Mediterranean that, whilst Swordfish from *Illustrious* attacked Leros in the Dodecanese that night, Swordfish from *Eagle* attacked Tripoli, 750 miles to the west.

On the night of 24/25 November, the COLLAR convoy, of three merchant ships carrying motor transport, escorted by *Manchester* (flag of Vice-Admiral L.E. Holland, commanding 18th Cruiser Squadron) and *Southampton*, passed eastward through the Straits of Gibraltar, while Force H — *Renown*

(Somerville's flag), *Ark Royal*, *Sheffield* and *Despatch*, and nine destroyers — covered them to the northward.

MW.4 arrived safely early on 26 November. At noon, *Ramillies*, *Newcastle*, *Coventry* and five destroyers sailed from Malta, to be joined by *Berwick*, and rendezvoused with Admiral Somerville next day. A convoy of five empty ships, ME.4, sailed for Alexandria, to be escorted by the fleet.

ABC's ships had all returned to Alexandria by 30 November. Most unusually, no ship had fired a gun in the seven days spent at sea. But any pleasure ABC felt at this was dispelled when, to his great annoyance and indignation, he found that the Admiralty was to hold a Board of Inquiry into the recent actions of James Somerville.

ABC had a record of recent success, capped by the brilliant coup at Taranto. Somerville, on the other hand, was well aware that after Oran and Dakar his stock was not high in the Admiralty or in Downing Street. He knew he was considered to be too cautious, too ready to calculate the odds against. Even ABC, his friend, had said that he was 'unduly pessimistic' — an 'Et tu, Brute?' remark which infuriated Somerville.

The problem was that the Italians were very elusive opponents. Trying to engage them was like trying to hit quicksilver with a hammer. As Somerville said, 'The worst of the jobs I have to do is that it is always our object to avoid meeting the enemy if possible — we want nothing to interrupt the safe passage of whatever we have to pass through. It would be a welcome relief if we could go out with a high speed Force and just look for the toads and it would do us all a lot of good.'

At 8 a.m. on 27 November, Somerville's ships were about 100 miles south-west of Cape Spartivento (the southernmost point of Sardinia, not the similarly named point off Calabria), steering to cover *Manchester*, *Southampton* and the COLLAR convoy.

Somerville had had no intelligence information on the whereabouts of the Italian fleet for the previous fifteen days. But, early on the 27th, aircraft reported enemy ships off Cape Spartivento. In fact, having learned of the movements of forces from both ends of the Mediterranean, the Italian fleet was out in strength, with the battleships *Vittorio Veneto* (wearing Campioni's flag) and *Giulio Cesare*, seven 8-inch cruisers and sixteen destroyers.

This was a superior force to Somerville's, even after *Ramillies* and the other ships from Alexandria had joined him later that forenoon. However, Somerville ordered the convoy to continue towards its destination, steering south-east to keep clear of any action, whilst he concentrated his force in the classical manner, placed his cruisers in the van, and turned towards the enemy at high speed. As he said,

> An inconclusive action followed, lasting about an hour, in which the cruiser *Berwick* and the Italian destroyer *Lanciere* were hit and damaged, and two torpedo strikes by *Ark Royal*'s Swordfish both failed. The action then became a chase, with the Italian ships hauling off, steadily out-distancing the British pursuers and rapidly passing out of range.

Somerville now had to decide whether or not to continue the chase. So far as he knew, the enemy ships were undamaged, their speed undiminished. He signalled to Holland: 'Is there any hope of catching cruisers?' Holland replied: 'No'. The enemy had retreated out of range, behind a horizon obscured by a dense smoke screen. Beyond the smoke was the enemy coastline with the airfields of Sardinia and the submarine and motor-torpedo boat bases at Cagliari close at hand.

The main object was the safe and timely arrival of the convoy, which would still be within range of enemy torpedo bombers at dusk. Somerville decided to break off the chase and rejoin the convoy which was sighted later in the afternoon and escorted onwards to the east until dusk, passing through the Sicilian Narrows under cover of darkness. Force H, with *Ramillies*, *Berwick* and *Newcastle*, turned back to Gibraltar.

The objects of COLLAR had been achieved in full. The enemy had been driven off and the three ships carrying motor transport reached their destinations. MW.4 and ME.4 had passed without loss. *Ramillies*, *Berwick* and *Newcastle* had reached Gibraltar on their way home.

Nevertheless, Somerville was aware that there might be some disappointment in London that he had not brought the enemy to more decisive action. But he was quite unprepared for the furious reaction he did provoke.

'I felt like a pricked balloon,' Pound told ABC, 'when I read Flag Officer Force H's signal that he had given up the chase.' Pound was not the man to suffer such disappointment in silence or inaction. Somerville was astonished and angered to discover that the Admiralty had already — without asking for his written report and before he had even reached harbour — ordered a Board, chaired by Admiral of the Fleet the Earl of Cork and Orrery, to inquire into the reasons why the chase had been broken off and the failure of the second striking force to attack the Italian battleships.

The Admiralty was fully entitled to order an Inquiry and, if it was felt justified, to reprimand the officer concerned, but the manner, almost unprecedented in naval history, in which this Inquiry was announced was a grave reflection upon an admiral's leadership and professional reputation. Somerville's captains and staff were as astonished and angry as he was, while the wardrooms of Force H were reported to be 'seething with indignation at the insult'.

Somerville's predicament was even more perilous than he or his officers had supposed. It was only by a chance of timing that he was still flying his flag. 'We have not been very satisfied with James Somerville's outlook,' Pound wrote to ABC, 'and a letter had actually been approved, that he was to be relieved. When we got news that he was chasing the Italians we naturally had to hold the letter up.' In the end, all that saved Somerville was the lack of a suitable relief. 'We wanted Fred Collins to relieve him,' Pound went on, 'but the Politicians have only two people in mind — yourself and Harwood.'

The Board heard evidence for three days and brought in a finding which upheld Somerville and *Ark Royal*'s Swordfish strike leader and considered that the decision to break off the chase was correct.

Nevertheless, the Admiralty decided that Somerville had been 'overinfluenced by his anxiety for the security of his convoy' and that 'he could have continued the pursuit until it was clear beyond doubt that no possibility of the destruction of any of the enemy units remained'.

'I do not know whether you will have been surprised or not at the Inquiry,' Pound wrote to ABC, who replied in terms of swingeing criticism: 'You ask me if I was surprised at the Board of Inquiry on Force 'H''s action south of Sardinia. You will wish me to speak outright quite frankly and say that I was very sorry for this decision and did not agree with it, more especially as the Board was set up even before Force 'H' had returned to harbour.'

ABC 'thought it intolerable that a Flag Officer, doing his utmost in difficult circumstances, should be continuously under the threat of finding a Board of Inquiry waiting for him on his return to harbour if his actions failed to commend themselves to those at home who knew little or nothing of the real facts of the case. Such prejudgment is not the best way to get loyal service.'

ABC believed others besides Pound had been involved and wrote to Somerville, 'I don't believe he [Dudley Pound] is at the bottom of it but allows himself to be talked into these things, by W.C. and others.'

Pound told ABC of attacks on him in the papers and clearly was beginning to see himself as beleaguered and without a friend — except ABC. 'I have come to the conclusion,' he said, 'that by the time I have finished this job I shall have no friends left, but I am sure you will not be included in the number I have lost.'

One of the main intriguers against him, Pound was sure, was Admiral of the Fleet Sir Roger Keyes, the Director of Combined Operations. 'I am sorry to have to say it,' Pound wrote to ABC, 'but R.K. is just out for his own glorification — nothing else matters.'

This would not have concerned Pound much, had not Keyes begun to press for Operation WORKSHOP, the capture of Pantelleria, a small island in the Sicilian Channel, some 140 miles north-west of Malta.

Keyes had an almost legendary reputation — the Boxer Rising in China, the Dardanelles, Zeebrugge and the Dover Patrol. Now nearing seventy, but still vigorous in mind and body, he was still as thirsty as ever for glory, still brimming with ideas on how to take the offensive. Pantelleria, he told the Chiefs of Staff on 30 October 1940, had an excellent airfield, well placed for attacks on Italy and Sicily, and it could be used as a staging post for aircraft on their way to the Middle East.

The island controlled the Tunis-Sicily Channel, and its capture would be a threat to the Vichy Government at Tunis.

Churchill was immediately enthusiastic and continued so for months (although even he wearied of Keyes' importunity in the end) and wanted Keyes himself to lead the expedition.

As the Commander-in-Chief most closely involved, ABC was asked for his views. ABC thought WORKSHOP a 'wildcat scheme'. He had no doubt the island could be captured and held, but he could not see what possible use it would be. Also, ABC was 'frankly aghast' at the prospect of having to maintain another island, when he was already hard pressed to supply Malta. As he told Churchill in a signal of 12 December, 'the calls on my forces increase almost daily, for instance today I am arranging for the supply of the Army in the Western Desert and for the removal by sea of some 20,000 prisoners.'

There was a more personal cause for concern, which ABC was only able to express more bluntly after the war: 'Also, although I well knew Lord Keyes' ardent fighting spirit, I felt quite sure that to have an officer of his seniority operating independently within the area of my command would lead to difficulties.'

The exchange of signals continued, 'protesting from us and insistent from home', as ABC said, through November 1940 and into December. The Chiefs of Staff generally, and Pound particularly, disapproved of WORKSHOP for the same reasons as ABC did. But Churchill returned to the fray again.

Pound tried every argument. He even 'pointed out that employing R.K. was opposed to the policy of employing young officers at sea'. It was to no avail, 'the P.M. is as pigheaded as a mule over these things, and his reply was that R.K. was full of the flame of war etc. etc.'

Keyes and his 'flame of war' might actually have undertaken WORKSHOP, had not events elsewhere caused it first to be postponed, and finally to be cancelled, much to ABC's relief.

Meanwhile, much larger events had been taking place in the Mediterranean. On 4 December 1940, the three C-in-Cs had a conference in Cairo to discuss the COMPASS offensive in the Western Desert, due to begin on 7 December. This was the plan which, for secrecy's sake, Wavell had not communicated home, not even to Churchill, but only to Eden by word of mouth during his visit in October and only then because Eden was proposing to sap his strength in favour of Greece, thinking Wavell had only a defensive policy in mind.

To support COMPASS from the sea, ABC formed an Inshore Squadron, under Rawlings, of the monitor *Terror*, the gunboats *Ladybird*, *Aphis* and *Gnat*, and the Australian destroyers *Vampire*, *Vendetta*, *Voyager* and *Waterhen*, led by Captain H.M.L. ('Hec') Waller, RAN, in *Stuart*. ABC gave Rawlings one order: 'to help the Army in every possible way', which they did by bombarding shore targets and escorting the small merchant ships and craft which took stores, ammunition, food and water up to the front and brought back wounded and prisoners-of-war.

By mid-December, there were over 30,000 Italian prisoners-of-war, for COMPASS, commanded by Lieutenant-General Sir Henry Maitland-Wilson, with Major-General Richard O'Connor commanding in the field, had been a great success. The Italian Army under General Graziani was in full retreat. Supported by bombardments from the sea, O'Connor took a series of enemy positions and reached Bardia on 5 January 1941.

ABC was delighted by COMPASS, not just because of its success, but because it showed Wavell as the really great leader and soldier ABC knew him to be. It also had another result, hardly noticeable at the time but which was to be supremely important in other major operations later in the war: it brought the three C-in-Cs closer together, making them realise that success could only be obtained by continual co-ordination and co-operation, that each Service depended on the others, and that the campaign by sea, land and air was really one combined campaign. 'Before this time,' ABC admitted, 'we had been inclined each to pursue a vague and shadowy object, actually more or less the same; but each Commander-in-Chief using his own arm without much consultation with the others. After this offensive in Libya, in which perhaps the three Services proved each other, the closest consultation on all important moves became a *sine qua non*. I paid many more visits to Cairo, and Wavell and Longmore often flew to Alexandria to talk to me, sometimes at extremely early hours.'

It was proposed to send another convoy (codenamed EXCESS) through the Mediterranean before the end of the year. Five fast merchant vessels would sail from the United Kingdom with one of the WS convoys (which was going round the Cape of Good Hope to Egypt) and break away from it under cover of darkness when they passed Gibraltar.

However, EXCESS was delayed. Meanwhile, another series of closely connected and interlocking operations was planned, involving convoys to and from Malta and Alexandria and including a sweep by the main fleet into the Adriatic to bombard Valona, as well as attacks by carrier aircraft on the Dodecanese and on the Italian supply route to Tripoli.

These operations began at 1 a.m. on 16 December 1940, when ABC sailed from Alexandria, flying his flag in *Warspite*, with *Valiant*, *Illustrious*, *Gloucester*, *York* and eleven destroyers. Pridham-Wippell and the 7th Cruiser Squadron, with three destroyers, were to sweep up the Adriatic as far as the Bari-Durazzo line. *Malaya* and three destroyers escorted a convoy of four ships (MW.5) to Malta.

The next day, *Illustrious'* aircraft bombed Rhodes and Stampalia, but few aircraft found their targets in bad weather. By the 18th, the weather had worsened until night flying was impracticable. *Illustrious* was left behind while the fleet closed the coast to bombard Valona, the main supply port for the Italian Army in Albania.

By midnight, the skies had cleared, the winds had dropped and it was a calm, moonlit night. However, there was snow on the hills and it was bitterly cold. ABC was very glad of the balaclava helmet Nona had knitted for him.

The battleships opened fire just after 1 a.m. on 19 December. Intervening hills prevented anybody seeing what, if anything, was being hit. In fact, twenty aircraft on Valona airfield were damaged.

ABC had decided to visit Malta, for the first time since May. *Warspite* arrived in Grand Harbour in the early afternoon of 20 December. The news spread quickly and the harbour battlements were soon black with wildly cheering and waving Maltese.

ABC found Malta in good heart. Air attacks had slackened. The convoys arriving and sailing had heartened everybody. ABC was cheered and mobbed wherever he went. He toured the dockyard, which was working almost normally, and called at Admiralty House, which looked very bare and deserted. He had talks with Vice-Admiral Ford and the Governor of Malta, Lieutenant-General William Dobbie, and inspected naval establishments.

Warspite rejoined the fleet and returned to Alexandria on Christmas Eve. There was Christmas dinner at the Residency, with party games and Scottish dancing. The two nieces teased Hugh Lee, the new Flag Lieutenant who, ABC told Doodles, 'gets badly shaken up by Hilda, which is very good for him'. It was voted a very good Christmas, for wartime.

In spite of setbacks, 1940 was ending, as ABC said, 'in high hope'. On land, Wavell's Army had won a crushing victory The enemy had been driven out of Egypt and was soon to be expelled from Cyrenaica. At sea, the fleet had taken their chances and had sunk an enemy cruiser and four destroyers. Convoys were passing to and from Malta, and the Aegean. The enemy had been attacked in the Adriatic, the Dodecanese, Albania and at Taranto. Enemy convoys to Libya had been attacked, although more could have been done with more air reconnaissance from Malta.

However, ten submarines had been lost by the end of 1940, which was nearly half the number which had operated since the outbreak of war, for a comparatively small amount of enemy shipping sunk.

For ABC personally, there was news on 3 January 1941 that he had been confirmed in his acting rank of Admiral.

The EXCESS ships sailed with convoy WS.5, which was attacked on Christmas Day in the Atlantic 1,000 miles from Gibraltar by the German heavy cruiser *Hipper*. No serious damage was done, but one ship was hit, the convoy was ordered to scatter and the EXCESS ships were held at Gibraltar.

This delay had very unfortunate results. Mediterranean naval operations were so closely interlinked that a delay in one was likely to affect others.

Lofty Power had hit his head on a hatchway while running up a ladder when *Warspite* was at sea on 8 December. He was concussed and spent ten days convalescing ashore in the

Residency. Meanwhile, Captain DM. Lees prepared the plans for the operations connected with the EXCESS convoy. Power, who had been made OBE in the New Year's Honours List, the first honour awarded to ABC's staff, wrote later: 'I did not much like his plan. I thought the timing wrong which entailed our meeting the convoy further west than usual. I had a mild disagreement and was briskly told by ABC that it was a case of sour grapes and if I chose to go idling ashore etc. etc...'

Lyster, Boyd and the staff in *Illustrious* felt they were being called upon to operate too close to land and to other ships in the convoy and the fleet. With their aircraft's range, *Illustrious* could operate from a more discreet distance and still provide adequate air cover. But ABC, with his curious blind spot for the handling of air power, overruled them. He thought it would be good for fleet morale to see the carrier near them.

One EXCESS ship ran aground on 1 January 1941 and did not take part. Of the four remaining ships, one had 4,000 tons of ammunition, 3,000 tons of seed potatoes (just as vital to Malta's survival), and a deck cargo of twelve Hurricanes in crates. The others had urgent stores and supplies for the Piraeus. The ships also had troops and airmen for Malta.

Convoy and escort sailed on the evening of 6 January, steering west into the Atlantic, hoping to deceive the watching spies in Spain, and then turning east under cover of darkness to go through the Straits, being joined next morning by Force H: *Renown, Malaya, Ark Royal, Sheffield* and six destroyers.

The convoy was to be met west of Sardinia by *Gloucester* (flag of Rear-Admiral E. de F. Renouf, commanding 3rd Cruiser Squadron) and *Southampton* who were to take over from Force H and escort the convoy through the Sicilian Narrows. The two cruisers, with some 500 soldiers and airmen for Malta, sailed from Alexandria on 6 January, disembarked their passengers in Malta on the 8th, sailed again and joined the convoy the next day.

For the first ten days of January 1941, the air effort from Malta had concentrated on the enemy's sea traffic to Libya and Albania. This had resulted in some successful air raids on Tripoli, Palermo, Naples and Messina, but at the expense of reconnaissance of Sicilian airfields. So the convoy's first warning of approaching aircraft was from *Sheffield*'s radar, at its extreme range of forty-three miles. Bombs fell close to *Malaya* and *Gloucester*, and a Fulmar from *Ark Royal* shot down two bombers.

There were no more air raids and so, that evening of the 9th, Force H and *Malaya* turned back for Gibraltar, while *Gloucester* led the convoy to the east.

On 7 January, ABC had sailed from Alexandria in *Warspite*, with *Valiant*, *Illustrious* and seven destroyers. Also sailing that day was a fast westbound convoy (MW.5½) from Alexandria to Malta.

ABC's daily routine at sea in *Warspite* hardly ever varied:

I never took my clothes off at sea except for my daily bath, and never left the close proximity of the bridge. I had a sea cabin and bathroom one ladder down, and here I had my meals unless some urgent situation compelled me to have them in the Commander-in-Chief's charthouse on the bridge. The five Commanders on the staff, Dick, Carne, Barnard, Brownrigg and Power, kept watch day and night and conducted the routine movements of the fleet. By day I was practically always on the bridge and if I was not, the Chief of Staff, Rear-Admiral Willis, was there. If things were quiet he would be on the bridge until midnight, when he was relieved by the Captain of the Fleet, Richard Shelley, until 3 or 3.30 a.m. Then I came up, and was always on the bridge at dawn. I was on call, of course, at any time during the night.

Everything was reported to me, and I was invariably up for any alterations of course other than the normal zigzags.

Early on 10 January, *Warspite* and the other ships were north-west of Malta, steering to close the convoy. At dawn, the cruiser *Bonaventure* signalled that she had sighted two enemy destroyers. ABC himself sighted gun flashes to the westward and ordered the fleet to increase to full speed in case the convoy escort needed support.

Bonaventure and the destroyer *Hereward* were off Pantelleria pouring shells at close range into the burning and crippled Italian destroyer *Vega* — the other destroyer having escaped. *Vega* finally blew up, which, apart from the prodigious amount of ammunition *Bonaventure* had expended, was a satisfactory outcome.

ABC's ships had gone past the convoy and turned to the south-east to follow when, in ABC's words, 'things started to go wrong'. He was watching the destroyers changing their stations on the radar screen — a sight of which he never tired — when *Gallant* struck a mine. Her bows were blown off, sixty of her ship's company killed, and another twenty-five wounded. Towed stern first by *Mohawk*, she reached Malta later that day.

Meanwhile, *Warspite*, *Valiant* and *Illustrious*, with five remaining destroyers, and the convoy, with three more destroyers, were highly exposed, still more than 100 miles west of Malta, in broad daylight. They were sighted and reported by an enemy aircraft at 10.15 and a shadower was shot down. Two Savoia S.79s dropped torpedoes and were engaged by ships' gunfire and chased by Fulmars.

Unfortunately, the Fulmars were still down near sea level when, at 12.35, large formations of aircraft were sighted approaching from the north. They were Junkers Ju.87 Stukas and Ju.88 bombers — with German markings.

It had always seemed inevitable that sooner or later the Germans would come to the assistance of their Italian allies. Hitler had written to Mussolini on 20 November 1940, proposing that German bombers should operate from bases in Italy against British shipping. Field Marshal Erhard Milch, the German Secretary of State for Air, went to Italy early in December 1940 to make the arrangements for Operation MITTELMEER.

The force chosen for MITTELMEER was *Fliegerkorps* X, the *Luftwaffe's* antishipping specialists, who began to move down through Italy at Christmas, 1940. There had been some prior indications of the move, including fragments of decrypts of *Luftwaffe* messages in Enigma code referring to a transfer of *Fliegerkorps* X to bases from which it could attack the Mediterranean Fleet, but British Air Intelligence was deceived by the sheer rapidity of *Fliegerkorps* X's build-up. Air reconnaissance of Sicilian airfields on 5 January had shown nothing unusual. But by the 8th, ninety-six bombers had arrived, and the numbers rose to 120 long-range bombers, 150 dive-bombers and forty fighters by the end of January.

Illustrious' 'Y' Officer, who listened in to enemy W/T broadcasts, managed to give an hour's warning of the attack (although he could not have been familiar with the newly arrived *Luftwaffe's* W/T procedures, and indeed might not have been able to speak German fluently). But otherwise the Mediterranean Fleet was given no intelligence warning. The *Luftwaffe's* arrival on 10 January therefore came as a complete surprise.

The bombers deployed into three groups, two concentrating upon *Illustrious* and the third on the battleships. It was soon clear that this was flying of a skill and aggressiveness which ABC's ships had never experienced before. ABC himself recognised fellow professionals:

> One was too interested in this new form of dive-bombing attack really to be frightened, and there was no doubt we were watching complete experts. Formed roughly in a large circle over the fleet they peeled off one by one when reaching the attacking position. We could not but admire the skill and precision of it all. The attacks were pressed home to point-blank range, and as they pulled out of their dives some of them were seen to fly along the flight deck of the *Illustrious* below the level of her funnel.

The ships opened fire with every anti-aircraft gun they had, but they could do nothing to save *Illustrious* whose long hull and island superstructure were completely hidden for minutes at a time in leaping curtains of water thrown up by near-misses. Eventually a direct hit from a 500 kg bomb penetrated the armoured flight deck, blew out the after lift, destroyed or damaged every aircraft in the hangar, killed or wounded most of the men there, and started numerous fires. Other direct hits, six in all, with three near-misses, crippled the ship's steering gear, and reduced the after part of the ship to blackness, lit only by the fires raging along the main deck. But for her armoured flight deck, *Illustrious* must have been lost. Fortunately, she was still able to steam, and steering by main engines (altering the revolutions on the shafts) she headed for Malta.

Warspite and *Valiant* closed to give *Illustrious* all the support they could, but at about five o'clock, when *Illustrious* was making about 17 knots towards Malta, she was attacked and near-missed again, but not hit. Some of her Fulmars flew into

Malta to refuel and now returned to engage the Stukas and claim six of them.

Illustrious arrived in Malta at 9 p.m. that evening with casualties of thirteen officers and 113 men killed, seven officers and eighty-four men wounded. No longer the fleet carrier, her main preoccupation was now survival. *Valiant* had casualties from splinters, and *Warspite* was hit a glancing blow on the starboard bower anchor by a bomb, but it was only a partial detonation and little damage was done.

The warships might be damaged, but the conveys were arriving and sailing as planned. On 10 January MW.5 and one EXCESS ship arrived in Malta. Two eastbound convoys sailed from Malta the same day, joining the remaining three EXCESS ships, which reached the Piraeus on 12 January. Thus, all fourteen merchant ships in EXCESS and the ME and MW convoys eventually arrived safely at their destinations.

But the ordeal by air attack continued. On 11 January, *Gloucester* and *Southampton* were ordered to overtake and support the escort of the slow convoy ME.6 and by 3 p.m. were about thirty miles astern of the convoy. Neither ship had radar, and the Stukas which dived out of the sun were undetected. One bomb hit *Gloucester*'s gun-director tower and penetrated through five decks but failed to explode. *Southampton* was hit by two bombs which did tremendous damage and started major fires.

Southampton continued to steam at a surprising 20 knots for another hour, and actually beat off a high-level bombing attack, while the fires raging inside her steadily gained the upper hand. Loss of boiler feed water gradually reduced her speed until at 4.40 p.m. she stopped. For another two hours her ship's company fought the fires, which were now so large it was impossible to reach the magazines and flood them. The time was approaching where the ship herself might blow up and take all her people with her. She was abandoned at 7 p.m., after ABC had given his permission. At 10 p.m., Pridham-Wippell arrived in *Orion* and fired three torpedoes into *Southampton*, who sank with casualties of eighty killed and eighty-eight wounded. Her survivors were embarked in *Diamond* and in *Gloucester.*

Next morning, Pridham-Wippell joined ABC off the western end of Crete where they were also joined by Rawlings, flying his flag in *Barham*, with *Eagle*, *Ajax* and destroyers. ABC had intended, once the convoys had arrived safely, to carry out strikes against enemy shipping, but without *Illustrious* these were no longer practicable. So, it was a somewhat subdued fleet, lacking its much-loved aircraft carrier, which ABC led back to Alexandria.

For ABC's staff, there were the inevitable post-mortems. Power, in particular, felt that

> I had not pressed my objections sufficiently strongly. Had we followed my usual plan and not gone so far to the west away from Malta's air umbrella, it would not have happened. ABC did not help matters, on the evening of the 11th [the day after the attack on *Illustrious*] by attacking me for making such a stupid plan. When I pointed out mildly that I hadn't, that he had approved it anyway and that I *had* objected to it, he merely said 'You didn't make your objection strong enough.' I said 'I did not wish to be insubordinate,' to which he replied 'that bang on the head must have changed your nature and not for the better. I *hate* Staff Officers who agree with me.' We had quite a blazing row in front of several interested spectators. I was left, however unjustly, with a feeling that I had let the side down owing to a mistaken loyalty to my temporary relief (my senior anyway) and a failure to fight the C-in-C hard enough to change his mind.

ABC took a philosophical, if somewhat rueful, view of matters. 'Well, we have had a set-back,' he wrote to Pound, 'but we have been in the same position before, and I have no doubt we shall overcome our present difficulties.'

9: 1941: THE CAMPAIGN IN GREECE, AND MATAPAN — THE FIRST MOVES

ABC PUT A brave face on this 'setback'. 'We have been properly in the wars lately,' he told Doodles. 'We ran into some German air gentlemen. Rather a different proposition to their Italian confreres and we got a bit knocked about. So did they!'

Four of *Southampton*'s midshipmen were staying at the Residency 'while they kit themselves up again. They lost everything, and want a bit of rest and looking after. Nona is in her element putting stuff on burns etc. etc. and Hilda also who is keeping them in order.'

The midshipmen were badly in need of rest and recuperation, but the Residency was no rest cure. Having to talk to the C-in-C at breakfast every morning was as much of an ordeal as any *Luftwaffe* attack. Not surprisingly, they broke out, hired cars and went for a drive around Alexandria. 'I don't believe there was a driving licence amongst the lot,' wrote ABC. 'Nona was in a fit that they'd break theirs or somebody else's neck.'

Meanwhile, Malta dockyard worked frantically to repair *Illustrious*, while *Fliegerkorps* X tried as hard to sink her. They attacked in strength on 16 January and hit *Illustrious*' quarterdeck. *Essex*, from the EXCESS convoy, was hit by a heavy bomb. By a miracle, the thousands of tons of ammunition still on board did not explode but many stevedores were killed or wounded. The rest, showing the first cracks in Maltese morale, refused to work. Unloading was completed by soldiers and sailors.

Despite more heavy air attacks, *Illustrious* was ready for sea on the 23rd and sailed after dark that evening. She was able to make such good speed, of 24 knots, that she evaded the air and cruiser escort sent to meet her, who then themselves suffered the air attacks intended for her. Battle-scarred but triumphant, she was cheered into Alexandria on 25 January and went on to the United States for permanent repairs.

Recognising what a triumph *Illustrious'* escape was for Malta dockyard and the Royal Corps of Constructors, ABC sent them a congratulatory signal and also, characteristically, signalled his gratitude to the RAF for their efforts to help *Illustrious* by bombing airfields in North Africa during her passage.

However, this did not mitigate the hard truth that the loss of *Illustrious* was, as ABC was soon to find out, rather more than a 'setback'. The Admiralty took immediate steps to try and rectify the situation. On 12 January, before ABC had even returned to harbour, the new aircraft carrier *Formidable*, *Illustrious'* sister ship, which was to have relieved *Ark Royal* in Force H, was ordered to join ABC instead. Going round by the Cape, she was expected to arrive in March. The old unarmoured *Eagle*, which had become increasingly defect-prone, could then leave.

The lack of a carrier severely restricted the fleet's activities in the central Mediterranean for the rest of January and February. No convoy could be run to Malta, although later in February it was possible to send two infantry battalions in cruisers to Malta and to bring out a small convoy for Alexandria.

Attacks on the Suez Canal by German aircraft on the night of 18/19 January 1941 showed that, as expected and feared, the *Luftwaffe* had arrived in the Dodecanese. ABC had been considering some form of operation in the islands to forestall just such an eventuality. He much preferred action in the Dodecanese to WORKSHOP, which was still Mr Churchill's favourite.

Two operations were planned to seize the small island of Kaso, which dominated the Kaso Strait, east of Crete, but the first was vetoed by the Chiefs of Staff and the second was a failure.

A much larger operation, codenamed ABSTENTION, was planned to seize Castelorizzo, an island in the eastern Dodecanese off the southern coast of Turkey. Two hundred Commandos, in the destroyers *Decoy* and *Hereward*, left Cyprus just after midnight on 23/24 February. Guided in to land by the submarine *Parthian*, they were to land in ten whalers in the early hours of 25 February. But almost everything went wrong. The island was quickly secured, but the gunboat *Ladybird*, which was to have provided ship-to-shore W/T communications, was damaged in an air attack and had to withdraw.

The Commandos were to have held the island until reinforced by a battalion of the Sherwood Foresters. But owing to a misunderstanding, the Sherwood Foresters were sent to Alexandria, arrived at Castelorizzo three days late, in only company strength, and, in the end, were not landed at all.

The Italians, reacting with unexpected vigour, mounted several bombing raids and dispatched two destroyers which bombarded the Commandos with disconcerting accuracy and also landed some 300 Italian troops. The Commandos, by now very short of food and ammunition, held their positions until they were taken off by the two destroyers on the 28th, having suffered about fifty casualties.

A Board of Inquiry was held. The Commandos, who were themselves criticised, had done what they had been ordered to do. It was not their fault that they had not been relieved as planned, nor could they possibly have prevented the enemy landing on the island. The whole operation had been mounted and carried out with a lack of proper forward planning and reconnaissance and a shortage of intelligence, compounded by a failure to reinforce the initial landing force in time. The Navy had left the island, and allowed the enemy time and space to counter-attack. ABC and his staff must share the blame for the fiasco.

By contrast, the main offensive on land continued to go extremely well. On 19 January, ABC reported to the Admiralty that in spite of bad weather the Inshore Squadron had ferried 35,000 Italian prisoners-of-war to Alexandria in the last ten days. They had also cleared both the harbours of Solium and Bardia and were supplying stores to them at the rate of 500 tons a day.

Tobruk fell on 22 January and the harbour was open for sea traffic by the 27th. ABC and Willis flew there on the 29th, to inspect the harbour and shore defences. There had been considerable damage to cranes and wharves, but there were more sheltered berths than ABC had expected, so there was ample room for store ships.

Derna fell on 30 January, Benghazi on 6 February. On the 7th, the British armour dashed across the desert to Beda Fomm, some fifty miles south of Benghazi, to cut off the Italians' retreat. This lightning stroke, 'This desert variety of the naval manoeuvre of crossing the enemy's T', as ABC described it, 'greatly delighted the Navy.' It also brought the campaign to an end, with the capture of 130,000 Italian prisoners, 400 tanks and 850 guns, after an advance of 500 miles. The victory was both intellectually satisfying and militarily complete.

The victorious General, Sir Richard O'Connor, paid a generous tribute to the Navy's part in his victory and wrote personally to ABC who invited him to lunch on board *Warspite* and to dine at Admiralty House.

After the capture of Benghazi, ABC signalled the Inshore Squadron:

> The feat of the Army in clearing Egypt and occupying Cyrenaica in a period of eight weeks is an outstanding achievement to which the Inshore Squadron and the shore parties along the coast have contributed in no small measure. All officers and men who took part in these operations may well feel proud, as I do, of their contribution to this victory.

But, as always, there was a price. The minesweeper *Huntley* and the destroyer *Dainty* were dive-bombed and sunk. The South African whaler *Southern Floe*, and the trawler *Ouse*, were mined and sunk. The old monitor *Terror* was dive-bombed, and then mined. Finally she had to be abandoned, and sank.

Mines and aircraft were the two greatest dangers. The most vulnerable place for mining was the Suez Canal, the Mediterranean Fleet's lifeline. The first aerial mines were dropped on 31 January 1941, closing the Canal at a very awkward time, with *Formidable* in the Red Sea, waiting to join ABC's flag, and *Illustrious* and *Eagle* both waiting to go south.

It was often difficult to decide which types of mine were being dropped. Twenty-four ships had passed over one mine before the twenty-fifth detonated it. Minesweepers were improvised to sweep magnetic mines, and mine-watching was organised. In parts where an unexploded and undetected mine would be particularly inconvenient, huge nets were stretched across — not, as popularly supposed, to catch the mines, but to show by the holes where a mine had dropped through.

By prodigious efforts the Canal reopened on 11 February, although *Formidable* did not reach Alexandria until 10 March, having been squeezed, literally with only feet to spare, past one especially awkward wreck which had sunk across the channel.

But the main danger was still from the air. By mid-February 1941, ABC was becoming increasingly concerned about the lack of RAF co-operation with the fleet. Longmore did his best, but he simply lacked the resources. When ABC showed him the text of a message he proposed to send to the Admiralty, Longmore did not object, knowing that it was not intended to be critical of him personally.

ABC spelled out the problems in stark terms: *Formidable*, when she arrived, would not be able to operate against the *Luftwaffe* with the same degree of immunity which *Illustrious* had enjoyed against the *Regia Aeronautica*. She would have to carry more fighters for her own protection, at the expense of reconnaissance aircraft and torpedo-bombers, which meant that her striking force would be reduced.

Many more aircraft were needed, in Malta, in Crete, Cyrenaica and the Epirus, to reinforce the long-range reconnaissance aircraft already working from Malta and Greece and the Swordfish from the aircraft carrier, strike at enemy shipping and shore targets and give fighter protection to the convoys to Malta and the Aegean. Above all, ABC concluded, what was particularly needed was an organisation similar to Coastal Command with aircraft equipped and trained to work over the sea.

On 4 March, ABC was created a Knight Grand Cross of the Most Honourable Order of the Bath. 'This was highly gratifying,' he said, 'as showing that the work of the Mediterranean Fleet was appreciated; but my remark on hearing of this honour — "I would sooner have had three squadrons of Hurricanes" — came from the bottom of my heart. I was thinking of the way our little ships were being pounded on the supply route along the Libyan coast.'

ABC and Pound took every chance to send letters care of officers flying home or out to the Mediterranean. On 11 March 1941, ABC told Pound of the 'pounding' off the Libyan coast and stressed his lack of aircraft:

> There seems to be some bad misunderstanding about the state of our Air Force out here. I feel the Chiefs of Staff are badly misinformed about the number of fighter squadrons available. Longmore is absolutely stretched to the limit, and we seem to have far fewer than is supposed at home. We are getting sat on by the Germans in Cyrenaica. The figures there are over two hundred German and Italian fighters against thirty of our own. It seems to me that if the fighter situation is not taken in hand drastically and speedily we are heading straight for trouble…

Malta was again being heavily bombed. The windows of Admiralty House were blown out. 'Well I don't suppose I shall ever occupy it again,' ABC told Doodles. To Pound, he painted a much grimmer picture:

> Malta is in a very bad state… I have just seen the Air Vice-Marshal, who is here to report. He tells me that the Germans are right on top of them. He has only eight serviceable Hurricanes left, and the German fighters are coming over in droves and machine-gunning people in the streets of St Paul's Bay and other outlying villages. He ought to have two full squadrons and at once. I am really seriously concerned about Malta. I am running a convoy there in about ten days' time; but with their defences in the present state I am quite expecting some of the ships to be damaged. The Grand Harbour and the creeks are also being mined whenever the

enemy cares to come. This is a gloomy picture; but someone is misinforming the Chiefs of Staff about the real state of affairs out here. We must have large numbers of fighters rushed out to us if we are to make any headway, and, indeed, they are needed to save what may be a serious set-back.

ABC also discussed changes in personnel. Rear-Admiral Renouf had been, in ABC's opinion, unfortunate in that four cruisers of his squadron had been damaged, although he personally had been rather lucky; twice, the bridge structure had been hit by a bomb which failed to explode. ABC had had his doubts about Renouf as early as October 1940, when he told Pound he was 'not *quite* happy about Renouf. He has too much imagination and always thinks the worst is going to happen at sea...' He had been in charge at Castelorizzo when 'he, poor man, cracked in the middle of it. I should have stepped in and straightened things out.' His relief was Rear-Admiral I.G. Glennie.

Lumley Lyster went home, to become Fifth Sea Lord and Chief of Naval Air Services. ABC was sorry to lose him, because he was 'unshaken by his experience in *Illustrious*. Boyd *was* a bit shaken but has bobbed up again splendidly.' Boyd was given command of the aircraft carriers, as an acting Rear-Admiral.

It was also time Willis was relieved. 'Towards the end of February [1941], I was beginning to feel exhausted, mentally and physically, and felt keenly I wasn't pulling my weight,' Willis said. 'Three years on the Station and two as the Chief of Staff, I had run out of ideas, and felt ABC ought to have a fresh mind.'

ABC felt his going as a great personal loss, 'but I could well see that for his own sake he must have a rest'. When Willis left in April, ABC wrote:

My dear Com, I am as you know very bad at expressing myself verbally and so have not been able to tell you how grateful I am and how much I owe to you for all your help, wise guidance and *forbearance* in the last nearly two years.

I am glad you are going because it is time you were on your own doing valuable work for the country and I know you will if they only give you a chance. I shall miss you very badly and there will be a gap in our family circle which no one can fill.

I have the feeling I shall not be long after you, I don't feel I can let the sailors down by consenting to this B (in more ways than one) business.

Goodbye old boy and God bless you.

Yours affectionately, Andrew Cunningham

Willis' relief was Captain John H. Edelsten, whom ABC had marked as a very fine officer as Deputy Director of Plans during his own short sojourn in the Admiralty.

Meanwhile, the Italian Army was no more successful in Greece than it had been in North Africa, making the arrival of the *Wehrmacht* all the more likely. On 11 February 1941, Wavell received a new directive from the Chiefs of Staff: no serious advance to be made beyond Benghazi; Cyrenaica to be held with the minimum force; all possible land and air forces to be sent to Greece; and preparations to be progressed for an attack upon the Dodecanese, which was of such importance that it was to be undertaken at once.

Of this Dodecanese attack, ABC thought that 'the authorities at home were living in a land of optimistic dreams'. Nobody was keener to attack the Dodecanese than ABC but his fleet was already stretched to its utter limits and he simply could not take on yet another commitment.

On 19 February ABC attended a conference with Anthony Eden, General Dill, the Chief of the Imperial General Staff, Wavell and Longmore in Cairo, at which he said that the forces available for Greece could be safely transported there. He thought the decision to support Greece was right, but he had his doubts about the outcome. (Significantly, when the decision to send troops to Greece was finally taken, ABC and his staff started at once to think of how they would bring the troops back.)

Wavell, Longmore, Dill, Eden, and Royer Dick, representing ABC, flew to Greece on 22 February. It was decided to send three infantry divisions and an armoured brigade, with RAF reinforcements, in an operation, codenamed LUSTRE, which began on 4 March 1941. On that day, ABC signalled the Admiralty that, although he was convinced that the right policy was being followed, he wanted to make it clear that a big risk was being taken, because of the weakness of the convoys and the ports of disembarkation against air attacks. He was going to run a convoy to Malta as soon as *Formidable* arrived, but, apart from that one operation, LUSTRE would take up the whole resources of his fleet for at least the next two months, and longer if the Germans managed to keep the Canal closed through mining.

ABC reported to the Admiralty on the 6th that the first convoy had sailed and that there would be a convoy every three days. Most of the troops were carried in warships, with the bulk of their equipment and stores in merchant ships. Almost every convoy was bombed by the *Regia Aeronautica*. The antiaircraft cruisers did their best and kept the bombers high and at bay but, like all Cunningham's ships, they were feeling the strain of months of hard and almost continuous action.

On 6 March ABC attended a conference in Cairo with Wavell, Longmore, Eden, Dill, General Pierre van Ryneveld, Chief of the South African General Staff, and General Smuts. It was ABC's first meeting with Jan Smuts. He was 'most impressed by his youthful energy [Smuts was then seventy years of age], his quick grasp of a situation and his calm wisdom in counsel'.

With Smuts, having joined him *en route*, was ABC's brother Alan, now a lieutenant-general, who had commanded the East Africa Force since 1 November 1940. Alan Cunningham was then one of the very few successful generals on the Allied side at that stage of the war. Supported by the South African Air Force, he had begun an advance from Kenya into Italian Somaliland early in 1941. By March, when the two brothers met in Cairo, his forces were engaged in pursuing the rapidly retreating Italian Army over some 1,000 miles, to reach Addis Ababa itself early in April.

LUSTRE continued until 24 April 1941 and, in spite of the risks, it was a success. Though there were some minor casualties among ships proceeding with the convoys but not going to Greece, or in ships returning empty, no soldier nor any equipment was lost during the transport to Greece of some 68,000 troops with their mechanised transport, full equipment and stores.

Pound had asked ABC to be frank with him and to say whenever he disagreed with anything. The two men corresponded as often and as fully as they could. But an edgy and somewhat acrimonious exchange of signals at this time shows that both men had a tendency to believe that the other did not fully appreciate his own difficulties.

On 16 March, when *Formidable* had 'squeezed through' the Suez Canal and ABC's staff were planning for a convoy to Malta, ABC sent a signal to the First Sea Lord:

> Secretary of State informs me that owing to risk to carrier the delivery of Hurricanes to Malta by aircraft carrier has been abandoned.

I hope you may be able to reconsider this, particularly as I wish to run a convoy on 23 March to Malta, risking the *Formidable* and to a greater extent the convoy, both during the approach and while unloading. This risk will be much accentuated if Malta's fighters have not been reinforced by then with Hurricanes.

The same day, ABC had what he called the 'somewhat tart reply' in a personal signal from Pound, telling ABC, 'I am not sure you fully appreciate events outside the Mediterranean, the Battle of the Atlantic is of supreme importance over all other commitments,' and ending: 'I trust you will disabuse Longmore that the reinforcement of Malta with Hurricanes will become a routine affair, which I suspect he hopes for. Although glad to use carriers as air transports in grave emergency I feel this is wrong when it can be avoided by looking ahead sufficiently.'

After such a broadside, ABC 'felt constrained' to reply in a personal and, he hoped, a 'mollifying' message to Pound. 'I feel I should be failing in my duty if I did not point out our difficulties in the Mediterranean with suggestions for meeting them, but at the same time I fully realise the difficulties you have in the Atlantic; and believe me I have no wish to add to your anxiety.'

Whether or not Pound was as mollified as he hoped, ABC went on with preparations for the next Malta convoy, of four store ships, which left Alexandria on 19 March. The battle fleet and *Formidable* sailed to escort it the next day The passage was uneventful, neither convoy nor covering force being attacked. The battle fleet turned back on 22 March and the convoy reached Malta the next day, where they were bombed: two of the merchant ships were hit, and *Bonaventure* and the destroyer *Griffin* were damaged by near-misses. The battle fleet returned to Alexandria on 24 March.

On 26 March, the Italian Navy carried out one of those daring attacks for which they were to become famous. Six fast one-man torpedo boats penetrated the rudimentary harbour boom at Suda Bay, and one of them severely damaged the cruiser *York*, the Mediterranean Fleet's only 8-inch gun cruiser, which had to be beached and eventually became a total loss.

Meanwhile, there had been indications from intelligence that the Italian Navy, under severe pressure from the Germans, was at last preparing to take action to interrupt the flow of British convoys to Greece. ABC had longed for another fleet engagement. His chance was at hand.

On 15 March 1941, Admiral Angelo Iachino, the Italian Commander-in-Chief Afloat, was summoned to Rome to discuss an immediate operation against the British in the eastern Mediterranean. The Italian plan, as it eventually evolved, was for a major fleet offensive against the British convoys to Greece. Cruisers and destroyers, accompanied by a battleship force, were to penetrate deep into the waters south of Crete to intercept the convoys. On 25 March, D-Day for the operation was fixed: 28 March.

The date was well chosen. On that day, there were to have been two Allied convoys at sea, AG.9 from Alexandria to the Piraeus, and GA.9 southbound from the Piraeus to Alexandria. The Italians knew that the British fleet had been to sea to escort a Malta convoy on 20 March, returning to Alexandria on the 24th, when it could be expected to stay in harbour at least for a few days. Thus on D-Day, attacks could be made on convoys escorted by forces very much inferior to the striking force the Italian Navy planned to use, and at times and places when the Italians expected that Allied forces at Suda Bay would be too disorganised (by the attack on *York*) and those at Alexandria too far away to be able to intervene.

It was an excellent plan, which might well have succeeded. But it was betrayed. A marked increase in enemy air reconnaissance to the south and west of Greece and Crete from mid-March, together with almost daily-attempts to reconnoitre Alexandria harbour, had already warned ABC that something was afoot. Of the possibilities, it seemed to him that the most likely was an attack upon the convoy routes, most probably south of Crete.

It was ULTRA (although that codename for Special Intelligence was not yet in general use in the Navy) which, in one of the earliest cryptanalytical successes for the Allies in the war at sea, was to reveal the enemy's true intentions.

At that time, March 1941, the Government Code and Cypher School (GC&CS) at Bletchley Park had still had little success in breaking into the German Navy's Enigma codes, and almost none at all against the Italian Navy's book cyphers, used for most of the important signal traffic. In fact, these codes were never read after their introduction in July 1940, except for very brief 'fitful gleams of light' gained from captured documents.

However, GC&CS had had some success against an Italian naval machine cypher, after the Italians had used a version of the Enigma coding machine somewhat carelessly during the Spanish Civil War. This gave a 'toe-hold' in that cypher, an improved version of which the Italians brought into use for the Italian Navy in 1940. GC&CS broke into this code in September 1940, but unfortunately it only carried one or two messages a day until the summer of 1941, when it was withdrawn from naval use and used solely for Italian Secret Service signal traffic. But its naval messages, though few, proved to be of vital importance to ABC's preparations in March 1941.

The first ULTRA signal giving notice of the enemy's intentions was sent by the Admiralty on 17 March to ABC, Vice-Admiral Malta, Flag Officer Force H and other addressees authorised to receive ULTRA signals, informing them that ten motorised SS ferries, forty *Landungsflossfähre* (landing ferries fitted with floats), one landing battalion and one *Trossengerät* (windlass apparatus) were to be made available from German sources in the central Mediterranean on 26 March. The next ULTRA, on 21 March, said that these ferries and landing troops were going to be used for supplying German air and military forces along the North African coast.

On 25 March, the Admiralty sent two ULTRA signals, the first derived from a *Luftwaffe* Enigma intercept: available heavy German fighters were being flown from North Africa to Palermo, a.m. on the 25th, for a special operation. The second was from an Italian Navy Enigma intercept: 'Rome has informed Rhodes that today 25 March is D-Day Minus 3.'

An ULTRA on 26 March, which began 'following presumably refers to my signal 1705/25', revealed that there was to be air reconnaissance of Alexandria and Suda Bay and traffic routes on D-2 and D-1, attacks on Cretan aerodromes on the night of D-1, and intensive air reconnaissance between Crete and Athens from dawn to noon on D-Day itself, with attacks on Cretan aerodromes at dawn on D-Day and further reconnaissance of traffic routes between Crete and Alexandria.

A second ULTRA signal of 26 March gave more detail about D-Day: intensive reconnaissance over an area bounded by the coast of Crete, the east coast of Greece, the Gulf of Athens, and the line Kea-Milo-Cape Sidero from dawn to noon, dawn reconnaissances of routes from Gavdo to Alexandria and Kaso to Alexandria, and a dawn attack on Cretan aerodromes.

Thus forewarned by ULTRA, ABC was able to make his preparations, and began to mobilise naval and air forces over the whole of the eastern Mediterranean. There was no longer any chance of the Italian Navy being able to descend with greatly superior force upon surprised and weakly escorted troop convoys.

ABC signalled his intentions to Pridham-Wippell, Vice-Admiral Land Forces (VALF), and to the Admiralty on the evening of 26 March. Force B, the 7th Cruiser Squadron, of *Orion* (wearing VALF's flag), *Ajax* and *Perth*, with *Gloucester*, and destroyers, was to complete with fuel and sail from the Piraeus, p.m. the next day, 27 March, and to rendezvous at 0630 on 28 March at a position thirty miles south of Gavdo (a rocky island twenty miles south of Crete) with Force C, the five destroyers *Nubian*, *Mohawk*, *Havock*, *Hotspur*, and *Greyhound*, who were to sail from Alexandria p.m. on the 27th. Two more destroyers, *Hereward* and *Vendetta*, would be ordered to Suda Bay; to join Pridham-Wippell on the 27th, while the destroyers *Juno*, *Jaguar* and *Defender* would be kept at immediate notice at the Piraeus. The submarine *Rover* was ordered to patrol off Suda Bay, *Triumph* south of Milo.

Convoy AG.9 was ordered to steam onwards to the north until after dusk on the 27th and then turn back to Alexandria. GA.9 was to be held in harbour until the situation became clearer. *Carlisle* was ordered to Suda Bay to reinforce the air defences. The Swordfish of 815 Squadron, then at Maleme in Crete, were to stand by to be airborne from dawn on the 27th. The RAF were to provide maximum air reconnaissance of the south Ionian Sea, the south-western Aegean, and the sea south of Crete from first light on the 28th. Thirty RAF bombers were to stand by in Greece.

Meanwhile, the Admiralty had concluded that the Italians intended only to make attacks on the convoys. However, it was possible, as signalled to ABC in an ULTRA of 27 March, that military forces were also to be employed, because some of the Enigma intercepts had been signed by a high official in the Italian War Office. There was also the information about the ferries and the landing force, which could still mean that a military operation was being planned. The only piece which would not fit into the general jigsaw was the concentration of heavy German fighters at Palermo.

ABC and his staff considered the general situation during the forenoon of 27 March. ABC signalled the Admiralty that 'our appreciation is much the same', and that he now intended that his battleships and the carrier *Formidable* would be south of Crete by dawn on Friday 28 March.

ABC also signalled to Pridham-Wippell: *Warspite*, *Valiant* and *Barham*, with *Formidable*, would now sail after dark that night, Thursday 27 March, and proceed westward south of Crete; the five Force C destroyers would now screen the battle fleet and would not now be joining him; AG.9 would be turned back only sufficiently to be to the eastward of the battle fleet at dawn, and would then resume its passage; if there were no further developments, Pridham-Wippell was to rendezvous with the Commander-in-Chief at a position [given] south of Crete at 5 p.m., Friday 28 March.

At 12.30 p.m. on the 27th, a Sunderland from Malta sighted three enemy cruisers and a destroyer some eighty miles east of the south-eastern corner of Sicily, steering south-eastward towards Crete, a course which suggested they were heading for the convoys to Greece.

ABC believed that if he could conceal the departure of his fleet for as long as possible he would encourage the enemy to come on. The plan was to make everything appear normal during the day and then slip away under cover of darkness. Staff officers left by air during the day so as to deceive Italian agents. *Warspite*'s awnings were still spread and ABC invited guests to dinner. But as soon as it was dark, the awnings were furled, the officers returned and the dinner was cancelled.

ABC had his own 'cover plan', to give the impression he was spending the night ashore (thus, to a certain extent, conflicting with *Warspite*'s dinner invitations). He was known as a keen golfer. So too was the Japanese consul in Alexandria, who was on the course most afternoons where, as ABC said, he was an 'unmistakeable, indeed a remarkable sight, short and squat, with a southern aspect of such vast and elephantine proportions when he bent over to putt that the Chief of Staff dubbed him the blunt end of the Axis'.

That afternoon ABC went ashore with his golf clubs and an ostentatiously large suitcase, obviously intending to play a round and then spend the night at the Residency. He played the round but, in the evening, quietly retrieved his suitcase and returned on board.

The fleet sailed at 7 p.m. that evening of 27 March, ABC flying his flag in *Warspite*, with *Valiant* and *Barham* (wearing Rawlings' flag in command of the 1st Battle Squadron) and the newly arrived *Formidable*, wearing Boyd's flag as Rear-Admiral, Aircraft Carriers, escorted by nine destroyers: *Jervis*, *Janus*, *Nubian*, *Mohawk*, *Stuart*, *Greyhound*, *Griffin*, *Hotspur* and *Havock*. 'What the Japanese consul thought and did when he saw the empty harbour the next morning', said ABC, 'was no affair of mine.'

ABC was not entirely convinced that the Italians were coming out. In spite of ULTRA (obliquely described in his memoirs as 'some unusual Italian wireless activity'), the increased and persistent Italian air reconnaissance over Alexandria in the previous few days and the Sunderland's sighting report, he bet Power ten shillings that they would see nothing of the enemy.

In fact, the Italians were out, and in strength. Iachino sailed from Naples at 9 p.m. on 26 March, flying his flag in the new, fast (30-knot) and powerful (nine 15-inch guns) 35,000-ton battleship *Vittorio Veneto*. He was joined on passage southward by the 10,000-ton, eight 8-inch gun cruisers *Trieste* (flag of Vice-Admiral Sansonetti), *Trento* and *Bolzano* and the 8,000-ton, ten 6-inch gun cruisers *Abruzzi* (flag of Vice-Admiral Legnani) and *Garibaldi*, all from Brindisi, and by three 10,000-ton, eight 8-inch gun cruisers *Zara* (flag of Vice-Admiral Cattaneo), *Fiume* and *Pola*, from Taranto. The Italian destroyers, thirteen in all, were some 1,600 tons, and armed with four, five and some even six 4.7-inch guns.

Iachino disposed his ships in three groups: Force Y (as it was called by the British when it was first sighted), of his flagship and four destroyers; Force X, of the three *Trieste* cruisers and three destroyers; and Force Z, of the three *Zara* and the two *Abruzzi* cruisers, with six destroyers.

At 12.25 on 27 March, *Trieste* signalled Iachino that she had been sighted by a Sunderland. Italian cryptanalysis was excellent at that stage of the war, and Iachino soon had the Sunderland's decyphered report. He was glad to see that only three cruisers and a destroyer had been sighted. Fortunately, mist had hidden the rest of the Italian fleet. Their course was given as 120°, so Iachino altered further to the south, to 150°, to suggest they were heading for Cyrenaica.

Later that afternoon, Iachino received a reconnaissance aircraft's report of three battleships, two aircraft carriers and some cruisers still in Alexandria. This was accurate (*Illustrious* was still in Alexandria, having not yet sailed for the United States). Iachino later complained that air reconnaissance was lacking or misleading but, certainly in the early stages, he did have adequate information which all tended to suggest that his enemy was still in harbour, that the Italian plan was about to be successful and that, if he could press his advantage with skill and determination, he was on the brink of a smashing victory.

At dawn on 28 March, Iachino's fleet was some sixty miles south of Crete, steering 130° in three groups, the *Trieste* cruisers ten miles ahead of *Vittorio Veneto*'s port bow, with the *Zara* and the *Abruzzi* cruisers some twenty miles to port of the *Trieste*. They had spent a quiet night, steaming east at 23 knots. There had been no enemy air activity and the fleet had not been sighted again.

The flagship catapulted her RO.43 reconnaissance seaplane at 6 a.m., to sweep an area of 100 miles by twenty miles ahead of the fleet, and then land at Leros (it was another of Iachino's complaints, that his aircraft could not be recovered but had to land ashore). Iachino had decided that, if nothing had been seen by 7 that morning, he would call off the operation and return to base.

But, at 6.43 a.m. the RO.43's observer reported four cruisers and four destroyers steering south-east at 18 knots, only fifty miles from *Vittorio Veneto*. Iachino's ships increased to 30 knots and steered to close.

Pridham-Wippell had reached the rendezvous as ordered at 6.30 a.m. At that time ABC in *Warspite*, with the rest of the battle fleet and *Formidable*, were some 150 miles to the south-eastward, steaming north-west at 20 knots. At 6.45 Pridham-Wippell turned to a course of 200° at 20 knots, steering away from what he judged to be the most likely direction of Italian reconnaissance. In fact, it was his ships which had already been sighted and reported by *Vittorio Veneto*'s R0.43.

Formidable had launched a reconnaissance flight at dawn. At 7.20, Albacore 5B reported four cruisers and four destroyers, steering 230°. At 7.39 a second Albacore, 5F, reported four cruisers and six destroyers, steering 220°. Both positions were within thirty miles of Pridham-Wippell, so he assumed that the aircraft had sighted his ships and reported them as the enemy by mistake. ABC and Boyd both reached the same conclusion.

Their mistake was dramatically exposed at 7.45 when one of *Orion*'s lookouts reported smoke astern, bearing 010°. A minute later the smoke was seen to be coming from a force of enemy ships, identified at 7.55 as three cruisers and three destroyers. They were, in fact, the *Trieste* cruisers and destroyers of Force X.

At 8.02 *Orion* made an enemy sighting report: three unknown vessels, distant eighteen miles, bearing 009°, steering east. This signal was intercepted by *Warspite* at 8.24. On the flag bridge, ten shillings changed hands.

Pridham-Wippell, correctly believing that the enemy were 8-inch gun cruisers which could outrange and outstrip his cruisers, hauled round to 140° and increased to 28 knots, hoping to draw the enemy toward ABC's battleships.

At 8.12 *Orion* made a second sighting report: three cruisers and an unknown number of destroyers, range thirteen miles, bearing 010°. At that moment, the *Trieste* cruisers opened fire, having sighted Pridham-Wippell's ships at 7.58 a.m. and reported them as 'evidently bound for Alexandria'.

The first Italian salvoes were short, but as the range closed because of the Italians' superior speed, so too did the shell splashes. The Italians appeared to concentrate upon the rearmost ship, *Gloucester*, who had been suffering from a main-engine defect the night before. But a few shells close alongside worked wonders, and *Gloucester* was able to keep her place in station, and to avoid salvoes by 'snaking the line' and steering for the latest splash.

By 8.29, when the range had come down to 23,500 yards, *Gloucester* opened fire and her Walrus was catapulted at 8.30, to spot the fall of shot. *Gloucester* fired three salvoes, all short, but they caused the enemy to turn away for a few minutes. By 8.37 the enemy was once more steering parallel to the British cruisers and opened fire again, but once more they were short. Their salvoes continued to be short until they suddenly broke off at 8.55, turned to port and withdrew to the north-westward. Sansonetti had allowed a good opportunity to go begging. His steps were heavier and faster than his opponent's but he had achieved nothing, not a single hit, and, unknown to him, he had been drawn some fifty miles nearer to the British battle fleet.

Meanwhile, *Formidable*'s Albacores were still reporting the enemy. At 8.04, 5B amended his earlier report to four cruisers and six destroyers and, a minute later, 5F reported three Italian battleships. Pridham-Wippell did not receive this report until almost an hour later, when he said it was 'manifestly incorrect' because he himself had been only seven miles from the position given at 8.05 and would have seen the battleships.

The Albacores had reported two groups of cruisers, and two there were. At 9.17, *Gloucester*'s Walrus sighted and reported Admiral Cattaneo's *Zara* group, by then also steering north-west, like the *Trieste* group. Unfortunately, this report got no further than *Gloucester*.

Pridham-Wippell was not aware for some time that the enemy was retiring. His force continued to steer south-east under cover of a smoke screen, until everybody suddenly noticed the silence. The enemy had stopped firing.

Pridham-Wippell had just received the 'manifestly incorrect' report of three Italian battleships. At 9.21 he turned his ships back to the west and at 9.36 he reported three enemy cruisers and three destroyers still in sight, steaming 320°, at 28 knots, range sixteen miles.

At 10.58 one of *Orion*'s look-outs sighted an unknown vessel, bearing 002°, range sixteen miles. The ship was identified a minute later as a battleship of the *Vittorio Veneto* Class. She opened fire at that same moment. Pridham-Wippell's ships altered course to the south and increased speed to 30 knots. Once again, *Gloucester* had been having main-engine trouble. Once again, the first salvoes had a dramatically encouraging effect and *Gloucester* kept up with no difficulty.

The urgent tone of Pridham-Wippell's signals — 'Make smoke by all available means', 'Turn together to 180 degrees', 'Proceed at your utmost speed' — when they were intercepted in *Warspite*, caused what Barnard called 'The usual chat among the lower orders of the staff: "Hallo, what's up?" "What on earth is VALF up to?" ABC took one look at the signals and said "Don't be so damned silly. He's sighted the enemy battle fleet, and if you'd ever done any reasonable time in destroyers, you'd know it without waiting for the amplifying report. Put the enemy battle fleet in at visibility distance to the northward of him." A few minutes later the confirming report arrived.'

Barnard was able to observe ABC at close quarters at these times when action might be imminent:

Whenever enemy forces were reported at sea in a position which gave us a possible chance of interception before they could get back home, ABC's burning desire to get at them and utterly destroy them would at once become evident to those

238

of the staff who knew the form. He would pace one side of the Admiral's bridge, always the side nearest the enemy; the speed of advance of the battleship was never fast enough for him and every second was grudged when a turn from the main line of advance was required for operating aircraft. This mood was known colloquially among the staff as the 'caged tiger act' and we adjusted our actions accordingly; there were many times and places when ABC would allow his junior staff officers to 'speak out of turn', but these occasions were not one of them. It was always, for all beholders, an inspiring example of single-minded concentration on the one object of getting to close grips with the enemy.

On this occasion, the speed of advance of the battle fleet was not bad, in spite of the *Warspite* having slight condenseritis and the *Barham*, as usual, having to cut corners on the zig-zag, or when the *Formidable* was operating aircraft. At intervals a smile could be seen on the face of the tiger... ABC was on the top of his form, and pulled the legs of the staff officers on duty.

ABC may have been on the top of his form but, possibly because he himself had not believed that the Italians would really come out, the advance of his battle fleet was comparatively leisurely, in the circumstances. At 7 a.m. on 28 March, twelve hours after leaving harbour, the fleet was 240 miles from Alexandria — an exact average of 20 knots. *Warspite* and *Valiant* had a top speed of 24 knots but the unmodernised *Barham* could barely make 23 knots.

Whilst leaving Alexandria, *Warspite* had passed too close to a mudbank, and mud had clogged her main condensers. Her speed was reduced to 20 knots, which appeared to satisfy ABC for that night. Certainly he did not urge *Warspite* to go any faster. As Power recalled, 'It must be remembered that we were in no particular hurry as we had not appreciated any threat which was not within the capacity of the cruisers to handle. It was a latish decision that the battle fleet should go to sea at all.'

But at 8.32 a.m. on the 28th, after *Orion*'s sighting report, ABC ordered the fleet to increase to 22 knots and detached *Valiant*, escorted by *Nubian* and *Mohawk*, to go ahead at utmost speed to join Pridham-Wippell. ABC thought Pridham-Wippell's position, under fire from Italian 8-inch gun cruisers, was 'not unduly alarming', but clearly he needed support.

There had been that puzzling report of Italian battleships. It would be reasonable for Italian cruisers to have a battle squadron in support. But Italian cruisers had been confused with battleships in the past. ABC ordered *Formidable* to range a striking force of torpedo-bombers, but made up his mind to hold it back until he had more information about the Italians' strength and position.

ABC looked to the Fleet Air Arm to slow down the enemy sufficiently for him to be able to catch up and apply the *coup de grâce* with his heavy guns. Until that happened, he did not wish to reveal the presence of his battle fleet or the carrier.

Meanwhile, ABC wanted *Warspite* also to go to Pridham-Wippell's assistance but was annoyed by her low speed. Her Commander (E) was sick on shore, but the Fleet Engineer Officer was on board. ABC sent for him and 'told him to do something about it'. Evidently a word from ABC had the same effect upon ships' main engines as a near-miss from a 15-inch Italian shell, for shortly afterwards ABC was gratified to see that *Valiant*, which had been coming up from astern, was no longer gaining.

However, when ABC heard at 9.18 a.m. that the enemy cruisers had broken off, he cancelled the order to *Valiant*, and reduced the battle fleet's speed to 22 knots, to allow *Barham* to regain station.

After Sansonetti's cruisers broke off at 8.55, the whole of Iachino's fleet turned to the north-west and by 9 a.m. were steering a course of 300°. Iachino himself was surprised that Pridham-Wippell had turned away to the southeast and 'considering the equality of force had refused to fight'. Iachino appeared to count the twenty-four 8-inch guns of Sansonetti's three cruisers as equivalent to the thirty-six 6-inch guns of Pridham-Wippell's four ships. He made no allowance for Sansonetti's advantage in speed, which allowed him to choose the range at which the action was fought and thus keep Pridham-Wippell out of range.

If Iachino was, as he claimed, surprised that Pridham-Wippell's cruisers did not stay to fight, then he or his staff might have been expected to look for some reason for their retreat. For instance, was it conceivable that the British cruisers might be falling back upon the British battle fleet?

Apparently, it was not. Iachino later said that he believed that the British battle fleet was still in Alexandria, because he had been given no reason to think otherwise from any aircraft sighting reports.

But, in fact, Iachino did have accurate and timely warning. Shortly after 9 a.m., he received a signal from Rhodes: 'At 0745 No. 1 aircraft of the Aegean strategic reconnaissance sighted one carrier two battleships nine cruisers fourteen destroyers in sector 3860/0 course 165 degrees 20 knots.' This was as good and as up-to-date a description of Cunningham's fleet's strength, position, course and speed as any fleet commander could possibly have wished for. But Iachino calculated that he himself had been in that area at that time and therefore the report must refer to his own ships. He replied to Rhodes to that effect, saying that a 'gross blunder' had been committed.

It could be said, with hindsight, that Iachino and his staff should at least have considered the possibility that the ships referred to might be the enemy. Ironically, it was Iachino himself who was to commit the grossest blunder of all that day, by persistently discounting reasonable evidence, from more than one source, that the British battle fleet was at sea.

But Iachino did know, from Sansonetti's reports, that he was being shadowed by Pridham-Wippell's ships. Although Iachino had not yet seen the British cruisers for himself, he estimated that they were some way to the south of *Vittorio Veneto*, but vulnerable to a trap.

At 10.30, Iachino ordered the flagship to reverse course and steer east. His object was to reach a position to the north of the British cruisers and on their starboard quarters. When he had achieved this, he could order Sansonetti also to reverse course and steer east. Pridham-Wippell's ships would then be caught advancing into a trap, with a 15-inch gun battleship to the north, and three 8-inch gun cruisers to the south of them.

It worked. Surprised, Pridham-Wippell's ships turned away and fled to the southward, with Sansonetti's cruisers on their starboard quarter and *Vittorio Veneto*, only twelve miles away on their port.

Vittorio Veneto concentrated upon *Orion* and her fire was dismayingly accurate. *Orion* suffered at least one near-miss which caused minor damage. Pridham-Wippell ordered his ships to make smoke. When the smoke screen took effect, only *Gloucester* remained visible to the enemy and *Vittorio Veneto* shifted target to her. *Gloucester* was still having trouble with her main engines but, as ABC said, 'The sight of an enemy battleship had somehow increased the *Gloucester*'s speed to 30 knots.'

At this moment, when Pridham-Wippell's ships were being pursued by bigger and faster opponents and in mortal peril, ABC was still some seventy miles to the eastward, too far away to intervene. Pridham-Wippell's cruisers would have been annihilated, but for the fortunate intervention of *Formidable*'s strike aircraft.

In spite of ABC's earlier intentions, the decision had been made not to hold back the strike. *Formidable* turned into wind at 9.56 and flew off her striking force of six Albacores of 826 Squadron, led by their CO, Lieutenant-Commander Gerald Saunt, with one Swordfish of 826 as action observer, and an escort of two Fulmars. ABC had signalled to Pridham-Wippell that the striking force was on its way, but in spite of Saunt's Albacores' attempts to identify themselves, they were vigorously taken under fire by every one of the cruisers as they flew past.

When the Albacores were sighted, Iachino was told they were Italian Fiat CR.42 fighters and was delighted. Here, at long last, was the air escort he had always begged and prayed for. But the six supposedly friendly aircraft split into two groups and, diving from 9,000 feet, attacked at 11.27. They dropped their six torpedoes and Saunt was convinced they had at least one hit. In fact, *Vittorio Veneto* was turning to evade the attacks and all six torpedoes narrowly missed, two running just ahead of *Vittorio Veneto*, and four astern.

However, the Albacore attack did have what ABC called the 'unfortunate effect' of making Iachino break off his pursuit of Pridham-Wippell who, still making good his escape to the south under cover of his own smoke screen, did not notice the air attack nor *Vittorio Veneto*'s turn away.

When the smoke eventually cleared and Pridham-Wippell could look again to the north, from where *Vittorio Veneto* had had him under an unpleasantly accurate straddling fire, and to the north-west, where Sansonetti had been closing rapidly, the horizon was miraculously clear from side to side. Astonishingly, the enemy had vanished. The whole Italian fleet was once again steering 300° at 28 knots, this time heading for home. *Vittorio Veneto* had fired ninety-four 15-inch shells in twenty-nine salvoes and, though they had straddled the target repeatedly and observers had made the usual claims of definite hits, in fact there had not been a single hit.

ABC was now only forty-five miles away to the east-south-east, but still much too far away to intervene. At 12.24 *Gloucester* sighted the forward destroyers in the British battleship screen. ABC was at last about to concentrate his forces. But the enemy was now in full flight for home. The only hope of catching him was another air strike.

10: MATAPAN — THE DUSK APPROACH

FROM PRIDHAM-WIPPELL'S signals, ABC judged that action must be imminent. *Warspite*'s plot showed that Pridham-Wippell was steering towards *Warspite*, hotly pursued by the enemy. By 12.00, ABC was waiting expectantly for the enemy to appear over the horizon at any moment. All ships were closed up at action stations. The battleships had their guns ready trained to starboard, to the northward. The destroyers were sent ahead, to form up by flotillas on their Captains (D). The relative closing speed of the two fleets was about 50 knots. The enemy was due to appear at about 12.40.

Previously, when the enemy battle fleet had been sighted in daylight, off Calabria in July, *Warspite* had delayed launching her spotting Swordfish and the aircraft had been caught still on the catapult when the first salvoes were fired. With that bitter memory in his mind, Barnard 'on this occasion begged to get spotting aircraft off in plenty of time, and off they went, just as an ominous silence was beginning to fall on the plot'. By 12.25 there had been no more news, either of Pridham-Wippell or the enemy.

Thus, when Pridham-Wippell's ships appeared at an unexpected angle on the battle fleet's port bow at about 12.30, he and ABC were both surprised. There was a considerable discrepancy in the calculated positions of the two forces. Pridham-Wippell was ten miles to the north-west of the position calculated by the flagship.

Pridham-Wippell was convinced he was in the right. As he stated in his report, his position had been confirmed by a fix at noon within one mile. (Much work was later required to reconcile the two differing track charts. Commander Fisher, Pridham-Wippell's Staff Officer (Operations), and *Orion*'s Navigating Officer were both quite certain theirs was right and Brownrigg's was wrong, but they had to distort theirs in deference to the Commander-in-Chief's seniority.)

Pridham-Wippell's signal, sent at 12.10, that he had lost touch with the enemy, was received in the flagship at about the same time as Pridham-Wippell himself was sighted. 'Where is the enemy?' ABC signalled. 'Sorry don't know; haven't seen them for some time,' was the reply. Once again, it was time for everybody to keep clear of the 'caged tiger'.

By 12.50 p.m. it was clear that the enemy battleship must have turned to the westward after the Albacore attack — exactly the outcome ABC had feared. 'So,' said Barnard, 'we were back again in the normally-to-be-expected Mediterranean situation of attempting to catch a much faster enemy with a good start on his way home. It was a bitter anti-climax, and no prudent staff officer approached the "caged tiger" without good cause, while signals were being made for the *Warspite* to reduce speed to enable *Barham* to catch up.'

At 1.05 Pridham-Wippell was ordered to proceed ahead of the battle fleet with his four cruisers and keep station on a bearing of 290 (the battle fleet's course) at maximum visual signalling distance.

For the second air strike, the wind was in the north-east, so that *Formidable*, which had been detached earlier that forenoon, with two destroyers to escort her, had to haul out of line to operate her aircraft. Acting independently, she could turn into the wind to fly her aircraft on and off without delaying the battle fleet who were then in full pursuit of the enemy.

At 12.22 *Formidable* began to fly off the strike, of three Albacores and two Swordfish of 829 Squadron, led by their CO Lieutenant-Commander Dalyell-Stead, with a fighter escort of two Fulmars. As soon as they had gone, Saunt's first strike landed on, with their news that at 11.45 the enemy battleship was steering west, with cruisers twenty miles to the south of her.

By this time, *Formidable* was some distance astern of the fleet and came under torpedo attack herself by two Savoia Marchetti S.79s. ABC watched anxiously as she manoeuvred to avoid the torpedoes. One torpedo hit now would put her *hors de combat*, with incalculable consequences in any coming action. He was very relieved to see her successfully avoiding both torpedoes and steering to rejoin his flag. He sent two more destroyers to her assistance and slowed to 21 knots, to allow her and *Barham* to catch up. The northeasterly wind dropped, and it became almost calm with a light westerly breeze, which meant that *Formidable* could now operate aircraft without leaving her place in the line.

Meanwhile, a Sunderland from Malta had reported another enemy force, of two *Cavour* Class battleships, one *Pola* and two *Zara* cruisers and five destroyers, steering 315° at 25 knots, thirty-five miles west of Gavdo Island. This raised the possibility that the aircraft had sighted *Vittorio Veneto* and Force Y. It was, in fact, Cattaneo's Force Z, of the *Zara* and *Abruzzi* groups and six destroyers. This was checked when the aircraft made a landfall and gave an accurate own position, so that at 1.42 p.m. ABC was able to signal the positions of all three enemy forces to his fleet.

Iachino, now steaming to the west, having seemingly given up the operation, was still receiving information about his opponent. 'At noon,' he said, 'I was brought two signals stating that the carrier *Formidable* had sailed from Alexandria and had flown off aircraft to attack us.' From this, Iachino deduced that the carrier must still be a long way off, and that the battleships were still in harbour.

At 2.25 p.m. Iachino received two more signals which seemed to confirm that there was no immediate danger. The first was from Rhodes, much delayed, that at 12.25 p.m. reconnaissance aircraft had reported one battleship, one carrier, six cruisers and five destroyers, in a position which Iachino's staff plotted as some eighty miles to the east. The second was from the Italian Naval High Command, based on Radio Direction Finding bearings, that at 1.15 enemy ships had been in a position some 170 miles to the south-east.

Of the two, Iachino was inclined to believe the D/F bearings. 'Positions fixed by the intersection of D/F bearings', he said, 'were generally more accurate than those given by aircraft as the latter were greatly influenced by meteorological factors.' In fact, positions reported by aircraft and those indicated by D/F were both liable to error, and Iachino should have allowed for both.

Throughout the day, Iachino rightly feared air more than surface attack. After 826 Squadron's attack on *Vittorio Veneto* had been beaten off, three Swordfish of 815 Squadron, flying from Maleme in Crete, attacked Sansonetti's *Trieste* cruisers just after noon. The cruisers dispersed and put up an intense anti-aircraft barrage. The three aircraft dropped their torpedoes from long range and scored no hits. Sansonetti thought, wrongly, that he saw one of the Swordfish shot down.

After the Swordfish had gone, three Blenheims of 84 Squadron RAF bombed *Vittorio Veneto* from high level at 2.20 p.m. They scored no hits but their bombs dropped very close alongside. Half an hour later, six Blenheims of 113 Squadron

RAF attacked *Vittorio Veneto* again. Between 3.10 and 5 p.m. Blenheims of 84, 113 and 211 Squadrons returned to score near-misses on *Zara* and *Garibaldi* in Cattaneo's force, and on *Trento* and *Bolzano* in Sansonetti's force.

No ship was hit but these attacks all served to aggravate Iachino's sense of grievance and anger that his ships were being repeatedly attacked by British bombers with no German or Italian fighters to defend them. 'I felt pretty well deceived by the lack of co-operation,' he complained. 'We continued to remain for the rest of the day without any fighter cover.'

Iachino had even greater cause for complaint at 3.19 p.m. when what he himself called the most important attack of the day developed on *Vittorio Veneto*, 'conducted this time with particular ability and bravery in aircraft which had evidently come from an aircraft carrier'.

The knowledge that there was an aircraft carrier within striking distance was a very unpleasant shock. At 3 p.m. Iachino had considered all the information available to him and had concluded that, in addition to the four *Orion* Class cruisers which had already been in action, there was another force of a battleship, an aircraft carrier, cruisers and destroyers at sea, but it was at least 170 miles away and, being much slower than his own force, had no chance of engaging.

But now, here was the carrier at least, much nearer than he had estimated. With hindsight, Iachino should have considered the possibility that the battleship might also be closer than he had been led to believe.

The attack by carrier aircraft was made simultaneously with one of the Blenheim bombing attacks, so, as Iachino said, 'Whilst everyone was busy with the high-level bombers, three torpedo aircraft approached without being sighted until very close.'

Lieutenant M. Haworth, the observer in an Albacore which had found *Vittorio Veneto* at 3 p.m. and continued to report her position, course and speed, watched Dalyell-Stead's aircraft making their attacks: 'The attack was delivered in two waves because the Albacores in the striking force climbed at higher speed than the Swordfish. Diving out of the sun, the leading sub-flight appeared to achieve a degree of surprise and the enemy made a turn of 180 degrees to avoid.'

After seeing *Vittorio Veneto* make her first sharp turn, Haworth saw

> an emission of smoke rings from the funnel, and a further 180 degrees turn to revert to the original retreating course, at which time it was observed that the formation was proceeding at such a speed that the destroyers made no noticeable wake. There can be no denying that enemy speed was very materially reduced.

Dalyell-Stead had managed to get down to 5,000 feet before his sub-flight was observed by one of the two screening destroyers ahead of the flagship. His three Albacores attacked from ahead and fired at *Vittorio Veneto*'s port side as she turned sharply to starboard, while the two Swordfish dived from 8,000 feet and attacked *Vittorio Veneto*'s starboard side.

Vittorio Veneto had been caught unawares and was temporarily overwhelmed by the variety of the attacks. While the Blenheims' bombs were exploding alongside, the two escorting Fulmars machine-gunned the surprised look-outs, guns' crews and men in exposed positions on *Vittorio Veneto*'s upper decks.

As the ship began to swing unbearably slowly to starboard, 'we all had our hearts in our mouths and our eyes fixed on the aircraft,' Iachino said. He himself could not forbear to admire the prodigious skill and courage of the attackers as he saw the torpedo drop from the leading Albacore, flown by Dalyell-Stead, at a range of only 1,000 yards. He could actually see the torpedo's track in the sea, racing towards his flagship's port side.

The leading Albacore crossed only a few yards ahead of *Vittorio Veneto*. As the aircraft turned, showing its underbelly, it caught the full fury of the battleship's anti-aircraft batteries. 'He was hit many times,' said Iachino, 'as we saw him roll a little and then dive suddenly across our bows, only a few dozen metres away and finally crash into the sea about a thousand metres to starboard. So died a brave pilot without the satisfaction of knowing that his attack had been successful.'

Dalyell-Stead and his crew were killed, but their torpedo hit *Vittorio Veneto* port side aft, about fifteen feet below the water-line, and just above the port outer shaft. In Iachino's words, 'the whole ship shuddered violently. *Vittorio Veneto* shook like a bar struck by a hammer, and rolled heavily.' The shaft was severed and the propeller sheared off. Thousands of tons of water flooded into compartments aft. At that very moment, a bomb from an RAF Blenheim scored a near-miss close by the stern which sent tons of discoloured water crashing onto the quarterdeck. From above, this looked like another certain hit.

By 3.30 p.m., *Vittorio Veneto* had stopped dead in the water. She listed some degrees to port and began to settle noticeably by the stern. Lieutenant A.S. Whitworth, 829's Senior Pilot, also saw Dalyell-Stead's attack. He reported that 'the column of water off the port quarter was seen by nearly all crews. I consider it a hit.' So too did Haworth, still observing and shadowing. At 3.58 p.m. he signalled: 'Enemy has made a large decrease in speed.'

The surviving aircraft from 829 returned to *Formidable*, after some four hours in the air. Dalyell-Stead and his crew were, of course, missing but it was thought still possible that their aircraft might have diverted ashore, or that they might have ditched and might still be picked up. His squadron claimed three possible hits on *Vittorio Veneto*.

When these claims were passed to ABC, he replied, 'Well done. Give him another nudge at dusk.' His battle fleet was now about sixty-five miles astern of *Vittorio Veneto*. Enemy reports were still coming in from shadowing aircraft and there were the reports from all the attacking aircraft — the Albacores and the Swordfish from *Formidable* and from Maleme; the RAF Blenheims from Greece and Alexandria — but they were all, not surprisingly conflicting.

Vittorio Veneto had, in fact, got under way again only a few minutes after the torpedo hit. In a short time she was making 16 knots and by 5 p.m., according to Iachino, she was doing 19 knots. But this was not immediately clear from *Warspite*'s plot. Many of the observers in *Formidable* were newly trained and lacked the experience necessary to spot and report ships at sea accurately. Even Haworth, a very experienced observer, said of the Italian fleet's dispositions that 'The close formation that they adopted defied the vocabulary of the Naval Aircraft Code.'

Thus, as Barnard said, 'the main impression of the afternoon chase was the obscurity of the situation owing to conflicting reports of the enemy squadrons... At the time the plot was most obscure, however, a fortunate mistake brought the *Warspite*'s spotting aircraft (catapulted about noon when Battle Fleet contact appeared imminent) back to the *Warspite* instead of going to Suda Bay.'

The 'mistake' was more fortunate than Barnard knew. The spotting aircraft had not been told to go to Suda Bay. It had had no instructions at all.

Of the two spotting aircraft launched from *Warspite* at about 12.15 pm., one had orders to go to Suda Bay and did so. The other, which had the Fleet Observer Officer Lieutenant-Commander A.S. Bolt on board, had no such orders. Bolt was a very experienced aviator who had already won the DSC for his work with a squadron of Wellingtons specially equipped to detect magnetic mines. He was very probably the only decorated officer in *Warspite*, apart from ABC himself, and thus he attracted ABC's approval.

Bolt assumed that he would be given his instructions while in the air, according to the tactical situation as it developed. The Captain of *Warspite* assumed that orders for the aircraft's return to base would be given by Edelsten, who was making his first trip as Chief of Staff-elect, in place of Willis.

The endurance of Bolt's aircraft was about 4½ hours. As time went by, Bolt continued to make routine reports of the fuel remaining, which 'evoked no response' from *Warspite*. At last, the point was reached when the aircraft had only fifteen minutes' fuel remaining, and Suda Bay was over an hour's flying time away. The aircraft either had to be recovered or destroyed.

According to Power, ABC was furious when he discovered no orders had been given to Bolt and 'the aircraft turned up at about 5 p.m. wanting to be recovered. ABC said one of the destroyers could pick up the crew, and abandon the aircraft. I pressed strongly for recovery. An experienced observer like Bolt could be invaluable later on. Recovery would be worth a few minutes lost. ABC agreed reluctantly.'

Bolt's pilot, Petty Officer Rice, landed his aircraft about two cables (400 yards) ahead of *Warspite* and 'in the grain of the fleet', which was at that time in hot pursuit of the enemy. Rice taxied at about 10 knots whilst *Warspite* overtook him with her starboard crane extended. Although they had never practised this form of recovery before, all went well: the sea was calm, the aircraft came smoothly under the crane hook, Bolt gave the signal 'hooked on', and the aircraft was rapidly hoisted clear of the water. 'The ship lost only one mile through the water during the recovery,' Bolt said, 'and I do not believe she was doing less than 18 knots at any moment during the operation.'

While his aircraft was being repositioned on the catapult and refuelled, Bolt went to 'make my peace on the Admiral's bridge'. As Powder said, 'Bolt was nonplussed, having arrived on the bridge after a five-hour flight, and had to get off again as soon as he was refuelled! But he cheerfully agreed and this was done.'

Pridham-Wippell had been ordered at 4.44 p.m. to press on at full speed and regain visual touch with the enemy. *Nubian* and *Mohawk* were stationed ahead of the battle fleet, to act as visual links between Pridham-Wippell and ABC.

The RAF Sunderland was still transmitting reports of Force Z (reported to include battleships) which it now said was in two groups, each making 30 knots, the battleships steering 310° and the cruisers about sixty miles to the south-east of them, steering 325°. However, the plot was unclear and it was possible that this force was actually Force X (Sansonetti's cruisers) which at 5.27 p.m. was seen to turn back and take station some five miles to the south of *Vittorio Veneto*.

The general situation was still somewhat obscure when ABC signalled his night intentions at 6.10 p.m.:

If cruisers gain touch with damaged battleship, 2nd and 14th DFs will be sent to attack. If she is not then destroyed, Battle fleet will follow in. If not located by cruisers, intend to work round to the north and then west and regain touch in the morning. *Mohawk* and *Nubian* join the 14th DF at dusk and destroyers form, 2nd DF and 14th DF, 45 degrees, one mile on either bow. 10th DF ahead.

Bolt was catapulted in *Warspite*'s second Swordfish for the second time at 5.45 p.m., his task 'to clear up the situation caused by conflicting reports about the position, course, speed, composition and disposition of the enemy fleet'.

Bolt sighted *Vittorio Veneto* at 6.20 p.m. and eleven minutes later made the first of what Power called 'impeccably concise and accurate reports'. Even Iachino, who soon had decrypts of Bolt's signals, admired their accuracy. 'This aircraft's appreciation', he said, 'was singularly exact.'

Bolt passed his messages

> by W/T direct to Alexandria W/T station at a distance of some 400 miles. We had carried out a great deal of practice with this station during dawn anti-submarine patrols from Alexandria and it was very satisfying that Petty Officer Pace, my telegraphist-air gunner, was able to clear some dozen Operational Immediate messages in a matter of minutes. These signals repeated by Alexandria W/T to Malta and Gibraltar were received immediately in Whitehall W/T and the Admiralty had them nearly as soon as the Commander-in-Chief in *Warspite*.

In Barnard's words,

> Bolt proceeded to make a complete series of enemy reports and amplifying reports exactly according to the perfect observers' 'copy book' and using various signal book groups

which we had met in peace exercise, but which we had grown to believe were most unlikely to be used in war. It was a classic example of air reporting, and the many hours spent on observers' training in peace would have been worth it for this one hour alone.

But Bolt's messages also made it disappointingly clear that the enemy was still about fifty miles ahead of the battle fleet, and still making good between 12 and 15 knots, on a course of 300°. The British speed advantage was therefore not more than 10 knots and was much more likely to be only seven. At this rate, it would take more than four hours to bring the enemy down to gun range of twelve miles. The enemy would have to be slowed again by another torpedo attack, either by destroyers or aircraft.

At 6.55 p.m. Bolt reported: 'Enemy are concentrating. Total enemy force sighted up to time indicated consists of 1 battleship 6 cruisers 11 destroyers.' Iachino had had a signal from the Naval High Command at 4 p.m. reporting one battleship, four cruisers and twelve destroyers in a position some 170 miles to the south-south-east of him. He concluded that this single battleship, which would only make 20 knots, had no chance of catching him before nightfall and had indeed probably given up the chase already. Therefore, his main dangers were another air attack before dark, or a night attack by destroyers.

Iachino therefore concentrated his ships, as Bolt had noticed, in five columns, the damaged *Vittorio Veneto* in the centre column, with two destroyers ahead and two astern of her. There was a column of cruisers immediately on either side of her: *Zara*, *Fiume* and *Pola* to starboard, *Trieste*, *Trento* and *Bolzano* to port (*Abruzzi* and *Garibaldi*, with two destroyers, were ordered to return to Brindisi). There was also an outer column of destroyers on each flank. Any attacks would have to penetrate two columns of ships to reach *Vittorio Veneto*.

Later, Iachino described with some emotion his feelings as his ships took up their night formation.

> My heart was with those grand and lovely ships and with their captains, officers and crews whom I knew so well, and to whom I felt bound by so many memories of peace and war. As I watched these ships, which, from the simplicity and harmony of their lines, gave an impression of virile beauty and strength, many memories of the past crowded in on me, memories of times spent aboard them, and which were dear to my heart. Who would have imagined that I was seeing them for the last time?

Iachino could still see the aircraft astern of him, waiting for their chance to attack.

> They looked like giant vultures, flying slowly round their prey until a favourable moment should present itself to descend upon it. It was a truly sinister spectacle, and its mysterious fascination, combining menace with fear, drew our attention to them like a magnet.

Formidable began to fly off her dusk strike of six Albacores of 826 Squadron and two Swordfish of 829 Squadron at 5.30 p.m. Led by Saunt, they took departure ten minutes later. By 7.15, they were in position astern of the Italian fleet, where Iachino had spotted them, and where they were joined by two Swordfish of 815 Squadron from Maleme. At first, they thought the two Swordfish were Italian biplanes and spent some time avoiding them. All ten aircraft waited for the sun to set.

By 7.30 it was almost dark and the rearmost Italian destroyer *Alpino* reported aircraft flying in towards the fleet. Iachino had ordered all ships to make smoke and ships in the port and starboard columns to switch on their searchlights and shine them into the eyes of the pilots as they approached.

High above, Bolt saw

> the attack develop from a position about 5 miles astern of the Italian Fleet and regretted very much that we had to jettison our two 500-lb bombs before our previous recovery by the ship. The attack was most spectacular, the Italian Fleet pouring out vast quantities of coloured tracer from their close-range weapons.

'Most spectacular' was the understatement of the day. Every anti-aircraft gun in the rear of the Italian fleet opened fire on anything the gunners could see but, most frequently, put up an intentional 'blind barrage' into the night. The uproar quickly spread almost by contagion until every part of the Italian force was involved. The sky for miles around was lit by gun flashes, streams of vividly coloured tracer, and the glow of exploding shells. Dazzling searchlight beams trained wildly to and fro, lighting up the superstructures of ships and the dense banks of funnel smoke.

Saunt's observer, Lieutenant-Commander F.H.E. Hopkins, said that when

> we eventually went into attack from the dark side with the Italians silhouetted against the last glow of light in the west, we found that we had been spotted at long range and were met with an impassable barrage of fire. We were forced to withdraw, and split up and came in again individually from different angles. The barrage of fire put up by the Italians was immensely spectacular but not very effective.

The attacking aircraft searched for *Vittorio Veneto* through the glare of the lights and the dense smoke screens. Several observers reported a hit on one of the cruisers in the starboard column which had been attacked from its starboard side. The last of *Formidable*'s aircraft to attack, Albacore 5A piloted by Sub-Lieutenant C.P.C. Williams, approached through heavy fire and dropped its torpedo from very close range at 7.46, and scored a hit amidships, on the starboard side of the cruiser *Pola*. Three major compartments were flooded, all electrical power failed, and the main engines stopped. *Pola* hauled out of line and gradually lost all way. The rest of the Italian fleet carried on, unknowingly, at 19 knots.

Saunt reported that 'The results were difficult to assess in the light conditions prevailing but one hit on a cruiser was observed.' *Formidable* informed her aircraft that she could not recover them on board because she might be about to be involved in a surface action. Saunt and the rest of the strike returned to Maleme or to Suda Bay, or ran out of fuel and ditched in the sea at various points on the coast of Crete and were picked up. Bolt was relieved by an aircraft from *Formidable* at 7.50 and also went to Suda Bay, where he landed at 9.20 p.m. He and his crew had been airborne for more than eight hours. It had been a long day.

Pridham-Wippell had also seen the dramatic pyrotechnics of the attack, lighting up the horizon some ten miles to the west of him. His ships had been pressing on to the west at 30 knots to try and regain touch with the enemy. At 7.07 p.m., just after sunset, he ordered his cruisers to spread out on a search line of bearing of 020°, seven miles apart. His ships were still taking up their stations when at 7.15 he sighted two unknown vessels bearing 295°, ten miles. His sighting signal was intercepted in *Warspite* at 7.18.

With Bolt's stream of accurate reports, and Pridham-Wippell's latest sighting, and the knowledge that *Formidable*'s aircraft had probably scored torpedo hits, ABC had a much clearer idea of the situation. He had also reached the point at which, as he said, there

> came the difficult moment of deciding what to do. I was fairly well convinced that having got so far it would be foolish not to make every effort to complete the *Vittolio Veneto*'s destruction. Some of my staff argued that it would be unwise to charge blindly after the retreating enemy with our three heavy ships, and the *Formidable* also on our hands, to run the risk of ships being crippled, and to find ourselves within easy range of the enemy dive-bombers at daylight. I paid respectful attention to this opinion, and as the discussion happened to coincide with my time for dinner I told them I would have my evening meal and would see how I felt afterwards.

'Respectful attention' to their opinions was not how ABC's staff recalled it. Barnard remembers:

> The well-known steely blue look was in ABC's eye and the staff had no doubt that there was going to be a party Nevertheless, on paper the compact mass of the enemy fleet looked to the staff a pretty formidable proposition for any form of night attack. I think that ABC had probably made up his mind by about 8 p.m. to send the light forces into attack and to follow up with the battle fleet, but he nevertheless, on this occasion, went through the formality of asking the opinion of certain staff officers. Neither Power nor Brownrigg liked the idea much, and said so in their very different ways. I said I was keen to let the guns off, but the battleships hadn't had a night practice for months and there might well be a pot mess with star-shells and searchlights if we got into a confused night action. ABC took one look at his

supposed helpers and said 'You're a pack of yellow-livered skunks. I'll go and have my supper now and see after supper if my morale isn't higher than yours.'

Power's recollections differ from those of Barnard who, Power said,

> is particularly inaccurate. What with being slightly deaf and a notorious exaggerator to book make (*sic*) him a very suspect witness. Brownrigg suggested eight destroyers join Pridham-Wippell and Pridham-Wippell conduct the attack while we followed at a reasonable distance in support. I did not favour this because I did not trust Pridham-Wippell (though I couldn't say that) and did trust Mack (D.14) in any situation. I rather think ABC shared my views about Pridham-Wippell but also couldn't say so. I outlined all the difficulties facing us (disparity of numbers, lack of recent training, lack of flashless cordite) because I wanted to make sure that ABC, who was in an exalted frame of mind, would weigh all the factors properly. I ended 'but I think we should have a crack at them'.

Expecting action at any time, Pridham-Wippell decided to concentrate his cruisers again and reformed them in line ahead. At 7.30 p.m. his ships saw the flashes of guns, the tracers and the searchlights in what Fisher called 'a brilliant Brock's Benefit of tracer'. 'They must', said Pridham-Wippell in his report, 'have been very gallant men who went through it.'

After ABC's 'night intention' signal of 6.10 p.m., the four destroyers of the 14th Flotilla, led by Captain P.J. Mack, DSO, in *Jervis*, had taken up station a mile ahead and on the port bow of the battle fleet. Similarly, the 2nd Destroyer Flotilla, with five destroyers, led by Captain H.St.L. Nicholson, DSO, in *Ilex*, stationed themselves on the starboard bow. This left the four destroyers of the 10th Flotilla (classified by Barnard as 'the old, the halt, the maimed and the blind') to screen the battle fleet.

Meanwhile, Pridham-Wippell had reduced speed at 7.45 to 20 knots 'to reduce bow waves'. Five minutes later, searchlights and gunfire were seen again to the westward, but by now visibility had dropped to four miles, and there were no ships in sight. It seemed that the enemy had slipped away yet again.

At 8.14 p.m. *Orion* altered course to 310° and, a minute later, her radar got a contact of an unknown ship, about six miles ahead. Speed was reduced to 15 knots and the ranges and bearing of the unknown ship plotted. *Orion*'s radar was an early type of ASV [Anti-Surface Vessel] which, as Fisher said,

> you could use by pointing the ship at the target. The only person who could work it was the flag lieutenant. As we came up on the enemy he was in the ASV office calling out ranges and bearings to me in the plot, and I pretty soon bowled out that the nearest ship was lying stopped, and told the Admiral.

At the same time as *Orion*'s 'stopped ship' radar echo, a dark object low in the water was sighted by *Gloucester* on her port bow. But *Gloucester* did not report it, and it was not seen from *Orion*. Pridham-Wippell ordered speed reduced further to 15 knots while the mysterious radar echo was plotted over a period of eighteen minutes. It was seen that the vessel was large, bigger than any cruiser, either stopped or moving very slowly. *Ajax* also reported the same object by W/T.

By 8.33 p.m. *Orion* was within three-and-a-half miles of the vessel. Although it could still not be seen, Pridham-Wippell had decided it was the battleship because of her size. At 8.40 p.m. Pridham-Wippell reported 'Unknown ship 240° five miles apparently stopped' and gave his own position. He decided to lead his ships clear to the north of the contact and carry on with his search for the rest of the enemy. He reasoned that if this was the battleship then she was now 'fixed', and it was up to the destroyers to go in and administer the *coup de grâce*. If this contact were not the battleship, then it was even more necessary for him to press on and find her.

When ABC returned to the bridge after supper, his morale had been 'reasonably high', although, as the battle fleet settled down to a steady pursuit, he did wonder how his four remaining destroyers would cope with any enemy destroyer attacks. But otherwise, with the enemy now only an estimated thirty-three miles ahead, his own destroyers must have a good chance.

Ajax's signal was just the news ABC wanted. Using the enemy position exactly as given by *Ajax*, ABC released his dogs of war with an IMMEDIATE signal at 8.37 p.m. to Mack and Nicholson: 'Destroyer flotillas attack enemy battle fleet with torpedoes. Enemy course 295 degrees, speed 13 knots. Estimated bearing and distance of centre of enemy battle fleet from C-in-C 286° 33 miles at 2030.'

There had been one understandable error in Bolt's reports. He had underestimated the enemy's speed. Italian ships, with their fine lines, made less wake than British ships, and were going faster than he thought. *Vittorio Veneto*'s damage control had been excellent and Iachino's ships had been making not 15, but 19 knots since 7.45 p.m. Iachino was not thirty-three miles but actually fifty-seven miles ahead of ABC.

Iachino was reasonably satisfied with events. His flagship had been damaged, but the damage had been controlled, the ship had picked up speed and there was now a good chance of reaching Taranto safely. At about 8 p.m. he received a signal from Naval High Command: 'From D/F bearings, it is learnt that an enemy flagship at 1745 was transmitting to Alexandria in a position 40 miles by 240° from Cape Crio.' Plotted, this position put the enemy flagship some seventy-five miles astern of *Vittorio Veneto*.

Iachino had had no other information about a large enemy force during the course of that afternoon and evening and he concluded, not unreasonably, that this message referred to the cruiser force he had engaged earlier that day, or to destroyers pursuing him for a night torpedo attack.

The news that *Pola* had been torpedoed, and had come to a stop, therefore came as a most unpleasant shock. Cattaneo signalled: 'Request I may turn back to go to the help of the *Pola*.' Clearly Iachino could not leave *Pola* to her fate. At 8.18 p.m. he ordered Cattaneo to turn back with the remainder of the 1st Cruiser Squadron and the four *Alfieri* destroyers to assist *Pola*. But his signal crossed another from Cattaneo suggesting that only two destroyers should turn back.

At 8.35 Iachino received a signal from *Zara*, repeated from *Pola*: 'Hit by torpedo amidships. Three compartments, forward engine room, boilers 4-5 and 6-7 flooded. Request assistance and tow.' Iachino kept to his original decision, and confirmed it with a signal at 8.38 p.m., to become effective at 9 p.m.

Iachino was much criticised for this decision, on which the outcome of the battle was to turn. He had a cool reception in some quarters, when he returned to Rome. But he defended himself vigorously in his own account. With hindsight, as he says, it may be obvious that he was detaching *Zara* and *Fiume* and four destroyers to steam directly towards the British battle fleet, only about fifty miles to the south-east. But with the information available to him *at the time*, it seemed a perfectly sound decision. 'It never occurred to me', he said, 'that we were within a relatively short distance of the entire British force. I thought the British cruisers had decided to turn back leaving only two destroyers to deal with us.'

From the information he had of *Polo*'s predicament, it seemed to Iachino that difficult decisions would have to be made, on what kind of assistance to render, on whether or not to try and take her in tow, or sink her. These decisions should not be left to the junior commanding officer of a destroyer. An officer of Cattaneo's ability, seniority and experience was needed, to assess the situation on the spot.

Furthermore, as Iachino pointed out, he had reported his intentions to detach the 1st Cruiser Squadron to the Naval High Command, who had raised no objections at the time, even though the matter was eventually to be taken as high as *Il Duce*, Mussolini himself, for a decision.

At 9 p.m., *Zara* and *Fiume* turned back, with their four destroyers. Iachino himself with the rest of his force continued to the north-west, steering 3230 at 19 knots, heading for Cape Colonne.

This speed was higher, and the course more northerly, than the searching destroyers expected and threw them off the scent. Mack and his flotilla were steaming at 28 knots on a course of 300°. The situation on *Jervis*' plot at that time, according to Commander Walter Scott, her First Lieutenant, showed

the battleship many miles ahead steaming at about 12 knots to the north-westward, flanked by two cruisers about five cables on each beam, and two destroyers a further five cables away on each side. Captain Mack's intention was to work round ahead and then, dividing his force into two divisions, to come down on opposite courses, each division to pass between the battleship and the cruisers, one division passing at a range of 500 yards on each side. Thereby it was hoped that the enemy might be thrown into confusion and might fire on its own side. It was a bold plan, and in keeping with the Commander-in-Chief's known views that the nearer you got to the enemy, the better.

Jervis had not intercepted *Orion*'s 8.40 p.m. report of an 'Unknown ship, apparently stopped' and the destroyers continued to steer 300°, a course which took them towards Pridham-Wippell. Those on *Orion*'s bridge realised that the destroyers were converging. Fisher said:

> 'That stopped ship may be the battleship. Wonder whether we ought to go in and see? But Philip Mack and his destroyers will be going in to attack just about now and there could well be an all-British battle. The destroyers are better fitted for this sort of night attack than we are. We'd better leave them a clear field.' With that we cleared out.

Pridham-Wippell therefore led his ships first to the north-east and then back to north-west and at 9.19 p.m. increased to 20 knots.

There then occurred one of the misunderstandings which afflicted both sides during the battle. *Ajax* had the most modern radar set of all the cruisers and had been making regular radar reports until a communications failure. Pridham-Wippell was unaware that *Ajax* was still transmitting radar reports and that he was not receiving them. But at 9.55 p.m. *Ajax* reported three unknown ships bearing between 190° and 252°, distant five miles of her own position.

Mack plotted these ships and saw that they were steering approximately his own course, and were about four miles ahead of his own 9.55 p.m. position. He therefore decided that *Ajax* was merely reporting his own flotilla. In fact, there was a discrepancy in the plotted positions of Pridham-Wippell's ships

266

and Mack's ships, so that *Ajax*'s 'three unknown ships' were not four miles ahead of Mack at 9.55 (at which time Pridham-Wippell and Mack actually passed close to each other), but about ten miles on Mack's port bow, to the south-westward. Pridham-Wippell also thought *Ajax* was reporting Mack's destroyers and at 10.02 p.m. altered course further north, to 340°, to keep clear of them. *Ajax*'s 'unknowns' were, of course, Cattaneo's ships coming back to *Pola*'s assistance.

At 9.11 p.m. Pridham-Wippell had reported *Ajax*'s radar contact of a stopped ship five miles to the west. This put the unknown ship only some twenty miles away from ABC. He ordered the battle fleet to alter course in succession to 280°, ships remaining in line ahead. As Barnard said, 'ABC turned the battle fleet together to investigate, handling the fleet from this moment until midnight in the same way that he would have handled a division of destroyers.'

ABC had decided that he could not see enough from the admiral's bridge and went up to *Warspite*'s 'monkey island', alongside the Flag Captain. As Barnard commented,

> *Warspite*'s upper bridge design resulted in considerable congestion, even for a private ship at night action. To add the Commander-in-Chief, chief of staff, staff officer operations, fleet signal officer and fleet gunnery officer was not easy. The three latter officers were accustomed to improvise, and had taken some precautions with alternative wandering leads and voicepipes so that they could conduct their respective businesses; but by no stretch of imagination could the result be called satisfactory, least of all for the ship's officers of the *Warspite*.

At 10.03 p.m. *Valiant*'s radar detected a stopped ship, eight to nine miles on the port bow, bearing 2240 (*Warspite* was not fitted with radar and ABC had to rely on *Valiant*'s reports). At

10.10 p.m. *Valiant* reported that the contact was a large ship, more than 600 feet in length, some six miles away on the port bow.

Three minutes later, ABC turned his battle fleet 40° to port to close the enemy, each ship steering 240° on a line of bearing of 280°. This was contrary to his staff's advice and took them by surprise. 'It was widely assumed on the bridge', said Brownrigg, 'that enemy destroyers would be in company with the large enemy ship, and the Commander-in-Chief was recommended a turn away: BLUE FOUR. But he said: "If that's the enemy we will turn towards and find out what sort they are and how soon we sink them: FOUR BLUE." It thus occurred that for the first time in a night action either in peace or war a battlefleet turned towards an unknown force of enemy ships.'

'Our hopes ran high,' said ABC. 'This might be the *Vittorio Veneto.*'

11: MATAPAN — THE NIGHT ACTION

THROUGHOUT THE ACTION, the Italians continued to intercept many of the signals passed between ABC and Pridham-Wippell. At 10.25 p.m. they decrypted a message from an unknown British ship: 'J — 300 — 6'. This was, in fact, from *Valiant*: 'Jig (unknown ship radar contact), bearing 300°, range six miles.' It was thought to be of no importance (although, if nothing else, its format suggested that at least one British ship had radar) and was not passed to Iachino at the time. One of Iachino's staff showed the signal to him days later.

But, in any case, it was already much too late to save Cattaneo and his ships. At 10.20 p.m. *Valiant* reported the stationary ship bearing 191°, 4½ miles. With the battle fleet steering 240°, this put the target broad on the port bow. All guns were trained accordingly to port. *Greyhound* and *Griffin*, screening on the port side, were ordered to take station to starboard to clear the range.

The target bearing continued to draw aft, and the guns trained aft to follow, as the battle fleet pressed on. By about 10.20 p.m., by Barnard's reckoning, the enemy was drawing abaft *Warspite*'s port beam, at about three miles' range, and it began to appear to Barnard on the bridge that ABC was 'going to pass this one by'. But — 'so occurred a glorious fluke'.

Power and Barnard both saw the turrets creeping round until they were abaft the port beam, and both felt 'a bit uncomfortable that "there might be more stuff ahead" especially since intercepted reports from VALF's force had indicated that some other ships might be dropping back'.

Using the authority delegated to him as Fleet Gunnery Officer, Barnard made a signal on the Gunnery Control wave length and, by what he called 'a most fortunate fluke', made a 'look-out bearing' to bring the turrets right ahead. It was only just in time.

At 10.23 p.m. *Stuart*, on the starboard bow of the battle fleet, gave the night alarm. Fine on her starboard bow, bearing 250°, were the shapes of darkened big ships, steaming across her bows so as to pass ahead of the battle fleet, from right to left, at a range of only about two miles. They were Cattaneo's two cruisers, *Zara* and *Fiume*, with the destroyer *Alfieri* leading them, and three more destroyers, *Gioberti*, *Carducci* and *Oriani*, in that order, bringing up the rear. They were all coming back to help the stricken *Pola*.

But before *Stuart*'s night alarm was received, the enemy had been seen from *Warspite*. ABC said:

> Rear-Admiral Willis was not out with us. Commodore Edelsten, the new Chief of Staff, had come to gain experience… At 10.25, when he was searching the horizon on the starboard bow with his glasses, he calmly reported that he saw two large cruisers with a smaller one ahead of them crossing the bows of the battle fleet from starboard to port.
>
> I looked through my glasses, and there they were. Commander Power, an ex-submarine officer, and an abnormal expert at recognising the silhouettes of enemy warships at a glance, pronounced them to be two 'Zara' Class 8-inch gun cruisers with a smaller cruiser ahead.
>
> Using short-range wireless the battle fleet was turned back into line ahead (course 280°).

This course was almost the reciprocal of the oncoming Italian cruisers who were steering 130°.

I shall never forget the next few minutes. In the dead silence, a silence that could almost be felt, one heard only the voices of the gun control personnel putting the guns on to the new target. One heard the orders repeated in the director tower behind and above the bridge. Looking forward, one saw the turrets swing and steady when the 15-inch guns pointed at the enemy cruisers. Never in the whole of my life have I experienced a more thrilling moment than when I heard a calm voice from the director tower — 'Director layer sees the target'; sure sign that the guns were ready and that his finger was itching on the trigger. The enemy was at a range of no more than 3,800 yards — point blank.

At 10.28 p.m. *Greyhound*, ahead of the battle fleet, switched on her searchlight and illuminated *Fiume*, the third ship, with the great grey silhouette of *Zara* clearly visible to the left. According to Barnard,

> *Warspite*'s director layer (who was already on, but waiting for a perfect point of aim) fired at once... The events of the next few seconds will not readily be forgotten by those who witnessed them. The *Greyhound*'s searchlight revealed the enemy caught completely by surprise with their turrets still fore and aft and men running along the upper deck. The *Warspite*'s first salvo was probably one of the most spectacular of the war, five out of six fifteen-inch shells hitting at intervals along the enemy's length below the upper deck, the right-hand hit apparently lifting most of Y turret-gunhouse over the side.

ABC continues:

> It must have been the Fleet Gunnery Officer, Commander Geoffrey Barnard, who gave the final order to open fire. One heard the 'ting-ting-ting' of the firing gongs. Then came the

great orange flash and the violent shudder as the six big guns bearing were fired simultaneously [Y turret would not bear]. At the very same instant the destroyer *Greyhound*, on the screen, switched her searchlight on to one of the enemy cruisers, showing her momentarily up as a silvery-blue shape in the darkness. Our searchlights shone out with the first salvo, and provided full illumination for what was a ghastly sight. Full in the beam I saw our six great projectiles flying through the air. Five out of the six hit a few feet below the level of the cruiser's upper deck and burst with splashes of brilliant flame. The Italians were quite unprepared. Their guns were trained fore and aft. They were helplessly shattered before they could put up any resistance. In the midst of all this there was one milder diversion. Captain Douglas Fisher, the captain of the *Warspite*, was a gunnery officer of note. When he saw the first salvo hit he was heard to say in a voice of wondering surprise: 'Good Lord! We've hit her!' [ABC ordered this remark to be recorded immediately after the action, in case, as Barnard said, 'he should require to pull the legs of Whale Island'.]

The *Valiant*, astern of us, had opened fire at the same time. She also had found her target, and when the *Warspite* shifted to the other cruiser I watched the *Valiant* pounding her ship to bits. Her rapidity of fire astonished me. Never would I have believed it possible with these heavy guns. The *Formidable* had hauled out of the line to starboard; but astern of the *Valiant* the *Barham* was also heavily engaged.

The plight of the Italian cruisers was indescribable. One saw whole turrets and masses of other heavy debris whirling through the air and splashing into the sea, and in a short time the ships themselves were nothing but glowing torches and on fire from stem to stern. The whole action lasted no more than a few minutes.

Power remembered what he called 'an astonishing spectacle. For a few moments there were two beautiful silver cruisers

272

steaming along looking as though they were going to a review — guns trained fore and aft. Three minutes later they were both shattered and burning wrecks.'

Warspite fired her first two salvoes at *Fiume*, the second cruiser in the line, leaving her listing heavily to starboard in a mass of brilliant orange fire; *Fiume* veered out of line and stopped, burning furiously, and sank some forty-five minutes later, at about 11.15 p.m.

Griffin had been caught in plain view by *Greyhound*'s searchlight whilst still attempting to take up her ordered position to port. She was sped on her way by a 6-inch salvo from *Warspite*, which straddled her, and by a characteristically brusque signal from the flagship: 'I only remember', said her Captain, Lieutenant-Commander John Lee-Barber, 'that *Griffin* found herself in the unenviable position of being smack in the line of fire when the "battle-boats" opened up, and received a very curt "Get out of the way, you b.f." from ABC.'

After *Warspite*'s first two salvoes, ABC leaned over the bridge rail and shouted: 'Good! Give the next bugger some of the same!' *Warspite* shifted target left to engage *Zara* at a range of about 3,000 yards. *Zara* was also under fire from *Valiant* who had fired her first broadside at *Fiume* and then, finding that her two after 'X' and 'Y' turrets would not bear, also shifted left and, as ABC had remarked, poured broadsides into *Zara* with great rapidity — five full 15-inch broadsides inside three minutes.

Barham, bringing up the rear of the battle fleet, had actually sighted two red rockets, fired by *Pola* to identify herself to the approaching *Zara* and *Fiume*. *Barham* had trained her guns on *Pola* but was ordered back into line. Just as she trained her guns forward, *Greyhound*'s searchlight illuminated the Italian ships. In its glare *Barham* saw the destroyer *Alfieri* leading the Italian line and opened fire at a range of 3,100 yards. Hits were seen along the length of the destroyer's hull whose hard silhouette dissolved, as Fiume's had done, into a bright orange glow. *Alfieri* was seen to turn away, burning from end to end, until she disappeared behind thick smoke.

Barham then turned her attentions to *Zara*, firing six 15-inch broadsides and seven 6-inch salvoes. *Zara* was now under fire from the main 15-inch and secondary 6-inch armament of all three battleships. No ship could stand such punishment for long. *Zara* suffered a direct hit on her forward 8-inch turret, which was blown bodily over the side, on her bridge structure and in her main machinery spaces, where there was a huge explosion. She was on fire from end to end and listing to port. She was losing way, but completed a turn to port, showing her starboard side to her enemies.

At 10.31 p.m., the three destroyers astern of *Fiume* turned to port, towards the battle fleet, and a minute later the three of them were seen to turn away under cover of smoke and at least one fired torpedoes. 'Handling the fleet as he would a division of destroyers,' as Barnard said, 'ABC turned the three battleships 90° to starboard together by fixed-light manoeuvring signal…'

Warspite's 6-inch batteries had shifted aim from the cruiser *Zara* to the Italian destroyers. *Havock* had a lucky escape. She was closely engaged with the enemy destroyers and, as she had not switched on her fighting lights, she was mistaken for an enemy. *Warspite* fired two 6-inch salvoes at *Havock*, one of which actually straddled her and seemed to have sunk her. ABC saw this 'and in my mind', he said, 'wrote her off as a loss'. However, *Havock* survived.

Having turned to the northward to avoid torpedoes, the battle fleet was now steering a course of 010°, with *Formidable*, who had earlier hauled out of line, some five miles ahead of them and on their starboard bow. Such were the risks inherent in night-fighting that *Formidable* had also just had a narrow escape.

Chief Yeoman of Signals Freestone, whose action station was on *Warspite*'s bridge, had been blown by the first blast of the guns over the top of the chart table and into the back of the bridge. Getting to his feet and pulling himself together, he looked out to starboard and saw *Warspite*'s searchlight illuminating what seemed to him to be the bridge and funnel of an Italian ship. Estimating the bearing he called out: 'Green 60, enemy cruiser.' ABC walked over to join Freestone, took one look and said: 'Don't be a bloody idiot! It's the *Formidable*!'

Those on *Formidable*'s bridge had been horrified to find themselves suddenly dazzled by the blinding beam of *Warspite*'s searchlight, sweeping the sea on the disengaged side, in case there were other enemy ships present. ABC heard *Warspite*'s 6-inch control officer of the starboard battery get his guns on to her, and was only just in time to stop him from opening fire. To *Formidable*'s intense relief, the searchlight beam swept away and left them in very welcome darkness.

The battleships ceased fire at 10.35 p.m. and reformed in line ahead, steering 010°. The action had lasted less than ten minutes. Six minutes after the emergency turn of 90° to starboard, to a course of 010° to avoid torpedoes, ABC turned the battle fleet back to a course of 280° in line ahead. At 10.38 p.m., ABC released his screening destroyers *Stuart*, *Havock*, *Greyhound* and *Griffin*, with orders to finish off the two enemy cruisers which could be seen, still afloat but on fire, bearing 150°, range four miles.

At 10.45 when the two cruisers were right astern, bearing 190°, starshell and 'heavy firing with tracer ammunition' were seen on a bearing of 230° and it lasted for ten minutes or a quarter of an hour. ABC put it down to the enemy firing upon each other, since none of his own ships were on that bearing. The firing went on for some time longer and ended at about 11 p.m. with a heavy explosion.

At 10.43 p.m. *Orion* and *Gloucester* both sighted a red pyrotechnic signal on their port bow, bearing 320°. Pridham-Wippell broadcast the General Alarm Bearing signal, formed his cruisers into line ahead and altered course to the northward at 10.55 p.m. *Hasty*, one of Mack's destroyers, also sighted and reported the red signal on a bearing of 010°. Mack also made the General Alarm Bearing signal, but did not turn aside to investigate. He carried on to the north-west, intent on getting in front of and then attacking *Vittorio Veneto*. It seems virtually certain now that the red signal was burned by Iachino trying to get in touch with Cattaneo. Thus Pridham-Wippell and Mack must both have been within at least signalling range of *Vittorio Veneto*.

ABC's handling of his fleet up to this point had been exemplary. But he now made what turned out to be a mistake, although he could hardly have known that at the time. When, at about 10.50 p.m., he received alarm signals from both Mack and Pridham-Wippell, now several miles to the north-west of the battle fleet, ABC naturally thought that some of his ships were in contact with the rest of the Italian fleet. Intending to give his destroyers a free hand in their 'mopping up' operations, he decided he would himself withdraw to the northeast and, to prevent his own ships engaging each other, he would signal to all forces not actually engaged to withdraw to the north-east also. This he did, at 11.12 p.m. *Formidable* had been ordered to rejoin the line at 11.10 p.m. At 11.30 p.m., the battle fleet altered course to 070°, speed 18 knots. ABC intended to return to the scene of the battle in the morning.

But that signal had a most unexpected effect. Pridham-Wippell's exact intentions after he sighted the red pyrotechnic signal remain somewhat unclear, even with the benefit of his report to ABC, in which he wrote,

> I kept on to the north-west so as not to be silhouetted against the star shell that were being used during the night action then in progress astern. During this time a red pyrotechnic signal was sighted to the north-west at what seemed a long range, though it was difficult to judge its distance. I was about to spread when your signal was received ordering all forces not actually engaged to withdraw to the north-east.

In short, Pridham-Wippell broke off the pursuit of *Vittorio Veneto*, altering course to 060° at 11.32 p.m. *Vittorio Veneto* was then thirty-five miles to the west-north-westward of Pridham-Wippell and thirty miles to the north-north-westward of Mack. This was, in fact, the closest any of ABC's ships had been to her all day.

Pridham-Wippell's withdrawal was not at all what ABC had intended, as he later wrote:

> The objects of what I now consider to have been an ill-considered signal were to give our destroyers who were mopping up a free hand to attack any sizeable ship they saw, and to facilitate the assembly of the fleet next morning. The message was qualified by an order to Captain Mack and his eight destroyers of the striking force, now some twenty miles ahead, not to withdraw until he had attacked. However it had the unfortunate effect of causing Vice-Admiral Pridham-Wippell to cease his efforts to gain touch with the *Vittorio Veneto*.

Pridham-Wippell was universally criticised by ABC's staff. Brownrigg had seen that in the general melee which was about to take place, the battleships would be in the way and were quite likely to be torpedoed by destroyers of either side.

> For that reason, I wrote out a signal saying 'all ships not engaged in sinking the enemy steer to the north-eastward'. The Commander-in-Chief agreed and we led the battle fleet round to the north-eastward. In the event this was a most unfortunate signal since it led Admiral Pridham-Wippell whose cruisers were shadowing the enemy battleship also to steer to the north-eastward and give up his shadowing task; this had never been envisaged by me or the Commander-in-Chief, since all peace-time training had stressed that in no circumstances should cruisers give up touch.

Power had actually advised against the 'steer north-east' signal:

> ABC was very cock-a-hoop and said 'Make a signal "All forces steer north-east".' I said at once 'No, Sir, some of them are still engaged.' Brownrigg also demurred. ABC was in no mood to be argued with and said, 'Well, change it to "All forces not engaged in sinking the enemy steer north-east."' Brownrigg was writing it down on a pad. I said, 'That won't do either.' ABC said furiously, 'Leave this to me will you. Go and get the *Formidable* back into the fold, blast you, at once too.' I then told the Chief of Staff that the C-in-C was making a muck of things (Edelsten, brand new, 1st trip with us). He said 'He must handle it in his own way — and it's high time you had some rest — you're dead on your feet.'

Power did not mince his words. It was, he said,

> most disappointing, but in fact — since nobody could have imagined VALF being so stupid — none of us could have

done anything in time. ABC afterwards admitted his withdrawal signal was ill judged. When I said that, bad signal or no, VALF ought to be court-martialled for losing contact ABC got cross (he didn't like Admirals being criticised) and told me I ought to be court-martialled for disrespect. I fancy he tore a pretty big strip off VALF in private.

When Power took Edelsten's advice and got some rest he 'slept until 0400. When I woke I found that the cruisers had broken off contact. *Vittorio Veneto* had escaped.'

It was true enough, although it was not the fault of the destroyers who, in ABC's words, 'had a wild night'. It was certainly a night of confusion when possible targets could be sighted on any bearing, when the silhouettes of ships, enemy or friendly, were sighted in the glow of starshell and the flashes of gunfire. There were head-on encounters, when ships approached each other at high speed, passing within feet. Captains had to decide in split seconds whether or not to open fire.

At 10.40 p.m., *Griffin* and *Greyhound* steered to the south-west to pursue the escaping enemy destroyers. They sighted them and opened fire and thought they had hits, but the enemy turned to the southward and disappeared behind thick smoke at 11.20 p.m.

Meanwhile, *Stuart* and *Havock* had sighted two ships, almost certainly *Zara* and *Fiume*, at 10.59 p.m. One was apparently stopped and on fire, while the other appeared to be circling her in a protective manner. *Stuart* fired all her eight torpedoes at both targets and reported a 'dim explosion' which she believed was a torpedo hit, very probably on *Zara*. *Stuart* opened fire on the stopped *Fiume* but seeing the other ship begin to move off, followed and opened fire on her. There was a very loud explosion and large fires which silhouetted the ship and confirmed that she was a *Zara* Class cruiser.

Stuart now found herself in the centre of a maelstrom of action. As she was firing at the cruiser, suddenly another ship appeared at high speed on the port bow. *Stuart* had to alter sharply to port to avoid colliding with her. The other ship, almost certainly the destroyer *Carducci*, passed only some 150 feet clear of *Stuart*'s starboard side. *Stuart* fired a couple of salvoes, at 11.08 p.m., to speed *Carducci* on her way and in the glare sighted the *Zara* cruiser again, some distance away to the south-west. Approaching the cruiser for the second time, *Stuart* saw yet another destroyer, *Alfieri*, which had been caught and crippled by *Valiant*'s fire earlier in the action. She was lying stopped, listing and burning. At 11.15 p.m., *Alfieri* was seen to capsize and sink.

Two minutes later, *Stuart* sighted the cruiser for the third time and, as she was firing at her, sighted a third enemy destroyer at about 1,000 yards range, steaming very fast on a parallel course. This was *Oriani*, which had been hit in her forward engine-room by a 6-inch shell from *Warspite* whilst making the torpedo attack on the battle fleet. However, her speed seemed unimpaired and she escaped to the north-west without any further damage. Finally, just before retiring to the north-east, *Stuart* made one last sweep to the west and north and at 11.25 p.m. saw a ship, very probably the destroyer *Gioberti*, with a small fire burning on board her. *Stuart* gave chase but the ship escaped, also at high speed.

Meanwhile, *Havock* had also seen *Alfieri* capsize and sink, and had also engaged *Carducci*, firing a salvo of four torpedoes at her at 11.15 p.m., one of which hit. At the same time, *Havock* noticed two burning cruisers, one of them a wreck, stopped and just about to blow up. The sea all around her was littered with boats and floating debris and the heads of survivors. This was clearly *Fiume* who sank at about 11.15 p.m.

Havock then closed *Carducci* and continued to engage her with gunfire. *Carducci* lost way, and sank lower in the water until her upper deck was awash. Fires could be seen burning along most of her length and she sank at about 11.30 p.m. Having dispatched *Carducci*, *Havock* continued on to the south and fired her remaining four torpedoes at the surviving cruiser, *Zara*, as she passed. But all the torpedoes missed.

Havock turned again to look for *Zara*, still somewhere over to the west, and at 11.45 p.m. fired starshell to illuminate the target. But there, in the pale light of the starshell, on about the same bearing but very much closer than *Havock* had expected, was yet another large ship, stopped and apparently unharmed.

It was, in fact, *Pola*, the original cause of the battle. She had been lying stopped since the torpedo hit from *Formidable*'s Albacore at 7.46 p.m. Unable to raise steam, without power and without lights, her turrets still trained fore and aft, *Pola* had been untouched and unnoticed since *Barham* had seen her two red lights at 10.25 p.m. and had been about to fire when ordered to alter course to rejoin the line.

From *Havock*'s bridge, *Pola* looked enormous. This could only be *Vittorio Veneto*. *Havock* shone her searchlight on *Pola*, opened fire and scored two hits, causing two fires, one on *Pola*'s bridge, the other aft. *Havock* withdrew to the north-east and at 00.20 a.m. made the sensational signal that she was in contact with a battleship of the *Littorio* Class, which was lying 'undamaged and stopped'.

Captain Mack was then some sixty miles to the west-north-west and steering, as he thought, to cross ahead of *Vittorio Veneto*'s probable track. But when he received *Havock*'s signal, at about half past midnight, Mack naturally assumed that he had badly overshot his target, and at once altered course to the east-south-east, going back the way he (and, as it happened, Iachino) had just come. But at 00.30 a.m. *Havock* transmitted a correction, substituting '8-inch cruiser' for 'battleship', giving her own position and saying that she was returning to shadow the cruiser.

Mack had received the first, incorrect signal promptly but, by some Murphy's Law of naval battles, did not get the correction until 1.34 a.m., by which time he and his eight destroyers had been steaming at full speed to the east — away from Iachino — for over an hour. Mack decided that he had now lost too much ground on the Italian fleet ever to regain it — at least before dawn — and he would therefore stand on to the east.

Mack and his destroyers reached the scene of the battle fleet action just after 2 a.m. Everywhere, there were boats, rafts, floating debris and swimmers. There was a bright glow on the eastern horizon, and the destroyers headed for it. As they neared the source of the glow, they could see that it was one of the Italian cruisers, with fires burning on her upper deck. She was still afloat but had in fact been abandoned.

Mack did not want a torpedo 'free-for-all', with everybody firing and endangering each other as much as the enemy. He signalled that only *Jervis* was to fire torpedoes, and ordered the destroyers astern of him to pick up survivors. *Jervis* closed the cruiser, which turned out to be *Zara*, and fired five torpedoes, three of which appeared to hit. There was another tremendous explosion, and a towering column of flame and smoke. A moving mass of fire spread across the surface of the sea for a distance of several hundred yards in each direction. The waiting rescuers in Mack's destroyers could see the boats, life-rafts, baulks of wreckage, packed masses of debris, and the heads of swimming men, all clearly outlined in the flames.

Zara finally sank at about 2.40 a.m. Hugh Hodgkinson, in *Hotspur*, saw her go:

> She was at her most awe-inspiring as we steamed past. The flames seemed to make her gigantic. She was turning over gradually so that she showed us her whole deck. One could see the carnage the battle fleet had inflicted. One turret just was not there, and the others were pointing heedlessly fore and aft. The bridge was enveloped in mountainous flames and above hung a pillar of smoke with its underpart aglow from the light below. Like some fabulous animal breathing fire, she slowly rolled over and sank.

Mack's destroyers steamed at dead slow speed through her remains for some little time, picking up survivors with scrambling nets.

At about 2.50 a.m. Mack saw recognition signals to the eastward. His destroyers stopped the rescue work, to steam some two miles to the east. There they found *Pola*; *Havock* was in close attendance, with *Griffin* and *Greyhound*, who had hurried to the scene in response to *Havock*'s signal and reached it at about 1.40 a.m., Lee-Barber in *Griffin* remarking that until then their movements 'were unfortunately very dull as we saw nothing until we came upon the *Pola*, stopped and longing to surrender'.

Of all the events of that eventful night, *Pola* was perhaps the most astonishing. As Hodgkinson said, 'This was getting too fantastic. They made no effort to fight, but just lay there. The *Jervis* put a searchlight on her and saw a large number of men still on board...'

At 3.11 a.m., Mack signalled to ABC and Pridham-Wippell: 'Have sunk *Zara*. Am about to sink *Pola*. Large amounts of survivors which I shall be unable to pick up.'

Mack had been as surprised as anybody to see *Pola*, as Commander Walter Scott, *Jervis'* First Lieutenant, said:

Just as the blast of the *Zara* explosions subsided, the flotilla gunnery officer remarked to Captain (D) [Mack] 'Don't look behind you, sir — but there's another whopper.' All eyes turned to the port quarter and another cruiser (the *Pola*) was seen. She appeared to be undamaged, and lay wallowing in a slight swell. After circling round, Captain Mack suddenly said 'I am going alongside — tell the first lieutenant to fall out the guns' crews, except the pom-pom, and prepare wires and fenders starboard side.' I received this order whilst aft, and sent for the chief bosun's mate who, emerging from the director, received the orders with incredulity, but quickly got things organised. 'A' gun's crew, scenting fun, armed themselves with cutlasses kept for such an occasion in the fo'c'sle locker, and prepared to capture by boarding.

A perfect approach, and over went a heaving line thrown by the captain of the fo'c'sle and accompanied by the cry 'Take this, you buggers.' Take it they did, and our wires were hauled in with alacrity and the ship secured alongside [at 3.25 a.m.]. Uttering blood-curdling cries, 'A' gun's crew swarmed on board the *Pola*. Only 257 of a ship's company of 1,000 remained, and they were huddled, cowed, on the fo'c'sle...

The 257 Italian ratings filed on board in an orderly fashion over a brow hastily put out, and were followed by the commander and captain of the *Pola* [Officially, 22 officers and 266 ratings were taken off *Pola*]. Meanwhile *Jervis's* gunner's party had crossed the other way with a few tools, to remove small arms and, in particular, 20mm Breda guns, with which we were ill-supplied. The task proved beyond them in the limited time, but they came back with a story of chaos on board. The officers' cabins had been looted by the ship's company and empty Chianti bottles lay everywhere. Verification of this came when a number of the prisoners showed unmistakeable signs of inebriation.

284

Jervis slipped from *Pola* at 3.40 a.m. Mack toyed with the idea of towing his prize 500 miles back to Alexandria but dismissed it as being impracticable because of the certainty of air attack the following day.

Meanwhile, the other destroyers were almost queueing up to administer the *coup de grâce*. *Havock*, with no torpedoes left, had already signalled at 3.14 a.m. to Captain Nicholson in *Ilex*, asking permission to 'board or blowoff her stern with depth-charges'. Nicholson merely told her to 'Get clear'. *Jervis* fired one torpedo at *Pola* which hit but had no visible effect. Mack then told *Nubian* to fire a torpedo into *Pola*. She did so, and followed with a second to make sure. *Pola* blew up and sank at 4.03 a.m.

Mack then formed up his destroyers and departed at 20 knots, course 055°, to head for the signalled rendezvous position with ABC the next morning. ABC had asked for some details about the number of prisoners and wounded on board. 'Six cot cases,' Mack replied, 'fifty slightly injured; one senior officer has piles.' To which ABC replied: 'I am not surprised.'

Of Cattaneo's splendid 1st Cruiser Division, and the 9th Destroyer Flotilla, only *Gioberti* and *Oriani* had survived. *Zara*, *Fiume*, *Pola*, *Carducci* and *Aljieri* had all been sunk, with the loss of 2,400 Italian officers and ratings, including Cattaneo himself.

ABC was quite sure that at least one of his own destroyers had been sunk by *Warspite* the night before. He suspected that it was *Hasty* (instead of *Havock*) who had been straddled and when she appeared in the morning he signalled: 'You got a couple of salvoes from *Warspite* which should "larn" you to put your fighting lights on.' *Hasty* replied: 'I think I am being confused with another destroyer. I was in company with D.2 all night and no salvo fell near me.'

By 7 a.m. everybody had rejoined. 'To our inexpressible relief,' ABC said, 'all twelve destroyers were present. My heart was glad again.' In fact, the fleet's only loss was one Albacore, with Dalyell-Stead, Lieutenant Cooke, his Observer, and PO Blenkhorn, his Telegraphist-Air-Gunner.

At 8 a.m. ABC led his fleet back to the scene of the action the night before. There was no mistaking the place. From some distance away, they could see and smell the thick scum of oil covering the sea. Boats and rafts, some burned and smashed, and clusters of floating debris, stretched as far as the eye could see. There were a great many floating corpses, and wounded men in the rafts, many of them at the end of their tether. 'The sailors were in pathetic little groups on the rafts,' said Hodgkinson. 'The whole thing gave one the same feeling as when, out shooting, you find you have done a left and right with a couple of thrushes by mistake.'

It was a fine spring morning, the sea was calm and the destroyers were able to go to work. They rescued more than 900 men in just over an hour, before a German aircraft appeared and the rescue had to stop. The fleet was well within range of German air bases. But, as Barnard said in a revealing comment, 'ABC showed once again the knightly and very humane heart under his iron exterior' by flying off an aircraft from *Formidable*, with a message giving the position of the two or three hundred remaining survivors, to be taken to Suda Bay for transmission to Malta, where it was broadcast in plain language to the Chief of the Italian Naval Staff. Two days later, the Italian hospital ship *Gradisca* picked up thirteen officers and 147 men.

A flotilla of Greek destroyers picked up a further 110 Italian survivors during the night of 29 March. This flotilla could have played a part in the battle but for a cyphering error which

286

unfortunately substituted the word 'oilers' for 'orders' in a signal which was received in *Warspite* as: 'Seven Greek destroyers proceeding at once through Corinth Canal to await oilers between Cephalonia and Zante.' Thus no orders were sent. But quite possibly this was for the best in the end; the presence of destroyers of another nationality might have piled even more confusion on an already confused night action.

The fleet had been sighted by a reconnaissance aircraft during the forenoon of 29 March and the expected air attack developed at about 3 p.m. in the afternoon. Twelve Junkers Ju.88 bombers were detected by radar, approaching the fleet. Their bombing, which was disconcertingly accurate, concentrated upon *Formidable*, who only escaped damage by some adroit evasive manoeuvring. As it was, she was near-missed four times, but her Fulmars shot down two of the attackers.

The fleet reached Alexandria that evening of 29 March, Passion Sunday, after one last excitement. 'When on the very last lap of the return journey,' said Barnard, 'just as we were approaching the Great Pass into Alexandria Harbour, a submarine contact was reported right ahead. As there was no sea room to manoeuvre, ABC ordered the destroyers to "clear the area ahead of the Fleet with depth charges" — a spectacular end to an eventful three days.'

ABC ordered a special Thanksgiving Service for the victory to be held on board all ships on 1 April. Meanwhile, the messages of congratulation flooded in, from His Majesty King George VI: 'My heartiest congratulations to all ranks and ratings under your command on your great victory.' From Churchill: 'The War Cabinet desire me to express to you our admiration of the brilliant victory gained in the Mediterranean by the conduct and proficiency of the officers and men in your

Fleet and of the Fleet Air Arm under your own skilful and audacious leadership.' Nor did Churchill forget the RAF: 'We also express our gratitude to the squadrons of the RAF who so intimately and effectively prepared, aided and confirmed the success of these memorable encounters.'

From the Admiralty:

> Their Lordships offer you and your officers and men their sincere congratulations on the success of your recent operations against the Italian Fleet. The conduct of all Forces and especially the determined and successful attacks made by the Fleet Air Arm, the high standard of night fighting by the Battle Fleet and the work of destroyer flotillas combined to deliver a crushing blow on the enemy and demonstrated unmistakeably the high state of fighting efficiency which the Mediterranean Fleet has attained under your determined and able leadership.

There was even a plaintive letter from Admiral 'Jock' Whitworth in *Hood*. 'How the devil do you get in touch with the blighters? Please let me into the secret. *Scharnhorst* and *Gneisenau* are the most elusive devils, so if you can give me a hint or two about how to catch them, I shall be your devoted slave for all time.'

Finally, a message which ABC probably appreciated most of all, congratulations from his *Britannia* term-mates, sent by Charles Little on behalf of those who passed out of *Britannia* in June 1898. Sending a copy of this to term-mates, 'Tiny' Little wrote, 'I am sure he will appreciate hearing from us all. I can so well remember his frequent Sunday afternoon fights in the "Brit" and bloody face, "meat phaz". It does not surprise us that his determination, natural gifts, and love of battle have ranked him with our greatest naval leaders.'

By contrast, Iachino had an understandably cool reception from Admiral Riccardi when he arrived in Rome. According to Iachino's own account, his ships had been quite unprepared for night action between big ships, did not keep their big guns manned, and consequently had their turrets still trained fore and aft when they were first sighted. As ABC said, the enemy 'had good ships, good guns and torpedoes, flashless ammunition, and much else; but even their newest ships lacked the radar which had served us so well, while in the art of night fighting in heavy ships they were no further advanced than we had been at Jutland twenty-five years before'.

But Mussolini, perhaps surprisingly, was much more understanding and sympathetic, and he showed a good grasp of Iachino's main points, that he had lacked proper air support throughout the three days, and that it was now essential that the fleet have an aircraft carrier. So impressed was Mussolini with this argument that he gave orders for work to be progressed on the Italian Navy's sole aircraft carrier, *Aquila* (although she was still only partly completed by the time of the Italian surrender in September 1943).

In his dispatch, ABC wrote, 'Five ships of the enemy fleet were sunk, burned or destroyed as per margin [10,000 ton cruisers: *ZARA, POLA, FIUME*. 1,500 ton destroyers, two, probably: — *GIOBERTI, MAESTRALE*]. Except for the loss of one aircraft in action, our fleet suffered no damage or casualties.'

Nevertheless, ABC concluded his report with reservations:

> The results of the action cannot be viewed with entire satisfaction, since the damaged VITTORIO VENETO was allowed to escape. The failure of the cruisers and destroyers to make contact with her during the night was unlucky and is much to be regretted. Nevertheless substantial results were

achieved in the destruction of the three ZARA Class cruisers. These fast well-armed and armoured ships had always been a source of anxiety as a threat to our own less well armed cruisers and I was well content to see them disposed of in this summary fashion. There is little doubt that the rough handling given the enemy on this occasion served us in good stead during the subsequent evacuations of Greece and Crete. Much of these later operations may be said to have been conducted under the cover of the Battle of Matapan.

After Matapan, as after Taranto, there was a controversy about awards. What Barnard called

a legend gained wide currency in the Mediterranean Fleet, which is probably entirely apocryphal… to the effect that 'ABC's' first list of recommendations for honours and awards for Matapan was microscopic and that it was queried by some unnamed high authority, who was alleged to have pointed out that the Home Fleet had occupied several columns of the *London Gazette* for sinking the *Bismarck* and 'was A.B.C. sure he hadn't forgotten anyone?'

To which the reply, according to the bar gossip in Alexandria, was supposed to have been 'Certainly not. No officer did other than his bare duty. If they had done any less I would have had them dismissed for incompetence or shot for negligence.' So perhaps there are some officers alive today, whom His Majesty the King was ultimately pleased to honour for this action, who keep to themselves the salutary thought that their Commander-in-Chief might very justifiably have had them shot for negligence if they had acted other than as they did. (Chief Yeoman Freestone was awarded the DSM, in spite of being called a 'bloody idiot' in the heat of battle.)

As Fleet Gunnery Officer, Barnard was in the difficult position of being the staff officer representing a branch of the Navy about which ABC always had his reservations. In his own most valuable commentary upon Matapan, Barnard said,

> 'A.B.C.' had a healthy respect for the gun as a weapon *if properly used*, and an almost boyish delight in the sound of guns going off in a good cause; but he must have suffered much from earnest gunnery officers in the course of his Service career. As a result anything savouring of long range gun actions, with 'black magic' about curvature of the earth, canted trunnions and all that, was an anathema to him.
>
> It was the custom in pre-war days for the main fleets to send in long-winded and somewhat technical annual reports of 'Progress in Naval Gunnery'. In 1940 and 1941, these reports were neglected owing to the pressure of current operations. When a lull occurred in the autumn of 1941, and hastening inquiries from the Admiralty became pressing, 'A.B.C.' gave verbal directions for a report to be written in the following sense:
>
> 'There has been *no* progress in gunnery in the Mediterranean in the years 1940 and 1941, but certain old lessons well known to Noah and the Armada have been relearned at much trouble and expense. The most notable lesson is that the right range for any ship of the Mediterranean Fleet, from a battleship to a submarine, to engage an enemy ship with gunfire is *point blank* (now adays 2,000 yards or less) *at which range even a gunnery officer cannot miss.*'

'To understand this,' said Barnard, 'is to understand a lot about Matapan.'

291

12: THE BOMBARDMENT OF TRIPOLI AND THE EVACUATION FROM GREECE

AFTER THE CHASTENING experience of Matapan, there was to be no interference with the LUSTRE convoys to Greece by the Italian Navy. However, in March and April, the convoys were still subjected to heavy air attack. On 31 March, *Bonaventure* was torpedoed and sunk whilst escorting a convoy by the Italian submarine *Ambra*.

On 3 April, *Eagle*'s Swordfish, flying from Port Sudan, attacked an Italian destroyer flotilla based at Massawa. They bombed and sank two ships and caused two more to beach themselves, where they were abandoned and finally destroyed by the destroyer *Kingston*. A fifth Italian destroyer turned back to Massawa on being sighted and scuttled herself in the harbour. The threat of surface attacks on Red Sea convoys, admittedly never great, was thus removed and ABC was glad to get back the three destroyers he had sent into the Red Sea.

Eagle left for home through the Suez Canal on 13 April 1941. She had been a very popular and successful ship — in ABC's own phrase 'finely-manned and commanded'. He sent her a graceful farewell signal, which gave her people great pleasure.

In North Africa there was now a new Axis army commander in the field — General Erwin Rommel — who lost no time in making his presence felt. The strength and vigour of his offensive, ably supported by the *Luftwaffe*, caught the British in the desert off balance. By mid-April Tobruk had been cut off and the enemy had advanced to Solium, on the Egyptian border. All the previous British gains in Cyrenaica had been lost and a withdrawal had become a full retreat.

ABC was now under strong and continuing pressure from Mr Churchill to take action to stop the Libyan convoys. On 14 April, Churchill ordered that the highest priority was to be given to operations against the enemy supply routes to Libya. In February and March 1941 over 200,000 tons of Axis shipping was sent from Italian ports to Libya. Between March and the middle of May, convoys for Tripoli were leaving Naples every three or four days, with individual ships sailing from Palermo and Trapani.

Special Intelligence, codenamed ULTRA later in 1941, was not as full or as timely as it was to become. The Italian naval codes, using the Enigma enciphering machine, were never read, except in fits and starts. There was as yet no information from the German Navy's Enigma in the Mediterranean. The main source was the *Luftwaffe* Enigma, which was being read but contained only occasional information about the Libyan convoys.

On 7 April, the Admiralty informed ABC in an ULTRA signal that 'Advanced elements of German 15th Armoured Division were embarking at Palermo on or after 9 April probably for Tripoli.' ABC sent Captain Mack with *Jervis*, *Nubian*, *Mohawk* and *Janus* of the 14th Destroyer Flotilla to Malta.

On 17 April, ABC had an ULTRA signal: 'A consignment of 400 tons of B4 and 250 tons of C3 aviation fuel is due to arrive Benghazi on or after 20/4.' On the 18th there was another ULTRA: 'Further 150 tons petrol and 500 tons bombs left Naples 16th April in two ships for Benghazi possibly calling at Tripoli en route.' Finally, on 21 April, the Admiralty signalled the demand, clearly inspired by Churchill: 'Was information received in time to intercept these ships and if so with what result? Reply when W/T silence permits.'

In fact, the signals had arrived too late but nevertheless action had been taken, of which Churchill and the Admiralty must surprisingly have been ignorant. Reconnaissance aircraft from Malta had sighted a convoy of five enemy ships, escorted by three destroyers, at about noon on 15 April, approaching Cape Bon and steering south, at about 9 knots, obviously bound for Tripoli.

Mack's ships sailed that evening and in what Mack called the 'Skirmish off Sfax', in the early hours of the 16th, sank three Italian destroyers (of which one was later salvaged), all five merchant vessels and 350 men, 300 vehicles and 3,500 tons of stores and ammunition intended for the 15th Panzer Division. But *Mohawk* was hit by two torpedoes and sank with the loss of two officers and thirty-nine ratings.

In spite of this brilliant coup, only twenty-one Axis ships were sunk in April and May 1941. This was an improvement on the meagre ten ships sunk in January, February and March, but not enough to cause the enemy serious damage.

Mr Churchill now called for much more dramatic action — nothing less than the use of a battleship to block the entrance to Tripoli harbour. Mr Churchill's proposals, and ABC's objections to them, provided one of the sharpest of all the exchanges between *Warspite* and Whitehall.

The Admiralty suggested a bombardment of Tripoli from the sea and offered the old battleship *Centurion*, now a wireless-controlled gunnery target ship at Scapa Flow, as a blockship. ABC and his staff were sceptical both about the value of a bombardment and the use of *Centurion*. As ABC said, signals passed to and fro, until finally on 15 April he received a long and what he called an 'extraordinary message' from the

Admiralty, 'apparently dictated by somebody who appeared to know little of Tripoli or to have any true realisation of our circumstances in the Mediterranean'. Briefly, ABC was told that 'drastic measures' were needed 'to stabilise the position in the Middle East', which would interrupt the Axis 'communications drastically and for a considerable time'. Therefore, it had been decided that 'an attempt must be made to carry out a combined blocking and bombardment, the latter being carried out by blocking ships at point blank range' as they approached Tripoli harbour. ABC was told that, after careful consideration, it had been decided that the battleship *Barham* and a 'C' Class cruiser (actually *Caledon*) should be used for this operation.

The more ABC and his staff studied these proposals, the less they liked them. Power, who never minced his words, called it 'a peculiarly stupid and dangerous operation which had been imposed on us from Home'. ABC expressed his misgivings in carefully worded signals to the Admiralty. It would, he said, be extremely difficult to manoeuvre *Barham* into the right place. She drew thirty-two feet of water, which made many of the channels too shallow for her. Even in the main channel, she would be unhandy with less than two feet under her keel. Some channels had been mined by our own aircraft. Even if *Barham* did make her approach successfully, and were then 'wedged' into position, and did block the harbour, the enemy could still unload ships over the reefs, using lighters. In fact, the enemy was already doing that.

These were practical objections. There were others. This was a measure which would show the enemy just how desperate the Allies must be in Cyrenaica. Even if successful, it would still mean the total loss of a first-class capital ship in fighting trim, giving Italian morale an 'inestimable fillip'. Normally, a blockship would be manned by a skeleton crew of volunteers, but in this case the need for secrecy precluded the possibility of calling for volunteers.

Barham and *Caledon* would have to make the approach at top speed, which would require the presence on board of all their engine-room personnel and, because they were to carry out bombardments, they would also need at least two thirds of their guns' crews. There could be no possibility of getting survivors away afterwards. Thus, ABC calculated, nearly 1,000 officers and men would be lost, all of them sent on an operation quite 'unaware of what they are in for'.

The response was another personal message from Pound:

> H.M. Government has given instructions that every possible step must be taken by the Navy to prevent supplies reaching Libya from Italy and by coastwise traffic even if this results in serious loss or damage to H.M. ships. Failure by the Navy to concentrate on prevention of such movements to the exclusion of everything not absolutely vital will be considered as having let side down… Every convoy which gets through [to Libya] must be considered a serious Naval Failure.

The phrasing of this message, and particularly its conclusion, stung ABC to reply that he was fully aware of the need to stop supplies reaching Libya but that it could not be considered to the exclusion of all other commitments. In fact, he said, 'No less than four operations are in train for next 24 hours, including two landings. We are not idle in Libya and nobody out here will say the Navy has let them down.'

After further exchanges of signals, a compromise was reached. Tripoli was to be bombarded by the battle fleet at close range (a plan which ABC had also previously opposed).

If a ship were damaged, an attempt would be made to run her in so that when she sank she blocked the harbour.

In the event, it all went much better than ABC had expected or had dared to hope. The main fleet sailed from Alexandria at 7 a.m. on 18 April. Some of ABC's staff had mixed feelings. Barnard, who had entered in his diary for 17 April 'An AWFUL DAY', wrote for the 18th, 'Went to sea. Thank Gawd. Starting a cold and feeling mouldy. Lofty and Tom both under weather. What a party but grand to be at sea.'

The 'party' was in two groups: the bombarding force of the three battleships, *Gloucester* and screening destroyers; and the carrier force of *Formidable*, with three cruisers and four destroyers, under Pridham-Wippell, who was already operating in the Aegean.

ABC and Pridham-Wippell met about halfway between Malta and Crete on the morning of 20 April, and the bombarding force steamed south at high speed to close Tripoli after dark. RAF Wellingtons and Fleet Air Arm Swordfish from Malta were to bomb Tripoli before the bombardment. *Formidable*'s aircraft would drop flares and spot the fall of shot during the bombardment.

To help navigation, the submarine *Truant* was stationed some four miles offshore, shining a light to seaward. The bombarding ships duly rounded her at 4.45 a.m. and opened fire at ranges between 14,000 and 11,000 yards at 5.02 a.m. They had been given specific targets, but in the clouds of dust and smoke left by the bombing spotting was not easy, and many corrections were passed to the wrong ships. The enemy appeared to be taken completely by surprise. Wild and sporadic fire from the shore batteries only began after about twenty minutes, when the bombarding ships turned back to the east for their second runs. The bombardment lasted forty-two minutes, during which 478 15-inch and 1,500 smaller shells — some 530 tons in all — were expended.

Results were disappointing. There was some damage to the port and the city, but many 15-inch shells failed to explode. Although the bombardment did have an effect upon civilian morale, Axis shipping was only held up for one day. More damage was done to Tripoli when an Italian merchant ship blew up in the harbour on 3 May.

To ABC's astonishment, the bombarding force got away scot free. Not a ship was hit, from shore or from the air. Perhaps, as he said in his signalled report, the *Luftwaffe* was preoccupied elsewhere. Communications between Tripoli and Italy could have been disrupted by the attack, or perhaps *Fliegerkorps* X did not react quickly enough to the situation. Or maybe the fleet was lucky.

ABC had been totally opposed to the bombardment of Tripoli from the outset, and was equally against another bombardment which seemed to be in the minds of the authorities at home. He expressed these views in a continuing exchange of thunderous signals between himself and Churchill, with Pound acting as a kind of go-between:

> I wish to make it quite clear that I remain strongly opposed to this policy of bombardment of Tripoli by Mediterranean Fleet. We have got away with it once, but only because the German Air Force were engaged elsewhere. Thus we achieved complete surprise. It has taken the whole Mediterranean Fleet five days to accomplish what a heavy flight squadron working from Egypt could probably carry out in a few hours. The fleet had also to run considerable and in my opinion unjustifiable risks in this operation, which has been at the expense of all other commitments, and at a time when these commitments were most pressing.

To me it appears that the Air Ministry are trying to lay their responsibilities on Navy's shoulders, and are not helping us out here on naval side of the war as they should.

On 23 April, the Admiralty touched ABC on the raw with more ideas as to how they thought enemy convoys to Tripoli should be attacked by day and by night. They suggested sending a battleship to Malta. The Admiralty had decided that it would be worth a battleship for the sake of disrupting the convoys.

This suggestion was perilously similar to the earlier proposal to use *Barham* to block Tripoli harbour. ABC, as he said, began 'to feel seriously annoyed. This constant advice, not to say interference, in how to run our own business from those who seemed to be unaware of the real facts of our situation did not help us at all. They were a mere source of worry.'

The key to a successful offensive against the enemy convoys to Libya, indeed the key to Malta and to the situation in the whole Middle East, was air power. In a signal of 26 April, ABC made this point as bluntly as he could:

If we consider that six or even sixteen destroyers can be certain of intercepting Libyan convoys without proper air support to enable them to work by day we should be blind to the facts. The situation is analogous to that in the English Channel, which has many advantages we have not, and where interception distances are much less. Despite this, enemy vessels seem to pass freely there. The great difficulty of intercepting these convoys is a fact that must be squarely faced, and I therefore feel it wrong to expect much from a few destroyers at Malta.

When Winston Churchill recollected in latter days these exchanges between the Admiralty and ABC, and the whole anxious debate over the blocking or bombarding Tripoli, he thought the story reflected 'credit upon both the high Admirals concerned... It may well be that the Admiralty, with my cordial agreement, forced their Commander-in-Chief to run an unnecessary risk; and the fact that no loss was sustained is not absolute proof that they were right.'

But, at the time, Churchill intervened in a way which brought no balm to ABC. It appeared to Churchill that 'We at home alone could measure the proportion of world events and final responsibility lay with us.' However, he felt he owed ABC some sort of explanation and what he described as a 'wider view of the war scene than was possible from Alexandria'. In a message to ABC of 24 April, the Prime Minister said:

> There can be no departure from the principle that it is the prime responsibility of the Mediterranean Fleet to sever all communication between Italy and Africa.
>
> About your air support: you should obtain accurate information, because no judgment can be formed without it. The Chief of the Air Staff tells me that the same weight of bombs as you fired into Tripoli in 42 minutes, viz., 530 tons, might have been dropped (a) by one Wellington squadron from Malta in 104 weeks, or (b) by one Stirling squadron from Egypt in about 30 weeks.

Churchill added that the

> main disposition of forces between the various theatres rests with the Defence Committee, over which I preside, and not with the Air Ministry, who execute our decisions. Ever since November I have tried by every method and every route to pump aircraft into the Middle East. Great risks have been run and sacrifices made...

He reiterated his view that the primary aim of the air force in Malta was to defend the naval base against air attack, so that surface ships could operate against enemy convoys.

Finally, evidently feeling that the 'gallant Cunningham' deserved some special consideration, Churchill ended on a conciliatory note:

> I have taken the pains to give you this full account out of my admiration for the successes you have achieved, your many cares, my sympathy for you in the many risks your fleet has to run, and because of the commanding importance of the duty you have to discharge.

But ABC was not particularly consoled. He disagreed that the primary duty of the RAF in Malta was to defend the island. In his opinion, the RAF had the equally important function of offensive action against the enemy. Recalling Churchill's message in later years, he wrote, 'I need not refer to the rest of the message, to which I did not reply. We were far too busy with our other commitments.'

To the points about air power and Malta, ABC did reply, in another strongly worded signal of 29 April, which must have annoyed Churchill considerably. He said that a high degree of air reconnaissance should have been available, because for weeks on end he had no knowledge of the whereabouts of the Italian fleet.

ABC had not answered the rest of Churchill's message because 'we were far too busy with our other commitments'. No sooner had the fleet returned from the bombardment of Tripoli than, on 24 April, the evacuation of the Army from Greece began.

The Germans had launched a new offensive in Greece and Yugoslavia on 6 April 1941 and, to coincide with the advance on land, the *Luftwaffe* carried out very heavy air raids on the Piraeus, the Allies' only major supply port.

The ammunition ship *Clan Fraser* was hit by three bombs in quick succession and caught fire. She could not be moved because the harbour waters were infested with magnetic mines. After burning for about two hours, the ship blew up in the early hours of 7 April with a colossal detonation which sank another eleven adjacent ships of 42,000 tons and virtually destroyed the Piraeus as a port. For the purposes of the evacuation, codenamed Operation DEMON, the Piraeus was to be almost useless.

Wavell, Longmore and ABC had a conference on board *Warspite* on 15 April and agreed that the only sensible course of action would be to withdraw British troops from Greece. By the 18th, the Yugoslav Army had surrendered and the Greek Army which was operating in Epirus, on the border with Albania, was on the brink of collapse, after six months of campaigning, first against the Italians and then against the *Wehrmacht*. The New Zealand, Australian, Greek and British troops commanded by General Sir Henry Maitland Wilson, known as W Force, who had been fighting in the Olympus mountains, fell back, with the enemy almost hard on their heels, to the Pass of Thermopylae, the scene of the historic defence of 480 BC. But the local topography had changed since Leonidas' day; the pass was now several miles from the sea, and no longer a narrow defendable defile. In fact, W Force was already in an irreversible retreat which was only to end at the water's edge.

Operation DEMON, originally planned to begin on 28 April, was brought forward to 24 April. ABC put Pridham-Wippell in command of all operations afloat, with his headquarters at Suda Bay, and Rear-Admiral H.T Baillie-Grohman, who had arrived in Athens on 17 April to work with General Maitland Wilson, in charge of naval arrangements ashore.

ABC got matters under way with his customary briskness, as evinced by Commander R.L. Fisher, Pridham-Wippell's Staff Officer (Operations):

> We in the staff office had over the past weeks frankly discussed the likelihood that we might have to evacuate all the British forces from Greece, but this was a subject not to be hinted at to our admiral. Back in Alexandria one afternoon a signal came that the C. in C. wished to see my admiral or, failing him, his S.O. (O). The admiral was ashore so I went over to the *Warspite* and was shown into the cuddy. A.B.C. said gruffly, 'Where's your admiral?' 'Ashore playing golf, Sir.' 'Get him back at once and you are to sail tonight with all the cruisers and all the destroyers and take the army out of Greece. Four assault ships and eight troop transports now in the Canal will join you and come under your orders. Captain Crooks, the Sea Transport Officer from Port Said, will join your staff to help deal with the merchant ships.' I gulped and began to ask questions: 'How many soldiers, Sir? What about air cover?... and fuel?... and anti-aircraft ammunition? and (remembering Dunkirk) boats?' Drooping one eyelid (a well known danger signal I had heard about), he said, 'Don't stand there telling me you can't do it, Boy! Get out of here! Raise steam and sail as soon as your admiral is on board!' We did; and brought away 50,000.

However, it was not quite as simple as that. For DEMON, Pridham-Wippell had four cruisers, three anti-aircraft cruisers, nineteen destroyers, three sloops, the Infantry Assault Ships (later to be known as LSIs — Landing Ships, Infantry) *Glenearn*, *Glenroy* and *Glengyle*, which had special powered landing craft instead of boats, nineteen medium-sized troopships, and what ABC called 'various miscellaneous units', including a number of 'A' lighters which were the forerunners of tank landing craft or LCTs. Every destroyer was needed to ferry troops, with none to spare for escort, so the battleships had to stay in Alexandria.

Lacking harbours, the evacuation had to be carried out from whatever beaches had reasonable road access. After reconnaissance, beaches were chosen at Megara, Raphina and Raphtis near the Piraeus, and Nauplia, Tolon, Monemvasia and Kalamata in the Peloponnesus (some ostensibly superb beaches, shown on local maps to have excellent access, were actually found to have no approach roads at all).

Small craft were needed to take the soldiers out to the waiting ships. A dozen caiques, with motor-boats and local craft of all kinds, were chartered and fitted out by the 'Caique and Local Craft Committee' (although the caique captains demanded payment in gold, and not all of them turned up in the event).

This Committee was one of the measures taken by Baillie-Grohman to restore order out of a state of virtual chaos ashore. The salvage of the damaged cruiser *York* at Suda Bay was abandoned. Her officers and ship's company, with officers and men from Alexandria, were sent up to act under Baillie-Grohman as beach parties and communications numbers, and to crew the 'Committee's' craft. Gradually, as the evacuation progressed, Baillie-Grohman took over the control of all Greek shipping in local waters and eventually the conduct of all local naval affairs.

The *Luftwaffe* ruled the sky by day, but fortunately did not fly at night. Baillie-Grohman therefore ordered the ships not to approach the beaches until one hour after dark, so as to prevent enemy aircraft spotting which beaches were being used and bombing them by the light of flares. Ships were ordered to leave by 3 a.m. at the latest, so that they would have some chance of getting well clear of air attack by daylight.

For some days, the soldiers had been fighting rearguard actions by day under almost constant bombing and machine-gunning from the air, and marching by night over strange country and unfamiliar roads towards a problematical destination. They were dirty, hungry, thirsty and very tired. But they were not dispirited. Their morale remained high, and their organisation in the rear of the beaches and their discipline were described by Baillie-Grohman (writing his report, hiding in an olive grove, while the *Luftwaffe* searched overhead) as 'magnificent — especially considering they have been fighting a rearguard action from Salonika almost to Matapan'.

On the first night, 24/25 April, *Phoebe*, *Glenearn*, *Voyager* and *Stuart* and the corvette *Hyacinth* took off 6,685 personnel from Tolon and Nauplia, while *Glengyle* embarked 5,000 and *Calcutta* 700 from Raphtis and Raphina. But unfortunately *Ulster Prince*, an Irish Sea ferry of the Belfast Steamship Co., now commissioned as a troopship, ran aground across the fairway at Nauplia, preventing destroyers from using the wharves there on subsequent nights; she was found and bombed by the *Luftwaffe* the next day and became a total loss.

As with all such evacuations, DEMON followed a pattern of alternate success and disaster. On 24 April, the large Greek yacht *Hellas* arrived quite unexpectedly in the Piraeus, announcing that she could do 18 knots and take 1,000 passengers. Some 500 of the British community and walking Australian wounded embarked but the yacht was bombed that evening before she could sail, and a serious fire broke out. The single gangway to the shore was destroyed. There were no hoses on board, and none on the jetty for an hour. Most of the passengers died.

On the night of 25/26 April, at Megara, SS *Thurland Castle*, *Coventry*, *Wryneck*, *Diamond* and *Griffin* took off 4,600, and *Decoy*, *Hasty* and *Havock* another 1,300. Seven caiques did good work, but the transport SS *Pennland* was bombed twice and sunk while on her way north towards the beaches. Furthermore, some 250 men, many of them wounded, who had been waiting on the beaches for four days, were left behind. The LCT which was to have taken them off had her propellor fouled by a wire; the LCT, too, was lost.

The night of 26/27 April was the best of all: *Glengyle*, SS *Salween*, *Carlisle*, *Kingston*, *Kandahar* and *Nubian* took 8,223 from Raphina and Raphtis; *Orion*, *Perth*, *Calcutta*, *Stuart*, *Isis*, *Hotspur* and SS *Slamat* 4,527 from Tolon and Nauplia; and SS *Dilwara*, SS *City of London*, SS *Costa Rica* and *Defender* 8,650 from the southern harbour of Kalamata — a total of 21,400.

At dawn on the 26th, German parachutists landed on the Corinth Canal and captured the road and rail bridge, cutting off Morea from the rest of Greece. The final evacuations from north of the Corinth Canal were therefore made on the night of 27/28 April, when *Ajax*, which had joined from Alexandria the day before, *Kimberley*, *Kingston* and *Havock* embarked 4,640 from Raphtis and Raphina Cove.

The evacuation was now in its fourth day, longer than had been planned. But another 4,320 were taken off from Monemvasia on the night of 28/29th by *Ajax*, *Havock*, *Hotspur*, *Griffin* and *Isis*. Many of these were New Zealanders, and among them were General Freyberg, VC, commanding the New Zealand Forces, and Baillie-Grohman, who sailed in *Ajax* at 3.45 a.m. on the 29th. Meanwhile, at Kithera, *Auckland*, *Salvia* (towing one of *Glenroy*'s LCAs) and *Hyacinth* embarked 820, including 700 RAF personnel.

That same night, *Kandahar*, *Hero*, *Kimberley* and *Kingston* took off 332 from Kalamata. Evacuation from there continued for the next two nights, when another 235 were lifted. Thousands of troops were still in the town and more might have been done to rescue them. But a sudden attack by German forces, which was actually driven off, caused a misunderstanding of the situation. Hearing that the town was in enemy hands, the ships withdrew. Some ships did return, but the Brigadier commanding some 800 New Zealanders, 380 Australians and about 300 of the 4th Hussars decided that resistance was useless and surrendered; 7,000 men, including about 2,000 Palestinians and Cypriots and 1,500 Yugoslavs, were taken prisoner. Finally, *Hotspur* and *Havock* visited Milo on the last night, 30 April/1 May, and took off 700 British and Palestinian troops.

DEMON lasted seven nights during which a total of 50,732 were evacuated, including an uncertain number of Greeks and Yugoslavs. About 500 soldiers were subsequently lost in *Slamat*. Only some 14,000 embarked from wharves and jetties. The rest were ferried from open beaches out to the ships in anything that could be collected or commandeered — landing craft, ships' boats and small craft.

British casualties from all causes were about 12,000, but many of the sick and wounded returned to duty later. *Diamond* and *Wryneck* and *Ulster Prince*, *Pennland*, *Slamat* and *Costa Rica* had been sunk. *Glenearn* was twice bombed and damaged but was towed to Suda Bay by *Griffin* and then to Alexandria by the sloop *Grimsby* (whose Captain, Commander K.T D'Arcy, was, in ABC's phrase, 'a man of resource', having previously towed another bombed and damaged merchantman, *Scottish Prince*, into Suda Bay). Of six LCTs, only one survived. Great quantities of guns, armour, vehicles (including 8,000 lorries), ammunition and stores had been lost, with 209 aircraft lost or abandoned. The Italian battle fleet made no attempt to interfere with DEMON at any time, another dividend from Matapan.

Misunderstandings such as happened at Kalamata were excusable, indeed it is surprising there were not more. Throughout DEMON, Pridham-Wippell and Baillie-Grohman both had to grapple with frequent changes of plan at the shortest of notice and a continual lack of accurate, up-to-date information. Ships intended for a particular beach were bombed and sunk. Troops to be embarked were diverted or delayed. There were constant difficulties with poor communications, shortages of fuel and food and political uncertainties, while the enemy advanced relentlessly on land and maintained an almost incessant daily harassment from the air. Not surprisingly, ABC spoke in the warmest terms of the achievements of Pridham-Wippell and Baillie-Grohman and their staffs.

He also praised the officers and men of the merchant vessels who, he said, 'behaved magnificently, their masters never hesitating to take their ships into unfamiliar, unlighted and difficult anchorages, with no navigational marks and often without adequate charts. They acted throughout with the greatest courage, skill and determination.'

The Greek Navy now came under Cunningham's command. One cruiser, six destroyers and four submarines escaped from Greece before the end and arrived at Alexandria on 25 April.

Shortly before German troops entered Athens on 27 April, Alexandria and Malta received a message from Athens radio: 'Last night with you — Happy days with victory and liberty — God with you and for you. Good luck.' Malta replied: 'Very grateful for your message. The Medes and the Persians could not make it. How shall the modern Attila?' The last transmission from Athens was, 'We shall not forget you and look forward to the day of freedom,' followed by silence.

It was a very tired fleet which brought the last convoy from Greece back to Alexandria at the end of April. Every ship was desperately in need of repair and refit, and there was not an officer or man who did not long for leave and a respite from the sea and the almost constant air attacks. But there was no let-up, except a few hours in harbour, and those were fully occupied in refuelling, ammunitioning and storing, before putting to sea again.

At sea, 'by day and night gun crews and look-outs lived at the maximum tension of vigilance', wrote Bartimeus, the Mediterranean Fleet's own historian:

> Engine room staffs nursed their overdriven machinery like anxious seconds plying sponge and towel, patching up a battered champion to stick it for another round. Captains and navigators and defence officers were afraid of dozing off on their feet, betrayed by the weary flesh into a treacherous moment of oblivion. The anti-aircraft cruisers had worn smooth the rifling of their gun barrels; the destroyers, after the embarkations from the beaches of Attica and the Peloponnisos, had no boats left.

ABC, who was much more sensitive to the state of morale in his fleet than the sailors ever gave him credit for, was well aware of this state of affairs. When Longmore was called to London early in May for discussions on air matters generally, he took with him a letter from ABC to Pound, written on board *Warspite* and dated 3 May. 'We are not having too good a time out here,' ABC wrote, 'and it can all be put down to lack of air support.' Two or three days ago, he said, there were only thirteen fighters in the Western Desert. Tobruk had no fighter defence at all. There had been steady losses amongst the little ships supplying Tobruk.

He had, said ABC, noticed 'signs of strain among the officers and ratings especially in the anti-aircraft cruisers, but also in the destroyers. The former have had a gruelling time ever since the move of the Army to Greece started on March 4th, never a trip to sea without being bombed.' The CO of *Coventry* had 'gone under', as he put it, and he had had to relieve some officers and men in *Calcutta*.

But there were many other concerns. The mining of Alexandria, for instance, which was 'a nuisance'. This was an understatement. Enemy aircraft were regularly laying mines actually in Alexandria main harbour and near the entrance, known as the Great Pass, though fortunately not in the fairway Mines had also landed and exploded ashore.

ABC was also 'worried to death about Malta and the mining situation there. I don't feel that they do everything possible there.' The morale of the dockyard workmen was going down. The minelaying attack on Malta was what ABC called 'the most virulent kind'. He had had to withdraw Captain Mack and his flotilla. They were replaced by the 5th Destroyer Flotilla, of *Kelly*, *Kipling*, *Kelvin*, *Kashmir*, *Jackal* and *Jersey*, under Captain Lord Louis Mountbatten, who had just come out from England. But within five days, on 2 May, *Jersey* was mined and sank in the entrance to Grand Harbour. ABC sent one of his favourite ships, the cruiser *Gloucester*, to support the destroyers. But she too was often either bottled in or, as when *Jersey* was sunk, prevented from entering by mines. Furthermore, she was repeatedly attacked from the air and was hit by a bomb — for the third time.

Benghazi was also 'a very difficult problem. I hope it's realised that it is 500 miles from Alexandria and it is not easy to keep anything permanently stationed off it except submarines.' However, he concluded his letter, 'I hope I haven't drawn too gloomy a picture. We'll hold on somehow I am sure, but this air superiority is the devil. Personally, though much harassed, I have never been fitter.'

ABC was astoundingly fit, in body and mind. No matter how bad the news, or how gloomy the outlook, ABC remained outwardly cheerful and optimistic, seemingly utterly confident of success in the end. He played tennis or golf every day he could in harbour. He and Nona, 'that unworthy woman' as he called her, continued to entertain and be entertained. ABC loved going to the cinema in Alexandria. He particularly enjoyed a musical called *Balalaika* and when an air raid interrupted the performance he insisted on going back after the 'All Clear' and seeing the end of the film.

James Munn, who had served in *Coventry* when ABC was Rear-Admiral (Destroyers) and had been his Flag Lieutenant in *Hood* in 1937, and who was now commanding the destroyer *Hereward*, was able to compare the Cunninghams, past and present, when he stayed at Admiralty House at about this time, while his ship was boiler-cleaning.

Munn noted that ABC seemed to have mellowed slightly since his destroyer days, but the kindness and hospitality of ABC and Lady Cunningham were just the same.

> At Alexandria their house was often full of people who were tired, or who had lost their ships, or were in need of a rest. I remember Denis Boyd being there on one occasion and he could not stop talking about and blaming himself for the damage to *Illustrious*. ABC was always in good form and after dinner made us all lie down on the floor and throw ping-pong balls into the electric light bowl hanging from the ceiling. I

wrote home to my family saying I felt certain we would win the war.

ABC and Nona much enjoyed entertaining guests. 'We're always glad to see them,' ABC told Doodles, on 5 May, 'it keeps us young.' He knew what the newspapers and news broadcasts were saying about the situation in the Mediterranean and was at pains to reassure Doodles.

> Well we are not very happy out here, very hard pressed but keeping our end up all the same. My little ships — destroyers and such like — have just finished bringing off the men from Greece. Some wonderful stories of courage and determination have come in both by our lads and the men of the merchant ships to whom I take off my hat. But I lost some valuable ships and even more valuable men.

It was ABC's devoted staff who bore the brunt of the times. They had recently ended what Barnard had called 'this muck-up with a floating office' and moved to offices ashore at Gabbari House, with a floating catwalk across to *Warspite*. But life was still a great strain on their bodies and nerves. Power wrote:

> ABC was always at his greatest in adversity and was extraordinarily understanding of my bloody-minded fury at some of the orders I received. I tried very hard not to clash with him unnecessarily because I had no wish to add to his burden; but we did have a lot of rows and the unfortunate Chief of Staff spent a lot of time soothing us both down.

Commander Sir Charles Madden, *Warspite*'s Executive Officer, wrote:

ABC was a determined and aggressive exponent of the art of 'one-upmanship'. 'I'll see him off' was one of his favourite sayings. He couldn't abide people who didn't stand up to him. We were coming out of dock in Gabbara, Alexandria, and had to ammunition ship. As a gunnery officer I had spent half my life ammunitioning ship and it was one thing I did know about. We were way ahead of the record for the ship when ABC came alongside in his barge and looked at the scene on the quarterdeck. Commander, he said to me, this is disgraceful, get going and get the thing shaken up! I said, I think it's going very well, sir. We're ahead of past records for this ship. He looked at me as if he was going to strike me but then turned away!

13: MAY 1941: THE TIGER CONVOY AND THE BATTLE FOR CRETE

ON 21 APRIL 1941, the Defence Committee in London considered the implications of a most alarming signal from Wavell to the CIGS, stating that the British in the Western Desert were greatly inferior to the Germans in armour, upon which desert warfare depended, and that he had just received disquieting intelligence that a fresh German armoured division had arrived in Tripoli and would be in the fighting line by the end of the month.

When Churchill read this, he resolved, as he said, 'not to be governed any longer by the Admiralty reluctance, but to send a convoy through the Mediterranean direct to Alexandria carrying all the tanks which General Wavell needed'. There was already a large convoy with armoured reinforcements sailing for the Middle East round the Cape. Churchill decided that this convoy should turn off at Gibraltar, thus saving nearly forty days' passage time. The operation was codenamed TIGER.

The TIGER convoy consisted of five 15-knot ships carrying 295 tanks and fifty-three Hurricanes. Escorted by Force H, and by reinforcements for ABC, the battleship *Queen Elizabeth* and the cruisers *Naiad* (flag of Rear-Admiral E.L.S. King) and *Fiji*, the convoy passed through the Straits of Gibraltar on the night of 5/6 May. They were also to be escorted by *Gloucester* and the 5th Flotilla from Malta.

It was to be a complicated 'cross-over' operation, of a kind which had not been tried since EXCESS in January. ABC was to sail from Alexandria, flying his flag in *Warspite*, with *Barham*, *Valiant*, *Formidable*, *Orion*, *Ajax* and *Perth*, every available destroyer and *Breconshire* with oil fuel and ammunition for Malta.

In *Warspite* as a passenger and ABC's guest was Admiral Sir Walter Cowan, now with the rank of Commander and serving with a unit of Commandos in the desert. ABC was naturally deferential to his old chief, while Cowan himself, a stickler for discipline and protocol, could not forget that ABC was now the Commander-in-Chief. ABC's staff spread the tale about that the two men had the greatest difficulty in passing through a bulkhead door, each persisting in saying 'After you, sir' and trying to give the other precedence.

ABC also took the chance to sail a slow convoy of two large 10-knot tankers with 24,000 tons of fuel for Malta, escorted by two anti-aircraft cruisers, three destroyers and two corvettes, which left Alexandria on 5 May, and a fast convoy of four supply ships, escorted by three cruisers and three destroyers, which sailed with the fleet the following morning.

At dusk on 8 May, the TIGER convoy reached the entrance to the Skerki Channel and Force H withdrew, leaving their destroyers to refuel in Malta, and *Queen Elizabeth* and Admiral King's cruisers and destroyers to take the convoy on.

There was the danger of minefields in the Narrows and some mines were swept and exploded. After two mines had exploded close to *Empire Song*, she reported that she had a fire on board. She fell astern, and blew up and sank at about 4 a.m. Her crew were taken off by a destroyer, but fifty-seven tanks and ten Hurricanes were lost.

On 8 May, ABC received a signal from Vice-Admiral, Malta, that all the island's harbours were mined in and the four remaining destroyers of the 5th Flotilla would not be able to join the TIGER escort. ABC sent for the Fleet Torpedo Officer, 'the rather silent, imperturbable and never defeated'

Commander 'William the Silent' Carne, and told him to 'do something about it'.

Carne himself once said that 'Many people found ABC a difficult chap to get on with but when I got to know him and he had realised that my brain only worked at a third the speed of his, we got on pretty well.' Carne pondered for about an hour and then came back with 'a long signal' in which Vice-Admiral Malta was advised to blast a channel into Malta with depth-charges so as to countermine the magnetic mines in the fairways, or at least disrupt their working mechanisms.

It seemed to work. At 8 a.m. on 9 May, the Mediterranean Fleet was about 120 miles south of Malta and the TIGER convoy and escort some ninety miles to the west. The slow and fast convoys approached Malta in unusually thick weather and, preceded by *Gloxinia*, a corvette fitted for magnetic minesweeping, entered harbour on 8 May.

The 5th Flotilla was able to sail to join the TIGER convoy which met the fleet at 3.15 p.m. on 9 May, some forty miles south of Malta. Visibility was still poor, with fog and occasional rain showers. Brownrigg had been unable to get star sights that morning, or the night before, and was uncertain about the fleet's position, and had in fact been afraid of collisions with friendly forces during the previous night.

Everyone on *Warspite*'s bridge therefore tensed when the shape of a big ship was sighted, with her powerful signalling light flashing through the fog. Freestone read the signal: '"Dr Livingstone, I presume", sir.' At once ABC said, 'Reply, On Stanley, On'. To the Fleet Signal Officer, he said: 'Turn 120 degrees to starboard together.' Thus, by eye and in hazy weather, ABC took *Warspite* precisely into position ahead of *Queen Elizabeth*. Convoy and escort and the fleet then steered eastward while *Breconshire* went on to refuel destroyers in Malta.

The visibility continued to be amazingly, almost miraculously, poor for that time of year in the Mediterranean, with mist patches and larger fog banks down to masthead height. Enemy aircraft were on the radar screens and could be heard searching overhead throughout the day, but the unseasonable fog persisted. Aircraft finally found the fleet at about 4 p.m. that afternoon, but though they accurately reported the fleet's position, course and speed, surprisingly no attacks developed.

Providentially, the thick weather lasted while the convoy steered eastward on 10 May. Again, enemy aircraft were overhead, and could be heard making reports but they failed to find the fleet again until the night of 10 May, when the sky cleared and a full moon appeared. Aircraft flying down moon attacked the convoy but heavy anti-aircraft fire from the cruisers, and the radar-directed barrage put up by the combined fire of the four battleships and *Formidable* drove them off.

During the night, the 5th Destroyer Flotilla was detached to give Benghazi a 'pasting'. ABC was not pleased with the outcome. He wrote to Pound, on 18 May:

> I was a little disappointed with the 5th Flotilla when they shelled Benghazi. They were divebombed by moonlight and legged it to the Northward. If they had gone south in accordance with their orders I think they would have picked up 4 ships which arrived at Benghazi next day. They might quite easily lose a destroyer but as at the moment you get bombed daily outside a hundred miles from Alexandria and sometimes nearer, it doesn't seem to matter whether you go north or south.

More enemy aircraft approached the TIGER convoy during 11 May but they were thwarted by the continuing bad weather and by *Formidable*'s Fulmars. Convoy and fleet arrived in Alexandria in the forenoon of 12 May.

The Admiralty sent ABC a signal congratulating him on the 'memorable achievement' of the TIGER convoy's safe passage but ABC was under no illusions. He knew that the success was due to bad weather and he feared that the 'apparent ease' with which the convoy had been brought through from one end of the Mediterranean to the other would cause Churchill to draw the false conclusion that ABC and his staff had been exaggerating the dangers.

A delighted Churchill was indeed eager to repeat 'the brilliant success of TIGER', convinced that his own judgement had at last been vindicated. He would have pressed the matter to a Cabinet decision, had not Wavell himself taken the other side. This, said Churchill, 'cut the ground from under my feet'. The next convoy, with 100 tanks, went round by the Cape and did not arrive at Suez until 15 July.

ABC returned to the perennial subject of enemy air superiority:

> We are short of fleet fighters, and look like being short of A. A. ammunition. There is practically no reconnaissance, whereas the Germans and Italians report us as soon as we put our noses out of port. We really must get something analogous to a Coastal Command out here.
>
> I am afraid you will think this letter full of moans but we are not having too good a time out here. Everyone is at very high pressure and we are having some failures of personnel. Gilmour of *Coventry* has cracked up and I am a little unhappy about *Gloucester*'s ship's company. They have been a long time from home and taken more bombs and mines than any other ship out here. However I am going on board as soon as they get a day in and I don't doubt I can cheer them up.

ABC rarely made such speeches and, when he did, he nearly always had that particularly ship's state of morale in mind. When returning across Alexandria harbour to *Warspite* one night, the C-in-C's barge passed close to a motor cutter full of libertymen who had, clearly and audibly drunk deeply of the local beer. They recognised ABC and shouted abuse at him. ABC visited that ship the next day, had lower deck cleared so that he could address the whole ship's company and there was no more trouble.

Supplying Tobruk had become an increasing strain upon the fleet. Normally two destroyers ran in every night with supplies, sailing before daylight to return to Alexandria with wounded. With virtually no fighter defence of their own, the Tobruk garrison had to rely upon gunfire. The Stukas normally had the freedom of the air over the beleaguered port, and many merchant ships and warships were sunk.

ABC regularly visited the wounded in hospital in Alexandria and was greatly impressed by their cheerfulness. He took a much closer interest in his sailors' welfare than they knew of and jealously looked after their rights.

With two new Rear-Admirals, E.L.S. King and I.G. Glennie, ABC rearranged his flag officers' duties. Pridham-Wippell, who had just been made KCB, was given command of the battle fleet, flying his flag in *Queen Elizabeth*, while ABC himself, with the very greatest reluctance, transferred his flag ashore. Rawlings became Rear-Admiral, 7th Cruiser Squadron, with his flag in *Orion*. Rear-Admiral King, in *Naiad*, was Rear-Admiral, 15th Cruiser Squadron, while Glennie became Rear-Admiral (Destroyers).

ABC had thought that Longmore's absence in the United Kingdom would be only temporary, but to his disappointment he heard on 19 May that his old friend had been relieved as AOC-in-C and would not be returning.

It did seem, as ABC said, that no one at home realised how meagre Longmore's resources were and how well he had done with what he had. There is the suspicion that to some extent Longmore was the scapegoat for this ignorance in high places. His constant requests for more aircraft had been at first discounted and then disapproved of at home. Churchill even complained of the length of Longmore's weekly summaries.

Longmore was shocked to be told suddenly that he was being relieved. He was not allowed to return to the Middle East and thus had no chance to say farewell to his fellow Commanders-in-Chief or to the officers and men he had commanded. He was to be appointed Inspector of the RAF This was a high and responsible post but it did not, of course, compare with an operational theatre command.

It was announced on 1 June that Longmore was to be superseded by his Deputy AOC-in-C, Air Chief Marshal Tedder ('replacing a first class man with a second class in my opinion', ABC told Pound). Relations between the Navy and the Air Force in the Middle East were never to be as close again as they had been in Longmore's time.

But ABC's misgivings about Tedder were matters for the future. He had other more immediate concerns, in Crete.

'The next phase in the Mediterranean was the zenith of effort and the nadir of hope,' wrote Lieutenant-Commander Hugh Hodgkinson, First Lieutenant of the destroyer *Hotspur*. 'For months we had been working and fighting day and night. Four hours on, four hours off. Perhaps one day a week in harbour, or rather one night of real sleep.'

Hodgkinson spoke for all the ship's companies, and especially the destroyers, of the Mediterranean Fleet. 'We were tired and jaded,' he said. 'The physique of the ship's company was falling off. Even boats took a long time to hoist; and now the effort demanded of us rose to a crescendo.'

The 'crescendo' was Crete. At first, it had seemed that the Commanders-in-Chief in the Middle East had no clear directions about the defence of the island. On 16 April Wavell had signalled that he assumed Crete would be held. Mr Churchill replied that it certainly would. On 18 April the Chiefs of Staff signalled Churchill's decision on priorities in the Middle East. They were, broadly, that 'Victory in Libya counts first; evacuation of troops from Greece second; Tobruk shipping, unless indispensable to victory, must be fitted in as convenient; Iraq can be ignored and Crete worked up later.'

But once British troops had been evacuated from Greece, Crete became of prime importance. Crete was, as Churchill said, the last foothold for the Greek King and Government. Some 30,000 personnel evacuated from Greece had in fact been taken to Crete, so as to shorten the turn-round time of the ships; but these troops were armed only with rifles and light machine-guns, their artillery and their vehicles having been left behind. Eventually nearly 7,000 men, mainly from non-fighting units, with about 6,000 Italian prisoners-of-war, were shipped to Egypt to reduce the number of useless mouths.

Writing years later, Churchill was bitterly critical of the handling, in Cairo and in Whitehall, of the preparations in Crete where, he said, 'Everything had proceeded in a halting manner.' He complained that six successive commanders had been appointed in as many months and there had been 'neither plan nor drive'. But he did concede that it would only have been possible to supply guns and troops to Crete at the expense of somewhere else, where the needs were even more urgent, that there was no labour locally to develop the airfields, and there was no question of having a strong garrison or strong air forces in Crete while Greece was still in Allied hands. But, in his view, Middle East Command should still have foreseen coming events more accurately and should have made everything ready to receive reinforcements.

In fact, Crete was a very difficult island to defend, even with the benefit of hindsight. It stretched for about 160 miles from east to west, varying in width from north to south between thirty-five and seven-and-a-half miles. There was a backbone of high mountains, rising to 7,000 feet, running down to usable beaches and plains suitable for airfields only on the northern coast, and sloping sharply down to the sea in the south. There were no railways and one suitable road for motor vehicles, along the northern coast. There were only rough roads, ending in mule tracks, across the mountains to Sphakia and Tymbaki on the south coast.

The three landing strips, at Maleme, Heraklion and Retimo, were all on or near the north coast. The two 'major' ports (both of them tiny by mainland European standards), Suda and Heraklion, were both on the north coast, so that ships from Egypt had to pass round the island, through the Anti-Kithera Channel to the west or the Kaso Strait to the east, before they could unload. The whole island seemed to face in the wrong direction for the Allies. As ABC said, 'It would have suited us much better if the island could have been turned upside-down.'

There was no time to bring large numbers of extra troops to Crete by sea and in the event the defence of the island was undertaken by the 26,800 troops who were there at the beginning of May. A few British units did arrive in Crete from Egypt during April and May. They included a Mobile Naval Base Defence Organisation (MNBDO) of some 5,300 Royal

Marines, with their own anti-aircraft guns, searchlights, booms, nets and all the gear necessary to establish and defend a naval base.

Originally intended for an assault on Rhodes which never took place, the MNBDO had come round the Cape and arrived at Suez on 21 April. Their CO, Major-General E.C. Weston, RM, arrived in Crete to take command of British troops on the island on 22 April. Later, after General Freyberg's arrival, Weston took over command of the defence of the Suda sector.

But the MNBDO's ships had not been 'operationally' loaded, with items stowed in the order they would be required, and the MNBDO had first to go to Haifa to reorganise and restow their equipment. About 2,000 Marines of the MNBDO arrived at Suda Bay on 9 May, with some of their guns, so that the number of anti-aircraft guns in Crete had risen by 19 May to thirty-two heavy and thirty-six light guns, and twenty-four searchlights.

It was decided that the danger of losing ships to enemy air attack at Suda was so great that no more MNBDO ships were sent. Some 3,000 Marines of the MNBDO were thus held back, to the chagrin of Churchill who felt 'they might have got there'.

But some further reinforcements were brought in by ship. On the night of 15/16 May, *Gloucester* and *Fiji* embarked the 2nd Battalion of the Leicester Regiment and all their equipment at Alexandria and landed them at Heraklion. *Glengyle*, escorted by *Coventry*, *Waterhen*, *Voyager* and *Auckland*, embarked 700 men of the Argyle & Sutherland Highlanders at Alexandria on the night of 18/19 May and took them to Tymbaki. They guarded the Mesara Plain against parachute landings for some days before marching over the mountains to Heraklion.

The only ports suitable for shipping were Heraklion and Suda, which Churchill had often pressed to have fortified into what he called a 'second Scapa'. It was far from that. There was one small stone pier, where two ships of shallow draught could berth. Large ships had to lie off at anchor and unload into lighters (as they also had to do at Canea and Retimo). Nevertheless, Captain J. A. V. Morse arrived on 23 April to take charge of the base and through his exertions and those of his small staff, and of Captain M.H.S. MacDonald at Heraklion, some 25,000 tons of army stores were unloaded from fifteen ships between 29 April and 20 May, in spite of the difficulties and the increasing weight of air attacks. But eight ships were sunk or seriously damaged.

Operation MERKUR (Mercury), as the Germans codenamed the capture of Crete, was the first assault by airborne troops in military history. It was to be carried out by *Luftflotte* 4, of *Fliegerkorps* VIII and XI, under General Lohr. *Fliegerkorps* VIII had 228 Heinkel He.111s and Junkers Ju.88 bombers, 205 Junkers Ju.87 'Stuka' dive-bombers, 114 Messerschmitt Me.no twin-engined fighters, 119 Messerschmitt Me. 109 fighters, and 50 reconnaissance aircraft. Of this total strength of 716 aircraft, 514 were reported serviceable on 17 May. *Fliegerkorps* VIII could also call on certain aircraft from *Fliegerkorps* X. *Fliegerkorps* XI, who were to carry the airborne troops for the first assault, and follow up with reinforcements, had over 500 three-engined Junkers Ju. 52 transport aircraft and 72 gliders.

Against this, the Allies had the remains of Nos. 33, 80 and 112 Squadrons RAF — what Major-General Bernard Freyberg, VC, who had arrived on 30 April to take command as GOC Crete, described as six Hurricanes and seventeen obsolete aircraft. There were also three Sea Gladiators and three Fulmars of 805 Squadron Fleet Air Arm, based at Maleme.

The RAF and naval pilots in Crete flew with great gallantry against tremendous odds. ABC himself paid tribute to the Fleet Air Arm participants at Maleme, especially Commander G.H. Beale, Lieutenant-Commander Alan Black, Lieutenant (A) R.A. Brabner and the observer Lieutenant (O) A.W.F. Sutton. Theirs, he said 'was an example of grand personal courage… under the worst possible conditions which stands out brightly in the gloom of the Cretan affair…'

Allied Intelligence had for some time been suggesting that Crete was the enemy's next objective after Greece. As early as March, Enigma decrypts of Axis diplomatic traffic had revealed that the Germans were assembling airborne forces in the Balkans. By the end of April, it appeared probable that the Germans intended an airborne assault on Crete, although the possibility remained that the preparations for Crete might be a cover for an attack on Syria or Cyprus. But, on 5 May, the Enigma confirmed that Crete was the real target.

Later decrypts revealed the enemy's progress in building up forces, the arrival of *Fliegerkorps* XI in the Athens area, the assembly of 27,000 tons of shipping, the results of the *Luftwaffe*'s 'softening up' bombing raids on Crete which began on 14 May, and the likely scale of the attack, which could come on any day after 17 May. Finally, and crucially, the Enigma revealed that the attack had been postponed to 20 May.

ABC's object was to ensure that the enemy did not land in Crete from the sea. The indications were that the attack would begin on 15 May and ABC had his ships at sea from the 14th onwards. By 15 May, they were south of Crete, ready to steam to any threatened point. Force C, of *Dido* (flag of Rear-Admiral Glennie) with *Coventry*, *Nubian*, *Kingston* and *Juno*, was ready to go to Heraklion and Sitia; Force D, of *Naiad*, *Phoebe* and two destroyers, was to deal with any landing west of Retimo; and Force B, of *Gloucester* and *Fiji*, was ready for enemy forces north-west of Crete and to go to the support of Force D. The ships were to carry out sweeps on the night of 16/17 May: Force B along the west coast of Greece from Matapan, Force C from Kaso towards Leros, and Force D from Anti-Kithera to the Piraeus. All the forces were ordered to retire from their sweeps in time to be close to the north of Crete by dawn and to stay south of Crete in daylight.

Meanwhile, Force A, of *Queen Elizabeth* (wearing Pridham-Wippell's flag) and *Barham* and five destroyers, was to the westward of Crete, to cover the other forces and to guard against any intervention by the Italian battle fleet.

By 19 May, the RAF's strength in Crete had been whittled down to four Hurricanes and three Gladiators. It was decided that keeping them 'for the day' would just be sacrificing them to no purpose. The seven survivors were sent away to Egypt that day, with the full agreement of General Freyberg. After the operational losses of the bombardment of Tripoli and the passage of the TIGER convoy, *Formidable* had only four aircraft left. There were no reserves, either of aircraft or aircrew. Thus the battle for Crete was to open with no Allied fighter cover at all.

Lacking *Formidable*'s fighters, ABC's ships could make only very limited use of Suda Bay as a base by day, and had to refuel and reammunition in Alexandria, which was more than 400 miles from Suda Bay. In reserve at Alexandria was Force A, of *Warspite*, *Valiant*, *Formidable*, *Orion*, *Ajax* and the rest of the available destroyers. ABC himself, to his deep regret and with the very greatest reluctance, shifted his flag to offices ashore, deciding that he could best control events from Alexandria.

No enemy forces were sighted on any of the night sweeps, and the ships withdrew south of Crete where, on 18 May, ships had to be relieved to return to Alexandria and refuel, sailing again on the 19th. Rawlings shifted his flag to *Warspite* and sailed from Alexandria on the evening of 18 May with Force A1, of *Valiant*, *Ajax*, and eight destroyers to relieve Pridham-Wippell's Force A.

At dawn on 20 May, Force A1 was about 100 miles to the west of Crete, where they were shortly joined by Glennie in *Dido*, with *Orion*, *Greyhound*, and *Hasty*, who had all fuelled in Alexandria, sailed again on the 19th and had reached the Anti-Kithera Strait during the night. King, in *Naiad*, with *Perth* and four destroyers, had also fuelled in Alexandria, sailed on the 19th and patrolled the Kaso Strait during the night. They were now withdrawing to the southward. *Gloucester* and *Fiji*, who had refuelled, were on their way to patrol up as far as Cape Matapan and then to join Rawlings.

As anticipated from the Enigma decrypts, the Germans began their main assault upon Crete on 20 May. Heavy air raids on the AA batteries around the airstrips at Maleme, Heraklion and Retimo on the north coast had begun on the 19th and continued on the 20th. Untroubled by any fighter opposition, the bombers were able to descend to low altitude and bomb and machine-gun the guns' crews in their gunpits.

At 8 a.m., when the majority of the guns had been put out of action and their crews driven to take cover, convoys of gliders with fighter and dive-bomber escort appeared through the thick palls of dust and smoke overhead. Landings by paratroopers or by gliders or both were made around Maleme, at several points south-west of Canea and on the Akrotiri peninsular.

More German troops landed during the day, bringing the total on the island by nightfall up to about 3,000. There was fighting at Retimo and Heraklion in the afternoon. Aircraft gave German troops on the ground close support with bombing and strafing. But the defenders — British, Australian, New Zealand and Greek — fought back fiercely. The German paratroopers suffered huge losses, especially amongst their officers.

All three airstrips, obviously prime targets for the enemy, were held throughout that first day. The New Zealand defenders at Maleme had suffered heavy casualties and withdrew during the night of 20/21st to a position just south-east of the airfield, leaving it as a kind of no-man's land for the next day. The battle for Crete was to become very largely a battle for Maleme airstrip.

As soon as ABC heard that the attack had begun, he ordered his ships to move up towards Crete, but, if nothing developed, to keep out of sight of land. He had planned night sweeps by cruisers and destroyers to the north of the island. But air reconnaissance reported caiques (local sailing craft) in the Aegean. These might be part of the expected invasion by sea and so, at 6 p.m. on 20 May, ABC ordered his ships to move north of Crete at once.

As there was a chance that his ships might miss southbound enemy convoys in the darkness, ABC cancelled the night sweeps. Instead, he established patrols on either side of Longitude 250 East. Force C, under King in *Naiad*, with *Perth*, *Kandahar*, *Nubian*, *Kingston* and *Juno*, was to patrol off Heraklion, and Force D, under Glennie in *Dido*, with *Orion*, *Ajax*, *Isis*, *Kimberley*, *Imperial* and *Janus*, off the Maleme-Canea-Kissamo area.

During the night, King's ships met six Italian motor-torpedo boats in the Kaso Strait and damaged four of them in a short night encounter. Meanwhile, Captain Mack (D.14) in *Jervis*, with *Nizam* and *Ilex*, closed the island of Scarpanto to the east of Crete and bombarded the airfield there.

At daylight on 21 May, it appeared to ABC and his staff that the general situation in Crete was under control and that the main German assault of 20 May had been contained. At sea, Rawlings' ships were some sixty miles west of the Anti-Kithera Channel, steering south-east to meet Glennie who was retiring to the west after his patrol. King was withdrawing to the south where he was joined by Mack from Scarpanto. *Gloucester* and *Fiji* had patrolled off Cape Matapan and were about to join Rawlings.

At this point the *Luftwaffe* took a hand. Their attacks began soon after daylight and continued almost incessantly until dusk. There was high-level bombing by squadrons of bombers or single aircraft, low-level attacks from a few hundred feet, massed bombing by Junkers Ju.88s and Heinkel He.111s, dive-bombing by Ju.87 Stukas, and low, fast machine-gun strafing runs by Messerschmitt Me. 109s. Finally, there were torpedo attacks at dusk.

The *Luftwaffe* found almost all ABC's ships at some time during that day. The battleships with Rawlings were attacked during the forenoon, again for two-and-a-half hours in the afternoon, and in the evening. Glennie's ships were also attacked heavily during the forenoon, when *Ajax* was damaged by near-misses, again for two-and-a-half hours in the afternoon, and a third time that evening when they had joined Rawlings' Force A1.

King's ships were bombed continuously from 9.50 a.m. for four hours. The destroyer *Juno* was hit by two bombs at about

12.50 p.m. A third bomb detonated in the after magazine. *Juno* broke in half and sank within two minutes. *Kandahar*, *Nubian* and *Kingston* picked up six officers and ninety-one men.

Amongst all the signals of that day's hectic doings, there was one personal message of loss and tragedy for ABC and his family. Walter Starkie, *Juno*'s First Lieutenant, was not among her survivors.

Hillie, whose married life had lasted only just over a year, took the news with great bravery. 'She is a lion-hearted little mortal,' ABC wrote to Doodles, 'and after the first blow she has stood up to it well, but it's very tragic for her. Fortunately a baby is on the way which will make all the difference.'

On 21 May; the battle on land took a decisive turn against the Allies. German paratroops had established themselves near the western end of the runway at Maleme, but they had by no means secured the airfield, nor were the Germans particularly successful elsewhere on that day. However, during the afternoon of 21 May, German transport aircraft began to land boldly at Maleme, although under artillery fire, and disgorged load after load of troops. By 5 p.m. the Germans had taken the airfield.

The defending Allied Commander in that area decided that any attempt to retake Maleme could only be made in darkness. But reinforcements were delayed. The counter-attack did not begin until 3.30 a.m. on 22 May and went on in a confused and localised series of engagements until daylight, when the airfield perimeter was finally reached. By then it was too late. The runway was being swept by a withering mortar and machine-gun fire which made any frontal attack impossible. By the afternoon of 22 May the Germans had a grip on the vital airfield which they never relaxed. They continued to fly planeload after plane-load of troops into Maleme.

The reinforcements which reached Crete through Maleme compensated for the Germans' lack of success at sea. Without Maleme the Germans could never have secured Crete, for they received almost no reinforcements by sea.

The German Admiral Commanding South-East Area, Admiral Schuster, had assembled enough shipping to transport one battalion, with all its heavy equipment and supplies. The troops were to cross in two convoys of caiques, which were the only sea transport the Germans were able to muster. The first, of twenty-five caiques, was to land 2,300 troops at Maleme beach on the evening of 21 May, and the second, of thirty-eight caiques, was to take 4,000 troops to Heraklion on the evening of the 22nd. The heavy guns and tanks were to follow in a third convoy of steamships.

On 21 May an Enigma decrypt and other Sigint revealed the enemy's preparations to send the first of these reinforcements by sea. A Maryland aircraft from Egypt was sent to confirm the report (and thus safeguard the intelligence source). The first convoy was delayed because British ships had been reported to the north of Crete. But the Maryland sighted the caiques, escorted by one Italian torpedo boat, heading for Crete from the direction of the island of Milos, on the afternoon of the 21st.

Force D steered to intercept and sighted the first caiques some eighteen miles north of Canea at about 11.30 p.m. on the 21st. Guided by radar, Glennie's ships penetrated into the midst of the convoy and in the next two-and-a-half hours caught and sank ten caiques, all crammed with German troops. The escorting torpedo boat, *Lupo*, was damaged by gunfire from *Dido* and *Ajax*, after firing torpedoes at the cruisers and trying with great bravery to defend her charges. Of the 2,300 troops in this convoy, about 800 were killed or thrown into the sea. Many were later recovered by the enemy's Air Sea Rescue Service but none reached Crete. Force D's ships had become scattered during the engagement and so at 3.30 a.m. Glennie headed west and gave his ships a rendezvous to meet him to the west of Crete.

When Schuster heard of the attack on the first convoy, he ordered the second to turn back. But his signal had probably not been received before the second convoy also came under attack from Force C. King's ships, which had been joined by *Calcutta* and *Carlisle* the day before, were off Heraklion at about 4 a.m. and had then steered north-west towards Milos in search of a southbound convoy. A single caique, carrying German troops, was sighted at 8.30 and was sunk by *Perth*. Meanwhile *Naiad* engaged large numbers of aircraft who had already appeared and begun to bomb the ships.

A confused and indecisive action followed. At 9.09 a.m. *Calcutta* reported a small merchant vessel ahead of her. The destroyers were ordered to sink it. By 10 a.m., when Force C was some twenty-five miles south of the eastern corner of Milos, *Perth* had rejoined after sinking the caique but *Naiad* was still some way astern. At 10.10, an enemy destroyer, with five or six small sailing craft, was sighted to the northward. Some destroyers gave chase while *Kingston* engaged the enemy destroyer at 7,000 yards and claimed two hits.

Kingston also reported sighting a large number of caiques (this was actually the thirty-eight-caique convoy) behind the smoke screen which the enemy destroyer was laying down whilst making its escape.

Although still in contact with the enemy convoy, King now broke off the action. His ships were being bombed almost continuously. He knew that AA ammunition was running low. He must keep his ships together, for their own protection; this meant a top speed of only 21 knots, which was all *Carlisle* could do on her one remaining shaft. King therefore reasoned that he would jeopardise his whole force if he went any further to the north.

Unfortunately, a signal from ABC, that this convoy was of considerable size, did not arrive until 11 a.m., by which time King's ships were withdrawing to the west towards the Anti-Kithera channel, being pursued by aircraft as they went. Bombing by waves of Junkers Ju.87s went on almost without respite from 9.45 until well after 1 p.m. *Naiad* suffered thirty-six misses, some of them very near, in ten minutes. Two of her turrets were put out of action, several compartments were flooded and her speed reduced to 16 knots. *Carlisle* was hit and set on fire. A Messerschmitt Me. 109 machine-gunned her bridge and killed her CO, Captain T.C. Hampton.

ABC did his best to make allowances for King, whose ships had had a 'gruelling time', had been in action with torpedo boats the night before, had been bombed continuously for more than four hours without any air cover, and had lost *Juno*. The sailors had been on the alert for more than forty-eight hours and everybody had been under tremendous strain. Ammunition was low and if King had pressed on to the north he would have been moving away from any help.

Nevertheless, ABC thought King's decision to retire

> was a faulty one. It is probable that the safest place was in amongst the enemy convoy and retirement could not better the most unpleasant position in which he found himself. Also, the destruction of that large convoy would have justified severe losses... I have always held that if the enemy is in sight on the sea air attacks and any other considerations must be disregarded and the risks accepted.

Writing to Pound, ABC said that, 'It is true that he [King] found it difficult to maintain a course towards the convoy due to dodging the heavy and persistent bombing attacks but I could cheerfully have put up with our losses had we had some thousands more Hun soldiers swimming in the Aegean.' However, the German soldiers may not have been swimming in the Aegean, but they certainly turned back and, when they did eventually arrive in Crete, the battle was over.

Rawlings had been patrolling between twenty and thirty miles to the west of the Kithera Channel since dawn on the 22nd. He had been joined that morning by Glennie's Force D and by Force B, of *Gloucester*, *Fiji*, *Greyhound* and *Griffin*, who had been patrolling off Matapan. Force B had already been attacked by dive-bombers almost continuously for one-and-a-half hours from 6.30 that day. His ships were all, as Rawlings ruefully said, 'serving a useful purpose by attracting enemy aircraft' and, in fact, his main anxiety was now the severe shortage of anti-aircraft ammunition.

Rawlings had intended to meet King in the Kithera Channel at about 3.30 that afternoon. But when he had a signal from King at 12.25 that *Naiad* was badly damaged and in need of support, he boldly decided to enter the Aegean, increased to *Warspite*'s maximum speed of 23 knots and steered east, coming under further air attacks as he went.

Shell bursts of anti-aircraft fire to the westward were seen from *Naiad* at 1.12 p.m., as the two forces approached each other, and Rawlings' ships came into sight some ten minutes later.

So far, Rawlings' ships had been lucky, considering the intensity of the air attacks upon them and the absence of any air cover. For instance, *Gloucester* and *Fiji* had been damaged that morning, but not seriously. At about 1.30 *Warspite* was hit by a bomb on her starboard side which wrecked the starboard 6-inch and 4-inch gun batteries, started large fires, caused one boiler room to be temporarily abandoned and casualties of one officer and thirty-seven men killed and thirty-one wounded. From that moment, matters began to go disastrously wrong.

Greyhound was detached from Rawlings' force at 1.20 to sink a large caique between Pori and Anti-Kithera islands. Having done this, she was returning to take up her station in the destroyer screen when, at 1.51 p.m., she was hit by two bombs. She sank by the stern fifteen minutes later.

King was senior to Rawlings and was thus the senior officer of forces present at that time. He ordered *Kandahar* and *Kingston* to pick up *Greyhound*'s survivors and *Fiji* and *Gloucester* to give them anti-aircraft fire support, and also to stand by *Greyhound* until dark.

This, in ABC's view, was a second serious mistake by King. 'The sending back of *Gloucester* and *Fiji* to the *Greyhound* was another grave error, and cost us those two ships,' he told Pound. 'They were practically out of ammunition but even had they been full up I think they would have gone. The Commanding Officer of *Fiji* told me that the air over *Gloucester* was black with planes.' Certainly, the rescuing ships and *Greyhound*'s survivors in the water were bombed and machine-gunned almost continuously.

But, at the time, King did not know how short of AA ammunition *Gloucester* and *Fiji* were. He asked Rawlings to give him close support, as his own ships had practically no ammunition left. Rawlings, who was already, in the words of ABC's dispatch, 'feeling uneasy about the orders given to *Gloucester* and *Fiji*', closed King at *Warspite*'s best speed of 18 knots and informed him of the state of *Gloucester*'s and *Fiji*'s high-angle ammunition. Whereupon at 2.57 p.m. King ordered them both to withdraw, with ships in company, at their own discretion. At 3.30 *Gloucester* and *Fiji* were sighted coming up from astern of the force at high speed. They were still engaging enemy aircraft.

At about 3.50, *Gloucester* was hit by a bomb, and then by a second, and was then hit several times. She came to a standstill, with a huge fire burning on her upper deck, which had been smashed into a shambles. *Fiji* devotedly closed her and dropped all her own Carley floats and as many boats as possible. *Fiji*'s Captain, P.R.B.W. William-Powdett, then decided that because of the constant bombing he must take his ship away. The *Gloucester*'s company in the water, fully expecting to be machine-gunned at any moment, cheered *Fiji* as she left. King decided, with Raw lings' agreement, that to take the battle fleet back to help *Gloucester* would only be risking even more ships.

'Thus went the gallant *Gloucester*' ABC wrote, in his own elegy for this much-loved ship:

> She had endured all things, and no ship had worked harder or had had more risky tasks. She had been hit by bombs more times than any other vessel, and had always come up smiling. As she left Alexandria for the last time I went alongside her in my barge and had a talk with her Captain, Henry Aubrey Rowley. He was very anxious about his men, who were just worn out, which was not surprising, as I well realized. I promised to go on board and talk to them on their return to harbour; but they never came back. I doubt if many of them survived, as they, too, were murderously machine-gunned in the water. Rowley's body, recognizable by his uniform monkey jacket and the signals in his pocket, came ashore to the west of Mersa Matruh about four weeks later. It was a long way to come home.

Air attacks continued through the afternoon and into the evening. *Valiant* was hit twice during a high-level bombing attack at 4.45 p.m. Two hours later, it was *Fiji*'s turn. She had survived twenty attacks in the previous four hours, miraculously weaving her way as though protected by some magic spell through storms of spray and splinters from near-misses. In fact, she had beaten off so many attackers she had expended all her live AA ammunition and was down to practice rounds when, at 6.45 p.m., a solitary Messerschmitt Me. 109 dived down through low cloud and dropped a bomb close alongside which blew in the ship's bottom and flooded one boiler room.

Fiji struggled on at slow speed for a time but finally came to a stop, with a slowly increasing list to port. Half an hour after the first, another solitary aircraft dropped three more bombs which hit and penetrated the upper deck. The masts collapsed, the list rapidly increased and, at 8.15, *Fiji* rolled over and sank.

Kandahar and *Kingston*, who were in company and who already had *Greyhound*'s survivors on board, dropped floats near *Fiji* (whose own had, of course, been left for *Gloucester*) and withdrew until darkness. When they came back, they spent two hours searching for survivors, being guided by flashing torches from the rafts. *Kingston* eventually rescued 339 of *Fiji*'s people, and *Kandahar* another 184.

Kandahar and *Kingston* had themselves been subjected to twenty-two air attacks since 2.45 that afternoon and ABC paid warm tribute to their ships' companies and to the outstanding examples of their COs, Commander W.G.A. Robson (*Kandahar*) and Lieutenant-Commander P. Somerville, DSO (*Kingston*). He also praised the CO of *Greyhound*, Commander W.R. Marshall A'Deane, himself a survivor, who dived from *Kandahar*'s upper deck to rescue a man from *Fiji* some distance away and was not seen again. He was awarded a posthumous Albert Medal.

That night of 22/23rd, the destroyers continued patrols off the north coast of Crete. *Jervis*, with *Ilex*, *Nizam* and *Havock*, patrolled off Heraklion, and then withdrew to Alexandria the following day. The 5th Destroyer Flotilla, of *Kelly*, *Kashmir*, *Kipling*, *Kelvin* and *Jackal*, had joined Rawlings at 4 p.m. on the 22nd. He first sent them that evening to look for survivors from *Gloucester* and *Fiji* but then ordered the search to be abandoned and instead sent the flotilla to patrol inside Kissamo and Canea Bays. *Kelvin* and *Jackal* withdrew independently after investigating some shore lights at Canea Bay. *Kipling* was ordered to turn back because of a steering defect. *Kelly* and *Kashmir* found a troop-carrying caique which they engaged with gunfire, and went on to carry out a short bombardment of Maleme airfield. On their way back out to sea they found another caique and set it on fire.

Also during that night, Rawlings detached *Decoy* and *Hero* to Agriarumeli, on the south coast of Crete, to embark the King of the Hellenes, the British Minister, and other important personages. The next day, as the two destroyers passed the battle fleet, Rawlings firmly ordered them to join the battleship screen instead of going on to Alexandria by themselves and perhaps being caught alone by aircraft.

This was a very wise precaution, but His Majesty objected, and told ABC so when he did eventually reach Alexandria. ABC could not agree. On the contrary, experience off Crete had shown, as it already had off Norway in 1940, that it was

a golden rule which we had long since found in all our previous encounters with aircraft, and that was never to detach ships for any particular tasks. The fleet should remain concentrated and move in formation to wherever any rescue or other work had to be done. *Greyhound, Gloucester* and *Fiji* might not have been lost if everybody had stayed together. Together, the fleet's volume of anti-aircraft fire might have prevented some of our casualties.

Many times ABC regretted the necessity which had forced him to shift his flag ashore. 'I did not dare to go to sea myself,' he later wrote to Willis, 'so as to keep my finger on matters here. Oh! that I had. I am sure two good cruisers and two destroyers would now be afloat if I had been there. These Home Fleet admirals don't know what fighting means. I like King but these are two most glaring mistakes of his.'

Others also believed that matters would not have gone so badly if ABC had been there. In Brownrigg's opinion, 'quite certainly there would have been half the losses if ABC had been at sea. King was ghastly and Rawlings' staff poor.' The lower deck, some of whom would be calling ABC 'The Butcher' before long, were sure that they would have been safer if the Old Man himself had been there. When Edelsten joined *Warspite* just before Matapan, he actually overhead somebody saying: 'The Old Man's aboard, we'll be all right!'

During that day, 22 May, ABC signalled to his ships at sea: 'Stick it out. Navy must not let Army down. No enemy forces must reach Crete by sea.'

The message was much more confident in its tone than either ABC himself or his staff were feeling, as the afternoon gave way to evening, and evening to night, and news of ever more casualties kept coming in. The positions of all the ships, plotted hour by hour on a large-scale chart in the war room next to ABC's office, showed the gravity of the situation. By the end of that dreadful day, during which ABC had had the shocking news of *Gloucester, Fiji* and *Greyhound* sunk and *Warspite, Valiant, Naiad* and *Carlisle* all damaged, he had reached the stage where he dreaded the arrival of every fresh signal, every knock on his office door and every ring of the telephone.

Nevertheless, ABC never gave the slightest outward sign that he was at all worried or perturbed. Power was normally the chosen bearer of bad news and giver of unwelcome advice because very often, as he wrote, although 'the whole staff including the Chief of Staff felt as I did, they left it to me because he might listen to me whereas they'd only be ordered out of the room'.

Thus it fell to Power to go in and

report the loss of *Gloucester*, our favourite, battle-scarred and immensely gallant cruiser. ABC said, 'All right, it's no use looking like a bloody undertaker.'

I said, 'Well, I don't think we're going to achieve anything to justify losses on this scale. We had much better withdraw.'

ABC said, 'You're a pusillanimous bugger (favourite expression for anyone who counselled caution), what the hell's the matter with you?'

I said, 'If you go on knocking your head against a brick wall you'll get knocked right out.'

ABC replied, 'Probably, but what has escaped your notice is that it may also loosen a brick!'

That was precisely the spirit which the Mediterranean Fleet was going to need so badly in the next seven days.

14: CRETE: 'THE THREE HUNDRED YEAR TRADITION'

THE 22 MAY, a day of disasters, was followed by another, whose shocks and losses were aggravated for ABC by interference from home.

The 5th Destroyer Flotilla completed their short night bombardment of Maleme airfield on the 23rd and by dawn were retiring from Canea at full speed. But at 7.55 a.m., when they were south of Gavdo Island, they were attacked by twenty-four Junkers Ju.87s.

Kashmir was hit and sank in two minutes. *Kelly* was hit as she was turning hard to starboard at 30 knots. She continued her heel to port and, still going at considerable speed, turned over and finally sank after floating upside down for half an hour. *Kipling*, the only surviving ship, was subjected to six divebombing attacks while she picked up 128 officers and men from *Kelly* and 152 from *Kashmir*; 210 officers and men were lost from the two ships. *Kipling* then headed for Alexandria, surviving another forty attacks and eighty-three bombs between 8.20 a.m. and 1 p.m. She ran out of fuel and was towed for the last fifty miles by the net-layer *Protector*.

At Suda Bay, five MTBs of the 10th Flotilla were all sunk. Captain J.A.V. Morse, the Naval Officer in Charge, began to consider the possibility of evacuating. Elsewhere on the island, the situation of the Allied defenders was steadily deteriorating under unopposed heavy air attacks, whilst the enemy continued to land reinforcements through Maleme.

Some Allied reinforcements were on their way. *Glenroy* embarked 900 men of the Queen's Royal Regiment and sailed from Alexandria for Tymbaki on the afternoon of 22 May, escorted by *Coventry*, *Auckland* and *Flamingo*.

Because of the air attacks *Glenroy* was likely to have to undergo off Crete, ABC decided (after consulting Wavell) to recall her and so, on the 23rd, he signalled *Glenroy* and escort to return to Alexandria. But then, to his amazement and fury, the Admiralty sent a direct order to *Glenroy* to turn back to the north, pending further instructions.

Later the Admiralty sent a signal to ABC urging him to land *Glenroy*'s troops, if it could be done that night. ABC replied that it was much too late for *Glenroy* to reach Tymbaki that night and that, if she had continued to go north, she would have been in the most vulnerable position possible for air attacks at daylight. It was out of the question to disembark troops and he had ordered *Glenroy* back to Alexandria. ABC was understandably angry: 'The less said about this unjustifiable interference by those ignorant of the situation the better.'

By now ABC was convinced that those at home were ignorant of the true situation in Crete. His temper, always on a short fuse, was severely tested by an exchange of signals to the Admiralty that the last four days had

been nothing short of a trial of strength between the Mediterranean Fleet and the German Air Force... In the coastal area we have to admit defeat and accept that losses are too great to justify us in trying to prevent seaborne attacks on Crete. This is a melancholy conclusion, but it must be faced. As I have always feared, enemy command of air, unchallenged by our own Air Force, and in these restricted waters, with Mediterranean weather, is too great odds for us to take on except by seizing opportunities of surprise and using utmost circumspection...

ABC was never one to magnify difficulties or dwell on disasters and those uncharacteristic phrases — 'admit defeat', 'losses too great', 'too great odds', 'utmost circumspection' — should have warned the Admiralty that the situation must be extremely grave. But the Admiralty responded at once by telling ABC what he already knew only too well: if it were just a matter of a duel between the fleet and the German Air Force then indeed it would 'probably be necessary' to accept the restrictions on the fleet which ABC suggested.

'There is however' the Admiralty signal went on, with plodding insistence, 'in addition the battle for Crete.' If the fleet could prevent seaborne reinforcements reaching the enemy until the Army had dealt with the airborne troops already on the island, then the Army might be able to deal with seaborne attacks. 'It is vitally important therefore to prevent a seaborne expedition reaching the island during the next day or two, even if this results in further losses to the Fleet. Their Lordships most fully appreciate the heavy strain under which your fleet is working.'

On 24 May the Chiefs of Staff called for an appreciation of the situation in Crete. The Commanders-in-Chief in the Middle East replied that in their opinion the scale of enemy air attack now made it impossible for the Navy to operate in the Aegean or near Crete by day. ABC could not guarantee to prevent seaborne landings without suffering losses which, added to the losses already sustained, would seriously prejudice the command of the eastern Mediterranean.

ABC, Wavell and Tedder would never have used language like this unless the situation was desperate. But the Chiefs of Staff, with Churchill's impatience and anger urging them on, replied that if the situation was 'allowed to drag on the enemy will have the advantage because unless more drastic naval action is taken than is suggested in your appreciation, the enemy will be able to reinforce the island to a considerable extent with men and stores'.

The message continued that, if enemy movement by sea or any collection of craft at Milos be reported, 'it will be essential for the Fleet to operate north of the island by day'. Losses would probably be considerable, and only experience would show for how many days the situation could be maintained.

ABC found this message 'singularly unhelpful'. As for losses, he said,

> Surely we have already sufficient experience of what losses are likely to be? In three days two cruisers and four destroyers were sunk, one battleship is out of action for several months, and two other cruisers and four destroyers sustained considerable damage. We cannot afford another such experience and retain sea control in Eastern Mediterranean.
>
> In point of fact, supply by sea has not yet come much into the picture, as, despite loss and turning back of his convoys, enemy is so prolific in air that for the moment he is able to reinforce and keep his forces supplied by air at will. This process is quite unchecked by air action on our part, and sight of constant unhindered procession of Ju.52's flying into Crete is among factors likely to affect morale of our forces.
>
> I feel that Their Lordships should know that the effect of recent operations on personnel is cumulative. Our light craft, officers, men, and machinery alike are nearing exhaustion. Since LUSTRE started, at the end of February, they have been kept running almost to the limit of endurance, and now, when work is redoubled, they are faced with an air concentration beside which, I am assured, that in Norway was child's-play. It is inadvisable to drive men beyond a certain point.

While the paper battle raged, the real war continued. The

Luftwaffe were using an airfield on Scarpanto, east of Crete. It was decided to attack it using aircraft from *Formidable* who now had twelve Fulmars, although some of them, according to ABC, 'were of doubtful reliability'.

Pridham-Wippell, flying his flag in *Queen Elizabeth*, with *Barham*, *Formidable*, and eight destroyers, sailed from Alexandria at noon on 25 May. *Glenroy* also sailed that evening for Tymbaki, escorted by *Stuart*, *Coventry* and *Jaguar*, with the same troops as she had tried to land before.

At 5 a.m. on 26 May, from a position 100 miles south-south-west of Scarpanto, *Formidable* flew off four Fulmars and four Albacores to attack the airfield. Four more aircraft should have taken part but two were unserviceable on deck and two returned to the carrier early because of defects.

Four bombers escorted by four fighters were a puny force compared with the air armadas the *Luftwaffe* mounted daily, but this was the first Allied air attack on Scarpanto and it achieved complete surprise. A number of aircraft were destroyed or damaged.

The *Luftwaffe*'s response was swift and savage. *Formidable* was dive-bombed twice and badly damaged. Her 'seaguard' destroyer *Nubian* was also hit and had her stern and rudder blown off but, somewhat to her Captain's surprise, she was still able to maintain 20 knots. So, steering by main engines, *Nubian* headed for Alexandria, with *Jervis* standing by her.

Formidable and four destroyers were detached after work, to return to Alexandria at daylight on 27 May and, after temporary repairs, she followed *Warspite* and *Illustrious* to the United States at the end of July. The damage her aircraft did to Scarpanto was not worth the loss of the fleet's only aircraft carrier.

The rest stayed at sea for another day in which they suffered more air attacks. In a raid early on 27 May, *Barham* was hit on 'Y' turret and two of her torpedo bulges were flooded by near-misses. The ships had to steer downwind whilst the fire on board *Barham* was put out.

On land the situation had continued to deteriorate for the Allies. On 26 May General Freyberg sent a signal to Wavell saying that the troops under his command at Suda Bay had reached the limit of their endurance and that, no matter what decision the Commanders-in-Chief reached, his troops' position was hopeless.

On the morning of 26 May Wavell and Tedder went to Alexandria for a meeting with ABC on board *Warspite*. General Sir Thomas Blamey, commanding the Australian Forces in the Middle East, and the Rt. Hon. Peter Fraser, the Prime Minister of New Zealand, were also present, both understandably anxious about their troops in Crete.

The joint planning staffs in Cairo had prepared a paper assessing the situation. It stated that the troops in Crete were defeated, disorganised and had no supply line. The air force had lost heavily and could not operate effectively over Crete. The Navy had lost half (*sic*) its operational ships, sunk or damaged. The paper recommended that the Commanders-in-Chief order the Army in Crete to surrender.

After they had considered the paper, Wavell said that the remainder of the fleet might well be lost if they persisted in trying to evacuate the beaten Army from Crete. If the fleet were lost, the Allies would lose control of the eastern Mediterranean, the Germans would reach Syria and then go onwards to the Persian oilfields. Without Persian oil, Wavell feared we could not win the war. It would take three years, he said, to build a new fleet.

Blamey and Fraser joined Wavell and Tedder in agreeing to accept the unanimous advice of their staffs. There seemed no alternative. The only dissenter was ABC, who spoke last and, Brownrigg recalled, along these lines:

> It has always been the duty of the Navy to take the Army overseas to battle and, if the Army fail, to bring them back again.
>
> If we now break with that tradition, ever afterwards when soldiers go overseas they will tend to look over their shoulders instead of relying on the Navy. You have said, General, that it will take three years to build a new Fleet. I will tell you that it will take three hundred years to build a new tradition. If, gentlemen, you now order the Army in Crete to surrender, the Fleet will still go there to bring off the Marines.

ABC's own recollections of this time when 'evacuation was in the air' were equally firm. 'My view was perfectly clear. I needed no persuasion. It was impossible to abandon the troops in Crete. Our naval tradition would never survive such an action. Whatever the risks, whatever our losses, the remaining ships of the fleet would make an all-out effort to bring away the Army.' However, he did make the point to Wavell that 'with the enemy's complete command in the air the moment might come when, with the terrible losses among the troops during their embarkation and their passage to Alexandria, lives might be saved if they surrendered where they were.'

Late that night of 26 May, Wavell replied to Freyberg that indeed the longer Crete could hold out the better. He had repeated Freyberg's signal to London, and Churchill's response was to signal to Freyberg himself: 'Your glorious defence commands admiration in every land. We know enemy is hard pressed. All aid in our power is being sent.' To the Commanders-in-Chief, Churchill telegraphed: 'Victory in Crete essential at this turning-point in the war. Keep hurling in all aid you can.'

But the time was past for such messages, however inspirational, or for 'hurling' in any aid, although attempts were still made to run troops and supplies to Crete. *Glenroy*, with the Queen's Regiment (who must have felt themselves old sea-dogs by now) still embarked, was first bombed and then attacked by low-flying torpedo-bombers on 26 May. Petrol in cans on the upper deck caught fire. In a ship with nearly 1,000 troops embarked and a large cargo of petrol, a fire could cause a major disaster. *Glenroy* had to steer south down wind while the fire was put out. But there was then no time to disembark the troops at Tymbaki, so *Glenroy* and her escort turned back that evening of 26 May. Later that night, *Abdiel, Hero* and *Nizam* landed 750 Commandos, under Colonel Laycock, in Suda Bay.

These were the last reinforcements to reach Crete. Convoy AC.31, of two merchant ships, had sailed from Alexandria for Suda Bay early on 26 May. But next day it was realised that the convoy had no chance of reaching Crete under the prevailing conditions of air attack and it was ordered to turn back.

Had that convoy arrived, its stores would only have benefited the enemy. On 27 May, Wavell sent a message to the Prime Minister: 'Fear that situation in Crete most serious. Canea front has collapsed and Suda Bay only likely to be covered for another twenty-four hours, if as long.'

That evening the Chiefs of Staff replied, 'You should evacuate Crete forthwith saving as many men as possible without regard to material and take whatever measures you think best whether by reinforcements or otherwise. C-in-C Mediterranean should take any steps to prevent seaborne landings which would interfere with evacuation…'

Seaborne landings by the enemy were now among the least of ABC's problems. He wrote in his dispatch:

> That the fleet suffered disastrously in this encounter with the unhampered German Air Force is evident, but it has to be remembered on the credit side that the Navy's duty was achieved and no enemy ship, whether warship or transport, succeeded in reaching Crete or intervening in the battle during those critical days. Nor should the losses sustained blind one to the magnificent courage and endurance that was displayed throughout. I have never felt prouder of the Mediterranean Fleet than at the close of these particular operations, except perhaps, at the fashion in which it faced up to the even greater strain which was so soon to be imposed upon it.

The position on land, when the order was given to evacuate, was that two battalions of Australians were holding out at Retimo, although surrounded and cut off. An RAF aircraft was sent to drop a message for them to retreat to Plaka Bay. The aircraft never returned and the message never got through. The garrison continued to resist until their CO decided it was useless to go on and surrendered on 30 May.

At Heraklion, some 4,000 troops of the 14th Infantry Brigade and the 1st Battalion Argyll & Sutherland Highlanders were also cut off but had suffered fewer air attacks than the troops in the west and they still held the airfield and the harbour.

The majority of the garrison of Crete, over 20,000 men, were in and around Suda Bay, from where they could not be evacuated. They would have to cross the mountains to the southward as best they could and be lifted off the beach at Sphakia.

ABC did not blink at the difficulties. 'We were not really in favourable condition to evacuate some twenty-two thousand soldiers, most of them from an open beach, in the face of the *Luftwaffe*. But there was no alternative. The Army could not be left to its fate. The Navy must carry on.'

There were some long faces amongst some of the 'pusillanimous buggers' on ABC's staff when they came to plan the evacuation. But to his staff and especially to his 'Inner Circle', of Edelsten, Dick, Brownrigg and Power, ABC went on insisting that they must not let the Army down. When Edelsten tried to argue with him, saying 'that the Fleet was played out, that we had few ships left, and that we must think of the future, ABC shut me up by saying that the Fleet's job was to go on trying to get the soldiers out, until the Army said enough'.

Without ABC's determination, the Crete evacuation might never have taken place. He pressed it forward against the opposition of the other Commanders-in-Chief and their staffs, of his own staff, and the Australian and New Zealand governments. It was ABC *contra mundum*.

The evacuation began on the night of 28/29 May. Captain S.H.T. Arliss (Captain (D) 7th Destroyer Flotilla) in *Napier*, with *Nizam*, *Kelvin* and *Kandahar*, with extra whalers, and food and small arms for the troops ashore, arrived off Sphakia just after midnight. In the next three hours they embarked nearly 700 troops, as well as unloading rations for the 15,000 who were expected to arrive in the next two days. The destroyers sailed before dawn and, although they were attacked by Junkers Ju.88s during the forenoon and *Nizam* was damaged by a near-miss, they reached Alexandria safely at 5 p.m. on 29 May.

Arliss' ships had got off lightly. Rawlings was not so lucky. Flying his flag in *Orion*, with *Ajax*, *Dido*, *Decoy*, *Jackal*, *Imperial*, *Hotspur*, *Kimberley* and *Hereward*, Rawlings sailed from Alexandria for Heraklion at 6 a.m. on 28 May. Air attacks began at about 5 p.m. when the ships were some ninety miles from Scarpanto. High-level bombing, dive-bombing and torpedo attacks went on until dark. *Imperial* and *Ajax* were near-missed. *Imperial* appeared unharmed but *Ajax* had a small fire, twenty men seriously wounded and some damage to her ship's side.

Rawlings knew that all his ships would have to be fully fit and operational to carry out the evacuation ahead of them and to survive the air attacks which were bound to follow the next day. It seemed to him that *Ajax* was already something of a lame duck and at 9 p.m. he ordered her to return to Alexandria.

Rawlings' ships arrived off Heraklion at 11.30 p.m. Destroyers went into the harbour to embark the soldiers and ferry them out to the cruisers. Ferrying was completed by 2.45 a.m., *Kimberley* and *Imperial* had embarked the rearguard by 3 a.m., and by 3.20 a.m. the force had left, having taken off the whole garrison of some 4,000 troops.

But the ships had been on their way just twenty-five minutes when *Imperial*'s steering gear failed, evidently as a result of the near-miss the previous evening. She only narrowly missed colliding with *Kimberley* and then with both *Orion* and *Dido*. She just had time to flash 'My rudder' to *Orion* before dropping astern.

It was the worst possible moment for such a mishap. At any other time *Imperial* could probably have been towed home, but now it was vitally important that Rawlings' ships be as far from enemy air bases as possible by dawn. Rawlings therefore had to decide whether to wait and hope that *Imperial*'s steering gear could be repaired or to sink her at once and press on.

When he heard that *Imperial* was unable to steer, Rawlings reduced speed to 15 knots and ordered *Hotspur* to go alongside

Imperial, take off her troops and her ship's company, and then sink her. 'There she was,' wrote Hodgkinson, in an account which moved ABC himself, 'a beautiful destroyer with engines, guns, torpedoes, everything, in perfect condition — lying utterly alone like some haunted thing.'

Hotspur hit her with one torpedo. 'But she was made of good stuff. She heeled over and then righted low in the water. Her Captain [Lieutenant-Commander C.E. de W. Kitcat] must have felt a glow of pride in her silent obstinacy... One could hear her quiet labours as she fought for buoyancy.' *Hotspur* fired a second torpedo. 'With a shudder she turned over towards us, and disappeared into the black sea. We did not talk to her Captain, as one does not talk to a man who has just lost his wife.'

The ninety minutes' delay was fatal. At daylight, when *Hotspur* with 900 men on board was just rejoining, Rawlings' ships were only just turning south through the Kaso Strait. The inevitable air attacks began at 6 a.m. and were to continue at intervals for the next nine hours.

The first ship lost was *Hereward*, hit by a bomb which caused her to reduce speed and fall away from her position in the screen. Once again Rawlings had to make a difficult decision — that to stay and help *Hereward* would only invite further casualties, and he must therefore leave her. She was last seen heading towards the coast of Crete some five miles away and firing her guns at aircraft. Her Captain was Lieutenant-Commander James Munn, who had been ABC's Flag Lieutenant in *Hood* before the war. Munn, his crew and the troops on board became prisoners-of-war.

More mishaps followed thick and fast. *Decoy* had suffered a near-miss and at 6.45 a.m. she reported fractured turbine feet and main circulator damage. Rawlings' ships had to reduce to

25 knots. Fifteen minutes later, *Orion* herself also had a near-miss which caused another reduction, to 21 knots.

At about 7.30 *Orion* was dive-bombed and machine-gunned and her Captain, G.R.B. Back, was mortally wounded by an explosive bullet. He died two hours later. Rawlings himself was wounded. At 8.15 *Dido* was hit by a bomb on 'B' turret. Three-quarters of an hour later *Orion* was attacked again and hit by a bomb on 'A' turret. Both turrets were put out of action.

At 10.45 *Orion* was attacked a third time. A large bomb hit her bridge, passed down through the superstructure and exploded in a stokers' messdeck crowded with soldiers. *Orion* had nearly 1,100 troops on board and there were very heavy casualties: 260 killed and 280 wounded.

High-level bombing attacks continued in the afternoon until the final raid at about 3 p.m. when the ships were within 100 miles of Alexandria. The first and only friendly aircraft of the day were two naval Fulmars sighted at about noon. Tedder had warned that air cover for the evacuation would be only meagre and spasmodic because of the distance from the air bases. The RAF provided some fighter cover on 29 May but the fighters were only able to stay on patrol for a short time. Despite several attempts, they were unable find Rawlings' ships, although they did engage and shoot down some enemy aircraft.

Rawlings' ships entered Alexandria harbour at 8 p.m. on 29 May *Orion* herself had only ten tons of oil fuel and two rounds of 6-inch H.E. ammunition left. ABC watched them come in. 'I shall never forget the sight of those ships coming up harbour,' he said, 'the guns of their fore turrets awry, one or two broken off and pointing forlornly skyward, their upper decks crowded with troops, and the marks of their ordeal only too visible.'

ABC went on board *Orion* at once. He found her 'a terrible sight and the messdeck a ghastly shambles'. Rawlings was 'cheerful but exhausted'. He had had an almost sleepless night, and had endured several air attacks. His Flag Captain had been mortally wounded at his side and he himself had been wounded.

Apart from the casualties in *Orion*, 103 officers and men out of 240 of the 2nd Black Watch — Wavell's own old battalion — were killed in *Dido*. Thus, of the 4,000 troops embarked from Heraklion, 800 — one in five — had been killed, wounded or captured since leaving Crete.

At times, as the saga of Crete unfolded, ABC had to take a very tough line with one or two ships. Brownrigg recalled

a well-known cruiser whose reputation as a fighting unit under a fighting Captain was one of the highest in the Med. When ordered to sail to evacuate the troops from Crete, the Captain asked if he could 'wait upon the C-in-C'. He explained that his ship's company were so worn out by some 36 days continuously at sea under air attack that he very much doubted if they would sail again that evening for Crete; he asked for them to have 48 hours in harbour to recoup. ABC explained the necessity to evacuate troops from Crete and the reasons for sailing that night. He ended 'Because you have a fine ship with a fine ship's company which have done magnificent work in the Med., I will come on board your ship and address your ship's company, but, if there is then a mutiny, I shall be no more backward than Lord St Vincent in making you hang your own ring-leaders from your own yard arm.' To underline his point — we were all very worked up in this moment of defeat so that his action did not seem so melodramatic as it does now in peace — he rang for his Secretary and said 'Bring me some Warrants for hanging; you know the forms.'

ABC addressed the ship's company and the ship sailed, but four men jumped over the side at the breakwater entrance rather than go to Crete again. In due course they were brought to Court Martial. The regulations say that the President of a Court Martial is to report the result in person to the Convening Authority, but we had the usual standing Station Order that the Commander-in-Chief did not wish to see Presidents of Courts Martial after the Court unless they had something special to report.

On this occasion, however, ABC made a signal to the President of the Court Martial saying 'C-in-C does not require you to wait upon him at the conclusion of the Court unless, if the accused are found guilty, the sentence should be less than three years' imprisonment.' This caused a furore among the barrister RNVR officers who often acted as 'Prisoner's Friends'. Nevertheless, the accused were sentenced to three years' imprisonment.

The night of 29/30 May was what ABC called 'the really big effort'. King, flying his flag in *Phoebe*, with *Perth*, *Glengyle*, *Calcutta*, *Coventry*, *Jervis*, *Janus* and *Hasty*, sailed from Alexandria for Sphakia at 9 p.m. on 28 May.

ABC had actually been out of touch with events in Crete from about 9 p.m. on 27 May until 10 a.m. on the 28th. Captain Morse and his Staff Commander C. Wauchope had shared headquarters with General Freyberg under a tree at Suda Point. On the evening of 27 May, they abandoned this HQ, destroyed their Wireless Station and loaded their kit, including a portable wireless set, into lorries for the drive to Sphakia.

The road across the mountains was rough and congested with traffic. The portable W/T set was irreparably damaged by the jolting of the lorry. Another set had been sent in ML 1011 but it was lost when the ML was sunk with all hands on 27

May. But Captain Morse recalled that the RAF at Maleme had had a W/T set which they had sent to Sphakia. He found it during the forenoon of 28 May in a cave about a mile from Sphakia. Here, in the cave, the three Services made their joint headquarters for the final stages of the evacuation.

That night Morse signalled to ABC that up to 10,000 troops would need evacuation on the following night (29/30 May). But Freyberg had already signalled that he thought it unlikely that the troops could hold out until then, and that 'an optimistic view' of the fighting troops which could be evacuated was under 2,000, with a number of stragglers.

From these signals it appeared that the situation in Crete was very bad, that 10,000 troops remained to be evacuated, with only about 2,000 of them in organised units, and that the night of 29/30 May would have to be the last.

On 29 May, when King's ships, including *Glengyle*, were at sea (and already being bombed) ABC's Military Liaison Officer Major-General Evetts flew to Cairo to brief Wavell on the naval situation. After consulting Blamey and Tedder, Wavell sent a personal message to ABC suggesting that the *Glen* ships and the cruisers should not be risked further, but destroyers could go on with the evacuation.

ABC's response was as resolute as before. He sent a 'Most Immediate' signal to the Admiralty, stating that three cruisers and one destroyer had already been damaged during the evacuation and there had been some 500 casualties (actually an underestimate) among the troops in the ships. More heavy casualties could be expected the next day, particularly if *Glengyle* with 3,000 troops embarked should happen to be hit. ABC asked if he was justified in accepting a similar scale of loss and damage to his already weakened fleet. But, he concluded, he was 'ready and willing to continue the evacuation as long as a ship remained to do so. It was against all tradition to leave troops deliberately in enemy hands.'

The Admiralty replied that evening, ordering *Glengyle* to turn back and the other ships to go on. But ABC then told the Admiralty he considered it was too late for *Glengyle* to turn back and he was sending three more destroyers [*Stuart, Jaguar* and *Defender*, who left Alexandria p.m. on 29 May] to join King's Force. They would give extra protection to King's ships and, having no troops on board themselves, would be able to take off troops from any ships which might be damaged by air attack.

It was under thirty miles from Suda to Sphakia by road — not a great distance by Army marching standards. But this was over a single narrow mountain road, much of it no more than a track with an appallingly rough surface, which wound through steep, waterless and almost barren countryside. The march would have been an ordeal for fresh, rested men. For the exhausted, thirsty; footsore New Zealanders, weighed down with kit and small arms as they clambered up the steep slopes, it was torture — a *via dolorosa* indeed, as Freyberg himself described it.

Enemy air activity was surprisingly light, although occasional Me. 109s would fly along the road, raking everything in sight with machine-gun fire. Some men hid by day and marched only by night. Others decided to take their chance and plodded onwards, doggedly putting one foot in front of the other. Discipline varied according to the quality of the surviving officers and NCOs. Some continued to march smartly in disciplined, soldierly fashion, keeping in their proper ranks as fighting units. Others degenerated into a disorganised rabble, especially as the sea came nearer.

The road finished in a series of acute hairpin bends before finally ending abruptly at the edge of a 500-foot cliff. From there, a precipitous goat track led down the almost sheer cliff face to the tiny fishing village of Sphakia where there was only one beach, with one stretch of shingle less than two hundred yards long suitable for embarking men in boats. The soldiers had to stay up on the cliff top, hiding as best they could from observation from the air, until they were called forward to embark. There was no communication between beach and cliff top except by runners. All instructions therefore took a very long time to pass.

King's Force arrived at 11.30 p.m. on 29 May and the main evacuation began. *Phoebe*, *Perth* and *Glengyle* anchored off Sphakia, whilst *Calcutta*, *Coventry* and the destroyers patrolled to seaward. The soldiers were ferried off to the ships in *Glengyle*'s landing craft and in two Assault Landing Craft which had been brought in *Perth*. The beach was so small that there was no room for ships' boats to be used as well as the landing craft. But, with the destroyers coming in later to embark their quota of troops, about 6,000 men had been embarked by 3.20 a.m. when the Force sailed for Alexandria. Three landing craft were left behind for use the next night.

Stuart, *Jaguar* and *Defender* joined soon after dawn, as did the *Luftwaffe*. In the first of three attacks, *Perth* was hit by a bomb which put her forward boiler room out of action. But RAF fighters put in an appearance and covered the Force for most of the day, driving off or breaking up formations of Ju.87s, Ju.88s and Heinkel He.IIIs.

During 29 May it became clear from interviews with senior officers who had just returned from Crete, and from more optimistic signals from Freyberg and Morse, that the situation ashore was not quite as bad as had been thought. ABC decided to send four destroyers to embark men on the night of 30/31 May. Captain Arliss in *Napier* sailed again from Alexandria on the morning of 30 May; with *Nizam*, *Kelvin* and *Kandahar*, bound for Sphakia.

Kandahar reported a mechanical defect some three hours out and was ordered back to Alexandria. At 3.30 p.m. *Kelvin* was near-missed by bombs from three Ju.88s which reduced her speed to 20 knots. Arliss had to order her, too, to turn back. He himself went on with his two remaining destroyers and arrived off Sphakia at 12.30 a.m. on 31 May. Using the three motor landing craft left there, *Napier* and *Nizam* embarked the prodigious number of 700 troops each and sailed again at 3 a.m. They arrived in Alexandria, after *Napier* had been near-missed and her speed reduced to 23 knots, at 7 p.m. that evening.

On 30 May Freyberg asked for one last lift, of 3,000 troops, to be taken off from Sphakia on the night of 31 May/1 June. This was a much larger number than had been estimated. But ABC decided to send more ships, although the number of troops embarked was to be restricted to 2,000. King, with *Phoebe*, *Abdiel*, *Kimberley*, *Hotspur* and *Jackal*, sailed from Alexandria at 6 a.m. on 31 May to carry out the last evacuation from Sphakia. But Arliss had signalled on his way back that some 6,500 troops still remained to be evacuated. So ABC authorised King to increase his maximum number to 3,500.

During the night of 30/31 May, Freyberg and Morse, acting on instructions from Wavell, embarked in a Sunderland flying boat at Sphakia and flew to Egypt, leaving Major-General Weston, Royal Marines, in command in Crete.

Wavell, Fraser, Freyberg, Blamey and Evetts had a meeting in Cairo on 31 May and decided they could not ask the Navy to do anything more. They flew down to Alexandria and met

ABC and his staff at a conference hut on the airfield. There, Wavell gave ABC

> our decision and absolution from further effect on behalf of the Army. I saw the faces of his staff light up with relief. I heard afterwards that they had been trying to impress on him that any further losses by the Navy and even the Italians could not help being masters of the Eastern Mediterranean. Then Andrew C. spoke briefly. He thanked us for our effort to relieve him of responsibility but said that the Navy had never yet failed the Army in such a situation, and was not going to do so now; he was going in again that night with everything he had which would float and could bring off troops.

This, Wavell said, was 'a very gallant decision'.

ABC signalled to King to fill his ships up to capacity. He also sent a message to the Admiralty that he had called a halt to evacuation after the night of 31 May/1 June; even if King's ships suffered no losses, ABC said, he would still be left with a fleet of only two battleships, one cruiser, two anti-aircraft cruisers, *Abdiel* and nine destroyers fit for service.

At about 8 p.m. on 31 May, ABC received a personal message from Wavell to be passed to Weston informing him that this was the last night and authorising the surrender of any troops left behind. As this meant an 'irrevocable decision' to end the evacuation, ABC considered it very carefully before sending it on.

But even then, it was not quite the end. Almost at once, ABC had a message from General Blamey who was disturbed by the small number of Australians who had been evacuated. Blamey asked for a ship to be sent to Plaka Bay. ABC had to tell him that it was too late to change the destinations of any of the ships. (In any case, although Blamey was unaware of it, the

Australians who might have reached Plaka had already surrendered on 30 May.)

King's Force arrived off Sphakia at 11.20 p.m. on 31 May; having survived three air attacks *en route*. The three motor landing craft were again invaluable. In fact, embarkation went so well that at one point the beach was actually empty of troops. But this unfortunately caused a last-minute rush and some troops had to be left behind, including some Special Service troops and, to the Navy's particular regret, some 1,000 Royal Marines.

Medical stores were landed, the three landing craft were sunk or disabled, and the ships sailed at 3 a.m. on 1 June with nearly 4,000 troops. During the night, on Wavell's instructions, General Weston embarked in a Sunderland at Sphakia and flew to Egypt. He handed written orders to the senior British Army officer remaining to come to terms with the enemy.

To give King's ships added anti-aircraft protection on their return journey, ABC ordered *Calcutta* and *Coventry* to sail early on 1 June to meet them. *Calcutta* had been in King's first Force which had returned to Alexandria in the middle watch of 31 May. Immediately after breakfast her Captain, D.M. Lees, went to the C-in-C's office:

> Knowing that the final evacuation was to be made that night I was confident of at least two days and nights in harbour, during which my ship's company and I would be able to get some much needed rest and sleep.
>
> Imagine my feelings therefore when, in the Operations Room, I was told I was to sail again at 2300 that night, meet the party returning from Crete and escort back to Alexandria any ships whose speed might have been reduced, thereby enabling the main body to carry on at high speed. I must have been fairly near the end of my tether because I'm afraid I let fly a torrent of vituperation and abuse at the staff.

ABC, whose office adjoined the Operations Room, must have heard, as the door opened and, without saying a word, he beckoned me to come into his room. Having sat me down he said, 'Now, what's the matter?' I replied, 'I know tonight is the final evacuation. My ship's company is tired out. I'm tired out. And now I hear we have to go to sea again at 2300 tonight.'

Most Commanders-in-Chief would have given a very severe 'ticking-off' to a very junior Post Captain for such an outburst; not so ABC. He understood the strain we had been under for long weeks. He talked to me quietly, like a father, explaining everything, including his own misery at being shore-bound whilst the ships of his Fleet were being decimated. After about a quarter of an hour he asked, 'Now are you happy to go out tonight?'

Of course I was.

At 9 a.m. on 1 June, *Coventry* detected aircraft on her radar and some minutes later two Ju.88s dived out of the sun. A stick of bombs from the first Ju.88 narrowly missed *Coventry*, but two bombs from the other hit *Calcutta*. She settled fast and sank in a few minutes. *Coventry*, now commanded by Captain William ('the Silent') Carne, picked up twenty-three officers, including Lees, and 232 men.

ABC was waiting on the jetty when *Coventry* returned and he came on board as soon as she had secured. He felt the loss of every ship deeply, but *Calcutta* had been special. He had commanded her himself in the West Indies before the war. She had served in his fleet since September 1940 and had been in action almost every time she went to sea. 'As we walked up and down the quarterdeck,' said Lees, 'ABC was in tears.'

ABC was disappointed to learn that there were still some 5,000 troops left in Crete. He had hoped, and had been given to understand, that King's last trip had brought everybody off.

Certainly Pound felt that still more could be done. In the early hours of 1 June ABC received a message from him saying that if there was a reasonable chance of taking off any substantially formed body of men on the night of 1/2 June he thought the attempt should be made.

This convinced ABC, if he had needed convincing, that nobody at home understood what had been accomplished in Crete and what his ships had endured to achieve it.

But now, even for ABC, enough was enough. He replied that Weston had said that the 5,000 troops in Crete were not capable of further resistance because of strain and lack of food and they had been instructed to capitulate. Therefore, no more ships would be sent.

In a later message ABC pointed out that the only ships available for an evacuation on the night of 1/2 June were *Queen Elizabeth* and *Valiant* and five destroyers. Every other ship was either too slow or damaged. Fighter protection was 'thin and irregular'. In view of the situation developing in the Western Desert and in Syria any further reduction in the strength of the fleet was out of the question. In other words, it was all over and nothing more could be done.

In fact, a great deal had been done. Some 16,500 British and Imperial troops had been evacuated. Provisions and stores had been landed for those who were left behind. The price for the Navy was 1,828 killed and 183 wounded. The cruisers *Gloucester*, *Fiji* and *Calcutta*, and the destroyers *Greyhound*, *Kashmir*, *Kelly*, *Hereward* and *Imperial* had been sunk. *Warspite*, *Barham*, *Formidable*, *Orion*, *Dido*, *Kelvin* and *Nubian* had been damaged beyond the capacity of local resources to repair. *Perth*, *Naiad*, *Carlisle*, *Napier*, *Kipling* and *Decoy* would be under repair in Alexandria for some weeks, *Havock*, *Kingston* and *Nizam* for a fortnight.

There had also been serious losses among the flotilla of little ships, based at Suda Bay, who had carried out local defence duties in Crete: the minesweeper *Widnes*, the South African-built whalers *Syvern*, *KOS 22* and *KOS 23*, the Tank Landing 'A' Lighters A.6, A.16 and A.20, and the MLs 1011 and 1030 were all either bombed and sunk or beached.

Such losses in ships and men would, as ABC said, 'normally only occur during a major fleet action, in which the enemy might be expected to suffer greater losses than our own'. It all made ABC feel

> very heavy-hearted. We had been fighting against the strength of the *Luftwaffe*, and once again it had been borne in upon us that the Navy and the Army could not make up for the lack of air forces. In my opinion three squadrons of long-range fighters and a few heavy bombing squadrons would have saved Crete.

In the final peroration of his dispatch, ABC wrote,

> It is not easy to convey how heavy was the strain that men and ships sustained. Apart from the cumulative effect of prolonged seagoing over extended periods it has to be remembered that in this last instance ships' companies had none of the inspiration of battle with the enemy to bear them up. Instead they had the unceasing anxiety of the task of trying to bring away in safety thousands of their own countrymen, many of whom were in an exhausted and dispirited condition, in ships necessarily so overcrowded that even when there was opportunity to relax conditions made this impossible. They had started the evacuation already overtired and they had to carry it through under conditions of savage air attack such as had only recently caused grievous losses in the fleet.

There is rightly little credit or glory to be expected in these operations of retreat but I feel that the spirit of tenacity shown by those who took part should not go unrecorded.

More than once I felt that the stage had been reached when no more could be asked of officers and men, physically and mentally exhausted by their efforts and by the events of these fateful weeks. It is perhaps even now not realised how nearly the breaking point was reached, but that these men struggled through is the measure of their achievement and I trust that it will not lightly be forgotten.

Possibly, the realisation of just how many ships and men had been lost under his command, and the tone of some of the signals he had been receiving, suggested to ABC that his own position was in question. In his letter to Pound of 30 May, in which he had discussed *Ajax*'s morale, he said: 'It may be that he or the Admiralty would like a change in command of the fleet out here. If this is so, I shall not feel in any way annoyed more especially as it may be that the happenings of the last few days may have shaken the faith of the personnel of the fleet in my handling of affairs.' Although it is true that some of the Lower Deck did call ABC 'The Butcher' because of his handling of the battle of Crete, they would have regarded any suggestion that he should be relieved with incredulity and dismay.

Wavell had no doubt about the achievements of ABC and his fleet. Their work, he said, was beyond all praise. On 2 June, he sent ABC a personal message, which was promulgated throughout the fleet:

I send to you and all under your command the deepest admiration and gratitude of the Army in the Middle East for the magnificent work of the Royal Navy in bringing back the troops from Crete. The skill and self-sacrifice with which the difficult and dangerous operation was carried out will never be forgotten, and will form another strong link between our two services. Our thanks to all and our sympathy for your losses.

If ABC needed any reassurance, he could take it from the shoals of mail he regularly received from complete strangers. One letter in July 1941, economically addressed to 'Admiral Cunningham, Middle East, Egypt, Please Forward', was from a Mrs Palmer, of Taupo, New Zealand. She had three sons on active service, two of them in the Greek and Crete campaigns. She thanked Cunningham for saving her sons: 'Pray God may bless and keep you,' she wrote, 'and bring you victorious and unharmed till this ghastly war is over.'

But the best endorsement of ABC's handling of affairs was from the men who were there. Some of the New Zealanders who took part in the retreats in Greece and Crete later recorded their absolute faith that, if they could just reach the sea, the Navy would surely be waiting to take them off. One wrote, 'With a torch we flashed an S.O.S. and, to our tremendous relief, we received an answer. It was the Navy on the job — the Navy for which we had been hoping and praying all along the route.'

15: THE SYRIAN CAMPAIGN AND CONVOYS TO MALTA

IN LATER YEARS ABC wondered whether the loss of Crete after only ten days' fighting was really as serious a disaster as it seemed at the time. Had Crete been held, with its airfields, Malta would certainly have been much easier to supply from the east but it would be difficult to maintain a large garrison and an RAF contingent on the island.

Crete had cost the Germans some 6,000 men killed, missing or wounded, with particularly heavy casualties amongst the elite airborne troops and their senior officers. The *Luftwaffe* had lost 220 aircraft destroyed and 148 damaged. The Balkan campaign was to affect coming events in Syria and delayed the start of Operation Barbarossa, the German attack on Russia, by a critical few weeks.

ABC visited the hospitals in Alexandria and Cairo and was deeply distressed by the 'terrible sights' of sailors badly wounded and burned. The Residency was full of convalescing young men. 'We're always glad to see them, it keeps us young,' ABC wrote to Doodles. 'One poor lad with both eyes gone. It gives little Hilda something to do looking after him. A lot of friends went under. That charming boy James Munn my flag lieutenant in the *Hood* has I fear gone west. Added to the loss of Walter Starkie it has made Nona and I very sad hearted.'

For ABC's staff, May 1941 was the worst time. Power said 'it was the most miserable period of my life'. The 'pressure of work was intense day and night' and there was a 'sense of impending and actual disaster'. The fleet 'had been reduced to rags'. But 'ABC maintained a bold undaunted front, sparkling with energy and humour. We did our best to respond.'

While ABC turned a cheerful face to the world, he confided his doubts and misgivings in his letters. On 30 May he sent a letter to Pound by hand of Mountbatten (himself a survivor).

> There is no hiding the fact that in our battle with the German Air Force we have been badly battered. I always thought that we might get a surprise if they really turned their attention to the fleet. No anti-aircraft fire will deal with the simultaneous attacks of 10-20 aircraft.
>
> Our losses are very heavy... I would not mind if we had inflicted corresponding damage on the enemy but I fear we have achieved little beyond preventing a seaborne landing in Crete and the evacuation of some of the Army there. I feel very heavy hearted about it all.

ABC and his staff had now 'to sort out our ideas, and to consider what could be done with the greatly reduced fleet that remained to us'. They had two battleships, *Queen Elizabeth* and *Valiant*, two cruisers, *Ajax* and *Phoebe*, the anti-aircraft cruiser *Coventry* (though she had only a makeshift temporary bow) and some seventeen destroyers 'in various states of effectiveness'.

The main commitments were still the supply of Malta and Tobruk, and attacks on the enemy's supply line to Libya. But all three objectives were hamstrung by the lack of air cover. In his report to the Admiralty, ABC stressed that 'The lesson of recent events was quite definite and repeated that of France and Norway, which was that military operations in modern war could not be conducted without air forces which would allow at least a temporary air superiority.'

He asked that all obstacles be swept aside somehow so that a Coastal Command Force of torpedo-bombers, bombers and reconnaissance aircraft could be formed, to find convoys and sink the enemy, and take over the function of carriers.

It could be argued that the Navy should have provided its own air cover, over Crete and elsewhere. After all, the Navy had the Fleet Air Arm, with aircraft carriers, aircrews and aircraft, specially equipped and trained to operate over the sea. If there were no aircraft over the fleet, surely that was as much, if not more, a failure of the Navy as of the RAF?

Nevertheless, the Royal Air Force were, rightly or wrongly, widely held to have let the Navy and the Army down by failing to give proper air support. 'I was soon conscious', Tedder wrote in his post-war memoirs, 'of a first class hate working up against the RAF for having "let them down in Greece and Crete".'

ABC was aware of the prevailing atmosphere. 'I am not very happy about our relations with the Air out here,' he wrote to Pound on 11 June. 'Since Crete, about which they came in for much criticism and odium, largely undeserved, they have been very touchy and difficult.'

The heart of the problem was ABC's own uneasy relationship with Tedder. The main bone of contention was ABC's proposal, to which he returned again and again, to set up a Naval Co-Operation Group in the Mediterranean, 'analogous to the Coastal Command at home' as ABC told Pound in the same letter carried by Lees, 'with its HQ down here'. Tedder had accepted the idea in principle but, according to ABC, was being 'most dilatory in setting up the organisation and he particularly refuses to allot aircraft for the sole duty of Naval Co-Operation'.

The real difference was that Tedder thought it a waste of time to train aircrews for the time they would spend flying over the sea, whereas ABC thought they should fly over the sea *all* the time.

In July 1941, ABC complained to Pound that 'I haven't had a [recce] report about the Piraeus or Suda for over a week.' However, there had been 'a slight stirring of the bones' about 'a Coastal Command organisation out here'. Tedder was 'on the whole sympathetic' but 'the chief n****r in the woodpile is a man Drummond [Air Vice-Marshal Peter Drummond], now Deputy AOC-in-C. He obstructs on principle and is a thorough non-co-operator. He was delighted when Longmore was relieved as Longmore kept him in order.'

ABC's staff were well aware of his opinions about his fellow C-in-Cs. 'Unfortunately,' Power noted, 'ABC did not like or get on with either the Auk [Auckinleck] or Tedder. ABC thought Tedder "capable but crooked", interested in the "glorification of the RAF first, co-operation to win the war second".'

Tedder had other demands upon his resources. In April 1941 there was a German-inspired revolt in Iraq and in June a new campaign began in Syria, where the Vichy French authorities were suspected of being sympathetic to the Axis.

To support the sea flank, ABC scraped together a force of *Phoebe* and *Ajax* and four destroyers under King, based at Haifa. A second force, of *Glengyle*, *Coventry*, *Hotspur* and *Isis*, sailed with troops from Port Said on the night before the operation began on 8 June. Fulmars were based in Palestine to give air cover, and Swordfish in Cyprus to forestall any attempt to reinforce Vichy forces by sea.

Admiral Godfroy assured ABC that nothing that happened in Syria would affect the agreement they had made in July 1940, but the reaction of Vichy forces on the spot was still uncertain.

The affair did not start well. Two French flotilla leaders caught *Janus* alone off Sidon and badly damaged her. On 15 June *Isis* and *Ilex* were bombed and damaged whilst supporting the Army. Thus another three irreplaceable destroyers were out of action. 'Heard ye ever the like?' wrote ABC disgustedly (in the letter to Willis criticising King).

On land, the Allied forces under Maitland Wilson were outnumbered at the outset by the defending Vichy French, whose resistance stiffened as time went on. But after Wavell had sent in reinforcements, the French asked for an armistice, which was agreed in due course.

British control of Syria enormously improved the Allies' strategic position in the Middle East. However, as so often, dealings with the Vichy French were greatly complicated by the Free French. 'We have had a lot of trouble with de Gaulle,' ABC wrote to Pound. De Gaulle 'became almost unbalanced and wanted to denounce the Armistice terms and threatened all sorts of trouble. Lyttleton succeeded in quietening him down but he is a bad man, I am afraid.'

Oliver Lyttleton had recently come out from England as Minister of State in the Middle East. He not only dealt effectively with de Gaulle but took an immense political burden off Wavell's (and later Auchinleck's) shoulders. He immediately earned the approval of ABC (who liked him and called him 'the Commissar') by agreeing that it was impossible to run the fleet from Cairo. The pressure for ABC to move to Cairo intensified in June 1941 after *Warspite* left for repairs in the United States and ABC and his staff moved ashore to the Gabbari Docks in Alexandria. But ABC still felt passionately that his proper place was with his fleet. He thought it was enough that he flew to Cairo with Royer Dick at least once a week to attend meetings, and he still had Captain Norman as an additional Chief of Staff.

Wavell also appointed his own personal 'go-between', Lieutenant-Colonel R.B. Moseley, to liaise with ABC's staff. 'Babe' Moseley actually joined the Navy as a cadet and went to Osborne in 1913, but he had resigned as a sublieutenant to join the 1st Royal Dragoons. 'I was shown to a desk in an office used by the more junior staff officers, and allowed to see an assortment of signals,' said Moseley. 'I found it difficult to find out what was going on and was not informed about C-in-C conferences etc. After a few days I went to ABC and said, "I realise, sir, what you are thinking of me. Either I was a failure in the Senior Service and axed or I wilfully deserted and converted myself into a 'Pongo' in which case I must be mad. In neither case would I be of any use to you. I would like you to know I deliberately made myself a horsed soldier and have no regrets!" He roared with laughter and seemed to understand immediately. Very soon I was seeing the most top secret papers and signals and attending intelligence meetings etc. I was an immense admirer of ABC,' Moseley added. 'He was a very salt sailor but a great man of few words but staunchly loyal to his service and country. I enjoyed the twinkle in his watery eye and his great sense of humour.'

Longmore had been the first 'Lord of the Middle East' to depart. Unknown to ABC or Wavell, a second departure was imminent. Mr Churchill regarded the successful passage of the TIGER convoy, achieved with the help of a meteorological miracle, as his own special coup and ever afterwards took a fierce paternal interest in the welfare of his 'Tiger cubs', subjecting Wavell to constant pressure to use them in a counter-offensive in the Western Desert.

The 'Cubs' suffered from numerous mechanical defects, about which Churchill was displeased to hear. They, and the tanks already in Egypt, needed much work (some of it done by about ninety naval artificers and blacksmiths) to make them desert-worthy. Many of the crews had hardly had enough time for training in what to them were new weapons.

Furthermore, Wavell was bedevilled by political badgering. He was preparing an offensive in the Western Desert which he was told was to have absolute priority over Syria, yet he was constantly being urged to take air squadrons and troops away from the Western Desert for Syria.

Nevertheless, Wavell was induced to undertake the counter-offensive, codenamed Operation BATTLEAXE, its principal objective being the relief of Tobruk. It would also gain airfields along the Libyan coast to provide desperately needed fighter cover for convoys to Malta and for the fleet at sea.

The Army would have welcomed naval gunfire support along the coast, but every available fighter was to be used to support the Army and there were not enough left over to cover naval forces. Thus, the Navy took no part in BATTLEAXE, except to prepare for the opening of the port of Solium and to increase the flow of supplies to Tobruk.

BATTLEAXE began on 15 June 1941, and failed. After three days, the BATTLEAXE forces were back more or less where they started, after heavy losses in armour.

There were reasons for the failure. The operation had been mounted in a hurry; many crews had not been in a tank since February; the infantry and the tanks had not trained together; the two tank brigades, each equipped with different types of tank, had had no joint exercises; there were mechanical breakdowns; and there was a shortage of artillery.

Meanwhile, the enemy had Rommel, better tanks, better mutual understanding between tank units, good and timely intelligence of British movements and, last but not least, the formidable 88mm anti-aircraft gun, used as an antitank weapon in the desert for the first time.

Had BATTLEAXE been a success, it might have saved Wavell, but even that is not certain. Churchill had made up his mind on 19 May to replace Wavell with General Auchinleck, the C-in-C in India. The failure of BATTLEAXE prompted him to act.

ABC 'was desperately sorry to see Wavell go. We had come through a lot together, triumphs and set-backs. We were great friends, and I think trusted each other fully. Though naturally we did not agree on everything, we both knew that the other would go all out to help his opposite number. I had the greatest admiration for Wavell.'

The other news on 22 June 1941 was that Germany had invaded Russia. ABC thought it very satisfactory. Power had bought a 'Russian-style' fur hat when he was in Bucharest and put it on that day. ABC immediately impounded it and put it on. Thereafter it was kept on a hook and donned by any officer who mentioned Russia.

Wavell left Cairo by air at 7 a.m. on 7 July. ABC got up at 4 a.m., caught a plane from Dekheila, was on the airfield at Heliopolis to say farewell, and was back in his house in Alexandria for 8.30 breakfast.

Hillie had decided to go home at last. 'Poor child, she is a bit stunned,' ABC wrote, 'and it was very trying for her to see the young men come in daily to tea and her lad not coming. My goodness, Doodles, that child has courage. She is as brave as you are and that's saying no small thing! I wish you knew her better, she is streets ahead of the rest of the family I hope she doesn't get caught up in the Edinburgh set. If her baby turns out a boy she plans to come South I know so that in due course he may become known to her husband's friends.'

There was news of Hillie from Cape Town early in August (when ABC also heard that James Munn was a prisoner-of-war) and a cable in September saying she had arrived safely in England. She had her baby, a boy, in December.

Late in July 1941 ABC sent a letter to Pound by hand of Auchinleck who, he presumed, 'is going home to explain why the Western Desert offensive must be delayed till November'.

ABC's relationship with Auchinleck was not easy. Although he was never 'in a state of continual war' with him, as he once told Willis he was with Tedder, ABC found Auchinleck a somewhat aloof and unapproachable character. Writing in September 1941, ABC told Willis that 'the order of precedence in India is C-in-C Army at the head of the Viceroy's council and the Naval C-in-C East Indies the bottom of it after all the Indians!! I feel he has not yet got this out of his head though he will before I've finished with him.'

But the task of educating Auchinleck proved to be more difficult than anticipated. By November ABC was writing, 'Having served in India all his life he views himself as a heaven-born and does not lightly tolerate other heaven-borns such as the C-in-C Mediterranean. As you know, although naturally most sweet-tempered I have a vein of "tenacity of purpose" (rude people call it pig-headed obstinacy) and when my feet are firmly planted I have found him to give way I like him but I liked his predecessor better!!'

In May 1941 U-110 was captured in the Atlantic, with its Enigma coding machine, code books, tables and settings intact. It later sank under tow, but the material taken from it was a major intelligence coup, brilliantly exploited. With this and material from other sources, GC&CS at Bletchley Park began to read some of the German Navy's Enigma machine cyphers currently from June 1941.

The Special Intelligence thus gained was codenamed ULTRA (replacing the name HYDRO, used since January 1940). ULTRA material was distributed only to specially selected and severely restricted numbers of recipients by means of one-time pad cypher (an additive table used once only and then destroyed, giving total protection).

In the Mediterranean, the Navy had an Operational Intelligence Centre (OIC) at Alexandria. The only indoctrinated members of the 'ULTRA Club' were ABC himself, Willis, Dick and Power. Vice-Admiral Ford, at Malta, was also an ULTRA recipient.

At first, the flow of ULTRA was meagre. The Italian naval cyphers were not being read and the main source of ULTRA in the Mediterranean until the summer of 1941 was the *Luftwaffe* Enigma. This, for example, revealed the Vichy Government's naval movements and intentions in Syria. But, understandably, it contained only occasional instructions and information about convoy escorts.

Characteristically, Mr Churchill was eager to make the most of ULTRA, or BONIFACE, as he called it, using an earlier codename. In July 1941, after he had been briefed on the Admiralty's arrangements for sending ULTRA about Axis shipping movements in the Mediterranean out to ABC, Churchill minuted to Pound: 'I hope Admiral Cunningham realises the quality of the information. If he cannot intercept on this we do not deserve success… I wish I knew what he *did* when he received these messages.'

This was a somewhat unfair jibe. By mid-1941 the balance of success regarding convoys to North Africa had tilted dramatically in the enemy's favour. Between March and the middle of May, convoys for Tripoli were leaving Naples every three or four days, with individual ships sailing from Palermo and Trapani. Only ten Axis ships were sunk in the first three months of 1941, and only twenty-one in April and May, including those sunk by the 14th Destroyer Flotilla on 15 April.

Churchill's remark also seemed to ignore a fundamental truth: the most accurate and timely intelligence is useless without adequate forces to take advantage of it. ABC did not for the time being have enough ships seriously to interrupt enemy convoys. The run to Tobruk still took a steady toll — the sailors called the jetty in Alexandria where they loaded stores for Tobruk 'The Condemned Cell'.

In July, ABC decided it was asking too much of the same ships to go on this hazardous trip week in and week out, and that the work should be shared by all the destroyers in turn. Because of enemy aircraft on the Egyptian border at Solium, the runs to Tobruk had to be precisely timed, so that the ships arrived by night and were away by daylight. There was some competition to achieve the fastest unloading times; the destroyer *Jervis* claimed the record, unloading fifty tons of stores into lighters in twenty minutes.

The one branch to have some success against the enemy at this time were the submarines. The 8th Flotilla, based at Gibraltar, the seven 'U' Class in Malta (designated the 10th Flotilla in September 1941), and the larger 'T' Class boats based at Alexandria all had good months in June and July 1941. ABC asked the Admiralty to send him all the submarines that could be spared. As he said, 'each boat was worth its weight in gold'.

Knowing that the constant bombing of Malta was giving the submarines there little rest in harbour, ABC sent a signal 'to cheer them up a little': 'The strain of continuous and arduous duties you are being asked to carry out is fully appreciated, but your fine actions clearly indicate that their necessity is very apparent to you and I am certain that you will carry on with the same ready efficiency.'

The submarine campaign against enemy shipping in the Mediterranean was very much helped by an unexpected stroke of good fortune for the Allies on the cryptographic front. Ironically, the Germans, whose own Enigma naval machine cyphers had been penetrated, criticised the vulnerability of the Italian naval machine cyphers, which remained secure. The Italians eventually yielded to German pressure and began to use for most of their communications about shipping in the Mediterranean a medium-grade cypher known as 'C38m', based on a Swedish C38 coding machine.

GC&CS had broken the C38m settings for May and June by the end of June 1941 and the July settings by the 10th of the month. Thereafter the C38m was read more or less currently in the United Kingdom and transmitted to the Middle East until the Italian armistice in September 1943. The first intelligence from the C38m, sent out on 23 June, was the news of a convoy of four liners with troops bound for North Africa. The convoy turned back because all available aircraft at Malta were concentrated against it. It sailed again on the 27th and reached Libya safely. But there would be other chances to attack those ships.

The C38m intelligence was so plentiful and so promising that as early as August 1941 Churchill and ABC were discussing the possibility of basing surface ships in Malta again. But, meanwhile, no supplies had reached Malta since May, apart from the essential stores brought in by minelaying submarines. By mid-July the situation in Malta was very grave. Clearly, something had to be done about the beleaguered island.

As it was not possible to run a convoy from the east, ABC suggested that the July 1941 convoy be mounted from the west.

The main object of the Operation, codenamed SUBSTANCE, was the safe passage of an eastbound convoy of seven large transports to Malta. Other objectives were to transport nearly five thousand troops, embarked in cruisers and destroyers of the escort, to Malta; pass a second convoy of empty transports from Malta westward to Gibraltar; fly off a small force of Swordfish to Malta; and, finally, the safe return of the convoy escorts to Gibraltar.

SUBSTANCE was commanded by Somerville with Force H, with the battlecruiser *Renown* wearing Somerville's flag, *Ark Royal* and the cruiser *Hermione* (temporarily replacing *Sheffield*) as a covering force; the convoy escort, of the cruiser *Edinburgh*, wearing the flag of Rear-Admiral Neville Syfret, commanding the 18th Cruiser Squadron, with the battleship *Nelson*, the fast minelayer *Manxman*, and five destroyers; and the cruisers *Manchester* and *Arethusa*, the personnel ship *Leinster* and three destroyers, which would embark the troops from the French troopship *Pasteur* in Gibraltar and then sail, on 21 July, to join the convoy.

ABC put to sea with his battle fleet, steaming west during daylight, and submarines were stationed ahead to transmit signals west of Crete, all to try and convince the enemy that the convoy was to be run right through the Mediterranean to Alexandria.

Elaborate arrangements were made to conceal the convoy's intentions from the watchers in Spain but there was thick fog in Gibraltar harbour which delayed sailings. *Leinster* ran aground in the early hours of the 21st. The 1,000 troops she carried (which, by ill fortune, included the RAF ground crews for the Beaufighter squadrons in Malta) had to be left behind.

But otherwise, SUBSTANCE was a resounding success. With ABC's manoeuvres to the eastward, which drew enemy reconnaissance, the combined gunfire of Somerville's ships and fighter cover provided by *Ark Royal*'s Fulmars, the remaining six transports reached Malta on 24 July. Another six merchant vessels and *Breconshire*, which had been stuck in Malta since April because of the danger of air attack, were brought out. The troops were disembarked and the Swordfish flown off to Hal Far.

On the debit side, the destroyer *Fearless* was torpedoed and had to be sunk. *Firedrake* was bombed but was towed to Gibraltar. *Manchester* was torpedoed and badly damaged but succeeded in getting back to Gibraltar.

Fighter reinforcements were flown off to Malta from carriers in August and September, and more personnel were sent there (Operation STYLE) in August. Another convoy was planned for September, codenamed HALBERD.

The HALBERD convoy contained nine 15-knot ships, with about 2,600 troops divided between the transports and the warships, under Rear-Admiral Burrough, flying his flag in the cruiser *Kenya*. They were covered by three battleships, *Nelson* (wearing Somerville's flag), *Rodney* and *Prince of Wales* (Rear-Admiral A.T.B. Curteis), *Ark Royal*, five cruisers, including Syfret's flagship *Edinburgh* (Somerville exclaimed at the number of admirals in his force), and eighteen destroyers.

Again, measures were taken to mislead the enemy and a special route was chosen, to surprise and evade enemy aircraft by hugging the south coast of Sicily. ABC again sallied out on a diversionary sortie, breaking radio silence so as to draw attention to himself. Every long-range fighter from Egypt and elsewhere was sent to Malta and every submarine was on patrol off Naples, Taranto and the north coast of Sicily in case the Italian battle fleet attempted to intervene.

The Italian battle fleet put to sea but played no part. All but one of the merchant ships — the *Imperial Star* was torpedoed and had to be sunk — reached Malta. The only other casualty was *Nelson* who received a torpedo hit right forward on her stern, which considerably reduced her speed, so that Somerville had to delegate authority to Curteis.

Nevertheless, HALBERD had been a success and ABC signalled Somerville, commiserating on *Nelson*'s torpedo hit: 'I hope that these my congratulations will compensate for a slap in the belly with a wet fish.' To which Somerville replied: 'Thank you. At my age kicks below the belt have little significance.'

The exchanges of ribald signals between the two admirals were much appreciated by the fleet. ABC signalled on Trafalgar Day, a few weeks later, when Somerville, already a KCB, was appointed KBE: 'Fancy, twice a knight and at your age. Congratulations.'

ABC was not so preoccupied by these events at sea as to neglect his sailors' welfare. In September 1941, he became aware of gross inefficiency in the delivery of the fleet's mail. He summoned two GPO officials to his office and told them of 'one poor woman' whose son was missing. She had paid 1/3d for air mail but her letter had taken *eleven weeks* to get to Alexandria. 'They looked a bit uncomfortable,' ABC told Doodles, 'and took the envelope away with them.'

Given the conditions of the Mediterranean in 1941, the Navy's achievement in reprieving Malta, if only temporarily, seemed hardly to be realised at home, where Pound had been receiving prodding minutes from the Prime Minister, remarking that the Mediterranean Fleet did not appear to have been doing much fighting since Crete.

Pound was therefore concerned about publicity for the Navy, and especially for the submarines in the Mediterranean. 'I feel it absolutely essential from so many points of view,' he wrote to ABC, 'that we should publicise the Navy in future much more than we have done in the past. I know that, on the whole, you do not like this and I wish myself that it was not necessary.'

ABC certainly did not like publicity. He believed that it was anathema to most naval officers, and he himself was no exception. 'I could not see how it would help us to win the war,' he said.

There was, of course, a fine line between publicly praising the feats of one's own side, and giving away important information to the enemy. ABC particularly complained of one BBC bulletin which reported that a convoy had passed through the Mediterranean and safely reached its destination. The result was that the enemy called off the large air forces then searching the eastern Mediterranean, at a time when ABC actually wanted the enemy to waste aircraft searching fruitlessly at sea, instead of using those resources to bomb Suez and the Red Sea. 'This was only another example of injudicious publicity from those at home', he wrote, 'who did not understand the local implications.'

The point was fair. Nevertheless, ABC was wrong. Publicity could help to win the war. ABC himself might abhor anything that smacked of self-advertisement, but he grossly underestimated the morale-boosting effect of newspaper stories on the sailors and their families at home. Whatever the officers might say or think, the sailors loved to read about themselves. The only thing that could annoy a ship's company was to see their own doings attributed to some other ship.

The Admiralty were especially reluctant to make public the efforts of the submarines. Earlier in the war, the exultant German media had trumpeted the triumphs of the U-boats abroad and in so doing had given away priceless information about the U-boats, their commanders and their crews.

Admiral Sir Max Horton, Admiral Submarines, came out to visit ABC and discuss publicity for submarines. 'I saw him, of course,' ABC said, 'and we more or less reached a measure of agreement.'

'A measure of agreement' was not how Power remembered it. 'ABC and Max had a row,' he said. 'Max was so furious that he said he would have the letters S/M expunged from my name in the Navy List — and did.'

In the event, Lieutenant-Commander Ricci, a well-known writer on naval affairs under the pseudonym of 'Bartimeus', was deputed to write up the Mediterranean Fleet's doings in two excellent little books, *East of Malta West of Suez: The Naval War in the Eastern Mediterranean September 1939 to March 1941*, published by HMSO in 1943, and *The Mediterranean Fleet Greece to Tripoli: Naval Operations April 1941 to January 1943*, published in 1944.

Although news was often delayed, for security reasons, communiqués released by the Admiralty in the latter half of 1941 show that naval operations in the Mediterranean were not as neglected as ABC and Pound supposed.

News of the attacks on the SUBSTANCE convoy (though not the codename), including the loss of *Fearless*, was released on 25 July, only a day after the convoy arrived in Malta (possibly the convoy ABC complained of). *The Illustrated London*

News of 2 August carried two pages of drawings of SUBSTANCE by their artist G.H. Davis 'from information given by the Admiralty', under the headline 'The Convoy Must Go Through' — quoting Somerville's final words in a signal to his ships.

As if the supply of Tobruk were not already difficult and dangerous enough, towards the end of August 1941 there was a requirement to relieve the Australians in the garrison. Churchill and the C-in-Cs in the Middle East protested in the strongest terms, but had to bow in the end to political pressure from Australia, where there had recently been a change in government.

Sailing in the dark period of the moon, the fast minelayers *Latona* and *Abdiel* and destroyers took about 6,000 Polish troops and some thousands of tons of stores into Tobruk and brought 5,000 Australians out. The cruiser *Phoebe* was torpedoed by an aircraft but was able to reach Alexandria under her own steam.

ABC was wholly opposed to a second exchange of troops in September, because it disrupted many other arrangements, and only agreed to it under great pressure from the Australian Government. Churchill was anxious to avoid public disagreement with the Australian Government, and was also acutely conscious that world opinion might accuse the United Kingdom of fighting all their battles in the Middle East with Dominion troops.

So, the relief went ahead, again on moonless nights. The minelayers and the destroyers took out 6,000 Australians, and took in 6,300 troops from Syria and 2,100 tons of stores, in eleven days.

ABC opposed even more vehemently a further replacement of Australian troops in October, after there had been another change of government in Australia. He showed General Blamey, the Australian Army Commander, the long list of ships sunk and damaged on the Tobruk run. He also wrote to Pound to tell him that the diversion of such effort to Tobruk might delay the forthcoming offensive in the Western Desert for two to four weeks.

But it was all to no avail. General Blamey insisted and had his way. Between 12 and 26 October, 7,100 troops, and an average of 103 tons of stores a day were landed at Tobruk and about 7,900 men brought back to Alexandria.

ABC was convinced, with some reason, that not enough credit was being given by those at home to the ships who had continued, despite their grievous losses, to supply the garrison. Tobruk was relieved on 8 December 1941. On the 11th, ABC made a signal giving some statistics on the Navy's effort. In the 242 days — from April to December 1941 — that Tobruk had been under siege, seventy-two tanks, ninety-two guns, 33,946 tons of stores and 108 sheep had been transported to Tobruk; 32,667 men had been taken into Tobruk and 34,115 taken out, with 7,516 wounded and 7,097 prisoners-of-war.

The cost to the Navy had been 469 killed and missing, and 186 wounded. Merchant Navy casualties were seventy killed and missing, and fifty-five wounded. Twenty-seven ships were sunk, including one fast minelayer, two destroyers, three sloops, seven anti-submarine vessels and minesweepers, seven HM store carriers and schooners, six 'A' lighters and one gunboat. Twenty-seven ships had been damaged: seven destroyers, one sloop, eleven anti-submarine vessels and minesweepers, three 'A' lighters, three gunboats, one schooner and HMS *Glenroy*. Six merchant ships and one schooner had been sunk, and six more damaged. Yet, as ABC remarked more than once, all this fine work was largely unrecognised.

He remained very sensitive on the subject of the supply of Tobruk, and was particularly incensed by a speech of Churchill's in the House of Commons in December 1941 when, as he told Doodles, 'he talked a lot about the enormous stores in Tobruk and gave no credit to those who put it there. Every 50 tons of stores cost a sailor his life and every 1000 tons cost the Navy a ship! And not a word of acknowledgement. Well, well, it is our job to supply the Army and perhaps we should take it as a compliment that it is all taken for granted.'

ABC wrote to Pound in equally strong terms. 'I fear the Prime Minister's speech on the supplies at Tobruk made all out here in the Service very angry. I sent a signal to the Admiralty showing the losses. Do you think that even at this late hour the Admiralty might make a signal recognising the work of these small ships? It would I think be very well received. I hear the men are a bit sore-hearted at receiving no official recognition of what has been as gallant work as has ever been done… I issued a message to the little ships myself, but it is not the same thing.'

However, there were two pieces of good news in October 1941. The first was that, after what ABC called considerable resistance on the part of the Air Ministry, agreement was finally reached on the equivalent of an RAF Coastal Command in the Mediterranean.

No. 201 Group at Alexandria was renamed No. 201 (Naval Co-Operation) Group — the renaming being done (according to the RAF) in deference to ABC. Air Commodore L.H. Slatter, who had already distinguished himself in air operations in the Sudan, was in command, with Group Captain Scarlett-Streatfield as his Senior Staff Officer.

ABC was delighted. He thought both officers quite splendid. Matters improved from the moment they arrived. Now ABC and his staff had 'someone on the spot to whom we could refer immediately, while they provided a most convenient channel of communication with the Air Officer Commanding-in-Chief at Cairo'.

The second piece of good news was the arrival in Malta from the United Kingdom on 21 October of the cruisers *Aurora* and *Penelope* and the destroyers *Lance* and *Lively*, who were to operate together as Force K.

In the next six weeks, the combination of high-grade intelligence from the C38m and the activities of Force K was severely to hamper Axis supplies to Libya. Events fell into a pattern: advance information about the route and timing of an enemy convoy was decrypted from the C38m at GC&CS, transmitted to Vice-Admiral Ford in Malta and sent by him in the form of operational orders to Captain W.R. Agnew, the Senior Officer Force K in *Aurora* (who was not himself an authorised recipient of ULTRA). Air reconnaissance was arranged, to provide an aircraft sighting as a 'cover story'. Force K then sallied out to attack the convoy. The C38m later provided information on the damage done.

The first chance came on Saturday 25 October, but the C38m information did not arrive soon enough. Force K did sail and steamed hard for Benghazi but was unable to intercept a group of Italian destroyers carrying troops to North Africa. But on 8 November (another Saturday: Force K's sailors began to call their sorties 'Saturday Night Club runs') the C38m decrypt was received in time for a Maryland aircraft to fly out and sight a large enemy convoy, some forty miles east of Cape Spartivento, in the afternoon.

The convoy consisted of seven merchant ships, escorted by six destroyers, with a covering force of the heavy cruisers *Trieste* and *Trento* and four more destroyers. The convoy also had an air escort and submarines were stationed off Malta to report the sailing of any Allied warships.

Force K sailed, unreported by enemy submarines, just before dark that evening. Although radio and radar failed in the Wellington which was to guide Force K to the target, the nearest enemy ships were first sighted from *Aurora*, where they were expected, shortly after midnight on the 9th.

Force K's captains had often discussed the action they would take when attacking a convoy. Everybody now knew what to do. Agnew had to make only two signals: one to reduce speed, the other to avoid wasting ammunition. *Aurora* led the way round to the northward, to silhouette the enemy ships against the rising moon. The Italian ships were caught utterly by surprise. All seven merchant ships, totalling 39,000 tons, and the destroyer *Fulmine*, were sunk. To complete a bad night for the Italian Navy, *Upholder*, on patrol in the area, torpedoed and blew off the stern of a second destroyer, *Libeccio*, who had returned to pick up survivors. She later sank under tow.

The C38m revealed that this 'Saturday Night Club run' had indeed destroyed the entire convoy which had been carrying fuel for the *Luftwaffe* and badly needed equipment, including a large consignment of motor transport, for the Afrika Korps. A decrypt later on 9 November revealed that Rommel had reported that transport to North Africa had completely stopped and, of 60,000 troops expected at Benghazi, only just over 8,000 had arrived.

Force K returned triumphantly to Grand Harbour to well-earned praise and plaudits from all sides, after what ABC called a 'brilliant example of leadership and foresight.'

By 15 November the C38m had revealed that another convoy, of four large supply ships and seven destroyers, covered by three heavy and two light cruisers and another seven destroyers, was due to sail for Tripoli on the 20th, which was two days after the new Allied offensive in the Western Desert, Operation CRUSADER, was due to be launched.

The convoy was duly sighted, to provide a 'cover story', by a Sunderland as it emerged from the Straits of Messina on 21 November and it was attacked that evening by RAF Wellingtons, Swordfish of 830 Squadron and Albacores of 828 Squadron from Malta. The cruiser *Duca degli Abruzzi* was torpedoed and had to return to harbour. During the night the submarine *Utmost* torpedoed *Trieste* which also had to turn back. The whole convoy was then recalled to Taranto (as revealed by the C38m the next day), clearly for fear of another attack by Force K.

Force K sailed for another 'Club run' two days later to attack a convoy of two German ships, *Maritza* carrying ammunition and *Procida* carrying high-octane fuel for the *Luftwaffe* to Benghazi, escorted by two Italian torpedo boats, *Lupo* and *Cassiopaea*. These cargoes were obviously of the utmost importance to Rommel and Mr Churchill pressed unusually hard, even for him, for the ships to be sunk, going so far as to ask whether Cunningham had seen the decrypts which had described the ships' safe arrivals as 'decisive'.

Force K found and sank the two ships, although the torpedo boats did their gallant best to protect their charges, only leaving the scene when it was clear both ships were doomed. On 25 November the *Luftwaffe* Enigma revealed that the loss of those two ships had placed German operations in North Africa in 'real danger'. Fuel now had to be ferried across in any available craft. By the end of November the C38m revealed that Italian destroyers were transporting petrol in drums on deck and floating them ashore at Derna, so as to shorten their time in harbour and reduce the risk of air attack.

The combined efforts of Malta-based surface ships, submarines and aircraft, assisted by advance warnings from the C38m, had a dramatic effect. Between June and October 1941, only about 16 per cent of the cargoes failed to arrive. But in November this figure soared to 62 per cent. There were further delays caused by ships turning back or hesitating to sail at all, and by bombing and mining of the convoy assembly ports.

But there were losses to be set against the gains. On 13 November an ominous signal gave the news that the aircraft carrier *Ark Royal*, returning after yet another trip to fly off fighters to Malta, had been torpedoed. She was still afloat, though listing, and was attempting to reach Gibraltar. But, by the next morning, she had sunk. She had often been claimed sunk by German propaganda. Now she really was gone.

This was only the beginning of the bad news. The last few weeks of 1941 were to be the absolute nadir of the Mediterranean Fleet's fortunes during the war.

16: THE LOWEST POINT OF THE WAR

WHEN THE C38M revealed the *Maritza* convoy, Force B, of five cruisers and four destroyers led by Rawlings, sailed from Alexandria on the morning of 24 November to support Force K. Force A, of *Queen Elizabeth*, wearing ABC's flag, *Barham*, wearing Pridham-Wippell's flag, *Valiant* and eight destroyers sailed later the same day, to support Rawlings if Italian heavy ships appeared.

Some twenty German U-boats had entered the Mediterranean in October 1941 and had made their presence quickly felt with the sinking of *Ark Royal* by U-81 on 14 November.

At about 4.30 p.m. on 25 November, Force A was cruising between Crete and Cyrenaica, some sixty miles north of Solium, when U-331, one of three U-boats patrolling the route to Tobruk, penetrated the destroyer screen and hit *Barham* from close range with three torpedoes of a salvo of four. U-331 broke surface after firing and passed so close down *Valiant*'s side that her guns could not be depressed enough to fire.

ABC was having tea in his bridge cabin when he heard and 'half-felt' the cabin door give three distinct rattles. He thought the ship had opened fire with anti-aircraft guns. 'I went quickly up the one ladder to the bridge, and then I saw the *Barham*, immediately astern of us, stopped and listing heavily over to port. The thuds I had heard were three torpedoes striking her.'

Barham made a slow circle to port, quickly heeling inwards as she did so, and then blew up with an appalling detonation about four minutes after the initial torpedo hits. ABC said:

The poor ship rolled nearly over on to her beam ends and we saw the men massing on her upturned side. A minute or two later there came the dull rumble of a terrific explosion as one of her main magazines blew up. The ship became completely hidden in a great cloud of yellowish-black smoke, which went wreathing and eddying high into the sky. When it cleared away the *Barham* had disappeared. There was nothing but a bubbling, oily-looking patch on the calm surface of the sea, dotted with wreckage and the heads of swimmers. It was ghastly to look at, a horrible and awe-inspiring spectacle when one realised what it meant.

Barnard was the duty staff officer on the bridge:

The juddering of the door had ABC up before I could call him. It was then he showed such a speed of decision and action as I have never seen before or since. He increased the speed of the fleet and altered the zigzag. He detailed destroyers to hunt and those to pick up survivors, and gave attention to many other items. He asked no advice and required no reminders from the whole staff who were up by this time, and there was nothing he forgot.

Despite a hunt by the destroyers, U-331 got clear away, after a most skilful and daring attack. There were 450 survivors, including Pridham-Wippell; 861 of *Barham*'s people and her Captain, G.C. Cooke, were lost.

Queen Elizabeth's Chaplain, the Reverend Launcelot Fleming, knew that many in *Queen Elizabeth* had friends in *Barham*, and he asked if he could say some prayers over the broadcast in the bridge lobby. ABC had misgivings about the effect of broadcast prayers, however sincerely meant, on *Queen Elizabeth*'s sailors, cooped up as most of them were at their action stations, able to see nothing.

However, ABC gave his permission, on the understanding that if it was necessary to broadcast an order it must have priority over the prayers, and that the look-outs were on no account to relax their concentration. He made no comment to Fleming about the prayers, then or later, but Fleming himself felt 'the sense of the whole ship's company being united'.

After Pound had sent a signal of condolence, ABC wrote:

> I very much appreciated your signal about the *Barham*. She is indeed a heavy loss. We blundered straight on to the submarine. There was no necessity for us to be there any more than anywhere else. At first we thought the submarine had not been pinged but on investigation it was found that she came in under the screen and was actually pinged by one of the destroyers, who unfortunately disregarded it as a non-sub echo. It was a most daring and brilliant performance on the part of the U-boat, which fired from a position about two hundred yards ahead of the *Valiant*. If there is anything to be learned from it, it is that our anti-submarine vessels are sadly out of practice. I am withdrawing the *Otus* from operational duty to run her as a 'clockwork mouse'. She is of little value anyway as she is constantly breaking down. Pridham-Wippell had a bit of a shake-up but I hope he will be alright in a few days.

(In fact, Pridham-Wippell's recovery took some time.)

The sinking of a battleship was a major success for the enemy and might prompt the Italian battle fleet to be more venturesome. The C38m decrypts were therefore anxiously studied, to gauge enemy reaction. To everybody's relief, it was clear that the enemy did not know that *Barham* had been sunk. The CO of U-331 had understandably been more concerned with making good his escape than with lingering at the periscope to admire his handiwork. This was one instance where ABC was grateful for reticence about the Mediterranean Fleet and its doings.

On 2 December 1941 the fleet had some good news: a Victoria Cross, albeit posthumous, for one of their shipmates. On 20 September, ABC had written to Admiral 'Jock' Whitworth, the Second Sea Lord,

> there is one particular case to which I wish to draw your especial attention, that of Petty Officer Alfred Edward Sephton, Portsmouth JX130821 of H.M.S. *Coventry*. Among many things done I think this PO is quite outstanding. Poor man he died of his wounds and so can only get a VC or be mentioned in dispatches. I think the most serious consideration should be given to awarding him a VC. Entirely beside the fact that I think he thoroughly deserves it, it would have a wonderful effect on the troops out here. They are all going strong again but at one time some of them were near the cracking stage.

Sephton's Victoria Cross was awarded for an exploit on 18 May 1941, south of Crete, when the hospital ship *Aba* signalled that she was under attack by Stukas (although the red crosses painted on her sides were clearly visible). *Coventry* closed her to assist.

Coventry's anti-aircraft guns were controlled from two director towers, one on the foremast and one on the main, whose crews observed enemy aircraft, estimated their height, speed, course, range and rate of change of bearing, and passed the predictions to the guns. Sephton was the director-layer in one of the towers.

As *Coventry* approached *Aba*, one Stuka penetrated the anti-aircraft barrage and raked *Coventry*'s upper decks and superstructure with machinegun fire. A bullet passed through Sephton's body and wounded the able seaman sitting behind him. Though Sephton was in great pain, losing blood rapidly and partially blinded, he stuck to his instruments and carried on with his duty until the attack was over. He then insisted that the wounded sailor be carried down first. He himself died of his injuries the next day and was buried at sea.

The Victoria Cross, announced in the *London Gazette* of 2 December 1941, seemed to the fleet to be recognition at last for all the blood and agony of Crete. ABC wrote to Pound — 'I am very grateful for your assistance in getting Petty Officer Sephton the VC. He was a very fine man and undoubtedly deserved it and I feel that the effect on the personnel of the fleet will be very marked.'

On 7 December the Japanese attacked Pearl Harbor, introducing another global dimension to the war, and on the 10th there came the shattering news that *Prince of Wales* and *Repulse* had both been sunk by Japanese aircraft in the South China Sea off the east coast of Malaya: 513 of *Repulse*'s people and 327 from *Prince of Wales* were lost, including Vice-Admiral Sir Tom Phillips, the C-in-C, Eastern Fleet, who flew his flag in *Prince of Wales*, and her Commanding Officer, Captain John Leach.

On 16 December, there was some good news: another Victoria Cross, this time to a submariner, Lieutenant-Commander Malcolm John Wanklyn, CO of the submarine *Upholder*, of the Malta 10th Submarine Flotilla.

Upholder had sailed on her first patrol in January 1941, with little success. After five patrols with not much to show for them, Captain (S) at Malta, Captain G.W.G. ('Shrimp') Simpson, began to doubt Wanklyn's competence; there was even a possibility he might be relieved. Torpedoes were too rare and valuable in Malta in 1941 to waste on a CO who could not hit anything.

It was on his sixth patrol, in April, in the Lampedusa Channel, that Wanklyn at last got his eye in and sank three transports. On 24 May, on his next patrol, Wanklyn brought off the exploit which was picked out for his VC. It was a dusk attack on a convoy of four large liners, packed with troops for Libya, with a destroyer escort. They had cleared the Straits of Messina and were heading at high speed for Tripoli.

Through the periscope, Wanklyn saw the silhouette of a very large ship outlined against the afterglow of the sunset. He fired two torpedoes which sank the 18,000-ton *Conte Rosso*, with 2,800 men on board, of whom 1,300 were drowned. Wanklyn made his escape, after a sharp counter-attack.

Wanklyn had already won the DSO, gazetted in September 1941, and he went on to win two Bars. His final score was nearly 140,000 tons of enemy shipping, including a destroyer, two U-boats and over a dozen troopships, tankers and store ships.

On 6 April 1942, *Upholder* sailed on her twenty-fifth patrol, her last before she was due to go home. But she was lost with all hands. The Admiralty announcement on 22 August read: 'The ship and her company are gone, but the example and inspiration remain.'

In December the C38m revealed that the Italians were going to try again to pass ships across to Tripoli on 12 December. A convoy of several ships was to sail from Taranto in three groups, each with battleship cover, and the battleship *Littorio* giving distant cover to the whole operation.

The 15th Cruiser Squadron, of *Naiad*, *Galatea* and *Euryalus*, with nine destroyers, sailed from Alexandria to intercept, while Force K sailed from Malta to support them.

ABC could not take *Queen Elizabeth* and *Valiant* to sea to cover the cruisers because he lacked destroyers for escorts.

Instead, he resorted to a trick. The C38m decrypts had given much insight into the way the Italians studied British W/T procedures and what their reactions were likely to be to any ruse. Strict radio silence was imposed at Alexandria, while the minelayer *Abdiel* put to sea to broadcast radio traffic supposedly from the Battle Squadron on its way towards Tripoli.

It worked. The Italian convoys and covering forces were recalled on the evening of 13 December. During the return to Taranto, the battleship *Vittorio Veneto* badly damaged by a torpedo from the submarine *Urge*, and two merchantmen were sunk by the submarine *Upright*. Two more were damaged in collision. However, as *Galatea* was returning through the swept channel some thirty miles west of Alexandria at midnight on 14 December, she was torpedoed and sunk by U-557. There were only 144 survivors from a complement of over 500.

The 15th Cruiser Squadron was now led by Vian, who assumed command on 1 November in place of King, who went home in October.

ABC knew Vian of old, of course, and was delighted to have him, regarding his arrival as a considerable addition to the fleet's strength. He had been much less enthusiastic about King. Pound had already written in June to ask: 'Are you satisfied with King as CS15? If you are not, let us shift him. We cannot afford to use second class material when first class is available.'

ABC replied, when King had left, that

> I was not very happy about him. I was much upset that he failed to utterly destroy that convoy full of Hun troops south of Milo particularly when his destroyers and the two little anti-aircraft cruisers *Carlisle* and *Calcutta* were getting in well among the caiques. He did better in the evacuation of Crete

and off the Syrian coast but I have always had the feeling that he was a better office wallah than sailor. He wants everything cut and dried and most precise orders. He doesn't exhibit much initiative at sea.

ABC's opinion of an officer can be construed from coded language in his memoirs. Those he thought had done well received their due tribute when they left his command. Others were either not mentioned at all or had the briefest of notices. King, according to ABC, simply 'went home to take up an appointment at the Admiralty'.

This contrasts vividly with ABC's comments in the same paragraph about Vice-Admiral Sir Wilbraham Ford, Vice-Admiral, Malta, who was to be relieved at the end of the year. 'I feel it was only right,' ABC wrote, 'as he had been five years there and ever since the outbreak of war with Italy had had a particularly onerous time, especially after the advent of the *Luftwaffe* and the intensive bombing of Malta. He was a sterling officer undaunted by any difficulties, of which he had plenty. His courage, unflagging energy and helpfulness provided shining examples to everyone in that hard-pressed island. I was glad to think that his services were not to be lost to the Navy in his new appointment as Commander-in-Chief, Rosyth.' ABC was delighted to see that Ford got a KCB in the 1942 New Year's Honours.

Malta was now dangerously short of fuel. *Breconshire* sailed with fuel and other stores from Alexandria late on 15 December, accompanied by Vian's two remaining cruisers, *Naiad* and *Euryalus*, with *Carlisle* and eight destroyers. The plan was for Vian's force to be met off the 'bulge' of Benghazi on 17 December by the cruisers of Force K and four destroyers from Malta, who would remain with *Breconshire* and escort her into Malta, while Vian turned back to Alexandria after dark on the 17th.

Meanwhile, on 16 December, the C38m and the *Luftwaffe* Enigma had both revealed that the enemy was going to try yet again to pass over his convoys, with battleship support, between 16 and 19 December.

ABC now decided that Vian's main object would still be the protection of *Breconshire* but that he should also try to attack the Italian convoy that night, while Force K took *Breconshire* to Malta. Having sent *Carlisle* back because of her lack of speed, Vian pressed on with *Breconshire*, hoping to cross ahead of the main Italian force and then deliver his charge to Force K.

Force K, of *Aurora*, *Penelope* and four destroyers, joined Vian on the morning of 17 December. Air reconnaissance reported the enemy ships at 10.25 that forenoon: two battleships, two cruisers and seven destroyers, 150 miles to the north-north-west.

The Italian force actually consisted of the battleship *Littorio*, wearing the flag of Admiral Iachino, with two more battleships, *Andrea Doria* and *Giulio Cesare*, two heavy cruisers, and ten destroyers. Some sixty miles to the west of Iachino, but not located by the aircraft, was the convoy, with yet another battleship, *Caio Duilio*, three cruisers and eleven destroyers.

Iachino also learned of Vian's ships from reconnaissance aircraft (which first identified *Breconshire* as a battleship and continued to report her as such) and steamed south-west at 24 knots, the most his two older battleships could do, hoping to intercept the British ships before sunset.

Vian's ships were attacked by Italian bombers and torpedo-bombers more than twenty times that day but survived untouched. The C38m gave some information about *Littorio*'s course and speed, but not her position. Air reconnaissance could not give continuous information about the Italian fleet throughout the day. However, Vian did know enough about the enemy's whereabouts to keep *Breconshire*, his main responsibility, out of danger until he turned her over to Force K, who took her safely to Malta.

Vian's cruisers and destroyers met the main Italian fleet at sunset on 17 December. It was a great chance for Iachino, who had overwhelming strength. But the Italians, now knowing themselves to be much inferior at night-fighting, were reluctant to take risks. When Vian's destroyers raced forward to try and deliver a torpedo attack, Iachino turned away and this brief engagement, known as the First Battle of Sirte, was over. Contact was lost in the darkness, with Iachino content to go back to covering the convoy, which had turned back but now resumed its course.

After losing contact with the Italian fleet, Vian patrolled for a few hours either side of midnight across what he had previously been informed by ULTRA signal was the route for the Benghazi-bound section of the convoy.

However, the Benghazi section, with the valuable merchant ship *Ankara*, carrying tanks, was not detached until late on 18 December. Vian was not aware of this. He had only an ULTRA signal, received late on 17 December, informing him that Iachino had been allowed to alter the convoy's route. It was this news which probably made Vian decide that the convoy was not coming his way and he broke off the search.

When Vian was halfway back to Alexandria, the C38m revealed the positions of the enemy convoys and the news that the Italians had decided to send their main naval force back to Taranto at 2 p.m. on 18 December. This changed the situation completely.

The enemy convoy, having enjoyed a night and day of most unexpected peace and quiet, arrived at Tripoli after dark on 18 December during a raid by Wellingtons laying magnetic mines in its path and a torpedo attack by Albacores of 828 Squadron from Malta, who hit and disabled the merchantman *Napoli*, which had to be towed in.

This convoy, with 300 vehicles, large stocks of 88mm ammunition, fuel and other stores, anchored for the night and entered Tripoli on 19 December. Its safe arrival was to have an important effect on the war in the desert and in particular on the outcome of Operation CRUSADER, for which ABC's brother Alan had been placed in command of the newly named 8th Army. 'To ensure that nothing was lacking in the liaison between his head-quarters and mine,' ABC sent Captain Guy Grantham, a 'brilliant and most capable officer', whose ship *Phoebe* had been torpedoed, to join his brother's staff.

ABC had misgivings about the numbers of aircraft available to support CRUSADER. Even including Fleet Air Arm aircraft, it seemed to him that the Desert Air Force would not have much, if any, air superiority over the enemy. 'However, if the Air Officer Commanding-in-Chief was satisfied, it was not for me to complain.'

CRUSADER began at dawn on 18 November 1941 and went well at the start. Some days of confused fighting in the desert followed. The Tobruk garrison made their attempt to break out on 21 November but were thwarted by the enemy, and failed to join the main advance.

On 26 November, when CRUSADER was still in its early stages, Alan Cunningham was summarily relieved of his command and replaced by General Ritchie, Auchinleck's Deputy Chief-of-Staff. ABC received a letter from Auchinleck dated 26 November 1941, marked

Personal. Most Secret. Commander-in-Chief's House, Gezira, Cairo: My dear Admiral, I am very sorry to have to tell you that I have had to replace Alan in command of the 8th Army. I find that the tremendous strain of the past week has been too much for him and I can no longer be sure that he is capable of viewing the situation in its true perspective and of gripping it as he should. This is a hard thing to say but I know you will realize that I would never have contemplated such a step were I not absolutely convinced it is necessary. It is most painful for me to do this as I have a great respect and affection for Alan.

Auchinleck added that it was essential it should not become known that Alan had been removed from his command, and to that end he would allow himself to be placed on the sick list.

Auchinleck's letter was meant to soften the blow, but the news was as big a shock to ABC as it had been to Alan himself. He wrote to Auchinleck to thank him for his 'understanding letter'. However, he sent a cable to Doodles to assure her that Alan was fit and that his dismissal was not due to sickness. But when he saw Alan he was not reassured. 'Having to give up smoking so suddenly on account of his eyes may have had more than a little to do with the change in him,' he told Doodles, 'for there is a change.'

Whatever he said to Auchinleck, ABC still rankled under a sense of injustice. 'Alan has in my opinion been most disgracefully and unjustly treated,' he wrote to Doodles, in a letter of 16 December. Nor did he think Auchinleck alone was to blame. 'I was quite furious', he told Doodles a fortnight later, 'when I read Churchill's speech about Alan's relief. He was made the scapegoat for Churchill's boasting before the battle opened.' ABC did not mention his brother's dismissal in his memoirs.

Ironically, CRUSADER prospered after Alan's departure. The 8th Army regained much of Cyrenaica. Rommel was forced to retreat or lose his Afrika Korps. Tobruk was relieved on 8 December, Derna captured on the 19th and Benghazi on the 24th. CRUSADER ended at El Agheila on 6 January 1942, except for the capture of Bardia eleven days later. It was meant to be a short sharp campaign. It had turned out a long and costly one. It was a victory, thanks to Auchinleck's leadership, but not a decisive one.

For the fleet the task was, as before, the supply of the Army. According to ABC,

> Tobruk, when relieved and opened up, required 1,100 tons a day of stores and petrol; and Derna and Benghazi, when captured, 200 and 600 tons a day respectively. These quantities may not sound enormous; but the small ships carrying them had to run the gauntlet through an area still dominated by enemy aircraft and infested by U-boats.

In the New Year, ABC had a letter from Alan who had by then returned to the United Kingdom, mentioning the 'Prime Minister's brutal statement on my removal', and the gutter press headlines 'Cunningham Sacked'. Alan 'had the feeling I am being ostracised. No-one has suggested that my experiences might be some value and are worth having!' It had been a humiliating ordeal: 'I had to go into hospital unnecessarily, remain incognito for nine days, move about in mufti, and travel back under an assumed name.'

Alan's fate added to ABC's feeling of resentment towards Churchill. Most galling of all was the almost constant stream of prodding signals demanding more action. There was yet another barrage during the opening days of CRUSADER, including a personal signal for ABC on 23 November about enemy ships arriving at Benghazi. 'I shall be glad to hear through the Admiralty what action you propose to take. Stopping these ships may save thousands of lives apart from aiding a victory of cardinal importance.'

This signal came after successes by Force K. ABC could only reply that enemy air activity against the fleet had not diminished, as it might have appeared to have done from home, and our own air reconnaissance was comparatively weak.

Force K's run of successes was about to end. When the C38m information that the enemy convoy was on its way to Tripoli and Benghazi had been confirmed by aircraft sightings, Force K, who had only just arrived in Malta with *Breconshire*, sailed again at 6.30 p.m. on 18 December to try and intercept the four ships of the Tripoli section.

But at about 1 a.m. on the 19th, Force K ran into a minefield some twenty miles east of Tripoli. *Neptune* (Captain Rory O'Conor) struck two mines, which disabled her. *Aurora* and *Penelope* both struck mines. *Penelope*'s mine exploded in her paravanes, but *Aurora* was badly damaged, although she was able to reach Malta under her own power. *Penelope* stayed to help *Neptune* who struck a third mine. *Kandahar* entered the minefield to give assistance but she too struck a mine which blew off her stern.

Finally, *Neptune* detonated a fourth mine and sank. Admiral Ford sent out *Jaguar* which found the crippled *Kandahar* some thirty-six hours later and rescued most of her ship's company, but the ship herself had to be sunk.

The sole survivor from *Neptune*, Leading Seaman J. Walters, later told how only Captain O'Conor, himself and fourteen men remained on a raft at daylight on the 19th. They died one by one until Walters was picked up by an Italian torpedo boat on the afternoon of 24 December, five days later.

Some hints about this minefield, which had effectively destroyed Force K in a few hours, had been given by the C38m in October. Captain Agnew, Senior Officer Force K, was not an ULTRA recipient and received ULTRA information transmuted and rephrased through signals and orders from Vice-Admiral, Malta. He may never have been told of the possibility of a minefield, or its existence may have been discounted by the staffs in Malta and Alexandria. It was laid close to the 100-fathom line, a depth of water in which the Royal Navy had considered it was impossible to lay moored mines.

But this was not the only disaster that day. At 4 a.m. on 19 December ABC was woken in his cabin in *Queen Elizabeth* to be told that two Italians had been found clinging to the bow buoy of *Valiant*. They had been taken on board and questioned but they had given nothing away and had been sent ashore under arrest. ABC ordered them to be brought back and put in a forward compartment well below the water-line.

It seemed the prisoners had laid a time-fused charge beneath *Valiant*. As the time of detonation drew nearer, the men grew restive and asked to see the Captain. But again they said nothing and were taken below again. As the minutes passed, they again asked to see the Captain and this time advised him to clear the ship, as there was about to be a big explosion.

It later transpired that at about 9 p.m. on the evening of 18 December 1941, the Italian submarine *Scire* surfaced off Alexandria, about 1V2 miles from Ras el Tin lighthouse, and launched three two-man submersible 'chariots', or 'pigs' as they were called.

The three 'pigs', with their helmeted, rubber-suited and goggled crews sitting astride them, set off towards Alexandria, their objective being to penetrate the harbour entrance and lay explosive charges under major units of the British Mediterranean Fleet. It was a very dark night, with a clear sky and a calm sea — perfect for their enterprise.

The C38m had already given warnings of some form of raid. By 17 December decrypts had shown the Italian Navy's interest in some undertaking, as yet undefined, at Alexandria. An ULTRA signal on the 17th informed ABC that an Italian reconnaissance sortie that day had reported two British battleships at their usual berths and — an odd and possibly significant detail — that the sea was calm.

A general warning was issued to the fleet at 10.25 a.m. on 18 December: 'Attacks on Alexandria by air, boat or human torpedo may be expected when calm weather prevails. Lookouts and patrols should be warned accordingly.'

Had Italian naval book cyphers been readable during the previous year, before the C28m was adopted, British intelligence would have known that it was the Italian 10th Light Flotilla, who had carried out the attack on *York* at Suda Bay in March 1941, and the abortive EMB attack on Grand Harbour in July, who now manned the 'chariots' launched from *Scirè*.

The charioteers boldly took the chance in the early hours of 19 December to pass through the entrance when the anti-torpedo nets were drawn aside to permit destroyers to return to harbour. Despite the increased vigilance, the extra patrols and the deterrent charges being dropped in the water, the chariots succeeded in penetrating to the main anchorage.

ABC was on the quarterdeck of *Queen Elizabeth* just before 6 a.m. when there was a violent explosion under the stern of the tanker *Sagona* (mistaken by the charioteers for an aircraft carrier) who was lying close by, with *Jervis* alongside her. She was holed aft, with rudder and screws badly damaged. *Jervis* was also badly damaged.

About twenty minutes later, ABC saw another heavy explosion under *Valiant*'s forward turret, and four minutes after that, when ABC himself was aft by *Queen Elizabeth*'s ensign staff, he felt a dull thud and was tossed five feet into the air by the whip of the ship and 'was lucky not to come down sprawling'. He 'saw a great cloud of black smoke shoot up the funnel and from immediately in front of it, and knew at once that the ship was badly damaged. The *Valiant* was already down by the bows. The *Queen Elizabeth* took a heavy list to starboard.'

The charge had been fixed to *Queen Elizabeth*'s starboard bilge keel. Three boiler rooms were flooded and the ship was unable to raise steam. Submarines were brought alongside to provide power with their main engines. With a hole about forty feet square in her hull and several thousand extra tons of water on board, *Queen Elizabeth* was very low in the water, and out of action as a warship.

The charioteers had been unable to fix their charge to *Valiant*'s hull. It had dropped to the bottom, about fifteen feet below the ship. Nevertheless the explosion did extensive damage along some eighty feet of *Valiant*'s keel. She too was put out of action and had to go into dock for two months for temporary repairs.

At about 7.30 a.m. flaming smoke-candles were seen burning in the water all around *Queen Elizabeth* and *Sagona*. These were intended to ignite oil escaping from ruptured ships' tanks. It was this aspect of the attack, the astounding, almost impertinent forethought, which most impressed ABC. As he said, 'one could not but admire the cold-blooded bravery and enterprise of these Italians'. In one sublimely brave exploit, those six men, who were all captured, had rendered both the Mediterranean Fleet's remaining battleships *hors de combat.*

However, ABC was determined not to give anything away to the enemy. When boats had gone round the harbour and gathered up all the floats, he said: 'We must go and clean up, or we shall be late for Colours.'

It had not entered anybody else's head that there would be a Colours ceremony that morning, with the ship listing fifteen degrees to starboard and in danger of sinking. Always prickly in the early mornings, ABC surpassed himself that day. He astonished *Queen Elizabeth*'s officer of the watch and gangway staff by roaring at them to ask why they were not preparing for the ceremony of hoisting the Colours at 8 o'clock that morning as usual? He demanded the immediate appearance on the quarterdeck of the duty staff officer, the Royal Marine guard, band and bugler, and the signalman with a clean ensign for the day.

Colours were duly hoisted on time and at the normal staff meeting at 9.30 that morning, ABC presided as though nothing untoward had happened. All he said was: 'Now we've got to bluff them that we've got a Fleet. Under no circumstances are the prisoners to be allowed into a prisoner-of-war camp or anywhere where they can pass on any news whatever.'

Both battleships finally settled on more or less even keels, so it was possible to conceal the full extent of the damage done to them. ABC continued to occupy the admiral's quarters and daily life and ceremonial carried on more ostentatiously than usual. A photograph was taken, widely reproduced in the press at home and abroad, reassuringly showing an unruffled ABC standing at the salute while the White Ensign was ceremoniously hoisted on the quarterdeck of a seemingly unharmed *Queen Elizabeth*. It needed a knowing eye to discern that the admiral's stern-walk was several feet nearer the water than was originally designed.

It was always possible that a reconnaissance aircraft would evade the fighter patrols and take a picture of *Queen Elizabeth* with the two submarines alongside her. Once again, the C38m decrypts were anxiously studied and showed that the enemy, for the time being, did not realise how successful the charioteers had been.

The six Italians were segregated, allowed no communication with the outside world by letter or other means. 'They will just die for six months,' ABC told Pound, 'and I hope give the Italians the impression that they perished in their attempt.'

When Pound wrote back in January, he mentioned that the promotion to Rear-Admiral of Captain Charles Morgan, *Valiant*'s Commanding Officer [due for that month] was being held up while the report of the Board of Inquiry was reviewed, 'in case he was found to blame in any way'. As always, ABC was quick to defend his captains and replied by return: 'He [Morgan] is clear of blame. I myself was the senior officer afloat.'

Once more, ABC and his staff were left to pick up the pieces and see what could be done. The fleet had now been reduced effectively to three cruisers, *Naiad*, *Euryalus* and *Dido*, under Vian, with *Carlisle* and some destroyers at Alexandria; and two cruisers, *Penelope* and the damaged *Aurora*, at Malta. *Ajax* was out of action owing to defects. 'And so the year 1941 closed with our naval forces in the Mediterranean at their lowest ebb,' ABC wrote.

The last day of 1941 ended on another note of deep gloom: the loss of the submarine *Triumph*. This was particularly sad news for Commander Wilfrid Woods, *Triumph*'s previous Captain, who had just relieved Power as Staff Officer (Operations). It fell to Woods to report to ABC at a staff meeting that *Triumph* was overdue and must be considered sunk. 'He looked at me for a long time,' said Woods, 'his eyes sad, and then said very quietly, "Poor *Triumph*". He never referred to her again.'

Power went home round the Cape in *Ajax*. Like Willis before him, he was mentally exhausted. The seemingly indestructible, tireless worker had had enough. 'Until recently,' he said, 'I used to say "What can I do?" Now I say "Oh my God, what have I *got* to do?"' He was both surprised and immeasurably consoled by ABC's soothing reaction. 'You've done more than could be expected of any man, so don't worry.'

One bright note at the end of the year was the arrival of the first of many drafts of Wrens to the Middle East. A party of W/T Chief Wrens had set out round the Cape earlier in the year but got as far as Cape Town where they stopped on ABC's orders. Half went to Singapore and the rest went back home. After the war ABC admitted to the Director WRNS that he had been wrong. 'I thought women could not stand up to the rigours of a war zone,' he said. 'But they could and did.'

For lack of ships, ABC now had to rely on shore-based air power to intercept enemy convoys to Tripoli. It was not enough. Also, there were personality problems in the air. Slatter was still doing well. The trouble was Drummond who, as ABC told Pound early in February 1942, 'appears to have run true to form. He is absolutely crooked, a trouble maker and a determined opponent of the Navy. He has been the thorn in our side ever since I have been here.'

The Italian Navy did not learn of their success in Alexandria harbour until as late as 30 January 1942 (and then from a prisoner-of-war). Meanwhile, the C38m indicated from 29 December onwards that the Italians were getting ready to sail another convoy to Tripoli under battleship escort, and also gave details of the convoy's size — nine merchant vessels of 10,000 tons — and its exact route.

But in this case timely and accurate ULTRA intelligence could not be effective because there was insufficient force to make use of it at sea. Force K was now reduced to *Penelope* and three destroyers.

Between 30 December and 5 January, preliminary to the convoy's sailing, massive air raids by more than 400 aircraft of *Fliegerkorps* II from Sicily rendered Malta's airfields largely unusable. Lack of reconnaissance from Malta meant that the convoy was not sighted until it was near Tripoli. An air strike was launched, but it failed to find the convoy. On 5 January, the C38m reported the convoy's safe arrival in Tripoli (but did not reveal that it had also included fifty-four tanks).

ABC intended to run one convoy to Malta every month. The first convoy, of four ships, sailed from Alexandria on 16 January, escorted by *Carlisle* and eight destroyers, with Vian's cruisers as a covering force. One merchant ship with engine defects turned back, was bombed and set on fire, and had to be sunk. The destroyer *Gurkha* was torpedoed by U-133 on 17 January and later sank. But the remainder, effectively escorted by Beaufighters of No. 201 Naval Co-Operation group and by Hurricanes from Malta, arrived safely.

Vice-Admiral Ford was relieved on 19 January 1942. He had written to ABC on 3 January: 'I want you to know that I have done nothing about leaving this island — i.e. in asking to go.

Much the reverse, as I told the powers I was more than willing to stay on for the duration.'

ABC sent Ford an appreciative signal, and praised him again in his memoirs. 'I was truly sorry to see his departure. It is no exaggeration to say that he was one of the main stays of the defence of Malta through one of the most grievous periods of its eventful history.'

Ford was certainly leaving Malta at one of its greatest times of trial. In the same letter to ABC he wrote: 'I've given up counting the number of air raids we are getting. At the time of writing, 4 p.m., we have had exactly seven bombing raids since 9 a.m., quite apart from a month of all night efforts. The enemy is definitely trying to neutralize Malta's effort, and, I hate to say, is gradually doing so.'

Fliegerkorps II sustained its onslaught upon Malta throughout January 1942, when not a single day, and only eight nights, passed without an air raid. There were 262 raids during the month, seventy-three of them by night. Malta's Swordfish, Wellington and Blenheim squadrons had therefore been reduced to only a few serviceable aircraft when, on 22 January, the Italians sailed another convoy with battleship cover.

Again, the C38m disclosed the convoy's sailing, its movements, the strength of its covering forces and the fact that it would be carrying a large quantity of motor transport.

The convoy, codenamed Operation T.18, sailed in two sections: four merchantmen, escorted by six destroyers and two torpedo boats, left Messina on the morning of 22 January, with a covering force of three cruisers and another four destroyers. The 13,000-ton former Lloyd-Triestino liner *Victoria*, described in Count Ciano's diary as 'the pearl of the Italian merchant fleet', but now a troopship and carrying some 1,600 men of a Panzer division, sailed from Taranto escorted by the battleship *Caio Duilio* and four destroyers at 5 p.m. the same day.

The passage of this convoy coincided with another run to Malta by *Breconshire*, and the bringing out of *Glengyle* and a second ship, between 24 and 28 January. It all passed off safely, with a certain amount of bombing which caused no casualties.

The three cruisers in the T.18 convoy were sighted by a reconnaissance aircraft from Malta early on 23 January. The *Duilio* group was also sighted shortly afterwards and, at 11 a.m., the three merchantmen (one having already turned back) and their escort. The two convoy sections joined up at 1 p.m., that afternoon and were shadowed, despite their escort of eight (later increased to twelve) Junkers Ju.88s.

In the next hour-and-a-half there was a series of attacks by Wellingtons, Blenheims, and torpedo-carrying Beauforts (making their operational debut in the Mediterranean) involving fifty-three aircraft in all from No. 201 Group.

At sunset *Victoria* was hit and brought to a standstill by a torpedo from a Beaufort. In the gathering darkness, as the troops were getting into the lifeboats, two out of a strike of five Albacores of 826 Naval Air Squadron, flying from Berka, an airstrip near Benghazi, attacked with torpedoes. Their CO, Lieutenant-Commander J. W.S. Corbett, was shot down and he and his crew became prisoners-of-war. But the torpedo from the second Albacore, flown by Lieutenant H.M. Ellis, hit and finally sank the 'pearl'.

The C38m later revealed that over 1,000 of the troops on board *Victoria* survived and reached Tripoli, as did the rest of the convoy, on 24 January, despite very persistent efforts by 830 Naval Air Squadron from Malta, determinedly led by their CO, Lieutenant-Commander F.H.E. Hopkins. Swordfish from

830 flew two sorties through a full gale during the night to make torpedo attacks, claiming two hits.

The arrival of this convoy, the convoy earlier in January and the convoy of 19 December, with their loads of tanks, vehicles, fuel, ammunition, troops and stores, enabled Rommel to launch and sustain his counter-attack on 21 January. It began as a reconnaisance in force, which surprised and drove back the British outposts, and was swiftly turned into a full scale offensive when Rommel realised his opportunity.

Rommel's forces took Agedabia the next day, 22 January, and advanced on Msus to keep the pressure on the 8th Army. Msus was taken on the 25th and Rommel wheeled west towards the sea to cut off Benghazi.

On 25 January, ABC received the message: 'Army Commander has ordered the evacuation of Benghazi.' ABC said,

> It was particularly galling. We had just got the port running again, and apart from other stores had actually landed some 3,000 tons of petrol. But there was no help for it. We had to bring away the small craft and the naval personnel, and with the Royal Engineers did our best to demolish the port again. Nevertheless, not everything could be destroyed, and I fear the enemy acquired considerable and valuable supplies.

Rommel captured Benghazi on 29 January and began a two-pronged advance to the east to recapture Cyrenaica. Derna was evacuated on 1 February; the port was demolished, and the ships and naval base party left for Tobruk.

Rommel called off the pursuit on 5 February, having recaptured the whole 'hump' of Cyrenaica. The new front stabilised just to the west of Gazala, not far from where the 8th Army were when CRUSADER began.

ABC was bitterly disappointed. 'To think we should be had twice in the same way is just too frightful,' he wrote to Pound on 6 February. 'I don't know the reason. I know it was not due to any naval shortcomings (we had just landed 2,500 tons of petrol and over 3,000 tons of other stores at Benghazi and had doubled the amount we had guaranteed to land daily at Tobruk). When one thinks of the efforts that we've made and all the losses, it's just too sickening.'

With the airfields of Cyrenaica once more back in Axis hands, the situation at sea again changed very much to the Allies' disadvantage. On 7 February, ABC sent a personal message to Pound 'setting out the situation at Malta in all its grim bleakness'. It was imperative to run a convoy into Malta, whatever the risk.

Events underlined the gravity of ABC's assessment. The destroyer *Maori* was bombed on 12 February and sank in Grand Harbour. The submarine base at Manoel Island in Lazaretto Creek was hit by two land-mines in a daylight raid which did great damage to the submarine crews' living quarters. Submarines had to lie submerged in the harbour during the day, putting an extra strain on their crews.

The February convoy to Malta, codenamed Operation MF.5, sailed from Alexandria after dark on the 12th, in two sections: MW.9A, the fast merchantmen *Clan Chattan* and *Clan Campbell*, escorted by *Carlisle* and four destroyers; and MW.9B, a third fast transport, *Rowallan Castle*, with another four destroyers.

Despite fighter cover from shore, the convoy came under heavy air attack on the next day. *Clan Campbell* was hit, her speed was reduced and she was diverted to Tobruk, escorted by two destroyers.

Vian's cruisers, *Naiad*, *Dido* and *Euryalus*, with eight destroyers, joined on 14 February, the critical day, when the convoy would be beyond fighter cover. By that time, anti-aircraft ammunition was already being rationed. High-level and dive-bombers made a series of attacks in which *Clan Chattan* was hit and caught fire. The ammunition on board began to explode. Her crew and service personnel were taken off and she was sunk by the destroyers.

That afternoon the convoy met Force K, of *Penelope* and six destroyers, who were escorting convoy ME.10, of *Breconshire* and three merchant ships, from Malta. Vian turned back for Alexandria with the four 'empties', while *Penelope* and her destroyers took *Rowallan Castle* on towards Malta. But she, too, was bombed and disabled. The destroyer *Zulu* took her in tow, but when it became clear that she could not reach the 'umbrella' of Malta's Hurricanes by daylight, ABC reluctantly gave the order for her to be sunk.

Penelope and her two destroyers, *Lance* and *Legion*, returned to Malta on 15 February, while Vian's cruisers, the rest of the destroyers and the four 'empties' reached Alexandria safely.

The enemy might not have the benefit of ULTRA, but they did have their own decrypting service, agents in Alexandria and Cairo, intensive and continuous air reconnaissance and, most important of all, the certain knowledge that every Allied convoy which left Alexandria had to be going to Malta. The Italians knew of the sailing of the MW convoys, and a powerful force, of *Caio Duilio*, four cruisers and eleven destroyers, sailed from Taranto to intercept. They lay in wait for some time to the north-east of Malta but eventually returned to Taranto on 15 February. By that time their objective, the convoy, had simply ceased to exist.

By contrast, a week later, in Operation K.7, the Italians passed across two convoys of three ships, from Corfu and Messina, with battleship and cruiser cover. The convoy sailings and details of the covering force were again revealed by the C38m and some of the ships were located by a radar-equipped Wellington on the night of 21 February. Next day, and during the following night, attacks were made by Flying Fortresses, Beauforts, Blenheims, Wellingtons and Albacores. But the Albacores failed because of a navigational error of 100 miles in the locating report. Of the other aircraft, some turned back, some had engine troubles or radio failures and some failed to find the target. Only one Fortress and one Wellington found and bombed the convoy. Both missed. The convoy reached Tripoli unscathed.

ABC may have confided his true feelings in his letters to Pound, but outwardly he was the same as ever. 'Of course,' said 'Wilf' Woods, 'we all realised the gravity of the situation [early in 1942], but nobody could have guessed it from the C-in-C's demeanour.'

Woods was virtually a stranger to ABC and almost completely unaware of the problems he would have to face on ABC's staff. But, as a 'new boy', having been as he said 'abruptly removed from the "sheltered" submarine world', Woods was particularly anxious to find his feet quickly; so he studied his new chief with more than usual care and was thus in an excellent position to describe ABC at this time of troubles.

Although ABC continued to sleep in *Queen Elizabeth*, his staff were established ashore at Gabbari. Woods himself slept in a cubicle behind a partition in the Main Signal Office, where he was deafened by the constant clatter of typewriters and teleprinters and was woken several times every night to be shown almost every signal that arrived.

Often Woods then had to telephone ABC and propose some action, only to find that there was sure to be some point which he himself had not appreciated but which ABC 'would be on to in a flash'. It took Woods some little time to gain the confidence to deal with these 'nocturnal crises', while the morning staff meetings held in ABC's office were a daily ordeal.

First, Woods had to report on any operations in progress. Then, he had to undergo a 'regular grilling' about the 'Daily State', when he had to know the exact whereabouts, condition and employment of every ship in the fleet, 'down to the smallest local defence patrol boat or harbour minesweeper', and be prepared to answer questions about any of them.

Like Power before him, Woods found himself

> frequently acting as the champion of various destroyers and other small ships whose turn for boiler-cleaning had come round, and were so shown on the Daily State. The C-in-C never accepted this question — indeed without a positive inquisition. He demanded chapter and verse in every case — how long since the last boiler-clean, what other defects she had, how long since her last operation, what was planned for her next, and so on. In fact he usually knew all the answers even better than I did, but his unswerving aim was that the fleet should always be ready for sea, and he expected it to 'live on its fat' as far as maintenance was concerned.

During what Woods called 'these dreaded boiler-cleaning contests', ABC's eyes would assume 'their most baleful expression'. He would make 'curious gestures with his hands down the front of his monkey jacket', thus polishing it to a high degree.

Woods gradually learned to take the staff meetings in his stride:

Often they were a riot of laughter, and enlivened by two little games of which he was extremely fond. He loathed the Signalese expression 'come up', and any staff officer unguarded enough to report that so-and-so had 'come up' with a signal would be greeted with roars of delight and ordered to put a piastre in the 'comeuppance box' which he kept on his desk. Similar fines were imposed on anyone referring to No. 201 Naval Co-operation Group RAF (HQ at Ras-el-Tin at that time) as '201 Group'. The words 'Naval Co-operation' were obligatory and were, indeed, a reflection of the battle he had fought with his fellow Cs-in-C in Cairo to get an RAF Group specifically detailed and equipped for Naval Co-operation.

I don't know what he did with the fines, but I suspect he used them to buy the boiled sweets which he always kept in a tin on his desk, and which he sometimes used as a peace offering after a stormy scene. I shared an office with Tom Brownrigg (Master of the Fleet), Michael Culme-Seymour (SOO2) and Douglas Alston (misleadingly entitled Staff Officer Intelligence Afloat). This adjoined the C-in-C's office, with a connecting door and another door onto a balcony which ABC used as a 'stern walk', and which gave him a good view of the harbour. We never knew when he wasn't going to erupt into our office. Often enough it was to take one of us to task about something, eyes gleaming, hands massaging his monkey jacket, language pungent. Equally abruptly he would be gone, nearly always to return a few minutes later with his box of boiled sweets, his blood pressure perceptibly lower, to offer one to his late victim.

I never knew ABC to use Christian names or nicknames. He referred to people, and addressed them either by their job title (e.g. COS, FEO, RA(D), etc.), or by their surnames. From the time I joined his staff he always addressed me as 'Woods', but previously I had always been '*Triumph*', which, I confess, gave me a considerable feeling of pride. The only exception to this rule was Captain Boustead (Chief of

Intelligence Staff). ABC professed to treat all intelligence as somewhat lunatic guesswork. 'No deductions,' he would say. 'Give me the facts. *I* will make the deductions.' He had such a gift for getting the essentials out of signals and documents that he really knew it all. He could never resist pulling COIS's leg, and every morning he would ask him, 'Well, Bouser, any dirty stories this morning?' COIS was usually able to oblige, but if he failed, out came the 'come-uppance' box.

While ABC expected, and got, the utmost loyalty, he was equally loyal to those who served him. In any contest between the men in his fleet and bureaucracy, ABC always took the men's part. On 16 February 1942, the submarine *Thrasher* (Lieutenant H.S. Mackenzie) was on patrol north of Crete when she was bombed by aircraft and depth-charged by destroyers while attacking an Axis convoy. In the early hours of the next morning, when *Thrasher* surfaced to recharge her batteries, unusual banging noises were heard against the hull. A bomb was found lodged inside the casing.

The First Lieutenant, Lieutenant P. Roberts, and the Second Coxswain, PO T. Gould, succeeded in manhandling the bomb to the bows and dropping it overboard. Whilst doing so, they discovered a second bomb. They had to lower themselves through a narrow metal grating and crawl on their stomachs some twenty feet to reach the bomb. It took them forty minutes to extricate it and drop it over the side.

If the bomb had exploded, they and the submarine would have been lost. *Thrasher* was off an enemy coast, and the enemy knew there was an Allied submarine in the area. If an aircraft or a surface vessel had been sighted, Mackenzie would have had to dive, and the two would have drowned.

ABC recommended both men for the Victoria Cross, and was amazed and angered when the Honours and Awards

Committee argued that the George Cross would be more appropriate, as the submarine 'had not been in the presence of the enemy'. As ABC wrote to Edelsten in June 1942, 'I have been having a round or two with the decorations board on the subject of the Thrasher. I found the No. 1 and 2nd coxswain were being given George Crosses as it was agreed their action was only equivalent to that of a bomb disposal squad. I managed to stop that and I hope the result will be VCs.' Roberts' and Gould's VCs were gazetted a week later.

Characteristically, ABC wrote of this time of grievous losses that

> our greatest loss at this period was Rear-Admiral H.B. Rawlings, who struck his flag in the *Ajax* on January 15th and went home to England for a well-deserved rest. He was a man of many fine qualities, and no failings that I ever discovered. Rather quiet and retiring he never obtruded himself; but was quite fearless in discussion and in expressing his occasionally unorthodox opinions. Highly strung, I feel sure he had difficult moments and had sometimes to drive himself relentlessly; but with his capability of rapid and courageous decision in tight corners he seemed instinctively to do the right thing. With his great sense of humour and very humane understanding he was a grand and inspiring leader much liked, respected and trusted by those who served under him. As for me, I have the greatest affection for Rawlings as a friend and a comrade, coupled with admiration for his great qualities as a leader and a fighting seaman.

Rawlings replied modestly but from the heart. 'I don't suppose you have time to realise what you give to those who go paddling in your wake,' he wrote to ABC from *Ajax* before going home. 'It happens to exceed any bit of ribbon and the last sixteen months has shown one something one's got to try to pass on to those following.'

17: FROM THE MEDITERRANEAN TO WASHINGTON DC

JUST AS THE Allies intended to pass one convoy a month to Malta, so the Axis, too, intended to pass at least one convoy a month to Tripoli. In the first week of March 1942, the C38m began to give details of an operation, codenamed V.5, involving three convoys to Tripoli, sailing from Brindisi, Messina and Naples, and two return convoys. The whole undertaking, which lasted from 7 to 9 March, was covered by cruisers, destroyers and torpedo boats.

A northbound convoy was sighted by an aircraft from Malta on 9 March, some 200 miles south-east of Malta and steering north-west, and it was attacked by Beauforts. A southbound convoy of eight destroyers and five merchant ships was sighted later off the African coast, steering west for Tripoli. Although hits were claimed, all the convoys reached their destinations without mishap. As ABC said, 'this was by no means satisfactory'.

Cruisers and destroyers, with Vian flying his flag in *Naiad*, sailed from Alexandria at 4 a.m. on 10 March, so as to be off Tobruk by dusk and then pass through the most dangerous area to the west under cover of darkness. They did not meet the enemy but did rendezvous with the damaged destroyer *Kingston* and the cruiser *Cleopatra* from Malta.

Cleopatra was new, just out from England, and had had what ABC called a 'rude reception' to the Mediterranean, when a bomb hit her fo'c'sle as she entered Grand Harbour for the first time. The sailors of the 15th Cruiser Squadron believed that whenever four *Dido* Class cruisers were in company, one of them would be sunk or badly damaged. Experience showed there was some basis for this belief. When therefore Captain Guy Grantham, now commanding *Naiad* after four months' liaison duty with the 8th Army, cheerfully said over the ship's broadcast after *Cleopatra* joined the Squadron on 11 March 1942, 'Once more the 15th Cruiser Squadron is all the same class', a shiver of apprehension ran through *Naiad*'s ship's company.

Within minutes of *Cleopatra* joining, the Squadron was under attacks by German bombers and Italian torpedo-bombers which lasted almost without a break for the next nine-and-a-half hours. The ships sustained no damage until the evening, when *Naiad* was hit amidships on the bulkhead between her two engine-rooms by a torpedo from U-565, about sixty miles north-east of Solium. She took a heavy list and sank in twenty minutes. Vian, Grantham and most of her ship's company were picked up but eighty-two of her people were lost.

ABC had formed no great opinion of *Cleopatra*, or of her Commanding Officer, Captain Matthew Slattery. 'Cleopatra arrived here in a poor state,' he told Pound, in a letter of 19 March. 'She apparently was prevented by weather from doing any working up at home, and after her lively reception at Malta, Slattery had some trouble with his ship's company. He told me they were inclined to be "yellow" and that his officers were poor. She is, in fact, in a state of gross inefficiency. Slattery of whom I know nothing did not impress me.'

ABC took immediate action with brutal ruthlessness. Vian hoisted his flag in *Cleopatra*, with Grantham as his Flag Captain. Slattery was summarily dismissed from the command of his lovely new ship and sent to a 'backwater' appointment as Chief Staff Officer to the Commodore Eastern Station, to investigate the possibilities of establishing airfields in East Africa. His Executive Officer and his Gunnery Officer were also replaced.

The losses of *Naiad* and other ships to U-boats were to some extent counter-balanced by the successes of the 'U' Class of the 10th Flotilla under 'Shrimp' Simpson, running from Malta, and the larger 'T' Class of the 1st Flotilla, under Captain S.M. Raw, based at Alexandria.

The submarines were particularly effective against enemy U-boats, sinking seven between January and March 1942. In March, submarines sank six ships of 17,298 tons, and Lieutenant-Commander A.C.C. Miers in *Torbay* capped a series of bold patrols with a daring sortie into Corfu Roads on the night of 3/4 March, for which he was awarded the Victoria Cross.

Miers was a ruthless, aggressive submarine captain, a man after ABC's own heart. In *Torbay*'s third war patrol off Crete in July 1941, *Torbay* sank a caique carrying German troops. The German survivors were not made prisoners-of-war but shot, in circumstances which gave rise to some post-war (and posthumous) criticism of Miers' behaviour. But at the time, ABC endorsed Miers' patrol report: 'A brilliantly conducted patrol. Lieutenant-Commander Miers is an outstanding Commanding Officer.'

But, on the debit side, twenty submarines were lost in the Mediterranean from the outbreak of war against Italy to the end of March 1942. At one point the chances of survival of a submarine of the 10th Flotilla were put at 'no better than even money'.

Vian's ships, less *Naiad*, returned to Alexandria on 12 March. It was now time for the March convoy to Malta, codenamed MW 10. *Breconshire*, *Clan Campbell*, *Pampas* and the Norwegian *Talabot* sailed from Alexandria at 7 a.m. on 20 March, escorted by *Carlisle* and six destroyers. This close escort was to be joined at sea by six *Hunt* Class destroyers who, however, were first sent on a submarine 'hunter-killer' operation along the North African coast towards Tobruk. They did find one U-boat, U-652, which torpedoed *Heythrop* on the 20th. *Heythrop* later sank while under tow by *Eridge*. The five remaining *Hunts*, and a sixth from Tobruk, joined the convoy on the 21st.

Vian, flying his flag in *Cleopatra*, with *Dido* and *Euryalus* and four destroyers, sailed at 6 p.m., to overtake the convoy on the 21st. Force H, under Vice-Admiral Syfret, flying his flag in *Malaya*, sailed from Gibraltar with *Hermione*, nine destroyers and the carriers *Argus* and *Eagle* with nine Spitfires to fly off to Malta.

The convoy was sighted and reported by Italian submarines and attacked by German aircraft late on 21 March. Just after midnight on the 22nd, three Italian cruisers and four destroyers sailed from Messina, and *Littorio*, wearing the flag of Admiral Iachino, and six destroyers (two of which soon turned back), sailed from Taranto. *Littorio*'s sailing was revealed by a C38m decrypt, and was reported by the submarine *P.36*, on patrol in the Gulf of Taranto, in the early hours of the 22nd.

Penelope and *Legion* joined Vian from Malta early on the 22nd. By then, Vian had *P.36*'s report and the C38m ULTRA decrypt and knew that he was likely to encounter enemy heavy ships later in the day. It was *Euryalus* who first made the signal 'Enemy in sight' at 2.27 p.m. that afternoon. (As Captain Eric Bush, commanding *Euryalus*, later recalled, it was the frigate *Euryalus* who first sighted the combined French and Spanish fleets before Trafalgar.)

Superbly led by Vian himself in two engagements that day which together made up a brilliant action known as the Second Battle of Sirte, Vian's cruisers and destroyers held off a vastly superior force. Making judicious use of the weather gauge, as in the days of sail, with timely and skilfully laid smoke screens, advancing to open fire with guns and to threaten with torpedoes, then retreating as though to lead their adversaries into a trap, and advancing again, they frustrated and fought off first the Italian heavy cruisers and then *Littorio* herself.

Vian's leadership was so bold and decisive that all his captains knew what to do and he made very few signals. But those he did make were, of course, intercepted in Alexandria and studied by ABC who followed the battle's progress closely.

Towards the evening, when *Littorio* had made her appearance, Vian ordered the convoy to steer south away from the enemy at their best speed, while he and his ships laid another smoke screen in front of the enemy. The situation, in ABC's own words,

> was still fraught with danger. My feelings and those of my staff in our offices at Alexandria while the battle was in progress are better imagined than described. Never have I felt so keenly the mortifying bitterness of sitting behind the scenes with a heavy load of responsibility while others were in action with a vastly superior enemy force. We could visualize so well what was happening — the Italian battleship and cruisers to the northward; Vian's four cruisers and destroyers laying their smoke-screens and dodging the enemy's 15-inch and 8-inch salvoes; the violent air attacks upon the *Breconshire* and the three merchant ships upon which, for all we knew, the fate of Malta depended; the heavy and rising sea which so greatly hindered the work of the destroyers. We could imagine it all, yet there was nothing we could do to help.

Colonel Moseley was an enthralled spectator in the operations room throughout the battle.

The excellence of naval communications meant that ABC had his operations table plotted with the movements of both forces and he received all signals and sightings as they were made. Never once did he interfere though continually making such comments as 'Good boy!', 'That is correct', then 'Now is the time for a daylight destroyer attack', 'One hit on a *Littorio* and they will all group round in protection'. A few minutes later came the signal from Vian for his destroyers to attack. 'There you are, he is right again.' No other comment while he paced up and down. Then the dramatic claim of a hit and ABC's great joy. The Italians did as he said. Finally Vian's 'night dispositions' and intention to withdraw. Here ABC intervened for the first time. 'The convoy will need the *Carlisle*'s anti-aircraft protection entering Malta, we must instruct Vian to detach her'. It was a great experience to be at his side during so thrilling and important an occasion. His confidence and infectious enthusiasm kept his entire staff at their best.

The prospect of penetrating a smoke screen to find destroyers waiting to attack him with torpedoes on the other side was apparently too much for Iachino's nerve. *Littorio* had indeed suffered one hit aft, but it did no serious damage. At dusk Iachino was persuaded to break off the action and retire.

As ABC said, 'Our relief at Alexandria was indescribable when we heard that the Italians were withdrawing.' To try and take some of the responsibility off Vian's shoulders, ABC signalled to him that he might consider dispersing the convoy and letting them make their own ways to Malta at best speed. But he had already done so. At 7.20 p.m., with darkness falling and the convoy out of sight, Vian decided to turn back to Alexandria, while the convoy went on. The Italians were somewhere to the north, but it was most unlikely they would make a night attack.

Cleopatra had suffered one shell hit on her bridge which had killed fourteen men, and *Euryalus'* upper deck had been swept by splinters from a near-miss. *Lively* and *Havock* had both been damaged by near-misses and *Kingston* had been crippled by a direct 15-inch shell hit. *Penelope* and *Legion* went back to Malta with *Kingston* and *Havock*, who were unable to steam with the rest of Vian's ships into a rising gale from the east. *Lively* was also detached later to Tobruk.

Vian's ships arrived in Alexandria, after more air attacks, at 12.30 p.m. on 24 March and were given a tremendous reception by the rest of the fleet. Every ship in harbour manned the side to cheer. When ABC heard that Vian's ships were entering harbour, he brought a staff meeting in progress to a quick end, saying: 'Come on, come on, we must get out of here and give a proper welcome to my magnificent Fleet.'

Woods stood with ABC on the stern-walk of *Queen Elizabeth* as Vian's ships passed, 'and a moving moment it was. ABC was unnaturally silent at first, but then all his delight burst out, and he cheered with the rest of us.'

ABC himself always thought that the Battle of Sirte on 22 March 1942 was

one of the most brilliant naval actions of the war, if not the most brilliant... It sounds easy; but it is against all the canons of naval warfare for a squadron of small cruisers and destroyers to hold off a force of heavy ships. The determination and team-work of all the ships engaged more than fulfilled the high standard expected of them. This, combined with the fine leadership and masterly handling of his force by Philip Vian, produced a heartening and thoroughly deserved victory from a situation in which, had the roles been reversed, it is unthinkable that the convoy or much of its escort would not have been destroyed.

Penelope and *Legion* had joined the convoy after dark on 22 March, with the damaged *Kingston* and *Havock*. The four ships were no longer in convoy, in the strict sense; the Commodore, Captain C.A.G. Hutchison, in *Breconshire*, had ordered them to steer diverging courses, each with one or two destroyers as escort.

Unfortunately, the detour to the south during the Battle of Sirte had delayed the ships, so that they were still at sea at daylight on the 23rd. Ships and escort came under heavy and frequent air attacks and were by then very short of anti-aircraft ammunition.

Talabot and *Pampas* entered Grand Harbour, each accompanied by a destroyer, just after 9 a.m., to the tumultuous cheers of the Maltese gathered on the ramparts. But *Clan Campbell* was still fifty miles from Malta at daybreak and was bombed and sunk at about 10.30 that morning. Some 120 of her people were saved, but *Legion*, who had been ordered to join her, was damaged by a near-miss and had to be beached in Marsaxlokk, a bay on the south-east coast of Malta.

At 9.20 a.m. *Breconshire* was only eight miles from Grand Harbour and had survived many attacks when she was hit and disabled. A full gale was blowing but first *Carlisle* and then *Penelope* tried to take her in tow whilst still fighting off enemy aircraft. As *Breconshire* was drifting towards the shore, she anchored with three destroyers to cover her, although one, the *Hunt* Class *Southwold*, was mined and sunk. *Breconshire* was towed into Marsaxlokk during the night of 24/25 March. She was bombed and set on fire on the 26th, and finally rolled over and sank on the 27th.

The air onslaught on Malta grew ever more ferocious. *Legion* was bombed and sunk on 26 March, having reached Grand Harbour from Marsaxlokk. *Talabot* and *Pampas* were also hit;

Pampas was largely flooded and *Talabot* had to be scuttled in case her cargo of ammunition exploded. Much of the fuel in *Breconshire* was recovered by fitting valves in her exposed hull. But, in the end, only some 5,000 tons of the nearly 26,000 tons in the convoy were safely unloaded in Malta.

March 1942 was 'indeed a month of misfortune'. Such was the ferocity of air attack that all the remaining surface ships had to leave Malta. *Havock* ran aground near Cape Bon on her way to Gibraltar and had to be destroyed by her crew who were interned and abominably mistreated in prison camps by the Vichy French.

Woods had noticed that ABC was 'unnaturally silent' while watching Vian's ships return. Possibly it was because ABC knew that this was the last time he would watch his ships enter Alexandria. He had received in mid-March a message from Pound that it was proposed to send him to Washington DC to head the Admiralty delegation and to be the First Sea Lord's representative on the Combined Chiefs of Staff committee.

ABC was not pleased by the prospect. He disliked leaving his fleet at a time when their fortunes were at their lowest ebb. However, he had made it a rule never to question any appointment. His relief was the victor of the Battle of the River Plate, Admiral Sir Henry Harwood — an appointment of which ABC strongly disapproved, and later told Pound as much. But by then it was too late to change. ABC would haul down his flag on 1 April 1942. Pridham-Wippell was to act as C-in-C until Harwood arrived.

So as not to give the slightest comfort to the enemy by letting them know that their old adversary had left the Mediterranean, ABC's departure was kept secret. He took this as a great compliment but, of course, it also meant that he could not go round his ships and say goodbye to the sailors and thank them for their marvellous efforts over the years.

However, ABC did draft three messages, one to the fleet, one to the Merchant Navy and the third to Malta, to be broadcast as soon as the news ban on his departure was lifted. He told his fleet of the deep regret with which he laid down the command in the Mediterranean. It had, he said, been his greatest pride that throughout the war the Mediterranean Fleet had consistently shown itself the master of the enemy in every branch of naval warfare, whether in the air, against submarines, or in surface fighting.

To the officers and men of the Merchant Navy, ABC said:

> There is probably no theatre of war in which more tenacity and courage has been required of the Merchant Navy than in the Mediterranean. During my tenure of command I have seen innumerable instances of the unobtrusive yet sterling work of the Masters, officers and crews under conditions often of great difficulty and danger. It has been possible to keep an Army and Malta supplied only because the Merchant Navies have surmounted these difficulties... I thank you for your good work which we in the Royal Navy fully appreciate and which we greatly admire.

To the Vice-Admiral, Malta, ABC signalled that he wanted to draw attention to the enormous damage done to the enemy by the submarines, air and surface forces based in Malta:

> The record has been magnificent, and I heartily thank every officer and man who has taken part, not forgetting those who have the less spectacular, but none the less exacting, task of maintaining and bringing back into action our ships and aircraft to the discomfiture of the enemy...

The flag officers and captains dined ABC out on board *Queen Elizabeth*. 'I felt poignantly overcome at leaving all my faithful friends and comrades,' ABC recalled, 'rather as though I had lost everything.'

ABC and Nona travelled *incognito*, as Mr and Mrs Browne, with ABC in plain clothes. They left Cairo for home on 3 April 1942. ABC felt that he was leaving part of himself behind. 'My heart remains in the Mediterranean,' he wrote to Willis. 'I was told the other day that Nelson once said "Waking or sleeping Malta is always in my thoughts" and that exactly describes my case.'

ABC's staff, too, felt an aching sense of personal loss. Norman wrote a fortnight later that he had just visited the Residency, for the only time since ABC left, 'and I walked with ghosts'. Bartimeus said that 'When you had gone everybody felt like Fore Street Devonport on a wet Sunday afternoon.'

Mr and Mrs Browne flew to Khartoum, and then across Africa to Sierra Leone, spending a night at Genefra and landing next day at Kano in Nigeria. Mr Browne noticed that wherever they went they were usually met at the airfield by an ADC and taken to Government House, so 'our *incognito* did not appear to be impenetrable'. After a delay in Lisbon, when their flying boat was commandeered for HRH The Duke of Gloucester, they landed at Bristol on 9 April 1942.

At Paddington Station, ABC was surprised and touched to find the whole Board of Admiralty, except Dudley Pound, on the platform to meet them. But Pound had sent a note: 'Welcome back. I cannot give you the official welcome you deserve but the longer the I.T.s are in ignorance of your having left the better. Betty [Lady Pound] had another major operation yesterday and I am seizing the only chance of going down and seeing her.'

After so long an absence, ABC found wartime England a strange place. He spent the first ten days in London, and went frequently to the Admiralty, where he was most uncomfortable in the atmosphere of intrigue. He found that Pound was well aware of it. Years later, ABC wrote to Admiral John Godfrey: 'In 1942 I found Pound in great distress. He asked me if I thought he ought to resign and I said certainly not. He also told me that Winston Churchill was thinking of getting rid of him and putting Mountbatten in as First Sea Lord! I told him to glue himself to his chair but he was much worried about it.'

At last, ABC managed to shake himself clear of London for some badly needed leave and a chance to see his family. He and Nona went to stay with the aunts at Dolgellau in North Wales and then with relatives in Edinburgh where there was a family gathering. They all had a good gossip and played games, including one of ABC's favourites — lying on their backs on the living room carpet and throwing ping pong balls into the centre light. From Edinburgh, they went north to Aberdeenshire, for a ten-day fishing holiday.

Back in London in May 1942, ABC interviewed anyone who had any ideas on the line he should take in co-operating with the US Navy. He himself was in no doubt about his main task. 'I was suddenly told I was wanted at Washington', he wrote to Willis, 'to deal with the U.S.A.'s rather truculent and didactic Chief of the Naval Staff. A great tribute to my charming manners…'

Waiting for ABC when he came back to London was a letter from the Prime Minister, saying that he intended to recommend ABC to the King for a baronetcy. ABC said he never set much store by titles, but there was no reason for him to refuse this. Yet he did actually go to see Pound to ask if he could refuse it, only to find that Pound had been pressing for it. Pound pointed out what ABC must surely have known already, that the honour would be seen by the Mediterranean Fleet as a tribute to their work under his command. ABC therefore accepted. (Years later, having no children of his own, ABC tried unsuccessfully to have the baronetcy transferred to a nephew, showing that contrary to his protestations he set *some* store by titles.)

The journey to the United States was postponed again and again. There were difficulties with the flight and then an unforeseen snag about ABC's pay and allowances. The 'powers that be', as he called them, proposed to pay ABC less than the Naval Attaché in Washington.

ABC was determined to get the matter settled before he left London, knowing that once he was in Washington he could write as many letters as he liked but they would merely be pigeon-holed. He refused to leave until all was cleared up and went so far as to write a letter asking permission to withdraw from the appointment. He showed the letter to Pound but did not actually send it, to give Pound a chance to see what he could do. 'Of course, as usual,' ABC wrote to Doodles, 'it is W.C. who is the n****r in the woodpile and he has undoubtedly some ulterior motive — which prognosis was to prove close to the mark.' Churchill's plan was to put ABC in command of the Home Fleet, relieving Admiral Tovey, and it was only reluctantly, and after one of the strongest campaigns of protest Pound had ever mounted, that Mr Churchill eventually dropped his efforts to have Tovey; of whom he had 'a poor opinion', replaced by ABC.

Finally, after their air passage had been put back several times, ABC and Nona took off from Bristol for the New World on 23 June 1942.

In the first few days, Little took ABC on what seemed an endless round of official calls on high-ranking political, naval and military figures in Washington, to introduce ABC to his new colleagues and to a certain extent *pour prendre conge* for Little himself. Churchill, who had flown to the United States on 17 June, himself took ABC in to meet President Roosevelt.

There was bad news from North Africa. Rommel had secretly transferred much of his armour from the north to the south of his line and, on the night of 27 May, by the light of an almost full moon, launched a Panzer offensive across the desert towards Bir Hacheim, where a furious tank battle was soon raging. Tobruk fell on 21 June 1942. Thousands of men and many valuable supplies were captured by the enemy. Bardia, Solium, Sidi Barrani and Mersa Matruh were all taken one by one. By 30 June, the 8th Army stood at El Alamein, only seventy miles from Cairo.

But, from Washington, the war seemed to be on another planet. 'It's really terrible how far we are from the war here,' ABC wrote to Doodles. Early in July, ABC gave a cocktail party for about 250 people. 'I would not have believed that there were so many people in the British Admiralty Delegation.'

ABC and Nona soon decided their hotel was too expensive and moved, after some house-hunting by Nona, to a house at 2819 McGill Terrace, Washington DC, in the suburbs of the city near the Zoological Gardens, on 1 August. There, they had what ABC called 'rather a curious *ménage*' of a new flag lieutenant, a young RNVR officer, 'who had served as a signalman in a trawler, had been excellently brought up and was unsurpassed at washing up and cleaning white shoes'; Chief Steward Sackett, who had been with ABC at Chatham; Chief Petty Officer Percy Watts, ABC's Coxswain; a Chinese steward, Ah Ping, 'stranded from a British cruiser'; a Cockney steward; a black cook, and a mixed-race maid.

Not surprisingly, there were some household problems. ABC eventually had to send the Cockney steward home for being 'much too familiar with coloured people'. The black cook in a few days had quite fallen for Sackett. When Nona said she hoped the kitchen would be kept clean, Cook said 'Mam, cleanliness comes next to Godliness and I am a Christian woman.' Nona tried to get her to 'cook English', but without much success.

Washington was very social and ABC and Nona found this side of their work a definite burden. In July and August the capital was very hot and sticky. ABC acquired an eight-cylinder Buick saloon and had to accustom himself to driving on the right (i.e. wrong) side of the road.

ABC's duties 'were not particularly exacting'. 'It is an interesting but amazing job this,' he wrote. 'You haven't anything at all under your command and all you do is to sit out on deck and on committees.' His main duty was to keep in close touch with the Navy Department. 'Whether we have the best organisation for winning the war is another question. I don't myself think we are close enough together yet, but it will doubtless come.'

The combined Chiefs of Staff Committee consisted of Admiral William D. Leahy, the chairman, who also chaired the US Joint Chiefs of Staff and was the President's representative; Admiral Ernest J. King, the Chief of Naval Operations and Commander-in-Chief, US Fleet; General George C. Marshall, the Chief of Staff of the US Army; and General Henry ('Hap') Arnold, head of the US Army Air Force. On the British side, Field Marshal Sir John Dill, chairman of the British Joint Services Mission to Washington; ABC, representing the First

Sea Lord; Lieutenant-General G.N. Macready, representing the CIGS; and Air Marshal D.C.S. Evill, representing the Chief of the Air Staff.

There were difficulties from the outset with Admiral King, of whom ABC was to see a great deal. After the first formal call, ABC asked for an interview to discuss naval matters. But he was told that King was very busy and could not give him an appointment until a date six days ahead.

ABC's response was to call a Combined Chiefs of Staff meeting and then pointedly to tell the Army and Air Force members that he was sorry to have wasted their time but he had important naval matters to discuss with Admiral King.

ABC got his interview, but relations hardly improved. By the end of July ABC was writing to Pound, 'King I have not found very easy. He announces his decision without giving reasons which I find a little trying. I will doubtless in time wean him from this bad habit.'

But the bad habits persisted. ABC said of King, in his memoirs,

> A man of immense capacity and ability, quite ruthless in his methods, he was not an easy person to deal with. He was tough and liked to be considered tough, and at times became rude and overbearing. It was not many weeks before we had some straight speaking over the trifling matter of lending four or five American submarines for work on our side of the Atlantic. He was offensive, and I told him what I thought of his method of advancing allied unity and amity. We parted friends.

ABC used much stronger language in August 1942, in his account to Pound:

I have just had a very stormy interview with King about the submarines for the Mediterranean. He was abominably rude and I had to be quite firm with him and I told him that the remarks he had made got us no further in winning the war. I do not think the breeze did any harm and he made a lame sort of apology when I left, but if he says the same things about us to his underlings, as he said to me, as I have no doubt he does, it makes things very difficult.

It seemed that King was smarting from ABC's remarks made at a press conference, that the US Navy's contribution to the Battle of the Atlantic was wholly inadequate. 'I therefore interpreted Cunningham's inquiry as a "needle" directed at me,' King said, 'and I was indeed very abrupt and rude with him — and purposefully so... I was very rough with him.'

'Apparently there had been an agreement', said George Russell, King's Flag Secretary, 'that the British would provide the submarines for the Mediterranean, and they wanted to go back on that agreement and have the United States Navy provide the submarines. King refused to do it, and Cunningham got insistent and started pounding on the table. King stood up and said, "Britannia may have ruled the waves for three hundred years, but she doesn't any more. There's the door."'

Very probably, King had heard a somewhat garbled account of a speech ABC made in July when he was the guest of honour at an Overseas Press Club lunch. The US Navy had been slow to introduce convoy in the first half of 1942. German U-boat captains had enjoyed what they called 'a happy time' against shipping which was still behaving as in peacetime along the eastern seaboard of the United States.

ABC took the shipping losses caused by submarines as the principal theme of his lunchtime speech, implying that all was not well with the US Navy's anti-submarine organisation and stressing that what was needed was an all-out effort and a unified system of command.

ABC was aware of the stir his words caused in his audience. 'Unfortunately,' he wrote to Doodles, 'there were two or three US naval officers there and they did not like hearing that there were shortcomings. They don't over here, they always like to see and comment on the moats [*sic*] in their neighbour's eye quite regardless of the many and great beams in their own.'

The contrast in appearance, and the similarities in temperament, between ABC and King were well described by Rear-Admiral G.A. Thring, at that time a commander in the Operations Division of the British Joint Services Mission.

> Both were tough, both had been successful in different ways, both were dedicated but to different causes. I believe they admired each other for their toughness but differed in almost everything else.
>
> ABC was broad, stocky, and wore immaculate full whites, and had been a 'salt-horse'. King was tall and wore US Navy Air uniform, and was very wedded to Naval Air. ABC had a great sense of humour. King appeared to have very little of that commodity.
>
> ABC had led a Fleet to victories in the Mediterranean, and was the admiration of his country. King had put the US Navy on its feet again after Pearl Harbor, building up morale and ships by his own leadership and untiring energy, for which his country was justly proud and grateful.
>
> King was naturally bent on revenge for Pearl Harbor, and throughout his period of office he never really appeared to accept the agreed priorities, always trying to direct the available effort to the Pacific.

ABC could not help remarking the bitter rivalry between the

US Navy and the US Army which was, he said, 'an eye-opener to me and was carried to extraordinary lengths'. He even wondered whether it was 'drilled into embryo officers at West Point and Annapolis'. The senior Navy and Army officers ABC himself largely dealt with, such as General Marshall and Admiral Stark, were 'above this constant and acrimonious bickering'. But many others were not. It was, ABC said, 'a great pity'.

But generally, ABC got on well with the Americans, as did Rear-Admiral Patterson, ABC's Chief of Staff, and Royer Dick, his Deputy Chief of Staff. Marshall, ABC liked and admired immensely. Leahy, he thought 'a charming and courteous man and an excellent chairman, smoothing out difficulties and calming any approaching storm'.

When ABC arrived in Washington, Allied plans for future operations in Europe were still undecided. One plan, a somewhat desperate measure to help relieve the pressure on the Russian front, codenamed Operation SLEDGEHAMMER, was a cross-Channel expedition in the autumn of 1942, to capture the Cherbourg peninsula. But, if SLEDGEHAMMER was not practicable (Churchill said: 'No responsible British general, admiral or air marshal was prepared to recommend it'), then a major invasion, Operation ROUND-UP, to end the war in Europe, would be undertaken by September 1943. Meanwhile, the build-up of American forces in Europe, Operation BOLERO, would continue.

In July 1942 President Roosevelt ordered the US Chiefs of Staff to 'undertake some kind of offensive ground action in Europe in 1942'. King, Marshall and Mr Harry Hopkins flew to London to confer with Churchill and the British Chiefs of Staff. The Americans continued to press for SLEDGEHAMMER. But the British did not believe an invasion of north-west Europe was possible before 1944 and favoured a landing in North Africa in October 1942, Operation GYMNAST, later christened TORCH by Churchill.

To the Americans, this was at least preferable to sending American troops to serve under a British C-in-C in Egypt. Thus TORCH was agreed on, to take place under an American Supreme Commander not later than 26 October.

But the US Chiefs of Staff remained unenthusiastic. Their lack of keenness, as ABC wrote to Pound,

> reacts on TORCH, for which there are few signs of enthusiasm, and they do not seem to be getting down to it though they pay lip service to the usefulness of the operation. I am sure that King is dead against it, and that he has given it as his opinion that it is of no value to the war effort of the United States, and this opinion of his is reflected all through the Navy Department.

On 14 August 1942, Lieutenant-General Dwight D. Eisenhower, US Army, the Commandant General, European Theatre of Operations, was appointed Commander-in-Chief, Allied Expeditionary Force, with General Mark Clark as his Deputy and Brigadier General Walter Bedell Smith, Secretary to the US Chiefs of Staff, as Chief of Staff. Bedell Smith was one of the Americans whose sense of humour and ready wit ABC particularly liked. A day after his appointment, Bedell Smith came to have what ABC called 'a heart to heart talk with me'.

Bedell Smith said he himself was enthusiastic about TORCH but he was getting little encouragement from the US Navy Department. He wanted an independent naval opinion on the effect of the occupation of North Africa on the naval and shipping position as a whole. King said it would have little or no effect. What did ABC think?

ABC said that

> the gain accruing from complete success was just incalculable from every point of view. If we could occupy the whole North African seaboard from Egypt to Spanish Morocco, Italy at once lay open to invasion. She was what the Prime Minister later referred to as the 'soft under-belly of the Axis'. Airfields along the whole stretch of the North African coast would eventually give us dominance in the air, and enable us to pass convoys through the Mediterranean.

As for TORCH itself, ABC repeated the gist of a signal he had sent to Pound on 21 July: 'It would go a long way towards relieving the shipping problem once the short route through the Mediterranean was gained. It would jeopardise the whole of Rommel's forces and relieve anxiety about Malta. It would shake Italy to the core and rouse the occupied countries.'

That was exactly the reassurance Bedell Smith needed. But he had another point to put: would ABC take on the job of Naval Commander for TORCH? It was very important to get a naval officer who was whole-heartedly in favour of the operation.

ABC certainly was wholly in favour of TORCH, but he replied very guardedly, not knowing the views of the British Government or of the First Sea Lord. But he did say that he would be proud to serve under an American Supreme Commander. To Pound on 31 July, ABC wrote, 'You probably have someone already in your mind, but if it was considered that I could be of use I should be more than willing. At the same time I don't want to push myself forward'.

In fact, ABC was very keen. He had had more than enough of 'the detached atmosphere of Washington and my office desk' and he 'really yearned to be up and doing again'. But first there was much discussion and some disagreement, in London and in Washington, over the overall naval command structure for TORCH.

There were three elements: first, the command of the naval expeditionary force; second, the command of the battle fleet and other ships in the covering force; and, third, the command of the western Mediterranean including the fortress and harbour of Gibraltar, which would play a major part in planning, launching and supplying TORCH.

Command at Gibraltar also involved the operation of some Atlantic convoys and ABC suspected this was why Pound was reluctant to have only one C-in-C — because Gibraltar would then come under the TORCH Supreme Commander. But ABC thought it unreasonable to expect the Supreme Commander to deal with three separate naval commanders and urged Pound to have a single Naval C-in-C.

Eisenhower also wanted to achieve what he called overall unity and insisted that there should be a single Allied Naval Commander, directly responsible to himself.

With ABC's support, Eisenhower won his point. Vice-Admiral Sir Bertram Ramsay had been appointed Naval Commander-in-Chief, Expeditionary Force, for ROUND-UP in July. On August Bank Holiday, he was directed to leave the planning for ROUND-UP and concentrate upon TORCH instead.

Washington might seem remote from the war, but into it poured a torrent of signals and reports, and sometimes ABC caught sight of a sad reference to a ship who had once served in his fleet. 'I have just seen with a pang', he wrote to Pound, 'about the loss of the *Eagle* [torpedoed and sunk on 11 August in the PEDESTAL convoy to Malta]. It is a wonder she has lasted so long and she has paid a very handsome dividend.'

Washington also had the attentions of the very active and aggressive American news media. ABC still held his somewhat contradictory views about publicity, being unconvinced that it was at all necessary, yet being furious when it was bad or incorrect. After seeing Mr Butler, head of British publicity in the States, 'It's frightful,' he told Doodles, 'that we have to go in for that sort of thing.' But after the failure of the Dieppe raid in August 1942, he wrote: 'One would think that Great Britain was taking no part in the war at all. The Dieppe raid was headlined in the papers here as American troops land in France. Nothing about the British or Canadians.'

No sooner had Ramsay been appointed than there were second thoughts, especially in America. The obvious man to be Naval Commander-in-Chief for TORCH was surely ABC. He had been a firm supporter of the project from the start. He was very well liked and respected by the Americans. 'Cunningham was my favourite,' said Admiral Leahy, 'because, in the first place, he was a splendid sailor. He was a daring, experienced and successful British sea commander, worthy of the tradition of Britain's Nelson. Cunningham was also the best expert in the Allied navies on strategy and tactics in the Mediterranean theatre.'

The choice of ABC was also approved by Eisenhower. He and ABC took to each other at once. They became firm friends for life. Yet, it might not have been so. ABC was a war celebrity. Matapan had made him as internationally famous as Nelson after the Nile, and he was one of the very few Allied commanders of any nationality or service with victories to his credit at that stage of the war.

Eisenhower, on the other hand, had no battle experience. He had not served in Europe in the Great War. In fact, he had never commanded troops in the field. He was virtually unknown to the British Army and, although he had been in command of the build-up of US Forces in Europe (BOLERO) since June 1942, he was not much better known in the US Army. But ABC supported Eisenhower from the start. If ABC had done nothing else in the war, the Allies would still owe him gratitude for the generous and whole-hearted way he backed Eisenhower.

Even Admiral King approved of ABC's appointment, but he had a rooted aversion to US naval forces being placed under British command (although, as ABC noted, he did not object to British naval forces being placed under US command 'whenever he thought fit and proper'). King wanted the US Naval Task Force for the Casablanca landing under Vice-Admiral H. Kent Hewitt to be independent of the main expedition, under the command of the US C-in-C, Atlantic.

This would put ABC, as Naval C-in-C for TORCH and Eisenhower's principal naval adviser, in an impossible position. There was another acrimonious meeting. Eventually General Marshall, who was in the chair, said he wondered what the US Admiral concerned thought about it. Kent Hewitt, who was sitting at the back, said in a quiet voice, 'It would be a privilege to serve under Admiral Cunningham.'

A compromise was reached. The US Task Force would be under the US C-in-C Atlantic's command until passing a certain Longitude West, when command would pass to the Supreme Commander. As ABC said, the chain of naval command was 'always a little nebulous', though I always took it that the Casablanca naval force was under me. In the Mediterranean itself there was no question about it.'

King made one other major concession. Not only did he agree to Hewitt's force being placed under ABC's command, but he also authorised ABC to send home any American flag officer whom he thought incompetent because he [King] 'would know that Cunningham was right'!

Thus, early in September 1942, ABC heard definitely that his appointment as Allied Naval Commander-in-Chief of the Expeditionary Force (ANCXF) was to be confirmed, but the appointment was to be kept secret for the time being. Ramsay was to be ABC's deputy.

Ramsay was understandably disappointed, although he appreciated that a flag officer of ABC's stature would be more acceptable to the Americans. But 'I now understand', he told his wife, 'how Moses must have felt when leading the people to the Promised Land but no farther.'

Ramsay had previously asked ABC if he could recommend any good staff officers. Not surprisingly, ABC advised Ramsay to collect as many of his old team from the Mediterranean as were available. Geoffrey Barnard and Tom Brownrigg joined Ramsay's staff. Rear Admiral Patterson was required to stay in Washington, so ABC asked for Royer Dick because he 'knew me and my methods, or perhaps I should say lack of method'. Dick became ABC's Chief of Staff, with the rank of Commodore.

Ramsay and Brownrigg flew over to Washington early in September. On their first night, ABC and Nona took them to a restaurant twenty miles out of Washington for dinner. Fresh from rationing in wartime England, one ordered a chump chop and the other steak. 'Their faces,' said ABC, 'when they were served with gargantuan helpings were worth seeing.'

ABC and Ramsay made an interesting contrast of styles and personalities. ABC was apt to be impatient with the small print,

446

to leave matters to 'come out in the wash', believing that many problems would solve themselves on the day. Ramsay, however, had a very tidy mind and hated to leave any loose ends untied. An officer who worked with them both said: 'I had to deal more with Cunningham than Ramsay. The latter was very polite and meticulously accurate in his planning; the exact opposite to the former!'

ABC and Ramsay were invited to the White House one night after dinner. They sat talking with the President and Harry Hopkins for three hours. The President had just, on 5 September, cabled one word to Churchill, 'HURRAH', and Churchill had replied, 'O.K. FULL BLAST'. So the conversation that evening was mostly about TORCH. The President said that the US Navy were still doubtful about maintaining forces as far east as Algiers. ABC, with his mind ever on Malta's parlous predicament, suggested that a landing might be made even further east, at Bizerta.

On 20 September, ABC, Ramsay and Royer Dick flew to Great Britain in a bomber — 'not the most comfortable form of transportation,' ABC said. His part in TORCH was still secret, and he was supposed to be in England on ordinary business. He spent about twelve days in England, 'very busy conferring, planning and so on' but found time to go up to Dolgellau to see the two aunts.

He flew back to Washington early in October 1942, settled all outstanding business, and left America on 11 October, 'delighted to be away from the hothouse atmosphere of Washington and actively back in the war'. He left Washington having earned the respect of Admiral 'Ernie' King. 'Then they got a *man*,' King said later. 'A fighter. He would fight like hell. When I had something to say against the British he would stand up and say, "I don't like that".'

ABC, for his part, said of King, 'On the whole I think Ernest King was the right man in the right place, though one could hardly call him a good co-operator. Not content with fighting the enemy, he was usually fighting someone on his own side as well.'

Because ABC's appointment as ANCXF was still secret, Nona had to stay in Washington, much to her disgust, to maintain the fiction that ABC would be coming back.

The flight back to England was even more uncomfortable than the one before. The bomber was unheated, so it was bitterly cold, and ABC could hear the ice rattling off the wings. When he arrived at Prestwick, he found his sponge had frozen hard inside his suitcase. It reminded him, he said, 'of the old days on the bridge of a destroyer in the North Sea in mid-winter'.

ABC now threw himself into the preparations for an operation which 'if successful, would mean the end of Malta's trial, and our freedom of the Mediterranean'. The TORCH was about to be lit.

18: THE TORCH IS LIT

D-DAY FOR TORCH was 8 November 1942 — the last day it was considered feasible to land troops on the open beaches around Casablanca, where the surf rolled in from the Atlantic (ABC had misgivings about the choice of Casablanca for that reason).

The basic plan, issued on 20 September 1942, was for convoys of American troops to sail from Portland, Maine, and from Hampton Roads, Virginia, to land in French Morocco, either side of Casablanca, at Port Lyautey, Fedala and Safi, and for convoys of American and British troops to sail from the Clyde, to land at Oran and Algiers.

ABC's command extended across the Atlantic to 40°W, north to the latitude of Cape Finisterre, and south almost to the Cape Verde Islands; in the Mediterranean, east to a line between Cape Bon and Cape San Vito, the north-western tip of Sicily.

By the time ABC arrived, Ramsay had done a great deal of preliminary planning. The naval forces and the troop-carrying ships had been allocated. The ports of departure had been arranged and shipping was being concentrated at them. But the naval plan for TORCH had not been written, nor had any of the operational orders for the hundreds of complicated convoy, squadron, flotilla and individual ship movements. For this 'monumental task', ABC decided, special treatment was needed.

The only, obvious man was 'Lofty' Power who was then in command of the destroyer *Opportune* in the Home Fleet. ABC knew Power would not be pleased to leave his ship but was sure he would agree to help. With the Admiralty's permission, ABC asked Tovey for Power to be released. 'There was only one possible answer,' Tovey said to Power, 'so I have given it for you — Yes!'

Power's reception when he arrived at the Admiralty at 9.30 one morning was vintage ABC. 'Hello, you unshaven bugger, what do you want?' 'I understand you wanted me, sir.' 'The Chief of Staff does anyway. Says he can't get on without you. Go and see him, it's Royer Dick. Don't hang about now, there's a lot to be done. I'm delighted to see you.'

Planning for TORCH was a new experience for ABC. In the lean and dangerous years of 1940 and 1941, he had had to make do with what little he had. Now, there was an abundance of ships and men. Although ABC quickly adjusted his thinking to the much larger scale of TORCH, he could never quite throw off his ingrained habit of examining everything, every plan and suggestion, with a view to economy. Anything he thought too lavish was dubbed 'Too velvet-arsed and Rolls Royce!'

For TORCH, ABC's staff had to organise the sailing, routeing, exact timing and arrival at Oran and Algiers of two advance convoys of some forty-five ships, followed by a main body of more than two hundred vessels and a hundred escorts, carrying some 38,500 British and American troops. The orders laid down the movements and duties of all the naval forces inside the Mediterranean, which, apart from more than 100 vessels at Gibraltar, meant another 176 vessels of all types.

The orders also had to provide for the passage of more than 400 ships through the Straits of Gibraltar, which were only eight miles wide, in a limited time, and to arrange for the smaller ships to refuel at Gibraltar.

Royer Dick, Brownrigg, Barnard, Power and Durlacher, the Signal Officer, set to work at Norfolk House, St James's Square, in London, the pre-operational headquarters of the Allied Commander-in-Chief. According to ABC, 'I think Power dictated for about four days almost without stopping with four Wren stenographers on duty and another four standing off and waiting to come on.' The orders were completed, printed and distributed to the ships just before they sailed.

No matter how hard ABC's staff worked, they got little or no sympathy. When told that someone was overworked and needed an assistant, ABC would say: 'I've never heard of a staff officer dying of overwork, and if he does I can easily get another one!' 'This was said most genially and with a broad grin,' said Power, 'and of course nobody did die, that was really the maddening part!'

ABC disliked information being passed to him second-hand, always preferring to talk to the man directly involved. Concerned about U-boats interfering with TORCH, he asked for a briefing from Commander Rodger Winn, RNVR, in charge of the Submarine Tracking Room at the Admiralty.

ABC arrived with Ramsay and Dick, a full half-hour before he was expected (deliberately, Winn suspected, because he wanted to speak to Winn without his Admiral, whom ABC forbade Winn to send for). After dealing with some questions, Winn suggested that another officer should answer one particular point.

> This brought forth a torrent of apparently violent abuse, to the effect that it was my answer that he wanted and not that of some so-and-so lieutenant. When, however, I persisted in asserting that Lieutenant X's answer would be more up-to-date and precise than any I could give, without notice, and

that I took full responsibility for such answer, ABC turned to the others, roared with laughter, and said: 'These buggers in the RNVR seem to have picked up quite well the important Service traditions,' and added 'come on, Lieutenant X, tell me what the answer is!'

ABC's initial liking for Eisenhower warmed into a lasting friendship. 'Ike' struck ABC as 'being completely sincere, straight-forward and very modest'. At first, it seemed to ABC that Eisenhower was unsure of himself

> but who could wonder at that. He was in supreme command of one of the greatest amphibious operations of all time, and was working in a strange country with an Ally whose methods were largely unfamiliar. But as time went on Eisenhower grew quickly in stature, and it was not long before one recognized him as the really great man he is — forceful, able, direct and foreseeing with great charm of manner, and always with a rather naive wonder at attaining the high position in which he found himself. We soon became fast friends and I can only hope that he had for me some of the great esteem and personal affection I had for him.

ABC need have had no doubts. 'I personally considered him one of the finest individuals that I ever met,' Eisenhower said of ABC, years later, 'and I had the utmost respect for his military judgement as well as for his great human qualities.' Of ABC's contribution to TORCH, Eisenhower wrote,

> He was the Nelsonian type of admiral. He believed that ships went to sea in order to find and destroy the enemy. He thought always in terms of attack, never of defence. He was vigorous, hardy, intelligent and straightforward. In spite of his toughness, the degree of affection in which he was held by all grades and ranks of the British navy and, to a large extent, the

452

other Services, was nothing short of remarkable. He was a real sea-dog.

Eisenhower was determined to have complete unity between the Americans and the British on his staff. He once told his staff: 'You can call a man a son-of-a-bitch and that's OK. But if you call him a *Limey* son-of-a-bitch, you're out!' 'The staffs were closely integrated,' said ABC, 'and it was not long before its British and American members ceased to look at each other like warring tom-cats, and came to discover that the nationals of both countries had brains, ideas and drive.'

ABC was still supposed to be in London for conferences before returning to Washington, so he wore plain clothes when he took the train to Plymouth on 28 October 1942. Driving through the city to Millbay Docks, he was greatly shocked by the devastation wreaked by bombing. He wished that some of his American friends in 'peaceful Washington' could see it.

The Commander-in-Chief, Plymouth, Admiral of the Fleet Sir Charles Forbes, saw ABC off in his barge for the cruiser *Scylla*, lying in Plymouth Sound. Her ship's company were not told where the ship was going or why ABC was on board. Her Captain, I.A.P. MacIntyre, left a 'dummy' signal lying casually on his desk, stating that ABC was going to the Far East after calling at Gibraltar.

Ramsay stayed in London to act as a 'rear link'. When ABC wanted anything in the weeks to come, he signalled direct to Ramsay who arranged it with the Admiralty. This procedure worked so well that it was repeated in future operations.

Ramsay was naturally disappointed to be left behind, but he gave ABC his full support. 'There is no one I would rather have done my work for than you,' he wrote, 'and I have done it with real pleasure. I'm confident that success awaits you...'

Scylla arrived in Gibraltar on 1 November and ABC hoisted his flag as Allied Naval Commander. He and his personal staff stayed at the The Mount, the residence of the Flag Officer, Gibraltar, Vice-Admiral Sir Frederick Edward-Collins. The Mount was comfortable enough, but ABC's staff were not impressed by Edward-Collins. 'Fat Fred,' Power called him, 'a fat, stupid, pompous man, His Pregnancy the Panda.'

ABC had an office in the dockyard, from which he could watch the ships coming and going, and receive the calls of their commanding officers. He was thrilled to be in the seagoing Navy again, feeling as though he had been away from it for years instead of only seven months.

As the advanced base, Gibraltar was the hub of Operation TORCH. The harbour was so congested by convoys with personnel for the Rock, and by a never-ending stream of vessels of all kinds, that ABC sent for Captain Geoffrey Oliver, his Gunnery Officer in *Rodney* in 1930. Oliver was on leave, 'rather dolefully waiting for an expected appointment to a dreary desk at Bath,' when he received ABC's joyful summons to come out as Commodore (Flotillas) and organise matters. His services, ABC said, were invaluable.

Gibraltar has always been a favourite of sailors and those who were about to take part in TORCH enjoyed its facilities to the full. ABC disapproved. 'Things are damned slack in this place,' he told Ramsay. 'I want to lay my hands on some of the young officers to be seen in ½ dozens drunk in the streets at night. It is reported to me that they are worse than the sailors.'

Eisenhower arrived on 5 November, his Flying Fortress *Red Gremlin* having taken off in England in conditions of rain, fog and zero visibility so abominable that the pilot (Major Paul Tibbets, the man who was to drop the atomic bomb) had been reluctant to fly. But Eisenhower insisted. Even when they arrived over the Rock, they had to circle for an hour, because of crosscurrents and congestion on the runway.

Eisenhower and his personal staff were accommodated by the Governor, Lieutenant-General Frank Mason-Macfarlane, at the Governor's residence, The Convent. Eisenhower's offices were also in the tunnel, on the opposite side to ABC's.

ABC was critical of the state of security in the fortress and ordered Lieutenant Lord Ampthill, who was on the staff in Gibraltar, to arrange for a Royal Marine detachment to guard the tunnel and institute a system of passes. One of the first to be stopped and asked for his pass, which he did not have, was Eisenhower.

Lord Ampthill said:

> It was at this time that I first saw ABC with Ike, and I was tremendously impressed with the way that ABC made it clear to Ike, and everyone else anywhere near, that he, Ike, was the Supreme Commander. It seemed to me that ABC went out of his way to hoist Ike into his proper position as Supreme Commander and that ABC did as much or more than anyone else to give Ike confidence, and also to blend the British and US staffs into a reasonably smoothly working Allied team.

The RAF, under Air Marshal Sir William Welsh, also had offices in the tunnel and there was a Combined Naval and RAF Operations Room, with wall charts on which ABC and the others could watch the progress of the TORCH convoys, now approaching the Straits of Gibraltar.

The Western Task Force, for the Casablanca landings, was wholly American. But the landings at Oran and Algiers were under the charge of the Royal Navy. The Central Naval Task Force, for Oran, was commanded by Commodore Thomas Troubridge, flying his broad pennant in the headquarters ship

Largs, with two escort carriers, two cruisers, the anti-aircraft cruiser *Delhi*, an anti-aircraft ship, thirteen destroyers, two sloops, two cutters, eight minesweepers, six corvettes, eight trawlers, ten motor launches, two submarines (to act as navigational markers off the assault beaches), nineteen landing ships and twenty-eight transports, carrying the 1st US Infantry Division, and half of the 1st US Armoured Division, comprising 39,000 troops.

The Eastern Naval Task Force, for Algiers, was commanded by Vice-Admiral Sir Harold Burrough, flying his flag in the headquarters ship *Bulolo*, with the aircraft carriers *Argus* and *Avenger*, the cruisers *Sheffield* (wearing the flag of Rear-Admiral C.H.J. Harcourt), *Scylla* and *Charybdis*, the monitor *Roberts*, three anti-aircraft ships, thirteen destroyers, three sloops, four corvettes, seven minesweepers, eight trawlers, eight motor launches, three submarines, seventeen landing ships and sixteen transports. The land forces were the 34th US Infantry Division, a third of the 9th US Infantry Division, half of the 1st US Armoured Division and the 78th British Infantry Division, comprising 33,000 troops.

The British Task Forces and the 'follow-up' convoys were covered by an enlarged Force H, of the battleships *Duke of York* (wearing the flag of Vice-Admiral Sir Neville Syfret) and *Rodney*, with *Renown*, *Victorious* (wearing the flag of Rear-Admiral Lyster), *Formidable* and *Furious*, the cruisers *Bermuda*, *Argonaut* and *Sirius* and seventeen destroyers, with a fuelling force of four tankers, a corvette and four trawlers.

Meanwhile, there had been encouraging events at the other end of the Mediterranean. The 8th Army under Montgomery had launched their offensive at El Alamein on 23 October and, after some days of hard fighting, broke through the enemy positions on 4 November and began the chase to the west, with the Afrika Korps in full retreat.

The Mediterranean portion of the TORCH convoys and their escorts, some 340 ships in all, passed through the Straits of Gibraltar between 7.30 p.m. on 5 November and 4 a.m. on the 7th. Many warships had to refuel in Gibraltar and all had to sail in their correct sequence and to a precise time-table. They arrived unscathed, although the UK convoys had been sighted by the enemy no fewer than five times during their passage.

When the enemy realised that an invasion of North Africa had begun, many of the U-boats were deployed off the disembarkation ports. But by then air and surface defences were strong enough to keep the U-boats in check.

But the one imponderable was the attitude of the French, and in TORCH, as in everything connected with the French throughout the war, there were difficulties.

On 6 November, General Giraud was picked up by the submarine *Seraph* at a rendezvous some twenty miles east of Toulon. Much was hoped and expected of him, as the French leader under whom all Frenchmen in North Africa could unite and end any opposition to the TORCH landings.

When Giraud arrived in Gibraltar on 7 November, he was taken straight to a conference with Eisenhower and Clark. ABC was not present but guessed that things were not going well when he saw Eisenhower that evening 'looking desperately tired and worried'.

ABC took Eisenhower off to dinner at The Mount, to try and cheer him up, and to be told the whole sorry story. Giraud flatly refused to play any part in TORCH, except as Supreme Commander of the whole expedition. Furthermore, he wanted some sixty thousand troops to be diverted so as to land in the south of France.

ABC reckoned that Giraud had, of course, started by pitching his demands at their highest; in time, he would be more reasonable. But when Eisenhower went back with Clark after dinner for more talks, Giraud was as stubborn as before. However, at a conference at Government House the next morning, 8 November, at which ABC was present, Giraud 'finally came off his high horse' and after some further talk agreed to do what was wanted of him, that 'Roughly he should be recognised as Commander-in-Chief of all the French troops and be in general charge of North Africa.'

ABC and his staff spent the night of 7/8 November in the tunnel offices. The first landings were timed for 1 a.m. on the 8th and there was an anxious wait for the early reports. The fiercest resistance at all three landing ports was put up by the French Navy, who manned most of the coastal defences in North Africa. Many senior French naval officers looked to Admiral Darlan as their leader and were loyal to Marshal Pétain as head of the French Government. They were still bitter towards the Royal Navy because of Oran and Dakar in 1940.

TORCH had had to go ahead before the landing craft crews could be trained as thoroughly as ABC would have liked, and some landing craft flights missed their proper beaches. A few were sunk by gunfire and rising seas wrecked others. There were some communications difficulties and unforeseen obstacles such as a sand-bar overlooked by photo-reconnaissance. But, in general, the landings went well and the watchers in the Gibraltar tunnels had cause to be satisfied. Power, in particular, had the peculiar sensation of watching on a radar screen the convoys behaving just as he had prescribed in his orders. 'It seemed unbelievable', he recalled, 'that these four hundred ships should be doing so exactly what I had intended.'

'... the long lad Power is just a marvel,' ABC wrote to Whitworth. 'To see him weaving his webs of convoys, escorts and ships movements completely unmoved by triumph and disaster is a constant astonishment to me.'

There were disasters as well as triumphs. On Power's advice, the largest liners were routed independently after they had discharged their troops, relying on their speed to avoid trouble. Three were sunk. Power apologised to ABC for having 'caused him to back the wrong horse over the independent sailings'.

'Never mind,' ABC replied, 'you can't make omelettes without breaking eggs.'

'Goose's eggs, I'm afraid.'

'More like an ostrich.'

'I'm not hiding my head in sand.'

'You ought to be hiding it in shame, go away and forget it.'

It was vitally important to capture the harbour installations and facilities at Algiers and Oran before the defenders could destroy them. At Oran, two ex-US Coast Guard cutters, *Walney* and *Hartland*, chosen for their American appearance and with US Rangers on board, crashed through the harbour boom early on the morning of 8 November. But both ships were taken under heavy fire, blew up and sank. Captain F.T Peters, who led the expedition in *Walney*, was one of the few who survived, though wounded, but he was killed in an aircraft crash on 13 November. He was awarded a posthumous VC in May 1943.

There was some reaction from the French Navy at Oran. On 8 November, the destroyers *Tornade* and *Tramontane* were sunk and the flotilla leader *Epervier* damaged, by *Aurora* and two destroyers. On the 9th, *Aurora* and *Jamaica* engaged *Epervier* and *Typhon* who were trying to escape. They drove *Epervier* ashore in flames while *Typhon* went back into Oran harbour with damage and was scuttled there.

According to ABC's report, *Aurora* 'polished off her opponents on each occasion with practised ease'. 'The performance of HMS *Jamaica*' he went on, 'in expending 501 rounds to damage one destroyer was less praiseworthy.' *Aurora* was, of course, an old Mediterranean hand, while *Jamaica*, who had served with the Home Fleet, was new to the Station. ABC was always ready to criticise ships fresh out from home for not realising what a very dangerous theatre of war the Mediterranean was.

Meanwhile, operations in and around Oran were proceeding. *Rodney* gave heavy gun support to the troops going ashore. Carrier aircraft strafed and bombed the airfields at Tafaraoui and La Senia and put an estimated 80 per cent of the aircraft there out of action. Aircraft were operating from Tafaraoui by the evening of 8 November. Fighting continued next day and into the morning of 10 November. American tanks entered the city at 11 a.m. The French capitulated at noon.

In Algiers, the destroyers *Malcolm* and *Broke*, each with US troops on board, attempted to seize the harbour. *Malcolm* was hit in a boiler room and was forced to turn back, but *Broke* got alongside at the fourth attempt and put her troops ashore. Four hours later, heavy fire made her position untenable. She was hit on the way out, and sank under tow the next day. ABC supported the decision to retire, but felt that *Broke*'s damage had been underestimated, which meant that she foundered at sea when she could by then have been safely berthed in Algiers harbour.

By the end of the first day, the airfields at Blida, some twenty miles inland from Algiers, and Maison Blanche, east of Algiers, had been captured. In the evening, it was reported that all resistance in the city had ceased. By dark more Allied troops had been landed and Commodore J.A.V. Morse, of Suda and Beirut fame, was installed as Naval Officer in Charge, Algiers.

On the evening of 8 November, Admiral Burrough had a message from the American General commanding the troops ashore in Algiers, which was passed to Eisenhower and ABC at Gibraltar: 'Darlan wishes to negotiate immediately. He will not deal with any Frenchman.'

General Mark Clark and other American officers flew to Algiers on 9 November. ABC sent Royer Dick with them because his French would be useful. General Giraud had also flown to Algiers independently.

The French in Algiers had recovered from the first shock of the landings, and realised how comparatively few troops the Allies actually had ashore.

French troops were occupying key points in the city and there was a real danger of a counter-attack against the Allies.

Eisenhower had instructed Clark to direct Giraud to use all his influence to stop French resistance to the Allies. But it transpired that Giraud had no influence. To his own amazement and annoyance, nobody of any importance rallied to his lead, but he continued to insist that he should be made Commander-in-Chief of all French forces in North Africa, as he had been promised. When it was impressed upon him that this was not practicable, Giraud left the meeting in a huff. At a further conference later that evening, attended by Robert Murphy, the American State Department's representative in North Africa, who had himself only just been released from house arrest, it was decided to meet Admiral Darlan the next morning.

Admiral of the Fleet Jean Louis Francois Xavier Darlan was widely respected in the French Navy and had the absolute allegiance of its officers. Since April 1942 he had been

Commander-in-Chief of the French Armed Force and was now the second man in Pétain's regime, with authority which far outweighed that of anyone else in North Africa. It was only by chance that he was in Algiers. He had returned to France on 30 October after a tour of inspection of North Africa, leaving his son in hospital recovering from an attack of infantile paralysis. But the boy had a relapse, and Darlan flew back to Algiers on 4 November.

Darlan was no friend of the British (his great-grandfather had been killed at Trafalgar). 'Darlan is a snake but a useful viper if we can use him,' ABC wrote to Whitworth. Snake or not, he was the man the Allies would have to deal with.

At last, agreement was reached: Darlan was to be Governor-General in French North Africa, Giraud was to command the French Army and Noguès was to be Resident General of French Morocco.

ABC was naturally very interested to meet Darlan, about whom he had heard so much, 'though generally with a few qualifying and uncomplimentary adjectives'. Writing to Doodles, he reverted to his reptilian metaphor: 'Darlan was most embarrassingly cordial to me but he looked rather a snake and I would not trust him.'

Darlan did indeed greet ABC 'most effusively', shaking him warmly by the hand and saying: 'Thank you for Admiral Godfroy.' He also said that, although Admiral de la Borde might not obey his orders, he did not think that de la Borde would allow the French fleet to fall into German hands.

Eisenhower and ABC flew back to Gibraltar after the conferences very late on the evening of 13 November, arriving in darkness and thick weather, with cloud almost down to ground level. It seemed the radio in their Flying Fortress was unserviceable, because Gibraltar air control tried unsuccessfully for several hours to divert them. At last, said ABC, 'We eventually picked up some lights, and after milling around for some time at 500 feet and having a dummy run or two at the aerodrome, I being fully aware that the Rock was 1,400 feet high, we made a perfect landing, much to the relief of the reception committee who had been throwing fits since sunset.'

On 14 November, Pétain again publicly repudiated Darlan, saying he had already appointed Noguès. But much less attention was now being paid to Pétain. Much more important were the storms of protest the agreement with the notorious Vichyite Darlan aroused in the United States and in Great Britain.

The brunt of the criticism fell upon Eisenhower, who justified his decision on military grounds. Washington and London had completely misjudged feelings in French North Africa. The co-operation of the French on the ground would reduce Allied casualties (as indeed it was found to have done very effectively when the figures were added up).

Eisenhower had the support of Churchill, Roosevelt and ABC who thought the deal with Darlan 'the only possible course and absolutely right. Darlan was the only man in North Africa who could have stopped the fighting and brought the authorities and people of North Africa in to help us in the struggle against the Axis.'

Unopposed landings were made at Bougie, 100 miles east of Algiers, on 11 November and at Bône, 125 miles east of Bougie, on the 12th. But there was a costly delay of nearly forty-eight hours in capturing the airfield at Djidjelli, thirty-five miles east of Bougie, because the landing was hindered by heavy swell on the beach. At Bougie, enemy aircraft bombed and set on fire the monitor *Roberts* and sank three transports and the anti-aircraft ship *Tynwald*.

ABC hoisted his flag in *Aurora* on 15 November and sailed for visits to Oran and Algiers. At Oran, the inner harbour was still blocked by sunken wrecks but some ships were unloading in the outer roads. ABC made advance arrangements for the heavy ships of Admiral Syfret's Force H to berth at Mers-el-Kebir, the naval base of Oran.

The next day, *Aurora* went on to Algiers where ABC found 'some things were good and some bad'. Morse was in charge, working well with the French, and stores were being unloaded, but there were difficulties in moving stores away from the harbour because of lack of transport.

There was also inadequate defence for the large number of ships in Algiers. There was an anti-submarine patrol to seaward but the air defences lacked proper radar. The RAF warning set had not arrived because it had not been given high enough priority in loading. For the time being, ships' radar sets had to provide air raid warning.

The TORCH plan had called for a rapid Allied advance eastward, to capture Tunis and Bizerta. But torrential rain storms turned the few narrow coastal roads into quagmires and prevented Allied aircraft taking off from several of the airfields. By 15 November, the 1st Army was at Tabarka, a small port some sixty miles from Bizerta, and the campaign finally paused on a line about thirty-five miles west of Bizerta. Meanwhile, the Germans were daily flying more troops into Tunis. Once again, ABC bitterly regretted that the TORCH planning had not been bolder and included a landing further east, at Bizerta.

Eisenhower moved his headquarters to Algiers on 24 November and ABC followed him the next day. Both had their offices on the first floor of the Hotel St Georges. ABC found that his and Eisenhower's staffs were competing amongst themselves for the same villa for their respective masters.

Eisenhower, although already installed, offered to give the villa up to ABC, but ABC 'refused any such thing' and preferred another house, the Villa Kleine, in the same garden.

After a foray into the countryside, Watts came back with six hens and a cockerel. Every morning, the steward would ask ABC what he wanted for breakfast and the reply invariably was: 'A boiled egg'. When the egg appeared, ABC would ask: 'Which hen laid this?' 'The speckled one, sir.'

The villa had a spectacular view of the harbour and the Bay. One evening ABC took a guest out on to the balcony after dinner to admire the view. Instead of saying how magnificent it was, as ABC expected, the visitor said: 'Well, sir, I understand now what you mean when you say it's "Too velvet-arsed and Rolls Royce!"' ABC roared with laughter at having one of his own favourite sayings so neatly turned against him.

But, as ABC said, 'Algiers at that time was no bed of roses.' There were air raids every day, for while enemy aircraft could take off from all-weather airfields, Allied aircraft were hampered by the bad weather which turned their airfields into swamps. This state of affairs was to last through most of the winter, until weather-proofing material arrived.

On 18 November, the Germans suddenly demanded that all French troops withdraw from the fortified area of Toulon which, they said, could only be garrisoned by naval units. This was clearly suspicious and when, on 27 November, the Germans tried to seize the fleet, the French Navy was ready and reacted quickly. One battleship, two battlecruisers, four heavy and three light cruisers, twenty-four destroyers, sixteen submarines and some smaller craft were scuttled or seriously damaged by their crews. Only six destroyers and six submarines remained undamaged. Of the warships at Toulon, only three submarines eventually reached Allied ports.

There were still one battleship, three 8-inch cruisers, one 6-inch cruiser and three destroyers under Admiral Godfroy at Alexandria. But, as ABC said, Godfroy 'was still obstinate in refusing to come in with us'.

Allied intelligence before and during TORCH was excellent. ABC himself said that the intelligence information about the landing beaches, defences and the general terrain gave the whole operation 'a flying start'. Nevertheless, the Allied commanders underestimated the speed and scale of the German reinforcement of North Africa. After some early advances, the 1st Army met stiffening resistance. The leading units were within fifteen miles of Tunis on 28 November but were repulsed by the enemy. By the end of 1942, the front had stabilised in the mountains overlooking the Tripolitanian plain, some thirty miles from Tunis. The Allies had lost the race for Tunis.

Malta's long siege was finally relieved by the arrival of the STONEAGE convoy in November. *Dido* and *Euryalus* and four destroyers from the convoy's escort made up a reconstituted Force K on the 27th. Force Q, of *Aurora* (wearing the flag of Rear-Admiral C.H.J. Harcourt), *Argonaut*, and *Sirius* and the destroyers *Quentin* and *Quiberon*, was formed a day later, to be based at Bône, where they arrived on the 30th, when it was considered that the fighter defences were adequate.

The Enigma decrypts were continuing to reveal the timing and routes of enemy convoys. Force Q intercepted and sank all four ships of a convoy bound for Bizerta and one escorting destroyer about forty miles north of Cape Bon on the night of 1/2 December. But the destroyer *Quentin* was sunk by an aerial torpedo.

This sortie had been planned and ordered by Power without telling ABC who, when he heard, at once fastened upon *Quentin*'s loss. 'You've lost one of my destroyers. See what happens when you take things into your own hands like that. Still, it's just as well someone was attending to business — well done.'

On the next night, Force K sank three ships from a four-ship convoy off Sfax and also sank one ship and an escorting destroyer from a convoy to Tripoli, of which the decrypts had given full details on 28 November.

Decrypts also revealed two enemy minefields laid between 21 and 26 November, one west of Bizerta, the other from Cape Bon, east of Tunis; both extended almost to the Sicilian coast, to form a 'corridor' down which the enemy intended to pass convoys by night to Bizerta and Tunis. The minelayers *Welshman* and *Abdiel*, and the minelaying submarine *Rorqual*, closed the 'corridor' with mines laid across and between the two enemy minefields, as ABC said, 'rather like fitting rungs into a ladder'. One 'rung' sank SS *Menes* on 4 December. Her cargo included thirty-four tanks. This was equivalent to a major victory on land; the Enigma had shown that the total of serviceable tanks the Germans had in Tunisia on 30 November was sixty-four.

But these successes had not prevented the arrival of the 10th Panzer Division in Tunisia. Had they done so, it is probable that the Allies would have broken through to Tunis and the campaign could have been over by the end of the year.

The roads in Algeria were narrow and badly metalled and completely inadequate to carry the necessary traffic to supply the 1st Army. The single track railway was in poor condition and short of rolling stock. It was quicker and more efficient to transport men and supplies by sea. With Bône established as an advance port, a 'Bône Run' began, similar to that to Tobruk, and almost as dangerous.

It was too risky to send large ships east of Algiers because of the danger of air attack, so the burden fell on the smaller ships and landing craft. According to ABC's figures,

> in one period of seven weeks during the worst of the bombing these little ships discharged some 128,000 tons of supplies at Bône, while about 4,000 tons of food and petrol was reloaded into naval landing craft and taken forward to the smaller ports of La Calle and Tabarka to the eastward. All these convoys had to be fought through, and no passage was without incident.

A 'shuttle service' carrying troops from Algiers to Bône every third or fourth night was carried out by four cross-Channel steamers, *Queen Emma*, *Princess Beatrix*, *Royal Ulsterman* and *Royal Scotsman*, which had been converted into Landing Ships Infantry. Again, on ABC's figures, 'carrying between them some 3,300 troops on every trip, these four ships had ferried 16,000 men to Bône by December 5th, an outstanding achievement. By February 13th, 1943, they had carried another 36,000.'

The attack on enemy convoys was carried on by Force Ct and Force K, aircraft, motor-torpedo boats and by submarines but still it seemed to ABC that too many enemy ships were crossing to Tunisia by day without being attacked by Allied aircraft. ABC had a meeting with Eisenhower and General Carl A. Spaatz, who commanded the US Army Air Force and who was 'a grand little man, always ready for anything and a great friend'. Spaatz said he would deal with it.

ABC felt that Spaatz did not properly realise the problems. Flying over the sea required experienced navigators. Spaatz's pilots might have some difficulties in knowing where they were and in identifying friend from foe. Even telling the difference between a battleship and a destroyer was not easy from the air. But Spaatz brushed ABC's doubts aside 'and went off to do the job'.

For the next ten days, ABC and his staff watched results carefully. But nothing much seemed to be happening to Axis shipping. Then one day ABC had a message from Spaatz, asking if he could come and see him.

Spaatz came to the point at once. 'Admiral, I've just come to tell you that we don't know a damned thing about this business of working over the sea. Will you help us?' 'I already held Spaatz in high esteem,' ABC said, 'but that simple remark of his endeared him to me more than ever. There are not many men who are great enough to acknowledge error. Of course we helped him.'

Ten Fleet Air Arm observers were appointed to work with Spaatz's squadrons operating over the sea, and a very experienced observer, Lieutenant-Commander V.G.H. Ramsay-Fairfax, joined Spaatz's staff. Results improved so dramatically that ABC had to pay up several bottles of whisky which he had wagered with Spaatz on the destruction of some particular named vessels.

Early in December 1942, there was a serious breach of security concerning ULTRA Special Intelligence. Between 5 and 11 December, C38m decrypts indicated that the enemy was planning an operation of some sort against a North African port, probably Bône. A warning was given to the Mediterranean theatre in three signals, one on 5 December, mentioning an unspecified operation by the Italian Naval Command in Tunisia, and two signals on the 11th, specifying that the attack would be mounted from Bizerta, to take place after nightfall on 11 December.

But this Special Intelligence was shown to have been compromised when, on 18 December, the German Naval Command in Italy issued a signal that 'The enemy had prior knowledge of the planned M.A.S. [Italian motor boat] attack on Bône on 11-12 December.'

This was the result of a decrypt by the Italians and passed to the Germans of a signal made by Oliver, as NOIC Bône, on the evening of 11 December to the destroyer *Velox* and a range of interested addressees, instructing a convoy approaching Bône to delay its arrival because of an expected E-boat attack.

Oliver was not an authorised ULTRA recipient, but his signal had clearly been based on an ULTRA message which had been sent to him unparaphrased. Worse still, Oliver's signal was in Naval Cypher No. 3, which the Italians were known to have had some success in decyphering.

The Admiralty expressed their concern on 19 December: 'The information in NOIC Bône's signal unnecessarily disclosed our knowledge of enemy intentions to a wide circle and probably led to this leakage. The fact that the attack did not take place may lead the enemy to suspect the real source of our information.'

ABC could only reply that: 'This danger was realised and the matter taken up in the appropriate quarter immediately on receipt of NOIC Bône's signal. Error is regretted.' This was not much consolation to the OIC in the Admiralty. It now seemed only a matter of time before the enemy tumbled to the solution. But, miraculously, the ULTRA secret survived this and other security scares.

Just before dawn on 14 December, when Force Q was returning to Bône at 26 knots after another night sortie into the Sicilian Narrows, *Argonaut* was torpedoed by an Italian submarine. Her rudder was blown off, but her main engines and two of her four propellor shafts were still working, so she was able to steam. ABC watched her enter harbour, presenting 'an extraordinary sight on arriving at Algiers with portions of her bows and stern blown away'.

The Captain of the Fleet had just departed, so ABC suggested to Captain Longley-Cook, *Argonaut*'s Captain, that surely he would not be much interested in taking *Argonaut* to the United States for repairs and sitting on his backside until she was ready? Longley-Cook agreed to be Captain of the Fleet but with the proviso: 'I do want the *Argonaut* again when she's fit for action.'

Thus ABC secured for himself another good staff officer. Longley-Cook found it hard work, but was sustained by the

inspiration of his leadership, the excitement of success and his never failing sense of humour which, even in the most anxious moments, made us laugh about something. Every morning ABC held his staff meeting. I do not recall, in fact I am sure, there never was a meeting at which he did not raise a laugh — not a sycophantic one, a genuine belly-laugh. (He was always rude to Tim Shaw, the oldest of us, though of course they understood one another.) He used to pull my leg frequently about a certain mistake I'd made, and this got me on the raw after a time. Finally, after one staff meeting I stayed behind and told him I didn't like it, that it hurt. He put his arm round my shoulders and said: 'My dear chap, I'm *so* sorry, I'll never mention it again!' — nor did he.

When *Argonaut* was ready for sea again early in 1944, ABC arranged that Longley-Cook returned to her.

ABC often referred to Nona as 'that unworthy woman my wife', but he was very concerned about her. She had left

America in a slow convoy on 19 November and ABC was very anxious until he heard she had arrived safely.

His other concern was mail — or rather, the lack of it. On 13 December he wrote to Doodles that it was 'six weeks since I left [Gibraltar] and not a single letter from the UK has reached me. What an advertisement for the efficiency of the Admiralty mail department.' In the end, ABC complained to the Admiralty that he was waiting longer for his mail than Nelson, who had made the same complaint in about 1800.

ABC had a small dinner-party at his villa on Christmas night. By order of President Roosevelt Eisenhower presented ABC with the American Army Distinguished Service Medal. 'It was quite unexpected,' said ABC, 'and I was greatly touched at the kind things he said.'

On Christmas Eve, an appalling lapse of security allowed a young fanatic to get into Admiral Darlan's office and empty a revolver into him. The French announced that: 'Darlan was a victim of those who would not forgive him for having again taken up the struggle against Germany at the side of the Allies.' ABC did not believe it. 'The ultimate responsibility for the crime was never properly fixed. Many hands were in it, and it was of no service whatever to the Allied cause.'

Darlan was given a state funeral, which Eisenhower and ABC attended. 'I rather liked him,' said ABC, in a letter to Doodles, 'and certainly, whatever he did in France, in the last few weeks he worked for us as best he could, and did a lot for us.'

In general, ABC was optimistic about the progress of the war at the end of 1942. With the Russian counter-offensive beginning at Stalingrad, ABC 'began to see the shining dawn of final victory gradually creeping up over the dark horizon. "Far back, through creeks and inlets making,"' he quoted, '"comes

silent flooding in, the main." It will take us two more winters,'
he told Doodles; 'this one and one more.'

19: 'SINK, BURN AND DESTROY, LET NOTHING PASS' — RETRIBUTION

THE NEW YEAR of 1943 began badly at Bône, where there were heavy daylight air raids on 1 January, sinking or damaging several ships. It was suggested to ABC that it was unwise to keep cruisers and destroyers there in the face of such attacks. But he hardened his heart and made a signal to Bône, saying he knew they were having an unpleasant time but they must stick it out.

He himself visited Bône in the destroyer *Lookout*, 'to see the sailors in one port that had been having a poor time,' he told Doodles. 'It was grand getting into a little ship again. It was quite rough and I had difficulty in keeping myself in my bunk.'

ABC had a sharp eye for detail concerning the sailors' welfare. There was a shortage of naval uniforms in Algiers and many sailors who had just been released from Vichy prisoner-of-war camps were kitted out with army uniforms. Leading Telegraphist W. Humphries was going on watch in the naval headquarters in the Hotel St Georges one night when he saw ABC approaching and stood aside to let him pass. However, ABC

pulled me out of the crowd and stood watching — battledress blouse, bell bottoms, khaki shirt, 'pussers' flannels, army boots etc. and then he asked me why. I explained and he grunted 'Carry on my boy'. We were fully kitted within a couple of days with kit flown from Alexandria. Whenever he appeared in the wireless office we all felt that he took a personal interest in us. He never seemed tired — even at 2 a.m. when we changed watches, and in the early days we were under considerable pressure with constant air raids, very poor accommodation and heavy work. We felt that if the old man could stick it, so could we.

ABC closely followed the later careers of those who had served under him. In his opinion, the cruiser *Manchester* was 'a glaring example', he wrote to Whitworth, 'of HM Ships being abandoned prematurely' (she was scuttled after being disabled by a torpedo during the PEDESTAL convoy to Malta in August 1942).

The court martial, ABC said, 'disclosed a poor show'. But, he told Whitworth, 'I was much disturbed to hear that Dan Duff [who had served with ABC before the war] had been badly jumped on. Hadn't you better send him out here to me and I will put him in the way of rehabilitating himself.' (Duff had already won a DSC, the Croix de Guerre and the Legion d'honneur in the Norwegian campaign, and went on to win a Bar to his DSC in the Normandy landings.)

ABC took the trouble to put in good words for Lieutenant-Commanders Layard, of *Broke*, and Watkins, of *Havock*, who were court-martialled after their destroyers were lost. 'I will see that his [Watkin's] prisoner's friend has the relevant extracts from your letter,' Whitworth wrote back. 'No wonder these young fellows serve you well, when you take so great a personal interest in their affairs.'

ABC could be relied on to champion those serving at sea against unnecessary or insensitive interference from shore. On 29 January, the destroyer *Avon Vale* was very badly damaged by an aerial torpedo off the North African coast. ABC objected strongly to a signal about missing paperwork sent to the ship by a staff officer ashore. 'I am sure you will agree with me', he wrote to Whitworth, 'that this armchair warrior's tone is quite unjustified to a wretched CO of a destroyer, who had just had his bows blown off as far as the foremost boiler room bulkhead and lost half his ship's company (and probably his typewriter).'

If there was a solution, even an unorthodox one, ABC found it. The Fleet Naval Constructor, Constructor Captain I.E. King, was having difficulties pumping water out of an escort which had been driven ashore in Algiers in a storm when ABC

> arrived on the harbour breakwater and got his first glimpse of this sorry and embarrassing situation. After passing a few preliminary 'thoughts' by megaphone he departed.
>
> In less than half an hour he returned and with great gusto shouted 'FNC I've got the biggest pump in North Africa for you', and pointed to the shore end of the breakwater, where lo and behold I could see the city of Algiers' finest fire engine, resplendent in all its colourful and sparkling array, and 'rearing to go'.

On 2 January 1943, Harold Macmillan, the British Minister Resident at Allied Force Headquarters, flew to Algiers from Gibraltar with John Wyndham, his Private Secretary, and their two secretaries.

ABC got on well with Macmillan and was delighted to have him in Algiers. It 'was a blessing to me,' ABC said, 'as it took me out of the political business and allowed me to get on with my proper job of running the naval side of the war in the Western Mediterranean.'

For his part, Macmillan liked ABC and, after lunching and dining there, was particularly impressed by ABC's 'sumptuous villa (the Navy knows how to be comfortable)'.

Macmillan also noticed ABC's way with French naval officers. In February, Macmillan wanted Admiral Michelier, commanding French naval forces in Casablanca, to assist in trying to win Admiral Godfroy over to the Allies. Michelier had fought against the Allied landings at Casablanca. Macmillan remarked that Michelier 'has been slowly coming over to the opposition, first to a modified support and now, I think, to a really enthusiastic co-operation with the British Navy. This change of heart is largely due to Admiral Cunningham, who has managed him very well.'

ABC himself was always quick to praise a kindred spirit in a Frenchman. 'Boisson from Dakar [General Pierre Boisson, Governor-General of West Africa] I frankly like,' he told Whitworth. 'Three times he has tried to introduce trout into the French West African rivers — so he can't be a wrong'un!!'

In January 1943, Roosevelt, Churchill and the Combined Chiefs of Staff met at Casablanca to debate the future progress of the war after the end in North Africa which, it was optimistically assumed, could only be two or three months off. Eisenhower was summoned to attend and flew to Casablanca on the 15th.

Pound sent for ABC a day or two later. ABC stayed for two nights in General George Patton's 'sumptuous villa' and found him a most charming and interesting host.

ABC attended a meeting of the British Chiefs of Staff and several conferences with Pound and 'Ernie' King, finding the latter unusually amenable and understanding, possibly because of the success of TORCH, which he had at first opposed.

At Casablanca it was decided that the next major undertaking would be Operation HUSKY, the invasion of Sicily, rather than BRIMSTONE, a landing in Sardinia. ABC himself favoured Sardinia, because it could be captured more quickly and cheaply, and would give just as good air cover for shipping passing through the Narrows as Sicily. But he was almost alone in this opinion. The Chiefs of Staff argued that Sardinia would appear only a minor success, particularly to the Russians, who were still pressing for a Second Front, whereas Sicily was a strategic crossroads in the theatre. A landing there would be second only to an assault upon an Axis mainland.

Eisenhower was once again Supreme Commander, with Alexander commanding the land forces, including the 8th Army when it reached Tunisia. ABC was again the Naval C-in-C, Tedder the Air C-in-C. Tedder had long advocated a unified air command, like ABC's unified command of the naval forces. Eisenhower was sceptical but later agreed, knowing that Tedder had had eighteen months' experience of Mediterranean air warfare.

Relations between ABC and Tedder had improved over the past year. In January 1942 Tedder had thought ABC 'rather a trial' and said: 'I don't know how much longer we can carry on with him'. But now Tedder considered ABC 'the live wire' at Algiers.

One disappointment of the Casablanca Conference was the failure to achieve the hoped-for rapport between Giraud and de Gaulle. The two were totally different in temperament, and their supporters were mutually suspicious. 'To unite the pair', ABC said, 'was like trying to mix oil and water.'

There was not much scope for recreation in Algiers, but ABC much enjoyed walks along the beach with Oliver, an Airedale given to him by one of the French admirals. ABC was fond of dogs and usually had one as a pet. Oliver did not mind anti-aircraft fire and used to go out onto the balcony and bark during air raids. He had a friend, a Scottie belonging to Eisenhower, with whom he galloped around the villa's garden every morning.

On 15 January, twelve Wren officers and six Wrens, the forerunners of many, arrived in Algiers from Gibraltar in the destroyers *Penn* and *Pathfinder* — known as the 'Wrens' Special'.

'These most useful ladies', ABC called them in his memoirs, but that was not his opinion at the time. He had somewhat old-fashioned, almost romantic views of women and had strenuously opposed the employment of Wrens abroad, particularly under his command in Alexandria, which he thought was no place for British young women, and he arranged for them to be accommodated in a convent. However, as he conceded, in time the Wrens proved all his objections quite wrong.

On 21 January 1943, ABC was promoted to Admiral of the Fleet and exchanged the flag of St George, which he had flown in various versions since 1932, for the Union Flag, hoisted in the submarine depot ship *Maidstone* in Algiers harbour at 8 a.m. that morning. 'Now I am indeed a veteran admiral as the American newspapermen called me,' ABC told Doodles. 'But I am very pleased about it.' He was even more pleased when his Secretary reminded him that Admirals of the Fleet never retired.

When the Allied advance paused at the end of 1942, the enemy continued to pour supplies into Tunisia. In January 1943 about 15,000 Germans and 70,000 tons of equipment and supplies arrived by sea and 14,250 Germans and 4,000 tons by air. Some 12,500 Italians also arrived in Tunisia. As early as 6 January 1943, Eisenhower was reporting that unless enemy supplies could be 'materially reduced the situation both here and in Eighth Army area will deteriorate without doubt'.

In December 1942, the Allies sank over a quarter of the enemy ships sailing for Tunisia, including nearly half the known fuel and ammunition cargoes. In January 1943 the Allies still sank about a quarter of the enemy shipping but this included only about one-seventh of the fuel and about one-ninth of the ammunition. The enemy's fuel situation greatly improved when the tanker *Thorsheimer* arrived at Bizerta with 10,000 tons of fuel on 28 January.

There were some Allied successes. The 4,700-ton freighter *Ankara*, which had already made twenty-one crossings to Africa, usually carrying tanks, and had been a coveted target for ABC's ships for some time, struck one or more of the submarine *Rorqual*'s mines off the Cani Rocks on 18 January and sank with a large cargo of vehicles and 700 tons of ammunition.

The weather was bad in January, and the first air success did not come until the 20th, when US Mitchell bombers escorted by Lightning fighters sank the 5,000-ton German tanker *Saturno* north of Tunis. *Thorsheimer* escaped two bombing attacks in Bizerta but, betrayed by ULTRA, she was torpedoed and sunk by aircraft between Trapani and Cape Bon with another large cargo of fuel on 21 February. This alone raised the proportion of known fuel cargoes destroyed during February 1943 to 70 per cent. But otherwise, the percentage of enemy ships sunk on their way to Tunisia or on arrival there in February dropped to less than twenty. During the month some 16,000 Germans and 59,000 tons of equipment and supplies arrived in Tunisia by sea, and another 12,800 Germans and over 4,000 tons arrived by air. Some 7,000 Italians also arrived, most of them by air.

There were reasons for this: continuing bad weather; effective enemy defences, especially his strength in the air and his extensive minefields; and the change, on Hitler's personal orders, to transporting tanks only in smaller and safer ferries, and only from Sicily. Also, much Allied air effort was diverted from attacking shipping to supporting the Army ashore after the Afrika Korps' smashing success against the US 2nd Corps at the Kasserine Pass in southern Tunisia on 14 February.

Though not a decisive defeat, it was very damaging to American morale.

On 4 February, ABC and his staff were 'electrified' to hear that the Prime Minister was coming to Algiers the next day. He arrived by air amid the strictest security precautions. Eisenhower set out with the official procession to drive from Maison Blanche to Algiers by the most direct route. Meanwhile, Mr Churchill and ABC went to ABC's villa by another way in Eisenhower's heavily armoured car, while Churchill grumbled at the length of the circuitous drive he was being made to take.

Churchill, Eisenhower and ABC had lunch in Eisenhower's villa, with Macmillan, de Gaulle, Giraud and other senior French figures. Churchill was supposed to leave after lunch, but there was so much to settle that he delayed his plans for departure until late that evening, when a cavalcade of cars formed up outside Eisenhower's villa to give the impression Churchill was just about to leave.

The car cavalcade duly departed for the airport and an aircraft took off for Gibraltar. Mr Churchill stayed on in ABCs villa, virtually taking it over. 'You never saw anything like the house,' ABC wrote to Nona. 'Every type of hanger-on, detectives, valets, secretaries. The Foreign Office was set up in Roy Dick's bedroom!'

Near midnight Churchill was taken to the airport, and his party took their places in the 'Commando', Churchill's aircraft. But owing to a magneto failure, the aircraft could not take off, so Churchill was brought back to ABC's villa, where he arrived at about 2.30 a.m., 'not in the best of tempers'. He finally left late the next day.

On 22 February Macmillan injured both legs and suffered severe facial burns when the aircraft which was to have taken him to Cairo crashed and caught fire shortly after take-off. ABC visited him in hospital next day, bringing the good news that an Allied counter-attack on the evening of 22 February had forced Rommel back behind the Mareth line. ABC impressed the hospital staff. 'Nobody cares much about a poor old civilian minister,' Macmillan wrote to his wife, 'but an admiral of the fleet, with a white hat, and gold from his cuff to his elbow, and Flags with gold all over him, well, you can imagine how my stock has risen.'

ABC commiserated with Macmillan, saying he was not surprised by the RAF's failure to take anyone safely anywhere. 'For myself,' he said, 'I generally travel American.' 'This', Macmillan said, 'was just naughtiness and to tease the air chief marshal [Tedder] and others.'

On 20 February 1943, ABC was again appointed Commander-in-Chief, Mediterranean. As he told Doodles, ABC thought it: 'A strange turn of the wheel — to enter by the other door and get back to the same position.'

Admiral Sir Henry Harwood, whom ABC relieved, was to become Commander-in-Chief, Levant. But Harwood did not depart without bitterness. One ostensible reason for Harwood's removal was the Navy's supposed delay in clearing the port of Tripoli.

A small naval contingent had entered Tripoli on 23 January, five hours after the leading troops. The harbour entrance was completely blocked and there were numerous wrecks and burned out ships in the harbour. Facilities on the jetties had been demolished and many warehouses had been damaged by Allied air attacks.

At dusk that day Captain Wauchope, the SNO Inshore Squadron, arrived in Tripoli by air from Benghazi but unfortunately the Fleet Salvage Officer had to come later by sea because of the shortage of aircraft berths. Commodore Dundas, Harwood's Chief of Staff, was also delayed by a defective aircraft and did not arrive from Alexandria until 25 January. A salvage vessel, a mine-clearance force and a convoy of LCTs with supplies arrived that same day.

At first, ships were unloaded outside the entrance, but by the 28th a thirty-foot gap, to a depth of nine feet, had been opened through the obstructions.

Although it did not appear that the 8th Army's advance was at all hindered by the lack of supplies through Tripoli, General Montgomery told Dundas on the 26th, only three days after Tripoli was taken, that the Navy's arrangements 'for uncorking the harbour were totally inadequate both as regards personnel and equipment.' He complained, over the head of his C-in-C General Alexander, direct to the CIGS, General Sir Alan Brooke, who was in Cairo.

Mr Churchill himself interviewed Harwood in Cairo the next day, 27 January, in the presence of the CIGS, who had received Montgomery's complaints and told the Prime Minister of the Army's surprise that it was estimated that clearing the harbour would take fourteen days. In fact, Tripoli was being cleared as quickly as could reasonably be expected, but possibly the Navy did not put this truth across forcefully and convincingly enough to the Army. Mr Churchill and General Alexander visited Tripoli on 4 February and saw for themselves the first two large merchant ships entering through a 100-foot gap with a depth of twenty-four feet.

But, for Harwood, the harm was already done. The Admiralty had decided to relieve him. Although Pound told Harwood 'that the arrangements for the clearance of Tripoli harbour are largely responsible for this', Harwood believed that he was being relieved as much because of the Prime Minister's impatience with Godfrey's intransigence and Harwood's own policy towards the French ships at Alexandria.

ABC had much sympathy for Harwood. He wrote to Whitworth on 17 March, that Harwood Thinks he is being kicked out because of the Prime Minister and the French squadron and the clearing of Tripoli, and Montgomery's complaints'. Montgomery, ABC added, 'has a low opinion of the Navy, not realising how much he owed to it. I am just taking my coat off if Montgomery makes any more signals. I thought Tripoli was organised very well and extremely speedily. I never thought Harwood should have gone as C-in-C Mediterranean but once there he should have been supported.'

ABC had already written to Pound, mentioning that Harwood was upset about being relieved, and believed that the reasons were, first, because he had withstood the Prime Minister on the question of the French fleet at Alexandria, and second, because Montgomery had complained of dilatoriness in opening up Tripoli, which was quite untrue.

There was a sharp reply from Pound, emphasising that 'the French Fleet at Alexandria had nothing to do with Harwood's relief. I came to the conclusion that J.H.D Cunningham could do the job much better. Montgomery has been most appreciative of what the Navy had done and took the trouble to visit every ship at Tripoli. I am surprised', Pound went on, 'at your expressing such a definite opinion about his relief when you only know one side of the case.'

Ironically, Harwood's health was already failing and he had to be relieved before the intended date. On 27 March, Vice-Admiral Sir Ralph Leatham, who had been succeeded as Vice-Admiral, Malta, by Vice-Admiral Sir Stuart Bonham-Carter on 29 January, took over as C-in-C, Levant, until the arrival of Admiral Sir John Cunningham, on 5 June.

ABC was particularly gratified that his new area of command included Malta, and he visited the island, for the first time that year, at the end of February, in a Flying Fortress lent him by the Americans. He stayed with Leatham, who was Acting Governor, at San Anton Palace, where he admired the flowers in the garden. He visited the dockyard and all the naval establishments, finding the dockyard 'badly knocked about; but was going strong, not only in the upkeep and repair of ships, but also in rehabilitating its own docks, buildings and machine shops'.

Admiralty House was hardly touched by the bombing, except for some broken glass. Even the marble tablet in the hall, engraved with the names of all the previous Commanders-in-Chief, including ABC's own, had survived intact. ABC resolved to have his name carved there again.

As ABC told Macmillan, he 'flew American'. When he asked Bedell Smith for the loan of an aircraft to go to Malta, Bedell Smith had answered, 'Admiral, the whole of the American Air Force is at your disposal.' The remark was typical of ABC's relations with the Americans. He was touched and amused by one incident at about that time. He was in Eisenhower's office one morning when Eisenhower gave him two letters to read. One was from President Roosevelt. The other was from Harry Hopkins, the President's personal representative. Both letters began 'Dear Ike'. 'I never know how far to go with you Britishers,' Eisenhower said, 'but just how long will it be before you start calling me Ike?'

'Just half a second,' ABC replied, 'provided you'll call me Andrew in return.'

The news that ABC had been promoted to Admiral of the Fleet and was again to be Commander-in-Chief, Mediterranean, prompted a flood of correspondence which, fortunately, coincided with an improvement in the postal service to Algiers. ABC received a hundred congratulatory letters from all over the world.

He filled his own letters home with gossip. He had been elected a member of the Athenaeum ('I should be a bishop'). Alan had written from the Staff College to say that he had just had 'his brother outcast Godwin-Austen' (Major-General A.R. Godwin-Austen) to dinner. Watts had got ten chicks out of thirteen eggs. ABC secretly liked having his photograph taken or his picture painted; of his portrait for the National Gallery, he said: 'You should see the fine fierce looking admiral the portrait painter has made me.'

ABC wrote appreciatively of the villa's garden, which was a constant source of pleasure to him. In March, it was 'looking lovely, I never saw such a show as the ranunculus. Every imaginable colour. I am going to collect some seeds.' In April, 'the rain has revived the garden. There is a lovely light blue iris just coming out. The cinerarias are a wonderful show.'

He was concerned about his own garden at Palace House, and the whereabouts of Nona, whom he still called in his letters to Doodles 'that woman my wife' and 'that unworthy woman my wife'. 'I am wondering where that woman my wife has now got to,' he wrote in March. Nona had left America in a slow convoy on 19 November 1942 and was in fact now staying with Doodles in North Wales ('so many thanks for being so kind to that unworthy woman my wife').

In March 1943, the Allies began to exert a tighter grip on the enemy's supply lines to Tunisia. In the three months from March to May, 108 enemy ships of over 340,000 tons were sunk, either in port or at sea. Of these, sixty-three of over 211,000 tons were sunk by aircraft, the lion's share going to the US Army Air Force which sank fifty-three ships, of 168,000 tons. During the same period, submarines sank thirty ships of more than 86,000 tons. By comparison, surface ships had a lean time, sinking no enemy ships in March and four, of 11,000 tons, in April and May.

By the end in May, the enemy was living from hand to mouth. Monthly tonnage to Tunisia, which had averaged around 64,000 in December, January and February, dropped to 43,000 in March, to 29,000 in April, and to 3,000 tons before the surrender in May. German tonnage transported by air was 8,000 in March, 5,000 in April and 837 in May. In March, some 12,000 German reinforcements arrived by air and 8,400 Germans and 11,000 Italians by sea. But in May, only 300 German reinforcements arrived, by air.

Much of this success was due to ULTRA, which provided a continuous and often complete flow of accurate and timely information about enemy convoy sailings, escorts, casualties, port loadings and ports of arrival and departure, some of it being decrypted quickly enough for enemy ships to be attacked while on passage.

Great care was taken over security, with strict procedures for the distribution and disposal of ULTRA material and the provision of 'cover stories' — such as 'one of our submarines/aircraft has reported' — to account for the presence of Allied forces at the right time and place. But mistakes were made which compromised the secret. Had the enemy not had such faith in the invulnerability of the Enigma machine, they must have realised that some of their high-grade machine cyphers were no longer secure.

Early in March, the C38m and the *Luftwaffe* Enigma gave full details of the enemy's intention to sail four merchant ships and a tanker, with cargoes which Kesselring said were 'decisive for the future conduct of operations', to Bizerta on 12 and 13 March in two convoys but in a single interlocking operation.

Attacks by air and surface forces were carried out. Two merchant ships and the tanker were sunk. But there was a failure to provide a 'cover story' by making sure that air sightings were obtained beforehand. Unknown to the Allies, the enemy delayed the convoy and some British forces were then sighted by the *Luftwaffe* at the position on the route *where the convoy would have been* had it not been delayed.

The Enigma soon revealed that the enemy's suspicions were thoroughly aroused. A message to *Luftwaffe* Command in Italy from *Fliegerkorps* Tunis on 13 March said: 'The enemy activity of today in the air and on the sea must lead to the conclusion that the courses envisaged for convoys C and D were betrayed to the enemy.'

Reading the decrypts of these exchanges, the watchers in Whitehall became increasingly alarmed. Pound and Churchill both reprimanded ABC. Churchill went so far as to threaten to withhold ULTRA altogether unless it was 'used only on great occasions or when thoroughly camouflaged'.

On 14 March, Pound sent a personal message to ABC, repeated to C-in-C (Levant) and Vice-Admiral (Malta), stating: 'From the British sea and air activity he [*Fliegerkorps* Tunis] appreciated that the courses planned for convoys C and D must have been betrayed to the enemy. German suspicions are now aroused and great care will be required until these are allayed.'

ABC replied on 15 March that

> care was taken to arrange air reconnaissance in vicinity of both convoys. Reconnaissance could not in fact reach northernmost convoy, but arrangements were made for dummy enemy reports to be made from vicinity. The convoy

along north Sicilian coast was sighted by ASV aircraft at frequent intervals and the information provided was more accurate than that of Special Intelligence.

As regards movement of warships, there have been warships in vicinity of Skerki Bank on average every other day for the past fortnight. Enemy was aware of at least a proportion of these moves and reports of them.

While not minimising seriousness of arousing enemy misgivings, I consider his statement comes as much from a desire to cover his failure in protecting the convoy as from real base of suspicion.

Short of failing to make proper effort against the convoy which I suggest would have been inadvisable, there appears to be no other action that could have been taken. I share your anxiety in this matter which is extremely difficult one to handle, but I assure you it received the closest attention.

The episode demonstrated the difficulties of handling ULTRA material effectively. Fortunately for the Allies, the enemy did not follow up their first suspicions. They were still confident of the Enigma and blamed interrogation of PoWs, the cutting of ground lines by the Allies, Allied air and ground reconnaissance, intelligence derived by the Allies from the use of plain language or careless signal procedures by their own forces — anything but the Enigma.

In March, Willis came back to the Mediterranean to relieve Burrough as Flag Officer, Force H, flying his flag in *Nelson*. Vice-Admiral H. Kent Hewitt, USN, was appointed to command all the United States naval forces in the Mediterranean, under ABC. Hewitt was another American with whom ABC got on very well. They became the best of friends. Hewitt had his headquarters next to ABC in the Hotel St Georges where, said ABC, 'We worked together like brothers.'

Another welcome change was the appointment of Air Vice-Marshal Sir Hugh Lloyd to command the RAF units operating with the Navy. 'His arrival', ABC said, 'made a great difference to our air effort over the sea.' He also made a great different to ABC's own travelling arrangements by providing him with his own personal Beaufighter aircraft, with his own pilot, a most efficient young man, ABC said, 'who landed or took off with me at any hour of the day or night, though he did once get a wigging from the group captain at Lukka airfield, in Malta, for the dashing way in which he landed the Naval Commander-in-Chief'. He was also very good-looking, a 'beautiful young man', ABC called him, prophesying some broken feminine hearts.

ABC was also provided with a Douglas Dakota and a US Army Air Force crew, but usually preferred his 'less comfortable but twice-as-fast Beaufighter' which made it much easier to visit the far-flung parts of his command in a surprisingly short time.

ABC soon took a superstitious pride in his Beaufighter. He and Royer Dick were about to take off from Algiers for a flight to Bizerta when Vian, who had come out to North Africa early in May, asked if he could thumb a lift. Dick knew that ABC was very fond of Vian, so he was surprised to see that, for some reason, ABC only agreed with the greatest reluctance.

About an hour after take-off, Vian suddenly said, 'Is it all right that there is fuel and oil coming out over the port wing?' 'Nonsense, perfectly all right,' ABC retorted, furious that anybody should criticise his pet toy. At that moment, there was a call from the cockpit: 'Stand by for forced landing.' The pilot saw what looked like a landing strip and managed to put the aircraft down in the desert.

Dick thought 'having got away with what to put it mildly was a lucky escape there would be mutual congratulations all round. Not at all. ABC turned round in fury and said "There you are you see. I told you something would go wrong. Two lucky men in one place cancel out and this is the result." That was not said in jest.'

On land, the final break-through began on 6 May and within two days a routed and demoralised enemy was being driven up into the Cape Bon peninsula. At sea, ABC was determined that the enemy should not organise their own 'Dunkirk' evacuation. On 8 May, all available destroyers began a night and day patrol off Cape Bon, with coastal forces closer inshore, to foil any attempts at escape by sea.

ABC signalled to them: 'Sink, burn and destroy. Let nothing pass.' But Operation RETRIBUTION, ABC made clear, was not so named 'in any spirit of revenge or because we intended to slaughter defenceless survivors in the water, as the *Luftwaffe* had done in 1941; but because we hoped, and most earnestly, that those of the enemy who essayed the perilous passage home by sea should be taught a lesson they would never forget'.

In the event, very few tried to escape by sea in the 'Kebilia Regatta', as the destroyer captains called it. About 800 men in all were captured from small motor boats and sailing boats, some from rafts, some even from rubber dinghies.

On 12 May 1943, officially at 7.52 a.m., all organised enemy resistance came to an end. 'The whole of Africa was ours. Something like a quarter of a million Axis prisoners and vast quantities of material were in our hands. It was a stupendous victory.'

Minesweepers from Bône had swept a channel through to Bizerta from the west by 11 May. The French naval dockyard at Ferryville, near Bizerta, had been bombed by the Allies and what had not been destroyed by bombs had been methodically blocked and sabotaged by the retreating enemy. Bizerta was in ruins, with no electricity, water or drainage. The Germans had sunk twenty-six ships, using destroyers, large steamers, floating cranes, lighters and harbour craft, in the narrow entrance from the other basin to the inner berths.

The advance naval port party arrived in Bizerta on 9 May. By the 10th, small coasters and landing craft could discharge their cargoes and begin evacuating thousands of prisoners-of-war; 1,000 tons of stores were unloaded on 14 May. Commodore G.N. Oliver, who had already made one somewhat premature visit to Bizerta in an MTB on 8 May, when he had been fired on and forced to retreat hastily, arrived again by rail as Naval Officer in Charge. A team of salvage experts blasted the main channel clear with explosives so that 10,000-ton Liberty ships could berth by the end of May. On 20 May, Admiral Sir Gerald Dickens, ABC's old flotilla-mate in the Dardanelles, now serving in the rank of Rear-Admiral, hoisted his flag as Flag Officer in Charge, Bizerta and Tunis.

ABC now reorganised his fleet. *Nelson* and *Rodney* were relieved in Force H by *King George* Land *Howe*, Willis went home in *Nelson* and Force H was commanded by Bisset, flying his flag in *King George V*. When ABC visited Malta in April, he was shocked by Bonham-Carter's manner and appearance. 'He is a worrier and he hadn't even a smile,' ABC told Pound. Bonham-Carter was relieved by Rear-Admiral Arthur Power, who was himself relieved in command of the 15th Cruiser Squadron by Rear-Admiral Harcourt, flying his flag in *Newfoundland*. Captain Agnew became Commodore-in-Command of the 12th Cruiser Squadron, flying his broad pendant in *Aurora*.

Victory in Africa left the Navy with the task of clearing the Mediterranean, so that ships could pass through it to the

Middle East instead of having to go round the Cape of Good Hope, thus shortening the passage distance by six thousand miles and saving thousands of tons of shipping.

The approaches to Malta, the Galita and Sicilian Channels, and the whole area to the east of Cape Bon had been thickly mined by the enemy. At least six hundred miles had to be cleared, against bad weather, strong tides and a seabed strewn with wrecks. Many enemy mines had explosive anti-sweeping devices which parted wires and caused delay.

The work began on 9 May with the 12th, 13th and 14th Minesweeping Flotillas, two groups of minesweeping trawlers along with motor launches and motor minesweepers. By the 15th they had swept a channel two miles wide from the Galita Channel around Cape Bon as far as Sousse and from there on to Tripoli.

ABC signalled on 15 May that 'the passage through the Mediterranean was clear'. The first through convoy of four fast ships escorted by *Carlisle* and four destroyers passed Gibraltar on 17 May, rounded Cape Bon on the 21st and reached Tripoli on the 22nd. At Tripoli four more merchant ships and more destroyers joined and on 26 May, two years and fourteen days after the last convoy to make that passage in Operation TIGER, a through convoy again reached Alexandria. A regular series of through convoys now began in both directions. The first Malta convoy to reach the island unopposed since 1940 arrived on 24 May.

The minesweeping was finally completed on 9 June, for the loss of one minesweeper and damage to another. Having swept a total of 257 mines and cleared several hundred anti-sweeping devices, the minesweepers received well-earned signals of congratulation from ABC and from the Admiralty.

On 20 May, there was a Victory March in Tunis, at which Eisenhower took the salute and Alexander, ABC, Tedder, Giraud, Macmillan and Robert Murphy were on the saluting platform. Some 30,000 troops, British, American and French, took part in a parade timed to last one-and-a-half hours but which actually took nearly twice as long because, ABC said, the French had crowded in many more units than their proper allowance, naturally wishing to impress the local populace, especially the Arabs.

ABC was very impressed by the men of the 1st Army. 'They were in wonderful fettle — magnificent young men, fit, smart, and in great spirits; toughened by their hard fighting and trying winter in the cold and mud.' He told Macmillan, standing beside him, that the very sight of them made one proud to be British.

Afterwards, they all went to lunch and then to call on the Bey of Tunis, who presented Eisenhower and the others with the highest Tunisian honour, the Grand Cordon of the Order of Nichan-Iftikhar. The diplomats Macmillan and Murphy were also to be invested but, according to ABC, diplomatically lost their way to the Bey's palace and missed the investiture. (However, the pair were later presented with what Macmillan called 'a ridiculous star of tinsel with the sash in the M.C.C. colours, which will be fine for charades').

Not to be outdone, the Sultan of Morocco decided he would also honour the Allied Commanders. General Noguès arrived in Algiers to invest Eisenhower and the others as Grand Officers of the Order of Ouissan Alaouite. It was a 'gorgeous-looking decoration with a bright orange ribbon'. Eisenhower was invested first, and then ABC. But there proved to be only two stars and sashes so ABC's were removed and 'hung upon Tedder, finally coming to rest upon Bedell Smith'. It 'was known as the lion tamer's order', ABC wrote to Doodles. 'Lions are supposed to tremble in their eyes before the wearer. The colour of the ribbon is enough to make them. Did you ever hear such nonsense?'

In the midst of naval affairs, ABC found time to deal with private business. He and Nona had no children, nor would they ever have. On such evidence as remains, theirs was a curiously asexual marriage. In the old Service cliché, ABC was wedded to the Navy.

With no direct heir, ABC had enquired about a special remainder, to confer on his nephew the baronetcy conferred on ABC in 1942. The answer in May 1943 was that it was 'not possible, even for the Sovereign, to alter the descent of a hereditary dignity which has once been granted and the Letters Patent sealed. It would mean the conferment of a new Baronetcy bearing the Special Remainder.'

On 28 May, Mr Churchill, Marshall, Alan Brooke and Ismay arrived at Maison Blanche airfield, having come from the Washington Conference. Mr Churchill and his entourage took over ABC's villa, ABC going to live on board a cruiser in the harbour.

ABC had had one personal success late in May, when Godfrey at last agreed to bring his ships over to the Allies. Some destroyers came to Algiers, while cruisers and the battleship *Lorraine* went round the Cape of Good Hope to Dakar.

ABC drew Mr Churchill's attention to Ecclesiastes 11, verse 1: 'Cast thy bread upon the waters: for thou shalt find it after many days.' As ABC said, this remark was 'rather ill received'. But even ABC could not really have believed that such a veiled reference to events at Alexandria in 1940 was as innocent as he claimed.

Before he left for home, Mr Churchill agreed to ABC's suggestion that he visit the depot ship *Maidstone* and meet some of the submarine crews of the 8th Flotilla. Mr Churchill said 'exactly the right thing' to the sailors who gathered round him on the upper deck and then went down to the wardroom where he was soon surrounded by young officers to whom he 'chatted and joked in his inimitable way'.

One of the submarine COs Mr Churchill met was Lieutenant Ian McGeoch of *Splendid* (previously *P.228*, until Mr Churchill decreed that submarines should have names, not numbers). McGeoch had wanted to call his submarine *Scorpion*, unaware of the name's significance for his Commander-in-Chief. He was one of several submarine COs who were summoned to see ABC, and

> were ushered into the presence of our renowned C-in-C wondering what was in store. The not very tall, red-faced grey crew-cut admiral stood up and welcomed us warmly enough. Emerging from behind his desk he began to pace up and down the room as if it were the quarterdeck, paused, looked at us fiercely and said, 'One of you wishes to call his submarine *Scorpion*.'
>
> I instinctively tried to shrink from view and heard the great man go on, 'I have telegraphed [that was the archaism he used] to the controller that on no account should any submarine be named *Scorpion*. That is a destroyer name.'

A price had had to be paid for the submarines' recent successes. *Tigris* was lost with all hands, probably mined, on 10 March. *Turbulent* was sunk with all hands off Corsica two days later, on what was to have been her last patrol; her CO, Commander J. W. Linton, was awarded a posthumous Victoria Cross. On 14 March *Thunderbolt* (the pre-war *Thetis*) was sunk by an Italian corvette off the north-west coast of Sicily.

On 14 April, *Splendid* was sunk off Capri by the destroyer *Hermes*, which picked up thirty survivors, including McGeoch. On 24 April, oft the north coast of Sicily, *Sahib* was depth-charged, forced to the surface and scuttled, though all but one of her company were picked up. '*Sahib* and *Splendid*,' ABC said, 'two of our best COs.' Shortly before, or on, 1 May, *Regent* was lost with all hands off Brindisi.

ABC 'had never regarded Mr Churchill as emotional; but when we left the *Maidstone* the tears were streaming from his eyes as he talked of those fine boys walking in the valley of the shadow of death'.

Mr Churchill reluctantly left on 5 June, after Eisenhower and ABC had worked hard to dissuade him from coming with them to witness the rehearsal on 9 May for the forthcoming assault on Pantelleria.

Pantelleria is a rugged, mountainous island, about the size of the Isle of Wight, some 150 miles west-north-west of Malta. It had a sizeable Italian garrison, a small harbour in its north-west tip, an airfield and radar stations. It was supposed to be heavily fortified, although ABC doubted it. Ships had often passed quite close without ever being troubled by enemy fire.

The island's value to the Allies lay in its commanding position in the centre of the Sicilian Channel, where fighters would be able to use the airfield to cover some of the beaches in a future landing on Sicily.

The plan, codenamed Operation CORKSCREW, was for an intensive 'softening-up' bombardment from the air and from ships, followed by an assault in the harbour area, the only possible place for a landing, on 11 June.

Eisenhower, ABC and members of the staff flew on 8 June to Bône where they embarked in *Aurora* the same evening. The ship sailed early the next morning and escorted by the destroyer *Troubridge* steamed eastward to join the main force of *Newfoundland*, *Orion*, *Penelope*, *Euryalus* and eight destroyers.

Aurora was to have been a floating grandstand for the VIPs, but this did not satisfy ABC who ordered her to go within 7,000 yards of the island, hoping to draw the enemy's fire.

The ships were in position by 10.30 and the bombardment began, with *Aurora* joining in and ABC himself providing spotting corrections. Soon the target area was obscured by smoke and dust. When the bombardment ceased at about midday, at least one enemy battery had replied, pitching shells in *Aurora*'s wake. It was later learned that, although only two out of fifty-four gun batteries on the island were actually knocked out, the central control system had been put out of action.

The final bombardment was carried out by 100 Flying Fortresses. The whole island was blotted out by an impenetrable curtain of dust. The watchers in *Aurora*, three miles out to sea, could physically feel the reverberations of the bomb blasts.

It had been such an impressive rehearsal that ABC thought that if only they had had a few hundred troops in landing craft they could have taken the island there and then. He said to Eisenhower, 'With all the resistance we are getting, you and I could get into the captain's gig and capture the island alone.'

Pantelleria succumbed easily on n June. H-Hour for the landing was 12 noon, and white flags could be seen as the leading landing craft moved inshore a few minutes later. Soon a signal was received via Malta from the Italian commander: 'Pantelleria begs surrender, due lack of water.'

ABC did not believe there was any shortage of water: 'The truth was that the Italians, stunned by their defeat in Tunisia, had no stomach for further fighting.'

On 12 June, 'General Lyon' arrived by RAF aircraft at Maison Blanche. His visit had been arranged in the utmost secrecy but he was soon recognised as he was driven through the city. The news quickly spread that His Majesty King George VI was in Algiers.

Despite long hours of travelling and the afflictions of 'Desert Tummy', the King did not spare himself. He conferred with the British and American Navy and Army commanders and their staffs, inspected troops of the 1st Army at Bône, and went to Libya to inspect the 4th Indian Division.

King George V, *Howe* and two American cruisers were in Algiers harbour and ABC managed to

> assemble a most representative parade. There were about five thousand of our own seamen and Royal Marines; some six hundred of the United States Navy, very-smart and well turned-out, and best of all, about one thousand two hundred officers and men of the Merchant Navy from the merchant vessels in the port.
>
> Himself a seaman, His Majesty asked many shrewd questions. He met all the British and American Flag Officers, and visited the United States flagship and the *Howe*. Everybody was delighted to see him. On the Sunday he attended Divine Service in the church we had established in the dockyard, and one night he honoured me by dining at my villa.

During dinner the King said that he would very much like to visit Malta. Nobody knew better than ABC the effect such a visit would have on morale, in Malta and in the British Empire and the whole Allied cause. Malta was not entirely free from air attack, but ABC did not think that security would be a problem provided proper precautions were taken.

On 19 June ABC went to Tripoli to meet the King. Together they embarked in *Aurora* and sailed for Malta that evening, escorted by four destroyers. *Aurora* had only had forty-eight hours' notice of the King's arrival, which, as one of her officers wrote, 'had been preceded by tremendous exertions in the matter of scrubbing out, in a desperate attempt to look "tiddly"'.

Sunday 20 June dawned bright and clear. The Maltese people had only been told of the King's arrival on the radio at 5 a.m., but that was time enough. Every vantage point was packed with people as *Aurora*, wearing the Royal Standard, passed through the breakwater at 8 a.m., with the King himself standing at the salute on a special platform in front of the bridge superstructure.

The cheering swelled, thin at first, from a solitary Bofors crew, lined up by their gun on a harbour promontory, but growing to a tremendous crescendo as *Aurora* passed *Penelope*, her old comrade-in-arms of Force K, inside the harbour. It was the first time a Sovereign had visited Malta since 1911 and it resulted in what ABC called 'one of the most spontaneous and genuine demonstrations of loyalty and affection I have ever seen.

'I have never heard such cheering, and all the bells in the many churches started ringing when he landed. Incidentally, we had no ship-sized Royal Standard, and the one flown by the *Aurora* was made and painted on board the *Howe* at Algiers.'

The King toured the bomb-shattered streets and the countryside, saw the island's George Cross, lunched with Lord Gort the Governor and presented him with his Field Marshal's baton. The King re-embarked in *Aurora* that evening for the return to Tripoli, where he transferred to a Free French Motor Launch outside the breakwater, passed close down a line of ships all manned to cheer him, met officers and ratings of the 1st Escort Group, chatted to all the COs and ordered 'Splice the Mainbrace'. His Majesty flew home on 25 June, having travelled 6,700 miles in all.

In Algiers, Eisenhower, ABC and their staffs returned to the planning of Operation HUSKY, the invasion of Sicily, which had now become pressingly urgent.

20: OPERATION HUSKY — THE INVASION OF SICILY, JULY 1943

THE DECISION TO invade Sicily was taken at Casablanca in January 1943. It was planned for June, when it was assumed that the fighting in Tunisia would be over. But because of changes in plans, and shortages of shipping and landing craft, the date was delayed until the earliest favourable moon period in July. D-Day was eventually fixed for the 10th.

Eisenhower was once more the Supreme Commander, with Alexander as his deputy, ABC the Naval Commander and Tedder the Air Commander. The commanders of the land, sea and air forces of the two task forces were, for the American Western Task Force, Patton, commanding the US 7th Army, Vice-Admiral Hewitt, US Navy, and Colonel T.J. Hickey, USAAF; for the British Eastern Task Force, Montgomery, commanding the 8th Army, Ramsay, and Air Vice-Marshal Broadhurst, commanding the Western Desert Air Force.

Work began in February on an outline plan, but it soon ran into difficulties, not least because the planners were geographically separated by long distances. The planning staffs of Eisenhower, Alexander, Tedder, ABC and Hewitt were all in Algiers, but Ramsay's and Montgomery's were in Cairo, while Patton's staff were at Oran.

There were frequent changes in the plan. Alexander rejected the first, so that, as ABC said, 'All the preliminary work of our planners went for nought, and after a series of conferences and discussions another plan was produced.'

This plan, for British landings in the south-east and an American landing in the west, was approved in principle by

Eisenhower, ABC, Alexander and Tedder, although Tedder pointed out that an important airfield on the south coast of Sicily would be left untouched. ABC supported Tedder, saying that the risk of allowing the *Luftwaffe* to operate from airfields in the south-east of Sicily was unacceptable. The speedy capture of enemy airfields close to the landing beaches and one major port was crucial to success.

But the strongest objections were expressed by Montgomery, who called the plan a 'dog's breakfast' and told Alexander late in March that it 'has no hope of success and should be completely recast'. In his view, another division was required (which was eventually provided from the Middle East).

On the 24th Montgomery sent a message to Alexander: 'Planning to date has been on the assumption that resistance will be slight and Sicily will be captured easily. Never was there a greater error. If we work on the assumption of little resistance, and disperse our effort as is being done in all planning to date, we will merely have a disaster.'

ABC could not see how the dispersion of the assaults, so deprecated by Montgomery, 'would in any way have altered our overwhelming command of the sea'. On 28 April, he wrote to Pound:

> We are arriving at a state of deadlock out here over 'Husky'.
>
> Personally I think Montgomery's plan to concentrate on the South-east beaches is unsound as it leaves three aerodromes in the occupation of the enemy except for such force as the RAF can put on them, and we are landing a mass of shipping a mere thirty miles off. It also seems to surrender our greatest asset — that of being able to assault the island in numerous places at once at will.
>
> I am afraid Montgomery is a bit of a nuisance; he seems to think that all he has to do is say what is to be done and everyone will dance to the tune of his piping. Alexander

appears quite unable to keep him in order. But the seriousness of it all is that here we are with no fixed agreed plan, just over two months off D-Day and the commanders all at sixes and sevens, and even if we do get final agreement someone will be operating a plan he doesn't fully agree with. Not the way to make a success of a difficult operation.

At a conference in Algiers on 29 April, ABC again insisted that it was essential to capture the airfields at the earliest possible moment so as to protect the mass of shipping which would be lying off the beaches. Tedder said that the plan would leave thirteen airfields in enemy hands, far more than could be effectively neutralised from the air, and unless the airfields could be captured at the earliest possible moment, he was opposed to the whole plan. As ABC said, 'General Alexander was faced... with a complete contradiction between the Army view, on the one hand, and that of the Navy and the Air Force, on the other.'

On 3 May Eisenhower recast the plan more to Montgomery's framework. The American assault in the west was cancelled and the entire strength of the US 7th Army transferred to the south-east, on the left of the British 8th Army. The 7th Army would only have the use of a small port at Licata, supplying six hundred tons a day; the rest would have to be unloaded over the open beaches. But Eisenhower hoped for better weather on the beaches in July and in the event he was to have the inestimable assistance of the DUKWs, or 'ducks', a new type of amphibious vehicle which revolutionised ship-to-shore transport.

There was now the broad outline of a settled plan. But, as ABC wrote to Pound on 8 May,

I think it is well you should know of the atmosphere here after the acceptance of the final 'Husky' plan. The Admiral [Hewitt] and General [Patton] of the Western Task Force are very sore about it because they feel they have been made to dance to Montgomery's tune and have been given rather a raw deal. There is no doubt that the maintenance of three American divisions is a very tricky problem, involving the supply over beaches and perhaps one small port for some six weeks, of 3,000 tons a day and no one really knows whether he can do it or not.

Hewitt has told Patton definitely that he does not think he can, but Patton has taken up the attitude that he has been ordered to land there and he will do it.

I think myself that, barring accidents, it can be done, and I have assured them of all the assistance we can give them.

The only person unconcerned by the frequent changes in plan was Power, who had volunteered to 'see HUSKY through'. 'ABC loathed Monty (who was responsible for most of the changes),' Power said, 'and for some reason was bitterly jealous in his dealings with his contemporary Bertie Ramsay. I had to fly hither and yon soothing ruffled Admirals and Staffs and putting things on a basis.'

Ramsay had a frank and happy relationship with Montgomery, which may partly explain ABC's feelings towards him. Ramsay spent a week in Algiers in March, and stayed in ABC's villa. 'ABC has his own very definite views,' Ramsay wrote to his wife. 'His judgement is excellent but his facts are sometimes wrong. There may be trouble later on, owing to his way of centralising command, in the same way as when he and I play together in ping-pong, he takes 4/5ths of the balls. He's very good too...'

Some of ABC's signals to Ramsay were worded so strongly as to be very nearly offensive. One was delivered during a dinner party at the British Embassy in Cairo. After reading it, Ramsay put it in his pocket, saying: 'That can wait until tomorrow morning when I will have time to consider it and tempers have cooled down.'

Ramsay was well aware of the feelings between ABC and Montgomery, who had by now realised that he was no longer dealing with Harwood, against whom he could lodge complaints without fear of repercussions, but with a far higher calibre of a man.

Ramsay's letters record his difficulties. Late in April, he wrote: 'My latest proposals in conjunction with Monty bring me into conflict with ABC, which is most unfortunate, but with patience and understanding I do hope for a settlement of great importance whilst retaining our existing friendly and amicable relations.'

Ramsay's efforts at conciliation at last had their reward. The final plan was agreed, although not until 13 May.

HUSKY was the greatest amphibious operation ever undertaken up until that time. ABC summed it up:

> Some 160,000 troops, with 14,000 vehicles, 600 tanks, and 1,800 guns were to be landed in enemy territory in the face of hostile resistance. This initial landing was to be followed by a stream of reinforcements with huge quantities of stores and war material. Nearly two thousand vessels of all types, warships and merchantmen, were to take part in the first assault [in fact, the initial total was 2,590, including 1,614 British, 945 American and 31 Belgian, Dutch, Greek, Norwegian and Polish ships]. More than three thousand two hundred were to participate in the operations as a whole.

Over 1,000 British and 700 American major and minor landing craft took part. Providing them, and training their crews, were major undertakings. To guard against possible interference by the Italian fleet (although ABC personally thought that unlikely) there was Force H, with *Nelson* (wearing Willis' flag), *Rodney*, *Warspite* and *Valiant*, *Formidable* and *Indomitable*, the 12th and 15th Cruiser Squadrons and destroyer escort. *Howe* and *King George V* were in reserve at Algiers.

ABC had been under pressure to move his headquarters to Tunis where the RAF and USAAF had their headquarters and Eisenhower also had an advanced post. He resisted, preferring Malta which was in the front line only-sixty miles from Italy and with excellent naval communications. He won his point and although the Air stayed where they were, he, Eisenhower, Alexander, Ramsay and Montgomery all moved their headquarters to Malta for the actual operation.

ABC sailed from Algiers in the cruiser *Uganda* on 3 July, arriving in Malta next day. At once he had all the officers and their wives who had been using Admiralty House as a hostel cleared out to other quarters. He himself settled in on the ground floor, with Royer Dick, Shaw and the Flag Lieutenant. The rest of the staff used the large public rooms on the first floor, where Vice-Admiral (Malta) also lived.

ABC had an office in the Lascaris bastion overlooking Grand Harbour, where Vice-Admiral (Malta) and Ramsay also had offices. The combined naval and air operations room, with the huge wall chart and communications staff, was in a tunnel dug from Lascaris through the sandstone to the middle of the moat under Valletta. It was, ABC said, 'slightly better than the dank and dismal cavern at Gibraltar' which they had used for TORCH, but it was still 'extremely smelly and appallingly hot'. It was also infested with sandflies and many of the staff soon went down with sandfly fever.

On arrival in Malta on 4 July, ABC gave the order 'carry out Operation HUSKY' to start the great enterprise going. It was

American Independence Day and Eisenhower had mentioned to ABC that it was his countrymen's custom to fire a 'Salute to the Union' on the day. So, against the objections of his staff and the regulations, and on ABC's insistence, the salute was fired at noon from *Maidstone* in Algiers harbour, using forty-eight rounds of anti-aircraft ammunition, bursting at a height of about 5,000 feet.

Eisenhower and Alexander arrived in Malta on 8 July and stayed with the Governor, Lord Gort, at the Verdala Palace. By now, on quiet nights, ABC could hear the rumble of bombing as the USAAF and RAF pounded airfields in Sicily. Malta was bustling with activity. Grand Harbour and the adjacent creeks were filling up with landing craft. The airfields were all packed with aircraft, mostly fighters. ABC remarked on the fighter airstrip the Americans had bulldozed level on Gozo, the small island north of Malta. He ruefully recalled that he had suggested building an airfield there to the Defence Committee in 1938. The suggestion had 'met with no response'.

The first ships with troops and supplies for HUSKY had left the United States on 28 May 1943, to join ships assembling at Oran and Algiers. Eventually, fast and slow convoys left for their assault areas from Tunis, Bizerta and Sousse, from Alexandria and Port Said and from the Clyde. The continuous day and night cover given to the convoys by sea and in the air meant that the only losses were three ships from a slow convoy from the Clyde and one ship from a convoy from Alexandria, all torpedoed by U-boats off the North African coast.

Nevertheless, ABC sometimes had cold feet.

> Looking at that chart showing the carefully synchronized movements of hundreds of vessels in convoy, all steaming through certain points at their pre-arranged speeds, I often found myself wondering what might happen if things went

wrong. We hoped we had the measure of the U-boats and of the *Luftwaffe* as well; but the movement of this great mass of shipping must be known to the enemy. We had taken every possible precaution in the way of anti-submarine and anti-aircraft protection; but there was always the odd chance that the convoys might be attacked.

I had implicit faith in our planners; but what chaos and confusion might also arise if one single detail in our planning had gone awry? The time available for drawing up, co-ordinating, drafting and issuing the printed operation orders to each and every convoy and naval unit had been short enough; but a single error in calculation, a solitary false figure, might make the difference between success and failure. Mine was the ultimate responsibility for the landing of 160,000 troops and all their varied impedimenta. It is hard to describe one's feelings at such a time; but idle to suggest that one did not feel anxiety on the eve of a great operation. So much depended upon success in this, our first invasion of enemy territory in Europe.

Although, as ABC said, the enemy must know of the movement of such a great mass of shipping, efforts were made to mislead them. Early in May, in an operation with the grimly appropriate codename MINCEMEAT, the corpse of an unknown serviceman dressed as 'Major Martin', a Royal Marine officer on Mountbatten's staff, was dropped over the side from the submarine *Seraph* off the south coast of Spain where it would surely drift ashore and come to the notice of the Spanish authorities.

'Major Martin's' briefcase contained what purported to be secret documents, among them a personal letter to General Alexander from General Sir Archibald Nye, the Chief of the Imperial General Staff (and actually written by him), outlining Allied plans for the future, notably plans for an assault landing in Greece (codenamed HUSKY) and that the idea of using Sicily as a cover target for HUSKY had been rejected in favour of using it as cover for another operation, codenamed BRIMSTONE, target still unspecified [in fact, BRIMSTONE was the codename of the plan to invade Sardinia, rejected by the Combined Chiefs of Staff at Casablanca].

MINCEMEAT worked, up to a point. A signal on 14 May from the German Naval High Command to Kesselring and other German commanders in the Mediterranean included the 'absolutely reliable' information that the Allies were planning large-scale landings in the eastern and the western Mediterranean, and that the target in the east, codenamed HUSKY, was the Peloponnese.

A few days before D-Day, Force H made a feint appearance south-west of Crete to further the deception. However, the enemy never entirely ruled out Sicily as the possible target. In the week before D-Day, decrypts showed that the enemy regarded Sicily as the most probable target. On 4 July, the Germans still believed that there would be simultaneous landings in Sicily, Sardinia and Greece and that the danger was not imminent.

How ever, on that same day the Italian High Command in Sicily came to the accurate conclusion, from reconnaissance of Allied convoys and the movements of Allied warships, that Sicily, particularly eastern Sicily, was the real target and that the attack would come on 10 July. Thus, the decrypts made it clear that the Allies would not achieve surprise on D-Day. In the event, the most effective cover for the landings was provided by the weather, which lulled the enemy into a state of false security, believing that nobody would land in such bad conditions.

The weather had been very much on ABC's mind.

If it blew up I had visions of what might happen on some of those open beaches in Sicily. I had already told Eisenhower that up till twenty-four hours before zero hour [2.45 a.m. on 10 July] we could reverse the many convoys and delay the assault if the weather became too bad for landing. After that, I had said, whatever happened, the operations must take its course and we must risk the consequences. Actually, between ourselves — the Naval Staff — we had decided that noon on July 9th was the very last moment we could cancel the assault for next morning.

ABC's worst fears were realised on the morning of 9 July, when the weather began to deteriorate. Unusually for that time of year, it came on to blow hard from the north-west, raising a short, choppy sea. Wind and sea quickly increased until, by early afternoon, the weather was really bad.

By that time, the troop convoys were arriving and had begun to assemble at their rendezvous positions east and south of Malta. It was the very situation which ABC had hoped would never happen. He and Eisenhower had now to decide whether the weather was bad enough for the assault to be delayed for twenty-four hours.

The 8th Army in the east, and the Canadians in the extreme south, would be landing in the lee of the land and conditions for them would be favourable. But the wind would be blowing right across the beaches in the south-west where the US 7th Army were to land. Any beach there facing west would be a dead lee shore and the landing craft would have a very difficult time — that is, if they ever got to the beaches at all.

But if the convoys were turned around at that late hour, there was bound to be confusion. 'Our signals might not get through to all the units, so some might go on and some not.

Our attempt to land twenty-four hours later might produce a ragged and ill-timed assault.'

Eisenhower was in ABC's office when the meteorologists brought in their forecasts. These sudden Mediterranean blows often died away at sundown and the meteorologists predicted that this was likely to happen. So, said ABC:

> with rather fearful hearts we decided to let matters take their course. The landing-craft flotillas from Malta started to sail during the afternoon. Our anxieties were not at all relieved as we watched them literally burying themselves, with the spray flying over them in solid sheets, as they plunged out to sea on their way to their assault positions.

That afternoon, having nothing more to do, ABC and Royer Dick drove out to one of the airfields. 'It was the last place we should have visited,' said ABC. 'All the winds of heaven seemed to be roaring and howling round the control tower.' They returned to Admiralty House much depressed.

By about 8 p.m., though the wind was still blowing hard, it had noticeably decreased. After dinner, Dick and ABC went to Delimara Point, in the south of Malta, to watch the gliders and their towing aircraft go by, flying at about three or four hundred feet, 'sometimes in twos and threes, sometimes in larger groups, with their dim navigation lights just visible. In the pale half-light of the moon they looked like flights of great bats. Occasionally we could hear the drone of engines above the howling of the wind.'

Some 2,000 men of 1st British Airborne Division had taken off in 137 gliders towed by Halifaxes and Dakotas that evening. Their main objective was the strategic bridge of Ponte Grande, south of Syracuse. But the wind was still blowing at forty knots, half the gliders were cast off by their tugs at distances of two to ten miles from the coast and nearly fifty gliders crashed into the sea. Only twelve gliders actually reached their correct dropping zones. Some paratroopers were picked up by destroyers and small craft and some struggled ashore, but nearly a quarter of them were drowned. However, the bridge was captured.

After midnight ABC and Eisenhower turned in still wearing their clothes in their cabins in the Lascaris tunnel. 'The die was cast,' said ABC. 'We were committed to the assault. There was no more we could do for the time being.'

All HUSKY forces had been keeping strict radio silence. The first break came just before 5 a.m. on 10 July, when an intercepted message was brought to ABC reporting a successful landing by Royal Marine Commandos who had gone ashore on the left of the 1st Canadian Division. Soon, more good news began to pour in and by 5.30 a.m. 'success signals' had been received in the headquarters ships from every beach-head.

The bad weather of the night before had persuaded the enemy that, as ABC wrote in his report, 'tonight at any rate they can't come'. But, ABC went on, 'they came'. The wind moderated during the night. Dawn on the 10th saw the beginning of a perfect day, with a clear blue sky and steadily decreasing swell.

During the forenoon, ABC embarked in the minelayer *Abdiel* for a tour of the beaches. All was going well in the British sectors, with little sign of any fighting. The Americans had had more difficulties. ABC could see large numbers of landing craft washed up on the beaches. Rear-Admiral Alan Kirk, US Navy, had conducted a particularly awkward landing, on a dead lee shore. ABC could appreciate how well Kirk had done and sent him a congratulatory signal as *Abdiel* steamed by.

On land, the 8th Army advance in the east went briskly. Syracuse was occupied on the evening of 10 July and the large protected anchorage of Augusta was captured after some fighting two days later. But on 11 July the American 1st Division in the west had a setback near Gela when the Germans counterattacked and their tanks reached the beach.

Aided by naval gunfire, the Americans repulsed the Germans after some hours of hard fighting. However, Patton was soon on the move again and made a rapid advance to secure Palermo, Marsala and Trapani on 22 July; when 45,000 Italians surrendered in the west of Sicily.

The Navy was kept busy, landing supplies and reinforcements for the armies ashore and carrying out anti-submarine and anti-aircraft patrols outside and above the vast armada of merchant vessels lying off the beaches. Bombardments were laid on at specific times and places, as the 8th Army requested.

On 17 July, ABC received an urgent call for a bombardment of Catania. *Warspite*, *Euryalus* and a destroyer escort proceeded to the bombarding position. To get there in time, *Warspite* made good a speed of 23½ knots, remarkable for a battleship almost thirty years of age. ABC was so pleased he signalled: 'Operation well carried out. There is no doubt that when the old lady lifts her skirts she can run.'

Ship losses were light during the assault stages. Between D-Day and the end of July, the Western Task Force lost a destroyer, a minesweeper, two submarine chasers, two LSTs and one merchant ship. In the east, three landing craft and six merchant ships, totalling 41,509 tons, were sunk; the main loss was the hospital ship *Talamba*, bombed and sunk on 10 July although she was fully illuminated.

Early on 16 July *Indomitable* was hit by a torpedo dropped by an enemy aircraft fifty miles east of Cape Passaro. It was a fine clear night with a full moon, and *Indomitable* was surrounded by ships and had a destroyer screen. In his report, Willis admitted that his ships had been caught napping but said that there were almost always many friendly aircraft present, many of them failing to establish their identity by IFF (Identification — Friend or Foe). ABC was not impressed, saying: 'An aircraft in a position to menace the fleet must be instantly engaged unless it has identified itself in the most positive manner.'

Apart from four British merchantmen and two American LSTs sunk, and the cruisers *Cleopatra* and *Newfoundland* and three merchantmen damaged, all the ship losses were caused by aircraft or by shore batteries. Thus, the U-boats hardly affected the progress of HUSKY and were themselves subjected to a successful, ULTRA-assisted anti-submarine offensive. Between 11 July and the end of the month eight Italian and two German U-boats were sunk or captured in the Mediterranean, the majority of them in waters around Sicily and southern Italy.

The best day was 12 July when U-409 was sunk by the destroyer *Inconstant* between Algiers and Bougie, U-561 was sunk by MTB 81 in the Straits of Messina and the Italian *Bronzo* was captured by the minesweepers *Seaham*, *Boston*, *Poole* and *Cromarty* off Syracuse.

Bronzo was towed into Augusta Bay and later to Malta, with the White Ensign hoisted above the green, white and red of the Italian tricolour, and the towing minesweeper, looking extremely pleased with herself, being greeted with signals of 'Is That Your First Today?' from other ships in harbour.

Such a capture was, of course, a very good story. But it led indirectly to yet another fracas between ABC and the press. ABC genuinely wanted a good press for the Navy but always seemed unwilling or unable to achieve it. The trouble was mainly ABC's own fault. Unlike Montgomery, who handled his public relations superbly well, ABC's attitude towards the press was always prickly and suspicious, if not downright hostile. If anything went wrong, he was apt to sever relations completely.

In January, ABC had been prevailed upon by the Admiralty to give a press conference on the Navy's achievements in the Mediterranean, during which he remarked that he hoped Tripoli would soon be captured by the 8th Army and that the Navy would be able to use the port for supplying the Army.

It seemed an innocent and a harmless enough comment. As ABC said, the fact that the Allies had captured Tripoli and were using the port could not be concealed from the enemy. But it provoked a furious reaction at home, where the Chiefs of Staff took exception to the remark and issued an order that in future all Commanders-in-Chief, at home and abroad, were to have what they intended to say at any press conference approved by the Chiefs of Staff beforehand. 'I have to confess,' said ABC, 'I became irritated and retorted by signal that if the Commander-in-Chief himself did not know what he could safely say "on the record" and what he could not, he was not fit to be Commander-in-Chief. '

The upshot was that ABC refused to give any more press conferences, conceding that the Navy thereby lost some publicity. He maintained that it was impossible for him to signal beforehand exactly what answers he was going to give to 'the astute and agile questions of thirty or forty British and American gentlemen of the Press avid for news stories'. However, he did say 'how loyal ninety-nine per cent of them always were, and how carefully they guarded any secrets which were told them "off the record".' The Chief of Naval Information, Admiral Sir William James, who was also MP for

North Portsmouth, was sufficiently concerned about ABC's handling of publicity to make a visit to Algiers in May 1943.

Whitworth wrote to ABC in June that 'Bubbles James is just back from Algiers greatly impressed with the happy and apparently carefree atmosphere in your villa. He said that you must have hated the sight of him representing as he does three trades you abominate — Gunnery, the Press and an MP.'

James had enjoyed his three days' stay with ABC and had been immensely struck by the friendliness of his relations with Eisenhower. However, James was not so impressed by the prospects of publicity for the Navy, calling his visit 'not very profitable' in that respect.

Eisenhower had two Press Agency correspondents, one American, one British, to whom he gave the latest information, he himself deciding what could and could not be published. Thinking no harm of it, Eisenhower told the two journalists of the *Bronzo* capture. Not surprisingly, they promptly published it world-wide.

The first ABC heard of this was when he received a very sharply worded signal from the Admiralty, 'demanding to know why this tit-bit of news had been made public contrary to all rules and regulations'. The rule, unknown to Eisenhower, was that the destruction of enemy submarines must on no account be published, especially when a submarine had been captured and the enemy might get to know that codes and cyphers had been compromised.

It was impracticable and undesirable to conceal the news of all enemy U-boat sinkings, as the Admiralty must have known. This would give the impression that the Allies' anti-submarine forces were failing. Throughout the war news of U-boat sinkings was released.

ABC himself took much pleasure in seeing Malta once more functioning as a great naval base and watching all the ships arriving and departing. On 14 July he wrote to Nona: 'Today as I look out of my office window the Grand Harbour looks as it used to be. Two battleships [*Nelson* and *Rodney*] are lying down below, the first to come into the harbour since I paid a short visit in the *Warspite* in December, 1940. Willis told me he was quite thrilled coming in, and I must say so was I.'

One night ABC watched from the roof of Admiralty House an air raid on Malta, one of only ten that month (compared with 184 in July 1942). In ABC's account, 'it was a wonderful experience to see Malta's well-tried air defence going into action. The roar and thunder of the anti-aircraft fire, increased by that of the ships lying in the harbour, had to be heard to be believed. Everything worked like clockwork.'

By 19 July 1943 HUSKY was virtually accomplished, so far as the landing of the 7th and 8th Armies was concerned. Henceforth the supply of the armies in Sicily became what ABC called a 'routine operation' under the C-in-C, Mediterranean.

ABC flew back to Algiers on 25 July. Mussolini fell that day, to be succeeded by Marshal Badoglio, who announced that Italy would continue the war alongside her German allies — who, however, knew very well that the new Italian Government intended to negotiate an armistice as soon as possible. However, as ABC said, 'The end was not yet.'

Nor was it. Towards the end of July there was a lull on the Catania front, while the 8th Army regrouped for a change of plan. It was clear that the enemy were determined to defend Catania in earnest. Montgomery decided to abandon the direct advance along the coast road towards the town, as being likely to be too costly in casualties. Instead, he intended to make a circling movement to the west around the volcano Mount Etna.

To ABC, the absence of any plans to carry out coastal operations came as a surprise and a disappointment. He felt that a great chance was being missed to land troops along the coast behind enemy lines, to harass and unsettle the enemy. 'There were doubtless sound military reasons for making no use of this, what to me appeared, priceless asset of sea power and flexibility of manoeuvre,' he wrote in his Report, 'but it is worth considering... whether much time and costly fighting could not be saved by even minor flank attacks, which must necessarily be unsettling to the enemy. It may be that, had I pressed my views more strongly, more could have been done.'

Rear-Admiral McGrigor had landing craft specially equipped to work in support of the Army ready at Augusta, as part of his Inshore Squadron. Twice, McGrigor actually had a Commando force embarked and once even sailed to cut enemy road and rail communications along the coast. But the Army called off the operation each time.

British troops occupied Catania on 5 August and the first American troops entered Messina from the east on the night of 16 August; 40 RM Commandos from Scaletta entered from the south next morning. But the enemy had gone. The last enemy troops had left hours earlier.

Using an assorted flotilla of train ferries, small steamers, minesweepers, landing craft, naval ferry barges and miscellaneous small craft, the enemy had successfully evacuated an entire army of more than 100,000 men, with tanks, guns, vehicles and stores across the Straits of Messina to the Italian mainland, in the face of overwhelming Allied naval and air superiority.

This success, favourably compared by the enemy to Dunkirk, understandably caused some heart-searchings amongst Allied commanders. There were some mitigating circumstances. The Italians and Germans had each organised four escape routes across the Straits which were only some two-and-a-half miles wide at their narrowest point. Many of the ferrying ships and craft could cross in twenty minutes.

The Straits were also guarded by batteries of heavy guns which made it too dangerous for warships to operate close inshore for long. The batteries were small targets from the air and any low-flying aircraft had to run the gauntlet of an intense anti-aircraft barrage.

Alexander had signalled to ABC and Tedder as early as 3 August that there were signs that the Germans were preparing for a withdrawal to the mainland. 'You have no doubt co-ordinated plans to meet this contingency,' he said.

In fact, there were no such plans, then or later. To prevent the enemy evacuation of Sicily, a strategic prize well worth striving for, would have required a much closer co-operation between all three Allied Commanders-in-Chief than was ever achieved.

Writing of this period in his memoirs, ABC said, 'By the second week in August the Germans realised that the game was up and started to pull out. There was no effective way of stopping them, either by sea or air. The passage across the Straits of Messina, no more than three miles, could be made in less than one hour, and was covered by batteries and searchlights on both sides.'

ABC conceded that he did not pay enough attention to the matter. His staff believed that he did pay attention but always had in the back of his mind the fate of some of the heavy ships sent to bombard the batteries in the Dardanelles in 1915.

However, the fact remains that HUSKY was a success, and it was achieved with far fewer losses than had been anticipated. ABC said in his report, he thought it 'almost magical that great fleets of ships could remain anchored on the enemy's coast, within forty miles of the main aerodromes, with only such slight losses… as were incurred'. Royal Navy casualties were 314 killed, and 411 wounded, a comparatively low figure considering the numbers involved.

ABC paid his own tributes to those who had taken part: the young RNVR officers, new and inexperienced, who commanded the landing and other small craft and who 'on that shocking night of July 9th-10th, thrashing into a strong wind and heavy sea in which several were damaged, pressed determinedly on for their objectives'; the 'fine spirit, discipline and calm determination of the many officers and men of the Allied Merchant Navies who so greatly contributed to our success'; the 'gallant young men of the Combined Operations Reconnaissance and Pilotage Parties, the "C.O.P.P.s", who landed and reconnoitred the landing beaches beforehand in folboats sent in from submarines'; and 'Then there were the submarines themselves, the *Unruffled*, *Unseen*, *Unison*, *Unrivalled*, *Seraph*, *Shakespeare*, and *Safari*, which served as inshore beacons guiding the flights of landing-craft to their beaches in the dark and early morning of July 10th.'

ABC sent a message of congratulations to the officers and men of the landing craft. 'Quite apart from their rude buffeting during the passage to Sicily, they carried out their various tasks during the landings with a competence and courage that excited my warm admiration.' He also had good words for all his ships, the cruisers, destroyers, the bombarding ships including the twenty-eight-year-old river gunboats *Aphis* and *Scarab*, the minesweepers and the submarines and especially the

DUKWS, 'popularly "Ducks" — now well known, but then a complete novelty to us. It was amazing to see these ingenious amphibious craft loading stores alongside the ships in a swell, wallowing ashore, and then waddling dripping up the beaches to deposit their cargoes in the dumps inland.'

The Royal and United States Navies received a message of thanks and praise from Eisenhower, and ABC had a letter from Alexander which was promulgated around the fleet:

> Before leaving Malta for the mainland, I should like to take this opportunity of expressing, on behalf of the Fifteenth Army Group, our admiration for, and gratitude to the Royal Navy and the other naval units you command for the magnificent support and service you have given and continue to give to the troops under my command. It will gratify you to hear what I hear on all sides — namely, unstinted praise for the Senior Service.

ABC himself had more honours. The French awarded him the Grand Cordon of the Legion d'honneur. He was invested with the sash and star by General Giraud and had to submit to a kiss on both cheeks from the General. He and Hewitt were also made Honorary Members of the Seventh Spahis and were both presented with a Spahi's red woollen cloak lined with white.

ABC's Spahi cloak became 'a cherished possession which I have had some difficulty in retaining. My wife's covetous glances are often cast in its direction, for there is no doubt it could well be converted into a garment suitable for a lady.'

21: SALERNO AND THE ITALIAN SURRENDER, SEPTEMBER 1943

AFTER HUSKY CAME BAYTOWN, the operation to take the 8th Army from shore to shore, across the Straits of Messina to the 'toe' of Italy. But before BAYTOWN, there was a protest from ABC about the behaviour of Montgomery, whom he accused of going directly to the Allied C-in-C, suggesting a British Navy/Army squabble which they could not resolve among themselves.

On 26 August 1943, ABC addressed a handwritten letter to Alexander in which he said that at a C-in-C's meeting on the 23rd Monty had

> stated that the Army was ready to execute the BAYTOWN operation on 1 September but that they were held up by the Navy who refused to do it until 4/5th and furthermore that Navy was unwilling to do the operation by night. I have the right to assume that such a statement was authoritative. So serious did it appear to me that I decided, as you know, to fly to Sicily at once as the only means of clearing up the situation. I found that, not only were the statements incorrect, but that General Montgomery had at no time been in direct touch with the S.N.O. of the Expedition and that his statements were, in fact, completely unfounded. The object of this letter is to bring matters out into the open.

Alexander returned a non-committal reply and in fact BAYTOWN did take place. The first step was for warships to bombard enemy defences on the Italian side of the Straits. On 31 August, a force led by Admiral Willis, flying his flag in

Nelson, with *Rodney*, *Orion* and destroyers, bombarded Reggio at the southern entrance to the Straits; *Warspite* and *Valiant* carried out a second bombardment on 2 September.

At dawn on 3 September two divisions of the 8th Army, one British, one Canadian, began to be ferried across the Straits in twenty-two LSTs and some 270 landing craft, under the cover of a tremendous bombardment from batteries around Messina and from ships in the Straits.

ABC had embarked in the destroyer *Tartar* the night before and watched the assault. Never, he said 'since perhaps the time of Gallipoli, had I seen or heard such a bombardment'. In fact, it was something of an anti-climax and probably even a waste of ammunition.

> The Italians were not fighting, and the Germans had already pulled out to the north. There was no retaliation except for an occasional ill-aimed shell plopping harmlessly into the middle of the Straits. Indeed, except for the roar and thunder of our vast concentration of artillery it was more like Cowes Week than an assault on enemy territory. Our people called it the 'Messina Straits Regatta'.
>
> It was a bloodless victory, this, our first landing on the mainland of Europe; but the crews of the landing craft did excellent work. The Navy had promised the Army to ferry 5,000 vehicles in five days. By working all out, with some of the craft making as many as ten or twelve trips a day, 5,300 vehicles were transported across the Straits in *three* days.

ABC only remained long enough to communicate with Rear-Admiral McGrigor, who was in command of BAYTOWN, and then left for Malta. Planning was already well in hand for the next operation, AVALANCHE, a landing in the Gulf of Salerno, with the objective of capturing Naples.

On 15 August Sir Samuel Hoare, Ambassador to Spain on Special Mission, sent telegrams to the Foreign Office describing a conversation he had just had with high-ranking Italian officials in Lisbon who wished to begin negotiations.

The text of the telegrams was sent to Eisenhower on 17 August. Bedell Smith and Eisenhower's Chief of Intelligence, Brigadier Kenneth Strong, were fitted out with civilian clothes in what Macmillan called 'an atmosphere of amateur charades' and then flew to Lisbon for a series of melodramatic meetings which, as ABC said, 'would not have been out of place in a spy story'. They took with them a short list of Allied demands. ABC was not consulted and thus the list made almost no reference to the Italian fleet.

Bedell Smith and Strong came back with the news that the Italians desperately wanted to surrender but the Germans had taken over most of the important posts in the Government and the armed forces. The Italians, ABC said, 'could not think of capitulation unless it coincided with a large scale landing by the Allies on the Italian mainland'.

Such a major landing was, of course, in hand, but 'to cut short a complicated story', a document later known as the 'Shorter Instrument' was signed in Sicily on 3 September 1943. All Italian forces, wherever they were, would surrender on 8 September.

Royer Dick signed on ABC's behalf. 'I signed and thought no more about it,' he said, 'until about two months later when all the bells rang — "Commander-in-Chief would like to see you, sir". With a shaking hand, ABC was pointing his finger at this picture of me in some newspaper. "What do you mean", he demanded, "by signing an armistice wearing *shorts*?"

'He was really angry. I said, "Well, sir, to tell the truth, I haven't often signed armistices before and I didn't quite know what I should be wearing."'

'It was half fun. You had to fire back at ABC, and then the clouds rolled by.'

Eisenhower and his Commanders-in-Chief had decided on Salerno as the next objective at a conference on 17 August, and fixed the date as 9 September. Typically, ABC pressed for a bolder move. Just as he had suggested Bizerta as an objective for TORCH, so he now recommended that AVALANCHE should go for Rome. But it was known that the Germans were moving reinforcements into Italy from the north, and a landing in the Rome area would be beyond the range of Allied shore-based fighters. Even Salerno was beyond all but the most modern American fighters flying from Sicily, and even they could stay only twenty minutes over the battle area. The bulk of the fighter cover for the AVALANCHE landing beaches and support of the Army would therefore be provided from escort carriers sent out from Britain for the purpose.

Once again, there were some familiar names in AVALANCHE. The naval commander was Admiral Hewitt, the army commander was General Mark Clark. Commodore Geoffrey N. Oliver commanded the British landing of X Corps on the northern beaches, and Rear-Admiral John L. Hall, US Navy, commanded the landing of the US VI Corps in the south.

Vian, flying his flag in *Euryalus*, commanded Force V, of five escort carriers to provide fighter cover over the beaches. Force H, under Willis, would again cover against an appearance by the Italian battle fleet, and its two aircraft carriers, *Illustrious* and *Formidable*, would give fighter cover over Force V as well as provide anti-submarine patrols and CAPs for Force H itself.

It had been decided, much to ABC's annoyance, that the Commanders-in-Chief should have their headquarters for AVALANCHE at Bizerta. ABC thought communications there were quite inadequate to deal with the volume of signal traffic, the telephones were 'indifferent and insecure' and the facilities generally unsuitable, especially for a naval C-in-C who, unlike an army C-in-C, did not delegate operational or other important matters to anybody except possibly his Chief of Staff but dealt with all signals and signed all orders personally. ABC compromised by moving to Bizerta with some of his staff on 7 September, using the headquarters ship *Largs*. It was hot and crowded but it was the best that could be done, and it was not to last long.

The arrangements for the impending surrender of Italy had been kept so secret that some two days beforehand ABC and his staff became aware that there was nobody to cover the surrender of the Italian fleet. All the war correspondents, with their photographers and cameramen, were already embarked in their various ships, on the way to cover the landings at Salerno.

ABC thought this a pity and mentioned it to Eisenhower, who sent for Captain Butcher, his naval aide, and gave him the choice of going back to Washington with all the papers relevant to the Italian armistice or embarking in *Warspite* to see the Italian fleet. 'The decision was not hard to make,' Butcher said, 'because there are few times in the life of any man when he can witness the surrender of a fleet.' It was suggested that Butcher take his cameras.

Butcher joined *Warspite* in Malta on 7 September and the ship sailed later that day. He found that even Rear-Admiral Bisset, flying his flag in *Warspite*, had only the barest inkling of what was in store; he had sealed orders, not to be opened until later. Thus, said Butcher, 'I kept my mouth shut.'

At 1.30 p.m. on 8 September, *Warspite* and *Valiant*, escorted by five British, one French and one Greek destroyer, were detached from Force H to rendezvous with the Italian fleet. At 3 a.m. on the 9th, the main body of the Italian fleet, including the battleships *Roma*, *Vittorio Veneto* and *Italia* (formerly the *Littorio*), six cruisers and eight destroyers, sailed from Spezia under the command of Admiral Bergamini, flying his flag in *Roma*. Their route was down the west coasts of Corsica and Sardinia to a point some twenty miles north of Cape Garde, near Bône, where they were due to meet the Allied ships at 8 a.m. on 10 September.

To the Allies' surprise, on the afternoon of the 9th Bergamini's ships unexpectedly altered course to the east, steering to pass between Corsica and Sardinia, as though heading for Maddalena. But the Germans now had control of all bases and ports in Corsica and Sardinia, including Maddalena. Perhaps Bergamini heard of this, because at about 4 p.m. he turned back again to the west. At almost the same time, his ships were attacked by Dornier Do, 217 bombers armed with the new FX. 1400 wireless-controlled bombs. *Roma* was hit, caught fire, blew up and sank in twenty minutes, with the loss of many on board, including Bergamini himself.

One cruiser and some destroyers stayed behind to pick up survivors, but the rest met Bisset's ships the next morning. *Warspite* and the other ships, steaming east and steering to seaward so as to keep the Italians between them and the land, were at action stations, with all guns trained on the Italian fleet.

The cruiser *Eugenia di Savoia* was now the flagship, wearing the flag of Admiral Romeo Oliva who took over after the death of his C-in-C. Brownrigg boarded *Savoia* who took station, leading the Italian line, astern of *Warspite* and *Valiant*, with the Allied destroyers leading the Italian destroyers on each flank.

That afternoon, ABC embarked with Eisenhower and Dick in the destroyer *Hambledon* and went out to watch the Italian fleet go by. ABC was at his most carping and critical, constantly needling *Hambledon*'s Captain, Lieutenant-Commander G.W. McKendrick, on his ship's appearance and handling until Eisenhower eventually said: 'For heaven's sake, leave the boy alone.'

All criticism was stilled when the Italian fleet came over the horizon. 'To me,' said ABC,

> it was a most moving and thrilling sight. To see my wildest hopes of years back brought to fruition, and my former flagship the *Warspite*, which had struck the first blow against the Italians three years before, leading her erstwhile opponents into captivity, filled me with deepest emotion and lives with me still. I can never forget it. I made a signal congratulating the *Warspite* on her proud and rightful position at the head of the line.

The battleships *Andrea Doria* and *Caio Duilio*, two cruisers and a destroyer, sailed from Taranto on 9 September and arrived in Malta on the following day. *Savoia* and the others reached Malta on the 11th. ABC sent a signal to all ships and authorities under his command that 'the Italian fleet having scrupulously honoured the engagement entered into by their Government, officers and ship's companies are to be treated with courtesy and consideration on all occasions'.

On 11 September ABC flew to Malta to meet Admiral Alberto da Zara, who commanded the Taranto squadron, to give him instructions about the disarming and disposal of the Italian fleet. Da Zara came ashore at 4 p.m. that afternoon at

Custom House Steps in Grand Harbour, to be met by a guard of honour and Royer Dick, once again representing ABC, and to be photographed by Butcher.

ABC's office in the Lascaris bastion was almost above the landing stage, only sixty steps up a circular stairway. But ABC decided that da Zara should see some of the devastation done to Malta by Axis bombing and arranged for him to be driven to Lascaris by a roundabout route.

ABC found da Zara 'a pleasant-enough man speaking good English; but as was only natural felt his position keenly'. 'I wished he had been a German,' ABC told Doodles, 'so that I could have rough-handled him properly but there was little spirit left in this poor man.' Unsurprisingly, da Zara did not oppose any of ABC's proposals.

Later that day, 11 September 1943, ABC made his unforgettable signal (actually drafted by Royer Dick) to the Admiralty: 'Be pleased to inform Their Lordships that the Italian Battle Fleet now lies at anchor under the guns of the fortress of Malta.'

A third battleship from Taranto, *Giulio Cesare*, arrived in Malta on 13 September and other ships followed later in the month. By 21 September, five battleships, eight cruisers, eleven fleet destroyers, twenty-two escort and local defence destroyers, a seaplane tender, twenty corvettes, thirty-four submarines, five midget submarines, twelve E-boats and fifteen other miscellaneous warships were under Allied control, at Malta and other ports. The light cruiser *Attilio Regolo* and destroyers, who had stayed behind to rescue *Roma*'s survivors, reached the Spanish Balearic Islands. The cruiser went on to Gibraltar, but three destroyers were interned and two others scuttled themselves to avoid internment.

Also under Allied control were 101 merchant ships, totalling 183,591 tons. Another 168 merchant ships, of 76,298 tons, were scuttled to avoid capture by the Germans. Many Italian warships were also scuttled by their crews. When the Germans took Spezia, they shot the Italian captains who had scuttled their ships. 'That's the way to treat your late Allies!' ABC wrote to Doodles.

The news of the Italian armistice naturally aroused hopes, wholly unjustified in the event, amongst the assault troops on their way to Salerno. It also, as was later discovered, caused a stiffening of resolve amongst the defending Germans.

The first waves of troops touched down about an hour before dawn on 9 September, with no preliminary bombardment. This was at the request of the Army, who wanted to achieve surprise. The Navy would have preferred to land in daylight and to sacrifice surprise for a 'softening-up' bombardment.

There was stiff opposition to the first landings, but by the end of that day the Germans were withdrawing and the beaches at least were in Allied hands.

The Germans counter-attacked on the night of 11/12 September, trying to drive a wedge between the British and American beach-heads. Only the first and follow-up assault troops were ashore and although the beach-heads were held, very little penetration had been made inland. Artillery could not be properly deployed on the narrow strips of land already captured, whereas the Germans were making the most effective use of mobile guns in the hills inland and to either side of the beaches, so that every part of the Allied bridgehead came under sustained heavy fire.

The German counter-attack intensified during the 13th. By the end of the day a gap had been forced open between the

British and the Americans and the Germans had penetrated to within three miles of the sea. Next day, the Americans had to give more ground and the situation on shore deteriorated even further, so that Admiral Hewitt signalled to ABC asking if heavy ships were available for bombardment. ABC reacted with characteristic speed, replying that he would give all the help he could. *Warspite* and *Valiant* were on their way. *Nelson* and *Rodney* were also available, and had been ordered to Augusta in case they were needed.

The situation had become so grave on that day, 14 September, that General Clark requested Hewitt to order all available craft in the assault areas to prepare to transfer troops from the Southern Attack area to the Northern Attack area, or vice versa. Hewitt also halted the unloading of merchant ships in the Southern Attack area in case it became necessary to begin a withdrawal. Oliver was asked if he could accommodate General Clark and 5th Army staff in his headquarters ship *Hilary*.

Oliver was summoned to Hewitt's headquarters ship USS *Ancon*, when he was astonished to discover Hewitt's staff hard at work, not only on plans to transfer Clark's staff to *Hilary* but also to shorten the Allied front by moving units of the British X Corps from the Northern to the Southern Attack area, or by transferring units of the United States VI Corps in the opposite direction. Oliver had only just parted from Major-General Richard McCreery, the X Corps Commander, who had said nothing, and obviously knew nothing, of this change of plan.

Oliver said that in view of the enemy's strength ashore and the nature of the beaches for re-embarking troops, he thought that the idea of transferring troops from one attack area to the other was, as reported by ABC, 'quite impossible and not to be contemplated. Now that the troops were ashore, he [Oliver] insisted, the only thing that they could do was to stay and fight it out with all the support the Navy could give them in the way of gunfire.' As for the transfer of Clark's staff to *Hilary*, Oliver said he would gladly have them, if necessary, but as Clark's staff numbered nearly 2,000, with about 500 vehicles, it was impossible to accommodate them all.

Oliver hurried back to *Hilary* and hastened to get in touch with McCreery who, as ABC described him, 'to put it mildly, was horrified at the proposal to evacuate troops from one attack area to another,' especially as General Clark had made no mention of any such plan at that day's conference. By then it was 10 p.m. at night but McCreery at once signalled to Clark and Hewitt saying that no mention had been made that morning of any plan to transfer British units to the Southern Attack area and he thought there could be no question of it taking place.

On 14 September every available aircraft of the Mediterranean Air Force was switched from attacking targets inland to bombing German troops and guns near the beachheads. Next day, the 15th, *Warspite* and *Valiant* arrived and began bombarding at ranges of up to 21,800 yards. Every other ship available also joined in the bombardment.

The combination of air and sea bombardment brought the German advance to a halt. The naval bombardment sealed the enemy off from any reinforcement and, in ABC's words, 'helped to convert the spearhead of the German attack into a huddle of men, tanks, guns and vehicles which were mercilessly pounded'. By 16 September, the situation ashore had stabilised.

That afternoon of the 16th, when *Warspite* had just finished her third bombardment of the day, she was attacked by German bombers. One 3,000 lb radio-controlled bomb scored a direct hit and went down through six decks to explode below

No. 4 boiler-room, wrecking it and flooding four of the other five boiler-rooms. Two more bombs were near-misses close on the starboard side.

All power was lost, but the ship was taken in tow and, after an exciting passage through the Straits of Messina, when the tows parted and the southward current carried her helplessly broadside on through the Straits, she reached Malta on 19 September and Gibraltar for temporary repairs on 8 November.

On 17 September ABC embarked in the destroyer *Offa* for a personal tour of the operational area. He visited Hewitt's flagship to talk over the situation with him and then they both went to the British sector for lunch with Oliver in *Hilary*. 'As ever,' said ABC, 'Oliver was on the crest of the wave — calm, imperturbable, and completely optimistic as to the final outcome.

'By the 18th the crisis was well past. The enemy was showing signs of retiring and the Allied beach-head was secure.

'The assault had come very near to failure, and for a time the situation was precarious.'

In his official report ABC paid tribute to Hewitt and those who had served under him: 'That there were extremely anxious moments cannot be denied — I am proud to say that throughout the operation the Navies never faltered and carried out their tasks in accordance with the highest traditions of their Services.'

ABC also congratulated Vian on the performance of the carriers of Force V. Their Seafires had flown 265 sorties on D-Day, maintaining patrols of about twenty aircraft over the beach-heads. Originally the carriers were to have given air cover only for the first two days until the 10 September, but because of the delay in capturing Monte Corvino airfield and making it operational, they stayed until the 12th, for three-and-a-half days, in which their aircraft flew 713 sorties. An emergency landing strip was established in a tomato field at Paestum and twenty-six Seafires landed there on the afternoon of the 12th.

There were very few contacts with enemy aircraft; probably two were shot down. The main casualties were the Seafires themselves. Their numbers declined dramatically through accidents. The carriers' slow speed, the lack of wind, the Seafire's fragile under-carriage and a shortage of training amongst the pilots (which ABC criticised in his report) all contributed to the accident rate. By 15 September, when patrols were taken over by USAAF and RAF fighters and the carrier fighters were withdrawn, ten Seafires had been lost and thirty-two damaged beyond repair, mostly in deck-landing crashes.

On 22 September ABC sailed in a cruiser from Malta for Taranto, his first visit there since 1917. He was not there to renew old acquaintance but to clear up uncertainties about the Italian Navy and merchant ships caused by the 'Shorter Instrument' which had been signed in Sicily on 3 September without consultation with ABC or his staff.

ABC found Admiral de Courton, the Italian Minister of Marine, 'though very downcast, was pleasantly amenable' and 'a strictly honourable man who carried out all that he promised'. An agreement was drawn up, known as the Cunningham-de Courton Agreement, later signed on ABC's behalf by Rear-Admiral McGrigor.

The port of Salerno was under shell fire until 25 September when it was reopened for the use of Allied shipping. The British beaches and anchorages were at last freed from enemy artillery fire the next day. A violent storm swept the Bay of

Salerno on the night of 28/29 September, driving many small ships and landing craft ashore, especially in the American sector. It was as well it had not happened between 10 and 15 September when the situation ashore had been so critical; not even naval bombardment could have averted a disaster for the Allies.

On the forenoon of 29 September 1943, ABC joined Eisenhower, Bedell Smith, Alexander, Tedder, Lord Gort, Willis, Harold Macmillan and Robert Murphy on board *Nelson* in Grand Harbour for the formal signing of the Italian surrender. ABC had thought of holding the ceremony in his old flagship *Rodney*, but decided on Willis' flagship instead.

Marshal Badoglio, who was to sign on behalf of King Victor Emmanuel III, was received by a full Royal Marine guard and the whole of *Nelson*'s ship's company at divisions. After a private discussion between Badoglio, Eisenhower and Bedell Smith, everybody sat round the table in Willis' dining cabin and put their signatures to the 'Longer Instrument'. But, to ABC's disgust, the disposal of the Italian fleet was again left unsettled and a clause had to be added later to the Cunningham-de Courton Agreement.

The first British troops entered Naples on 1 October. The object of AVALANCHE, the capture of Naples, had been accomplished in twenty-one days. The Western Naval Task Force was dissolved at noon on 6 October and Admiral Hewitt's appointment lapsed. Naval operations off the west coast of Italy became the responsibility of Rear-Admiral Morse, flying his flag ashore in Naples.

Meanwhile, there was news from home that Dudley Pound was ill. This was bound to affect ABC's future. As he said, 'It would be false modesty to suggest that I was not intimately concerned, for more than once he had asked me whether he

536

should not resign and allow me to relieve him. I had always pressed him to stay on.'

Pound had gone to the Quebec Conference with Mr Churchill who had noticed what an uncharacteristically subdued part Pound had played in the proceedings. But it was not until Pound refused an invitation to go fishing, which Churchill knew he adored, that Churchill realised all was not well.

A few days later Pound came to Churchill and told him he had had a stroke. His right side was largely paralysed. He had hoped it would get better. Instead it was getting worse every day and he was no longer fit for duty.

Churchill accepted Pound's resignation at once and invited him to join his table for meals on the journey home in the battlecruiser *Renown*. But Pound said he would prefer to have his meals in his cabin with his staff.

From Quebec Mr Churchill had cabled to Vice-Admiral Sir Neville Syfret, the Vice-Chief of the Naval Staff, placing him in charge pending the appointment of a new First Sea Lord. Pound tendered his formal written resignation on the train to London after *Renown* had reached Plymouth. Mr Churchill now had to find a successor.

The obvious choice, proposed by the First Lord of the Admiralty, Mr A.V. Alexander, was Cunningham. But Churchill argued that Cunningham could not be spared from the Mediterranean, where so many operations were going forward.

Churchill's own choice was Admiral Sir Bruce Fraser, the C-in-C, Home Fleet. 'I have most carefully considered the question of filling Pound's vacancy,' he wrote to A.V. Alexander, the First Lord, on 9 September 1943, 'and I have no doubt whatever that we should offer it to Admiral Fraser.

[Cunningham] is an officer of the old school and the pre-air age. This epoch finishes with Pound's four years of splendid service. We must move forward to younger men.'

But when Fraser was summoned down from Scapa Flow and offered the post, Churchill was surprised and somewhat taken aback when Fraser refused. Fraser said he would of course serve wherever he was sent, but he thought that Cunningham was the right man. Fraser said he told Churchill, "'I think I have the confidence of my Fleet, but Cunningham has the confidence of the whole Navy. I haven't even fought a battle yet. If one day I should sink the *Scharnhorst*, I might feel differently." He more or less sat back at that, and said "Thank you very much". And then he decided, when I wouldn't take it, that he would ask Cunningham.'

It was true that much was happening in the Mediterranean where an able hand was needed to guide affairs. The recent crisis at Salerno had demonstrated that. But it is possible that Churchill hesitated to appoint ABC because of memories of sharp exchanges of signals in the past, and he might also have been reluctant to have such a strong character at home.

ABC certainly had reason to think so. Much later, he recorded in his diary for 19 February 1946 a conversation with A.V. Alexander. The First Lord, he said, was

> rather interesting and discussed the late Prime Minister's [Attlee was by then Prime Minister] fear of the Board of Admiralty. Churchill was apparently frightened that my advent to the Admiralty would mean a very independent line and when finally consenting he said 'You can have your Cunningham but if the Admiralty don't do as they are told I will bring down the Board in ruins even if it means my coming down with it!' It's quite good to know that some of my signals from the Mediterranean went home.

However, it was equally likely that Mr Churchill quite simply thought Fraser would make a better First Sea Lord than Cunningham.

ABC had a message from Mr Churchill on 28 September, telling him that a relief for Dudley Pound was being considered and asking him if he could come home for consultation. ABC was well aware of what that meant and next day, when they were all gathered in *Nelson* for the signing ceremony, he told Eisenhower that he might be leaving and asked him if he had any objection. Eisenhower said at once that if ABC was offered the appointment of First Sea Lord it was his duty to accept.

Leaving Willis to act as his deputy, ABC flew home on 1 October. He did not record all the places and people he visited in the next fortnight, which he recalled as 'a sort of mental whirl'. But his main purpose was to be reassured that it was really desired that he should become First Sea Lord. 'I knew that the office desk was not my strong suit,' he said. 'My own feeling was that however grieved I might be at leaving the Mediterranean, it was my duty to go to the Admiralty if it were felt throughout the Service that I should go.'

ABC did receive assurances on all sides, from many senior officers, and members of the Board of Admiralty, in particular the Deputy First Sea Lord, Admiral Sir Charles Kennedy-Purvis, who had assisted ABC in 1938, and Admiral Sir Jock Whitworth, the Second Sea Lord. Admiral Sir Percy Noble, writing from Washington on 1 October, expressed the general feeling:

> Now I see that Dudley Pound has gone sick — he has had a long bout in a most trying position, and if he should be unable to go on, I assume that you will, in due course, take his place... That is what the whole Navy would like to see, but I

know that you personally would view the suggestion with some distaste! All the same, I think for the good of everyone, you ought to do it if it comes your way.

ABC and Nona, who had come up to London from Palace House, were invited to Chequers. On Sunday 3 October, Mr Churchill asked ABC into his study 'where we had a heart-to-heart talk. He expressed his deepest regret at losing Sir Dudley Pound, and asked me if I would take on his place. I accepted.'

ABC's suggestion that his relief as C-in-C Mediterranean should be Admiral Sir John H.D Cunningham (who was no relation), the C-in-C Levant, was accepted. ABC's appointment was announced on 5 October 1943.

As soon as he could, ABC had gone to visit Dudley Pound in hospital. 'He was gravely ill, and I knew he was dying. He could not speak; but recognised me and pressed my hand. It was a sad moment. I was at a loss for words.'

ABC flew back to Algiers on 6 October and began packing up to leave. Other preparations were being made for his departure. 'For several days,' said Oliver, 'at set times there were unmistakable noises of military ceremonial from the lawn beneath his office windows. When one of the staff enquired what was afoot, his US opposite number proudly answered "We hev a liddle *sur*-prise for your Admiral Cunning-HAM".' The '*sur*-prise' was a full ceremonial march-past in ABC's honour of American and other Allied soldiers with guards and bands, at the Hotel St Georges on 14 October, the eve of ABC's departure.

He left Algiers by air on the 15th. Everybody was there to see him off: Eisenhower and Tedder, admirals, generals, air marshals, British, American and French, every member of his staff, all the senior officers he had worked with over the last year, and more guards and bands. He said:

I was greatly touched. With that peculiar constriction in the throat which comes of deep emotion, I found difficulty in expressing myself when saying farewell to all faithful friends and comrades. We had passed through troublous times together; but had won through in spite of everything. I was leaving after serving for the second time as Commander-in-Chief of the Mediterranean Fleet, and I knew the Mediterranean better than any other part of the world. I was leaving my beloved ships, and the gallant people who manned them. It was a great wrench.

ABC's Union Flag was hauled down in *Maidstone* at sunset on 17 October. He made a farewell signal to his fleet:

I leave you all in the Mediterranean with keen regret; but also with pride.

It has been my privilege for the last year to command a great fleet of ships of the Allied nations of every category from battleships to the smallest craft. We may well look back with satisfaction to the work which has been performed. You have caused grievous discomfiture to the enemy. You have carried and protected hundreds and thousands of men and millions of tons of supplies. You have taken a vital part in throwing the enemy out of Africa, in the capture of Sicily, and, finally, in the invasion of Italy and the re-entry of the United Nations to the mainland of Europe. It is a high achievement of which you may well be proud. To you all who have fought and endured with such courage, tenacity and determination, I send my heartfelt thanks and appreciation.

ABC's departure was deeply felt by his staff. 'I tried to write before but the letter was such a depressed one — just after you had gone — that it had to be torn up,' Royer Dick wrote. 'It was a pretty severe wrench to watch your aircraft take off and to feel that the end had come to over four years of working for you. A time of such intense interest and variety and so much that one will be happy and proud to remember.'

The keenest sense of loss was felt by Power. In one of his last conversations, or rather confrontations, ABC said: 'You should go far in the Service if you'd stop being so bloody argumentative.'

Power replied. 'I'm more interested in winning the war than in promotion.' 'Of you,' ABC said, 'I really believe that to be true. You've certainly done more to win the war in the Mediterranean than any other single man.' The remark left Power, as he said himself, 'speechless — red-faced'.

Power stayed on, to join John Cunningham's staff. He was constantly struck by the differences between ABC and his successor:

> It would be difficult to find two men less alike than 'ABC' and John D. Cunningham. The former fiery, aggressive, active and intolerant; the latter quiet, thoughtful, rather lethargic, very kind but possessed of an acid tongue. 'ABC' scintillating, successful and inclined to be schoolboyishly boastful. John D. with an unlucky series of operations — Norway, Dakar and the Dodecanese — behind him very cautious, cynical and suspicious of adventure. 'It's all very fine,' John D. would say, 'but it may go wrong and then they'll say...' I found myself translated suddenly from reining in a champing charger to goading a reluctant draft horse. John D. liked a large staff. ABC thought they would spend all their time writing to each other.

ABC arrived in London on Sunday, 16 October 1943, and joined the Admiralty at once.

22: FIRST SEA LORD

DUDLEY POUND DIED on Trafalgar Day, 21 October 1943, worn out in the service of his country and the Navy. ABC attended the memorial service in Westminster Abbey on the 26th and went down to Portsmouth the next day to join the procession from HMS *Victory* to the cruiser *Glasgow*, alongside South Railway Jetty. After a funeral service, the caskets with the ashes of Dudley Pound and Lady Pound were committed to the sea off the Nab Tower.

ABC wrote his own generous and perceptive obituary of his old friend and colleague. He had no doubt that

> Dudley Pound was the right man in the right place. For four most difficult years of trial and disappointment he bore the brunt and responsibility of the war at sea. Fearless and outspoken, he stood like a rock against the waves of adversity. They beat against him in vain, leaving him unshaken and unmoved, even in the face of criticism in Parliament and press, some of it cruelly unjust and bitter, when the tide of the war at sea was running against us.

In unexpected contrast to his powerful leadership at sea, ABC himself was curiously passive as First Sea Lord. In the Mediterranean he had been master of events and men. He had made things happen. In Whitehall, he let things happen to him. By his own testimony; there were Chiefs of Staff meetings at which he made no contribution, or remained neutral on a particular subject because in his opinion it did not concern the Navy.

ABC admitted that the office desk was not his strong suit. As one of his staff said, ABC had 'a blank spot' for administration. His only previous experience of the Admiralty had been a few months as Deputy Chief of the Naval Staff in 1938-9. When he arrived in October 1943, he brought with him Shaw, his Secretary, but otherwise he joined 'the strong team' already at the Admiralty. They were, as he said, a well-oiled machine, although he felt it might be too inclined to run in a groove. All the disasters, difficulties and disappointments of earlier years had been borne and surmounted by Pound. The Atlantic U-boat was still very dangerous but was not the mortal peril of the spring of 1943. Victory was not yet in sight but it was only just below the horizon.

The war certainly did look different when seen from a Whitehall desk. As one who had always thought of nothing but how to inflict further damage upon the enemy, ABC found the Admiralty tempo very slow. Accustomed to taking and acting upon his own decisions at once, he was appalled by the number of departments and people who had to be consulted before any action could be taken. For ABC the war had hitherto been literally a matter of life and death. Here, it was more a matter of daily routine.

To some, ABC's impact on the Admiralty was like a Force 8 gale blowing in from the sea and gusting tempestuously along the corridors of Whitehall. Years later, ABC heard that, within four days of his arrival, one senior officer was seriously considering asking to be relieved. 'I have no recollection of what lapse on my part produced this unfortunate desire,' he said.

But to many in the Admiralty, ABC must have appeared somewhat reactionary. He criticised the new large destroyers being built, saying they had become 'carriers of radar and radar ratings' and, while they could detect any enemy at any range, they could do nothing about it because they lacked the guns. He considered the battleship *Vanguard*, building at John Brown's, Clydebank, a waste of labour and money, unlikely to be ready for the war in the Far East (nor was she). He disapproved of ships being provided with 'American' amenities such as cafeteria messing, laundries and soda fountains, on the grounds that the Navy had done very well without them for hundreds of years. He felt that RNVR medical officers in escort carriers were too ready to pronounce aircrews unfit for flying duty. He was sceptical about trooping to the Far East by air and not by ship, viewing it as 'partially a method of keeping up the number of the RAF after the German war.'

ABC could sometimes misread events. For instance, he believed the Admiralty were too cautious about the enemy's air power which, in his opinion, was not the force it had been in the first three years of the war. Norway, Greece and Crete, he said, seemed to have left their scars on the Navy. Yet at the very time he became First Sea Lord the Navy was actually embroiled in a disastrous little campaign in the Aegean in which six destroyers were sunk, and two cruisers and two destroyers damaged, precisely because of lack of air cover. Far from leaving scars, Norway, Greece and Crete appeared to have been completely forgotten.

ABC's routine was a daily round of meetings, paperwork and social functions. He confessed that the countless official luncheons, receptions and cocktail parties to meet this personage or that, the mass of papers and dockets flooding into his in-tray and the endless stream of people coming to see him, made it physically impossible to give proper attention to all the matters brought before him. He had to delegate much to his staff and accept their opinions. He usually worked in the evenings after dinner, except on Mondays, when the COS attended a War Cabinet meeting to review the progress of the war. ABC liked to be in bed before 11 p.m. unless prevented by a summons to a meeting with the Prime Minister, who was an inveterate late-night bird.

ABC relied a great deal on Vice-Admiral Sir Neville Syfret, the Vice-Chief of Staff and an old comrade-in-arms from the Mediterranean, and Captain Charles Lambe, the Director of Plans, who had been on the staff when ABC was Rear-Admiral (D) in the Mediterranean in the 1930s, to brief him and support him in his dealings with the other members of the Chiefs of Staff Committee — General Sir Alan Brooke, the Chairman, and Air Chief Marshal Sir Charles Portal, the Chief of the Air Staff.

ABC was not the intellectual equal of Brooke and Portal. This was one of the rare occasions when he confessed to feelings of inadequacy. He knew he had had almost no staff training and felt that he was at a disadvantage in expressing himself in verbal debate round a table.

He knew, too, that the others had had far more experience in dealing with politicians and especially with Mr Churchill. ABC therefore looked forward 'with trepidation' to the meetings of the Chiefs of Staff Committee, with Mr Churchill often present. 'I was well aware', he said, 'that Mr Churchill was apt to overawe and bear down lesser beings by the sheer weight of his personality and persuasion. He did not care to be contradicted or thwarted.'

Brooke and Portal, for their part, were curious to see how ABC, the great sea captain and leader of men, would shape up to the council table. They need not have doubted his readiness as a colleague. Brooke wrote, after the war,

Andrew Cunningham's arrival in the C.O.S. was indeed a happy event for me. I found in him first and foremost one of the most attractive of friends, a charming associate to work with and the staunchest of companions when it came to supporting a policy agreed to amongst ourselves no matter what inclement winds might blow. I carry away with me nothing but the very happiest recollections of all my dealings with him. His personality, charming smile and heart-warming laugh were enough to disperse at once those miasmas of gloom and despondency which occasionally swamped the C.O.S.

ABC did take time to settle in. On 3 November 1943, Brooke wrote in his diary, 'This morning's C.O.S. Meeting took a nasty turn in the shape of a long discussion between Chief of Air Staff and the new First Sea Lord. Neither would give in and I had a difficult time. I wonder if this is the first of many more of this kind?'

It was not the first of many more, indeed the great strength of Brooke, Portal and ABC in their years together as COS was the united front they presented to the world and especially to the Prime Minister. They argued amongst themselves but once they had jointly decided on a policy they stuck to it and backed each other up.

ABC claimed that he was rather nervous about dealing with what he called the 'civil side of the Admiralty'. He knew the First Lord, Mr A.V. Alexander, a Labour politician, well and had cordial relations with him. For Admiralty civil servants ABC professed the greatest admiration, 'tempered perhaps at times with the impatience of an impatient man'.

The civil servants and the First Lord started work at 10 a.m. which was late in ABC's view. He conceded that some had distances to travel to work, but after years of attending Colours at 8 a.m., he was normally at his desk by 9. As he pointed out in one of the many historical references in his memoirs (which show that ABC was much more widely read and knew much more naval history than many give him credit for), 'I am reminded that in 1801, when the Earl of St Vincent was First Lord of the Admiralty at the age of sixty-six, his hours for interviewing all and sundry were from 5 to 7 a.m.!'

ABC had no house or flat in London. Mr Churchill, when he was First Lord, had offered Pound a flat in the Admiralty, which Pound had declined, possibly because of Lady Pound's poor health, and had lived instead in a bedroom with a bathroom in Admiralty House, the First Lord's official residence. ABC took over this bedroom, with his Coxswain, the faithful Watts, to look after him and cook his breakfast on an electric heater. (The morning routine never varied. Watts: 'What will you have for breakfast, sir?' 'A boiled egg.' 'Three and a half minutes, sir?' 'Yes.' 'May I borrow your watch, sir?' 'On my dressing table.')

Despite Watts' expertise, this arrangement was very unsatisfactory, and ABC and Nona were delighted when Mr Churchill renewed his offer. A flat was converted and furnished at the top of Mall House, which had once been the First Sea Lord's official residence but had been given up between the wars. ABC and Nona moved in February 1944 and stayed there for the next two-and-a-half years, with 'two most efficient Wrens' to look after them.

In October 1943, the principal enterprise before the COS Committee was the preparation for the invasion of Europe, provisionally planned for 1 May 1944. ABC's main concern was the choice of the Allied Naval Commander, Expeditionary Force (ANCXF). Churchill chose Admiral Sir Bertram Ramsay, who was also ABC's first choice. Besides being an officer of great and proven ability, Ramsay had, uniquely among the officers available, just carried out what Churchill called 'a great overseas descent' in the Mediterranean. Ramsay was duly appointed ANCXF.

In November 1943, the COS prepared for a meeting in Cairo with the US Chiefs of Staff. The particular problem was the Mediterranean. The British saw the Italian campaign as the best, indeed for the moment the only, way of continuing to exert pressure on the enemy in Europe, whereas the Americans suspected that emphasis on the Mediterranean would prejudice the eventual landing on the Continent.

On 1 November, the COS agreed on a document entitled 'OVERLORD and the Mediterranean Operations', which was the official British plan, to be submitted to the Combined Chiefs of Staff. Its main proposals were: unify the command in the theatre; maintain the offensive in Italy until the Pisa-Rimini line was secured; and intensify measures to supply and place on a regular military basis the Partisan and irregular forces in Yugoslovia, Greece and Albania. To sum up, 'Our policy is to fight and bomb the Germans as hard as possible all through the winter and spring; to build up forces in the United Kingdom as rapidly as possible consistent with this; and finally to invade the Continent as soon as the German strength in France and the general war situation gives us a good prospect of success.' To this, Mr Churchill added, 'I cordially agree.'

ABC sailed with Mr Churchill and his retinue in *Renown* on 14 November, and the conference opened in Cairo on the 22nd. According to ABC, the numerous discussions between the Combined Chiefs of Staff were harmonious. 'We discussed the war in all its aspects and phases,' he said, 'and came to full agreement on all matters of moment without any difficulty.' It was decided that Eisenhower should be Supreme Commander for the invasion of Europe — a very wise choice, in ABC's opinion.

Others remembered some of the meetings as anything but harmonious. On the second day, differences between the British and the Americans flared violently into the open. Brooke strongly opposed the American proposal to discuss the South-East Asia campaign before agreeing on the plans for the assault on Europe and the overall strategy for the war against Japan.

Brooke forcefully advocated the cancellation of amphibious operations in the Indian Ocean and retaining the assault shipping for operations in the Mediterranean. He deployed a formidable weight of statistics to prove that no landing craft could be spared for even the smallest operation in the Indian Ocean until after Eisenhower's and Alexander's coming attack on the German flank in Italy [at Anzio].

The Americans listened with scarcely concealed impatience. King in particular was infuriated by what he saw as Brooke's repeated attempts to renege on Britain's commitments in South-East Asia. 'Brooke got nasty,' said General Stilwell (known as 'Vinegar Joe', and no anglophile), 'and King got good and sore. King almost climbed over the table at Brooke. God, he was mad! I wish he had socked him…'

Apart from his approval of Eisenhower's appointment, and his debatable comments about 'full agreement', ABC said nothing in his memoirs about what was discussed or decided at the Cairo Conference. Although he was present at every meeting, he gives the impression of being more of an onlooker than a participant, who was not greatly involved in the arguments.

After the Cairo Conference, Brooke, Portal, ABC, Dill, Ismay and Colonel Brian Boyle, Brooke's Military Secretary, flew to Teheran after a stop at Habbaniyah, an airstrip near Baghdad, which had been the scene of an action earlier in the war.

ABC had not much more to say about Teheran than he had about Cairo, except to comment in a letter to Doodles that it was the furthest east he had ever been; curiously, ABC had never before been east of Suez, not even to the Red Sea which had for a time been under his command. He did not think anything very much came out of the Teheran Conference. He called it 'useful', as an exchange of views, and for some information on the war in Russia.

In fact, the British Chiefs of Staff achieved a great deal at Teheran, largely thanks to Brooke. The Americans had agreed that, to prevent the Germans transferring reserves to the Russian front, the campaign in Italy should be continued until Rome had been captured and the Pisa-Rimini line had been reached. The date of OVERLORD was postponed to the end of May 1944. The timing and scale of ANVIL, the proposed landing in the south of France, would be settled only when the amount of assault shipping available for it was known.

ABC and Nona spent as many weekends as possible in Palace House, motoring down in a large Bentley which on a good day could cover the distance to Bishop's Waltham in an hour and forty minutes. The duty officer in the Admiralty would ring ABC at about 9 a.m. every Sunday morning, to give him the latest news.

On 26 December 1943, the news was the battle off the North Cape of Norway. *Scharnhorst* had sailed from Altenfjord in northern Norway on the evening of Christmas Day, to attack convoy JW.55B on its way to Russia. In a day of long and anxious manoeuvring in Arctic cold and darkness on 26 December, *Scharnhorst* made two approaches to the convoy but was surprised and driven off by cruisers each time. Finally, she steered south-east to return to Altenfjord but was intercepted and engaged by the battleship *Duke of York*, wearing Fraser's flag, the cruiser *Jamaica* and four destroyers.

Scharnhorst sank at about 7.45 that evening, after sustaining at least thirteen 14-inch shell hits, possibly a dozen hits from the cruisers, and eleven torpedo hits. There were thirty-six survivors, from a ship's company of over 2,000.

ABC had presented the wardroom of *Scorpion*, a new destroyer, with a picture of himself which he had inscribed 'Captain, HMS Scorpion, 1911-1918'. He was delighted that the new *Scorpion* had played a prominent part in the sinking of *Scharnhorst*. 'You should ring a peal on the old bell to celebrate it,' he wrote to Doodles. (The old *Scorpion*'s ship's bell hung by the front door at Coed.)

After such success, ABC felt that 'the year 1943 closed with the Navy in great heart. The U-boat menace appeared to be held and the enemy's surface forces had been severely handled. We had some reason to feel optimistic in the New Year of 1944.'

ABC's letters to Doodles continued to record family and personal events. He had had his head sculpted by Epstein, and his portrait painted by Ewart. Hilda Starkie was engaged and then married to Lieutenant-Commander Gordon McKendrick. 'We are delighted she has chosen another naval officer, but I don't think Drumshaugh are quite so pleased.'

ABC had been optimistic about the war at the outset of 1944, but the year began with a major disappointment. Operation SHINGLE, the landing at Anzio, took place on 22 January. The enemy was caught by surprise. The road to Rome lay open. But the chance was not taken. Kesselring acted swiftly and vigorously to move part of the Rome garrison to isolate the bridge-head. In a short time, the Allied troops at Anzio were besieged and remained besieged for four months, during which they had to be supplied and reinforced by ship from Naples.

Every ship used at Anzio meant one fewer for the invasion of Normandy, codenamed OVERLORD but still in the build-up stage known as BOLERO. The date had not yet been fixed, but it had to be as soon as possible after the end of May when there was normally fine weather in the Channel.

In February 1944, Mr Churchill pressed for Ramsay to be returned to the Active List before OVERLORD. ABC demurred. He held that there were points of principle and expediency involved, particularly as Ramsay had retired at his own request. There were only a certain permitted number of flag officers on the Active List and if Ramsay were restored to it, others' promotions would suffer.

Mr Churchill had thought the matter settled, and had actually mentioned it to Ramsay at dinner. Ramsay was restored to the Active List, but not until 30 March, which suggested that ABC and the other Sea Lords were still unhappy about it.

The Chiefs of Staff were now grappling daily with the arrangements and decisions necessary for OVERLORD. When ABC saw the 'gadgets' needed for Normandy, every one of them 'essential', he could not help drawing somewhat rueful comparisons with the past and wondered 'how we had ever succeeded in any of our enterprises in the Mediterranean with our poor, austerity standards of assault equipment'.

The Chiefs of Staff were already looking beyond OVERLORD, at possible strategy and operations in the Mediterranean and the Far East. There was disagreement with the US Chiefs of Staff on plans for both theatres. The Americans still wished to carry out ANVIL, agreed at Teheran.

The British were against it, because it would virtually end the Italian campaign. After some acrimonious argument, ANVIL was agreed.

There was a general cooling of Anglo-American relations at this time. In Washington, Admiral Sir Percy Noble had detected a marked deterioration since Cairo. He had no doubt where the main problem lay. 'All the naval officers in the Navy Department are scared stiff of King,' he wrote to ABC. 'Any directive issued from him is obeyed literally and little common sense is used very often in interpreting his wishes.'

'King does not understand that his subordinates all take their tune from him,' ABC replied, 'and it is the absence of co-operation and the wish to cooperate on his part, which spreads itself through the whole American Navy.'

However, ABC did concede that there was some justification for the American view that the United Kingdom had not been pulling its weight in the Eastern war in 1943. The problem was that there were strong differences of opinion as to what British strategy in the East should be.

ABC believed that the main British fleet should operation in the Pacific alongside the Americans. Mr Churchill and the Foreign Office believed that the centre of gravity of British operations in the East should be in the Indian Ocean and directed towards the recovery of former British possessions. For years, Mr Churchill hankered after, and argued strenuously for, enterprises such as Operation CULVERIN, the forcing of the Malacca Straits, leading to the recapture of Singapore. The remote Pacific islands captured by the Americans might have tremendous strategic value, but they meant nothing to the peoples of Japanese-occupied Burma, Malaya and Indonesia. In short, the Japanese must not only be defeated, they must be seen to be defeated.

This view was supported by the US Chiefs of Staff, and of course by King, who wanted no British fleet in the Pacific. The alternative, favoured by the Americans, was the so-called 'Middle Strategy', in which the British concentrated on the reconquest of Malaya, Borneo and the Dutch East Indies, basing their forces on Brunei.

Nevertheless, the Admiralty went ahead with preparations to send a fleet out to the Pacific. The vast distances of the Pacific, and the distance from home, meant that a Pacific fleet would require something which the US Navy had developed and refined but which was quite new in the Royal Navy's experience — a 'Fleet Train', of tankers, store ships, depot ships, repair ships, hospital ships and other miscellaneous vessels, to support the fleet at sea.

A Fleet Train would need dozens more ships, of merchant types. This brought the Navy into direct conflict with Lord Leathers, the Minister of War Transport, who argued, not unreasonably, that it made no sense to allocate large numbers of scarce ships to support a fleet which might never go to the Pacific.

There were many meetings and much wrangling before an agreement in principle about the Fleet Train was reached at a meeting at Chequers on Easter Sunday, 10 April 1944. But this was only achieved in the face of what ABC called 'strong opposition' from Lord Leathers. In his private diary; ABC was more blunt. One meeting on 3 April he described as 'a fine exhibition of slipperiness by the Minister of War Transport over the Fleet Train'.

ABC was equally uninhibited in his comments on others, such as General Alexander. ABC had never had a high opinion of him since the Mediterranean days. After Alexander had attended a staff meeting with the Prime Minister on 11 April,

ABC noted that he 'appeared at first to be much on the defensive over the Anzio bridge-head operations. Personally I thought at times he talked sheer nonsense but I am used to his manner. I cannot believe he is much use as a general.'

ABC had begun his diary on 1 April 1944, writing on the first page of what was to be a series of school exercise books with ruled lines. 'So many interesting things are happening that I think it behoves me to keep a diary.'

One of the earliest entries concerned Bruce Fraser. It is not clear when ABC found out that Fraser had been Churchill's first choice as First Sea Lord and had turned it down in ABC's favour, but find out he obviously did, and he seems to have been mortally affronted. ABC and Nona had previously been very generous with their hospitality to Fraser, a bachelor, as Fraser himself gratefully acknowledged, and their relationships had been generally friendly. But from the beginning of 1944 onwards there was a sour note in ABC's references to Fraser.

The uneasy relationship between the two first emerged in ABC's diary for 13 April, after Operation TUNGSTEN, the strike by carrier-borne aircraft of the Home Fleet against the German battleship *Tirpitz* in northern Norway on 3 April. The first strike was moderately successful, but did not put *Tirpitz* out of action. ABC urged a second strike. Fraser decided against it. *Tirpitz* would not be caught by surprise again. The nights were shortening. There would be no convoy at sea to distract the enemy a second time.

ABC most emphatically disagreed, and urged a second attack as soon as possible, before the enemy had had a chance to recover. He telephoned Fraser on his return to Scapa Flow. ABC wrote in his diary:

> I called up Bruce Fraser about repeat 'Tungsten', and found
> him in a most truculent and obstinate mood. He had held a

meeting with his admirals and captains and made the decision that 'Tungsten' was not to be repeated. I reasoned with him and pointed out that Cs-in-C's decisions were not irrevocable and that the Admiralty must be allowed some voice in what operations were to be carried out. He did not admit this and said if we were not satisfied we must get another C-in-C, and in fact indicated that he would haul down his flag if ordered to repeat 'Tungsten'. I told him to sleep on it and call me up in the morning.

I do not know what the underlying reason for this attitude is, to me a most untenable position to take up, but it may be that he resented very much being practically bludgeoned into 'Tungsten' originally and is determined to resist further pressure.

The next day, 14 April, there were further telephone calls, when Fraser seemed to ABC to be as intransigent as ever, again threatening to haul down his flag, but later ABC 'found wiser councils had prevailed in the Home Fleet and some manoeuvrings on a lower level [had] made Fraser more tracticable [sic]'.

However, whatever their disagreements over TUNGSTEN, ABC championed Fraser's cause as the new C-in-C Eastern Fleet, to relieve James Somerville, and as C-in-C British Pacific Fleet (if a British fleet ever reached the Pacific). Somerville was to go to Washington to relieve Noble.

These appointments had been decided as early as March 1944, but were not made without another passage of arms between ABC and Churchill, who was still not convinced of the need for a British fleet in the Pacific 'for a good many months to come'. But they came just in time. Relations between Somerville and Mountbatten had reached the point where Mountbatten was about to ask for Somerville to be relieved.

557

ABC had had a high opinion of Mountbatten as a dashing destroyer captain in the Mediterranean before the war, but when Mountbatten was appointed Supreme Allied Commander, South-East Asia, ABC's attitude towards him began to change. ABC had in any case a low regard for the concept of a Supreme Commander, much preferring a triumvirate, such as Wavell, Longmore and himself in the Mediterranean.

Admiral Sir James Somerville, the C-in-C Eastern Fleet, ABC's contemporary and *Britannia* term-mate, eighteen years older than Mountbatten and several substantive ranks more senior, also thought highly of Mountbatten and at first welcomed his appointment. Yet, from the moment of Mountbatten's arrival in Delhi early in October 1943, things began to go wrong.

The 'Mountbatten-Somerville Controversy', in which ABC found himself playing the part of a long-range referee, was a complicated matter, whose main cause was that Mountbatten's position as Supreme Commander was never clearly defined, and thus a basic ambiguity over who exactly was in ultimate command of the Eastern Fleet was never resolved.

The initial Chiefs of Staff directive of 15 August 1943 had made Somerville responsible to Mountbatten only for the amphibious operations which it was then hoped would soon be taking place in support of a second campaign in the Burmese Arakan. At other times, except for the few specific ships allocated for specific combined operations, Somerville would continue to control all maritime operations in the Indian Ocean.

Yet Churchill's directive to Mountbatten of 21 October 1943 promised: 'At least four weeks before your first major amphibious operation you will be furnished... with a battlefleet to be based on Ceylon sufficient in strength to fight a general engagement with any forces... the Japanese could afford to detach from the Pacific.'

It would have saved much heart-burning had the directive used the words 'the naval commander' instead of 'you' and 'your'. But the damage was done. Such wording convinced Somerville that the fleet would be entirely under Mountbatten's command. He protested, to Mountbatten and to ABC.

ABC, and even Churchill himself, attempted to clarify the situation, but their efforts still left the basic anomaly in Somerville's position vis-à-vis Mountbatten. Somerville was responsible not only for the waters included in SEAC, but also for the Persian Gulf, Aden and much of the east coast of Africa, which were all outside SEAC. In practice, this meant that Somerville could be responsible either to Mountbatten, or to the Admiralty, for any of his ships, depending upon where they were and what they were doing.

All might still have been well, with some give-and-take, especially on Somerville's part. But ABC continued to receive complaints from Somerville, on everything from the size of Mountbatten's staff compared with his own, to the ceremonial Mountbatten laid down to be followed for his visits to ships of the Eastern Fleet.

Somerville particularly objected to Mountbatten's setting up a 'MacArthur style' War Staff, preferring to use his own planners rather than those of his Commanders-in-Chief. Mountbatten, for his part, was so exasperated by Somerville's behaviour he appealed to the Chiefs of Staff who, however, gave him a cool response, telling him they had more important things to think about than the precise definition of Mountbatten's powers. The upshot, largely brought about by the peace-making of Captain Charles Lambe, who had just come out to take command of the aircraft carrier *Illustrious* in the Eastern Fleet, was that Mountbatten disbanded his 'War Staff'.

Bruce Fraser arrived on 22 August. Somerville struck his flag the next day, and left by air on the first stage of his journey home on the 25th. Significantly, Mountbatten later wrote in his Report that matters, i.e. his relationship with the C-in-C, 'improved beyond recognition in August 1944'.

Meanwhile, events at home were hurrying towards OVERLORD. AS D-Day approached, every harbour in southern England was crammed with ships and landing craft. The south of England became a vast armed camp and a giant vehicle park.

On May 15 1944, ABC attended a final conference and presentation of the OVERLORD plan at St Paul's School, West Kensington, which had been requisitioned as Montgomery's headquarters (he was actually an old boy of the school). The King, Mr Churchill, General Smuts, the British Chiefs of Staff and the commanders of the expeditionary forces all attended, with their principal staff officers.

ABC sat between Mr Churchill and the American Admiral 'Betty' Stark, 'with Eisenhower and Admirals, Generals and Air Marshals by the score,' he said. 'Never in all my long experience have I seen a conference chamber more crowded with officers and others of high rank. The meeting had naturally been kept a dead secret; but I found myself wondering what might happen if the Germans made a daylight raid in force and landed a bomb on the building.'

Montgomery forecast the probable course of events and the immediate task before the Allied armies. Ramsay described the Navy's contribution, pointing out that the soldiers must not expect always to be landed exactly as shown in the diagram.

Then 'Bomber Harris explained what a nuisance this Overlord operation was,' ABC wrote in his diary, 'and how it interfered with the right way to defeat Germany, i.e. by bombing. Sholto Douglas, Coastal Command, explained how he was going to sink all the U-boats apparently without any assistance from the Navy.'

His Majesty, Mr Churchill and General Smuts all addressed the meeting and wished the commanders God Speed in their momentous undertaking.

Ramsay and his Chief of Staff, Rear-Admiral George Creasy, came to supper at Palace House on Saturday 3 June. ABC noticed Ramsay was showing signs of strain. His great responsibilities were clearly weighing upon him. ABC himself had such a sanguinary and optimistic temperament that he would have had no such cares had he been in Ramsay's position. He could see no reason why Ramsay should be so anxious. His plans were as near perfect as they could be. Given reasonable weather, he was sure to put the soldiers ashore at the right place and the right time.

The weather was now the main worry. For weeks it had been hot, dry and settled, perfect for a cross-Channel invasion. But as D-Day drew nearer, the weather became more unsettled. Early on 4 June, ABC was not surprised to have a message from the Admiralty that the invasion had been postponed for twenty-four hours.

Next day, Monday 5 June, the eve of D-Day, the Chiefs of Staff went to lunch at 10 Downing Street, where they found Mr Churchill 'very cracked up about Overlord,' ABC noted in his diary, 'and really in an almost hysterical state. He really is an incorrigible optimist. I always thought I was unduly so but he far outstrips me.'

Understandably, ABC could not sleep that night of 5/6 June. At about 3 a.m., an officer working at the Chart Table in the Citadel was surprised to see the First Sea Lord appear in pyjamas, reefer jacket and seaboots. After enquiring about progress, ABC said he would be back shortly and so he was, fully dressed. He spent the rest of that night in the War Room, watching the cross-Channel convoys being plotted on the chart. He hardly left the War Room for some days, following every movement until he was assured that the armies were safely ashore.

The chief danger to the great mass of shipping off the invasion beaches was expected from the U-boats. For two to three months prior to D-Day, most of the operational U-boats had been assembling in the Biscay ports, leaving the North Atlantic convoy routes almost entirely free of U-boats. On D-Day itself, there were forty-five U-boats in port, thirty-six in western France, twenty-one in south-west Norway and only twelve at sea.

In May 1944 ULTRA Special Intelligence revealed that the enemy had carried out a trial with half a dozen U-boats in the Channel, which had shown the difficulties, despite the benefit of the 'Schnorkel' device in some boats, of operating in the confined shallow waters and fierce tides there. But the trial indicated that the German High Command was prepared to send U-boats into the Channel again, which they had not done in any numbers since the first months of the war.

By D-Day ULTRA had revealed that the enemy's initial plan was to concentrate U-boats against the Channel by sending them right into the operational area, by attacking convoys around the coasts of Devon and Cornwall and by establishing U-boat patrols in the Western Approaches.

However, by concentrating the U-boats in a small area, the enemy allowed the Allies also to concentrate their anti-submarine forces in the same small area. Forewarned, the Allies assembled massive surface and air forces, including twenty fully experienced hunting groups of frigates and sloops, and almost the entire strength of Coastal Command, for the heaviest possible counter-attack.

Like other German authorities, U-boat Command was caught by surprise by the Allied landings and no U-boats were at sea anywhere near the invasion beaches. But U-boats began to leave the Biscay ports early in the evening of 6 June, and thirty-five had sailed by midnight. Nine 'Schnorkel'-fitted boats from Brest and La Pallice were ordered to a position twenty-five miles south of the Isle of Wight, to attack traffic crossing to and from the beach-heads, and seven Brest boats without 'Schnorkel' were to take up patrol positions between the Scilly Islands and Start Point, to attack shipping around the south-western coasts of Cornwall and Devon. The remaining nineteen boats were disposed in a defensive line off the west coast of France, while eight U-boats in the Atlantic, including five 'Schnorkel'-fitted boats, were ordered to proceed at full speed to the Channel.

There were never more than four or five U-boats at any one time in the 'Invasion Spout' area, but the 'Schnorkel'-fitted U-boats proved very difficult to detect. Nevertheless, the U-boats failed. They were simply overwhelmed. They sank six ships in June, four in July and eight in August. But thirty-five U-boats were sunk in those three months. By mid-August, they were evacuating their bases in northern France. By the first week in September, the bases were almost empty.

Meanwhile, there were almost nightly attacks by German E-boats from Le Havre and Cherbourg, which were engaged by

MTBs and MGBs. In the small hours of 9 June, the 10th Destroyer Flotilla, led by Captain B. Jones in *Tartar*, sank one German destroyer, drove another ashore and badly damaged a third. This removed the only enemy surface ship force capable of seriously threatening the Allied invasion convoys.

ABC had been hankering to visit the invasion beaches. Early on 16 June, he and His Majesty the King embarked in the cruiser *Arethusa* at Portsmouth and sailed for France. 'The whole way across,' ABC wrote to Doodles, 'almost ninety miles, was like Piccadilly in the rush hour. Convoys of every sort, and hosts of little ships as well. Nearer inshore it was very like Gallipoli over again.'

They arrived off the British beaches at about noon. The King went ashore to see Montgomery, while ABC transferred to the cruiser *Scylla*, Vian's flagship, and had lunch with Portal and Ismay before landing at Ouistreham. 'We landed in a DUKW,' said ABC, 'an amphibious vehicle, which was great sport, and it was quite thrilling to feel her take to her wheels in shallow water.'

They climbed a lighthouse which was being used for spotting for ships' gunfire. ABC wondered why the enemy did not knock it down. The spotters in the lighthouse thought the same and did not welcome their visitors' presence.

It might be the middle of an invasion, but ABC still insisted on proper standards and was displeased to see senior naval officers wearing battledress. Tom Brownrigg, *Scylla*'s Captain, knew ABC of old, of course, and saw to it that all his officers were correctly dressed and that his ship was as clean and 'tiddly' in every respect as the war permitted.

Early on the morning of 13 June, ABC awoke to the sound of an air raid warning and some gunfire. One enemy aircraft was reported. But that day ABC recorded in his diary, 'So Crossbow has come at last.'

CROSSBOW was the codename for the Allied attack on the sites producing and firing German V-weapons — the 'V1' pilotless flying bomb, which became known to Londoners as the 'doodle bug', or 'buzz bomb', because of the characteristic sound of its jet engine. The first V1s had been dispatched prematurely, as a reaction to Allied successes in Normandy. The main offensive, called '*Vergeltung*' (Retribution) began on 15 June 1944.

The V1s were small targets, very difficult to spot, and they flew at speeds of up to 400 miles an hour, faster than all but the most modern fighters, and at a height of about 3,000 feet. They carried about a ton of explosive.

There were more than two hundred V1s in the first twenty-four hours, and over three thousand in the next five weeks. London was the main target, but V1s fell all along the route between London and the south coast.

On 19 June, after 'not a very pleasant night' for ABC, a special meeting was held to discuss means of combating the V1s. Mr Churchill, who was in very good form because he felt that the V1s were putting everybody in the front line, said that the populace should be told that they ought to be glad to share in the soldiers' dangers.

That was as may be, but ABC continued to record some ominous statistics: casualties were already nearing 5,000, and some 136,000 houses had been destroyed. 'Another unpleasant night,' ABC wrote on 20 June. 'One flying bomb came roaring overhead and one found oneself waiting and listening for the engine to stop. I fear my nerves are not so good as they used to be! Old Age!' (The V1s had a small air-driven propellor which, when it had revolved the set number of times corresponding to the distance from the launching site to London, caused the controls to be tripped. The engine stopped dead and, in the eerie expectant silence which followed, the bomb plunged to the ground.)

After a few nights of 'sticking it out' in his flat at the Admiralty, ABC went down almost nightly to his cabin under the Citadel, while Nona and the two Wrens went to their bomb-proof quarters in the Admiralty. 'There is no question,' he wrote on 27 June, 'the London people do not like the uncertainty. The flying bombs may arrive at any moment day or night.'

The V1s were defeated in the end by a combination of fighters, guns, shells with proximity fuses, accurate radar, and balloon barrages. Their activities finally ceased in the first week of September 1944, when their launch sites in northern France were overrun by the advancing Allied armies. By then, over 8,500 V1s had been launched against London, and about 2,400 got through the defences. The total civilian casualties were over 6,000 killed and nearly 18,000 seriously injured. About three quarters of a million houses were destroyed or damaged.

On 8 September, only just after the V1 was defeated, the first two V2 rockets fell on London. Some 1,300 rockets were launched against England, of which about 500 landed in London, in the next seven months, before the advancing armies reached the launch sites, which were mostly around the Hague in Holland.

On average, each rocket caused about twice as many casualties as a flying bomb, because it gave no warning of its arrival, whereas the V1 could be heard from some way off, giving time to take cover. But, curiously, the rockets aroused far less apprehension than the flying bombs. The rockets, ABC said, 'actually came as something of a relief. They arrived at such a terrific speed that there was no minute or so of anticipation. The first thing one knew was the explosion, when one had either had it or escaped. My wife and I and our little household ceased to use the underground air raid shelters, and slept soundly in our beds in the Archway flat.'

ABC kept a sharp eye on the Navy's doings world-wide, and was quick to punish incompetence. On 8 August 1944, the Admiralty Floating Dock in Trincomalee, the large harbour in the north of Ceylon [Sri Lanka], suddenly collapsed with the battleship *Valiant* inside it. *Valiant* was badly damaged, with three of her four 'A' brackets (which supported the propeller shafts outside the hull) crushed. She had to go home round the Cape of Good Hope for refit and took no further part in the war.

ABC was suspicious, and his suspicions were confirmed when the docket on the accident reached him some months later. There had been what seemed to ABC a cover-up, with the three officers most closely concerned only receiving Their Lordships' displeasure:

> Here is a valuable capital ship put out of action for many months and a valuable floating dock completely lost, through the gross neglect and omissions of various officials and it is proposed that expressions of Their Lordships' displeasure in various degrees is a suitable penalty.
>
> It is indeed a mercy that the neglect of these officers did not result in a much greater disaster i.e. the total loss of the *Valiant* and a large number of her ship's company.

ABC ordered the Constructor Captain responsible to be relieved forthwith and stripped of the acting rank of Chief Constructor. The Constructor Commander involved was to revert to his proper rank of Inspector of Shipwrights, and the

Captain of the Dockyard 'merited Their Lordships' displeasure'.

ABC's diary entries, recording his discussions with visitors, show his ruthless conservatism. In July 1944, Lyster 'came in and we talked of carriers and fishing'. There was, it seemed, a problem with aircrew fatigue. The US Navy realised that carrier air groups tended to lose their offensive spirit and flying efficiency after prolonged operations, and relieved them with fresh air groups after a set period. By contrast, British air groups joined their carriers after commissioning and remained in the ships indefinitely, sometimes until they (literally) dropped.

The American practice did not appeal to ABC. To him, it smacked too much of the RAF. 'As I thought,' he said, of his talk with Lyster, 'our Fleet Air Arm pilots are getting contaminated by the RAF and want leave after so many operational hours. And I suppose a carrier with a crew of 1,500 lies idle while these temperamental young men go on leave.' Evidently it did not occur to ABC that there was no need for the carrier to lie idle. Fresh aircrew could have been flown on board.

His dealings often had a brutal directness. Captain Slattery, whom ABC had summarily relieved of his command of *Cleopatra* in the Mediterranean in 1942, came to see him, hoping for a sea appointment.

> I told him quite plainly that he would not go to sea in command of a ship again. He was much too valuable to the Fleet Air Arm in his present job [Chief Naval Representative at the Ministry of Aircraft Production] and at sea it was probable that he would only be a moderately successful captain. Judging by his showing in *Cleopatra* in 1942 it is very

doubtful if he would even reach that standard. He is a nice fellow and took his disappointment well.

By contrast, ABC never lost his mischievous sense of humour. After the Quebec Conference, the Chief of the Canadian Air Staff lent his aircraft to fly ABC to New York, there to embark in the *Queen Mary*, accompanied by Captain Guy Grantham and the female Admiralty and War Cabinet secretaries. While waiting to take off, ABC told the girls they were sure to be sick, and began ostentatiously feeling below his seat. When asked if he were looking for something, he said he was 'looking for that damned paper bag to be sick into!' The thoughtful silence which followed was broken when he added: 'Grantham, when I was a young lieutenant I was in the Sail Training Squadron. Do you know what the sailors had to do if they felt sick when they were out on yard?' Grantham tried to avoid replying but eventually had to say, 'No, Sir?' 'They had to be sick into their caps and put them back on their heads again!' That, Grantham said, 'finished the girls off'.

The great port of Antwerp fell to the Allies on 4 September 1944 with almost all its facilities intact. Amidst what ABC called 'the paean of triumph at its capture,' he himself provided the still small voice which pointed out that Antwerp by itself was worthless. It lay fifty miles from the sea and the Germans still held the approaches. ABC impressed on the other Chiefs of Staff 'that Antwerp though completely undamaged was as much good to us as Timbuctoo unless the entrance and other forts were silenced and the banks of the Scheldt occupied'. The powerful defences on South Beveland and Walcheren, on the north bank of the Scheldt, would have to be overwhelmed and the mines cleared from the fairways before Antwerp could be used for shipping.

So it proved. An amphibious assault, with bombardment support from *Warspite*, was launched on Walcheren on 1 November 1944. After a short campaign, with many casualties, enemy resistance ended on the 9th. Minesweeping began at once but the first ships did not berth in Antwerp until 26 November, some twelve weeks after its capture.

Although the strategy for the Pacific had not been settled, Fraser's appointment as C-in-C Eastern Fleet had been confirmed. On 5 July he came to see ABC and said that he saw no point in going out to his new command until the policy was settled. 'I disagreed with him,' said ABC, 'and told him so and took him off to tea.'

23: A STRATEGY FOR THE FAR EAST

THE FUTURE BRITISH strategy in the Far East was one of the two main subjects discussed when the US Joint Chiefs of Staff came to London in June 1944. ABC and the other Chiefs of Staff went to Euston Station to meet them off the train from Holy head. 'Marshall was as charming as ever, and King as saturnine,' ABC noted in his diary. 'I cannot bring myself to like that man.'

The other main subject was operations to assist OVERLORD. The Americans favoured the landing in southern France, ANVIL, instead of continuing with the campaign in Italy. Mr Churchill was obstinately and vehemently against it, but the Americans felt so strongly about it that he eventually gave way, albeit with a very bad grace.

ABC was hardly concerned about ANVIL. 'It was no debating point for a sailor,' he said. Renamed DRAGOON, the operation took place on 15 August 1944. It was, as ABC said, 'entirely successful'.

The second issue, British strategy in the Far East, did concern ABC deeply. He had never deviated from his opinion that a British contribution must be in the main thrust against the heart of Japan. A British fleet must operate in the central Pacific. He was therefore irritated to find Mr Churchill still harking on the Indian Ocean strategy, 'this island idiocy,' ABC called it; 'i.e. seizing an island and bombing Singapore from it.'

The Combined Chiefs of Staff Committee discussed the Pacific at length. The Americans agreed with a proposal that the British strategy should be based in North-Western Australia and directed towards Borneo. King had no objection to that, although he preferred the British and Australians to go for Sourabaya. ABC had no doubt why King was so in favour: 'He seemed quite determined to keep the Royal Navy out of the Pacific.'

Fraser came to tea again late in July, before he left for the Far East. ABC noted that he 'seems resigned to going out before the strategy is settled'.

The great strategy debate rumbled on through the summer and autumn of 1944. Of the seemingly interminable wrangling, ABC commented that the 'trouble is that the Prime Minister can never give way gracefully. He must always be right and if forced to give way gets vindictive and tries by almost any means to get his own back.'

Always, ABC tried to keep his temper with Churchill, to make allowances for the tremendous pressures on him, and to present as reasonable a front as possible. By and large, he succeeded, with the help of his diary which he used as a safety valve to vent his frustration.

At the Cabinet meeting on Monday 14 August, the Deputy Prime Minister presided. 'Such a change with Attlee in the chair,' ABC commented. 'Everyone who wished to gave his opinion and yet business was expeditiously accomplished.'

After an exhausting week, the Chiefs of Staff let the Vice-Chiefs take the Saturday meeting, whilst they took the day off. ABC drove down to Palace House, where he relieved his fraught feelings by wrestling with the motor mower. On Sunday, there was good news from the Admiralty: four Canadian and one British destroyer had sunk three enemy trawlers off Brest, and the cruiser *Diadem* and two destroyers sank a 7,000-ton ship near La Rochelle. Encouraged, ABC set about scything nettles under the walnut trees in the Palace ruins which, he discovered, soldiers in billets near by had been using as latrines in that summer's drought.

Mountbatten was in London that August of 1944, to try and settle future strategy and operations in Burma. He had two proposals: an advance by the 14th Army to Mandalay and eventually south to Rangoon, and the capture of Rangoon (codenamed DRACULA) by an amphibious assault from the sea.

Mountbatten was encouraged by the Chiefs of Staff's response. Only ABC was sceptical. He thought the forces proposed for DRACULA inadequate and the amphibious assault nothing more than wishful thinking.

ABC was no intriguer and he grew increasingly distrustful of Mountbatten and more testy in his manner towards him when he discovered Mountbatten's manoeuvres. For example, Mountbatten had gone directly to the Chancellor of the Exchequer about increased emoluments for the forces in SEAC, and had made proposals at variance with those of the Admiralty 'He cannot keep his finger out of any pie,' ABC said.

One possible reason for ABC's growing criticism of Mountbatten was that he disapproved of Mountbatten's skill in attracting publicity ABC himself remained incorrigibly conservative about publicity. He recognised, in some undefined way, that good publicity was good for the Navy, but he seemed to believe that it could be left to generate itself.

On 30 August, ABC had lunch with the press baron Lord Camrose, owner of the *Daily Telegraph and Morning Post*, who asked what the Navy was doing. ABC replied, 'Nothing, of course.' Lord Camrose then 'tried to argue that we did not advertise ourselves enough. I told him that I was not prepared to enter into an advertising competition with anyone and that the greatest compliment that could be paid to the Navy was that it should be taken for granted and that so long as those that mattered knew the truth I was quite content.'

On 5 September, ABC joined Mr Churchill's special train with the other Chiefs of Staff and travelled up to Greenock, where they embarked in the *Queen Mary* for the passage across the Atlantic to the second Quebec Conference. During the crossing, the Chiefs of Staff had meetings with Mr Churchill, when he was not in the best of tempers. At one, according to ABC, the Prime Minister was 'in his worst mood, accusing the Chiefs of Staff of ganging up against him and keeping papers from him and so on. He would not see that Italy after Kesselring is again defeated is a secondary front and the real work is on the Russian and Western Fronts. The worst of it is his feeling against the Americans whom he accused of doing the most awful things against the British.' Mr Churchill ended that meeting saying: 'Here we are within 72 hours of meeting the Americans and there is not a single point that we are in agreement over.'

Queen Mary arrived in Halifax on 10 September and the whole party went ashore after lunch to a special train to take them to Quebec where they arrived next morning. The President and Mrs Roosevelt had already arrived, and the Governor-General, the Earl of Athlone, and the Prime Minister of Canada, Mr Mackenzie King, were just arriving.

Conferences began at once, but ABC had a shock that evening when he received two cables from Nona. The first said that Doodles, his Aunt Helen, was very ill, the second that she had died during the night. 'Ever since my midshipman's days I had written to her every week, and she to me,' ABC said. 'Poor old lady. How we shall miss her. I thought her valiant and indomitable spirit would hold her up till the war was won but it was not to be. She was before her time and in some ways rather a wasted life for one of her advanced ideas, intelligence and courage.'

However, everything else went well. Next day, the US Joint Chiefs of Staff were 'in a most accommodating mood' and the first meetings brought full agreement on all the points that matter. Even the Prime Minister, ABC said, 'was in a mood of sweet reasonableness'.

The first plenary session on 13 September opened in what Mr Churchill called 'a blaze of friendship.' He reviewed the progress of the war in general, and went on to discuss a British fleet in the Pacific. He then surprised all three of his Chiefs of Staff by offering Roosevelt the British main fleet for operations against Japan in the central Pacific, under American supreme command.

After all Mr Churchill had said in previous months about the British fleet only being used to force the Malacca Strait and recapture Singapore and other British possessions in the Far East, ABC could hardly believe what he was hearing.

To ABC's great joy, the President interrupted to say, 'No sooner offered than accepted!'

Mr Churchill appeared not fully to realise at first the significance of what Mr Roosevelt had said and did not react immediately, but went on to say that a British fleet in the Pacific would not prevent the formation of a Task Force to work with General MacArthur in the South-West Pacific.

There was then some discussion on the contribution the RAF could make to the bombardment of Japan, before Mr Churchill returned to the subject of the British fleet and asked if he could have a more definite undertaking about its employment in the main operations against Japan. The President said that he would like to see the British fleet 'wherever and whenever possible'.

Here King intervened, as everyone in the British party had expected, to say that the question was being actively studied and a paper had been prepared for reference to the Combined Chiefs of Staff. But Mr Churchill again pressed the point. The offer of a British fleet has been made. Is it accepted? The President said: 'It is.'

Nobody expected King to let the matter rest there. Later that day, the British Chiefs of Staff received a memorandum from the Joint Chiefs of Staff welcoming a balanced and self-sufficient British naval task force in the Pacific to participate in the main operations against Japan, operating initially on the western flank of the advance in the South-West Pacific. The US Chiefs of Staff repeated their acceptance of the British proposal to form a British Empire task force in the South-West Pacific, though the timing of the formation of it would depend on the end of the war in Europe, on DRACULA and on projected operations in the South-West Pacific.

This memorandum had obviously been composed before the President's remarks of that morning, so the British Chiefs of Staff wanted to be sure that the situation really had changed and that the Prime Minister's offer of a British fleet had been fully accepted. They therefore raised the subject at a Combined Chiefs of Staff meeting the next morning.

Sir Alan Brooke opened by saying that the British Chiefs of Staff were disturbed by the statement of the United States Chiefs of Staff [in the memorandum] with regard to British participation in the war against Japan. He said he realised that the paper had been written before the plenary session on the previous day. He felt that it did not entirely coincide with the proposal put forward at that conference and accepted by the President.

Admiral Leahy asked if Sir Alan Brooke's point would be met if the words 'they consider that the initial use of such a force should be on the western flank of the advance in the South-West Pacific' were omitted. He said it might be that the British fleet would be used initially in the Bay of Bengal.

ABC said that the main fleet would not be required in the Bay of Bengal. There were already more British forces there than were required. He agreed to the deletion proposed by Admiral Leahy.

ABC was asked what was meant by the term 'balanced force'. He said that the British had in mind a force of some four battleships, five to six large carriers, twenty light fleet carriers and convoy escort carriers, and an appropriate number of cruisers and destroyers. ABC said this was what he would regard as a balanced force.

King intervened to stress that these forces must be self-supporting. ABC replied that if these forces had their Fleet Train, they could operate unassisted for several months, provided they had the necessary rear bases — probably in Australia.

It was now clear to all that a major nautical storm was brewing, with King and ABC as the main protagonists, and Leahy trying to pour oil on the waters.

The official minutes give some inkling of the argument, though not the full force of its animosity. ABC later recalled that stormy meeting:

> All went well till the use of the British Navy in the Central Pacific was raised. King flew into a temper. It couldn't be allowed there. He wouldn't have it and so on. I called his attention to the President's acceptance of the Prime Minister's offer. He tried to make out that the acceptance didn't mean what it said. Then he fell foul of Marshall on the Task Force

in the South-West Pacific and they nearly had words. King, having turned his guns on Marshall, was finally called to order by Admiral Leahy, with the remark: 'I don't think we should wash our linen in public.' In fact King made an ass of himself and having the rest of the United States Chiefs of Staff against him had to give way to the fact that the British fleet would operate in the Central Pacific. But with such bad grace.

The next day, the atmosphere was calmer. ABC noted that King seemed 'more or less resigned to having a British fleet in the Pacific'. However, he made it quite clear that the British ships must expect no assistance from the Americans. As ABC said, 'From this rather unhelpful attitude he never budged.'

The final plenary session on 16 September 'passed off happily' although ABC was distressed to see President Roosevelt looking 'very frail and hardly to be taking in what was going on'. He was also shocked by the appearance of his old friend Sir John Dill:

> He looked so ill that I besought him to give up and go home to restore his health; but this he utterly refused to do. This fine soldier and great gentleman died on November 4th. What he did for the Allied cause in Washington is just incalculable. The Americans well recognized his worth, and he was given an official state funeral in Arlington Cemetery and a special citation in Congress, most unusual honours for a foreigner.

ABC embarked in the *Queen Mary* that evening, 19 September. Mr Churchill and his party came on board the next morning, and the ship sailed at once.

ABC had lunch with the Prime Minister, Ismay and Lord Leathers on the first day out. Mr Churchill was in very good spirits and seemed thoroughly converted to the idea of a British fleet in the Pacific. ABC remembered this particular meal, of soft-shelled crabs and large beefsteaks, because during it Mr Churchill said 'that the fleet train for the Pacific must be done on a handsome scale and if we needed thirty-forty more ships we must have them!! Lord Leathers became somewhat pensive.' A great hollow laugh must have echoed down the corridors of the Admiralty. The provision of enough suitable ships for a Fleet Train in the Far East had been the subject of an ongoing war between the Admiralty and the Ministry of War Transport for months.

In October 1943 the Admiralty put in the first of a series of bids to the Ministry, for seventy-four ships, which by February 1944 had risen to 134 ships, including repair and depot ships; accommodation ships; maintenance ships; boom-defence vessels; store ships and carriers; distilling ships; hospital ships; tankers; tugs and miscellaneous small harbour craft. An alarmed Ministry replied somewhat obliquely, suggesting that a final decision should be deferred.

But fortunately an Inquiry headed by Sir John Anderson, the Chancellor of the Exchequer, to arbitrate between the Ministry and the Navy, reported in February and its findings were agreed by both sides. Most of the Fleet Train's requirements were met eventually.

ABC himself was somewhat sceptical about the number of ships required for the Fleet Train. With no advanced base and the main base in Australia over four thousand miles from the scene of operations, he agreed that 'we had, so to speak, to carry our shell on our backs'. Nevertheless, 'to the mind of one accustomed to the austere standards of the Mediterranean, some of the ships demanded appeared at first to be redundant, though the naval staff assured me that they were all essential. To fight alongside and with the same facilities as the

Americans, we had to some extent to adopt their scale of logistics, which was very lavish.'

The main base for the British Pacific Fleet, as it was called, was to be Sydney in Australia, where there was a magnificent harbour and extensive docking facilities, although, as ABC noted, the Australian Government 'were not too forthcoming at first'.

Fraser came back to London in October 1944 to discuss plans for his future fleet and meet some of his future staff. The fleet was to operate under Nimitz (although that had by no means been decided at that stage) and Fraser would be senior to any of Nimitz's sea commanders afloat. His duties as C-in-C would keep him in Sydney for much of the time. He would move up to an advanced base as soon as it was established, but that would clearly be some time in the future.

Meanwhile, a second-in-command was needed, to lead the fleet at sea. ABC suggested his old friend and proven sea commander from the Mediterranean, Bernard Rawlings, who was then Flag Officer, Eastern Mediterranean.

Rawlings had had a hard war and ABC wondered whether he was physically fit enough to undertake more arduous sea duty in the Pacific. He asked Fraser to call on Rawlings in Cairo on his way back out to Ceylon in November, and to report. Fraser did so and signalled at once that Rawlings was fit and well and he was delighted to have him. (Rawlings later told Fraser that he knew he was being 'vetted'!)

In October 1944 ABC was concerned by signals from the escort carriers about operational fatigue among the aircrews. ABC was sure the trouble was due to the ship's doctors, who he thought were too ready to diagnose operational fatigue.

ABC took the first opportunity to have a 'long talk' with the Medical Director General of the Navy. 'I put forward my view', he said, 'that the Medical Officer's duty was to keep them flying and not make reports that whole squadrons were suffering from operational fatigue and required leave.' ABC had the impression that the Medical Director General thought much as he did, but was 'rather frightened of some of his young doctors'.

At the Cabinet meeting on 2 October, Operation DRACULA, the assault on Rangoon, was postponed at least until November 1945. There simply were not the resources to carry it out. Mountbatten was understandably disappointed and many sympathised with him. But not ABC. 'I do not much care for Mountbatten's new plan, it seems to be sticking your neck out six months before you can bring forces to support it. He is as usual shouting for the moon.'

It did not improve ABC's relationship with Fraser that he supported Mountbatten. He thought Fraser spent too much time worrying about his staff. This was unreasonable and unfair of ABC. Fraser, after all, was going to operate what amounted to a separate Admiralty, 12,000 sea-miles from home. He would need a first-class staff if the British Pacific Fleet was ever to get into action.

Fraser was an instant success when he reached Ceylon. He felt it was essential to be on good terms with his Supreme Commander and did not insist upon any of the 'points of principle' which had so exercised Somerville. The atmosphere of antagonism and resentment between the C-in-C's and the Supreme Commander's staffs melted away almost overnight. 'What an improvement on his predecessor,' Mountbatten said.

The operations the British Pacific Fleet would carry out had not been decided. Fraser naturally wanted this settled quickly and he felt ABC was being unreasonably obstructive in turning down all his proposals. 'Therefore if I may be perfectly frank,' he wrote from Colombo on 14 November 1944,

> your signal summarily turning down all the proposals of Vice Admiral Eastern Fleet and myself has reacted most unfavourably. I had hoped to leave the Station in fine fettle both from my own point of view and from the fellows I leave behind, but the constant reverses one gets when I ask for things makes one mistrust one's own judgment. One cannot bicker with the Admiralty and it is obvious that I must now go and try to start things off in the Pacific, but one cannot continue as C-in-C unless one's inferiors think that he carries some weight (which I do physically I'm afraid!)
>
> I would be very grateful therefore if as soon as possible you would select someone whose judgment you could trust and advice you could follow, to relieve me and I will undertake any other task you desire.

In his diary, ABC called this 'an unpleasant letter from Fraser... I am in doubt myself if he is the man for the job the way he has behaved lately. He seems to think that he has only to put something forward and the Admiralty must agree. I decline to accept the idea of how things should work.'

However, ABC never seriously considered relieving Fraser. The main danger to Fraser's position was his old adversary, Admiral King.

On 12 November 1944 ABC had what he called 'rather a nasty signal' from King, which he feared foreshadowed trouble. It seemed that King objected to a signal from ABC formally nominating Fraser as Commander-in-Chief, British Pacific Fleet. King said,

This action sets up two naval C-in-Cs in the Pacific, which is an action not carried out in any other area or theatre of action, notably in the Mediterranean and in British home waters...

I contemplate initial employment of British Fleet units under Vice-Admiral Kinkaid, the Allied Commander of Naval Forces in the South-West Pacific Area. Subsequently employment to be under Admiral Nimitz and/or Vice-Admiral Kinkaid as operations may indicate...

This, ABC thought, was 'an attempt to try and put Fraser under any old American Admiral'. His answer to King was, he claimed, 'couched in sweet reasonableness but gave little away'.

However, King did agree to Fraser going to Pearl Harbor to meet Nimitz. From their first meeting, the two men liked and respected each other. Nimitz would have welcomed Fraser and his fleet at once. But that decision still rested in Washington.

At Pearl Harbor, it was agreed Fraser was to report his fleet for duty to King, who would assign the British either to Nimitz or MacArthur. The British Task Force Commander at sea would have the same status as an American Task Force Commander, but could be placed under American orders if the immediate tactical situation demanded it. The British would have an intermediate base anchorage and facilities at Manus, in the Admiralty Islands. The British would adopt American communications methods and procedures, just as American ships with the Home Fleet were already conforming to British practice.

Early in November 1944, there was discussion about replacing Sir John Dill in Washington with General Sir Maitland Wilson, the Supreme Allied Commander in the Mediterranean. ABC suspected an attempt by Mr Churchill to manipulate the Chiefs of Staff. 'Of course,' he confided to his diary on 4 November, 'the only reason for this is to get Wilson out of the way and appoint Alexander Supreme Commander in the Mediterranean, a post for which he is totally unfitted. We balked this in Cairo last year but it looks as though the CIGS and the Prime Minister have agreed this together. I may be maligning Brooke.'

ABC went down to Palace House for the weekend on 4 November and 'spent a profitable afternoon pruning the ramblers'. The next day, he was called to the telephone to be told that Dill had died.

The question of Dill's replacement now brought to a head, ABC voiced his objections about Alexander at a meeting on 7 November, but the 'upshot was the Prime Minister had his way'.

In spite of disturbed nights and the constant round of meetings and engagements, ABC's general health was very good, although he was troubled by rheumatism in one arm and shoulder. An X-ray showed there was not much wrong with the shoulder joint. An orthopaedic expert told ABC 'not to work it too hard and I'm afraid I just laughed at him'. However, a month later he went back to the same doctor who gave him a 'a rubber-tyred barrow wheel' to rest his shoulder on in bed.

ABC still had problems with his eyes. One visitor, Lieutenant-Commander Winn of the Submarine Tracking Room, found that ABC 'presented a startling and terrifying countenance since not only was he of ruddy complexion with bright blue eyes, but at that time the lower lids of his eyes had become so lax that they turned over and lay down towards his cheek bones showing the red lining exactly like the eyes of a bloodhound.'

As 1944 drew to a close, the employment of the British Pacific Fleet was still unresolved. The Australian Government had been assured that the fleet would reach Australia by the end of 1944. Clearly this promise could not now be kept. It was taking longer than expected to re-equip the four carriers' torpedo-bomber squadrons with American Grumman Avengers instead of Fairey Barracudas. There were also rumours that some of *Indefatigable*'s Seafire pilots were not 'match-fit.' With memories of aircrew being pre-maturely stood down from flying by what he thought were over-solicitous RNVR doctors, ABC was suspicious.

Fraser thought that any prospect of the fleet arriving in Australia by the end of 1944 was unrealistic. Furthermore, at Pearl Harbor, Nimitz had asked whether, on their way out to Australia, the British Pacific Fleet could carry out air strikes against the oil refineries at Palembang in Sumatra which produced much of Japan's aviation fuel. Fraser had been at pains to convince Nimitz of his fleet's worth. It would look bad if the fleet refused at the first time of asking. Eventually, as Fraser said, 'Everyone at headquarters gives in, when the man on the spot insists.'

But ABC had only given in with a bad grace. He noted in his diary a message from Fraser 'giving various alternatives, all delaying the fleet's arrival in the Pacific. The principal reason given being that Nimitz wishes Palembang attacked and it cannot be done in December.

'I confess I do not understand Fraser. There is no urgent desire to get to the scene of the action. It may be the climate but there has been dilatoriness in all his dealings particularly changing the carriers over to Avenger squadrons, since he has been in command of the Eastern Fleet.' However, to ABC's surprise, Mr Churchill fully concurred in the delay to the Pacific Fleet.

On 4 December 1944, the Board of Admiralty dined the Prime Minister on his seventieth birthday. During dinner, Mr Churchill told the Board that they must take the air into account. To ABC's horror, Mr Churchill finished by proposing ABC's health 'in very flattering terms'. ABC thus had to reply, which he did, assuring Mr Churchill that the Board 'did take the air into account, looked on it as our future principal weapon and would demand more of it'. ABC gave Mr Churchill a book of naval photographs. 'We were on "Andrew" terms at the end of the evening.'

The 21 December was the Cunninghams' fifteenth wedding anniversary. The same day, Hillie gave birth to a 'Miss McKendrick'. Christmas was spent at Palace House. Somebody's dachshund made a pool on the drawing room carpet and its owner allowed Nona to do the mopping-up. 'The young are pretty cool these days,' ABC commented.

Christmas Eve was a glorious frosty day. ABC made a large bonfire. The Prime Minister rang up to say that the President proposed a meeting at Yalta at the end of January and asked ABC to let him have a report on the place. But ABC knew nothing more about Yalta beyond the fact that it was in the Crimea.

On Christmas Day, they all drove over to Curdridge to visit Molly Somerville. ABC found her looking very white but on the whole better than he expected. Oliver, ABC's dog, disgraced himself by going for a large fluffy Persian tom. A cheerful Christmas dinner was washed down with 'Wehrmacht champagne' provided by Bedell Smith.

But Christmas was shadowed by an upsurge in U-boat activity. Midget U-boats were busy in the Scheldt estuary and off Ostend. On Christmas Eve, U-486 sank the troopship *Leopoldville* of Cherbourg; of 2,500 US troops on board, over

800 were lost. On Boxing Day, the same U-boat torpedoed two frigates searching for it, sinking one and blowing the stern off the other. 'He must be a first class man,' ABC noted in his diary. 'I hope we get him.'

On 12 December, ABC had attended a meeting of the War Cabinet. Later, the Chiefs of Staff, Eisenhower and Tedder dined with the Prime Minister. As they were leaving, at about 1.30 a.m., Mr Churchill called ABC alone into the Cabinet Room:

> He first asked if I was of Scottish ancestry, which I was easily able to confirm. He then said he had been looking into the precedence of the various Orders of Knighthood, and asked if I knew anything about the Order of the Thistle. I replied that it was one of the most ancient and honourable of all the Orders, and Scotland's own. He then said it was his intention to recommend to His Majesty that I should be created a Knight of the Thistle. It was so unexpected that I was rather at a loss for words; but realizing that the honour was even more a compliment to the Navy than it was to me, I thanked him warmly. I could remember no naval officer outside the Royal Family who had ever received this great distinction.

ABC's name was in the Honours List on New Year's Day 1945. He spent much of New Year's Eve at Palace House 'shifting frozen cowpats to the rose bed where I hope they will produce good roses' and then drove up to London. At a Board meeting on New Year's Day, Admiral Sir Charles Kennedy-Purvis, the Deputy First Sea Lord, referred to ABC's Order of the Thistle, and the news was greeted by the meeting 'with great and kindly applause'.

Letters of congratulation began to flood in, one of them from the Chancellor of the Order of the Thistle, the Earl of Mar and Kellie. The vacancy to be filled by ABC in the Order had been caused by the death of the Earl of Strathmore, the Queen's father. The Earl wrote to tell ABC of the cost of a coat of arms and recommending that he buy second-hand robes ('Get them off a dead knight,' the Earl said).

The congratulations were soon mixed with letters of condolence. On 2 January 1945, a Hudson with Ramsay on board crashed in France shortly after take-off. Ramsay and four others in the aircraft were all killed.

In ABC's memoirs there is little mention of Ramsay's personal qualities, although ABC claimed that Ramsay had been his friend for years. But they were certainly never close friends. In North Africa, ABC had frequently tested Ramsay's patience and forbearance to their limits. Ramsay 'was a fine sailor and a magnificent organizer', ABC wrote, 'with great personal charm of manner… For Dunkirk, Sicily and Normandy his name should be remembered.' ABC privately believed that Ramsay and Air Chief Marshal Sir Trafford Leigh-Mallory (also killed in an air crash) should receive posthumous GCBs or that their eldest sons should be made baronets, but no such awards were made.

ABC went down to Palace House on 6 January, where Churchill telephoned him refusing to confirm Vice-Admiral Sir Harold Burrough, ABC's nominee, as Ramsay's successor. Instead, Churchill wished to save staff by abolishing the post altogether. 'How he works in such complete ignorance and disregard for facts', an angry ABC wrote in his diary, 'beats me.' Disgruntled, ABC went out into the garden in the bitter cold to tie up roses, getting badly scratched.

On 8 January, ABC flew to Versailles to attend Ramsay's funeral at St Germain-en-Laye. It was very cold and the cemetery was covered in snow. ABC walked with Eisenhower in the procession. After a simple moving ceremony, all five who had been in the aircraft were buried together.

On 18 January, ABC had an appointment with 'the oculist', Sir Arnold Lawson, who told him he must have his eyes operated upon by a plastic surgeon. ABC then went to see Sir Harold Gillies, the 'grafting surgeon', and arranged to have his eye done on his return from Yalta. It would entail forty-eight hours in bed and then ten to fourteen days with a bandaged head.

ABC received the insignia of the Thistle, which he thought a 'fine example of enamel work', from King George VI at Buckingham Palace on 24 January. His Majesty talked for some twenty-five minutes and showed ABC the new medal ribbons.

The British Chiefs of Staff were to meet the Americans in Malta before going on to the 'Argonaut' Conference at Yalta. Brooke, Portal and ABC flew out of Northolt in an Avro York on 29 January and reached Malta in six hours, which for those days, ABC thought, 'was good going'.

ABC stayed at Admiralty House with John Cunningham. Somerville was also there from Washington, with Maureen Stuart Clark, who as a WRNS rating had been his personal assistant but who was now commissioned and his Flag Lieutenant — 'the things he says to the poor girl', ABC noted, 'are quite scandalous.'

Churchill arrived by air on the 30th and stayed in the cruiser *Orion*, in Grand Harbour. President Roosevelt was due to arrive in the US cruiser *Quincy*.

ABC was now weary of the seemingly endless round of conferences and social functions. His account of the preliminary meetings with the US Chiefs of Staff is perfunctory. They passed off satisfactorily, he said.

589

One dinner ABC did enjoy was given by John Cunningham at Admiralty House. The US Chiefs of Staff, Bedell Smith, Sir Alan Brooke, General Maitland Wilson, Admirals Stark and Hewitt and many others were present, also Lord Leathers, ABC's adversary over Fleet Train shipping, who was consistently described in ABC's diary as 'slippery' — 'Lord Leathers was his old slippery self.'

John Cunningham had brought out all the old furnishings that ABC and Nona had left behind in 1940. ABC had never seen the old house looking better. It would have delighted Nona's heart to have seen it again in all its glory, he said, for she was mainly responsible. 'Nona's ears would have burned at all the compliments.'

With Mr Bellizi conducting the C-in-C's string orchestra, it was like old times, and the dinner was a huge success. Sir Alan Brooke was profoundly touched by the atmosphere of Nelson's old headquarters. 'I felt swept off into the old ages, imagining him here with his romance and his wars.'

The Americans were also impressed. One Admiral, said ABC, 'looking at the tablet in the hall with the names of all the naval Commanders-in-Chief in the Mediterranean dating back to seventeen hundred and something, said to me: "It needs a British Admiral to live up to a place like this". I felt complimented, for here, in Malta, there was antiquity. There is something in tradition as it applies to the Royal Navy.'

President Roosevelt arrived on 2 February and there was a plenary session on board *Quincy* that afternoon. Once again, ABC was shocked to see how very frail and worn out the President looked.

Their aircraft took off from Malta early in the morning of 3 February and after a fairly comfortable flight during which ABC sucked on oxygen, they landed at Eupatoria in the

Crimea at 9.30 a.m. local time, to be received by Mr Molotov and various Russian admirals and generals. After a snack and a cup of tea in a tent, they were driven over the mountains to Yalta and then some miles along the coast to a villa which had belonged to Prince Vorontsov, a former Viceroy of the Crimea, and had been given by Hitler to General Manstein, commanding the German forces in the area, who had been so anxious to preserve his property that he had held on to it when every other house and villa was being blown up. Thus the house was more or less intact, even its library where ABC was interested to find a History of Hampshire with a description of the Old Palace at Bishop's Waltham, the ruins of which stood in the grounds of his own Palace House.

At Yalta, when the shape of post-war Europe was decided, much to the Soviet Union's advantage, ABC by his own account contributed very little. At the first plenary meeting on 4 February, Stalin said that the Allies had only to ask and the Russian Army would do all in its power to help. ABC was the only one who took him at his word and said that if the gallant Red Army wanted to make a striking contribution to the war at sea, they could push on and capture Danzig, where many of the latest types of U-boat were being built. It was intended as a perfectly serious suggestion, but for some reason it caused general hilarity. Even Mr Churchill laughed heartily, although he later congratulated ABC for saying what he had.

The Chiefs of Staff flew out of Yalta on 10 February, landed at Malta that afternoon and took off again at 1.30 the next morning. ABC spent an uncomfortable night at 12,000 feet, not sure whether his discomfort was due to lack of oxygen or over-indulgence in Russian hospitality, especially vodka and caviar. He drove to Bishop's Waltham from Northolt and then to the London Clinic on 12 February.

The operation on ABC's right eye was carried out next day. He found the Clinic very boring but was reading with one eye in two days. He was back at his desk a week later, looking out of both eyes, although 'the right one is not a very pleasant sight'.

ABC still had a stream of visitors. One was Lieutenant William Anderson, RNR, who had been relieved of his command of the submarine *Sturdy* and sent home for sinking a small Japanese coaster with women on board off the coast of Java in November 1944. Characteristically, ABC took the part of the man in the firing line and disapproved when the First Lord insisted on raising the matter at Cabinet on 26 February.

ABC also wrote in strong terms to Power, to say that he did not agree with his [Power's] summing up of the case, that he thought Anderson had been

> rather roughly handled and his Captain 'S' undoubtedly dealt with the matter very poorly. I think one has to take into consideration the situations in which these young Captains of submarines invariably find themselves, with full responsibility — and it is theirs alone — for the safety of their ships and the lives of all their men and, therefore, while I feel that Anderson acted on the whole very ruthlessly, I cannot find it in my heart to blame him.

In March 1945 there was an upsurge in U-boat activity, especially in home waters. Of fifteen ships lost during the month, twelve were in British waters or the English Channel. As ABC said, the Germans were starting to totter but clearly the U-boats were far from defeated and ABC sensed another approaching climax in the battle against them. He ordered six *Hunt* Class destroyers home from the Mediterranean and directed that no escort vessel that could run, even if only on one shaft, was to be paid off and that new escorts must be commissioned without paying off corresponding old ones. If necessary, reinforcements for the Far East and East Indies must be deferred.

On 6 March, ABC came back to the Admiralty after seeing *Private Lives* at the Apollo Theatre to find 'two infuriating signals', one from Fraser, the other from Mountbatten, 'the former ignoring the Admiralty and trying to be a law unto himself, the other allowing himself to be a catspaw to help the elements in the Navy Department who wish to prevent the fleet operating in the Pacific'.

The next day the Chiefs of Staff sent off what ABC called 'a pretty sharp rap on the knuckles' to Mountbatten for addressing the US Chief of Staffs directly. As for Fraser, ABC discussed with the First Lord Fraser's 'lapse' in making appointments without Admiralty approval and agreed to send off a 'pretty strong signal'.

ABC was now seriously concerned by the delay in deciding when and where the British Pacific Fleet should operate. At Yalta King had once again hinted at his misgivings about a British naval presence in the Pacific. There had been recent suggestions in the American press that the British Pacific Fleet was not wanted and was incapable of operating with the Americans. The British press were now demanding statements either confirming or denying American doubts about the worth of the British Fleet.

The British Pacific Fleet reached the fleet anchorage at Manus on 7 March and began a weary period of waiting, when the oppressive effects of tropical heat and high humidity were exacerbated by uncertainties about the fleet's future.

It may be that King succumbed to pressure from Nimitz and others who suspected that the forthcoming invasion of

Okinawa (Operation ICEBERG) was to be a far more difficult undertaking than anticipated; or he might have been influenced by a further spate of press reports that the British Fleet was about to be relegated ignominiously to a 'back area'; or he may simply have wearied of the whole argument. But, whatever the reason, on 15 March Rawlings was delighted to receive a signal from Fraser: 'In accordance with instructions received from COMINCH [King] you are to report Task Force 113 [the British Pacific Fleet] together with Task Force 112 [the Fleet Train] to C-in-C Pacific [Nimitz] forthwith for duties in operations connected with ICEBERG.' However, there was a reservation in the 'small print' of a second signal, timed three minutes later: 'COMINCH has directed that employment of Task Force 113 and Task Force 112 must be such that they can be disengaged and reallocated at seven days' notice from him.'

To Rawlings and the fleet, only the first signal mattered. Rawlings signalled to Nimitz that the fleet was reporting for duty and would be ready to sail at noon on 17 March, adding: 'It is with a feeling of great pride and pleasure that the British Pacific Force joins the US Naval Forces under your command.' Nimitz replied with typical generosity: 'The British Carrier Task Force and attached units will greatly increase our striking power and demonstrate our unity of purpose against Japan. The US Pacific Fleet welcomes you.'

The fleet refuelled at Ulithi in the western Carolines and, now designated Task Force 57 in accordance with US Navy procedure, sailed again and by dawn on 26 March was in position, stationed semi-independently on the left of the US 5th Fleet, off the islands of the Sakishima Gunto, south-west of Okinawa. The fleet's task, unglamorous and likely to be dangerous, was to prevent the Japanese staging aircraft reinforcements through the islands, which ran like a chain of convenient stepping stones between Formosa and Okinawa, by bombing their airfields.

Task Force 57 settled into a routine of two days of strikes, refuelling, and then returning to the flying-off position for more strikes. Despite difficulties and shortages, and several kamikaze suicide attacks, the fleet did very well, denying the enemy the use of the Sakishima airfields, certainly by day. When Task Force 57 reached Leyte on 23 April, it had been continuously at sea for thirty-two days, longer than any other British fleet since Nelson's day.

24: VICTORY

BY EASTER 1945, which fell at the end of March, the war in Europe was clearly drawing to its close, although ABC entered in his diary for 26 March that he had had rather a disturbed night with rockets and flying bombs. He had also suffered a violent nose-bleed and sent Syfret to represent him at the Cabinet meeting because 'I could not trust my nose.' But this was his last entry about V-weapons over London and on 20 April he attended what he hoped would be the last meeting about flying bombs and rockets. (A week later, ABC had his nose cauterised by 'a Dr Colledge of Wimple Street'.)

In March 1945, the Home Fleet carried out sorties by carriers to attack enemy shipping along the Norwegian coast, and to lay mines. One enemy ship was mined, but ABC was displeased with the outcome. 'The C-in-C Home Fleet [Admiral Sir Henry Moore] came in,' he wrote on 28 March, 'to explain why three carriers, a cruiser or two and attendant destroyers were used to drop seven mines. I remained unconvinced.'

ABC drove down to Palace House on Good Friday, 30 March. He spent Saturday at Broadlands, fishing with Sir Alan Brooke, but there was nothing moving. With his 'rheumaticky' right shoulder and 'tennis' left elbow, ABC found casting into the strong wind very difficult. Later, he saw a doctor about his shoulder and elbow and 'inferred it was old age'. He also had his neck X-rayed, revealing a certain amount of arthritis. 'Old age, I expect. One must just put up with it.'

On 10 April, ABC had a visit from Lord Keyes, who had just returned from a 35,000-mile goodwill trip round Australasia and the Philippines. ABC had never really forgiven Keyes for some of the adventures he had advocated in the Mediterranean, and he was unimpressed by Keyes' account of his doings in the East. 'There is something a little pathetic about these elderly admirals,' he wrote in his diary, 'who think they still have something to contribute but are really hopelessly out of date.'

On Friday 13 April, there was news of the death of President Roosevelt. ABC wrote:

> I cannot attempt to describe a world figure of immense stature, but we, who had seen a lot of the President in our various meetings, felt we had lost not only a wise ally but a firm and whole-hearted friend of Britain. We remembered how greatly he and America had helped us in the dark days when Britain was fighting alone; his fight against the desire for 'isolationism' among his own countrymen; his 'neutrality patrol' in the Western Atlantic which so greatly curbed the activities of the U-boats in our hour of stress and fell not far short of armed conflict with Germany before war was declared; the fifty destroyers we had been given in the autumn of 1940 in return for sites for the creation of American bases in the West Indies, Bermuda and Newfoundland; the plenitude of financial and military aid so freely granted under 'lend lease'.

ABC went to the US Navy's memorial service for the President the next day and then on down to Bishop's Waltham, to find that Nona had a bad throat, and an American lorry and trailer had taken the corner by the house too fast and fetched up in the moat of the Old Palace, removing most of the fence as it did so.

In mid-April 1945, there was a suggestion of assigning the South-West Pacific to SEAC or making it a separate command. Interestingly, if the latter ever came about, ABC considered that Fraser 'might do as Supreme Commander'. There was also what ABC called 'more talk' of sending the British Pacific Fleet to Borneo. When Rawlings arrived at Leyte and called upon Admiral Thomas Kinkaid, Commander of the US 7th Fleet, he was dismayed to discover that his fleet's future was once more in the balance.

King wished to invoke the 'seven days' notice' clause and allocate all or part of the British fleet to the South-West Pacific Area in support of the forthcoming Allied assault on Tarakan in Borneo on 1 May. This proposal was resisted by Nimitz and Spruance and, of course, by Fraser and Rawlings. MacArthur and Kinkaid were persuaded against it and the proposal was cancelled on 27 April.

The British Pacific Fleet was back on station on 4 May for more strikes against the airfields of the Sakishima Gunto, and continued until 25 May by which time they had been at sea for sixty-two days, broken by eight days at Leyte. All five British carriers taking part in ICEBERG were hit by kamikaze bombers, but their armoured flight decks prevented the very serious damage which the American carriers suffered. As the fleet retired to refit in Sydney, Admiral Spruance sent them a gracefully appreciative signal and concluded in his report of proceedings that the British Carrier Task Force was experienced and competent enough to take its place in the line with the Fast Carrier Task Force in future operations.

Operation DRACULA, the amphibious assault on Rangoon, was approved on 19 April, although ABC expressed considerable doubts about its feasibility, and it was carried out on 1 May, when the Japanese had already abandoned the city. In Europe, German resistance was collapsing. The Ruhr pocket was overrun by 18 April, with the capture of some 325,000 prisoners. As the Allied armies advanced, the horrors of the concentration camps were revealed. ABC had thought some of the stories exaggerated until he saw the pictures of Buchenwald in *The Times*.

ABC went to the Haymarket Theatre on 26 April to see John Gielgud, Leslie Banks and Peggy Ashcroft in John Webster's *The Duchess of Malfi*. ABC thoroughly enjoyed the 'wonderful cast and magnificent acting' and the 'full blooded Elizabethan language' which chimed with those tempestuous times.

On 30 April, there came the news of Hitler's suicide. The German armies in Italy surrendered on 2 May and all enemy forces in Holland, northwest Germany and Denmark surrendered unconditionally on the 5th. The unconditional surrender of Germany to the Western Allies and Russia was signed at Eisenhower's headquarters in Rheims at 2.41 a.m. on 7 May.

May 8 was 'Victory in Europe' — VE-Day. The Board of Admiralty had a meeting at noon when 'the principal business' was the demolition of a bottle of Waterloo brandy provided by the First Lord. At 4.30 that afternoon they all drove to Buckingham Palace to be present when His Majesty received the War Cabinet and the Chiefs of Staff. They had some difficulty getting through the excited crowds gathering outside the Palace. Mr Churchill, who was recognised sitting in his car and mobbed, had even more difficulty and arrived very late. The King made an excellent speech of appreciation and Mr Churchill responded with 'his voice full of emotion'.

From the Palace ABC drove to the Air Ministry for a cup of tea in Portal's office and then went on to the Ministry of Health, where Mr Churchill, the War Cabinet and the Chiefs of Staff appeared on the balconies. ABC 'had rarely seen such a crowd. Whitehall was packed from Trafalgar Square to Parliament Square.' Mr Churchill said a few words which sent the crowd wild with enthusiasm. ABC dined quietly at the flat with Nona and Alan, while outside the London night exploded with the sounds of fireworks and the constant cheering of the crowds.

The Navy had been ordered to 'Splice the Mainbrace' in honour of the victory. There was a plaintive signal next day from James Somerville in Washington:

> Poor B.A.D. can splice no brace,
> Because of rum there is no trace.

ABC made him what he hoped was a mollifying signal to the effect that Somerville was now promoted to Admiral of the Fleet.

The war in Europe was over, but the war in the Far East continued. On 15 May, ABC turned down Mountbatten's attempt to 'steal the light fleet carriers going to the Pacific.' But the same day there was very good news from SEAC. In a brilliant night action off Penang, five destroyers of the 26th Destroyer Flotilla under 'Lofty' Power intercepted, surrounded and sank the 10,000-ton 8-inch gun Japanese cruiser *Haguro* with torpedoes and gunfire. ABC, who had himself once described Power as having 'a genius for war', sent him a personal signal of congratulation.

The Government was dissolved on 23 May 1945. The King asked Mr Churchill to form a new administration, but it could only be a 'caretaker' one, pending a general election. On the 24th, the Board of Admiralty held its last meeting with Mr A.V. Alexander as First Lord. ABC made a short speech regretting his departure, knowing he must be careful in his choice of words, with the Financial and Parliamentary Secretaries to the Admiralty and the Civil Lord, all three Conservative MPs, 'sitting at the foot of the table'.

ABC had heard disquieting rumours that Brendan Bracken, the Minister of Information, was to be the new First Lord of the Admiralty. On 26 May the rumours proved to be true, and Brendan Bracken was appointed. 'I hope only temporarily,' ABC recorded in his diary. 'I dislike him, he is Winston's creature and this is Winston's way of trying to gain closer control of the Admiralty.'

ABC had his first meeting with Brendan Bracken three days later. 'He talked great sense,' ABC noted. 'I hope it was not put on for my benefit.'

General 'Bill' Slim, Commander of the 14th Army, was a welcome visitor. ABC knew, of course, of Slim's achievements in Burma, and his subtle and triumphant advance to Mandalay, and was keen to meet him. 'He impressed me very favourably,' ABC said, 'and I much liked his manner though we started with a disagreement when he said how SEAC had been neglected. I told him I knew they liked to take up that attitude. Anyway I liked him so much that I will certainly try and help him. I look on the capture of Singapore by the end of the year as the one big thing the British can do.'

The Fleet Train was still controversial. There was what ABC called 'a great fight' about the Fleet Train at a Cabinet meeting on 5 June. 'Leathers as slippery as ever and backed by Cherwell. The First Lord put up a good show and I backed him to the best of my ability. Finally the Prime Minister decided that the First Lord and Leathers under the arbitration of Anderson [Chancellor of the Exchequer] should fight it out.'

The Navy was represented at the meeting with Lord Leathers on 26 June by Brendan Bracken and the Fourth Sea Lord, Vice-Admiral Arthur Palliser, who afterwards bore a tale of woe to ABC, saying that 'The First Lord was a passenger and left half way through the meeting, being so occupied with electioneering that he pays no attention to Admiralty business.' ABC himself noticed the same behaviour at another meeting, to discuss the Navy's ship construction programme. 'He [Brendan Bracken] knew nothing about it. Everything except the programme was discussed and it was eventually put over on a wave of alcoholic verbiage.'

On 21 June Lord Trenchard wrote what ABC thought was a mischievous letter to *The Times*, in which he added the U-boats sunk by carrier-borne aircraft to those sunk by shore-based aircraft and claimed therefore that the RAF had won the war at sea. ABC and Brendan Bracken agreed at a meeting on 26 June that Trenchard's letter should be answered, but the reply was put off on 2 July because Brendan Bracken was still 'too busy collecting votes. He really pays no attention at all to Admiralty business.'

ABC always resented what he considered were the RAF's exaggerated claims. In June 1945 he wrote to Admiral Godfrey to commiserate with him on not being appointed Chichele Professor of History at Oxford. 'I am quite sure you would have made an excellent professor. I suggest you might start your historical work by a truthful and unexpurgated history of the real value of the RAF in the war. It would be a best seller even if the RAF bought up all the copies to burn them!'

What ABC called 'the final bill' for German U-boats, 3 September 1939—8 May 1945, was 785 U-boats sunk out of 1,200 commissioned: 246 were sunk by ships; 245 by shore-based aircraft; 43 by carrier-borne aircraft; 2 shared by shore-based and carrier-borne aircraft; 33 shared by ships and shore-based aircraft; 15 shared by ships and carrier-borne aircraft; 21 by submarines; 62 in bombing raids; 25 by mines; and the remaining 93 by other or unknown causes.

On 15 July 1945, the Chiefs of Staff drove to Northolt to catch a flight to Potsdam for the 'Terminal' Conference. Mr Churchill had, with difficulty, persuaded President Truman and Stalin to meet him in Berlin for one last inter-Allied conference, at which he hoped either to preserve some form of European independence or to convince the Americans that Stalin was not to be trusted. The Chiefs of Staff hoped to reach agreement with the Americans on Allied shipping priorities, on the Russian entry into the war in the Far East and on plans for the defeat of Japan.

The Chiefs of Staff were accommodated in a villa on the shore of a lake where they were besieged by clouds of mosquitoes. Each national delegation had its own zone, guarded by its own troops, but the whole area was occupied by the Russians who patrolled the lake and were liable to fire at anybody venturing upon it. Brooke and Portal, those indefatigable fishermen, went out in one of the villa's boats during their stay, but they were soon turned back by the Russians.

Once again, ABC's account glided over the actual conference. 'I need hardly mention all our conferences and discussions.'

Montgomery, who was also attending the conference, took ABC aback by calling him 'Sir'. 'A new departure, perhaps meant to placate.' ABC had in mind a recent incident when Montgomery inspected naval units in Hamburg and was reported to have ordered 'Splice the Mainbrace' — an order normally reserved for His Majesty. At further meetings, there were two main questions the British Chiefs of Staff wanted to settle: the British desire to take part in the direct attack on Japan, and the Supreme Command in the Pacific. ABC advocated the central strategy against Japan. This was amicably discussed. But the Supreme Command was more controversial. The British wanted some say in the control of operations. This the Americans were reluctant to concede. They were prepared to discuss strategy but insisted that final decisions must rest with them. If, for instance, the plan to invade the Tokyo plain did not suit the British, they could withhold their forces, but the Americans would still carry on.

On 22 July ABC went to Kiel, where he was impressed by the numbers of floating cranes, lighters, tugs and floating docks in the harbour — enough, he thought, to equip Portsmouth, Plymouth and Chatham. The massive concrete U-Boat shelters were still intact, despite the bombing. One of them contained about a dozen midget submarines and everywhere in the dockyard seemed to ABC to be littered with prefabricated sections of submarines. The cruiser *Admiral Hipper* was in dock, slightly damaged by Allied bombing, but much more badly damaged by her own crew who had dropped depth-charges alongside her. The pocket battleship *Admiral Scheer* was lying capsized in dock nearby, and there were many other damaged warships and merchant ships.

ABC went on to the German Navy's torpedo trials and research establishment at Eckernforde, across the Kiel Canal, where he saw a film of Dr Walther's revolutionary new type of U-boat, with a stream-lined hull and underwater speeds as high as 25 knots, powered by turbines and diesel-electric propulsion. ABC met Dr Walther himself, who demonstrated his hydrogen peroxide fuel, known as 'Engelin'.

The visit left ABC profoundly glad that the war had ended when it did and that no more than a few of these new U-boats had been built. Had U-boats with such high submerged speeds become operational in any numbers, they might have turned the Battle of the Atlantic against the Allies again.

On the following evening, the Prime Minister gave a dinner at the Palace where he was staying, attended by Truman, Stalin, Molotov, Eden, the Chiefs of Staff, Alexander, Montgomery and many others. There were what ABC termed the 'usual sloppy toasts. Leahy got very bottled and King very mellow, fell on my neck and besought me to call him Ernie!' Molotov was 'as oily as ever'. Truman 'looked and talked like a successful small grocer'. The Prime Minister 'was not at his best. I sat next to Zhukov whom I liked though we could not exchange a word. On my other side was Birse the interpreter and then Stalin. So I had a good look at Uncle Joe and did not much like what I saw. But he was in good form.'

General Marshall revealed to the Chiefs of Staff the existence of the atomic bomb, which had been tested in the New Mexico desert on 16 July, and told them that Truman and Churchill had agreed to use it against Japan on 6 August. The Combined Chiefs of Staff were not asked for their opinion, though, looking back, ABC said that

> I think it is fair to say that if we had been consulted we British would have been in favour of using it. The invasion of Honshu, the central island of Japan, defended by some 975,000 regular troops and 7,000,000 of the home guard, would have been a very tough proposition involving immense Allied casualties. Moreover, the dropping of an atom bomb and the resulting colossal devastation and casualties, would have given the Japanese a good excuse for surrendering, or at any rate a good point upon which to base their surrender.

Years later, ABC had changed his mind:

> looking back and being wise after the event, I think we rather failed to estimate the real significance of the heavy bombing attacks already being made upon Japan by shore-based and

ship-borne aircraft. Admiral Halsey's powerful American fleet with its carriers, and the British Pacific Fleet, were operating practically unmolested off the Japanese coast — bombing and bombarding. Hardly a Japanese city was out of range of the swarming Allied bombers; no coastal town was immune from shelling. With all these devastating attacks, and Russian action in Manchuria, I think Japan would have surrendered without either invasion or the use of the atom bombs. I consider now that it was a pity and a mistake that we ever dropped them.

The Chiefs of Staff flew back to England on 25 July. Next day, the results of the general election were announced. Polling day in the United Kingdom had actually been 5 July but the returns were delayed because of the problems caused by counting the postal votes of Service electors.

By noon on the 26th it was clear there had been a Labour landslide. That evening Mr Churchill resigned and Mr Attlee was called upon to form a Government. ABC attributed Churchill's defeat to the hardships people had undergone during the war, causing them to want to try someone else; the suspicion, which ABC thought not wholly without grounds, that Mr Churchill was becoming a dictator; dislike of Mr Churchill's 'favourite sons', Beaverbrook in particular but also Duncan Sandys and Randolph Churchill; and the Conservative Party's attempt to cash in on Mr Churchill's reputation as a war leader before it waned. This analysis was fair so far as it went, but ABC omitted the most likely reason for the Labour victory: the belief, rightly or wrongly, that Labour would 'get the boys home' more quickly than the Conservatives.

As for the general election, ever afterwards ABC thought it nothing less than a calamity that such artificiality and political rancour should have been forced on the country, dividing it into two political camps at a time when victory was already in sight and the country needed all possible strength and wise counsel to begin the difficult task of reconstruction after six devastating years of war.

ABC thought Mr Churchill's farewell statement to the nation that evening was very dignified. ABC himself said his farewells the following day. 'He was quite cheerful, though rather overcome with emotion when the time came to say good-bye.'

For ABC, the immediate concern was, who would be the new First Lord? When Syfret suggested Lord Strabolgi, who had served in the Navy to the rank of Lieutenant-Commander and had once been a Labour MP, ABC 'nearly fainted'. In fact, it was A.V. Alexander once again. He was glad to be back, but said Labour were having difficulty in replacing Lord Leathers. The Navy had in the end obtained the ships it needed for the Fleet Train, but ABC had not forgiven his 'slippery' opponent. He said 'it didn't much matter, provided he *was* replaced'.

On 30 July, ABC and Nona drove up to Scotland for a fishing holiday. ABC was fishing a loch on 6 August, the day the first atomic bomb was dropped on Hiroshima, and caught fifteen sea trout. They drove back next day, loaded with their catch, the car looking 'rather like a fish cart'.

On 9 August, ABC had a charming letter from Mr Churchill beginning 'My dear Andrew', saying that he had been granted the privilege of submitting his Resignation List of Honours and he hoped he could submit ABC's name to the King for a barony.

In his diary, ABC wrote: 'I fear it is just what I don't want. I have not the cash to sustain the dignity.' However, he did accept. Later Lord Lyon King of Arms wrote to ABC about his title. ABC found that 'Nobody can just be Lord Cunningham, he must be of some place.' Lord Lyon also wanted ABC to have albatrosses as supporters. ABC eventually settled on

Baron Cunningham of Hyndhope, in the parish of Kirkhope, in the County of Selkirk.

In his memoirs, ABC paid his own tribute to Winston Churchill:

> I had seen a great deal of Mr Churchill in many different environments and circumstances during my service as First Sea Lord and before. We had not always seen eye to eye, and had had our occasional disagreements and arguments. But never for a moment could I lose my profound admiration and respect for that most remarkable and courageous Englishman who by his energy, obstinacy and sheer force of character led Britain and her people through the greatest perils the country ever experienced. Who could forget his words over the radio, that speech of his when he told us he had nothing to offer but blood and sweat and tears? He was so pugnacious, so valiant, so filled with the spirit of offence, so unhesitant of risk if there was something to be gained, so ready to support anyone who took risks for some great object. He hated that hideous motto 'Safety First', which has always been anathema to me.

Soon after Mr Churchill left office, ABC wrote to tell him 'that I could never forget the kindness and consideration he had shown to me when I first joined the Chiefs of Staff Committee as something of a novice, and how privileged and honoured I felt in having worked under him. I said, too, how very deeply I regretted that what, to me, was a most proud association, had not been permitted to continue until the end of the war. Those words were not written in mere politeness; but from the bottom of my heart.'

The second atomic bomb was dropped on Nagasaki on 9 August and there were rumours that Japan was about to surrender. 'Well it looks like being all over,' ABC wrote in his diary for the 10th, 'for which we must be profoundly thankful.

I have now my own position to consider. I do not wish to hang on here keeping other people back so as soon as the fleet gets a bit sorted out I will go. My relief requires thought.'

The obvious choice was Fraser. But ABC seems to have had doubts. Early in July, Admiral Sir Geoffrey Blake called upon ABC and they discussed the subject. ABC thought it 'curious that he [Blake] agrees with me that John Cunningham would make a better First Sea Lord than Bruce Fraser'.

ABC continued to criticise Fraser. In July, after Fraser had suggested using some of the British Pacific Fleet to 'bomb Malaya', ABC commented 'I cannot make out why if he can't use it [the fleet]; he asked for it in such a hurry. I am against this attack on corpses like that on Truk [by a task group of the BPF in June 1945] or attacking another area where you are not wanted.'

The British Pacific Fleet sailed from Sydney again on 28 June and, designated Task Force 37, took its place on the right of the line of Admiral Halsey's 3rd Fleet. In the final operations against the mainland of Japan in July and August 1945, Task Force 37 played its full part in air strikes and bombardments and overcame its many handicaps to strike relatively blow for blow with the US fleet almost until the surrender of Japan. At the end, to their bitter disappointment, most of Task Force 37 had to withdraw for lack of fuel and missed the surrender in Tokyo Bay.

News of the surrender of Japan was received just after midnight on 15 August 1945 and that day was VJ — Victory over Japan — Day. The Prime Minister, this time Mr Attlee, members of his Cabinet and the Chiefs of Staff went to Buckingham Palace to congratulate HM the King on this final victory. The following night was very noisy but the illuminations were splendid. ABC went out on to the

609

Admiralty roof to look at them and was thrilled to see the figure of Nelson floodlit in Trafalgar Square, the only illuminated statue so far as he could see.

Admiral Stark had been relieved as Commander-in-Chief of the United States Naval Forces in Europe by Admiral H. Kent Hewitt, ABC's colleague from Mediterranean days. In the two years ABC had known him, 'Betty' Stark had become one of ABC's closest friends. They had worked together, as ABC said, without any trace of disagreement. 'Betty' Stark had been a very good friend to Great Britain and to the Royal Navy. He had worked hard to make sure that relations between the two countries and the two navies were as harmonious as possible. He had done particularly well, as ABC acknowledged, in smoothing over the worst effects of King's abrasive behaviour.

ABC made sure Stark was given a proper send-off. On 13 August the Board of Admiralty dined Stark in the Painted Hall of the Royal Naval College, Greenwich. The Prime Minister and the Foreign Secretary, Mr Ernest Bevin, were there and both spoke. ABC also made a speech in honour of his friend and received such a tremendous reception, with thunderous cheering and clapping, when he rose to his feet that he was unable to begin for some minutes.

On Sunday 19 August, the three Chiefs of Staff drove behind Their Majesties in a state landau with four bay horses to St Paul's for the Thanksgiving Service. It was an impressive service with beautiful music and the Archbishop of Canterbury's sermon, in ABC's view, 'put the atomic bomb in its proper place'. Afterwards they all drove back in the same order to Buckingham Palace. Talking on the steps of the Palace, ABC amused the King by pointing out 'the unseamanlike arrangements of the state landau, there being no method of slipping the tow in case of necessity'.

On the morning of VJ-Day the Chiefs of Staff had given orders for the immediate reoccupation of Hong Kong by ships from the British Pacific Fleet. There was a possibility that the Americans would try to prevent the British regaining Hong Kong as a Crown colony and there was no time to waste.

But there was a delay. Fraser was at sea, having been chosen by Mr Attlee to represent the United Kingdom at any surrender ceremonies. ABC thought it possible Fraser's absence was 'crossing the wires and making things difficult' but just as likely that his staff in Australia were being slow and pedantic and unable to appreciate the need for haste over Hong Kong. Two days later ABC was still chafing at their dilatoriness in getting the Hong Kong party away. Rear-Admiral Cecil Harcourt, who had been appointed Commander-in-Chief, Hong Kong, entered the harbour, flying his flag in the cruiser *Swiftsure*, at noon on 30 August.

ABC wrote to Bruce Fraser to congratulate him on being chosen to represent the United Kingdom Government at the Japanese surrender on board the battleship USS *Missouri* in Tokyo Bay on 2 September 1945. But, typically, ABC was very critical of the way Fraser dressed for the surrender. Instead of wearing full white uniform with tunic and trousers, as ABC himself would certainly have done for such a ceremony, Fraser wore an open-necked white shirt, *shorts* and long white stockings.

He was also critical of what he called Fraser's 'parochial' attitude, his habit of acting independently (Fraser visited Chungking in September 1945, for example, to discuss visits of HM Ships to China coast ports, without consulting or even telling ABC or the Foreign Office beforehand), his apparent belief that his own policies and decisions were better than the Admiralty's, and his way of making appointments locally and generally behaving as though he was running a miniature Admiralty of his own, 12,000 miles from home — which was, in fact, exactly what Fraser was doing.

One signal from Fraser in September 1945 gave his views on demobilisation — 'rather wild ones,' in ABC's opinion, 'and threatening us with unrest in the fleet unless the sailors could be assured that all was being done to demobilize them quickly'. When ABC discussed this signal with the First Lord, Mr Alexander remarked 'that Fraser's actions were making him doubt if he was fitted for the highest position in the Navy — First Sea Lord'.

Nevertheless, Fraser had a valid point. With world-wide commitments which had not diminished with the advent of peace, the Government were, in the matter of manpower, trying in ABC's words to have their cake and eat it. Demobilisation was a major problem. Now that the war was over, everyone — not only servicemen but thousands of recently released prisoners-of-war and internees — wanted to go home as soon as possible. Demobilisation schemes had been prepared, but it was not easy to put them into effect. Already, plans for Operation ZIPPER, the invasion of Malaya, had been affected by the 'Python' Scheme, whereby qualifying periods of service for the return home of men from the Far East had been considerably reduced.

While men waited for demobilisation, they were understandably unwilling to take further risks. Some Fleet Air Arm pilots, for instance, were now reluctant even to take off from a carrier's deck. Some submarine crews, hitherto notable for their devotion to duty and endurance, no longer wished to dive. Meanwhile, forces were required in the Mediterranean, in Germany, Greece, Italy, the Middle East, Indonesia and Malaya. Besides repatriation and demobilisation, there was also a huge variety of post-war tasks to be undertaken, from removing the armament and equipment from converted and requisitioned vessels and returning them to their civilian owners, to sweeping mines from waterways all over the world.

The Board's difficulties were increased by the sudden death on 24 September of the Third Sea Lord, Admiral Sir Frederick Wake-Walker, the very man who should have been best at seeing the Navy into the post-war era. As Controller, he would have been the Board member most closely involved in the provision of new ships for the Navy.

Wake-Walker was replaced by Charles Daniel who, in ABC's eyes, was too much Fraser's man. When he came to see ABC in October, ABC thought he 'had lots to say, obviously having been briefed by Fraser'. Daniel wanted to talk about the British Pacific Fleet and the effect the difficulties with demobilisation were having on the fleet's morale, but ABC 'rather shut him up. It's extraordinary how frightened some of these admirals are of their own men. Not having the facts of demobilisation they come in and talk nonsense.'

Officers who had been prisoners-of-war of the Japanese were returning, among them Captain Gordon who had commanded the cruiser *Exeter*, sunk by the Japanese in the Java Sea in March 1942: ABC thought he 'looked pretty well but with a strained look in his eye'. A Constructor Lieutenant-Commander who had been to Nagasaki described to ABC what he had seen. Any ship within 1,000 feet of the explosion, he said, would be burnt up and destroyed. 'An unpleasant form of death,' ABC said, 'to be roasted.'

A very welcome visitor, once again, was Rawlings, home from the Pacific. He had asked to put off his visit to the Admiralty for a month because of ill health and when he did come ABC found him 'not in good shape. Full of moans that the Pacific Fleet were not had home for a banyan at the termination of the Pacific War.'

This was a subject on which Rawlings had strong feelings. He had already written to the Admiralty, questioning the wisdom of dispersing the fleet in the way it was being done. He felt that at the very least a token force should have returned home to represent all that the British Pacific Fleet had achieved.

Rawlings wanted to retire. ABC tried to dissuade him, telling him 'not to be precipitate and wait and think about it for a month'. However, Rawlings was war-weary and did retire, 'to give younger men a chance'.

ABC was much less charitable to another officer home from the Pacific, Captain Q.D. Graham, who had commanded the aircraft carrier *Indefatigable* and who unwisely told ABC he was very tired. 'I rather jumped on him. Why a man with the frame of an ox should be tired after doing nothing for the last four months I fail to see.'

On 27 September, when the King and Queen visited Edinburgh, ABC was installed as a Knight of the Thistle in the Chapel of the Order in St Giles' Cathedral, in the presence of Their Majesties and all the Knights. The address was given by Dr Warr, the Dean of the Thistle. Admiral 'Jock' Whitworth read 'He rebuked the winds', from Matthew Ch.viii. There was an impressive rendering of 'Crossing the Bar' during which many members of the congregation showed signs of emotion. ABC said he could not remember hearing such singing.

ABC presented *Warspite's* White Ensign, and Captain C.M. Ford *Queen Elizabeth's* Red Ensign. As ABC said, these were the first flags of the sea to take their places among the tattered old Colours of famous Scottish regiments.

The Thistle was only one of the honours which, in ABC's own phrase, began to pour in on him. In June he was invited to become an Honorary Bencher of Lincoln's Inn. As ABC understood it, there were only ten such, headed by Queen Mary, and he accepted 'at some distant date.' The honorary degree of LL.D was conferred upon him by Edinburgh University in June, and then by the Universities of Birmingham and Cambridge in November. Later, he was conferred with the LL.D by Leeds, Glasgow, Sheffield and St Andrews Universities, and a DCL from Oxford University. He also received the Freedoms of Hove and of Manchester.

In his memoirs, ABC said he was overwhelmed and somewhat bewildered by all this kindness, but realised that it was not so much personal to himself as a tribute to the Royal Navy and the officers and men he felt himself to have been privileged and honoured to command. Privately, he had some misgivings. He accepted the honorary degree of laws from Birmingham, for example, 'rather against my will. I do not wish to be like Monty going round collecting these sort of things. I can't think when he does his job in Germany.'

ABC had to respond with many speeches, about which he still remained very nervous. Before his speech at Cambridge University, he had a sleepless night, getting up at four in the morning to write two paragraphs. In return he received a speech in his honour in Latin. He was 'little the wiser except that it began "Mare Nostrum"'.

The Board of Admiralty now had to address themselves to the shape of the post-war Navy. But such planning for the future, estimating the Navy's likeliest tasks and commitments, choosing which ships already building should be completed and which should be cancelled, weighing one ship design, aircraft marque or weapon system against another while they were all still on the drawing board, was not ABC's forte.

He was in any case growing tired, after six years in high command under the strain of war. The end found him supremely thankful, but mentally weary, after such a long time with no proper holiday. He compared himself most touchingly to Collingwood, who had had to serve on in the Mediterranean for five years after Trafalgar while longing for his home in Northumberland.

In short, ABC should have been relieved soon after the end of the war by a fresh personality with fresh ideas. As it was, he told the First Lord and the Cabinet in August 1945 that he wanted to leave the Admiralty between January and June 1946. He also told them that the Admiralty's choice of candidates to succeed him were James Somerville, Jack Tovey, John Cunningham and Bruce Fraser, and that he himself favoured John Cunningham.

25: RETIREMENT

ON 21 NOVEMBER 1945 ABC was introduced to the House of Lords. His supporters were Admirals of the Fleet Lord Chatfield and the Earl of Cork and Orrery. ABC had asked Lord Keyes, but he was too ill. However, they got 'through the drill without a hitch'.

ABC would not have been human if he had been quite as indifferent to honours as he so often claimed. But he felt very strongly about honours for the Navy and he fought the Navy's corner hard for a fair share against what he considered anti-Navy bias. In November 1945 Mr Attlee made his proposals for peerages in the armed services: three viscountcies to the Army, for Brooke, Montgomery and Alexander; to the RAF, a viscountcy for Portal and a barony for Tedder; and for the Navy, a viscountcy for ABC and a barony for Fraser.

ABC was outraged by this unfair distribution, grossly weighted in favour of the Army. 'I am personally concerned in this. If I accept the Viscountcy I will appear to my brother officers as a grabber of all the honours that are going about and also that I am satisfied that the Navy has been properly recognised.'

ABC wrote to the First Lord on 4 December, 'If that was the Prime Minister's last word I would feel myself compelled to refuse the Viscountcy.' Next day Mr Attlee gave way and proposed a barony for Tovey as well as Fraser. Mountbatten was also to be made a baron.

This was not at all what ABC had intended. 'I repudiated this absolutely,' he said, 'pointing out that MB had not been made a Supreme Commander because of his abilities as a naval commander but for political reasons. I refused to commit myself to withdrawing from the stand I had taken up until I had considered the new situation.

'Then came what was to me the astonishing offer of an Earldom for myself. I have told the man (AVA) time and again that I care nothing for these honours for myself and he evidently doesn't believe me. It's rather humiliating...' It was also, ABC thought, a bribe. Although Blake said ABC 'could now decently withdraw', ABC carried on, suggesting that some naval commanders whom Attlee refused to ennoble, such as Vian and Somerville, might receive baronetcies.

For a time it seemed that ABC had won. On 7 December he noted that '1st Lord told me that the PM had now come round on the question of baronetcies but I have a feeling that he is again going to weight the scales against the Navy.' So it proved. On the 10th the First Lord told ABC that Mr Attlee had changed his mind about the baronetcies and was now offering a barony to Tovey and Fraser but nothing to Somerville.

ABC decided that he had now done as much as he could for the Navy. 'So I wrote off and accepted the Viscountcy,' he wrote in his diary on 11 December. 'I don't want it. I am too poor for it to be of any use to me and I care not for these titles but I suppose for the good of the Navy one must take it.'

It seems that ABC was somewhat exaggerating his financial difficulties. Although he would have no table money or other allowances after he left the Admiralty, his expenditure on entertainment would surely be much less and, as an Admiral of the Fleet did not retire, he would remain on full pay for his lifetime.

Financial straits or not, ABC and Nona were at Palace House for Christmas 1945 ('Very good lunch with lots of Russian champagne; sawed wood in afternoon to work it off') — and for every subsequent Christmas.

On 1 January 1946, ABC wrote in his diary, 'Well, we start the New Year as a Viscount.' He had scores of letters and telegrams of congratulation, some from complete strangers. Tovey wrote: 'I have never visualised myself as a blinking baron and now that I am one I dislike the vision immensely. However I understand they have a backwoods contingent and I am applying for honorary membership.' Another letter was from Montgomery, who wanted a sailor and an airman to be his supporters when he entered the House of Lords. Trenchard was to be the airman and Montgomery asked ABC if he would be the sailor.

For ABC, the 'chief private thought', as he put it, was how soon he could get away from the Admiralty: '63 today!!' he recorded on 7 January. 'Well I don't feel it though I am a bit tired of this desk work.' He had suggested to the First Lord that he should bring up the matter of ABC's relief at the next Cabinet meeting. ABC recommended John Cunningham. 'After many protestations that he [the First Lord] did not wish me to go,' said ABC, 'which I accept at the face value of a politician's statements, he consented. I warned him to be sure and state that John Cunningham was no relation of mine.'

It only remained to break the news to Fraser. The First Lord thought, though ABC did not agree, that the letter to Fraser telling him the news was 'too clever and written to put him in a hole'. However, as would be expected from a man of Fraser's generosity of spirit, ABC had a nice reply from him. 'He has taken John Cunningham's appointment as my relief well.' Cunningham's appointment was officially announced on 1 March 1946.

Early in February 1946, there was mutiny in ships of the Royal Indian Navy in Bombay and Karachi. ABC claimed that the causes of the mutiny were 'rather obscure to us at home'. They should not have been, for the mutinies were symptomatic of growing unrest in India, where the Congress Party was mounting a campaign to oust the British from the sub-continent and there was great public turmoil over the future political shape of the country.

The cruiser *Glasgow* was rapidly deployed to Bombay, where sailors of the Royal Indian Navy were parading through the streets to support Congress. ABC's attitude was, if anything, somewhat flippant. 'I made the strict proviso that if there was any shooting to be done,' ABC wrote in his memoirs, 'it should only be carried out on the direct orders of the Indian authorities. I did not intend it to be said later that the brutal British Navy had fired on the poor Indian sailors.' Although there were riots in the city, in which the police opened fire and sixty people were killed, *Glasgow*'s arrival quietened matters down so far as the mutiny was concerned.

The subsequent Inquiry reached what ABC called sensible conclusions, but Vice-Admiral John Godfrey, in command of the Royal Indian Navy, was dismissed. Godfrey was the unluckiest of officers, having already been most unfairly dismissed as Director of Naval Intelligence by Pound in 1942. He was the only naval officer of his rank not to receive any award for his war service.

After discussions between the Treasury and all three Services, a new pay code was announced early in 1946. At first, it seemed that the new rates of pay were reasonable enough. But the sailors had expected their 'war service increments' to be consolidated as a permanent part of their pay. There was a great deal of discontent when it was found that this was not so.

The new codes attempted to pay men in all three Services the same, rank for rank, although conditions of service varied. The chiefs and petty officers pointed out that in the Navy, alone of the three Services, a man with a family had to maintain two homes, except in the comparatively short periods when he was awaiting draft in the naval barracks in his own manning port.

Furthermore, the chiefs and petty officers complained that there was not enough difference between their pay, considering their extra experience and responsibilities, and that of junior ratings.

At a meeting later in the month with the Commanders-in-Chief of the three manning ports, the First Lord was left in no doubt about the feelings of the sailors. Adjustments were made. But as ABC said, had the Admiralty been given more time to study the new rates before they were announced, many of the difficulties would probably never have arisen.

One possible solution to ABC's monetary problems was broached early in February 1946 — that he become the next Governor-General of Australia. 'A question of LSD,' ABC commented. 'I would have preferred anywhere but Australia but I don't suppose it will come to anything.' ABC talked it over with Nona, who pointed out that, although they might be able to live on the salary, the initial expenses would be daunting.

To find out more, ABC had Lord Gowrie, who had been Governor-General of Australia, to lunch. He learned that the Governor-General got £10,000 a year, free of taxes. He would need about sixteen domestic staff, and a Controller of the Household. Lord Gowrie said he paid his Controller £300 a year.

ABC wrote off that day to Lascelles, the King's Secretary; to say that he was a candidate for Australia. In April, the King wrote to him, hoping that he would take the appointment. Negotiations went on in a somewhat desultory way until August when ABC finally turned the appointment down, because of a recurrence of traces of the heart trouble he had in March.

In March, ABC drove up to Manchester, killing a sheep on the way on the A6 crossing the moors. 'The beast leapt out of a hedge in front of the car.' In Manchester he addressed the Luncheon Club, and he also paid a visit to Eaton Hall, near Chester, where the Royal Naval College had been evacuated for the duration. 'Some funny little chaps about,' he commented. 'Had a good argument with Stork [the headmaster] on education in general.'

ABC then went to Liverpool to embark in the destroyer *Solebay* which was to take him to Belfast for the launch of the aircraft carrier *Eagle* at Harland & Wolff's. *Solebay* was a new *Battle* Class destroyer, but ABC was not impressed by her. She was a fine enough ship 'which seemed to carry every mortal weapon and gadget except guns'. In his diary he noted: 'These "Battles" fulfil my worst anticipations. An erection like the Castle Rock Edinburgh on the bridge they call a director and all to control four guns firing a total weight of about 200 lbs. We must get back to destroyers of reasonable size and well-gunned.'

The launch on 19 March was carried out by Her Royal Highness Princess Elizabeth. It was a great success, according to ABC,

and the child did it all very well. She was for once well dressed in green and after a dummy run on a model in the office of breaking the bottle she did everything just right. I found the Princess very easy and we had many a laugh. She told me her speech was written by Anthony Kimmins and it was a very good one. Mine went well, particularly my reference to Northern Ireland's loyalty and contribution to victory.

ABC's diary ended abruptly on 25 March 1946 with a typically caustic entry: 'Dickie [Mountbatten] in Australia, I see. I have no doubt talking a lot. Still he has the film star technique and would make an excellent Governor General.'

The diary was never resumed. ABC had, as he said, fallen into the hands of the doctors and was sentenced to six weeks in bed in the Royal Naval Hospital, Haslar, after a minor heart attack.

ABC did not think his absence from the Admiralty was of much importance. The Admiralty Board carried on well enough without him. He had official papers sent down and his Secretary, Captain Shaw, and his Naval Assistant, Captain Sir Charles Madden, visited him regularly. Nona also came every day. He had a pleasant rose garden to look out on from his bed, letters, books and newspapers to read, and free cigarettes which, as he had never smoked in his life, he gave away.

In ABC's mail was a letter from His Majesty, offering him the Order of Merit. ABC accepted at once. 'It's a nice honour to have as it is HM's own gift,' he wrote to Aunt Connie, 'and has nothing to do with politicians. I hope it's the last anyway.'

It was not the last. In May 1946, Admiral Hewitt presented ABC with the US Navy Distinguished Service Medal (he already had the Army DCM, presented by Eisenhower in Algiers on Christmas Day 1942). 'How much had happened in the three and a half years that lay between,' ABC commented.

ABC also had a letter from 'Lofty' Power, now Director of the Joint Services Staff College, Latimer, asking him for his views on Supreme Commanders. 'A Supreme Commander', ABC wrote, 'must have great energy and ability, a knowledge of all three Services and be a man of great experience in war.

623

He must be a man acceptable to all three Services and able to hold his own with the politicians and finally he must be possessed of a supremely balanced judgment, which is probably the greatest need of all.'

But ABC still rather hankered after the great Mediterranean triumvirate, Wavell, Longmore and himself. 'I think, however, that there is very little that cannot be settled by the three Commanders-in-Chief around a table.'

Madden took notes of what ABC said and brought the completed typescript with him on his next visit to Haslar. ABC, he said, 'read it with zest and chuckled at his strong comments on the personalities. It does represent what he said and I believe what he thought at the time.'

For instance, ABC said Auckinleck's 'idea of co-operation was to dictate to the other services what was to be done!'

Wavell, ABC said, 'had all the qualifications we have listed, he had *learnt* about the three Services in the hard school of war, he could deal with the politicians, had energy, drive and was honest. He was a great and experienced soldier, had very good judgment and could discard the smaller things. An excellent choice with a hopeless job.' Eisenhower, on the other hand,

> had no military knowledge and knew nothing about the Navy, he was a pilot and knew something about the air; he was an untried man except that he was known to have great staff ability.
>
> What effect did he have on TORCH? Some on his American soldiery perhaps, otherwise none. I was never given any instruction or advice by him, nor was I consulted, nor did I consult him. He had no political experience and his negotiations with Giraud at Gibraltar were pitiable. Some Americans knew he was a good man who would probably develop. But what did Churchill and Roosevelt know of him when he was selected? It was purely a political appointment.

ABC's most stinging criticism was of Alexander, whom he called 'a mountebank'. 'He was not fit to be a Supreme Commander. He had no opinions of his own that he was not prepared to change and he took what the last man said. He had no knowledge of the sea and little of the air.'

Finally, of Mountbatten,

> He had energy and drive and a reasonable naval reputation as a young captain. He had shown great drive and ability and frightful extravagance in building up Combined Operations. He did not know much of the higher side of naval warfare and nothing of soldiery or of the air, *and he had no judgment*.
>
> In SEAC he fought with Somerville, Gifford and Peirse, but he was quick to learn. By the time Fraser arrived he was learning, and by the time Power arrived he had learnt.
>
> But what effect had he on the Campaign? If it had been left to Power, Park and Slim would not the results have been just the same?

ABC was back at the Admiralty by the middle of May; clearing a backlog of work and preparing to turn over to John Cunningham on 6 June. He had a parting audience of His Majesty the King at Buckingham Palace on 5 June. The next day he left the Admiralty for the last time. He had found it hard to say goodbye and was at a loss for what to say.

On 7 June, ABC had a letter from Alan Brooke:

> My dear Andrew; I could not say all I wanted this morning, I never can when I feel things deeply, but I cannot let you go without sending you a short line to give expression to some of my feelings.
>
> First of all, I should like to thank you from the very bottom of my heart for all your support during the past years, from the moment you joined the C.O.S. I was always certain that after we had reached agreement at a C.O.S. I had your full

support, no matter what turn the discussion took with Winston, and that in itself was worth anything. We went through some very difficult days with Winston together and I would never have got through them without all your help and staunch support.

Then I should like to thank you for the wonderful cordial and friendly atmosphere which you engendered at all our meetings, your patience when listening to points of view you did not agree with, and your constructive help throughout.

I thank heaven that I have only got a fortnight more to do after your departure, and therefore only a short time to miss you in.

I hope we may frequently join together on river banks, and discuss the far more attractive subjects of catching fish. With most heartfelt gratitude for all your help and friendship, Yours ever, 'Brookie'.

ABC and Nona were back in London on 7 June, staying at the Admiralty Archway flat which John Cunningham allowed them to carry on using until all the various farewell functions were over. They passed a restless night, kept awake by a man selling rattlers outside their window.

The rattlers were in honour of the Victory Parade through the streets of London on 8 June 1946. The Chiefs of Staff had places of honour on chairs to the right of the Royal saluting base in the Mall. ABC, representing the Senior Service, had the first chair, nearest the saluting base.

It was an impressive parade, which took nearly two hours to march and drive past the saluting base, with dispatch riders, many bands, men and women of every service and civilian organisation, representatives from all the Dominions and Colonies and from all the Allies, vehicles and tanks of every kind, followed by a fly-past of aircraft of the RAF.

As he watched, ABC's thoughts inevitably went back to the bronzed and battle-hardened young men he had seen marching in Tunis in May 1943. Since then, as he said, 'we had come a long and troublous way'.

ABC's Order of Merit, with Alan Brooke's, was announced in the Birthday Honours list and they both had an audience of the King at Buckingham Palace on 24 June when His Majesty invested them. ABC then drove down to Bishop's Waltham, feeling that he really had retired at last.

ABC looked forward to the prospect of a complete rest, although he did not pretend that 'it was not a great wrench to cease all active participation in the affairs of the Navy. Half a century is a long time, and it was a few months short of fifty years since I had joined the *Britannia* at Dartmouth as a small cadet, little realising what I was in for. None of my forebears had been at sea.'

In fact, ABC was as busy as ever in retirement. His personal mail remained very large and he was always punctilious about replying to letters. But now that he had no secretarial staff, he had to deal with his correspondence himself. He kept in touch with all his old friends, such as Walter Cowan, who exchanged letters and Christmas cards every year until his death in 1956, and Eisenhower, who never missed ABC's birthday, and wrote regularly over the years to congratulate ABC on every award or public mark of recognition that came his way. When ABC received his barony Eisenhower wrote, 'You well know that in my conviction there is no award, however great, that can ever symbolize the debt owed you by the United Nations.'

Amongst ABC's mail was a splendid embossed and coloured rendering of his coat of arms from Garter King of Arms. In heraldic language his coat of arms was: Argent, a shakefork Sable between a mullet in chief and two Dolphins descending, respectant, Vert, embouchee Gules. Supporters, Two Albatrosses proper, their wings elevated. The Motto was: Over Fork Over.

A high proportion of ABC's mail consisted of invitations to accept memberships and offices. ABC was particularly proud of his Presidency of the Royal Naval Pipers Society and allowed the Society to use his crest, surrounded by a strap and buckle, as a bonnet badge. 'All the Blue Bonnets are over the Border' was ABC's personal salute although he called it 'Brass Bonnets'. 'I am glad to hear', he wrote to Lieutenant-Commander Meilis, one Society member, 'that some of you have decided to introduce some decent music to the Sassenach.' Typically, he kept an eye on Meilis' career: 'Congratulations on your appointment in command of that large and useless ship,' he wrote, when Meilis became Captain of the *Battle*-class destroyer *St Kitts*. 'Remember — if you've got a bad First Lieutenant sack him, and many more ships have been aground than have reported it.'

As one of the chief participants, ABC was sent for comment and criticism the preliminary drafts of the official dispatches of various Second World War naval actions and operations which were to be published as Supplements to the *London Gazette*. He had many comments to make and the occasional old battle to be refought. He particularly resented the amendments proposed by the Air Ministry to his own criticisms of air cover in his dispatch on the Battle of Crete.

For example, the Air Ministry claimed that there had been very few ship losses to enemy air attack south of Crete. 'Evidence at the time', ABC retorted, 'went to show that the reason why losses were slight South of 37° North was because this was outside the range of JU.87s from the aerodromes where they were based. This consideration for the tender susceptibilities of the Air Ministry will no doubt be reciprocated when, for example, the dispatches of the Air Officer Commanding in Chief, Bomber Command, come to be published.'

But eventually ABC had to give in, though not without a parting shot. 'While for the purpose of publication I agree to the above alterations and emasculations of my despatch,' he wrote, 'I must insist that the despatch as originally written remains in the official record in the Admiralty archives.'

ABC also received from Captain G.R.G. Allen, Mr Churchill's principal historical assistant and researcher, 'the passages that affect you' of Mr Churchill's history of the Second World War which was published in six volumes from 1948 to 1954. Not surprisingly, ABC's recollection of some events differed sharply from Mr Churchill's. He was particularly concerned by Churchill's suggestion in Volume III that Dudley Pound had put forward the idea of sacrificing the battleship *Barham* in Tripoli harbour, a truly desperate venture which ABC had vehemently opposed at the time, merely as a trick to induce ABC to undertake the bombardment of the port.

ABC's strongly worded reply is marked, in his handwriting, 'Not what was sent but similar'. He said he did not think Pound was capable of such double dealing in his relations with any Commander-in-Chief 'and especially not with me'. In any case, there was no need for Pound to descend to such subterfuges. The Admiralty could simply have ordered the fleet to bombard Tripoli. Pound

> would have known the agony of mind the sacrifice, not so much of the *Barham*, but of well over 1,000 officers and men unwarned of their fate, would cause the Commander-in-Chief and he would never have adopted a ruse of this sort…

After all these years, my view remains as it was at the time; that is amazement at the ill-advised and reckless irresponsibility of those who ordered the bombardment or its alternative. The operation was successful but by good luck and the favour of Providence only.

ABC was working on his own memoirs, assisted by Captain Taprell Dorling, a contemporary of ABC's who went to the *Britannia* in 1897, served in South Africa and won a DSO in destroyers during the First World War. He was an experienced author, writing under the pseudonym of 'Taffrail', and he had also assisted ABC with some of his speeches in the past.

ABC's memoirs, *A Sailor's Odyssey*, were published in March 1951 and launched at a Foyles Literary Luncheon on the 28th, the tenth anniversary of Cape Matapan. Although ABC's book did give some indication of his disagreements with Mr Churchill during the war, his first draft was much more critical. After ABC sent it to the Admiralty for official approval, it is said that it took Sir John Lang, Secretary to the Admiralty, nearly a year to persuade ABC to tone down some of his criticisms of Mr Churchill.

Evidently ABC did not tone down his opinions enough about what he felt had been unwarranted interference in his professional conduct of the war or insulting imputations about his courage. He sent Mr Churchill a copy of *A Sailor's Odyssey*, which Churchill acknowledged and said he was looking forward to reading. But there is no record of anything further from Mr Churchill on the subject.

Living so near to Portsmouth, ABC kept in touch with the Navy and naval affairs. He attended as many naval dinners, especially Trafalgar Night dinners, as he could, and spoke in debates on naval subjects and the Navy Estimates in the House of Lords.

He had *Warspite*'s ship's bell hanging outside his front door. Nona struck it to summon him in from the other end of the garden to answer the telephone. One day he stopped on Portsdown Hill to look through binoculars at the ship herself, moored out in the harbour. Still awaiting removal to the shipbreaker's yard, she was stripped of her armament and seemed to ABC to be looking depressingly rusty and down at heel.

On 12 May 1948, ABC's HMS *Britannia* term held a dinner in London to mark the fiftieth anniversary of their going to sea. Twenty-four officers attended, with their Term Officer, Vice-Admiral Trewby. Present were two Admirals of the Fleet, ABC and James Somerville, six other admirals including Charles Little and two winners of the Victoria Cross, Rear-Admiral E.G. Robinson and Commander Basil Guy.

As an Admiral of the Fleet, ABC still had influence on the Navy's affairs and he was ready to use it where he felt the cause was just. He played a main part in the post-war campaign to restore the good name of Admiral Sir Dudley North, who in 1940 had been summarily ordered to haul down his flag as Flag Officer Commanding, North Atlantic Station, at Gibraltar for failing 'in an emergency to take all prudent precautions without waiting for Admiralty instructions'. The Admiralty blamed North for failing to stop six French cruisers from Toulon passing through the Straits of Gibraltar on their way to Dakar in French West Africa in September 1940.

The Admiralty were entitled to relieve North of his command if they had lost confidence in him, without giving any reason, but there seems no doubt that North was a political scapegoat for the disastrous failure of the Allied expedition to Dakar. He repeatedly asked for a court martial, so that he could clear his name. But successive First Lords refused his request, even when a deputation of five Admirals of the Fleet, including ABC, waited upon the First Lord, Mr J.P.L. Thomas. It was not until May 1957 that North was finally vindicated in a statement to Parliament by the Prime Minister Harold Macmillan. (Fraser had just taken part in a television programme on the subject: 'What an ass Fraser was,' ABC wrote gleefully to Geoffrey Blake, 'to appear on TV about North's affair!')

ABC's support of North may well have been part of the reason for the coolness between him and Mr Churchill, who seems to have regarded any effort on North's behalf as a personal criticism. Certainly, Churchill held up publication of the first volume of Captain Stephen Roskill's official history of the war at sea 1939-45 (in 1954, when Churchill was again Prime Minister) until he was satisfied with Roskill's account of North's dismissal.

ABC had no success with an appeal to Mr Churchill on behalf of his old colleague and staff officer from Mediterranean days, John Edelsten, who ABC considered should be promoted to Admiral of the Fleet. The promotion had been refused by the Treasury, on the grounds that there were customarily only ten Admirals of the Fleet and there were already ten at that time.

Knowing that such petty-fogging, penny-pinching arguments cut no ice with Mr Churchill, ABC wrote asking for his support. Mr Churchill replied from 10 Downing Street on 15 June 1954:

> My Dear Andrew, I should very gladly forward your letter to the Admiralty if you so desire. On the general question of numbers of Admirals of the Fleet it is not a question of saving a few hundred pounds but of lowering the prestige of the title by having too many.

I think Vian was hardly treated in being driven out of the service. In my opinion he fought the finest naval action of the war — four light cruisers against two or three Italian battle cruisers. I am sorry I allowed him to be so treated. Yours vy sincerely, Winston S. Churchill.

It was a curious, obliquely worded, letter. It was surely overstating the case to claim that Vian had been *driven* out of the Navy. He had been C-in-C Home Fleet from 1950 to 1952 and then, instead of being employed as C-in-C of a home command, as would have been usual, had gone on the retired list and had been promoted to Admiral of the Fleet. It is doubtful that Vian, who knew very well that, like his great friend ABC, he was not cut out for office work, ever regretted not becoming First Sea Lord. Possibly the reference to Vian's celebrated action [in the Bay of Sirte in March 1942] as the 'finest naval action of the war' was intended to nettle ABC: in short, Sirte had been better than Matapan.

ABC replied on 28 June: 'I fully agree with you that Vian's action off Sirte was the finest naval action of the war; in the Mediterranean at the time we were all very proud of it.' However, Edelsten was never promoted to Admiral of the Fleet.

Later that year of 1954, ABC himself was called upon to lend his support to a cause. The question of who should relieve Admiral McGrigor as First Sea Lord had been debated since 1953. One candidate was Mountbatten. The Navy, traditionally as a Service very bad at politicking, had reached a stage where it desperately needed as First Sea Lord some charismatic character who could charm the politicians. It was not a time for seamanship but for public relations. Mountbatten seemed ideal. The First Lord of the Admiralty, 'Jim' Thomas, was in favour of Mountbatten but he would not have gone against the

Admirals on the Board or the old guard of senior Admirals, including ABC, who opposed Mountbatten.

Mountbatten's appointment as First Sea Lord would have been unthinkable so long as ABC disapproved. 'Lofty' Power, who was on Mountbatten's side, went down to Bishop's Waltham to try and persuade ABC to change his mind. As Power well knew, ABC and Mountbatten had been friends. But, in Power's opinion, it was when Mountbatten became Chief of Combined Operations and then was 'jumped up' to Vice-Admiral that ABC took against him. When Mountbatten was made Supreme Commander, ABC became 'even more virulent. I can only put it down', Power said, 'to the ugly streak of jealousy which I knew to exist in ABC.'

ABC said flatly that 'Dickie Mountbatten has great gifts but lacks judgment. It would never do.' Power agreed that 'He is impulsive and impetuous, apt to go off half-cock but he *will* stop and listen to argument.'

'Well, there you are,' ABC retorted, 'he lacks judgment and needs someone to keep him on the rails.'

Power was sorely tempted to reply 'he's just like you in that respect', but forbore. Instead he used the analogy of 'a really first-class car', when one looks 'for enormous power and flashing acceleration. Brakes are provided by a separate make. That does not detract from the performance of the car.'

ABC said Power was talking nonsense. Power replied that on the contrary he was talking sense. Mountbatten would be invaluable to the Navy. Finally, ABC said he would think about it, but he was still sure that Power was wrong.

ABC did think about it and he did change his mind. It seems that a letter from 'Pug' Ismay on 18 October 1954, telling ABC of the difficulties the First Lord, who had always favoured Mountbatten, was having may have tipped the scales. Thomas had told Ismay that 'high professional opinion (he mentioned your name in particular) was against him [Mountbatten]'.

ABC replied, 'It is quite true that well over a year ago when Thomas asked me about it, I gave him my opinion as not Dickie for 1st Sea Lord, but the dire need of the Navy for a colourful personality well in the public eye has completely altered my views.'

To Thomas, ABC wrote on 22 October:

> You will perhaps remember that well over a year ago you asked my opinion as to who should be First Sea Lord when McGrigor's term of office comes to an end. I told you that I thought it would be a mistake for Mountbatten to be appointed.
>
> I have completely changed my views and I feel strongly that at the present time and in present circumstances the Navy requires as its professional head a man well in the public eye and whose opinion will carry great weight in high places both national and international. There is no one of the right seniority in the Navy so richly endowed in that respect as Mountbatten and I feel that the Navy is fortunate in having available at this time a man of his calibre.

That was a most generous retraction, and Thomas was grateful, although he now had problems of another kind. He was, he told ABC, having 'trouble with my own Party who want to know why I have appointed a socialist (but incidentally Dickie isn't)...' Mountbatten was duly appointed First Sea Lord. It was the last occasion when ABC played a decisive part in the Navy's history.

In 1951 ABC had had a recurrence of his heart trouble, which prevented him carrying out his ceremonial duties as High Commissioner of the Church of Scotland. 'I steam on about nine boilers out of ten,' he wrote to Royer Dick. In

December 1959 ABC had a serious car accident. As he wrote in a letter to Commander McHattie, who had served under him in the Mediterranean, it was 'a devil of a crash. A swine came out of a side road and rammed us under the windscreen which I think exploded and knocked both of us flat out — the car went on, crossed the road through the approaching traffic and we rammed the Post Office wall.'

It took both ABC and Nona some time to get over the accident. Even by February 1960, Nona was still affected, able only to use one eye at a time. ABC himself was writing to Godfrey in November that he was 'about 95% fit' but suffered from a deplorable lack of energy. 'But I always was lazy,' he said.

ABC still kept up with his old friends. In September 1961 he went to a dinner given by Ismay. Many of the distinguished war generals and airmen were there and ABC was glad, with an old man's glee, that apparently Montgomery had not been invited — 'just as well perhaps,' he told Godfrey, 'as Auchinleck was there'. Mr Churchill was also there — 'very far gone poor old man. We had great difficulty in getting him to leave. I thought we were in for one of our 2 a.m. Chief of Staff's meetings. We moved him at 1 a.m. with the bottle of brandy practically empty.'

In 1963, although he was eighty, ABC carried on with his correspondence and his gardening, went up to the Athenaeum, where he met all sorts of interesting people but thought the food very bad, and put in occasional appearances at the House of Lords. On 12 June he attended a meeting at the Admiralty in the morning and then lunched with Sir Edward Appleton, Vice-Chancellor of Edinburgh University, when according to Sir Edward, ABC was in the best of spirits and was 'the magnet of all eyes'.

After lunch ABC hailed a taxi in Parliament Square to take him to Waterloo to catch the train on his way back to Bishop's Waltham. He was dead by the time the taxi reached the station.

ABC's death was a great shock, but Nona, his family and friends were all glad that he had been spared a long illness. 'It was typical of his modesty', one friend wrote, 'that he just got into a taxi and went straight to heaven.'

ABC's body lay in the Chapel of the Royal Naval Barracks, Portsmouth, guarded by four lieutenants, keeping four-hour watches. Meanwhile, there was keen competition amongst senior ratings to be chosen for the honour of bearing the coffin at the funeral. Some 200 Chief Petty Officers of all branches and from various establishments in the Portsmouth Command assembled on the parade ground for inspection. Eventually all were eliminated, on grounds of size or stature, except six 'finalists', plus two spare numbers.

ABC's funeral, which was to be at sea, had a sub-plot which would greatly have amused ABC himself. The chosen six and the spare numbers rehearsed for the funeral parade, using a weighted 'dummy' coffin which, they were assured, was much heavier than the real thing would be.

However, there had once been problems before the war with the burial at sea of a distinguished admiral whose coffin had refused to sink and had had eventually to be sunk by gunfire, whilst the sorrowing relatives were consoled with tea and buns on the disengaged side of the ship. Ever since, precautions had been taken to weight the coffin, often by placing two 6-inch projectiles inside.

Thus, on 18 June, the day of the funeral, when the chosen six lifted the coffin from its stand on to their shoulders, they realised that it was in fact much heavier than the 'dummy' coffin. 'ABC's cocked hat was on top,' wrote one coffin bearer, 'and as we approached the exit door we bent our knees to negotiate the low doorway. I thought our knees would buckle and that we would never recover. It must have been sheer guts and determination but rise we did and eventually lowered the coffin on the gun carriage.'

In the march to South Railway Jetty in the dockyard, where the guided missile destroyer HMS *Hampshire* was waiting, the insignia of ABC's orders and medals were carried by Royer Dick. The pall bearers were Admiral of the Fleet Sir Caspar John, the First Sea Lord; Admiral Sir Wilfrid Woods, the C-in-C Portsmouth; Admiral Sir Royston Hollis Wright, Second Sea Lord; Vice-Admiral Sir John Villiers, Fourth Sea Lord; Vice-Admiral Frank Hopkins, Fifth Sea Lord; Lieutenant-General M.C. Cartwright-Taylor, Commandant General, Royal Marines; Vice-Admiral Sir Geoffrey Barnard; and Admiral of the Fleet Sir George Creasy.

It was a foul day, with a gale of wind blowing, which would also have caused ABC some wry amusement, when *Hampshire* slipped and proceeded to sea for the funeral service, conducted by the Chaplain of the Fleet and the Principal Chaplain of the Church of Scotland. For the family, Nona was supported by ABC's brothers, Lieutenant-Colonel John Cunningham and General Sir Alan Cunningham, and Lady Cunningham, Miss Mary Cunningham, ABC's niece, Commander and Mrs (Hillie) Gordon McKendrick, and Lieutenant J.C.K. Slater, Royal Navy, ABC's great-nephew. One of the wreaths which followed ABC's coffin into the sea off the Nab Tower carried a *Warspite* cap-ribbon.

ABC died a few days before the Royal Naval Pipers were due to 'Beat Retreat' at Edinburgh Castle. 'We toyed with the idea of cancelling it,' Meilis wrote to Nona, 'but came to the conclusion he wouldn't have approved, and that it was a splendid opportunity to pay tribute to him. So the programme was modified to include a lament and "Brass Bonnets", and we asked the crowd to stand up and take their hats off in his memory. I don't think "Rule Britannia" and the National Anthem in any Beat Retreat, even abroad, have meant so much to me, and I'm sure a lot of others felt the same.'

The Memorial Service for ABC was held in St Paul's Cathedral on 12 July 1963, and was attended by an almost complete muster of the senior ranks of the Navy, with representatives from the Commonwealth and the House of Lords. Her Majesty the Queen was represented by Admiral Sir Wilfrid Woods, Sir Winston and Lady Churchill by Captain G.R.G. Allen.

The address was given by the Rt. Revd Launcelot Fleming, who had been *Queen Elizabeth*'s padre in the Mediterranean, and was now Bishop of Norwich.

> For my own part, what impressed me when I first came to serve under him... was the quite remarkable devotion he so evidently inspired in his Staff; the persistent and undaunted determination and purpose he maintained when the Fleet which he commanded was suffering terrible losses at Crete, and in the months that followed: the demanding standards of duty and resolution that he set himself and expected from others: the alertness and distinction of his mind: and, through all this, a certain directness and simplicity; and a humanity which was kept in good repair despite the strain and burden of his responsibilities.
>
> After his retirement — (though I shall be reminded that an Admiral of the Fleet never retires) — he gave himself with immense relish and enjoyment to many interests and causes. He was such good company — so full of vigour; his older years appeared mellow and integrated and happy. He

remained outspoken in his views, generous in his judgement, and full of fun.

I would find it entirely fitting to interpret Cunningham's qualities and gifts as the outcome of a disciplined and thoughtful integrity of response to the Will and guidance of God — for it would seem that this lay at the heart and centre of his life... Thank God for giving our people and nation such a man at such a time.

On Sunday 2 April 1967, HRH the Duke of Edinburgh unveiled a bust of ABC by Franta Belsky in Trafalgar Square. The original design had been criticised by some who knew ABC. 'It was the bust of an amiable old gentleman,' said Sir Charles Madden, who had been Commander of *Warspite* in the Mediterranean and ABC's Naval Secretary at the Admiralty. 'ABC was *not* an amiable old gentleman. He was fierce and dangerous-looking with a firm mouth.'

On the afternoon of the same day, a service to dedicate a memorial plaque to ABC was held in the Nelson Chamber of St Paul's Cathedral. A memorial plaque to ABC was also unveiled in St Paul's Cathedral, Valletta. In 1968, one of the Cadets' Divisions at the Royal Naval College Dartmouth was named after Cunningham.

ABC summed up his own career in his memoirs:

I have little to regret. Fortune favoured me at every turn. How else could one with of such limited attainments have reached so far? I realize I have been lucky, and can think of others more talented and industrious than myself who fell by the wayside through sheer force of circumstance, not through any fault of their own. I am not, and never was, an expert in any of the technical subjects, or what Mr Churchill once called the 'instrumentalisms', of the Navy, which used to be one of the surest roads to advancement in peace. I think I was fortunate in obtaining command while still a young man, for it taught me much of what I know about sailors. After all, it is the men who win battles. I owe a great deal, too, to the fine example of the officers under whom I served, particularly in destroyers and later. Their names have been mentioned; but they, and others like them, were responsible for grafting the improved technique of an entirely new Navy on to the imperishable tradition of service and self-sacrifice of the old. The fighting spirit was never lacking.

I have no profound philosophy of life to propound. As perhaps I have shown, I have always been inclined to rebel and to speak out against decisions that I felt to be wrong. Otherwise, I think I have usually taken things as I found them, and tried to make the best of them.

Finally, to the end of my life, I shall remain convinced that there is no Service or profession to compare with the Royal Navy.

ABC concluded by quoting some lines from a poem by James Graham, Marquis of Montrose, 1612-1650, and which (though he actually misquoted them) hung over his desk for many years:

> He either fears his fate too much
> Or his deserts are small,
> That dares not put it to the touch,
> To gain or lose it all.

But these lines, favourites of ABC's though they were, are perhaps a little too solemn. Much more ABC's style were other verses, also favourites of his, which more closely reflected his attitude towards life, and his sense of humour, through his love of fishing:

641

I pray that I may live to fish
Until my dying day
And when it comes to my last cast,
I then most humbly pray:—
When in the Lord's great landing net
And peacefully asleep
That in his mercy I be judged
Big enough to keep.

CHRONOLOGY

1883

7 January: Born in Dublin.

1897

15 January: Joined HMS *Britannia* as Naval Cadet.

1898

18 May: HMS *Fox*, cruiser, Cape of Good Hope and East Africa.
15 June: Midshipman.

1899

May: Cruiser HMS *Doris*, Cape of Good Hope and East Africa.

1900

February-September: Serves ashore with Naval Brigade in the Boer War.
15 December: Battleship HMS *Hannibal*, Channel Squadron.

1901

15 December: Training brig HMS *Martin*, Portsmouth (attached HMS *St Vincent*).
1 November: Cruiser HMS *Diadem*, Channel Squadron.

1902

7 January: Acting Sub-Lieutenant, courses, Greenwich and Portsmouth.

1903

14 March: Promoted Sub-Lieutenant.

27 March: Battleship *Implacable*, Mediterranean.

16 September: Destroyer HMS *Locust*.

22 December: Destroyer HMS *Orwell*.

1904

31 March: Promoted Lieutenant.

June: Training ship HMS *Northampton*.

November: Training ship HMS *Hawke*, West Indies.

1906

May: Cruiser HMS *Scylla*.

3 July: Cruiser HMS *Suffolk*, Mediterranean.

1908

13 May: HMTB No. 14, in command, Home Waters.

1910

24 January: Destroyer HMS *Vulture*, in command.

15 August: Destroyer HMS *Roebuck*, in command.

1911

10 January: Destroyer HMS *Scorpion*, in command, Home Fleet, based on Harwich.

1913

November: To Mediterranean.

1914

August: Pursuit of German battlecruiser *Goeben*, action against Austrian torpedo boats in the Adriatic.

3 November: Bombardment of the Dardanelles forts.

1915

19 February: Naval attack on the Dardanelles, renewed 18 March.

25 April: Gallipoli landing, *Scorpion* in support.

30 June: Promoted Commander. Distinguished Service Order, for gallantry in the Dardanelles.

August: Mentioned in dispatches for service during Gallipoli landing.

1916

8-9 January: Evacuation of Gallipoli peninsula. Aegean patrols until July. *Scorpion* in refit. Temporary command, destroyer HMS *Rattlesnake*, August-October.

1917

Escort duty, *Scorpion*, Mediterranean.

1918

January: *Scorpion* returns home.

11 February: Destroyer HMS *Ophelia*, in command, Grand Fleet.

29 March: Destroyer HMS *Termagant*, in command, Dover Patrol.

May: Action with German destroyers.

November: Battleship *Swiftsure*, in command, for operation (cancelled) to block Ostend.

1919

17 January: Granted Belgian Croix de Guerre.

2 February: Bar to DSO, for services in destroyers of the Dover Patrol between 1 July and 11 November 1918.

28 February: Destroyer HMS *Seafire*, in command, for service in the Baltic.

1920

1 January: Promoted Captain.

8 March: Second Bar to DSO, for distinguished services in command of HMS *Seafire*.

29 September: President, Sub-Commission 'C', Naval Inter-Allied Commission of Control in Germany, for demolition of Heligoland fortifications.

1921

October: Returns from Heligoland.

1922

February: Senior Officers' Technical Course, Portsmouth.

2 May: Flotilla leader HMS *Shakespeare*, in command, and as Captain (D), 6th Destroyer Flotilla (in reserve). Port Edgar.

19 December: Flotilla leader HMS *Wallace*, in command, and as Captain (D), 1st Destroyer Flotilla, Istanbul.

1923

March: *Wallace* paid off and recommissioned in Atlantic Fleet.

1924

15 October: Captain-in-Charge, base HMS *Columbine*, Port Edgar.

1926

9 May: Cruiser HMS *Calcutta*, in command, and as Flag Captain and Chief of Staff to the C-in-C North America and West Indies Station.

1927
December: Returns to Chatham in *Calcutta*.

1928
January: Sails for Bermuda in cruiser HMS *Despatch*. North and South American waters, returns home, August.

1 October: Army Officers School, Sheerness.

1929
14 January: Imperial Defence College.

15 December: Battleship HMS *Rodney*, in command, Atlantic Fleet.

21 December: Marriage to Miss Nona Byatt.

1930
Fleet exercises in Atlantic and Mediterranean.

June: Visit to Iceland. Appointed Knight Commander of the Order of the Icelandic Falcon. Relieved 15 December.

1931
6 July: Commodore, RN Barracks, Chatham.

1932
24 September: Promoted Rear-Admiral.

1933
Senior Officers' Technical courses.

1934
1 January: New Year Honours. Companion of the Bath.

Rear-Admiral (Destroyers), Mediterranean, flag in cruiser HMS *Coventry*.

1935

July: King George V's Jubilee Review, Spithead. Returns to Mediterranean, flag in cruiser HMS *Despatch*. Abyssinian Crisis. Transferred to cruiser HMS *Galatea*, October.

1936

20 January: Death of King George V.

Mentioned by C-in-C for exceptional services during emergency 1935/36.

April: Returns home. On half pay. Leases Palace House, Bishop's Waltham.

22 July: Promoted Vice-Admiral.

1937

Chairman of Committee on Ventilation of HM Ships.

13 May: Coronation of King George VI.

20 May: Coronation Review, Spithead.

3 July: Vice-Admiral Commanding Battlecruiser Squadron, and Second-in-Command, Mediterranean Fleet, flying flag in battlecruiser HMS *Hood*. Spanish Civil War.

1938

17 October: Lord Commissioner of the Admiralty, Deputy Chief of Naval Staff.

1939

15 February: Invested with KCB.

6 June: Commander-in-Chief, Mediterranean Fleet, with acting rank of Admiral, flag in battleship *Warspite*.

3 September: Declaration of war against Germany.

By end of year, Mediterranean Fleet reduced to three 'C' Class cruisers and some Australian destroyers.

1940

10 May: *Warspite* returned to the Mediterranean.

11 June: Italian declaration of war.

22 June: Fall of France. French sign Armistice. Negotiations begin with French Admiral Godfroy over disposal of French warships at Alexandria.

3 July: Action against French warships at Mers-el-Kebir. Over 1,000 French sailors killed.

5 July: Neutralisation of French warships at Alexandria.

9 July: Action against Italian battle fleet off Calabria, Italy.

19 July: Cruiser HMAS *Sydney* and 2nd Destroyer Flotilla sank Italian cruiser *Bartolomeo Colleoni* off Cape Spada, Crete.

11 November: Fleet Air Arm Swordfish attack on Italian battleships at Taranto, seriously damage *Conte de Cavour*, *Caio Duilio* and *Littorio*.

1941

3 January: Promoted Admiral.

10 January: Aircraft carrier HMS *Illustrious* bombed off Malta.

11 January: Appointed GCB.

March: Operation LUSTRE. Fleet convoying army to Greece.

28 March: Battle off Cape Matapan. Italian heavy cruisers *Fiume*, *Zara* and *Pola* and destroyers *Vittorio Alfieri* and *Giosue Carducci* sunk.

24-9 April: Evacuation of the Army from Greece, with heavy fleet losses.

20 May-1 June: Evacuation of the Army from Crete, with further heavy fleet losses.

11 November: Awarded Medal of Military Merit First Class (Greece).

14 November: Aircraft carrier HMS *Ark Royal* sunk by U-81 east of Gibraltar.

17 November: Mentioned in dispatches for operations in the Middle East, July-October 1941.

25 November: Battleship HMS *Barham* sunk by U-331 off Libyan coast.

17 December: First Battle of Sirte. Passage of *Breconshire* to Malta and partial engagement with Italian battle fleet.

19 December: Battleships HMS *Queen Elizabeth* and *Valiant* badly damaged in Alexandria harbour by explosive charges laid by Italian Navy swimmers.

1942

22 March: Second Battle of Sirte. Defence of convoy MW. 10 to Malta by light cruisers and destroyers under Rear-Admiral Vian against a superior Italian force.

April: Cunninghams leave for London, travelling *incognito* as Mr and Mrs Browne. Appointed Head of British Admiralty Delegation, Washington DC.

11 June: Birthday Honours. Baronetcy.

October: Appointed Naval Commander-in-Chief, Allied Expeditionary Force (NCXF) North Africa and Mediterranean.

8 November: Operation TORCH. Allied landings at Casablanca, Oran and Algiers.

25 December: Presented with US Army Distinguished Conduct Medal by Eisenhower.

1943

January: Summit meeting, Casablanca.

21 January: Promoted Admiral of the Fleet. Appointed Chief Commander of the Legion of Merit (USA), Chevalier of the Legion d'honneur (France), Grand Officer of the Order of Ouissan Alaouite (Morocco), and awarded Grand Cordon of the Order of Nicham-Iftikhar (Tunis).

February: Reappointed Commander-in-Chief, Mediterranean.

20 April: Mentioned in dispatches for services as NCXF in Operation TORCH.

8 May: Operation RETRIBUTION. 'Sink, burn and destroy. Let nothing pass.'

10 July: Operation HUSKY, invasion of Sicily.

9 September: Operation AVALANCHE, landing at Salerno.

10 September: Surrender of the Italian fleet.

16 October: Joined the Admiralty as First Sea Lord.

November: Summit meetings, Cairo and Teheran.

1944

June: Visit to Normandy beach-head.

September: Summit meeting, Quebec.

1945

New Year: Appointed Knight of the Most Ancient and Most Noble Honours Order of the Thistle.

February: Summit meeting, Yalta.

July: Summit meeting, Potsdam.

17 August: Barony.

1946

New Year Honours: Viscountcy.

6 June: Leaves the Admiralty.

8 June: Victory March in London.

13 June: Birthday Honours. Order of Merit.

2 July: Awarded Distinguished Service Medal (USA). Receives Freedom of Edinburgh.

1947

Inauguration as Lord Rector, Edinburgh University.

15 April: Awarded Grand Cross of the Order of George I (Greece).

24 June: Awarded Special Grand Cordon of the Order of the Cloud and Banner (China).

25 November: Appointed Knight Grand Cross of the Order of the Netherlands Lion.

1950

Lord High Commissioner to the General Assembly of the Church of Scotland.

1951

Publication of *A Sailor's Odyssey*.

1952

Lord High Commissioner to the General Assembly of the Church of Scotland.

1953

Lord High Steward, Coronation of HM Queen Elizabeth II.

1963

12 June: Dies in London, aged eighty.

18 June: Buried at sea from the guided missile destroyer HMS *Hampshire*, south of the Nab Tower, off Portsmouth.

1967

2 April: Bust in Trafalgar Square and plaque in the crypt of St
Paul's erected by public subscription.

BIBLIOGRAPHY AND SOURCES

UNPRINTED SOURCES

British Library

Cunningham Papers Add MSS 52557-52584

52557, I., Correspondence with parents and sister, 1898-1917.

52558, II., Letters to Aunts Helen and Constance Browne, 1914-June 1941.

52559, III., Ibid., July 1941-1946.

52560, IV., Correspondence with Pound, Jan-July 1939.

52561, V., Ibid., August 1939-1943.

52562, VI., Correspondence with (1) Cowan, 1939-55., (2) Sir John Cunningham, 1941-60., (3) Admiral Sir Arthur Power, 1944-5.

52563, VII., Correspondence with (1) Somerville, 1940-5., (2) Roskill, 1952-7.

52564, VIII., Diary of Somerville, March-July 1944. Typewritten copy.

52565, IX., (1) Papers of Forbes, 1938-40. (2) Dispatch of Wavell, with map.

52666, X., Naval telegrams, 1940-6.

52667, XI., Ibid.

52668, XII., General correspondence, 1898-1939.

52669, XIII., Ibid., 1940-1.

52670, XIV., Ibid., 1942-June 1943.

52671, XV., Ibid., July 1943-1944.

52672, XVI., Ibid., 1945.

52673, XVII., Ibid., 1946.

52674, XVIII., Ibid., 1947-8.

52675, XIX., Ibid., 1949-53.

52676A, XX., Ibid., 1954-62.

52677, XXI., Diary, April-Dec. 1944.

52678, XXII., Diary, 1945.

52679, XXIII., Diary, 1946.

52680A&B, XXIV., Draft of *A Sailor's Odyssey* with related correspondence.

52681, XXV., Ibid.

52682, XXVI., Speeches, with related correspondence, 1946-58.

52683A&B, XXVII., Papers relating to the demolition of the defence of Heligoland 1919-26, inc. 'The Demolition of the Harbour and Defence Works of Heligoland', by Leopold Halliday Savile, CB, M. Inst.CE. Minutes of Procs. Institute of Civil Engineers, Vol. 220, Session 1924-6, Part 2.

52684, XXVIII., English translation of Admiral Angelo Iachino's *Gaudo and Matapan*, 1946. Typewritten.

Churchill College, Cambridge

Cunningham of Hyndhope, 1st Viscount, Admiral of the Fleet Andrew Browne Cunningham (1883-1963). Correspondence and materials from various sources for the biography by Oliver Warner.

Edelsten, Admiral Sir John Hereward (1891-1966). Papers, 1931-52.

Godfrey, Admiral John Henry (1888-1971). Memoirs.

Meilis, Captain David, BN, RN. Letters from Lord Cunningham of Hyndhope to Meilis, 1951-61.

Pound, Admiral of the Fleet Sir Alfred Dudley Pickman Rogers (1877-1943). Letters, cuttings, and notes collected for a projected biography by Donald McLachlan.

Power, Admiral Sir Manley, (1904-81). Autobiography.

Roskill, Captain Stephen Wentworth, RN (1903-82), historian, Fellow of Churchill College, 1962-82. Historical and family papers, *c.* 1912-82.

Somerville, Admiral Sir James Fownes (1882-1949). Naval and personal papers.

Willis, Admiral of the Fleet Sir Algernon Usborne (1889-1976). Naval papers, 1905-76.

Imperial War Museum

Admiral Sir Manley Power. Papers, 1942-70, inc. naval operations orders and MS notes for Operation TORCH, 1942, and MS minutes on Operation HUSKY, 1943, with notes by Power, Cunningham and others.

Admiral Sir William Whitworth, Vice-Admiral commanding the Battle Cruiser Squadron, 1939-41; Second Sea Lord, 1941-4; and C-in-C, Rosy th, 1944-6. Papers contain a series of letters from Admiral Cunningham.

National Maritime Museum, Greenwich

Cunningham Papers

'G.R.' Matriculation of Arms as Viscount; Viscountcy, Baronetcy and Barony warrants, with Royal Seals.

Scrolls: Oxford Degree Ceremony; Membership of Civil Engineers; picture of *Vanguard*; University of St Andrews Degree; N.E. Coast Institute of Engineers & Shipbuilders; Hon. Fellowship Royal College of Surgeons; Fishmongers Co; Shipwrights Co; Freedom of City of London; Warrant as Admiral of the Fleet 1943; Glasgow University LL.D; Edinburgh University.

Papers about military honours: career notes; First World War — 3 mentions in dispatches; DSO 1916; Icelandic Falcon 1930; CB 1935; KCB 1938; Second World War — 2 mentions in dispatches; GCB 1941; French Legion d'honneur, Algiers 1943; Legion of Merit (US) 1943 signed by President Roosevelt and permission to wear (US) DSM signed by President Truman; Tunisian Order; Greek Order; Netherlands; Chinese Order from Chiang Kai-shek; French Médaille militaire; Moroccan Order; Knight of Thistle 1945, appointment, ceremony and correspondence; Order of Merit.

Appointment as Lord High Steward for the Coronation; Appointment as Lord High Commissioner of the General Assembly of the Church of Scotland and consequential correspondence and material, inc. two 'Private Instructions' signed by King George VI and Queen Elizabeth.

Correspondence and notes for speeches for Hon. Degrees as Doctor of Laws at Universities of Edinburgh, Birmingham, Cambridge, Oxford, St Andrews, Leeds, Glasgow, Sheffield, Address as Lord Rector of Edinburgh, also inc. invitations, notes for speeches etc. for Freedoms of Cities.

Papers relating to Presidencies, Patronages and Hon. Membership of various Institutions.

Notes for speeches on various occasions at schools, boys' clubs, unveiling war memorials, dinners, inc. speech at Taranto Dinner, 11 November 1949.

Private

Bolt, Rear Admiral A.S. ('Ben'), CB DSO DSC*. Private papers, appreciation of ABC; notes on the planning of the Taranto Raid; comments on the Battle of Matapan.

Brownrigg, Captain Tom, CBE DSO RN. Private papers and memoir (by kind permission of Mr Henry Brownrigg).

Dick, Rear-Admiral Royer, CB CBE DSC. Private papers, appreciation of ABC. Lenox-Conyngham, Captain Alwyn, RN. Appreciation of Admiral Cunningham.

Macdonald, Vice-Admiral Sir Roderick, KBE. Extracts from Midshipman's Journal, HMS *Valiant*, 1 September 1940-14 January 1941.

Munn, Rear-Admiral W.J., CB DSO OBE. Reminiscences of A.B. Cunningham.

Rose, Lieutenant-Colonel, OBE Royal Marines. Notes on Middle East Commandos and Operation Pitch — Castelorizzo.

Wheeler, Lieutenant-Commander Sir Richard, KCVO MBE RN. Memoir of Admiral Andrew Cunningham.

Public Record Office, Kew

Documents ADM. 1 Series: Admiralty & Secretariat Papers, Second World War; Honours and Awards.

ADM. 53: Ships' logs.

ADM. 116: Admiralty & Secretariat Papers, Second World War.

ADM. 186: Admiralty Publications.

ADM. 199: War History Cases, 1939-45 War.

ADM. 205: First Sea Lord Papers.

ADM. 223: Intelligence Papers.

DEFE. 2: Combined Operations HQ Papers.

Royal Air Force Museum, Hendon

Papers of Air Chief Marshal Sir Arthur Longmore, GCB DSO.

PRINTED SOURCES

'A.G.P.', 'With "A.B.C." in the Med.': Memoirs of an RNVR Officer from Trawler to Destroyer, I-IV, *The Naval Review*, Vol. 65, Nos 2-4, April, July and October 1977, and Vol. 66, No. 1, January 1978.

'Amir', 'The Fighting Spirit': A Selection of Admiral Sir Andrew Cunningham's Signals, *The Naval Review*, Vol. XXXI, Vol. 4, November 1943.

Attard, Joseph, *The Battle of Malta*, London: William Kimber, 1980.

Bartimeus, *Malta Invicta*, London: Chatto & Windus, 1943.

——, *The Turn of the Road: Being the Story of the Royal Navy and Merchant Navy in the Landings in Algeria and French Morocco*, London: Chatto & Windus, 1946.

Beevor, Antony, *Crete: The Battle and the Resistance*, London: John Murray, 1991.

Bennett, Geoffrey; *Cowan's War: The Story of British Naval Operations in the Baltic, 1918-1920*, London: Collins, 1964.

Benstead, Instr. Lt-Cdr C.R., RN, *HMS Rodney: The Story of an Immortal Name*, Plymouth: Sellicks, 1931.

——, *HMS Rodney at Sea: Being the Story of the Second Commission of His Majesty's Battleship 'Rodney'*, London: Methuen, 1932.

Borghese, J. Valerio, *Sea Devils* (trans, from the Italian *Decima Flottiglia MAS*), London: Andrew Melrose, 1952.

Bradford, Ernie, *Siege: Malta 1940-1943*, London: Hamish Hamilton, 1985.

Bryant, Arthur, *Triumph in the West 1943-1946: Based on the Diaries and Autobiographical Notes of Field Marshal The Viscount Alanbrooke KG OM*, London: Collins, 1959.

Buell, Thomas B., *Master of Sea Power: A Biography of Fleet Admiral Ernest J. King*, Boston, Mass.: Little, Brown, 1980.

Butcher, Captain Harry C., USNR, *Three Years with Eisenhower*, London: William Heinemann, 1946.

Carver, Field Marshal Sir Michael (ed.), *The War Lords: Military Commanders of the Twentieth Century*, London: Weidenfeld and Nicolson, 1976.

Chalmers, Rear-Admiral W.S., CBE DSC, *Full Cycle: The Biography of Admiral Sir Bertram Home Ramsay KCB KBE MVO*, London: Hodder & Stoughton, 1959.

Chatterton-Dickson, Captain W.W.F., RN, *Seedie's Roll of Naval Honours & Awards 1939-1959*, Tisbury, Wiltshire: Ripley Registers, 1989.

Churchill, Winston S., *The Second World War*, I: *The Gathering Storm*, II: *Their Finest Hour*, III: *The Grand Alliance*, IV: *The Hinge of Fate*, V: *Closing the Ring* and VI: *Triumph and Tragedy*, London: Cassell, 1949-54.

Connell, G.G., *Mediterranean Maelstrom: HMS Jervis and the 14th Flotilla*, London: William Kimber, 1987.

———, *Valiant Quartet: His Majesty's Anti-Aircraft Cruisers* Curlew, Cairo, Calcutta, Coventry, London: William Kimber, 1979.

Connell, John, *Wavell: Scholar and Soldier, to June 1941*, London: Collins, 1964.

Corbett, Sir Julian, *History of the Great War, Naval Operations*, Vols I, II, London: Longmans Green, 1920-1.

Cunningham, Admiral Sir Andrew B., KCB DSO, Dispatch on 'Fleet Air Arm Operations Against Taranto on 11th November 1940', Supplement to *The London Gazette*, 24 July 1947.

———, Dispatch on 'Report of an Action with the Italian Fleet off Calabria, 9th July 1940', Supplement to *The London Gazette*, 28 April, 1948.

Cunningham, Admiral Sir Andrew B., GCB DSO, Dispatch on 'Battle of Matapan', Supplement to *The London Gazette*, 31 July, 1947.

———, Dispatch on 'Report of an Action against an Italian Convoy on the Night of the 15th/16th April, 1941', Supplement to *The London Gazette*, 12 May, 1948.

———, Dispatch on 'Transportation of the Army to Greece and Evacuation of the Army from Greece, 1941', Supplement to *The London Gazette*, 19 May, 1948.

———, Dispatch on 'The Battle of Crete', Supplement to *The London Gazette*, 24 May, 1948.

——, Dispatch on 'Mediterranean Convoy Operations (Operation "Excess", January 1941; Operation "Substance", July-August 1941; Operation "Halberd", September 1941; Operation "Harpoon", June 1942; Operation "Pedestal", August 1942)', Supplement to *The London Gazette*, 11 August, 1948.

Cunningham, Admiral of the Fleet Sir Andrew B., GCB DSO, Dispatch on 'Control of the Sicilian Straits during the Final Stages of the North African Campaign', Supplement to *The London Gazette*, 6 October, 1948.

——, Dispatch on 'The Landings in North Africa', Supplement to *The London Gazette*, 23 March, 1949.

——, Dispatch on 'Operation HUSKY, the Invasion of Sicily', Supplement to *The London Gazette*, 25 April, 1950.

——, Dispatch on 'Operation AVALANCHE, Salerno', Supplement to *The London Gazette*, 28 April, 1950.

Cunningham of Hyndhope, Admiral of the Fleet Viscount, KT GCB OM DSO, *A Sailor's Odyssey*, London: Hutchinson, 1951.

——, 'The Statement on Defence White Paper': Speech in the House of Lords, 10 March 1954, *The Naval Review*, Vol. XLII, No. 2, May 1954.

——, Speech in the Debate on the Address, House of Lords, 2nd December 1954, *The Naval Review*, Vol. XLIII, No. 1, February 1955.

Davin, DM., *Crete: Official History of New Zealand in the Second World War*, Wellington, N.Z.: Department of Internal Affairs, 1953.

Edwards, Kenneth, *Men of Action*, London: Collins, 1944.

——, *Seven Sailors*, London: Collins, 1945.

Ehrman, John, *Grand Strategy*, Vol. V: *August 1943-September 1944*, Vol. VI: *October 1944-August 194s*, London: HMSO, 1956.

Elliott, Peter, *The Cross and the Ensign: A Naval History of Malta, 1798-1979*, Cambridge: Patrick Stephens, 1980.

Fisher, Rear-Admiral R.L., CB DSO OBE DSC, *Salt Horse: A Naval Life*, Lochgilphead: by the author, 1986.

Fraser, Edward, and Leyland, John, 'HMS *Britannia*, Past and Present, The Story of the *Britannia* in War and Peace', *The Navy and Army Illustrated*, Volume V, No. 53, 24 December 1897.

Gordon, Ed, *HMS* Pepperpot: *The* Penelope *in World War Two*, London: Robert Hale, 1985.

Gretton, Vice-Admiral Sir Peter, KCB DSO OBE DSC, *Former Naval Person: Winston Churchill and the Royal Navy*, London: Cassell, 1968.

——, 'The Royal Navy in the Spanish Civil War of 1936-39', *The Naval Review*, Vol. LXII, Nos. 1-3, January, April, July 1974.

Harwood, Admiral Sir Henry H., KCB OBE, Dispatch on 'The Battle of Sirte of 22nd March 1942', Supplement to *The London Gazette*, 18 September 1947.

Hay, Ian, *The Unconquered Isle: The Story of Malta G.C.*, London: Hodder & Stoughton, 1943.

Heckstall-Smith, Anthony, and Baillie-Grohmann, H.T, *Greek Tragedy*, London: Anthony Blond, 1961.

Hewitt, Admiral H. Kent, US Navy, *Admiral of the Fleet Viscount Cunningham of Hyndhope K. T, G.C.B., O.M., D.S.O.*, Proceedings of the United States Naval Institute, Vol. 78, Jan-June 1952.

Hinsley, F.H., with E.E. Thomas, C.F.G. Ransom, R.C. Knight, *British Intelligence in the Second World War: Its Influence on Strategy and Operations*, Vols I, II and III, Parts I and II, London: HMSO, 1979-88.

Historical Section, Admiralty, *Naval Staff History, Second World War: Mediterranean*, Vol. I: *September 1939-October 1940*; Vol. II: *November 1940-December 1941*.

——, *Selected Convoys (Mediterranean)*, Battle Summaries Nos 18 & 32.

Hodgkinson, Lieutenant-Commander Hugh, DSC RN, *Before the Tide Turned: The Mediterranean Experiences of a British Destroyer Officer in 1941*, London: George G. Harrap, 1944.

Hogg, Anthony, *Just a Hoggs Life: A Royal Navy Saga of the Thirties*, Chichester: Solo Mio Books, 1993.

Howe, George F., *Northwest Africa: Seizing the Initiative in the West* (US Army in World War II: The Mediterranean Theater of Operations), Washington, DC: Department of the Army, 1957.

Humble, Richard, *Fraser of North Cape: The Life of Admiral of the Fleet Lord Fraser* [1888-1981], London: Routledge & Kegan Paul, 1983.

James, Robert Rhodes, *Gallipoli*, London: B.T Batsford, 1965.

James, Admiral Sir William, GCB, *The Sky Was Always Blue*, London: Methuen, 1951.

Jeans, Surgeon T.T, RN (ed.), *Naval Brigades in the South African War 1899-1900*, Part V: *From Belfast to Komati Poort, from the Diary of Lieutenant E.P.C Back, RN*, London: Sampson Low, Marston, 1902.

Jones, Geoffrey P., *Battleship Barham*, London: William Kimber, 1979.

King, Ernest J., and Whitehill, Walter Muir, *Fleet Admiral King: A Naval Record*, New York: Norton, 1952.

Langmaid, Rowland, *The Med: The Royal Navy in the Mediterranean 1939-1945*, London: Batchworth, 1948.

Laird Clowes, Sir William, *The Royal Navy: A History*, Vol. VII, Chapter 47, Military History of the Royal Navy, 1857-1900, London: Sampson Low, Marston, 1903.

Lane, G.R., 'The Dambusters who Never Flew', *Liverpool Daily Post*, 18 June 1968.

Le Bailly, Vice-Admiral Sir Louis, KBE CB, DL, *The Man Around the Engine: Life Below the Waterline*, Emsworth: Kenneth Mason, 1990.

Lewin, Ronald, *Ultra Goes to War: The Secret Story*, London: Hutchinson, 1978.

London Gazette, 12 March 1901, Letters from Back to Bearcroft, 15 June, 6 September and 7 October 1900.

Longmore, Air Chief Marshal Sir Arthur, GCB DSO, *From Sea to Sky: Memoirs 1910-1945*, London: Geoffrey Bles, 1946.

Lowis, Commander Geoffrey L., AFC RN, *Fabulous Admirals and Some Fragments*, IV: Rear-Admiral Reginald Charles Prothero, CB MVO, XIV: Rear-Admiral Sir Robert Keith Arbuthnot, Bt., KCB MVO, London: Putnam, 1957.

Macintyre, Captain Donald, DSO++ DSC RN, *Fighting Admiral: The Life of Admiral of the Fleet Sir James Somerville GCB GBE DSO*, London: Evans Bros, 1961.

——, *The Battle for the Mediterranean*, London: B.T. Batsford, 1964.

Macmillan, Harold, *The Blast of War 1939-1945*, London: Macmillan, 1967.

——, *War Diaries: Politics and War in the Mediterranean, January 1943-May 1945*, London: Macmillan, 1984.

Marder, Arthur J., *From the Dardanelles to Oran: Studies of the Royal Navy in War and Peace 1915-1940*, Oxford: Oxford University Press, 1974.

McGeoch, Ian, *An Affair of Chances: A Submariner's Odyssey 1939-44*, London: Imperial War Museum, 1991.

Ministry of Information, *East of Malta, West of Suez: The Admiralty Account of the Naval War in the Eastern Mediterranean, September 1939 to March 1941*, London: HMSO, 1943.

——, *The Mediterranean Fleet Greece to Tripoli: The Admiralty Account of Naval Operations: April 1941 to January 1943*, London: HMSO, 1944.

Morison, Samuel Eliot, *History of United States Naval Operations in World War II*, Vol. II: *Operations in North African Waters October 1942-June 1943*; Vol. IX: *Sicily-Salerno-Anzio January 1943-June 1944*; Vol. X: *The Atlantic Battle Won May 1943-May 1945*, Boston, Mass.: Little, Brown, 1950-6.

Naval Review, Vol. IV, 1916, 'The Proceedings of HMS *Amethyst* while at the Dardanelles'.

——, Vol. IV, 1916, 'A Narrative of HMS *Agamemnon* in the Mediterranean, January 1915 to March 1917'.

——, Vol. XXIII, No. 1, February 1935, 'Rear-Admiral Sir Robert Keith Arbuthnot, Bt.,KCB MVO'.

——, Vol. XXXIV, No. 1, February 1946, 'The First Sea Lord at Cambridge': a rendering into English (and the Latin text) of the speech of the Public Orator of the University of Cambridge, made in the Senate House at the conferment of Honorary Degrees, 29 November 1945.

——, Vol. LI, No. 3, July 1963, 'Admiral of the Fleet Lord Cunningham of Hyndhope', Tributes by 'D.M.L.' (Captain D.M. Lees), 'P.L.V' (Admiral of the Fleet Sir Philip Vian) and 'J.A.G.T' (Vice-Admiral Sir James Troup).

Newton, Don, and Hampshire, A. Cecil, *Taranto*, London: William Kimber, 1959. Obituary: 'Admiral of the Fleet Lord Cunningham: Taranto & Matapan Victor', *Daily Telegraph and Morning Post*, 13 June 1986.

——, 'Viscount Cunningham of Hyndhope: Victor of Cape Matapan', *The Scotsman*, 13 June 1963.

——, 'Admiral of the Fleet Lord Cunningham of Hyndhope', *The Times*, 13 June 1963.

Official Programme of the Victory Celebrations 8th June 1946, London: HMSO, 1946.

Ollard, Richard, *Fisher and Cunningham: A Study of the Personalities of the Churchill Era*, London: Constable, 1991.

Our Penelope, *by her Company*, London: Harrap, 1943.

Pack, S.W.C., *The Battle of Matapan*, London: B.T Batsford, 1961.

——, *Night Action off Cape Matapan*, London: Ian Allan, 1972.

——, *The Battle for Crete*, London: Ian Allan, 1973.

——, *Cunningham the Commander*, London: B.T. Batsford, 1974.

——, *The Battle of Sirte*, London: Ian Allan, 1975.

——, *Operation 'Husky': The Allied Invasion of Sicily*, Newton Abbot: David & Charles, 1977.

——, *Invasion North Africa, 1942*, London: Ian Allan, 1978.

——, 'Andrew Browne Cunningham', *The Dictionary of National Biography 1961-1970*, Oxford: Oxford University Press, 1981.

Playfair, Major-General I.S.O., CB DSO MC, and others, *The Mediterranean and Middle East*, Vol. I: *The Early Successes against Italy* (to May 1941); Vol. II: *The Germans come to the Help of their Ally* (1941); Vols III, IV: *The Destruction of the Axis Forces in Africa*, London: HMSO, 1954-66.

Pond, Hugh, *Salerno*, London: William Kimber, 1961.

——, *Sicily*, London William Kimber, 1962.

Poolman, Kenneth, *Illustrious*, London: William Kimber, 1955.

Richards, Denis, & Saunders, Hilary St George, *Royal Air Force 1939-1945*, Vol. I: *The Fight at Odds* (Richards); Vol. II: *The Fight Avails* (Richards and Saunders); Vol. Ill: *The Fight Is Won* (Saunders), London: HMSO, 1953-4.

Roskill, Captain S.W, DSC RN, *The War at Sea 1939-1945*, Vol. I: *The Defensive*; Vol. II: *The Period of Balance*; Vol. III: *The Offensive* (Part I, 1 June 1943-31 May 1944; Part II, 1 June 1944-14 August 1945), London: HMSO, 1954-61. *H.A1.S. Warspite*, London: Collins, 1957.

——, *Churchill and the Admirals*, London: Collins, 1977.

Schofield, B.B., *The Attack on Taranto*, London, Ian Allan: 1973.

——, *Silver Phantom: HMS Aurora*, by her Company, London: Frederick Muller, 1945.

Simpson, G.W.G., *Periscope View: A Professional Autobiography*, London: Macmillan, 1972.

Smith, Peter C., and Walker, Edwin, *The Battles of the Malta Striking Forces*, London: Ian Allan, 1974.

Somerville, Vice-Admiral Sir James F., KCB DSO, Dispatch on 'Action between British and Italian Forces off Cape Spartivento on 27th November, 1940', Supplement to *The London Gazette*, 5 May 1948.

Stevens, John, *Never Volunteer*, Emsworth: Woodleigh, 1971.

Stewart, I. McD. G., *The Struggle for Crete, 20 May-1 June 1941: A Story of Lost Opportunity*, Oxford: Oxford University Press, 1966.

Stitt, Commander George, RN, *Under Cunningham's Command 1940-1943*, London: George Allen & Unwin, 1944.

Taffrail [Captain Taprell Dorling DSO RN], *Western Mediterranean 1942-1943*, London: Hodder and Stoughton, 1947.

Thomas, David A., *Crete 1941: The Battle at Sea*, London: Andre Deutsch, 1972.

Thursfield, James R., 'British Naval Manoeuvres in 1906', *Brassey's Naval Annual*, 1907.

Times of Malta, 'Yesterday's Naval Wedding', 25 April 1940.

Vella, Philip, *Malta: Blitzed but not Beaten*, Valletta, Malta GC: National War Museum Association, 1985.

Vian, Admiral of the Fleet Sir Philip, GCB KBE DSO, *Action This Day: A War Memoir*, London: Frederick Muller, 1960.

Wade, Frank, *A Midshipman's War: A Young Man in the Mediterranean Naval War 1941-1943*, Vancouver, B.C.: Cordillera Publishing Company.

Warner, Oliver, 'Admiral Cunningham comes to Trafalgar Square', *The Times*, March 25 1967.

——, *Cunningham of Hyndhope Admiral of the Fleet: A Memoir*, London: John Murray, 1967.

Wemyss, Lady Wester, *The Life and Letters of Lord Wester Wemyss*, Chapter 3, HMS *Ophir*-Osborne College — HMS *Suffolk*, London: Eyre & Spottiswoode, 1935.

Whinney, Bob (Captain Reginald Whinney DSC and two Bars RN), *The U-Boat Peril: An Anti-Submarine Commander's War*, Poole, Dorset: Blandford Press, 1986.

Wingate, John, DSC, *The Fighting Tenth: The Tenth Submarine Flotilla and the Siege of Malta*, London: Leo Cooper, 1991.

Winster, Lord, 'Admiral Cunningham: His Move Next?', *Picture Post*, Vol. 19, No. 6, 8 May 1943.

Winton, John, *The Victoria Cross at Sea*, London: Michael Joseph, 1978.

——, *The Death of the Scharnhorst*, Chichester: Antony Bird, 1983.

——, *Convoy: The Defence of Sea Trade 1890-1990*, London: Michael Joseph, 1983.

——, *Ultra at Sea*, London: Leo Cooper, 1988.

——, *The Forgotten Fleet*, London: Michael Joseph, 1969; repr. Wadhurst, East Sussex: Douglas-Boyd Books, 1989.

Ziegler, Philip, *Mountbatten: The Official Biography*, London: Collins, 1985.

ACKNOWLEDGEMENTS

A GREAT NUMBER of people have contributed to this book, with letters, interviews, diaries, memoirs, pictures, reminiscences and anecdotes of ABC, and other material. I am particularly grateful to Mrs Hillie McKendrick (ABC's niece); Admiral Sir J.C.K. Slater, GCB, LVO (ABC's great-nephew); Mr Henry Brownrigg; Admiral Sir Charles Madden, GCB, Bt; the late Rear-Admiral A.S. ('Ben') Bolt, CB, DSO, DSC*; Air Chief Marshal Sir Kenneth Cross, KCB, CBE, DSO, DFC; Vice-Admiral Sir Roderick Macdonald, KBE; Mrs Desmond Davey; the late Rear-Admiral Royer Dick, CB, CBE, DSC; Mr Jim Dixon; the late Rear-Admiral W.J. Munn, CB, DSO, OBE; Captain Alwyn Lenox-Conyngham, RN; Lieutenant-Colonel Stephen Rose, OBE, Royal Marines; the late Lieutenant-Commander Sir Richard Wheeler, KCVO, MBE, RN; Mr Tony Ditcham, DSC; Bishop Launcelot Fleming; Captain Hugh Lee, DSC, RN; Mr James Longmore; Revd Kenneth N.J. Loveless; the late Vice-Admiral Sir Geoffrey Norman, KCVO, CB, CBE; Mr David Satherley; Lieutenant-Commander John Somerville, CB, CBE; Mr Philip Vella, of the National War Museum Association, Malta GC; Captain R.F. Whinney, DSC**, RN; and to Professor Mario Werner, MD, and Elsbeth, the present owners of the house ABC leased in Washington DC, for their generous hospitality.

A NOTE TO THE READER

If you have enjoyed this book enough to leave a review on **Amazon** and **Goodreads**, then we would be truly grateful.

John Winton

Sapere Books is an exciting new publisher of brilliant fiction and popular history.

To find out more about our latest releases and our monthly bargain books visit our website:
saperebooks.com

Made in United States
North Haven, CT
08 June 2023

37528546R00365